BEHIND CLOSED DOORS

The Tragic, Untold Story of Wallis Simpson

Hugo Vickers

arrow books

Published by Arrow Books 2012

2 4 6 8 10 9 7 5 3 1

First published in Great Britain in 2011 by Hutchinson

Arrow Books
Random House, 20 Vauxhall Bridge Road,
London SW1V 2SA

www.rbooks.co.uk

Addresses for companies within The Random House Group Limited can be found at:
www.randomhouse.co.uk/offices.htm

The Random House Group Limited Reg. No. 954009

A CIP catalogue record for this book
is available from the British Library

ISBN 9780099547228

Typeset in Erhardt by Palimpsest Book Production Limited, Falkirk, Stirlingshire

Printed and bound by CPI Group (UK) Ltd, Croydon, CR0 4YY

FOR GEORGE

(Sometimes known as George V)

WITH LOVE FROM HIS FATHER

The Duchess of Windsor in 1971.

She is wearing the jonquil diamond ring sold without her knowledge (but with the authority of Maître Blum) to Estée Lauder on 30 August 1977 – for $150,000.

Photograph by Cecil Beaton/*Vogue* © The Condé Nast Publications Ltd.

Contents

PART ONE – THE DEATH

PART TWO – THE LIFE

'The best way to keep someone as a prisoner is to surround him with love, affection and friendship.'

Maître Suzanne Blum to Carmel Offie
New York
22 September 1943

'Do you think we'll ever know the whole truth?' asked Diana Mosley.

Hugo Vickers' Diary
11 July 1986

Part One – The Death

I

Introduction

Schoolchildren put order on history by learning the names and dates of the kings and queens of England. It is not a bad method, and in a monarchical country it works as well as any. Some kings and queens make a great impact on their times – William the Conqueror, Edward III, Henry VIII, Elizabeth I and Queen Victoria. To others it would be hard to put a face or even to highlight a relevant fact or facet.

When I lecture about the monarchy, I spin through the curious succession from Charles I to the present day, showing how it came about, and mentioning the various ways that the power and influence of the Sovereign has been curtailed and modified.

These days one Sovereign follows another by succession. The days of the Wars of the Roses are over. Queen Elizabeth II is a constitutional monarch, with limited powers, because the power of kings has gradually been taken away, a process which began effectively when the barons confronted King John with Magna Carta in 1215.

Charles I believed in the Divine Right of Kings to rule and as a result he clashed with Parliament. The English Civil War followed and he had his head chopped off. There then occurred the only time in English history when we did not have a reigning monarch – the period of Oliver Cromwell's Commonwealth which lasted until 1660, and was an experiment not repeated. Charles II was restored to the throne and by the time the reign of the Stuarts ran out it had been decided that England's king should not be autocratic but should behave himself as far as Parliament was concerned.

Charles's brother James II had upset Parliament by professing the Roman Catholic faith and locking up the Archbishop of Canterbury. He fled to France and was deemed to have abdicated the throne. The crown was then offered to William and Mary of Orange and a parliamentary monarchy was established with the Bill of Rights of 1689.

One result of this bill was the decision that the English Sovereign must always be a Protestant: thus it excluded all the descendants of James II from the succession. This was followed presently by the Act of Settlement of 1701, which gave the throne to Sophia, Electress of

Hanover (a granddaughter of James I) and to her descendants provided they were Protestant.

Queen Anne – who succeeded William to the throne in 1702 – lost all her children while they were young, so in 1714 the throne went to Sophia's son, the King of Hanover, who arrived in England from Germany to be King George I. There followed four Georges in a row, whose lives were recorded in a rhyme by Walter Savage Landor:

> George the First was always reckoned
> Vile, but viler George the Second.
> And what mortal ever heard
> Any good of George the Third,
> But when from earth the Fourth descended
> God be praised the Georges ended.[1]

George I hardly spoke any English at all. During his reign he still presided over cabinet meetings with ministers, but in 1717 he ceased to do so regularly and the first minister did so instead, thus becoming the Prime Minister.

George I was succeeded by George II and then by his grandson, George III (who lost America to the Americans). George III is popularly thought to have gone mad and was confined to rooms in Windsor Castle, and so in 1811 his son became the Prince Regent. Though he built wonderful places like the Brighton Pavilion and Regent Street in London and greatly enriched the Royal Collection, he lived a racy life.

The Prince Regent had a daughter called Princess Charlotte. She married Prince Leopold of Coburg and was expecting a baby, but she died in 1817 while giving birth to a stillborn child. Thus the Royal Family lost their next two generations in one go.

Panic ensued. George IV (as he became in 1820) had no other children, but he had a number of fat, disreputable, syphilitic brothers, living ropy lives, drinking too much, and spending too much time in the arms of mistresses. There was now a huge rush to find an heir to the throne. As a result the brothers dropped their mistresses of long standing and hurriedly married German Protestant princesses much younger than themselves. So it was with the Dukes of Clarence (later William IV), Kent and Cambridge.

Of these, the Duke of Kent married a Coburg princess in 1818, had a daughter born in 1819, and died the following year. George IV died in 1830 and was succeeded by his brother, the Duke of Clarence, who reigned as William IV. During his reign the Reform Act of 1832 was passed, again reducing the powers and political influence of the monarch. When he died in 1837, the Duke of Kent's daughter – very much a designer baby – suddenly found herself queen at the age of eighteen.

Queen Victoria reigned for sixty-three years and proved to be a powerful and well-remembered ruler, becoming in time Empress of India. When she died in 1901, her son, Albert Edward, Prince of Wales, became Edward VII (1901–10), a flamboyant monarch who presided stylishly over the Edwardian era.

His son was the rather more serious George V (1910–36), whose great joys in life were stamp collecting and shooting whatever bird happened to be in season at the time of year. He was the present queen's grand-father.

This leads us to Edward VIII, the king who abdicated, the dates of whose reign are shown simply as '1936' and who was succeeded by his younger brother, the Duke of York, who reigned as George VI (1936–52), and whose daughter, Elizabeth II, has now been queen for sixty years. She descends from most, though not all, of the kings and queens of England and Scotland but, as can be seen, she arrived on the throne by a circuitous route.

I had been acutely aware of Queen Elizabeth II from an early age. I remember seeing her in her car driving along Beauchamp Place in London. I saw her in a carriage with the Shah of Iran in 1959 and with General de Gaulle in 1960. We were allowed the morning off school to watch Princess Margaret's wedding; I attended the Trooping the Colour as a youngster. I remember seeing the late Princess Royal coming out of Lord Roberts's Work Shop in Cromwell Road. At prep school I developed a keen interest in the Royal Family, began to work out who they all were with the help of *Whitaker's Almanack*, and the admirable two large volumes of the *Concise Universal Biography*, and later, at Eton, when I had access to St George's Chapel, the interest became more focused.

Inevitably the mysterious figure of Edward VIII captured my imagin-ation. He was the king who gave up his throne to marry 'the woman he loved'. In the 1960s it was still traditional to take a dim view of him, not to mention the shocking twice-divorced American, Mrs Simpson, who had lured him from his throne. I was given the distinct impression that these two individuals – the Duke and Duchess of Windsor – were somehow bad people, especially the Duchess. You did not talk about them. They belonged in the past tense.

As fresh in my head today as it was when it appeared forty-eight years ago is a photograph of the Duchess of Windsor visiting the New York

World's Fair in 1964. I cut it out of the *Sunday Express* and kept it. I
have it still: 'THEIR DAY AT THE FAIR' was the headline. 'The Duchess
of Windsor leads. The Duke follows, escorted by a man in dark glasses.
A woman in a sari passes. The flags of many nations flutter. The Windsors
are spending a day at the New York World's Fair, being staged by America's
chiefs of industry.'[2]

This evil temptress looked rather nice and was smartly dressed: a
Chanel coat, I would say in hindsight, and now I see the brooch – perhaps
in the famous sale, perhaps not. I remember thinking it extraordinary
that someone should have taken, let alone published, a picture of her.
Could she really be so awful? I was twelve at the time. I can be forgiven
for some naivety in the matter.

In those days, the press liked to publish informal photographs of
royalty. If they were intrusive, they were more charming. The Duke was
pictured in a series of four snaps, scything grass in his garden at the Mill,
and finally lighting his pipe. The Windsors were photographed dancing
at a party in Paris where the decor, the tents and the champagne were
pink. And then it all started to go wrong.

The Duke was in New York, heading for St Louis and Houston for
what was described as a 'check-up' – in fact, a hernia operation. The
Windsors were still rather distant figures in my imagination. Soon they
came much closer.

In 1965, while at Eton, I was able to buy a copy of the Duke's memoirs
in Windsor. I did not realise it at the time, but the copy I bought had
come from the library of Eric Hamilton, Dean of Windsor, who had died
three years before. It bore his signature. I read it eagerly. Almost simultaneously, the Duke came to London for an eye operation at the London
Clinic. He was there for many days, and almost every day there was a
photograph of the Duchess of Windsor arriving or leaving the hospital
to visit him in a variety of different outfits – a Chanel suit, a matching
dress and coat, or a sable fur coat. She usually had a smile for the cameras
before she returned to Claridge's.

Then, dramatically, the Queen went to the London Clinic to see the
Duke. She too was photographed leaving the London Clinic, her detective, Albert Perkins, at her side, her Private Secretary, Sir Michael Adeane,
and a lady-in-waiting following. The Queen saw him again at Claridge's.
The Duke's sister, the Princess Royal, also visited the hospital, only to
die unexpectedly some ten days later.

By that time the Duke had left the London Clinic, wearing a heavy
grey overcoat, with his eyes hidden behind the dark glasses that he would
wear more often than not for the rest of his life, and with supporting

hands either side of him. He began to take recuperative strolls in Regent's Park, muffled up in his overcoat, a trilby hat on his head, the Duchess at his side and a detective following. The Queen invited him to walk in the gardens of Buckingham Palace and on those occasions the Duchess did not accompany him. After the Duke's first visit to the Palace for many years, his spokesman said: 'When he came back he looked very refreshed and happy. His face was glowing.'³

I watched the televised memorial service for the Princess Royal that was held in Westminster Abbey. It was thought that the journey to Harewood House in Yorkshire for the funeral would be too much for the Duke after his operation. Instead he and the Duchess entered the Abbey by a side door (to avoid flashing cameras) and were seated in the stalls of the Choir of that great building, taking a very public place in a national service. It was the first time the Duchess had taken part in any public event in Britain. Before they returned to Paris the Duchess went with the Duke's Private Secretary, John Utter, to look at pugs at the Pug Dog Club show at Seymour Hall. Her dog Trooper had died, and she longed for another one. 'The Duke was terrified when he knew I was coming here because he knows I like them so much,' she told a reporter. 'He is afraid I will buy a houseful.'⁴

These were no longer the hated exiles. All the rules were being broken. There was more to come.

A better impression of the Duke of Windsor could be seen in the documentary film *A King's Story*, directed by Jack Le Vien and shown in cinemas in the summer of 1965. To watch it now is to view a somewhat dated production, the Duke reading from an autocue not very fluently, the Duchess likewise, marginally better. It is stilted and old-fashioned but at the time it was completely fascinating.

In 1967 came the celebrated public meeting between the Windsors and the Queen, one of the two things that the Duke had been asking for – especially from George VI and Queen Elizabeth – ever since the Abdication. The other request was for the title of Her Royal Highness to be given to the Duchess, a request which was not granted. The occasion of the meeting was the unveiling of a memorial to Queen Mary, set in the wall of Marlborough House. Photographs duly appeared of the Windsors standing in a royal line-up which included the Duke and Duchess of Gloucester, the Queen and the Duke of Edinburgh and the Queen Mother.

In August 1968 the Duke of Windsor materialised before my very eyes on what proved to be his last visit to England. By this time I was already involved in the life of St George's Chapel and for two years I had shown

tourists around on Sunday afternoons as one of the Eton guides. I had
made friends with Dr Sidney Campbell, the then chapel organist, and,
being aware of my interest in the Royal Family, he allowed me to come
to the organ loft on Friday 30 August to witness the funeral of Princess
Marina, Duchess of Kent, who had died of an inoperable brain tumour
the previous Tuesday morning. Her death was immeasurably sad as she
held a place in the hearts of the British people as a tragic and beautiful
princess, who had been widowed at the age of thirty-five and had raised
her young family on her own. She was only sixty-one when she died.

It was occasionally the custom at a royal funeral that the choristers
should be moved into the organ loft to sing there, thus liberating more
seats in the Quire for family mourners. On a bright late-summer afternoon the mourners began to gather, many of them Danish/Greek cousins
of the Princess who rather resembled her with their dyed auburn hair –
Queen Helen of Romania and others. To justify my presence (which
greatly irritated the then Dean, Chapter Clerk and Virger) I was to give
a sign to Dr Campbell when the Queen came into the Quire. She led the
Royal Family in through what are called the advance gates, on the north
side of the Quire, near the High Altar. In they came, one after another
– the Queen and the Duke of Edinburgh, the Queen Mother, the Prince
of Wales, Princess Anne, Princess Margaret and Lord Snowdon, the
Duchess of Gloucester and her son Prince Richard. And then, to my
astonishment, following them, in came the Duke of Windsor.

He was wearing what I later discovered to be the same morning coat
that he had worn at his wedding, having retained his youthful figure. He
looked like the young Prince of Wales of the photographs, except that
his hair was snow white now, and his face wizened by age. He had the
saddest eyes I think I have ever seen in a man.

He sat not far below me and I watched him throughout the beautiful
service. He did not look around with any curiosity. He followed the service,
rising and sitting at the appropriate moments. At the end of the service
the coffin was borne out of St George's Chapel to be buried at Frogmore.
The night before, the Duke of Kent's coffin had been conveyed to
Frogmore after the residents of the Lower Ward had been told to draw
their curtains and remain in their houses. Princess Alexandra held her
brothers' hands as she followed her mother's coffin, only letting go of
them when they came into view of the press photographers outside.

I watched the Duke of Windsor again as he followed the Royal Family
out under the organ screen directly beneath me to take his place on the
West Steps of the chapel. It was his last ever visit to England and I never
saw him in person again.

In January 1970 an interview with the Duke and Duchess by Kenneth Harris was shown on British television. It gave a vivid impression of both of them: he spoke with a slightly American accent, sanguine in old age, at times bitter, and was in reminiscing mood. The Duchess gave evidence of her quick humour and repartee. It remains one of the most telling of the interviews, and will be analysed a little later in the context of what was revealed.

After this the Windsors could be seen in occasional press photographs. The Duke began to use a stick to walk with and started to look older than his years. A friend told me that if you wrote to him and asked for his autograph and the Duchess's, you would be likely to receive them. If you asked for just his, either nothing came back or a card came with both signatures on it. I duly wrote to the couple in the autumn of 1971 and a card arrived signed by both of them in black felt-tipped pen. I was just in time.

All this unexpectedly became more relevant when my friend Hugh Montgomery-Massingberd rescued me from a short-term predicament. I had left school in December 1969 and had promptly been refused a place at Trinity College, Cambridge, the first time I had failed at an important step in life. Instead I spent a year in university at Strasbourg. I returned with no viable plans for the future. I rather think I did know what I wanted to do, but I could not do it, let alone justify my whims.

In July 1971 my father took me on holiday in the South of France, and as we drove back he enquired about my plans for a future career. I muttered something about going to art school, for which, in truth, I had no enthusiasm or talent. He listened. 'Shall we say three weeks? If not I am sure I can find something for you.' Of that I needed no convincing. He was the senior partner of thriving stockbroking firm Vickers, da Costa. The problem was that I did not understand a thing about what they did and had no inclination towards it. I knew I would fail miserably if I went near the place.

Luckily I met Hugh the very weekend of my return from France. He invited me to become a freelance contributor to the *Burke's Peerage*, which he had recently taken over following a coup which had resulted in the ousting of the then editor. I jumped at his offer in order to escape my father's three-week deadline, and intended to stay a few months. I stayed eventually for a year and a half.

During that time I helped rewrite some pedigrees for the third volume of *Burke's Landed Gentry*, which proved excellent training for a future biographer. Hugh had an encyclopaedic mind. He lived opposite Kew Gardens at the time, and as he commuted to the dingy *Burke's Peerage* offices not far from Waterloo Station he would peruse the births, marriages and deaths in *The Times* and *Daily Telegraph*, circling the names of people who belonged to families he was monitoring. He would throw the paper onto a desk and fledglings like me would try to find the entries for these newly born and newly deceased people in a series of vast interleaved books and mark them up so that we would be a step ahead when a new edition was in the offing.

Once the volume I was working on was edited and ready for the printers, I thought I should move on. But Hugh had an ambitious publishing programme laid out. Foremost was a reference book on the British Royal Family. Two genealogists would work on the pedigrees and Hugh would commission distinguished figures to write essays. My job was to create new reference biographies for all the living members of the Royal Family. Since I was only twenty when I was given this assignment it showed he had confidence that I could do it, and presently I was happily running in and out of Buckingham Palace, Clarence House, St James's Palace and Kensington Palace, meeting Private Secretaries and Press Secretaries, gathering my information. It led to a meeting with Princess Alice, Countess of Athlone, then eighty-nine and almost stone deaf – my first proper conversation with a member of the Royal Family. At that meeting I had to balance the need to be polite with almost shouting to make myself understood. It was no easy task.

Hugh also wrote to John Utter, the Duke of Windsor's Private Secretary, and received a letter back:

> His Royal Highness the Duke of Windsor has agreed to the suggestion in your letter of 12 April 1972 that Mr. Hugo Vickers come to see me to discuss the entry for H.R.H. The Duke of Windsor in your projected *Burke's Guide to the Royal Family*.

I was invited to ring 'so that we can decide on a date and hour for our discussions.'[5] I did so and was soon setting off to Paris to the Duke of Windsor's house. As I say, at the time I was only twenty.

In the early days I kept a five-year diary – which is not very informative since I was so young. But it has helped me put my story in order and I have relied on it and the later, rather fuller diaries to create my narrative or for direct quotes as I gleaned information from 1972 to the present day.

This is partly a personal quest. My interest in the Windsors grew from that time and has never flagged. I am one of many who has mulled over the events of the Abdication and sought the truth behind it, whatever that may be. Later, after the Duke's death, I monitored to the best of my ability the ongoing fate of the Duchess of Windsor. These are the two elements on which I now seek to impose order.

And this is how that story unfolded.

I quote from a letter I wrote in the early summer of 1972, which outlined the work and the visits to the Private Secretaries and continued:

> It's been tremendous fun for me to see inside all the Palaces. I saw the Topolski drawings in Buckingham Palace and actually went through the State Apartments. On one occasion as I came out, the Queen drove in, so I had a view from the inside, and as I went out I was photographed like mad by all the tourists, which was as amusing as it was disconcerting.
>
> Tomorrow I set off to Paris to visit the Duke of Windsor's Private Secretary and the letter suggested I *might* meet him, which would be fascinating. I'm then having a couple of days in Paris to watch a bit of the Queen's State Visit.[6]

By coincidence the date I proposed for the meeting with John Utter was the day before the Queen was due to visit the Duke during her State Visit to France. I flew to Paris on 16 May and booked myself into the Intercontinental Hotel on the rue de Castiglione. That evening I took up a position in the Faubourg St Honoré, opposite the British Embassy. Presently the narrow street filled with an impressive escort of motorcycles and I saw the Queen and Duke of Edinburgh and President and Mme Pompidou arrive at the Embassy for dinner.

The next day I set out in a taxi with a friendly driver to the Bois de Boulogne. It was not easy to find the Windsors' house, but I had left plenty of time. I knew I had come to the right place, for then, as now, at either side of the large gates there were lamp-posts with royal ducal coronets on them. Shortly before eleven a.m. I rang the doorbell and presently found myself walking up the drive towards the lovely house. There was one of those green signs with white letters urging visitors to beware of the dogs – more an exhortation not to run over one of them as they were small pugs. There were also two large stone dogs by the steps at the front of the house. (These disappeared at some point after the Duke's death.)

As I approached the front door there was some activity. The Private Secretary, John Utter, was surrounded by the Duchess's pugs and one mongrel, and was waving to a smart lady in a car. For a moment I wondered if this was the Duchess. In fact, it was a friend of hers called Mrs Gardner*, who happened to be staying at the time.

A small, smartly dressed man, Mr Utter wore a heavy grey suit, with French decoration ribbons in his buttonhole. He spoke with an almost imperceptible American accent. He was very friendly.

He led me into a dimly lit hall beyond which the light streamed in through the French windows of the downstairs drawing room. A magnificent staircase swept up on the left. He led me into the office, to the right of the hall. Here I met Miss Schütz, the Duchess's secretary, whose desk was to the left of his. Mr Utter and I went through the various points in the Duke and Duchess's biographical entries for the book. He agreed to my various suggestions. One of the sections concerned the Duke's foreign orders. (For some reason I felt it important that all these foreign orders should be listed with the dates on which they were received, something I took more seriously than the recipients.) He told me that all the Duke's orders were kept in the bank. I asked about dates.

Mr Utter said: 'I will ask him if I get the chance, but now he is so old, he's no longer interested. He'll just say: "Oh, I don't know".' I should have been quicker off the mark at realising how ill the Duke was as both the secretaries used expressions like: 'Up until last year, when he was all right . . .' Mr Utter spoke about the Duke's interest in fashion and his invention of the Windsor knot for ties. He spoke of larger collars, and how the Duke could wear the most outrageous clothes and look marvellous in them. 'You or I would look ridiculous,' he said, and went on to talk of baggy trousers, with a check pattern four inches by four.

When it came to the Duchess's entry in the book, he summoned her passport and we checked the date and place of birth. To assist her to pass through immigration control her passport was stylishly adorned with a Cecil Beaton photograph. I was considerably impressed.

Meanwhile Miss Schütz was fascinating. She rang up one of the fashion houses and informed the lady at the other end of the line that, '*Son Altesse voudrait voir les robes qu'elle a choisie de la nouvelle collection dans votre salon cette après-midi . . .*' and gave the time of arrival. Down went the telephone, leaving them to sharpen up fast in the couture house – Christian Dior if my memory is right. Miss Schütz was able to rattle out instructions on the Duchess's behalf in any number of languages. That morning she was wrestling with a problem. Mrs Gardner was staying and the Duchess was trying to organise a dinner party for that Saturday evening. I should have detected a further warning sign in the

* Susan, widow of Arthur Gardner (1889–1967), US Ambassador to Cuba 1953–7.

fact that as the two secretaries went through the list of guests the Duke was not among them.

'I ring up Lord Tennyson,' said Miss Schütz. 'Lord Tennyson, he never leaves Paris, but what happens? This weekend he leaves Paris.' Another name was suggested and rejected as being a bad bridge player. I thought how fascinating it was that even the Duchess of Windsor had a problem getting the right numbers for her dinner party. I longed to say that I would come and be the spare man, but wisely refrained from so doing.

On account of the Queen's impending visit there was a lot of activity in the house. I was lucky to see it running at its full pace for perhaps the very last time. There were a number of liveried footmen moving about in the hall, there was a profusion of flowers, and from time to time Mr Utter's telephone rang and he had to attend to some drama in connection with the visit. The British Embassy rang because someone the Duchess had spoken to had told them that she had given him permission to stand in the garden and watch the Queen arrive. Mr Utter's response to this was, 'The Duchess occasionally gives the impression she has said yes, when in fact she has said no.' So that was the end of that.

At the end of our meeting he took me back into the hall and then showed me the lovely pale blue salon. I saw the library and the dining room and went out onto the terrace to see the lawn stretching ahead, all beautifully manicured. I noticed the signed photograph of the Emperor and Empress of Japan on a table. They had visited the Windsors the previous October.

I was destined to see the house many times more in the years to come, although little did I know it then. I came to appreciate the different atmospheres, the heavy glass front doors with their wrought ironwork and bright yellow curtains, the subdued golden, honeyed light of the hall, to which one's eyes gradually adjusted, then the pale blue and silver brightness of the salon. It seemed to me a perfectly formed house, set in its large garden, on the edge of the Bois de Boulogne and yet a mere twenty minutes from the bustling traffic in the heart of Paris.

Upstairs in his bedroom was the Duke, cared for by nurses, while in her room the Duchess was preparing for her day and for the significant meeting that would take place on the next one. I saw neither of them. Yet there was an undeniable air of excitement. The two secretaries were friendly to me and to each other. Mr Utter, reserved, slightly dry, diplomatic, was supportive of Miss Schütz as she grappled confidently with the problems assigned to her. I detected no tension between them and felt privileged to have been allowed a glimpse into their lives. The house seemed happy. That the Duke was unwell was not a secret, but there was no hint of his impending demise. All seemed well.

Mr Utter asked me where I was staying. I assumed he would be as impressed as I was by the Intercontinental. 'Rather brassy,' he said dismissively. Then he despatched me to the gatehouse, where Germaine Bowyer, the nice concierge, rang for a taxi for me and I was whisked back to my hotel in the midst of the French capital.

2

Death of the Duke – 1972

The Duke of Windsor had been ill since November 1971. The Queen was aware of the gravity of his condition. Messages had reached the Palace in various ways, not least from Lady Monckton and Lady Alexandra Metcalfe, both of whom were old friends of the Windsors, the former as the widow of Walter Monckton, the latter the widow of the Duke's long-term equerry 'Fruity' Metcalfe. Edward Heath, Prime Minister since June 1970, was prompted to consider the Duke of Windsor's plight by a stray letter from a twenty-four-year-old. He raised this with his Principal Private Secretary, Robert Armstrong:

> Some of us have long been worried about various aspects of the Duke of Windsor's position, especially in the evening of his life.
> There will no doubt be some who will ask why, if the Emperor of Japan was able to visit the Duke and Duchess of Windsor in their home, it is not possible for The Queen to do the same for her uncle.[1]

An opportunity for the Queen to visit the Duke came during the State Visit to Paris in May 1972 – an invitation from President Pompidou to celebrate Britain being about to join the Common Market. The visit took place between 15 and 19 May.

The Queen duly arrived in Paris, was driven in an open car with the President to the Élysée Palace, attended a glittering ballet, a banquet at Versailles, and an equestrian performance by floodlight at the Champs-de-Mars. On the Wednesday, the Queen and Prince Philip were joined by Prince Charles for a tour of the principal sites of Roman Provence, visiting Arles and staying at L'Oustau de Baumanière at Les Baux.

The Queen came to the Windsors' house after an afternoon at Longchamp on 18 May, while on her way back into Paris. She was in her coat and hat from the races, while Prince Philip wore a camel-hair overcoat and Prince Charles a light grey suit.

By then I was back at my family home in Hampshire and in time to see the TV news bulletins of the Duchess of Windsor, elegant in dark blue, coming out of the house with the Queen, Prince Philip and Prince

Charles (looking upset and mournful). The Duke of Windsor was not seen. He was too ill to appear.

Reporting of the visit was predictable. *The Times* stated: 'The usual discretion is being observed about his [the Duke's] health, but it has not been denied that he has been unwell recently.'[2] *Paris Match* noted: '*Sur le perron, la Reine serre longuement la main de la duchesse qui fait une reverence. Mais dans les yeux, la même tristesse.*'[3] The French press over-dramatised it by talking of official reconciliation, while the British press speculated about the truth behind the British Embassy's reservations over the Duke's exact state of health.

It was now public knowledge that the Duke of Windsor was a very sick man, even if it was not admitted publicly. When a journalist asked Sir Martin Charteris, the Queen's Private Secretary, about the Duke's health, Sir Martin replied: 'I know he's dying, you know he's dying, but *we don't know* he's dying.'

Over the next few days, John Utter was frequently quoted in the news-papers, denying that there was cause for concern, explaining away the arrival of Dr Antenucci*, the Duke's doctor, from New York. 'The fact is that he is feeling weak after the operation,' stated John Utter one day. 'His health is not very good,' he said on another. 'Dr Antenucci is here for a while.' As the week went on the Duke's condition was described as 'unchanged' or even 'a little better'. The French papers printed that the Duke had cancer of the throat. This was politely denied.

By 1971 the Duke of Windsor was tired – or 'fatigué' as the French put it, and which means slightly more than that. That year the Duchess and he could not go to America. The Duke put his country house, the Moulin de la Tuilerie at Gif-sur-Yvette, always called 'The Mill', up for sale, and asked Miss Schütz to find him a house in the South of France, which the Duchess had always preferred. Latterly she hated being at The Mill, though she enjoyed entertaining there. Even if the Paris house was more or less closed down, she would find an excuse to return and would soon be back in Paris, staying there and going out to see the collections at the couturiers.[4]

A prospectus was produced advertising the eighteenth-century mill, its buildings and its twenty-three acres of surrounding gardens. It was offered through Previews Incorporated, New York, with a gardeners' lodge, guest cottage, bachelors' quarters, and a barn (or Trophy Room). It was to be sold with the contents, though some items were brought

---

* Dr Arthur J. Antenucci, MD (1906–87), Chief of Medicine, Roosevelt Hospital, New York 1957–70.

back to Paris, including the map of the Duke's world travels when he had been Prince of Wales*.

In Paris all the Duke wanted to do was to stay at home each evening. During the last years he hardly even knew where he was going when he went out. He used to ask Bowyer, the chauffeur, what the plan was. The Duchess liked to go out. In a sense she did not exist unless she was seen.

Neither the Duke nor the Duchess was well in 1971. She was under some stress due to ileitis and an ulcer – a nasty form of Crohn's disease which would affect her health for the rest of her life. Henry (Hank) Walter†, their American attorney, visited them and was saddened by the Duke's obvious concern for his ailing wife. Soon it was the Duke's health that gave the graver cause for concern. On 16 November he had treatment with Dr Fleury at the American Hospital. Three days later he was visited by Dr Antenucci. On 10 December he was treated for his throat condition.

On 4 February 1972 the Duke's cousin, Lord Mountbatten, called on the Windsors and was shocked by the Duke's decline. The Duke told him that he had been having deep X-ray treatment on his throat, thought that it had worked, but was now about to have a hernia operation.

At that time a film called *The Woman I Love* and starring Faye Dunaway was being planned by an American TV company.‡ Mountbatten thought it was garnering much unfavourable publicity. He came up with the scheme that the Windsors should allow themselves to be filmed seated side by side on a sofa, reading out a statement which he, Mountbatten, had prepared repudiating the film. Wisely, Hank Walter advised against this since it would only give more publicity to the film. Even then Mountbatten told the Duke that they must have statements prepared to issue to the press if any questions were asked.

On 20 February the Duke was admitted to the American Hospital under the pseudonym of 'Mr Smith'. The Matron decided that Miss Oonagh Shanley§ should look after him. She was an Irish nurse, who had learned

---

* The Duke introduced Edmond Bory of Fauchon to Miss Schütz as someone who would help try to find a buyer. By the summer of 1972 it was being advertised in the *Wall Street Journal*. It was sold in the summer of 1973.

† Henry G. (Hank) Walter, Jr (1910–2000), the Windsors' US attorney with Fulton, Walker & Duncombe since at least the 1940s. He always came to meet them at the quayside when they arrived in the United States. He dealt with matters such as US book contracts. Member of the Board of Trustees of the American Museum of Natural History from 1972, Vice-President 1981–88; Fellow & Trustee of the Pierpont Morgan Library; Fellow-Trustee of Long Island University.

‡ *The Woman I Love* was screened on ABC-TV in December, starring Richard Chamberlain as the Duke and Faye Dunaway as the Duchess.

§ Oonagh Shanley-Toffolo (b. 1929), author of *The Voice of Silence* (Rider, 2002). In her career, she also spent four years in India as a missionary, qualified as a midwife, obtained a nursing job at the American Hospital in Paris in 1970, and later married Joseph Toffolo, a musician and singer. Many years later she became a spiritual guide and healer to Diana, Princess of Wales.

healing powers from her father and had spent twenty years in a convent before seeking papal dispensation to go out into the world to do her nursing. She met the Duke in his room in the presence of the Duchess, of Perry Culley, the Governor of the hospital, and of the Duke's French doctor, Jean Thin.

The Duke was officially in the hospital for the hernia operation, but also for exploratory work on a throat tumour near the left carotid artery. The next day he had the operation at the hands of Dr Maurice Mercadier.* This was judged completely successful. But the doctors discovered that the tumour was inoperable. It was decided that it would be too distressing to the Duke and Duchess to tell them that the Duke was unlikely to live for more than six months.

The Duke stayed in hospital, his food being prepared by his chef and brought in from his house, until 26 February when he insisted, rather prematurely, on going home. As Oonagh Shanley had got on well with him, she went with him to nurse him. At this stage the Duke was able to do a lot for himself. Miss Shanley noted that his first question each morning was 'Is the Duchess awake?' and if he was told that she was he would go through to her room in his dressing gown.[5]

Later they would have brunch together in the sitting room between their two suites, invariably having scrambled eggs with thin slices of bacon, as well as toast and tea. The Duke would then attend to his correspondence and make his usual business telephone calls. In the evening they would have dinner together and sometimes Oonagh would join them. This would be served on a small table in the library downstairs. At night, Black Diamond, the Duke's pug, used to sleep on his bed.

In due course, the Duke needed no more post-operational care and Oonagh left, promising to return if needed. On her departure on 1 March, the Duchess gave her a brooch of an ivory eyelet, with sapphire rings, rod and ovals.[6]

On 2 March the Duke began to go into the American Hospital three times a week for treatment, but otherwise he was at home, wishing to spare the Duchess from having to visit him in hospital. If he knew how ill he was, he never addressed the subject.[†] He used to tell John Utter: 'It's the treatment that is making me feel so bad.'[7]

The Duke was well enough to attend a small dinner at Paul-Louis Weiller's[‡] house in the rue de la Faisanderie on 21 April at which his

---

* Maurice Mercadier (1917–2002), Chief of Surgery at the American Hospital in Paris.
† Dr Thin is on record as saying that by February 1972: 'He was clearly a dying man and knew it.' [Bloch, *The Secret File of the Duke of Windsor*, p. 301].
‡ Commandant Paul-Louis Weiller (1893–1993), First World War aviator, immensely rich Alsatian businessman, who housed the Windsors at 85, rue de la Faisanderie in Paris from 1948–53.

friend, Jean-Louis de Maigret, who painted well, was present. Dr Antenucci came over from New York to see the Duke on 29 April, and on 12 May there was a last joint dinner party – for ten people at the house. Lady Mosley recalled that the Duke 'went on coming down to dinner even though he could hardly speak and either barked or whispered.'[8] At the time she wrote: 'The last time we saw him his poor voice had almost gone & he looked so ill & made one feel miserably sad – yet *he* was marvellous & making jokes & interested in everything that's happening in the world, without a thought of himself.'[9]

By this time, a mere five weeks after she had left, Oonagh was back on duty at the house. She was saddened by what she saw. The duke was 'thinner, weaker, his voice hoarser.'[10] He underwent coughing spasms and suffered from fever, but all he ever wanted to know was if he would be well enough to dine with the Duchess. Likewise he wanted her to remain social, to entertain her friends and, above all, not to worry about him.

On the evening of 10 May Oonagh had the evening off. She returned at midnight and looked in on the Duke. She found him very agitated and then he suddenly suffered a total cardiac collapse. She injected cortisone into him and massaged his heart. His French physician, Dr Jean Thin, was summoned and the following day Dr Françoise Jacquin installed an intravenous drip. The Duke was aware that he had nearly died, but did not want the Duchess to be told of the heart attack.

By then the Duke was confined to his room. Diana Mosley wrote: 'We were invited to dinner on the eve of the Queen's visit to France & that night he was too ill to come down. I can't tell you how sad that was, one realised it must be terribly serious.'[11]

Throughout May daily bulletins concerning the Duke's health were sent to Buckingham Palace because if the Duke died, the State Visit would have to be postponed. Therefore the Queen Mother was aware how ill the Duke was, but made no attempt to contact him, just as she had not visited him at the London Clinic in 1965.

Dr Thin revealed later that he was summoned by the British Ambassador, Sir Christopher Soames, to be told that the State Visit was of enormous political importance. Bluntly, the Duke could die before it or after it, but preferably not during it. The Ambassador said 'it would be politically disastrous' if the Duke died during the visit.[12] Dr Thin succeeded in keeping him alive long enough for the visit of his niece, of whom he was fond. Each day during the State Visit, the British Ambassador telephoned Dr Thin to enquire: 'And how is our friend today?'[13]

The Duke's incentive to live was fuelled by his determination to see his niece, the Queen. He kept asking Oonagh how many days it was until they came. During the week of the Queen's visit, his condition remained stable.

On 18 May, the Thursday of the State Visit, the Queen went racing at Longchamp, her first ever visit to that course. On her way back, at 4.45 p.m., she called at the house in the Bois. With her were the Duke of Edinburgh and Prince Charles, the Duchess of Grafton (the Mistress of the Robes) and Sir Martin Charteris, her Private Secretary. The house had been filled with orchids and looked as festive as possible. The Duchess received her visitors and they had tea downstairs in the library. Sir Martin later recalled that the Duchess sat beneath her 1939 portrait by Gerald Brockhurst, looking hardly a day older than she had in the picture, thirty-three years before, and they talked about 'anything and everything except the one thing on everyone's mind – the poor man dying upstairs.'[14] Tea went well except that the Duchess's pugs were in evidence and jumping up, something of which the Queen did not much approve.[15]

Then the Duchess took the Queen upstairs to see the Duke. He had insisted on being dressed to receive his niece. As he pointed out, she was also his Queen, and he did not intend to receive her in his pyjamas. He was still on the intravenous drip. Dr Jacquin succeeded in keeping the apparatus well concealed behind the chair in which he was sitting.

As so often happens, the versions of the witnesses conflict. The correct one is that the Duke was seated in the yellow chair, with the medical equipment concealed behind it. The Duchess brought the Queen up and left her with the Duke. When the Queen came in, he made a great effort and rose from the chair to bow to his sovereign before kissing her on both cheeks. When the Queen asked him how he was, he replied: 'Not so bad.'[16] It was a short meeting and presently the Queen went down again. The royal party left.

Approved press photographers and news cameras were waiting outside as the Duchess led the Queen, the Duke of Edinburgh and the Prince of Wales out onto the steps. Photographs were taken. Georges Sanègre, the butler, stood to the left, and John Utter was also on hand to say goodbye. The Duchess waved as the royal cars departed.

Thus the world learned that the Duke of Windsor was dying. 'THE QUEEN VISITS SICK DUKE' was one headline. 'He was too ill to see his Duchess greet the Queen' said another.[17] The next day the Queen returned to Britain.

That night the Duke's black pug, Diamond, was restless and did not want to stay with the Duke, which he found upsetting.

*   *   *

During this time, as previously recorded, the Duchess had her friend Mrs Gardner staying with her. On the Saturday evening (20 May) there was to be the dinner party for her at which the Duke would not be present.

Earlier that day Dr Henry Shaw, an ear, nose and throat specialist,* visited the Duke, called in by their friend, Robin Beare† (who was also present) on the recommendation of Lady Monckton, in the hope that something could be done to help the Duke. When Dr Shaw arrived in Paris on the Saturday before the Duke's death, the first thing the Duchess said to him was: 'Would you like a bull shot?' He was obliged to drink two bull shots and eat a full and formal lunch before he could get near the Duke. He did not like the Duchess, describing her later as 'just a typical, rich, hard American'.

Dr Shaw went upstairs and found the Duke in the hands of Oonagh Shanley, an 'extraordinary Irish nurse, who had him completely in her spell', treating him with the care that might be given to a baby. Shaw observed the Duke and thought him 'pathetic, with huge childlike blue eyes staring at me from this old beaten-up frame of a body.' During the visit, Dr Shaw had to use the washbasin, but found that he could not turn off the gold taps because of their design. So the basin nearly over-flowed while they were talking. Oonagh intervened: 'Oh! Look now. They turn off this way. See.' The Duke said he was uncomfortable. After a few tests, it was clear to Dr Shaw that he was riddled with cancer and had no hope of surviving. All he could advise was: 'Just keep on with the treatment.'

Dr Shaw got the impression that the Duchess hardly ever went in to see the Duke. Later he resented not having been paid, nor receiving any thanks from the Duchess.[18] The reason was that the Duchess had not asked him to come. He had come at Lady Monckton's behest. It cost him the fare over and a day away from home.

The Duke gradually declined during his last week, though he still attempted to get up. On Tuesday (23 May) there was a dinner party for twelve at the house. In order to be on hand when the time came, John

---

* Dr Henry Jagoe Shaw (1922–2007), leading head and neck surgeon, and otolaryngologist; devoted his professional life to the care of those suffering from cancer of the head and neck, serving as consultant ENT surgeon at the RNTNE Hospital, and with a consultancy at the Royal Marsden.
† Robin Beare (1922–2007), Consultant Plastic Surgeon, St Mary's Hospital, London, and to the Plastic and Jaw Injuries Centre, Queen Victoria Hospital, East Grinstead (working with Sir Archibald McIndoe). A junior scholar at Radley, he joined RAF Bomber Command in 1940, and was shot down in World War II (Prisoner of War 1941–5). He and his wife became friends with the Windsors and stayed with them at The Mill. The Duchess consulted him on plastic surgery matters. He retired in 1986.

Utter moved into the house. He was frequently questioned by the press and conveyed vaguely reassuring messages which gave nothing away. Only on Friday, 26 May, did the Duke not try to leave his bed. That evening his temperature soared and he became delirious.

Dr Thin came to see the Duke every evening, noting that once the Duke had achieved the visit from the Queen, he sank rapidly. Usually Black Diamond, the Duke's pug, allowed the doctor to examine his master without moving. But on 27 May the doctor came in to find that the pug had left the Duke's bed and was sitting by himself on the floor near the bed, 'thus letting me know that the end was near'.[19]

Oonagh continued to care for the Duke. She noted that during those last days, the question of having been denied a 'worthwhile job' and the issue of the Duchess's title still played on his mind. According to Oonagh, in contradiction to Dr Thin, on the Friday evening Black Diamond came back to him. The Duchess spent some time with him on the Saturday, the last day of his life, and he continued to claim he was 'not too bad'.

On Sunday morning, 28 May, at 2.30 a.m. the Duke died peacefully, with Nurses Shanley and de Brun* on duty. As Oonagh put it: 'We witnessed the sight of relief and look of peace that descended upon him: he was home at last.'[20] The Duchess was awoken and came in to see the Duke in death. Oonagh thought that as Giselle Deberry, her maid, took her back to her room, 'she looked an old lady – though a proud one.'[21]

During the next days the newspapers, television and radio were filled with examinations of the life of the Duke, reassessments of the Abdication, and accounts of the Duke's life in exile.

Sir Charles Petrie made the point that at the time of the Abdication crisis there had been no objection to Mrs Simpson as a foreigner nor as a commoner. The objection was that she had previously been twice married. He told of Mrs Simpson's offer of withdrawal, but added: 'It was, however, at once clear that the King preferred abdication to the renunciation of Mrs Simpson.'[22]

Following the Duke's death, various distinguished figures called at the house in Paris, which was surrounded by the media for several days. King Umberto of Italy could be seen leaving in his car. The Mayor of Neuilly, Achille Peretti (who was also President of the National Assembly) was soon followed by Maurice Schumann, then Minister of Foreign Affairs, who had been a young reporter at the wedding of the Duke and Duchess in 1937.

Another who paid his respects was Gaston Palewski. Nancy Mitford

---

* Oonagh said the other nurse was 'Julie Chattard, from Baltimore.'

wrote to Kitty Mersey: 'Colonel went to see the Duke's body & came away very low – for one thing he loved him, & he says the Duke looks so worried. I've never seen a dead person but I know they generally look peaceful.' She also noted that her sister Diana Mosley was concerned that the Duchess had nobody to turn to – no intimate friends.[23]

Another inevitable visitor to the house was Mr Kenyon, the undertaker. He was irritated to find that the French police insisted on a gendarme being present at the embalming of the body.[24]

On the Wednesday, 31 May, the Duke's coffin left the house in the Bois for the last time. It was stated that the Duchess of Windsor was not well enough to accompany it. She witnessed it leave the house in Paris – with Paul-Louis Weiller hovering at her side. John Utter accompanied it to the airport at Le Bourget.

Arrangements for the Duke's funeral had been agreed between the Queen and the Duke of Windsor since as far back as 1961 and confirmed in private memoranda held at the Palace and Foreign Office since May 1962. Once the Duke died, the Queen's Private Secretary would inform the Prime Minister, the Lord Chamberlain, the Home Office, the Foreign Office, the Commonwealth Relations Office, and the Air Ministry. He would discuss a suitable date for the funeral with the Lord Chamberlain and the Duchess of Windsor. The Queen would offer an aircraft of The Queen's Flight to bring the Duchess over from Europe, or an RAF plane if she was in the United States*.[25]

In accordance with these long-laid plans, the coffin was flown to RAF Benson in an RAF VC-10. There were four hundred men on parade when it arrived, and the Central Band of the RAF. It was met by the Duke and Duchess of Kent, Lord Jellicoe and Lord Lambton (two ministers acting on behalf of the Government whose names were to be linked in a sex scandal that caused them both to resign a year later), Geoffroy de Courcel (the French Ambassador to Britain), Sir Denis Spotswood (Chief of the Air Staff), Sir Eric Penn (Comptroller of the Lord Chamberlain's Office) and others.

The Duke's coffin remained overnight at RAF Benson and early the next morning was driven to Windsor, arriving at seven a.m. to lie in the Albert Memorial Chapel in advance of the Lying-in-State.

One evening that week, at dinner at The Mitre, Hampton Court, I overheard a man at another table commenting that it was odd that nobody was wearing a black tie for the Duke of Windsor. He recalled that everyone had done so when the late King had died. I was wearing one.

* It was noted that the Duchess might prefer to travel by sea.

3

The Lying-in-State & Funeral – 1972

A clever photograph was taken of the Lying-in-State at Windsor. It showed the Duke's catafalque in the middle of the empty Nave of St George's Chapel, as seen from across the tomb of King George V and Queen Mary – the parents with whom he had so often been at odds.

As a new Lay Steward of St George's Chapel, I was on duty for many hours during the Duke's Lying-in-State, which took place throughout Friday 2 and Saturday 3 June.

My abiding memory of this is the atmosphere of solemnity and sadness. The queues stretched for miles down the hill and those that wished to pay their respects had to wait patiently in line for hours. One old soldier, looking reserved and stiff, surreptitiously dropped some flowers as he passed the catafalque. He wanted to pay this tribute, but he did not want to be seen doing it, for fear he might be thought sentimental. For one of my watches I was on the North Door through which came the disabled in wheelchairs. Many were intensely moved. Particularly harrowing was one lady who called out: 'My prince!' in a state of great emotion.

Whatever the media said, it was clear that for those who came to pay their respects their affection was undimmed. During those two days at Windsor, it was the young, charming Prince of Wales who was being remembered, not the Duke of Windsor who had deserted his subjects to take the supposed path of happiness.

Famous figures came to the chapel. Harold Wilson, then Leader of the Opposition, was one, Baroness Spencer-Churchill another.

Lord Mountbatten had been busy since he had heard the news of the Duke's death in a telephone call from Sir Eric Penn the previous Sunday morning. In his diary he recorded that the Queen asked him to help her with the Duchess since he was the only member of the family who really knew her. He noted that she was worried that Trooping the Colour would have to be cancelled and he took credit for thinking up the idea of a tribute to the Duke on the Parade Ground. 'She thought this a wonderful idea and said she would follow it up.'[1]

Then he was asked to do a tribute by the BBC and argued to Sir Martin Charteris that Presidents Nixon and Pompidou had given tributes to the Duke but there had been silence from the British Royal Family. The Queen gave her permission 'provided I spoke about him in a balanced way.'[2] There was then some doubt about whether the Duchess would be well enough to attend the funeral. She was in a state of shock after the Duke's death, for which she had not been prepared, and she was understandably nervous at the prospect of staying with the Royal Family, though she wanted to be at the funeral. Mountbatten was determined that she should come 'as she herself would be miserable if she missed the funeral, and the result on public opinion here would be disastrous.'[3]

Lord Mountbatten went to the Lying-in-State on his way to the airport to greet the Duchess of Windsor. He left a wreath with an exaggerated message: 'In happy memory of 53 years of friendship from his sorrowing but most devoted friend – Dickie'.

The Duchess overcame her fear of flying to arrive in Britain for the funeral. She travelled in an Andover of The Queen's Flight, accompanied by Lady Soames, wife of the British Ambassador in Paris, Grace, Countess of Dudley (widow of one of the Duke's oldest friends), Brigadier Douglas Greenacre (a former equerry to the Duke), and by John Utter, Dr Antenucci and her maid, Giselle Deberry. Monsieur Alexandre*, the famous Paris hairdresser, also went to London to ensure that the Duchess's hair was perfectly coiffed at all times. The Duchess was immensely elegant in black, with a small veil on her auburn hair. Mountbatten took her to Buckingham Palace in a royal Rolls-Royce, and told her about the Lying-in-State.

When Mountbatten met the Duchess at the airport, he found that she was nervous about having to confront the whole Royal Family and in particular the Queen Mother. He assured her that the Queen Mother was deeply sorry for her in her present grief. When he mentioned his proposed BBC tribute, he said he would have to say how much he had disapproved of the Abdication. She said: 'You are quite right. I disapproved of it too. I spent a long time over a bad telephone line from France begging him not to abdicate. I went so far as to say if he abdicated I wouldn't marry him.'[4]

The Duchess was shown to her suite of rooms on the first floor of Buckingham Palace, overlooking the Mall and the Queen Victoria memorial.† She lunched with the Queen in the Chinese Dining Room.

---

* Alexandre Raimon (1922–2008), first sent to the Duchess at the Chateau de la Cröe by Mme. David-Weill in the 1940s. Presently he took over doing the Duchess's hair from Antonio.
† These are the main guest rooms of the Palace. Prince Philip's mother, Princess Andrew of Greece, lived in them for two years from 1967 until her death there in December 1969.

John Utter was surprised to be placed on the Queen's right. Later he would tell his friends how immensely kind the Queen was to the Duchess during these difficult days. She said to the Duchess that she could come to the Palace or Windsor, stay as long as she liked, and that no demands would be made on her. The Duchess told Sir Martin Charteris: 'He gave up so much for so little.'[5]

That evening the Duchess had dinner with the Queen and Prince Charles, the Prince noting that she 'prattled away', so that he was not sure if it was 'a brilliant façade' or whether she was under such strain that she did not notice that the Duke had died.[6] Afterwards other members of the Royal Family joined them to watch Lord Mountbatten pay his tribute to the Duke of Windsor on television.

The following day was the Queen's Official Birthday. I was lucky to have been given tickets for Trooping the Colour, which this year included a roll of drums followed by a minute's silence, a further roll of drums and a lament – 'The Flowers of the Forest' – played by pipers of the Scots Guards in memory of the Duke. In those days the Queen still rode in the Parade, this time wearing a mourning band on her left arm. All members of the Royal Family were in black. A famous photograph was taken of the Duchess of Windsor looking out of her suite of rooms at the Palace as the procession returned. Much has been made of the sorrow on the Duchess's brow. This might have been deceptive. She was waiting for a telephone call from her banker in Switzerland.

Meanwhile the Royal Family appeared on the balcony, among them Prince William of Gloucester, soon to die in an air crash taking part in a race.

In the afternoon the Royal Family went down to Windsor, leaving the Duchess at the Palace. The Queen, Prince Philip and Princess Anne visited the Lying-in-State, entering the chapel via the Deanery.

Following the Trooping, I too made my way to Windsor for my last duty at the Lying-in-State in the afternoon. In due course the last of the 57,903 members of the public had filed past and the doors of the chapel were closed. I was still in the cloisters in Canon Verney's house when, late that evening, the Duchess, along with John Utter, was met by Prince Charles and Lord Mountbatten and witnessed the Lying-in-State. This part I did not see, as we were told by Admiral Davies, a Lay Steward and Warden of St George's House: 'This really must be private.' He himself was going to be there, of course.

Prince Charles walked down from the hill to St George's Chapel and Lord Mountbatten arrived by car. They were both there by the time the Duchess arrived from the Palace with her party, also including

Grace Dudley. The Duchess told Mountbatten that she was feeling 'very ill and sad' but went and stood at the head of the coffin for a few moments. She and Mountbatten then walked all round the Nave. Finally she took one last glance at the coffin and said: 'He was my entire life. I can't begin to think what I am going to do without him, he gave up so much for me and now he has gone. I always hoped I would die before him.'[7]

Then they walked round the Cloisters and looked at the wreaths. The Duchess came and went, but I did not see her. Some months later, John Utter said he wished I had been there – to help identify all the various wreaths from the foreign royal houses, from Prince Louis Ferdinand of Prussia and others.

On the following day John Utter replied to a great many letters and sent thanks for wreaths, all written on black-bordered Buckingham Palace writing paper.* The Duchess stayed quietly at the Palace. She was visited by Sir Eric Penn to be briefed about the plans for Monday. Evidently confused, she appeared not to remember having seen the Lying-in-State.

The Duke of Windsor's Funeral

My diary entry for Monday 5 June was slight, but made one significant point: 'Funeral of the Duke of Windsor. Deputed to meet the Duchess's secretary. V. Impressive ceremony. Long talk to her, re-invited to Paris. Back to London with crown on car . . . Watched *A King's Story*.'

I had been disappointed not to have been summoned for duty at the Duke's funeral but, on the Sunday before it, the call came to say they needed an extra Lay Steward. In order to be able to enter the castle I was to collect a black crown for my car from John Handcock, another Lay Steward, which would enable me to park in the castle car park. This was attached to the windscreen.[†]

Suitably attired in morning dress, I took my place at the briefing of the Queen's Gentlemen Ushers and the Lay Stewards, which took place in the South Quire Aisle. In those days the Gentlemen Ushers were terrifying figures – generals and air marshals, vice-admirals and colonels. In particular I remember General Sir Rodney Moore, an Osbert Lancaster

---

* A fair amount of this paper was taken back to Paris and sold in the Duchess's sale in New York in 1997. Grace Dudley also took the opportunity to write a number of letters to her friends, who did not fail to get the point.
† Many years later I was given a red one, as royal representative to Prince Michael of Kent at a memorial service.

version of a general, with a bristling white moustache. On other occasions he could be seen arriving at Smith's Lawn for the polo in an enormous old-fashioned Rolls-Royce, with a formidable-looking wife seated beside him. They were a daunting bunch.

Sir Eric Penn was issuing instructions and among the things he mentioned was that at the last moment the Duchess's secretary and some of the staff from Paris were coming over for the service. 'The trouble is,' he said, 'none of us know her or what she looks like.' I mentioned to the man next to me that I had met Miss Schütz and before I knew what was happening I was in the midst of that fearsome group and was instructed to look after her.

Sir Rodney Moore, forty-six years my senior, was intrigued to know how I knew her. He boomed at me: 'How did you manage that, old boy?'[8] After that, a more restrained Gentleman Usher, Air Marshal Sir Maurice Heath, overseeing proceedings in the Nave, took me under his wing.

So I spent the entire time before the service at the South Door and thus witnessed the arrival of all the invited mourners – Edward Heath (the Prime Minister), Harold Wilson (Leader of the Opposition), the Earl and Countess of Avon, the Duke and Duchess of Buccleuch, Lord Brownlow (who had accompanied Mrs Simpson on her dramatic drive to the South of France in 1936), now frail and leaning on a stick, accompanied by his wife, and other figures from the Abdication saga. Lady Diana Cooper came in with Cecil Beaton. They were placed in the Nave, but Lady Diana did not like their seats and nudged them both into seats closer to the central aisle.

Meanwhile, the Duchess arrived at Windsor via Frogmore Gate, with Grace Dudley sitting next to her. She was driven to the Deanery in Windsor Castle where Lord Mountbatten was again on hand to introduce her to all the Royal Family in turn. The royal ladies then took their places in the Quire, and the funeral procession made its way down the north aisles of the chapel to the Great West Door.

Miss Schütz herself did not arrive at the beginning of the service. Her plane was grounded in one of those summer smogs at the airport in France. So she only arrived after the service had begun, by which time we Lay Stewards were lined up at the back of the Nave.

From that position we saw the coffin come round the corner, past the tomb of King George V and Queen Mary. It was duly carried the full length of the Nave, followed by the Duke of Edinburgh walking with King Olav of Norway, the Prince of Wales alone, Princes William and Richard of Gloucester, the Duke of Kent with Prince Michael, and Lord Mountbatten with the Duke of Beaufort.

The service itself took place in the Quire. There came the historic moment when Garter King of Arms called out the styles and title of the Duke – ending with the words 'sometime the Most High, Most Mighty, and Most Excellent Monarch, Edward the Eighth, Emperor of India, Defender of the Faith . . . and uncle of the Most High, Most Mighty and Most Excellent Monarch, Queen Elizabeth whom God bless . . .' It was a reminder that it was one of Britain's Kings who was being laid to rest.

The most perceptive account of all this was written by Cecil Beaton. He had been reluctant to attend and only did so in order to describe it in his diary.* He summed it up as follows:

The service was short, and entirely noble. It even gave a departed nobility to a young man who once had such charm that everyone considered he was the ideal choice. But he lived on to keep his charm and little else, and one wondered how lucky we all were that even for such an unsuitable reason as the hard, brash and wise-cracking American, he had stepped down to make way for the Queen Mother, and now the very admirable and remarkable Queen.

Wonderful as the service was, I was not moved by the death of this man who for less than a year had been our King. History will make his love story into a romance. In fact, for us so close, it is hard to see that. Wallis has been a good friend to me, I like her. She is a good friend to all her friends. There is no malice in her. There is nothing dislikeable. She is just not of the degree that has reason to be around the Throne.

During these days of death, she has behaved with extreme dignity. She has by the simplicity of her silhouette made the rest of the Royal Family appear dowdier than ever, but she made me marvel once again that she should ever have become a figure in such a drama.[9]

During the service the Duchess appeared lost and wore a 'frown of worry and distraught bewilderment'. This confirmed the rumours that Cecil Beaton had heard from French friends that she was unwell. Lady Avon, seated directly behind the Duchess, told him that throughout the service, 'the Queen showed a motherly and nanny-like tenderness and kept putting her hand on the Duchess's arm and glove.'[10]

---

* For the full account, see Hugo Vickers (ed.), *The Unexpurgated Beaton* (Weidenfeld & Nicolson, 2002), pp. 254–7.

When the service ended, the Royal Family all left by the North Quire Aisle. I therefore saw a number of royal ladies pass by the coffin (which remained in its place in front of the High Altar). One of these was the Duchess. I cannot even be quite certain which one she was. Having seen innumerable photographs since, I can of course picture her in my mind, with her thick black-crêpe widow's veil. She was the only mourner who was heavily veiled that day.

After the service I found Miss Schütz, elegant in one of those smart black coats with large black buttons, and took her to see the coffin, along with the flowers outside on the lawns of the castle. I obtained a service sheet for her, and finally reunited her with Dr Antenucci in the Chapter Office in the cloisters. 'It's so sad for the Duchess,' she said.

My brief diary entry reminds me that she also said that I should come and see them again in Paris next time I was there. I now realise that this was just a courteous remark but I took it as a golden invitation – the green light to visit them again – and it was not long before I made a considerable detour in order to do so. Had I not done so, I would not have been able to write this book.

Only now, nearly forty years later, have I seen all the documentation for the Lying-in-State and funeral. The Duchess of Windsor sat between the Queen and Prince Philip. Next to them sat King Olav of Norway and then the Queen Mother. Those located in the Quire were largely members of the Royal Family, Cabinet ministers, senior representatives from the armed forces, the county, figures such as Harold Macmillan and Knights of the Garter – the Duke of Norfolk, the Earl of Avon, Sir Gerald Templer and Viscount Cobham – and their wives. Many of these would have had little if any personal contact with the Duke himself but were there for formal reasons*.

There were some figures from the Windsors' past: Sir John Aird, Sir Ulick Alexander, and Commander Colin Buist. Of friends, it was interesting to find Mr & Mrs Loel Guinness, Frances Munn-Baker, M. & Mme Bory (to the annoyance of the grand French since M. Bory owned Fauchon and they deemed him a grocer), and Reinhard Henschel†; of their staff there was Georges, (the butler), Gregorio Martin (the chauffeur), Lucien Massy (the chef), Henry Bertrand, Sydney Johnson (the valet), and of their lawyers, Sir Godfrey and

* See pages 383–7.
† Reinhard Henschel, German diplomat, anti-Nazi, Consul in Turkey during the war, and later based in Mexico running the family business concerned with diesel engines and lorries.

Lady Morley*, and Senateur Jacques Rosselli. Places were reserved for Dr Thin and Miss Schütz, and the household apothecary and a nursing sister were in the vestry throughout the service in case they were needed.

There was no mention of Maître Suzanne Blum, the Windsors' Paris lawyer. She was not on the list.

After the funeral there was a lunch for the Royal Family in the Castle. One member of the Royal Family was surprised when the Queen, speaking of the Duchess, said 'It's so difficult, because she hardly knows anyone.'[11] Lord Mountbatten looked after her, sitting next to the Duchess on the sofa before lunch. She kept saying 'how wonderful the family were being to her and how much better the whole thing had gone than she had expected.'[12] At the lunch itself she sat at a table between the Duke of Edinburgh and Lord Mountbatten.

On her return to Paris, the Duke's old friend, Walter Lees,† was one of the first to come to dinner with her.

'Wasn't that the most fine service?' she asked. He nodded, though he hadn't been there. She then told him that she was horrified by Prince Philip. He turned to her at the lunch and asked: 'Well, what are your plans? You going back to America, then?' She felt like saying 'Why should I?' In the end she said to him: 'I won't be coming back to England if that's what you're afraid of, except to visit the grave.' She was determined that they [the Royal Family] were not to see her grief and amused by the way they all tucked into their puddings.[13]

Another topic discussed was the fate of the Duke's papers. Prince Philip asked the Duchess what she intended to do with them. She was keen only to do what was considered right, and asked the Duke and Mountbatten what they thought she ought to do with them, and they replied that they should come to Windsor. To this she readily agreed.[14] As a result of this, as we shall see, the librarian, Sir Robin Mackworth-Young, paid two visits to Paris to collect such papers as were handed over.

John Utter was placed next to the Queen Mother, who asked him lots of questions about the Windsors' life in Paris. He was surprised how interested she was. Utter had been nervous of her because Lady

---

* Sir Godfrey Morley (1909–87), Senior Partner of Allen & Overy from 1960 to 1975.
† Major Walter Lees, LVO, MC (1919–2010), Assistant Military Attaché at the British Embassy in Paris in the 1950s, a social figure, sometimes described as a 'bouche-trou' at Windsor dinner parties.

Brabourne (Mountbatten's elder daughter, now Countess Mountbatten of Burma) had warned him that the Queen Mother had an iron fist in a velvet glove.

The original intention had been that the Queen Mother would not go to Frogmore for the Committal. But at the last moment she decided that she would. This took place in the afternoon. The Queen stood next to the Duchess as the Duke's body was lowered into the ground. 'Where would you like to be? To his right or to his left?' she asked. The Duchess thought for a moment. She considered it unlikely that many flowers would be placed on her grave, but she spotted a plane tree. She loved the leaves of plane trees and often collected these from her garden and placed them on her dressing table. She liked the idea that the leaves would fall onto her grave in the autumn. She also thought that so often in life she had been in the Duke's shadow. So she chose the side to the left, where she would be in the shade and under the spreading branches of the plane tree.

The same afternoon, in the House of Commons in London, tributes were paid to the Duke and an address of sympathy was voted to be sent to the Queen. After extolling the Duke's virtues, especially as Prince of Wales, and briefly as a modernising King, Edward Heath, the Prime Minister, expressed the House's sadness for the Queen. He then referred to the Duchess, 'the wife for whose love King Edward was content to give up his patrimony and who has repaid his devotion with an equal loyalty, companionship and love. His death has been above all her loss and to her the House will wish to extend its profound sympathy.'[15] Harold Wilson, Leader of the Opposition, concurred:

> We welcome that the Duchess has felt able to be in Britain to hear and sense the feelings of our people, and all of us appreciate the dignity she has shown not only over those tragic days but over all the years. We hope she will feel free to come among us and freely communicate with the people her husband – Prince, King and Duke – lived to serve.[16]

An amendment was moved to include the Duchess's name in the motion of sympathy and this was agreed to '*nomine contradicente*'.

Back at Windsor, it was time for the Duchess to leave. The entire Royal Family was gathered at the steps of the Castle to say goodbye to her as she got into her car. Mountbatten was disappointed that he had not been assigned the duty of escorting the Duchess to the airport, especially as the press next day made much of the absence of a member of the Royal Family at the airport to wish her goodbye.*

The Duchess was escorted to Heathrow by Lord Maclean, the new Lord Chamberlain, and the ladies-in-waiting assigned to look after her while in London. Thus there were images of Lord Maclean not bowing, and the ladies-in-waiting shaking hands, though pointedly not curtsying.

John Utter was another who was saddened that this image was the one that endured, as it appeared to contradict the Queen's consideration and kindness during the visit. The Duchess flew back to France, arriving at Villacoublay and then being driven to her home in the Bois.

The image of the Duchess, her crêpe veil blowing gently in the wind as she mounted the aluminium steps of the Andover, with the RAF officer saluting and the Lord Chamberlain standing rigidly at the bottom of the steps, gave Frances Donaldson a romantic, not strictly accurate, but nevertheless memorable last line for her book on the Duke:

> A fraction of a second in the Duchess's life had been immobilised by the camera, but it seemed entirely final. She would not turn again, one felt, for a last look at the land her husband had given up for her and this was the ending of an episode – an episode in the history of England and in the long life of its leading family.[17]

That should have been the end of the story. How very much better it would have been for the Duchess of Windsor to have followed her husband swiftly to his grave at Frogmore.

As Oonagh Shanley, who nursed the Duke in his last days, put it:

> The years that followed the Duke's death were unspeakably lonely for the Duchess. This period could fill many pages and could be compared to Dante's vision of Hell. She was a martyr at the hands of greedy people.[18]

---

* There is an impression that this was a mistake, the Lord Chamberlain being very new to his job. It was almost certainly correct etiquette – the same would happen when a State Visitor left – but it failed dismally on the public relations front.

4

The Duchess and Her Household – 1972

The Duchess of Windsor returned to Paris to face the predicament of widowhood. She had no relations of her own and – inevitably – a dwindling number of friends. She knew she would lose some of the friends that she had shared with the Duke. Widows were often deserted. She had dropped some widows herself. She felt the world hated her and resented her designated role as the woman who had caused the Abdication. She was anxious to do nothing to upset the Royal Family.

She was not without help, but while the Duke lived he had arranged everything. Now, after his death, she had to take control. She was frequently horrified by the cost of things. A dinner in Biarritz to thank those who had looked after her struck her as horrendously expensive.* It is not surprising that she found life bewildering. She was also in a state of shock, since she had scarcely ever been apart from the Duke since their marriage in 1937. As Monsieur Martin, her chauffeur, put it: 'She missed the space he occupied.'[1]

In those early days of widowhood there were numerous letters of sympathy, written either in English or French, that required her attention. Among those she thanked personally were President Pompidou and Maurice Schumann.

This is a good moment to look at the Duchess's household, staff, legal advisers and some of the other principal characters in the story, since they all play a part in the events that follow, some with less credit than others. It was not an easy time for any of them as they adapted to life without the Duke and with the Duchess far from well.

In 1972 the Duchess was looked after by two secretaries and a large staff in her house in Paris. She had an English lawyer, Sir Godfrey Morley of Allen & Overy, the American attorney Henry G. Walter in New York, a Swiss banker, Maurice Amiguet, James Fitch, the Duke's stockbroker (with E.R. Lewis & Co) in London, and in Paris a French lawyer, Maître Suzanne Blum.

While some of these were honourable figures, others were not. There

---

* Such bills were sent to Paris for payment.

are dangers for rich widows who have a considerable amount of worldly goods, if they are in frail health and have no blood relations of their own, the more so if their affairs are handled by a dishonest lawyer and an avaricious banker and they are served by a sly butler, their health overseen by a doctor acting on the instructions of the lawyer.

In the house were the two secretaries, and at this time they ran the Duchess's establishment between them.

John Utter had held the post of the Duke's Private Secretary since July 1962. He was a former diplomat who had left the American diplomatic service during the McCarthy purges, and had been recommended to the Duke by a friend, possibly the then American Ambassador. He was a kind and honourable man, but not forceful. The Duchess never really liked him, and hardly had the Duke died than she tried to dispense with his services. Nevertheless he was to remain in his post until early in 1975.

John Ellrington Utter was born in Elviria, New York in 1905, and educated at Harvard Business School (*magna cum laude*). He took the Foreign Service exam but failed the oral part, though later he spoke perfect French and had a good knowledge of German, Spanish and Italian. He then became a banker with the National City Bank of New York, first in the US and later in Paris. He was in Paris at the time of the German invasion and underwent a gruelling time escaping through France and Spain. He finally reached New York in the spring of 1941 and immediately applied to join the State Department.

He was sent to Africa, arriving in Tangiers with three fellow recruits as Vice-Consuls. Robert Murphy, President Roosevelt's personal representative and Minister to French North Africa, placed him and Harry A. Woodruff in Tunis to prepare the political ground for the Allied landings in North Africa. At one point Utter and Woodruff were sent to Oran to retain an American consular presence there.

Many years later he appeared in a book as a spy – one of FDR's 'Twelve Apostles'*. Utter was recruited by William Eddy onto William Donovan's OSS team. A fellow diplomat, Kenneth Pendar, recalled that they were 'an oddly assorted group for such a military job', and that in Tunis John Utter was 'the bravest man in Africa; he suffered an interminable series of boils, sheer torture in that humid climate; and no one ever heard him complain.'[2] Utter was one of those who identified among the local residents and French officers those who would help the Allied cause.

A group of resistance cells was formed in Tunis and Bizette. Details of comings and goings by air, sea and land, about what the Germans and

*Hal Vaughan, *FDR'S 12 Apostles* (The Lyons Press, 2006).

Italians were up to, and other activities were obtained by spying, all of which had to be done without the knowledge of the US Consul-General, Hooker A. Doolittle, who disapproved of this activity being conducted from behind the cover of diplomatic posts. Secret transmitters were established to relay information between the various Vice-Consuls.

John Utter was jailed for five days in Tunis, following the Allied landings, but he managed to escape to Constantine, in Algiers, where he and Woodruff worked with John Boyd on Robert Murphy's staff. There he made a new friend, Captain Andrew Robb*, later well known as the cartoonist Robb of the *Daily Express*. Robb visited him at La Maison des Femmes at Sidi bou Said after his return to Tunis, and described a meeting with Prince Ali Bey†, grandson of the last Bey of Tunis, and told how when Utter gave a picnic for the young prince a procession of eight or ten Arabs arrived in advance bearing what was described as a 'little contribution' but which amounted to nothing less than a magnificent feast.[3] For many years John Utter would stay with Robb at his mews house near Hyde Park Corner when he visited London.

Utter was awarded the Medal of Merit for 'exceptionally meritorious conduct in the performance of outstanding services between June 1941 and November 1942.'[4] It was stated that he had obtained information from French patriots of inestimable value to the Allied troops. He had been instrumental in setting up a clandestine radio station in Tunis which maintained contact with Allied Headquarters in Malta and Gibraltar. 'Throughout this period of eighteen months Mr Utter performed secret missions, often at risk to his life, in opposition to the German-Italian Armistice Commission.'[5]

Utter was also an adviser to General Eisenhower at Supreme Allied Headquarters. After the war he served as First Secretary at the US Embassy in Paris from 1948 until 1952. He occupied a splendid apartment in one of the Hotels des Maréchaux at the Arc de Triomphe. Later he was Head of African Affairs at the Department of State in Washington.

Being a confirmed bachelor, he realised that his diplomatic career was under threat from Senator Joe McCarthy and he resigned from the service. In December 1958 the Duke of Windsor discovered that his then Private Secretary, Victor Waddilove, who was based in an office in Buckingham Palace, had been embezzling his money. A prolonged series of negotiations followed, conducted by Walter Monckton, as a result of which, Waddilove (or 'Mr Light Fingers' as the Duchess now referred to him)

---

*Andrew Robb (1907–89) undertook fashion drawings and other illustrations for the *Daily Express*.
† Prince Ali Bey (1915–45), eldest son of Husayn En-Nasr, King of the Tunisians for a day in 1957, and grandson of Muhammad Al-Amin, Bey of Tunis 1942–57. Prince Ali died young of haemophilia.

was paid off, and the Duke decided to run his affairs from Paris instead. Some years later John Utter was recommended to the Windsors, and he brought the benefit of his banking and diplomatic experience to the job. Waddilove left in 1959, and Utter began work with the Windsors on 24 July 1962, his contract being finally signed by the Windsors on 9 November and witnessed by Sir Godfrey Morley. His salary was 2,000 new francs, and rose to 4,175 in 1973.

Needless to say, I knew none of this at the time I met him and nor did the Duchess of Windsor's personal secretary, Johanna Schütz, who shared an office with him for several years. He never spoke of his earlier career.

Mindful of what I took to be my golden invitation to revisit the Windsors' house next time I was in Paris, I flew in specially for an afternoon, from a holiday in the South of France, to have my *Burke's Guide to the Royal Family* article checked. It was Monday, 17 July, about five weeks after the Duke's funeral.

I do not think the Duchess was at home that day, but the office was a hive of activity as Mr Utter, Miss Schütz and others were busy answering the mass of letters of sympathy that had poured into the house since the Duke's death. A little printed card was being sent out to members of the general public to thank them for their messages of sympathy. If these were sent to friends, the Duchess sometimes added a few handwritten words of her own.

Mr Utter gave me iced tea on the terrace and we sat there for a while in the beautiful afternoon sunshine as he looked through my work.

Before my next visit to Paris in September, John Utter rang me in London and invited me for dinner. I was rather nervous before I went, being young and unsure as to what had inspired this invitation. But I need not have worried. On the evening of Sunday, 17 September I went to his small apartment at 16 quai de Béthune on the Île St Louis and he took me for a delicious dinner at a local restaurant.

This was the first time Mr Utter talked to me of the Windsors as real people, and they began to come alive for me in a wholly different way. He told me about the funeral and how kind the Queen had been to the Duchess. She had told her that she could come to Buckingham Palace or Windsor Castle and stay for as long as she liked, that she did not have to do anything she did not want to do. The strong implication was that both sides were keen to behave as well as possible in a situation that was difficult for both of them. The Queen hardly knew the Duchess.

He spoke of the Duke, how the people he most respected were tycoons and golfing professionals. He told me that on one occasion in 1966 the

Duke had called down and asked him to come up. He found the Duke in the study part of his room, enveloped in clouds of smoke from his pipe. The Duke had two bits of bad news. The first was a letter from his sister-in-law, the Duchess of Gloucester, telling him that his younger brother, the Duke of Gloucester, had suffered a bad stroke. The second was that Monsieur Boudin of Jansen was downstairs in the hall with the Duchess, proposing some expensive improvements. The Duke dreaded the cost.

John Utter said that the Duchess often varied her stories, saying whatever was in her mind at any given point. She was a typical Gemini. He had heard her relate stories that he had told about himself as if they had happened to her. He explained that her self-perception was as the heroine of *Rebecca of Sunnybrook Farm**.

John also talked of how Sir Martin Charteris, the Queen's Private Secretary, had suggested that he should write a memoir or some notes about the Windsors, which could be placed in the Royal Archives. Sir Martin told him that he could place an embargo date on this and it would be respected. But John was not keen on the idea. One of his often repeated lines was: 'They'll hate you if you destroy the myth.' He said that when the Windsors were alone at The Mill without guests, they would go through after dinner and a decanter of whisky would be brought in. They were not tired enough to go to bed but they had nothing to say to each other, so the contents of the decanter just went slowly down, down, down.

There were stories of the Duchess pressing her panic button and summoning the police in the night. She worried about security, despite the presence of a nightwatchman, cages on the windows, and four red panic buttons – one in the Duke's room, one in hers, one in Georges's room and one in the pantry. These buttons summoned the police. In these years of widowhood, the Duchess frequently pressed hers, though would never admit to having done so. The police then came, but charged for an unnecessary summons. They used to say they had never seen a more secure house. John Utter warned the Duchess that if she pressed the button too often it would become a 'cry wolf' situation. The Duchess

---

* *Rebecca of Sunnybrook Farm* by Kate Douglas Wiggin (1903) was a popular book amongst young American girls. The story concerns a girl whose father died when she was young, and who, in consequence, went to stay with a pair of stern aunts. They teach her to be a smart young lady, and she brightens the life of one of the aunts with her liveliness and curiosity. She tries to win over the other aunt, but finds her more resistant. Rebecca studies well and is sent to high school, maturing into a young lady, while retaining her high spirits and showing talent as a writer. Her mother falls ill and she nurses her. One of the aunts bequeaths Sunnybrook Farm to her and she sells it to a railway company. The novel ends with her becoming independent and in a position to help her siblings. I can see how the Duchess might have adopted her as a role model.

remained nervous, though, and used to say she never slept for fear that the nightwatchman might be asleep himself.[6]

He told me that the press had questioned the Duchess's use of the royal ducal coronet on the little card she sent out to those who wrote her sympathy letters, but by the end of 1972 the College of Arms had agreed that she was entitled to use a Royal Duchess's coronet.

John brought the Windsors to life in these stories, painting a picture of how they spent their time. A few days later I received a letter from him: 'It was so nice seeing you again, and I hope that you will come back often to Paris.'[7] So, my original misunderstanding of the 'golden invitation' had suddenly become the true state of affairs, and from that time on I always got in touch with John when I went to Paris, paid several more visits to the house in the Bois, and visited his country house at Osmoy three times.

Some years later he became yet more informative. He told me about the Duke's papers going to Windsor, how tiresome Lord Mountbatten was and how Winston Guest had tried to get his hands on some of the Duke's possessions. He spoke of how he sometimes berated the Windsors for going out too much. The Duchess was tired after a fortnight of parties. John said: 'You should only go out three nights a week.' The Duke looked up from behind his paper and said: 'Hear, hear.'[8]

Working with John was Johanna Schütz, the Duchess's personal secretary since 1 September 1970. She was then twenty-seven, vivacious and multilingual. When seen together, she and John Utter gave the impression that they were on excellent terms, and in the summer of 1973 I was present at a lunch at Osmoy when Johanna and her mother, and another friend of hers, were fellow guests. Later, perhaps, tensions increased as the Duchess became increasingly ill, culminating in John's 'retirement' in 1975, at which point Johanna was in sole control in the office for some three years.

John Utter said that in order for the Windsors to employ Johanna, Françoise Jacquet, the French secretary, had to be dismissed. The Duke used to write out his letters in longhand on yellow pads. Mlle. Jacquet would type them triple-spaced and he would correct them. She would then type a final copy. While John was in Wigan having his hip operated on, she was sacked on the grounds that she could not take shorthand. Mlle. Jacquet complained and the Duke called in lawyers. He was advised that a sum between $1,000 to $1,500 would be appropriate. The Ministère de Travail said something similar. So the Duke called in René de Chambrun, the husband of José Laval (Pierre Laval's daughter). He said that more should be paid, so the Duke hid his letter and eventually made a settlement.

John Utter said the Duke liked to talk German and Spanish ('*Usted habla la lengua de Cervantes*'). He often spoke German with Johanna Schütz though was careful not to do so when the Duchess was around.

I never had the chance in the 1970s to talk to Johanna for more than a few minutes about the Windsors but later she related her experiences, again bringing them to life vividly.

Johanna first met the Duke and Duchess in Portugal in 1968, when they stayed with the Patinos for whom her sister worked. The Duke wanted her to come and be his secretary, calling her once a month. Finally she and her sister went together to see them in Paris, Johanna wearing a short Courrèges skirt and even a short-haired wig. The Duchess encouraged the Duke to employ her, perhaps thinking that Johanna would add youthful sparkle to the house. She was offered the job.

Johanna Schütz spoke six languages – German, French, English, Spanish, Portuguese and Italian. She had been brought up by her father to count on a good education but to expect no further financial help. 'We are going to spend it,' he said. Her father had died in 1968. Meanwhile she had travelled the world and worked as a secretary at the Guatemalan Embassy in Switzerland from 1963 to 1968, fulfilling numerous roles including translating documents into Spanish, before taking a job preparing reports for scientific projects at Nestlé in La Tour de Peilz for a year.

When Johanna accepted the job with the Windsors she made it clear that she would take holidays. She knew what she wanted in life. She did not want a career or commitments, or marriage, children or security. Her aim in life was to explore the world, learning about different civilisations. She loved music and sport. She did not particularly want to do secretarial work, although she was very good at it, but one of the reasons she agreed to work for the Windsors was curiosity. She was intrigued by this couple, especially by the Duchess, who had mesmerising charm and used her eyes very well. She could get you to do anything she wanted. There was an aura around the Windsors and what Johanna saw as the devotion of an old couple to each other after their long years of marriage.

At the outset the Duke said he could not pay her Swiss salary but would put her in their will. Later $480 a month, payable in Switzerland, was agreed, with $20 a day travel expenses. Johanna would work from ten to six five days a week, was offered lunch and tea each day in the office as well as high tea (like John Utter), and this had appealed to her as she knew that the Windsors had the best chef in Paris.

The Duke told her that he wanted to get rid of John Utter and for her to take over, though this did not happen during his lifetime, nor did Johanna particularly want the additional commitment that would involve. But she said there came a time when the Duke no longer talked to John. She was told not to type his letters, and the Duke came to resent him using his chauffeur to take him to the country house.

She remembered that the Duke used to get very annoyed if proper respect was not paid to the Duchess. 'Her Royal Highness' was what he always called her. He asked Miss Schütz to stay on with the Duchess if anything happened to him and she promised: 'I will always stay with her as long as she needs me.'

Johanna acquired strong views about the Abdication. She believed, as I do, that the Duchess of Windsor was a victim. The Duchess told her that she never forgave the Duke for abdicating. She left for France in December 1936, thinking that she had left the King and would never see him again. She was horrified when he abdicated. She said: 'I aged ten years in that year.' Then they were separated for ages, but she was trapped. Evidently she used to berate the Duke about this.

The Duke had been spoiled as Prince of Wales. No one had ever said 'No' to him. Thus when it came to his wish to marry Mrs Simpson and suddenly they did say 'No', he was determined to have her no matter what the price. Johanna thought that for the Duke it was fine – he loved her – was always there to see her into her car – to meet her on her return. As long as the Duchess was there, he was happy. He was *not* happy to be effectively banished from his country. He loved England – of that she was sure. What the Duchess thought about all this was less clear. It is hard to live with that kind of devotion, and perhaps later it was hard to live without it.

Johanna had accompanied the Windsors on their last visit to the United States in 1971. The Windsors rented Apartment 40F on the thirty-seventh floor of the Waldorf Towers in New York. Also in the building was a new friend, Nathan Cummings, President of Consolidated Foods, whose apartment was on the thirty-first floor. The Windsors stored some furniture at the Waldorf for their annual visit and Nathan Cummings sent paintings up to adorn the apartment. Miss Schütz found a famous Renoir hanging in her office. She also found that the Windsors expected her to sleep in that office with maids walking through her room. To this she objected and so was assigned a proper bedroom.

Johanna was soon exposed to the spectacle of the Duchess getting her own way. The Duke was longing to go to Florida to stay with the Woodwards, while the Duchess, as ever, preferred to stay in New York.

A trip to Florida would be a considerable operation, with copious trunks of luggage preceding the Windsors to their next destination. Everything was in hand, and all was set for the journey until the night before the scheduled departure when Johanna received an anxious call from the Duke, asking her to come up. She found the Duchess in bed, peeping plaintively from behind the sheets. She said she was ill: 'Miss Schütz, you see I can't possibly go.' What could her secretary do but agree, and so the visit was cancelled. The next day the Duchess was up and about, and lunched with a school friend, declaring she could not disappoint her. At this point, Johanna realised what a great actress the Duchess was.

Nevertheless she thought she could help the Duke, aware that he needed a break. She thought that if she sent the Duchess's dresses on ahead of them, then the Duchess herself would have to follow. Johanna did so, but the same scenario was played out, and again the trip was cancelled. The Windsors stayed in New York and the Duke did not get his Florida holiday.

The Duchess always made an effort, even with her secretary. There came a time when Johanna used to have lunch and dinner with the Duchess unless a guest was expected. The Duchess often used to tease her as the evening drew on, saying she was sure she had a date. Johanna would deny it, never discussing her private life with her employer, but the Duchess had an uncanny instinct about it. Sometimes Johanna didn't escape until very late. 'We'll just have a nightcap,' the Duchess would say. Johanna recalled: 'I used to have two dinners – one with the Duchess and another at midnight.' She started work next day at ten a.m.

Johanna also detected the Duchess's irritation with John Utter, particularly when one night at dinner he placed himself in the chair that the Duke would normally have occupied. The Duchess was furious. Johanna thought Utter was weak and later blamed him for not standing up for the Duchess against her lawyer, Maître Blum.

The Duchess still maintained a considerable staff. Georges (officially Gaston) Sanègre had been with the Windsors as butler and major-domo since 1948. He was born in Narbonne and began to work for them at the Chateau de la Cröe on the Côte d'Azur. He ran the household's domestic affairs. He was a powerful figure, who listened in corridors and monitored everything that happened. He had the key to the silver safe, and knew where all the treasures were kept.

One of his duties was to count the gold knives, forks and spoons at the end of dinner parties. Occasionally it fell to him to have to suggest to a departing guest that – inadvertently, no doubt – a gold spoon might have jumped into his pocket.

Ofélia Baleni, who was born on the Isle of Elba in 1914, came to Paris when she was working for the Countess of Jersey and took the job of working as lady's maid to the Duchess in 1955. Georges married her in 1959 and they lived at the top of the house. Nothing happened in the house without Georges knowing about it.

Friends of the Duchess such as Lady Mosley thought him a saintlike figure in his devotion, but he was a devious man. John Utter, who had to work alongside him for many years, told me that Georges adored the Duchess 'and did everything in his power to strengthen his position with her'. This involved telling tales about others who were working in the house.[9] Georges was destined to stay to the bitter end. He told friends of the Windsors that he had promised the Duke on his deathbed that he would always look after the Duchess.[10] So too stayed Ofélia, though the Duchess did not like her and dismissed her three times. Georges always managed to get her reinstated.

In the early days Sydney Johnson was still working at the house. Born on Andros in 1923, he was taken on as a beach attendant by the Duke when he was sixteen. He worked at Government House in the Bahamas, and was with the Windsors at Ednam Lodge in 1946 when the Duchess's jewels were stolen. He was promoted to be the Duke's valet in the 1960s. Sydney had a French wife, something of which the Duchess had never approved – Sydney, a coloured man, marrying a white woman. 'My rich southern blood boils at the thought of a mixed marriage,' she told Major Gray Phillips.[11] As with John Utter, the first thing the Duchess wanted to do after the Duke died was to get rid of Sydney, and when his wife died soon after the Duke and he asked for more time to look after his small children the Duchess was furious. She dismissed him. John Utter was most disturbed by the way that Sydney was treated, after what he called 'thirty years of slavery to the Duke'. He described the dismissal as venomous*.[12]

There was a chef, Lucien Massy, a sous-chef, gardeners and chauffeurs, a nightwatchman, chambermaids and other figures. Germaine Bowyer, wife of the former chauffeur, was the concierge at the gatehouse and admitted visitors. She was the wife of David Bowyer, the Duke's

---

* Sydney went to work for the Chilean collector, Gerald Hochschild, and later for Mohamed Fayed, encouraging him to take on the lease of the Windsors' house in the Bois de Boulogne. He returned to work at the 'Windsor Villa' as it was called after the Fayed restoration. He operated as a kind of front man. He died in 1990, soon after the house was 'reopened.'

chauffeur, whom the Duchess had also sacked soon after the Duke's death. He too lived in the lodge, with a new day job, but somewhat aggrieved at his dismissal after 25 years of service. Gregorio Martin, the Duchess's chauffeur, would become an integral member of the household, travelling with her, and cooking for her when they were in America.

An intelligent man, he missed nothing, and remained loyal to the Duchess to the end. In his conversation, he recalled those who wished to 'profit' from the Duchess, and those who did not. He lived with Maria Costa, who had been a chambermaid and who took over as the Duchess's personal maid in 1974. She too was fiercely loyal to the Duchess. Maria was not a trained nurse, but when the Duchess fell ill it was she who helped the nurses to care for her, dyed the Duchess's hair and was the mainstay of the upstairs rooms. Nurses from the American Hospital came and went, but Maria was constant, the one person whom the Duchess knew from happier days. It must have been depressing to stay on in that house for those long years while the Duchess was ill.

Once the Duchess lost control over her affairs, the tensions became great. It was like a small court, with little for anyone to do and all kinds of machinations going on in the background. The once happy atmosphere deteriorated and the house descended into gloom and intrigue.

5

The Lawyer, the Librarian and the Cousin – 1972–1973

Helen, Lady Hardinge of Penshurst, was the widow of Alec Hardinge, the man who had warned Edward VIII that the press was about to break silence over the issue of Mrs Simpson. She heard of the Duke's death on the radio and observed: 'Now we shall have her as a *rich* widow being sought after by all the Royal Family.'[1] It was to be worse than that.

The Duke of Windsor's death meant that certain administrative matters had to be dealt with, not least his will. The Duke's last will had been signed on 6 January 1972. It was simple and straightforward. He appointed the Duchess the sole universal legatee of all his moveable and immoveable estate wherever situated ... in order that she should have immediate possession and enjoyment 'beneficially and absolutely' on all his estate when he died.[2]

In the event of the Duchess predeceasing him there were specific bequests for those still in his employ. The most generously treated were Sydney Johnson ($30,000), the Sanègres, the Bowyers, and Lucien Massy (the chef) ($20,000), Gregorio Martin ($15,000), Johanna Schütz*, Giselle Deberry, Ronald Marchant (former chauffeur), and Dr Antenucci ($10,000). Various others, including M. Alexandre and Jacky Orengia (Édouard) (the Duchess's hairdressers), Maurice Amiguet (the banker), and James Fitch (the London stockbroker) would get $5,000. The staff in the Duke's employ got an extra £100 for every year of service.

The Duke's plan was that the Duchess should enjoy the full benefits of his estate during her lifetime, and after her death the residue of the estate would go back to Britain to be distributed for charitable purposes. To that end the Duke created a company called Rossmore Assets, a company legally constituted in England, with its registered office at 9 Cheapside, London (the offices of Allen & Overy), this company becoming the Duke's 'universal legatee'.[3]

* Her $10,000 was increased to $25,000, though the estate only paid her $10,000 after the Duchess died. John Utter was meant to receive $10,000 but this was later revoked in a codicil.

Suzanne Blum, Sir Godfrey Morley and Ronald Edgar Plummer (another partner at Allen & Overy) were granted 'the seisin' of his estate.

The Duke's wishes were only fulfilled to the point that the Duchess benefited from the estate during her lifetime. The other provisions – and in particular the choice of universal legatee – were not adhered to.

Some years earlier, between 1953 and 1959, at a time when the Duchess was around sixty years old, and completely in control of her mental faculties, she made a note about what she wanted to happen to her houses, dogs and their various possessions. I have seen this document, much of which is written in the Duchess's own hand. I appreciate that the document has no legal authority, but it is indicative of her wishes. As with the Duke's will, the wishes expressed were not fulfilled.

The Duchess suggested that museums and galleries should be found to receive the two Cecil Beaton drawings of her, and her portraits by Alejo Vidal-Quadras, Ricardo Magni and René Bouché. Her portrait by Martin was to be destroyed.

Museums and galleries should also have the portraits of the Duke by James Gunn, Sir Alfred Munnings, Drian and Sir William Orpen, and the portrait of Queen Mary by Sir William Llewellyn. The paintings by Fantin Latour, Boudin, Stubbs and Bernard Lorjou should find similar homes.

Museums were to get the silver and silver gilt with monograms, the Duke's uniforms, decorations (presumably also including his Orders), his Field Marshal's baton, his dirk, the Abdication table, the illuminated addresses and the Augustus Rex (King of Saxony porcelain).

The Duchess singled out special friends to receive certain items. Mrs Robert Young, widow of the American financier*, who had advised the Duke so well over his investments, would receive a selection of four porcelain leaf dishes, the remainder of the porcelain and china to be sold. Jewellery was to go to Mrs Zachary Lewis (her first cousin)†, Princess Dmitri (the former Sheila Milbanke), Marjorie Amcotts Wilson, Mrs Brooks Howe, Mrs Cordelia Biddle Robertson (a very old friend)‡, Mrs Baker Senior, and Mrs Baker Junior. The remainder of the jewellery was

* Robert R. Young (1897–1958), Chairman of New York Central Railroad. A depressive, he committed suicide at his Florida mansion.
† Anita Warfield (1892–1969), daughter of General Henry Mactier Warfield, Jr. She married Zachary R. Lewis. They lived at the 700-acre Salona Farm at Timonium, Maryland, later moving Salona Farm to Monckton, Maryland. The Duke and Duchess visited both farms.
‡ Cordelia Biddle Robertson (1898–1984), Philadelphia-born philanthropist, who had been to school with the Duchess. Author of *My Philadelphia Father* (about Anthony J. Drexel Biddle), made into a Broadway play as *The Happiest Millionaire* (1958), and later filmed with Fred MacMurray; m. (1) 1915, Angier B. Duke (divorced); & (2) Thomas Markoe Robertson, architect (d. 1962).

to be 'sold by piece or broken up'. The Duchess wrote: 'Regarding the jewelry [sic] the ladies could choose between the smaller pieces – the large stones to be sold as well as valuable brooches or bracelets.'

The Duchess wanted another cousin, Mrs Herndon, to receive first choice of her clothes, the second choice going to Mrs Douglas. She wanted gold boxes to go to the Earl of Dudley, and a red box to his daughter-in-law, Lady Ednam (Stella Carcano). The remainder would go to a museum or could be sold if money was required.

The Mill should be sold and the furniture there be offered to the Baltimore Museum. The remainder of the lease on 4, route du Champ d'Entraînement should be sold. The Duke's clothes should be sold, but their photographs were to be offered to Lord Brownlow or to a museum. Their books (and in particular the books by figures such as Sir Winston Churchill and President Wilson) should be given to a library.

The Duchess loved her dogs. She wanted Sydney to take these, but in the event of no suitable home being found for them, then they should be put down.

This document was written at the time when Victor Waddilove was looking after the Windsors' affairs. He was to receive the two walnut chests in the entrance hall of The Mill and the flower painting over the mantelpiece in the entrance hall of The Mill (with Moulin de la Tuilerie painted on the picture).[4]

The Duchess's wishes were not fulfilled. Most of the items mentioned above were either sold in the 1987 sale of the Duchess's jewels in Geneva or in the Fayed sale at Sotheby's in New York in 1998. For example, the two Cecil Beaton drawings of the Duchess (Lot 50 – $134,500 & Lot 865 – $178,500), and her portraits by Vidal-Quadras (Lot 2496 – $9,000), Magni (Lot 2495 – $7,500) and two Bouchés (Lot 875 – $9,775; Lot 2098 – $27,000) were sold in New York; likewise portraits of the Duke by Munnings (Lot 1339 – $2,100,000), Drian (Lot 1335 – $3,500), and Orpen (Lot 1336 – $16,000), and the Llewellyn of Queen Mary (Lot 866 – $90,500) were sold in New York in 1998. Of the other items, the Lorjue painting (Lot 1607 – $26,000), the Abdication Table (Lot 843 – $415,000) and books by Churchill (Lot 1386 – $130,000; Lot 1387 – $22,000; & Lot 1388 – $36,000) and Woodrow Wilson (Lot 1393 – $31,000) also ended up in Sotheby's, New York in 1998.

As we shall see, the James Gunn portrait of the Duke and other items such as the Field Marshal's baton found their way into the Musée de la Légion d'Honneur by devious means.

* * *

Soon after her return to Paris, the Duchess had three visitors in quick succession – her lawyer, Sir Godfrey Morley, the Queen's librarian, Sir Robin Mackworth-Young, and the mainstay of her London visit, the Duke's cousin, Admiral of the Fleet Earl Mountbatten of Burma.

On 14 June, nine days after the funeral, Sir Godfrey Morley, came to lunch and talked to the Duchess about a number of plans. Since 1953 Sir Godfrey had dealt with all the Duke's important legal affairs. He had discussed the Duke's last will with him in 1971 and, as related, the Duke had signed it on 6 January 1972.

Sir Godfrey was a distinguished British lawyer, born in 1909, the son of a KC, and had been Senior Partner of Allen & Overy since 1960. He had served in the Rifle Brigade on staff in the Middle East and Italy during the Second World War, was awarded an OBE and the TD, had been a partner with Allen & Overy since 1934, had served as President of the Law Society and had been knighted in 1971. He sat on the Lord Chancellor's Law Reform Commission. He had assisted Sir George Allen with the Duke of Windsor's affairs since 1936.

The Duke was not always an easy client. It was Sir Godfrey who had had to deal with the Foreign Office when the Duke complained about lack of courtesy when he was in Texas for a check-up after his operation*.

It would have been hard to find a more honourable representative of the legal profession than Morley.

A few days after his visit to the Duchess, Sir Godfrey wrote her a letter marked 'Private and Confidential – To be opened only by the Duchess of Windsor.' His letter raised important points. She had told him that she wished to move from the house, a recurring theme over many years. And she added that she wanted to get rid of John Utter as her Private Secretary, but Sir Godfrey dissuaded her from this on the grounds that Utter would be of great assistance in the winding-up of the Duke's estate, and that she would need some help with her business affairs, travel arrangements and so forth. Miss Schütz, he pointed out, might not stay indefinitely.

The Duchess had raised the question of her will. Morley told her that there was 'no absolute necessity' to make a new will because her will provided that on her own death the legacies would be paid out, after necessary payments to staff, after which things would go to charities, except for historical objects which would go to regimental collections, archives and so on. He pointed out that what did need to be addressed was the question of legacies to servants who might leave during her

* *See* Part 2, Chapter 9.

lifetime, plus any decisions that she wished to make about leaving specific bequests to individuals rather than to charities, and again, whether she wanted her possessions all sold at death or whether some should be left to specific people.

Sir Godfrey was a reassuring presence. On 6 June he had advised her not to assist the *Daily Express* when they offered her £25,000 for extracts from her memoirs and some additional words from her: 'Very soon I hope for an opportunity to discuss financial matters with you, but I can assure you that you are very amply provided for and need have no worries at all on that score.'[6] The Duchess agreed that it would be undignified.

Sir Godfrey's advice was sound. It seemed that the Duke's wishes were to be fulfilled – but not for long.

The day after Sir Godfrey's visit, Sir Robin Mackworth-Young came to lunch. He came to collect the first consignment of the Duke of Windsor's papers to take them to the Royal Archives at Windsor Castle. This followed the discussion between the Duchess, the Duke of Edinburgh and Lord Mountbatten at the lunch after the Duke's funeral ten days before.

Sir Robin was a calm, scholarly man who ran the Royal Archives with quiet efficiency. He played no part in the actual decision to move the papers. It was his job to collect them and in due course to have them organised and catalogued for permanent housing within the Royal Archives, where, if permission were granted, they would be available for study by respected historians, and placed at the disposal of an official biographer.*

Sir Robin Mackworth-Young was born in 1920, was a King's Scholar at Eton, had served in the RAF in the Second World War, and had then joined the Foreign Service. He had been appointed to work on Sir Owen Morshead's staff at the Royal Library in 1955 and had succeeded him as librarian in 1958. To outsiders he could be aloof, as befitted the guardian of royal secrets, though one evening at a reception in the Norman Tower of Windsor Castle I observed him literally kneeling at the feet of Lady Diana Cooper, to press her for her views on the Windsors.

On the day of his visit, all the Duke's Orders of Chivalry, both the British and Indian ones as well as those awarded by foreign royal houses, were brought from the bank. They made an impressive display laid out in the office while Sir Robin went about his business. They were then taken to England with the papers, and were displayed in the National Army Museum in Chelsea for over twenty years before finding a final

---

* This commission was given to Philip Ziegler after the Duchess's death and his biography, *King Edward VIII*, was published by Collins in 1990.

home at Windsor Castle. The Duchess wanted them seen and it was generally felt that the Duke would have been pleased by this decision.

The first two visitors had been calm and quiet, and acting with good intentions, the lawyer advising what he felt was best for his client, the librarian fulfilling the Duchess's wishes. The following visitor was rather different.

Admiral of the Fleet the Earl Mountbatten of Burma was the next to arrive hot foot from Britain. He came to see the Duchess at five p.m. on 30 June 1972, seemingly on a social visit. In fact he was testing the ground before his full onslaught began.

Without doubt Mountbatten had been supportive to the Duchess during her stay in Britain for the Duke's funeral and had done much to make it easier for her and the Royal Family when they met at that difficult time. Unfortunately any good he did was soon undone as he took it upon himself to resolve what he perceived as the outstanding issues concerning the disposition of the respective estates of the Duke and Duchess.

A great-grandson of Queen Victoria, born in 1900, Mountbatten had been a youthful ally to the Duke of Windsor when he was Prince of Wales. In those days the Prince was at the very centre of the world to which young Dickie Mountbatten aspired. Mountbatten clawed his way onto *Renown* and sailed with him to India. There he met Edwina Ashley, reposing at Viceregal Lodge. She was rich and beautiful, he was dashing and ambitious, and he arrived in the Prince's suite. Much to his financial advantage, Dickie married her. The Prince of Wales was his best man.

With Mountbatten it is necessary to peel away layers of fabrication before you reach the truth. He claimed to have been at the Fort throughout the Abdication, advising the King. In fact he lunched there only once, with the brothers on 10 December – only then – by which time the matter was decided. He claimed to have taken the new George VI for a stroll and a chat soon after he ascended the throne. He also claimed to have offered to be best man to the Duke of Windsor at his marriage in France. On the contrary, he declined to attend, advising a fellow naval officer who was offered a job working for the Duke: 'The King is dead. Long Live the King.'[7] He naturally allied himself as quickly as possible with the new monarch.

Mountbatten's career advanced in leaps and bounds. He became the last Viceroy of India, he pushed the alliance between his nephew Prince Philip of Greece and the young Princess Elizabeth. He rose to the top of the Royal Navy, ending as Admiral of the Fleet and Chief of the Defence Staff. Much of his life was spent constructively, positively and forcefully.

He was also a bully. A look at the scene in his film, *The Life and Times of Admiral of the Fleet Lord Mountbatten of Burma*, when he orders his grandchildren about on a beach in Ireland, advising them of better ways to build their sandcastles, is indicative of his need to dominate all those around him.

Mountbatten's diaries make fascinating reading, since he was always firmly in the middle of them, always right. He never failed to take credit for any suggested idea, and (perhaps not uniquely) only took in what he wanted to take in. When he saw old friends, he invariably recorded that they were delighted to see him, even if evidence suggests the contrary.

So far as the Windsors were concerned, he considered himself their only true friend within the Royal Family. Certainly he was sure that he could help and at times ease a difficult situation. Unfortunately the Duke did not trust him, nor care for him much, and the Duchess bowed to the Duke's knowledge of him.

There came a point in the last years of the Duke's life when Mountbatten came over to France and showed the Windsors an extract from his film, the aforementioned *The Life and Times of Admiral of the Fleet Lord Mountbatten of Burma*, at a small cinema in Neuilly, taken over for the occasion. John Utter remembered the evening as the only time he ate caviar in hot pastry, a delicious dish devised by the Duchess. On that, or possibly a different evening, the Duke and Mountbatten sat down for a late-night chat. The Duke said to him: 'Dickie, I've got a bone to pick with you. Why were you not my best man?'[8] The Duke felt badly let down by Mountbatten over his wedding.

This was an issue that played on Mountbatten's mind over the years. He took every opportunity to press his version of events onto biographers, such as Frances Donaldson. When he met Lady Alexandra Metcalfe in Greece in 1953, she recorded: 'I sat by Dickie who got on his usual subject with me, the Duke of Windsor and the best-man story.'[9]

There is a hint in Mountbatten's diaries that there had been some cooling off between himself and the Windsors. Dining alone with the Duke in Paris in February 1970, he noted: 'We seem to have caught the old spirit really even more than in the 1930s, and I must say I thoroughly enjoyed the evening.'[10] A few weeks later there was another visit. 'So I went round and had an hour's further gossip and tea when he repeated for the third time how much he had enjoyed the dinner with me.'[11] On this occasion Mountbatten began to ask the Duke who he intended to leave certain objects to, suggesting the Prince of Wales. The Duke commented later: 'How dare he! He even tells me what *he* wants left to him!'[12]

Some years later, John Utter confirmed that Mountbatten was a pest. The Palace were always saying they tried to find things him for him to do. Otherwise he poked his nose into things. If Mountbatten telephoned, the Duke of Windsor would say: 'And what does *he* want now?'[13]

It was unfortunate that Lord Mountbatten should have begun his campaign about the disposition of the Windsors' property at a time when the Duchess was being harassed on all sides. As so often happens to widows, friends of the deceased began to make claims for objects they craved. Winston Guest, an American friend, was keen to take possession of some New Zealand jade merries for his collection. Then his wife, C.Z. – pronounced See Zee – some dubbed her 'Sleazy' – began to enquire about her jewellery. She expressed a particular liking for the Duchess's earrings, hinting how much she admired them and how sorry she was that Winston had never found her such a beautiful pair. The Duchess was extremely upset by this and, in her weakened state, cried about it. She felt under pressure that she could no longer even enjoy wearing her own jewels without her friends trying to purloin them.

The Duchess still had loyal friends like the Countess of Sefton, Lady Monckton, Robin and Iris Beare, Grace, Countess of Dudley and many in Paris who invited her to their homes, including some young people. But there were times when she appeared confused. Several guests attested over the years that sometimes they gathered for dinner and it seemed that dinner was being delayed. When someone asked why they were waiting, the Duchess would reply that they were waiting for the Duke to come down.

The Duchess's health declined steadily after the Duke's death. She had been suffering from ileitis and oncoming Crohn's disease. Nor did she eat properly, being determined to retain the figure of a young girl, which she achieved with considerable success but at the cost of her health. Digestive difficulties were a considerable problem. Shortly after the Duke's death, Diana Mosley wrote to her sister: 'She's ill, that's certain. I am glad he died first, he wd have been in total despair without her.'[14]

She was known to survive on nips of vodka which eventually took their toll. When pressed in a television documentary, made by Desmond Wilcox in 1997, Monsieur Martin said: 'The Duchess did not drink too much. The problem was that she did not eat enough.'[15]

A persistent story spread that she suffered from arteriosclerosis, that there were good days and bad days as a result, that sometimes she just sat there, unable to communicate, and then at other times would be quite normal. Johanna Schütz, who was with her closely during these years, is adamant that she suffered from no such illness, and that until November 1975 she was quite capable of coping with life. Her lapses of memory over whether the Duke was alive or dead resulted, she believed, from the Duchess being unable to fully register his death. He had been with her day and night more or less without a break since their marriage. He had spoiled her and done everything for her. The Duke had been worried about her memory before he died. All this combined to create these lapses.

Between 1972 and 1975 there were photographs of the Duchess at society occasions in Paris, going out for lunch or dinner, or arriving in New York for her annual visit. She was photographed strolling along the beach during her holiday in Biarritz that August. Snaps were taken of her sitting in her garden, and once there was a paparazzi sequence of her on her terrace, attempting to swat an annoying fly.

There were occasional interviews, and at least one photo session in the house in Paris, in which the Duchess was posed in her sitting room with her pugs, and even in her greenhouse in the garden.

Those who met the Duchess were concerned about her. Richard René Silvin had been hired by the State Department (USAID) to prepare a management analysis and assessment of the American Hospital. Perry Culley soon appointed him acting Administrator of the hospital. He saw the Duchess when she came for board meetings and he became something of a friend, occasionally escorting her on outings. He recalled: 'I worried about how frail the Duchess was, how little she ate and how much she drank. Ulcers were inevitable. It's not easy being alone, being widowed and, in her case, I think it was doubly hard.'[16]

On 3 August 1972 the Duchess went to the Hotel du Palais, Biarritz, with Grace Dudley, Carol von Radowitz, and John Utter. The Duchess took a suite with Grace Dudley, each having their own bedroom and sharing the drawing room.

Von Radowitz was a director of Moët Chandon with an unlimited expense account, travelling from San Francisco, to Nassau, to Palm Beach, to Biarritz and elsewhere. The Duke of Windsor had liked him as they could speak German together. He was good to the Duchess in Biarritz, which resulted in a curious incident at the end of her stay. The Duchess always gave a dinner party for the Mayor and others, and this time the Baron took it over for her and ordered all the food, so John Utter did not have to. The first course was a speciality of the house, a single lobster appearing before each guest – just one. For eight people these lobsters came to $125 and the whole bill was in the region of $500 – $600. Although this was an enjoyable evening, the Duchess was so out of tune with contemporary restaurant prices that she was most upset. She was convinced that she could not afford such extravagance.

On 5 September Diana Vreeland visited her, soon followed by Winston Guest. On 14 September she attended a farewell lunch at the Georges V Hotel for the retiring American Ambassador to France, Arthur K. Watson*, and on 29 September she dined with Paul-Louis Weiller at his large house in the rue de la Faisanderie. She signed herself in his book as 'The Duchess of Windsor'. Grace, Countess of Dudley and the Edmond Borys also dined.

In October there were visits from her banker, Maurice Amiguet, Lady Monckton with Robin Beare, and Ambassador Watson.

On 17 October the Duchess went into the American Hospital for an inspection of her leg. Three days later, with the Duchess's knowledge, Sir Godfrey Morley visited her Paris Lawyer, Maître Suzanne Blum, in the company of Jacques Rosselli to discuss a new will for her to take into account Sir Godfrey's advice over legacies for servants and others. Morley asked Rosselli to prepare a new will and to consult with Blum. This Rosselli did.

Hank Walter, the Duchess's American lawyer, had tea with her on 1 November and on 6 November she paid a final visit to the Mill before it was sold the following summer.

On 8 November the Duchess signed a new and different will. Only Maurice Amiguet was present when this was done, Sir Godfrey Morley being in London and kept in ignorance of this development. Amiguet was already quietly hostile to Morley, who, in July, had felt the need to ask him to clarify 'precisely the legal status of the operations which you and Jim [Fitch] conduct.'[17] This would have been a wholly reasonable request if made to an honest man. Maître Blum then got involved. On the same day, 8 November, she demanded sight of the articles of association of Rossmore Assets. She was particularly concerned that the French government should receive benefit from the Duchess's estate. Sir Godfrey was surprised. He explained that Rossmore Assets would have been the Duke's universal legatee if the Duchess predeceased him. She was now the universal legatee: 'In the case of the Will of the Duchess as it stands at present Rossmore Assets will become the legatee of the residue of the estate after payment of the legacies.'[18]

---

* The Hon Arthur K. (Dick) Watson (1919–74), former Vice Chairman of IBM, US Ambassador to France 1970–72; Governor of the American Hospital from 1973. A womaniser and a 'terrible drunk', he died as the result of a fall in New Canaan, Connecticut, after cracking his head open, on 26 July 1974.

Hot on the trail of this was Amiguet once more, anxious to close down all the Duke's former accounts and retain only her Morgan account in Paris. He wanted the Duchess to sell any residual mining rights she might hold in Canada, dispose of any financial assets still remaining in the USA, for the Duchess to renounce any royalties due from books in New York, to have the Queen's voluntary annual payment of £5,000 paid direct to Paris and in effect to sever any financial interests with Britain, Canada or the United States. Sir Godfrey dealt with these points.

On 20 November Blum told Sir Godfrey that she had excellent relations with the necessary French government departments and understood these better than he did. She said they wanted to know if the Duchess was free to dispose of objects in her possession to the French state, or whether these were controlled under the Duke's will. She proceeded to list benefits enjoyed by the Windsors in France since 1947.

While all this was going on, the Duchess went back into the American Hospital to have a cyst removed from her knee. Dr Maurice Mercadier performed this operation on 14 November. The Duchess nearly died on the operating table and was given strong drugs which affected her brain for some time. A nurse came to look after her and began to think she had a chance of inheriting some jewels from her patient. At one point, in terror, the Duchess hid in her bathroom and called Miss Schütz from there to ask her to come up and rescue her.

Soon after her return home, on 3 December, the Mosleys lunched with the Duchess in her house in the Bois. Lady Mosley described her as 'pathos personified, about nine people including a nurse (in a green silk dress) & she (Duchess) tried to set the ball rolling by saying nowadays people are only inter-ested in SEX, well as we were all well on the way to the grave the ball refused to roll. However it was all very jolly, & the food to dream of, she is a genius for food.'[19]

On 13 December she had a second visit from Sir Robin Mackworth-Young, who stayed for lunch, on which occasion, with her permission, he removed more papers to Windsor.

It was a feature of the way the press treated the Duchess of Windsor in the first year of her widowhood that they still tried to associate her with scandal. As time went by that became of less interest to them than the state of her declining health. *France Dimanche* and its reporter Baron d'Urdal (the pseudonym of a British journalist called Stephen East, a man with a vivid imagination) had long been the scourge of celebrities, especially at times of crisis. Towards the end of 1971 *France Dimanche* had prepared an edition concerning the death of Maurice

Chevalier, complete with his last words and intimate descriptions from his nurses, but the old star had rallied and the edition had had to be scrapped. They now concocted a fantasy that the Duchess was about to marry John Utter, pretending that they had first met in their youth, and that now they were free. 'Have they decided to unite and live together in the autumn of their years, and to achieve that dream of love which was forbidden them in the time of their youth?' mused the paper.

Maître François Alfonsi (in Maître Blum's office) complained on the Duchess's behalf, the French courts declared it an 'intolerable invasion of privacy' and some 1,200,000 copies of *France Dimanche* were seized. Sir Godfrey Morley stated that John Utter was 'greatly distressed' and there was 'not a shred of truth in it'. Miss Schütz, telephoned at the house, said that the Duchess had not been shown the story as 'she would have been too upset'.[20]

John Utter was in London when this story broke. On 20 December he was received by the Queen who bestowed an honorary CVO on him in recognition of his years of service to the Duke. During his audience at Buckingham Palace, the Queen told him that there was now another grave at Frogmore, not far from the Duke's – that of the Duke's nephew, Prince William of Gloucester, who had been killed while taking part in the Goodyear Air Race on 28 August.

The Duchess was ill at home between 16 and 22 December, and during that time King Umberto of Italy called on her (on 20 December at 6.30).

Over Christmas the Duchess fell out of bed and though in considerable pain, was not given proper assistance. When Miss Schütz came back to work on 2 January 1973, she realised that the Duchess had broken her hip and immediately called the doctor. So she was taken back to the American Hospital and underwent an operation on 4 January.

Ever since the death of the Duke, Maître Suzanne Blum had been advancing a campaign. Where Sir Godfrey Morley had protected and reassured the Duchess, Blum had worried her ailing client, persuading her that Morley's provisions were costing her too much money, that she needed to promise items to the great museums of France, including Versailles, the Louvre and the Musée National de Céramique-Sèvres in a new will, and worrying her that if she did not, she would be thrown out of the house in the Bois.

As we have seen, with the help of Sir Godfrey Morley, the Duke of Windsor's last will placed all his money in a trust of which the Duchess was the sole beneficiary during her lifetime, a simple and straightforward operation. The Duke had been anxious that the staff might leave her when he died, so they would not get their bequests unless they remained in her service.

The Duke did not inform Blum about this will. In January 1972 he was discussing business affairs with his secretary and said: 'Miss Schütz, I have not informed Maître Blum about my new will. She is only the Executeur Testamentaire and I am compelled to have her because we live in France.' Miss Schütz told him she saw no reason that Blum should know about the will: 'She will know about it when the will is opened.'[21] The will was probated in the London and Paris courts on 4 December 1972. Blum only found out about the will after the Duke died. She did not like what she found.

Widows traditionally think they do not have enough money, and in the Duchess's case, this was exacerbated by her ill health, and consequent fragile command over her financial affairs.

Blum informed the Duchess that an English trust would pay 70% in death duties and there would be little left. In reality what was given to the French museums proved to be larger than what would have been paid in death duties, but Blum did not tell her that. She finally clinched the argument by persuading the confused Duchess that her English lawyer was trying to get his own hands on her money.

So, while the Duchess was in hospital, Maître Blum and Amiguet took the first steps to assuming control over her. They dismissed Sir Godfrey Morley as her British lawyer.

6

Blum and Lord Mountbatten

Sir Godfrey Morley's dismissal was effected while the Duchess was in hospital. It appears that Amiguet instigated this, pressing the Duchess to sign a letter of dismissal. She did so on 13 January 1973. Six days later the Duchess signed a letter to Maître Blum appointing her as her sole legal representative.

On 22 January Amiguet wrote to Sir Godfrey to tell him his services were no longer required. Sir Godfrey replied:

> I still cannot understand what her reasons are for wanting the change. You mentioned on the telephone that she had suggested this as long ago as last summer and it is surprising that it has come round in this way, by her writing to you on 13 January, presumably from hospital, without having mentioned it to me on any of the occasions on which I saw her.

He recalled 'how insistent the Duke was that I should be involved.'[1]

Meanwhile Hank Walter, the Duchess's American attorney, informed Sir Godfrey that the American tycoon, Nathan Cummings, who had befriended the Windors*, had been advising the Duchess to cut down her staff, stay on in her house, consulting with Amiguet about her investments and suggesting the Duchess change her Will leaving half to charity and the other half to her servants on the premise that they would then take better care of her. Walter was deeply shocked and longed to point out the danger of promising bequests to those upon whom the Duchess depended for her food and drink.[2]

Only on 26 January did the Duchess write to Sir Godfrey to say there would now be no need for Maître Rosselli to prepare a new Will for her 'as I have already taken the necessary steps with regard to my will.' In a letter clearly prepared by Blum and signed in a shaky hand by the Duchess, she revoked 'any and all powers or charges heretofore given to you and Maître Rosselli.' She thanked him for past services to herself and the Duke.[3]

* See pp. 91–2.

Thus the Duchess left Allen & Overy and fell into the hands of Blum.*
John Utter and Miss Schütz were both aware of this changeover. Sir
Godfrey was left clearly suspicious, but only able to comment that 'the
Duchess of Windsor has gone a bit funny lately† . . . '[4]

Hardly had the ink dried than Blum requested sight of previous wills
and other legal documents. She took possession of a 'testament nuptique'.
In February the French Government confirmed that no tax would be paid
on the Duke of Windsor's estate and on 16 February the Duchess in turn
signed a codicil to her will which confirmed certain legacies designed to
show her gratitude for the generosity shown to the Duke and herself.[5]
Maître Blum was advanced in the Légion d'Honneur.

Within a month, on 8 February, Lord Mountbatten came to tea with the
Duchess. This was a mere week after she left hospital, following her
broken hip, so he was surprised to see her coming downstairs, walking
slowly with her nurse. Mountbatten was further surprised when she asked
him if he had seen David. A far from sensitive man, he replied quickly:
'How nice that you feel he is so close. I share your feelings that he is
very close to us now. Isn't it sad to think that he is actually dead and
gone?'

The Duchess replied: 'Yes, I suppose he has gone, but I feel he is
always with me and I can keep close touch with him.' After that exchange,
their conversation was 'more or less normal'.[6]

Mountbatten then thanked the Duchess for sending the papers and
decorations over to England, maintaining as ever that this had been his
idea, and said he thought Sir Godfrey Morley was doing a good job.

She then said that she had sad news for me because her French
lawyer, Maître Blum, a woman whom she had had for thirty years
and whom they had both liked very much, had bowled out that he
had been incompetent about a special private 'tax' company that
had been set up for them. When Maître Blum had disagreed with
him he had got a second French lawyer in who had proved equally
unsatisfactory.

The Duchess said that she had paid off Morley and his French friend,
following quite a row. Mountbatten realised he was getting nowhere on
the subject of Morley. Later she mentioned that this meant that Morley

* At the same time Blum terminated arrangements with James Fitch in London
† Sir Godfrey Morley remained Senior Partner of Allen & Overy until 1975. With his wife, he
attented the Duchess's funeral in 1986. He died in 1987.

would no longer be her executor, and Mountbatten 'reluctantly' volunteered his services as a member of David's family.

Mountbatten claimed that she consulted him about how various boxes and souvenirs should be distributed. His plan was that Prince Charles should have some say in where these items should go. Specifically he suggested that any items given by the Duke's brother, Prince George, Duke of Kent should go to members of the Kent family. He then advised the Duchess to appoint another English lawyer. He offered to find her one and thought she agreed. He suggested he should speak to the Queen, Prince Charles and Sir Martin Charteris and again thought she agreed.

The Duchess's doctor, Dr Thin, then rang up and managed to speak to Mountbatten. Apparently he asked Mountbatten to be a liaison. Thin told him that the Duchess's 'mind was rapidly deteriorating and it would not be very long before she would be incapable of making any decisions, though her physical health was quite good and she might live quite a while.' In his diary, Mountbatten justified his actions:

This proved to me that it is necessary to move quickly to get an English lawyer in and to get things settled while her mind is still in a reasonable condition. Dear, oh dear, I always seem to get involved in tricky matters. But I feel I must try and do something not only for the memory of David but after all for the sake of British history.[7]

Mountbatten got to work. On 13 February he wrote to John Utter, going over his conversation with the Duchess. He said he was surprised about Sir Godfrey Morley. 'However, this is entirely a personal matter for the Duchess to decide and I naturally didn't argue with her at all'. He said he was pleased that a new English lawyer could be appointed.

The Prince of Wales dined with me here on Sunday night, his last night in England before sailing aboard HMS *Minerva* for eight months in the West Indies. I told His Royal Highness about the departure of Godfrey Morley and he agreed that this was entirely a decision for the Duchess to make personally. However, he was extremely pleased at her decision to take a new English lawyer.

He was also relieved to hear that she was still so keen to set up a Trust Fund to commemorate the late Duke of Windsor and that she still wished the young Prince of Wales to be the principal trustee to decide how this money could best be spent in the way his greatuncle would have wished, probably for the benefit of people in

Wales, to ensure that his memory would be kept alive in the hearts of the people.

I also told him of the suggestion which I had made to the Duchess that personal souvenirs of historic importance bearing the Prince of Wales's crest or the Imperial cypher ERI or his own last cypher E, should only be given to people or institutions which we could feel certain that she and the late Duke would have approved of.

He was delighted with the suggestion I had made that I might be associated with him as a trustee to help him in choosing the right people and places for the souvenirs and for the disposition of the money, furniture, pictures and other belongings, made over to the Trust.

He said he would, of course, be very happy to work with any new English lawyer which she chose and of course with her French lawyer as well, and he thought that possibly the Senior Partner in the firm of personal solicitors which both he and his mother use might be appropriate. This is Mr Jo Burrell of 'Farrers'.*

Then on Monday night I saw the Queen and she expressed great interest and sympathy with the Duchess in her troubles. She said that she would be delighted if the Duchess cared to take Mr Burrell as her new English solicitor but felt strongly that the Duchess must be left complete freedom in choice. Her Majesty therefore recommended me to propose another solicitor as well as an alternative. I think a very good man would be Mr Arthur Collins of 'Withers'. He is very charming and regarded as a very helpful and tactful man. In fact, I think either of these two would do the Duchess very well; but if she wanted me to find yet another candidate I would, of course, be pleased to do so.

Neither of these has any connection with Allen and Overy or Godfrey Morley and whoever is chosen would start with a completely fresh approach to the whole problem.

If you would be kind and telephone me at this number with the Duchess's decision I will immediately get in touch with the solicitor of her choice and would be very happy to give him a briefing about the situation so as to make it as easy as possible for the Duchess to deal with him when he reports.

I would point out that he would have to work in complete harmony with her French lawyer.

---

* J.F. Burrell, CVO (1909–83), Senior Partner of Farrer & Co, & Solicitor to the Duchy of Cornwall 1972–6.

The Queen told me how touched she was that the Duchess had sent over the Duke's uniforms and Orders and decorations and so many of his private papers. Indeed, Her Majesty said that all the papers were lodged with great care in the Royal Archives at Windsor and that all had arrived except the last three volumes of letters which she understood the Duchess was arranging to have sent over.

You will remember that we also discussed the question of an English executor of her Will. I was distressed to hear that no single member of the Duchess's family was left alive who could act in this capacity and if she wanted a member of one of the families I would be happy to offer my own services as an Executor.

However, if the new English solicitor proves acceptable he might be more suitable than me as Executor if I were in fact nominated to be one of the Trustees of the Duke of Windsor's Trust under the Prince of Wales.

The Queen thought it was entirely understandable that the Duchess should wish to give some of the fine pictures in the Collection to the French Government in recognition of their having treated the Estate so generously by exempting it from death duties.

The Queen was also much touched to hear that the Duchess had refused Winston Guest's desire to buy those extremely historic New Zealand jade Merries and that she had also rejected the request of the New York Metropolitan Museum to acquire the Duke's plain clothes for exhibition.

However all these things could very easily be arranged according to her wishes at any time once Trustees have been appointed and the new Trust set up. I, therefore, urge very strongly that when the new English solicitor comes he should get together with the French solicitor and together they should set up the Trust which the Duchess herself had expressed such a strong desire to do.

If by any chance the Duchess wants me to come over and see her again I will always be at her service although it isn't always possible for me to get away easily as I have quite a number of engagements.

Anyhow, I shall look forward to your ringing me up as soon as you have taken the Duchess's wishes in this matter.[8]

On 19 February Mountbatten wrote to the Duchess, thanking her for putting him in touch with Maître Blum, who was 'charming and helpful on the telephone'. Blum had agreed to meet Joe Burrell in Paris the following week. Mountbatten continued:

> My only idea has always been to be as helpful to you as possible in the sad circumstances of David's death, but all the decisions rest solely with you. I know all David's family feel the same way and want to be helpful without interfering.
>
> Would it be any help my offering my services as one of the executors of your will? I was David's devoted friend and he was my best man and I would like to do this for you if you would like it.
>
> Please look after yourself and don't go breaking any more bones.
>
> Much love from your old friend, Dickie.[9]

Joe Burrell duly went over to see Maître Blum but she made it clear that his services would not be required. She explained to him that the Windsors had lived tax-free in France for thirty-five years and the Duchess had been exempted from paying any death duties. The rent of the Paris house was virtually symbolic, and as soon as the Duke died a number of people stepped forward to offer fifty times more. Blum's line was that if the Duchess appointed an individual, a Foundation, a trust or a company to operate for her, seventy per cent of her possessions in France or elsewhere would go in taxes. There would be the cost of an inventory and the French government might decide to recover taxes on the Duke's estate. Blum had other provisos, and expressed the hope that members of the Royal Family would not have to pay tax on historical objects or personal souvenirs that they received from the Windsors.

She told him that the Duchess knew exactly what she wished to do. She wrote that the Duchess, her friends and entourage did not need to be reminded constantly of her death, and urged that she be left in peace because, although the Duchess was courageous, these discussions were distressing for her and for them.[10]

Joe Burrell thanked Blum and told her he was communicating what she had said to Sir Martin Charteris in order that the Queen could be informed. He congratulated her for the way she had dealt with the French government and the consequent generosity with which the Windsors had been treated. He affirmed his wish to be able to keep in touch with her from time to time as the occasion arose. A few days later he sent Blum a copy of a letter from Sir Martin Charteris, which he thought she should have on her file.

Soon after the dismissal of Sir Godfrey Morley, Maurice Amiguet, the

Duchess's banker at the Société de Banque Suisse in Zurich, came to the house. Amiguet had been the Duke's Swiss banker and adviser since 1952. He had been involved in the crisis caused by the dishonesty of Victor Waddilove, the disgraced Private Secretary, particularly since these involved dealings in French francs on the black market. When the Duke made matters worse by criticising Amiguet for not looking after his interests, Amiguet turned over the necessary information to the Swiss bank.

Amiguet was a respected banker, many of whose clients were from the Middle East. His letters were peppered with light jokes, references to his meetings with royalty and descriptions of overseas visits – he enjoyed a world cruise with his wife, well armed with introductions in each country. He moved between Zurich, St Moritz and the South of France. When in London he stayed at the Dorchester. On 19 February 1973 he wrote to John Utter, confirming the new arrangements, expressing the hope that the Duchess would be well cared for by her office and nurses, and telling him that from now on Maître Blum would be directing matters.[11]

Blum had begun to take over. This process would continue over the next few years, since at this time John Utter and Johanna Schütz were still working in the house, and Blum was never able to take complete control, since Amiguet handled the Duchess's considerable funds in Switzerland.

The Duchess of Windsor and Suzanne Blum were two of the most unlikely people to have been thrown together in life. They had nothing in common, whether in background, temperament, style, mutual interest or anything else. The Duchess lived her life at the height of fashion, supremely elegant and with excellent taste. Blum was the opposite. She dressed badly and wore an ill-fitting wig, which caused the Duchess quiet mirth. Blum wore dowdy dresses or Gertrude Stein-ish tweed suits. The Duchess was light and social. Blum was austere and ruthless. Yet their lives became inexorably entwined from the 1970s onwards.

Blum's first connection with the Windsors was as the wife of their legal representative in Paris. Yet she rose to describe herself as the Duchess's '*Executeur Testamentaire*' and '*défenseur des droits moraux et des intérêts de la Duchesse de WINDSOR**'.[12] These phrases sounded important. They were meaningless. Blum was one of the executors of the Duke of Windsor's will, a will which contained stipulations that were never fulfilled. As to her role as defender, it was self-adopted.

The rise of Maître Blum coincided with the Duchess's fall. Presently

*Defender of the moral rights and interests of the Duchess of Windsor.

Blum would become the Duchess's captor, spokeswoman, keeper of the flame and of the keys. She would change the Duchess's will, altering the dispositions in it, lodge what I suspect to be a forged letter of authorisation with a tame notary, take the Duchess's name in vain in respect of what she wanted published, and pronounce herself to be the Duchess's friend and protector. It is one of the most sinister relationships ever formed between lawyer and client.

Blum was a woman of many contradictions. She was intelligent, and in later life formidable. She had her admirers, could inspire considerable loyalty, and yet many were horrified and repelled by her. She was intelligent, canny, hard-bitten, an intellectual radical, well read, with an incisive style and a sharp brain. But she was without humour, although capable of malevolent *bons mots*,* and she was jealous of others. She looked severe in her black dresses or tweed suits. Her eyes were as narrow as those of an old Mandarin. I had been warned about her, but I confess that the only time I met her (in December 1980), her attitude was charm personified, though with a hint of menace in her manner.

It is unlikely that Blum would have gained her position of supremacy had the Duke of Windsor outlived the Duchess. His links with the British court and his own family were always stronger than the general public were led to believe. Being a man, and a former King, he would have been better protected. But after his death, the Duchess was isolated, not only as a seventy-six-year-old widow without close blood relations but also as a woman in frail health.

I first heard the name of Blum in the summer of 1973. Mountbatten had paid the Duchess another of his visits. As he had a habit of telling the Duchess that 'David' had promised him certain items, John Utter asked her Paris lawyer to come and sit next to her during the meeting, to prevent such activities. Beyond that, Blum was politely invited to lunch once a year. The fact that the Duke did not take Blum into his confidence about his last will shows how little he valued her. At that time Blum was mentioned merely as a person to be summoned when needed.

Soon all that would change.

---

*During the war she described the journalist, Geneviève Tabouis as a 'de Gaulle digger'. [Blum to Carmel Offie, 17 June 1942].

7

The Early Suzanne Blum

Suzanne Marguerite Blumel was born in Niort, France, on 24 November 1898, the daughter of Joseph Blumel, a merchant, and his wife, Amélie Cahen. The family came from Alsace but, after 1870, Suzanne's father and two brothers, having been brought up by Jesuits during the German occupation, left their family and possessions and fled to France to avoid becoming Germans. Suzanne had a brother, André – also later a lawyer – to whom she was close. They later changed the family name to Blum. Suzanne was educated at the Universities of Poitiers and Paris, became a lawyer at the Court of Appeal in 1924, was Secretary of the Conference 'de stage' from 1925 to 1926, and lawyer at the Ministry of Foreign Affairs specialising in questions concerned with cinema.

It was not easy for a woman to get on in a professional world dominated by the opposite sex. She had apparently been the mistress of an important man, unlikely as such a relationship must seem to anyone who met her in later life. I speculate that this might have been another lawyer, President Joseph Paul-Boncour, born in 1873, briefly Prime Minister of France from December 1932 to January 1933, a man with whom she was by her own account a 'collaborator' for ten years. He was active in the Labour Movement, and became a Socialist, finally founding the Union Socialiste Républicaine which merged with the Parti Démocratique Républicaine to form the PDRS (Parti Démocratique Républicaine et Social). He was elected to the Senate in 1931. Among appointments held he was Minister of War and Foreign Minister. He opposed the formation of the Vichy Government.

In 1934 Suzanne Blum married Paul Weill, who was another lawyer at the Court of Appeal in Paris. Blum claimed that they were introduced to the Windsors by the United States Ambassador, William C. Bullitt, Weill later becoming the Duke's legal representative in France, dealing with his staff contracts and so on, while other more important matters were looked after by Allen & Overy in London and his US interests by his American lawyer – in later life, Hank Walter. Curiously, Blum went on to claim that she and Weill were 'reintroduced' to the Windsors by

Margaret Biddle* after the war. (If one has been already introduced, does one need another introduction?)

Nevertheless, Bullitt was to play an important part in her life. It says something about Blum that she admired a man like him.

Born in 1891, William C. Bullitt was a maverick figure, a brilliant graduate from Yale, who was taken to the 1919 Peace Conference by Woodrow Wilson, was made first US Ambassador to the Soviet Union by Roosevelt and served there from 1933 to 1936. Appointed to Paris in 1936, he rented the Chateau de St Firmin at Chantilly† – his time there was marked by some extraordinarily outspoken reports back to the President. In 1939 he quoted Édouard Daladier, the French Prime Minister, as describing George VI as 'a moron', and Queen Elizabeth 'an excessively ambitious woman'.[1] In turn Duff Cooper thought nothing of Bullitt: 'I have rarely met a man I dislike so much. He is both stupid and crooked.'[2]

Blum had reason to know the Ambassador since she acted for many American film companies in Paris. In February 1938 she courted him with the gift of a bottle of a particular aperitif from Martinique. Later he helped facilitate her passage through Immigration and Customs when she and Paul Weill arrived in New York in April 1938.

Blum also made friends with Bullitt's secretary, the sinister Carmel Offie. There is a devastating description of Offie in Burton Hersch's *The Old Boys*.[‡] Born in 1909, he was the son of an immigrant from Naples and later became a railroad hand in Pennsylvania but made his way to Washington where he became a typist and stenographer, rising to the position of clerk in the State Department. He joined Bullitt in Moscow when he was twenty-four and afterwards, in Blum's words, followed the Ambassador 'as his shadow'.[3] Swarthy and short, with a handlebar moustache, he looked a bit like Charlie Chaplin. A bachelor, he soon made himself indispensable, and did not mind when Bullitt summoned him to type a document at five in the morning or prevailed on him for an early-morning walk at the same hour.

In Paris in 1937 Bullitt recorded that Offie had become the Duchess of Windsor's favourite bridge partner, a curious addition to her table. In later life the descriptions of him became harsher. In his office he did not hesitate to fart loudly and without warning. One of his former colleagues

---

* Margaret Thompson Schulze (1897–1956), daughter of the Montana-based mining magnate William Boyce Thompson, m. 1931 Anthony Drexel Biddle, Jr (1896–1961), US Ambassador in various European countries, divorced; later a leader of American society in Paris after the war, columnist for *Woman's Home Companion*. She died of a cerebral haemorrhage in Paris.
† Later home of the Duff Coopers.
‡ Burton Hersch, *The Old Boys*, published in 1992 and revised in 2002, a gripping account of the CIA, of which Offie was later a member.

also described him as 'one of the ugliest men I've ever known, short and knobbly, with a long, swollen-looking face and a head made up mostly of lumps.' His teeth thrust forward through fleshy lips.[4]

Blum was soon on Offie's wavelength. She came to address him as 'Offie dear' or 'Darling Offie' and wrote to him in English when practising for her law course at Columbia University, telling him he could choose between receiving love letters from her or requests.[5]

Blum's involvement with the film world produced many important American contacts, most notably Jack Warner of Warner Brothers. It is odd to find such a dour creature as Blum involved in this magnetic and in some ways superficial industry but involved she was, and until late in life she was a respected guest at the Cannes Film Festival. On her evidence it is lucky for the film companies that they did not heed the advice she gave. She was doubtful about the success of certain American films dubbed into French, which she thought would not work or became simply ridiculous. She advised against the possible success of many films and was proved roundly wrong, notably over *Cavalcade*. She was also involved in censorship issues concerning films in France.

In 1939 she appealed to Offie for help when Universal Pictures suddenly dropped her as their legal representative after ten years, over an issue which loosely concerned the film star Danielle Darrieux returning to the USA to fulfil her contract.* Maurice Leon, a lawyer from Universal Studios, came to Paris and engaged the services of a M. Bétolaud to persuade the star to leave France. Blum was asked privately about Bétolaud and related the story of how this character had attacked Eugène Frot, the former Minister of the Interior under Paul-Boncour, from behind, on his return to the Palais after the political demonstrations of 6 February 1935,[†] and had even hustled Blum herself for no reason. She had set her husband onto the case, but when he found Bétolaud with a bloody face he decided not to press charges. Subsequently Bétolaud apologised to Frot, who agreed to forget the matter.

Blum related this story to Madame Bacheville, a young woman in charge of cinema matters at the Secretariat of the Presidency of the Council and she reported the conversation to Leon. He thought Blum had asked her to pass on the message; Bétolaud filed a complaint. There was an enquiry which cleared Blum, but nevertheless she was dropped by the film company. In turn Blum lodged a complaint against Bétolaud.

---

* Danielle Darrieux had made *The Rage of Paris* for Universal Studios, starring opposite Douglas Fairbanks Jr, but had then returned to Paris.
† Blum has accompanied Frot to these as a spectator, as he was a former Cabinet colleague of Paul-Boncour.

Offie was able to help Blum and presently she thanked him for having arranged everything for her. Blum sent further delicacies to the American Embassy for the Ambassador and his secretary.

Much can be learnt about the early Blum in her book, *Vivre Sans la Patrie 1940–1945*. It is a serious work but written with occasional wry asides, a style often adopted by a person who lacks a fundamental sense of humour. Its effect is to place Blum centre stage in a lot of wartime activities. She was clearly a friend of Léon Blum, and involved professionally with several film moguls and Hollywood stars. She drops a lot of famous names, yet these figures do not reciprocate in their own memoirs – with the notable exception of Virgil Thomson, the American composer, who knew and respected her, and Jean Cocteau, who made a passing reference to her in his own diaries.

I have an ingrained mistrust of Blum, based on the many contradictory statements she later issued and the many lies she told. In *Vivre Sans la Patrie* she claimed to have established a new fashion in the summer of 1933, when she arrived at the Miramar in Cannes wearing riding clothes. Evidently the sparsely clad guests of the hotel thought she had found an ingenious way of being noticed, and many imitated her. But is it true?

Blum was in New York in the summer of 1939, welcomed, so she claimed, 'with a fanfare'. She swept into the country without annoyance from Immigration and Customs, thanks to her prestigious friends, and was installed by these friends in some style at the Waldorf Astoria.

She and Paul Weill returned to France on 25 August. They lived through the bombing of Paris. She contemplated becoming an ambulance driver, but admitted she could not change a wheel. She toyed with the idea of taking a pilot's licence, but realised that was hopeless as she felt seasick if she read a newspaper in the back of a taxi. She made other attempts to be useful, but after 10 May 1940 she knew she had no hope. Ironically she obtained a visa to get out of France from the same Robert Murphy who sent John Utter to North Africa.

Before leaving Paris she asked Carmel Offie to house some of her possessions at the American Embassy during the war. This he did.

Blum left Paris with her mother on 9 June and made her way to Bordeaux. At one point on the journey, after a day without food, an *auberge* refused to serve them. She stole two steaks. As she described this in her memoirs, she took the steaks but left payment for them on the plate. She called this '*une vente forcée*'[6] and ruminated that she had never resolved the legal issues surrounding such an action. Reading this in 2000, I mentioned the '*vente forcée*' to Diana Mosley. She laughed and commented: 'That's very Maître Blum!'[7]

Presently Blum managed to cross the border with a number of other refugees and reached Lisbon. Here she found Schiaparelli, Jean Michel Frank and others. She had great difficulty in obtaining a visa for the United States, and only did so when Laudy Lawrence, Paris director of MGM, told her that William Bullitt, the US Ambassador in Paris, was in Portugal.

When the Germans invaded France in May 1940, Bullitt annoyed Roosevelt by deciding to remain in Paris, affirming: 'No American Ambassador in Paris has ever run away from anything, and that I think is the best tradition that we have in the American diplomatic service . . .'.[8] But on 30 June he left the capital with Carmel Offie, Robert Murphy and others. By 13 July they were in Madrid and then went on to Lisbon.

Blum claimed that Bullitt was there in connection with issues concerning the Duke and Duchess of Windsor but no evidence supports this and he was in Lisbon for less than forty-eight hours. Blum wrote in 1975: 'The Duke was going to take his derisory post as Governor of the Bahamas, which he accepted with dignity.'[9] According to her, Bullitt was delayed in Portugal, which gave him time to accompany her to the American Consulate and knock heads together. A fortnight later Blum got her visa. At the same time Offie gave her back some money she had entrusted to him, which helped her survive there and enabled her to give financial assistance to some refugee friends. Bullitt flew to New York in a Pan-American clipper on 15 July.*

Another who helped her to escape was Hugh Fullerton, the American Consul, an elegant man, who had worked under Bullitt in the American Embassy in Paris.† He had a difficult time in Marseilles, gradually unable to find meat to eat there and running out of shaving cream. He was to be quite an ally to Blum, serving as a conduit for messages from her to her brother André, at first over visa applications and later his imprisonment. Fullerton assisted many important figures to escape, including the tapestry collector Marie Cuttoli, and Max Adler of Sears, Roebuck.

But he and Blum differed over Varian Fry‡, who helped rescue some two thousand escaping Jews, including Marcel Duchamp, Leon Feuchtwanger and Heinrich Mann. Fullerton sided with the French Government in

---

* The widowed Empress Zita of Austria and John G. Winant were also on the flight.
† Hon. Hugh Stuart Fullerton (1892–1986), American diplomat from Clark County, Ohio, who served as Consul-General in Antwerp 1924, Cologne 1926, Kovno 1929–32, was at the US Embassy until transferred to be American Consul in Marseilles in 1940, and later served as Consul-General in Paris 1944–48. In 1949 he became Executive Governor of the American Hospital in Paris, and was later one of its honorary Governors. He was a much younger cousin of, and literary executor to Morton Fullerton (1865–1952), Chief Correspondent of *The Times* in Paris, who had had an affair with Edith Wharton. See Marion Mainwaring, *Mysteries of Paris* (New England, 2001).
‡ Varian Fry (1907–67), American journalist, later given a Yad Vashem award for his actions.

wanting Fry out of France. When Blum was in New York in 1941, she appealed to William Bullitt and Carmel Offie that Fry should be allowed to remain in France, but in vain. He was deported in August in that year. Despite this, Fullerton and Blum remained friends for many years.

Blum finally embarked in the *Excambion* on 8 August and sailed to New York. On this Noah's Ark of a ship were Salvador Dalí (thinking up jokes overnight to tell the next day) and his wife, the photographer Man Ray, the French film-maker René Clair* and other notables. On board too was Virgil Thomson who wrote in his memoirs that Blum was his 'warmest friend on board'. 'She knew that her safety lay in leaving France,' he continued, 'being Jewish and also prominent. And yet she worried over where her duty lay, to leave or not to leave her aging mother.'[10] She left her mother behind.

In her book, Blum claimed that she already knew Thomson, having met him with Gertrude Stein and Alice B. Toklas. It is not impossible but there is no evidence to support this in the correspondence between Thomson and Blum. Whatever the case, a firm and lifelong friendship was forged between them. As Thomson put it: 'So friends we became, and friends we have remained.'[11]

In New York Blum was once again received in some style, apparently. She related tales of staying in great houses, and how it suited her to borrow the family Rolls-Royce when it was offered to her. She introduced Virgil Thomson to Hervé Alphand[†], then serving as a financial attaché in Washington, and his wife Claude.

Blum settled finally at the Concord Hotel. She was far from idle. She made friends with Louis Rapkine[‡], the Jewish biologist who became famous for his efforts in helping thirty scientists to emigrate in secret from France during the Second World War. And she sent food parcels over to relatives and friends. She also managed to get her mother a visa, with the help of Hugh Fullerton. Her mother arrived in America, weighing thirty-eight kilogrammes.

Blum was in touch with François Piétri[§], Vichy Ambassador to Spain, as early as 1941 and thought he was helping her family. But her sister-in-law

---

* René Clair (1898–1981) was on his way to Hollywood. He was stripped of his French citizenship by the Vichy Government.
† Hervé Alphand (1907–94), French diplomat. He disapproved of the Vichy Government and resigned in 1941. He joined de Gaulle in London. He was French Ambassador to the US from 1956–65. Later he appointed Thomson a Chevalier in the Légion d'Honneur.
‡ Louis Rapkine (1904–48). The Rapkine French Scientist Fund was established in his name, and in 1985 became the Pasteur Foundation in New York, an arm of the Pasteur Institute.
§ François Piétri (1882–1966), French politician holding various ministerial positions. He was Ambassador in Spain from 1940–44.

and nephew were arrested and imprisoned at Perpignan*. Then her brother André was arrested in 1942 and imprisoned for twenty-one months, first at Perpignan and later at Évaux-les-Bains (Creuse). Piétri refused him funds that would have enabled him to eat adequately. At the time André wrote that Piétri was a cruel hypocrite who all but caused him to die from typhoid. After the war, Blum's brother wrote no more than an ironical letter to the priest who had denounced him. Blum herself recorded that she took a harsher line:

> Less 'Christian', I had sworn to chastise those on whose account my mother and I had spent years of anguish. But, contrary to the way the famous expression puts it, vengeance is a plate to be eaten warm. In the 1950s I had François Piétri at my mercy. He submitted to nothing bad. As for the others, for the most part, the justice of men or that of God had already descended on them.[12]

This passage shows something of the contradictions lurking in Blum's character.

During those years she supported and kept in touch with Léon Blum, then in prison in France, again pressing Bullitt to save him. She served in the American Women's Hospital Reserve Corps. We must give her her due. She worked nobly for the Resistance in France – but from the safe haven of the United States.

While in New York, Blum requested Carmel Offie that the Department should consult her as French adviser, since she was able to identify various undesirable people.[13] One such was a man called Alexandroff, a White Russian in Paris who was seeking a visa for the States. She denounced him as pro-Nazi and Fascist. Offie was by now a great admirer of hers. 'She is a grand girl,' he wrote, 'and as a lawyer in Paris did many great services for the USA and American businessmen.'[14]

It was during the war that Blum made a significant remark to Offie: 'The best way to keep someone as a prisoner is to surround him with love, affection and friendship.'[15]

While in New York, Blum earned an MA in international law at Columbia University. They asked for her diploma so that she could gain entrance. She produced a lawyer's card. They suggested she wrote to Paris for her diploma but she did not think it likely that General Von Stülpnagel, the Governor of Paris, would stir himself to send it. After May 1944 she

---

* Her nephew was later sent to work in a sulphuric acid plant in Poland.

worked for Jean-Michel Guérin de Beaumont when de Gaulle appointed him Consul-General of France.

Blum remained closely in touch with Offie and with Bullitt. After some uncertainties and indecision, the Ambassador finally quit the Diplomatic Service in 1941 but continued to crave political activity. He hoped to be Secretary of State but Roosevelt did not want him. He stayed in the limelight, making numerous speeches; he was sent to Africa and the Middle East to report on hostilities, but returned to inactivity in January 1942. He effectively dug his own political grave when, in April 1941, he went to see President Roosevelt to provide him with written evidence of the homosexual activities of his hated rival Sumner Welles, who had been serving as Under-Secretary of State with Cordell Hull since 1937.

Welles had got drunk in the special train to the funeral of Speaker William Bankhead* in Alabama in September 1940 and had propositioned a sleeping-car porter. The incident had been hushed up and from then on a Secret Service officer was detailed to accompany Welles at all times to keep him out of mischief – not always successfully.

Cordell Hull encouraged Bullitt to snitch on Welles to the President. He did so and the President was furious. He knew about the allegations and told Bullitt tersely that he did not see any danger of publicity. However, in 1943 Welles was asked to resign and never took public office again. Nor did Bullitt. He stood for Mayor of Philadelphia but, without Roosevelt's support, he lost.

One day in 1944 the former Ambassador came to see Blum at the Hotel Concord and told her that he was enlisting as a soldier in the Free French Army, Roosevelt having denied him a commission in the US armed forces. He crossed to France, where he was knocked over by a military lorry, which splintered a vertebra in his back and put him in hospital. Never again did he walk properly. In November 1944, in French uniform, he reopened the US Embassy in Paris. He also took part in General de Gaulle's victory parade.

After Blum's return to Paris she helped Bullitt with the French edition of his book, *The Great Globe Itself* (1946), a scathing attack on Roosevelt and his foreign policy, though she experienced delays with the publisher who was obstructed on account of using illegal paper. It was eventually published as *Le Destin du Monde* in 1948, but was somewhat eclipsed by Victor Kravchenko's *I Chose Freedom*. Ironically Blum's brother André Blumel, now at liberty once more, represented the Communist weekly

---

* Father of the actress Tallulah Bankhead.

Les Letters Françaises when Kravchenko sued them for libel in the 'trial of the century' of 1949. Kravchenko won.

According to Blum, Bullitt became bitter and ill in later life. He finally died in the American Hospital in February 1967. Only forty mourners turned up to his memorial service, amongst whom were Hugh Fullerton and Blum herself. No member of the French government was there, and only a few old generals. Blum was deeply shocked.

If Bullitt was a man hard to admire, Carmel Offie was worse. In 1948 he joined the CIA, working for Frank Wisner and assisting former Nazi collaborators to enter the United States with their dossiers sanitised, often with new identities. His activities caused James Angleton, a CIA official, to comment: 'Allen Dulles, Richard Helms, Carmel Offie and Frank Wisner were the grand masters. If you were in a room with them, you were in a room full of people that you had to believe would deservedly end up in Hell.'[16]

Eventually Senator McCarthy made public reference to a potential security risk in the CIA. Though he did not mention him by name, he was referring to Offie who had once been arrested in Washington for immoral loitering. J. Edgar Hoover monitored Offie, and there was suspicion of financial dishonesty and reports of further immoral behaviour. In 1953 Allen Dulles ordered Offie to be dismissed from the service. Offie continued to operate in business of one kind and another until he died in the BEA Staines air crash of 18 June 1972.*

In the spring of 1945, the war finally over, Blum returned to Paris in *Liberty Ship* and resumed her legal career there. In November 1946, when her re-entry permit ran out, she underwent a medical and a touch of tuberculosis was discovered.

Virgil Thomson used to send Blum welcome food parcels. Presently he asked her to help his friend, Bernard Faÿ[†], who had worked for Pétain during the German occupation of Paris. Pétain had appointed him Administrator of the Bibliothèque Nationale in place of the previous Jewish director. Secret societies were outlawed in France and it was Faÿ's job, as Director of the Anti-Masonic service of the Vichy Government,

---

* The BEA Trident took off on its way to Brussels on a Sunday evening, two weeks after the Duke of Windsor's funeral. I remember this well, my miniature diary referring to the 'ghastly accident'. All 118 people on board were killed in what was described as the worst disaster in the history of British aviation. Learning that Carmel Offie, a figure from the 1930s and 1940s, died in this way, he suddenly seems closer to a kind of contemporary reality.
† Bernard Faÿ (1893–1978), French historian & anti-Masonic polemicist, well known in French intellectual circles. Friend of Gertrude Stein and Alice B. Toklas.

to organise a list of some 170,000 files on Freemasons, which had been seized by the French police from Masonic lodges.

These names were organised into a single file by Faÿ's secretary and lover, Gueydan de Roussel*, the original purpose of which was to exclude Masons from public office. Later, however, the lists were used by the Gestapo. Sixty thousand were investigated. Six thousand were imprisoned, 990 deported and 540 were 'shot or died in camps'.[17] Faÿ was also the editor of *La Gerbe*, an anti-Jewish journal funded by the Nazis.

On 19 August 1944 Faÿ was arrested and, following his conviction for collaboration, sentenced to hard labour in December 1946. Virgil Thomson wrote of Faÿ:

> Gertrude Stein, to whom I had introduced him, had been wretchedly unhappy at his imprisonment. I shall not try his case in this memoir; suffice it to say that Suzanne Blum and Paul Weill, who had no reason to love him, but quite the contrary, had found the trial a travesty and Bernard pitiable ('digne de pitié'). For Gertrude's sake, and out of friendship too, I essayed what little power I could wield. It was Suzanne who helped the most, for she was legal counsel to a ministry. And it was she, unless I am in error, who procured his release from the Île de Ré, an island fortress where his health was being injured, to a prison hospital on the mainland near Le Mans; and it was from this easier situation that a year later he escaped . . .[18]

Thomson had appealed to Blum for help. She had been reluctant to take on the case. She respected Thomson's scruples concerning Faÿ, but, morally, felt she could do nothing for him. She was torn between her friendship for Thomson and her distaste for Faÿ. Nevertheless she accepted that the dossier against him was very bad.[19] By February 1947 she was advising Thomson how to help Faÿ. In December she sent him the trial documents. Later she heard that her name, that of her husband Paul Weill and of ten other lawyers were on one of Faÿ's lists of 'so-called freemasons' to be handed to the Germans. She mused that it might have been for that reason rather than for being 'members of the chosen race' that she and her husband were robbed of certain possessions while they were away in the United States.[20]

It is hard to prove that Blum was a Freemason but, given that she was a high-powered lawyer, it is not impossible. However, it would have been

---

* Gueydan de Roussel (1908–96). In 1944 he escaped to Switzerland and thence to Buenos Aires.

one of the minor lodges, and not an influential one since the main Masonic lodges did not admit women. Thomas Dilworth, co-editor of *The Letters of Gertrude Stein & Virgil Thomson*, suggested: 'I don't know whether Blum was a Freemason, but if BF put her on a list of Freemasons, then she probably was. Faÿ was a good scholar.'[21]

In October 1948 Faÿ's life sentence was reduced to twenty years, making him eligible for freedom in a general amnesty. But he was denied an amnesty, causing Alice B. Toklas to ask Thomson whether it was not now time for an intervention by Blum.

In January 1951 Blum was working on the case, seeking a pardon for Faÿ but, apparently due to an intervention by the Chief Rabbi in Paris, President Auriol himself vetoed it. 'I don't know how correct this report is,' wrote Thomson to Toklas. 'If so, that is where Suzanne Blum should have been on the job.'[22]

As he related in his memoirs, Thomson was not sure if Blum effected Faÿ's eventual transfer from the Île de Ré to the prison hospital at Le Mans, but it was most likely her work. The following September Alice B. Toklas secured Faÿ's escape from Le Mans by selling two Picassos and some drawings and hiring six men who entered the hospital dressed as nuns and removed him. He escaped to Spain and moved to Fribourg in Switzerland, where he worked as a lecturer under the name of 'Philippe Connaint'. In 1958 he was given a pardon by François Mitterand, then Minister of Justice, and allowed to return to Paris where he continued to lecture until forced to resign during the student revolts of 1968.

For Blum to have helped in the escape of a man like Faÿ is telling. She was a Jewish lawyer and possibly also a Freemason coming to the aid of a man who had endangered both Freemasons and Jews. This says much about Blum's pragmatic approach to life, putting her ambitions before moral or ethical concerns.

Blum acquired the reputation of being one of France's toughest lawyers. During her long career she represented Warner Brothers against the composer Igor Stravinsky, converting his damages from a million dollars to one franc. She represented Twentieth-Century Fox, MGM, Charlie Chaplin, and Walt Disney.

In 1947 she defended Aliki Weiller in complicated legal wranglings with her former husband, Paul-Louis Weiller, the man who housed the Windsors at the rue de la Faisanderie in Paris. When Weiller was imprisoned at the beginning of the Second World War he sent his wife and son, armed with money and a considerable cache of jewels, to seek sanctuary in the United States. Aliki Weiller, a former beauty queen from Greece, had been worn down by her marriage to this dynamic figure. In the 1930s she had sat for her portrait by Drian, but he told her that she was crying so much that he could not possibly paint her.[23]

Aliki went to Reno in 1943 and obtained a quick divorce. Weiller refused to accept this divorce, fearing that he might lose access to his son. When he heard that Aliki had married again* he attacked the divorce. In December 1948 Blum and Aliki Weiller lost the case and as a result Weiller succeeded in turning Aliki into a bigamist in France.

Blum was furious when Paul Reynaud, who had been in prison with Weiller at Pellevoisin, wrote to express his confidence and friendship in him. Weiller had obtained a similarly good reference from the President of France, Vincent Auriol. To the President himself Blum attacked Weiller ruthlessly, accusing him of moral crookedness and more besides. She described him to Carmel Offie as an abominable individual,[24] and was later delighted to learn that he was experiencing problems over American taxes.

The case went through appeal after appeal in France until a French divorce was granted in July 1959. Weiller was a formidable adversary, not accustomed to losing.† Again it was an interesting example of a Jewish lawyer pitted against a Jewish businessman.

Blum represented Rita Hayworth in her divorce from Aly Khan in 1958. She was lawyer to Jean Cocteau, Martine Carol and others. In one of her books she published photographs of herself with figures like Cary Grant, Charles Boyer, Michèle Morgan and Picasso, some of whom presumably she also represented. Ironically she also published a photograph of herself in the background during a reception for the Queen at the Louvre, given by President Coty of France in 1957. This is captioned in self-aggrandising style: '*entre la reine et le président Coty*'.[25]

In June 1949 Virgil Thomson thanked Blum for being hospitable to the American writer Mina Curtiss‡, who visited Paris when she published her edition of *Letters of Marcel Proust*. He wrote: 'You are a sweetie to send me a telegram. I think of you always and miss you always . . . Thank you for being nice to Mrs Curtiss. Thank you for existing.'[26]

By 1951 Blum was clearly doing well. For some years she had a home at la Gaiole, Chemin de l'Olivette on the Cap d'Antibes. Thomson wrote to her: 'I hear from visitors and mutual friends that you are very busy and

---

* In December 1945 she married the diplomat (Sir) John Russell, later British Ambassador in Ethiopia, Brazil and Spain.
† In 1983 Paul-Louis Weiller told me that he had tried to warn the Duchess 'gently' to be wary of Maître Blum, but to no avail.
‡ Mina Curtiss (1896–1985), sister of Lincoln Kirstein, another friend of Alice B. Toklas.

very famous. That changes nothing. I hope you are also very rich and very happy.'[27]

In November 1955 Blum intervened on behalf of Alice B. Toklas, again at the request of Virgil Thomson. Gertrude Stein's friend was living in virtual poverty in the apartment in the rue Christine. Her famous cookbook had not sold well. She had received a good sum for translating a children's story but those funds would not last long. A childhood friend, Mrs Corbett of San Francisco, formerly a Miss Lewis, had visited her and offered to present her with a substantial cheque, but Miss Toklas had declined on grounds of pride – 'to be asked . . . like a pauper . . . oh *NO*.'[28] But when Thomson told her that Blum had written to Mrs Corbett independently, her eyes lit up. In January 1956 Alice B. Toklas was able to write to a friend: 'Winter was mild until a week ago but it has commenced – there is a question of my having more adequate heat . . .'[29]

In 1966 Blum represented the Russian pianist Alexander Brailowsky, who specialised in Chopin, when a magazine urged its readers to boycott his performances. They claimed, possibly with some reason, that he was past his best. Blum sought support for her case from Thomson and he endorsed it.

Liliane de Rothschild lived at the centre of Paris life for many years. A wise and invariably positive person, she had no illusions about Maître Blum. She described her as '*dangereuse*' and was horrified that Blum went on to make the Duchess of Windsor her prisoner.[30]

Blum's first husband, Paul Weill, lived until 1965, after which Blum took on the role of representing many of his clients, including the Windsors. In newspaper interviews Blum sometimes claimed that she had met the Windsors at parties in the 1930s. This seems most unlikely.

In August 1967 she married General Georges Spillmann*, a widower, who had served with distinction for twenty-eight years in Morocco, Algeria and Indochina and as Secretary-General of the North Africa Committee under General de Gaulle. It would appear that Blum had been a close friend of General Spillmann's since at least the late 1940s, since she had arranged that he should rent Virgil Thomson's apartment at 17, quai Voltaire immediately after the war. In the letters between Thomson and Blum there are many cryptic references to the general as her friend. Even while Paul Weill was still alive the handsome general could be found

---

* General Georges Spillmann (1899–1980), first married to Marguerite Clément-Grandcourt, by whom he had four children, one daughter predeceasing him.

staying at Blum's summer home on the Cap d'Antibes. One of Spillmann's later posts was to be President of the Musée de la Légion d'Honneur in Paris, which is significant. He lived until 1980.

Blum enjoyed a secondary career as the writer of detective fiction. She published three books under the pseudonym L.S. Karen – *Le Billet Jaune* (1966), *Sillage de Rêve* (1967) and *Il n'y a pas de cheval dans le jury* (1968). Then, under her own name, she produced *Ne Savoir Rien* (1970). This was followed by *Quand Le Scandale Éclate* (1971), three historical tales of human passion, vanity, ambition, risk of torture. Her 1973 novel, *Le Printemps Foudroyé*, was generally believed to have been inspired by Daisy Fellowes, a well-known socialite and a client of Blum's, who had generously bequeathed her Nelson's desk on her death in 1962. Blum advertised this as 'a lucid if cruel book, which accuses, condemns and grants no pardon.' She denied that Mrs Fellowes had inspired it.

Caroline Blackwood left a memorable description of Maître Blum as she observed her in 1980.* A novelist and literary critic of distinction, Caroline possessed an almost witchlike perception of evil. Her approach to life was dark: 'Every silver lining has its cloud' was a favourite line of hers. Caroline captured the essence of Blum without the biographer's strict adherence to established facts.

Caroline was no great admirer of Blum's fiction. She was surprised that literary figures such as Julien Green, the homosexual novelist and diarist, and Jean-Louis Curtis, winner of the Prix Goncourt, had given them enthusiastic reviews – until she was told that Blum represented substantial elements of the French publishing world.

She noted that Blum favoured characters with aristocratic backgrounds and distinguished lineage, and told her stories with total lack of humour. Her characters were like cardboard cut-outs. She detected 'frightening violence' in these books. When Blum tired of a character, she killed them off 'in a moment of vicious caprice'. In *Ne Savoir Rien*, the heroine suddenly turns, with no prior warning to the reader at all, from being a well-mannered gentle creature into a violent murderess.

Caroline was equally disparaging of Blum's technical skills. The plot was careless to the point of risibility. The murder was committed by the heroine putting Nembutal into her husband's brandy. He gulps it down and drops dead on the spot. As Caroline pointed out, Nembutal tablets taste acidic and unpleasant. To kill a person by this method a considerable number of pills would have to be pulverised into the brandy.

* See *The Last of the Duchess* (1995).

The consistency would be like soup. No one could drink it without sniffing that something was wrong.[31]

Assisting Maître Blum in her office at 53 rue de Varenne were various other figures, notably Maître Jean Lisbonne.* He was born in Paris on 9 June 1912 and became a lawyer at the Court of Appeal in Paris in 1934. He specialised in the rights of authors and cinema. As such he was the lawyer attached to the Cannes Film Festival. He advised many embassies and Latin-American consulates in Paris, was President of the International Law Association in Paris from 1984 to 1986, and presided over the Iberian-American section of the Society of Comparative Legislation.

He is remembered in a number of different ways. Alastair Forbes† had a civilised conversation with him soon after the Duchess of Windsor died, when he was reviewing the Windsor letters for the *Spectator*. Sir Reginald Hibbert, British Ambassador to Paris from 1979 to 1982, believed him to be the notary who held the Duchess's power of attorney: 'He was certainly the one whose name had to be invoked whenever decisions had to be taken or implemented affecting the house, domestic staff or payments of any sort from the Duchess's funds. Maître Blum did what she could to interpose herself between me & him, as between me & Dr Thin, the Duchess's doctor, but she could never be wholly successful.'

Lisbonne was not in fact the 'mandataire' under the document of 1 February 1977. Hibbert described Lisbonne as 'a pleasant and apparently reasonable man.'[32]

Lisbonne never came to the Duchess's house in the Bois but Johanna Schütz saw him at Blum's office and remembered him as 'an old ugly man no taller than Blum and completely her slave'.[33]

---

* Maître Jean Lisbonne (1912–2004). He was an Officer of the Legion of Honour, Mayor of his village, Sonchamp, and Vice-President of Care-France.
† Alastair Forbes (1918–2005), journalist, raconteur and reviewer for the *Spectator*, noted for interminable Proustian sentences. He had a way of thinking up *bons mots*, not all of which were in good taste. His best was: 'Inside every bully there's a coward desperately trying to stay in.'

8

The Last Active Years – 1973–1975

Anyone who had seen the Duchess of Windsor at the Duke's funeral or in the press photographs of the next year or so would have been aware that she was in failing health.

Lady Donaldson, who was preparing an unauthorised biography of the Duke, was a friend of Lady Monckton and others. She asked me to help her with some aspects of her research and in the course of this she told me that the Duchess had arteriosclerosis, a theory much vaunted at the time but denied by Johanna Schütz, who pointed out that until November 1975 the Duchess was perfectly capable of taking decisions and was aware of what was going on around her.

Soon after this, *Burke's Guide to the Royal Family* was published. I set off to Paris with two copies, one for the Duchess of Windsor and one for John Utter. I went along to the house in the Bois on the morning of 9 March 1973.

John Utter and Miss Schütz were both at their desks as usual. There was no plan for me to present a copy to the Duchess in person, and I now realise that she was not particularly well at that time. But suddenly Miss Schütz got up from her desk and took a copy of the Duke's memoirs in French – which had lately been republished – and asked me to write my exact name on a bit of paper. She disappeared upstairs and presently returned with a copy inscribed to me by the Duchess. She apologised that the Duchess was not dressed and so could not receive me.*

There remained just over two years of active life for the Duchess. Since her decline is so much a part of what eventually happened to her, it is worth saying something of her activities, even at the risk of presenting some elements of social diary. However much it may seem to be that, intrigue was never far away.

On 15 May the Duchess went down to Cap Ferrat by train, taking her two pugs with her. She was accompanied by John Utter, who told me

---

* This treasure I took home with me, only to find that my family thought I had forged the inscription myself, since I had spent part of my adolescence learning how to copy famous signatures and had acquired some skill at this!

soon afterwards that the nine-hour train journey to Nice had proved something of a trial:

> John read half a page of a book he was longing to get on with, and she talked all the time, repeating the same thing constantly. In the Duke's day, there would be all the papers and he would hide behind one of these – then there would be John and the maid, so it was spread between all of them. On this occasion John got the entire barrage. Finally he said: 'Why don't you read the paper?' She glanced at it, but made no attempt to do so. In the end he became sleepy and the Duchess said: 'What's the matter with you, John? Are you tired?' He replied: 'Well, I guess I am, yes.'[1]

They went to stay at the Villa Roserie which was above Cap Ferrat and belonged to George Farkas, owner of the department store Alexander's in New York. Nearby was Mrs Frances Munn-Baker, a close friend of the Duchess's, who lived at Grasse. While the Duchess was in the South of France, Miss Schütz sold The Mill to a Swiss industrialist, Edmond Artar, for two million French francs, a sale which was completed on 27 June.[*]

On 28 May, by coincidence the first anniversary of the Duke's death, the American author Ralph Martin[†] came to lunch. He left a description of the Duchess as being alert and talkative, if small and frail. He noticed that her recent fractured hip had taken away some of her grace of movement, and she told him: 'It's because it's only partly plastic; if it were all plastic, I could move more smoothly.'[2] Martin was there to see the Duchess because he was writing a biography of her, though this was unauthorised.[‡] John Utter was anxious when he saw Martin steering the Duchess off alone into the drawing room to talk to her, fearing what she might say to him, but he felt unable to interrupt them.

Though her 'interview' gave Martin's book some added cachet, she did not say anything exceptional. He succeeded in getting some quotes from her about her childhood, and she told him how against the Abdication she had been:

---

[*] Edmond Artar (1921–77). After his divorce, he was much in the company of ex-Empress Soraya of Iran. He was found dead from an overdose in his villa at St Tropez. The Mill was again put up for sale.
[†] Ralph G. Martin (b. 1920), American author, who also wrote a best-selling biography, *Jennie: The Life of Lady Randolph Churchill*.
[‡] *The Woman He Loved* (Simon & Schuster, NY, 1974).

I told him it was too heavy a load for me to carry. I told him the British people were absolutely right about not wanting a divorced woman for a queen. I told him I didn't want to be queen. All that formality and responsibility. And I told him that if he abdicated, every woman in the world would hate me and everybody in Great Britain would feel he had deserted them . . . He said he didn't want to be king without me, that if I left him, he would follow me wherever I went. What could I do? What *could* I do?'[3]

This showed that the Duchess was still consistent to the views she held in later life, and perfectly coherent. On 4 June she travelled back to Paris.

Lord Mountbatten visited the Duchess on 14 June, after which she was scheduled to go to the British Embassy for a buffet dinner. He arrived for tea, which, because it was a hot day, proved to be a cold ginger beer. He suggested that she should form a Trust chaired by Prince Charles with Philippe de Gaulle, son of the General, as a French Trustee. He thought she liked the idea.

Mountbatten wrote to Blum on 18 June and she wrote back on 2 July with the same message – she had lunched with the Duchess who had arranged everything in accordance with the wishes of the Duke and herself and the French state. She hoped no one would be unhappy with the outcome. She was happy to hear any further suggestions from him, and would be willing to see the Prince of Wales if he came to Paris.

The day after Mountbatten's visit, on 15 June, the makers of the Sinclair plate in memory of the Duke presented her with the first of an edition of 1,000, one of the more tasteful commemorative items produced in his memory.

On 11 July the Duchess visited the Duke's grave, a visit which the press knew nothing about at the time. The Queen was in Edinburgh, at Holyroodhouse, but sent an Andover from the Queen's Flight for the Duchess. She travelled with John Utter, was met by the Duke of Kent and Lord Mountbatten and had lunch at Windsor Castle. A telegram was delivered to Mountbatten from Prince Charles, then serving at sea, about 'Uncle David's foundation', the plan hatched by Mountbatten by which the Duke's money might eventually be put into a charitable trust in England.[4]

The curious aspect to this is the arrival of the telegram, which the Prince of Wales had clearly sent to Broadlands some days before. Therefore Mountbatten had created a *coup de théâtre* on the occasion of the Duchess's only visit to her husband's grave in order to advance his cause over the money.

The Duchess changed into a blue dress and was driven down to the grave at Frogmore. Elizabeth Johnston, wife of the Assistant Comptroller of the Lord Chamberlain's Office, and a professional photographer in her own right, was asked at the last moment to come and take some photographs. The Duchess posed beside the grave between the Duke of Kent and Mountbatten. Mrs Johnston also took a photograph of the Duchess leaving the private royal graveyard, the last ever taken of her on English soil. The Duchess flew back to Paris in the early evening.

I happened to be in Paris and visited the house the next morning. While I was there the internal telephone on Miss Schütz's desk rang. It was the Duchess, and so the closest I ever got to her was to hear her voice on the telephone, discussing the previous day, how well the visit had gone, and the question of thanking the Queen. This conversation lasted a while, and as soon as it was over John Utter suddenly stopped talking to me and extended his hand, which hovered momentarily above his telephone. I wondered why he did this. His telephone rang as he knew it would. 'Good Morning, Your Royal Highness,' he said, and there then followed an exact rerun of the previous telephone conversation.

On 27 July Mountbatten came to see the Duchess at five p.m. I heard about this visit the following day, driving down to Osmoy with John Utter. John did not care for Mountbatten, nor for the way in which he ordered him about. 'You should have heard him yesterday,' he said, quoting Mountbatten: '"John, get your notebook out."'

As related, on such occasions John took the precaution of calling in Maître Blum to come and sit next to the Duchess to prevent Mountbatten from trying to walk off with gold boxes and other objects. Mountbatten had a habit of 'remembering' things that 'David' had promised him years before, as far back as the voyage to India in *Renown* in 1922. 'David always said that one day this would be mine,' and he would reach out and try to take a gold box.[5]

This was the first time I ever heard Maître Blum mentioned – she was summoned as any of us might when we needed the additional support of a lawyer. And that was her relationship to the household in those days: a lawyer to be summoned when required, nothing more. There was no hint that she would ever play a more substantial role.

This conversation took place in the car (driven by the Duchess's gardener, Roland Gougault) on the way to lunch at John's country house,

Le Prieuré at Osmoy, just outside Paris. It was rather like The Mill (which was not far away), with various outbuildings, and had belonged to a rich American lady, Miss Marion Kemp,* who had lived to the age of one hundred. She had left the house jointly to John and to a lady called Marcelle, who lived there full time while John visited at weekends. They were allowed to use it provided they housed musicians who were able to stay there and practise in another building.

We were joined for lunch by Johanna Schütz, her mother and a friend of hers. At the end of lunch Johanna gave me a lift back to Paris with them in her mini. My suitcase was so big that the boot did not close properly and had to be held shut as near as possible with a silk stocking. Less successful were my attempts to converse with my companions in French. I soon learnt that some of the expressions I had picked up on the beach in the South of France were not appropriate for a car journey back to Paris.

Johanna deposited me at Les Invalides. It was only just over a year since the Duke's funeral. I would never then have imagined, when we were walking round outside St George's Chapel, looking at the wreaths, that I would one day find myself in that car.

Mountbatten was not discussed on the journey back to Paris, but three years later Johanna Schütz gave me her version of Mountbatten and his visits, which I recorded on the day she told me:

> The Duchess of Windsor is very scared of Mountbatten and doesn't like to be in the room alone with him. This is because he goes round and says things like 'What a lovely gold box . . . Will you give it to me?' The Duke told the Duchess that he was 'Tricky Dickie' and the Duchess told Miss Schütz: 'That's enough for me.' . . . Now whenever he comes they have Maître Blum sitting in. With a lawyer present, what can he do? The awful thing is that the general public probably think: 'How nice of Mountbatten to go and see the Duchess of Windsor . . .'[6]

On his 27 July visit Mountbatten was clearly irritated by the presence of Maître Blum, but he wrote to her again on 3 September. This time the Duchess wrote back to say she did not wish to set up a Foundation as he had suggested:

---

* Marion Morgan Kemp (1862–1963) came from an Irish family of Kemps in County Cavan. Her father, George Kemp, had moved to New York and married an American wife. Miss Kemp was the aunt of Gladys Scanlon (who died in San Remo in 1964), a friend of the Duchess's, very much around at the time of the Abdication. At some point in the late 1970s the bequest ran out and John had to give the house up.

As you say in your letter, my decision will not affect our friendship in any way, I feel quite sure that David's memory will be preserved among his countrymen and others through the dispositions I have decided to make.[7]

The Duchess sent a copy of this letter to Prince Charles.

When Maître Blum returned to Paris after her summer holiday, she found Mountbatten persistently pursuing his idea for a foundation and in October she wrote to Joe Burrell, complaining that Mountbatten was still not accepting what he had been told the year before.[8]

Sometimes Lord Tennyson used to come and dine with the Duchess. He recalled that she liked to talk about old friends such as Eric Dudley, Perry Brownlow, Colin Buist, Sheila Milbanke and others. He was one of those who advised her not to lend the Duke's clothes to an exhibition in New York. Significantly, she never discussed the disposition of her papers with him. The Duchess hardly ever discussed anything controversial 'except once when she was in a towering rage and spoke of the impertinence of MOUNTBATTEN's visit when he attempted to dictate her bequests under her will.'[9]

Mountbatten's endeavours continued for another year and a half. But he did not see the Duchess again until November 1974.

Things did not go well for the Duchess that summer. She fell and broke some ribs on 1 August but was well enough to go to Biarritz as she had the previous summer to stay at the Hotel du Palais with her old friend 'Foxy', Countess of Sefton, her visit again made pleasant by the kindness of Carol von Radowitz. She came back to Paris on 5 September.

At the end of September she was destined to dine with Walter Lees. he contemplated the evening to come in a letter to Mona Bismarck: 'The Duchess of W (who cracked her ribs recently) is dining here in my apartment in a week's time and so I have asked some of her close friends. I *hope* she doesn't crack any more coming up my staircase!!'[10]

The last time I went to the house when both secretaries were there was on Monday, 15 October. My abiding memory of that visit was the butler, Georges, looking over the railing from the upper landing outside the Duchess's rooms and John saying: 'He'll want to know who you are and why you're here.'

On 22 October Princess Alexandra and Angus Ogilvy came to Paris and called on the Duchess for cocktails in the evening. The next day the Duchess went to Chanel and was then visited by Ashton Hawkins of the Metropolitan Museum in quest of clothes for the Costume Institute.

On 9 November it is recorded that there was some problem between Blum and John Utter.

The wedding of Princess Anne to Captain Mark Phillips on 14 November brought the Duchess into the British media spotlight once more, there being some speculation about whether she would or would not be invited. In fact she was not invited, and nor did she send a present. A few days earlier she was escorted to a dinner at Maxim's by Paul-Louis Weiller. It was a rare occasion when the whole of the restaurant was taken over by David Mahoney, of Norton Simon, who had recently bought Max Factor. There were two hundred guests, with Liza Minnelli as guest of honour.

As the Duchess left Maxim's on the arm of the doorman and another figure, she slipped and was photographed looking rather pathetic. This photograph found its way into Cecil Beaton's scrapbook and inspired him to sketch a wicked caricature, captioned 'The Widow Windsor arrives for her favourite entertainment – a night out at Maxim's.' Beaton sketched the Duchess in her little black dress with a huge Prince of Wales-feathers brooch, a necklace of enormous pearls, wild arthritic hands, and spindly legs. She was supported on either side. This was done for his own amusement and was never published.*

On the night of the wedding the Duchess was photographed at a party at the Wally Findlay Art Gallery in Paris, invited there by its Vice-President, Simone Karoff.

Hardly had Princess Anne's wedding passed by than the Duchess had to face more press trouble. She had been visited by Charles J.V. Murphy, the man who had ghosted the Duke's memoirs. He proceeded to write an article for *Time-Life*, which was widely copied by other papers and in which she was quoted as saying, 'It's a bombshell world full of violence and horror. I no longer understand or like it very much.' The impression given was that she had few interests in life and refused to take sleeping pills as she felt she needed to be alert at night, to see if the nightwatchman (a former French paratrooper) was doing his job. Her companions were her pugs. Among other quotes, she told Murphy: 'I don't dance any more.'[11]

Within days the Duchess complained in the courts about the serialisation of Ralph Martin's book *The Woman He Loved*, as a result of which

---

* Within a year Cecil Beaton had a stroke and was arguably in a worse state than the Duchess, at least for the next two years.

many copies of the *Ladies' Home Journal* were seized. The complaint concerned a reference to the Argentine diplomat Felipe de Espil* with whom it was alleged she had had an affair in the 1920s, the implication being that he was the man she really wished to marry – the true love of her life rather than the Duke. 'The excerpts that I have been told about do not deserve any comment on my part,' read the Duchess's statement. 'If some readers are naive enough to believe what is printed about me I can only feel sorry for them.'[12]

The Duchess won that battle, but Ralph Martin published the book containing his version of her affair with Espil. The relationship with Espil was something of an open secret. In 1943 *Time* magazine referred to Espil as 'London-tailored, expert at the tango, an escort of Wallis Spencer years before she became the Duchess of Windsor.'[13] The Duchess herself had made a veiled reference to him in her memoirs, *The Heart Has Its Reasons*,† and it has since been accepted by all her subsequent biographers that there had been an affair. The way the relationship was treated in the various books depended on the dignity or otherwise of her biographers, most, though not all, of whom veered to the sensational.

Martin was researching his book at a time when there were survivors who could tell him plenty of stories about Espil. Even Espil's widow, the former Courtney Letts‡, helped him, and he quoted one of the Duchess's friends as saying: 'She would kill me, if she ever knew I told you . . .'[14]

1974

In January 1974 the Duchess had X-rays in the American Hospital for intestinal problems. Her health was relatively stable, though her mind was now deteriorating. Once again Major Lees was a witness: 'I have dined with the Duchess one evening but I am not sure she knew who I was, and she makes up the most extraordinary stories. As Kitty Miller said – the blood isn't getting to her head!!'[15]

There were many visits from Maître Blum and Maurice Amiguet in 1974, and from 14 to 18 February Robin Beare and his wife came to Paris.

Amiguet and Blum conferred together and Amiguet issued instructions to the Duchess's office. Foremost, he was interested in her jewels. He wanted to reduce the insurance paid on them and limit those who

---

* Felipe de Espil (1887–1972), Argentine diplomat, later Argentine Ambassador to the US 1931–43, to Spain 1945–55, & to Brazil 1955–59.
† See *The Heart Has Its Reasons* (Michael Joseph, 1956), p. 98.
‡ Courtney Letts (1899–1995), one of Chicago's foremost debutantes, married (1) Wellesley H. Stillwell (2) John Borden, twice divorced, before she married Espil in 1933. After his death, she married (1974) Foster Adams. She died in Washington.

had access to them, particularly in light of the fact that the Duchess was going to New York. He wanted only John Utter and Miss Schütz to have a collective mandate with the Banque Morgan in Paris for access to the jewels.

Amiguet wanted an inventory created of all the furniture, pictures, rugs, objects of value, silver and utensils and even kitchen equipment in no. 4 Route du Champ d'Entraînement. He wanted everything to be photographed, especially the silver, porcelain, gold boxes, jade and the books in the library, copies to be given to himself and Maître Blum. He wanted to send a financial controller from the Société de Banque Suisse to check the household accounts. He wanted a copy of the last set of accounts (1972), as audited in London. Amiguet told John Utter that this was essential to protect the Duchess and also to safeguard Utter himself in his responsibilities towards her.[16]

I was back in Paris again in March 1974, on which occasion John Utter again invited me to Osmoy, this time to meet Sir Oswald and Lady Mosley, both of whom made a considerable impression on me. We were driven down there again (this time by Josef, the Duchess's gardener), accompanied by a talented pianist, Edward Auer, who was coming to stay at Osmoy to practise in advance of a concert he was giving at the Wigmore Hall in London.

Diana Mosley came in first, dressed fluffily, a tall lady with pure white hair and beautiful blue eyes. She was smiling broadly and gave me her hand with a slightly unnatural but graceful sweeping gesture. I thought her exactly like an 'Hon. in the cupboard' and she completely lived up to my concept of what a Mitford should be.

Then Sir Oswald entered. Though he was seventy-seven years old, he had the presence of a sixty-year-old – tall, confident and I thought how physically strong he must have been as a young man. The famous moustache had gone, his bright eyes looked directly at one, and his smile was generous (though it was not unlike that hewn on a pumpkin on Hallowe'en). His complexion was brown, and his skin had the dark spots of old age. His attitude was somewhat military, and the back of his head and neck reminded me of Erich von Stroheim.*

Before lunch we chatted about burglars. Lady Mosley said: 'People like the Duchess of Windsor who have nightwatchmen, one hears them talking about how one passed the other's house and saw them asleep.'

---

*Erich von Stroheim, Austrian film director and actor, who specialised in portraying villainous Germans, dubbed 'The man you love to hate'.

John told of how he had been at the Festival Internationale du Son for a concert, and someone had come from the Duchess's house to say there had been a burglary. He said that was impossible, only to find that it had been at his own flat.

After lunch Sir Oswald discoursed on British and French politics, the countries' attitudes to war, and Harold Wilson – 'Look at that little man with his pipe, hiding behind the smoke, saying nothing, holding his party together when they want to go this way and that. That's why all the other parties hate him so much.' He talked of the need in politics of 'the power of persuasion'. 'You can be successful in your affairs, but without this, you will never be a good politician.' Sir Oswald had it in full measure.

Later everyone walked in the garden. Sir Oswald had a confidential chat about a possible book on the Duke of Windsor that he hoped his biographer, Robert Skidelsky, might write. John said that he had contemplated writing one himself. Mosley said he could think of no one more suitable, but John again said: 'If you destroy the illusion, they'll hate you for it.' Mosley also said that John would be wise not to invite the Duchess to his lovely house as she would be covetous of it. John assured him that the Duchess had been there to lunch without there being any such issues.[17]

On 29 March the Duchess sailed to New York from Cannes on board the *Michelangelo*. Miss Schütz accompanied her on this visit as she would the following year. So did Maria, as maid, and the pugs, which lived below deck. Monsieur Martin flew to New York in advance in order to have the car ready and everything prepared for the Duchess's arrival.

The Duchess stayed mainly in her cabin and her name did not appear on the passenger list. Sometimes she dined in the dining room, largely out of consideration for Miss Schütz, to make the voyage more interesting for her. On these occasions the Duchess would get Maria to enquire whether Johanna wanted anything ironed so that she knew which colours she would be wearing.

During the voyage the Duchess always called Johanna 'Darling' rather than 'Miss Schütz' as she did not want the other passengers to think she was travelling with her secretary. When they entered the ship's dining room the whole room would immediately fall silent and the passengers would watch as the Duchess made her way slowly to her corner table.

The Duchess then liked to observe the other guests and speculate about their lives, sometimes all too audibly: 'Shall we invite that one tomorrow?' – 'Those two are pansies' – 'Maybe we'll go to the ball and see those two?' But she took little part in shipboard life. One evening the captain and first officers would invite her for cocktails and another evening she would reciprocate.

They arrived in New York on 9 April and again stayed at the Waldorf Towers, but this time in a different apartment. Nathan Cummings sent some fine paintings to cheer it up.

Cummings was the son of Jewish immigrants from Minsk in Russia, near the Polish border. Originally called Komiensky, his parents fled following a wave of anti-Semitism resulting from the assassination of Tsar Alexander II in 1881, and arrived in Saint John, New Brunswick, Canada, where Nathan was born in 1896. The family settled in Waltham, Massachusetts in 1905 and set up a shoe shop.

Young Nate worked in a store but when he was fourteen he was laid off. Cold, hungry and broke, he walked to Brooklyn. He made a resolution: 'The night I lost my job, I swore that one day I would be very, very rich and totally secure.'[18] In 1924, by now aged twenty-eight and with a wife and small family, Nate opened his own shoe shop and factory but went bankrupt in 1929. He rose from this setback and by 1939 had acquired McCormick's, a biscuit and candy factory in Canada. He sold this successfully and went on to manage and later acquire C.D. Kenny and Company, a Baltimore-based coffee, tea and sugar chain, then on the point of bankruptcy. He went from strength to strength, acquiring more and more companies, and in 1945 he formed the Consolidated Grocers Corporation in Chicago. In 1954 he changed the name to Consolidated Foods Corporation. (In the year of his death this was again changed to the Sara Lee Corporation.) Though he officially retired in 1968 he remained active in the company until the end of his life.

Cummings lived for work, expecting as much from himself as from those around him. His lifetime motto was: 'Nothing will ever be attempted if all possible objections must be first overcome.'[19] He had difficult relations with his sons and in 1948 his first wife Ruth, then in failing health, pleaded in vain with him not to take on any new businesses or commitments.

Cummings became interested in art when an advertising man suggested that he should have the view from his window painted. He was in Paris in 1945 and spotted a painting in a dealer's window. He bought it – a harvesting scene by Camille Pissarro. He went on to acquire an enormous number of paintings from the late nineteenth century and early twentieth century. He bought French Impressionists (Matisse, Gauguin and Degas), modern sculpture (including works by Giacometti), and works by Picasso, Chagall, Henry Moore and others. Douglas Cooper wrote that Cummings bought paintings entirely for their appeal to him. His choice was 'not determined by any aesthetic ideal, scientific plan or preconceived plan.'[20]

He collected ancient Peruvian ceramics, many of them dating back to the early Cuspinique time in the fourth century BC. In 1966 many of these were displayed at the Metropolitan Museum in New York. Like many American millionaire businessmen Cummings established charitable foundations, donated to major museums and galleries and helped hospitals and universities. He and his second wife, Joanne Toor*, gave more than six hundred pieces to the Metropolitan and a gallery was named after them.

When Cummings celebrated, he did so in considerable style. For his eightieth birthday in 1976 he took over the ballroom of the Waldorf-Astoria. As a grand finale to the evening, a twelve-foot, eight-tiered Sara Lee birthday cake weighing 1,000 lbs was wheeled into the room. A section of it opened and Bob Hope popped out to announce: 'I'm thrilled to be here on Nate's eightieth birthday – and so is he!'[21]

John Utter had already told me how Cummings became a friend of the Windsors. The Duchess had given an interview in which she said the one thing that she missed in Paris was bagels. Cummings read this and promptly sent her a giant deep freeze so that she could store frozen bagels in Paris. Presently he began to issue invitations to the Windsors. John said the Duke was 'like a small boy' in the presence of self-made men and golf champions. Thus he admired Arnold Palmer – 'The King' of golf – and so too did he esteem Nathan Cummings.

Cummings used to fly the Duke all over the place to visit his enterprises, obtaining publicity from this and sometimes giving the Duke money in return. After what the Duke thought was a private visit to a factory in New York, he was surprised to find a barrage of photographers. He was rewarded with a substantial unsolicited cheque, which was deposited in his Swiss bank account.

While the Duchess was in her apartment, Princess Margaret and Lord Snowdon were staying at the Waldorf Astoria. On 9 May they called on her on their way to the opera. Princess Margaret took the traditional line about the Duchess. I once heard her describe her as 'that ghastly woman.'[22] She blamed her for the Abdication and the consequent death of her father. But Lord Snowdon was more sympathetic and encouraged the visit, saying 'This has gone on too long.'[23] Photographs were taken of the Princess and

---

* Joanne Toor (1928–95), daughter of Harold O. Toor, owner of the United States Shoe Company. A sophisticated New York socialite, she left Cummings for a younger man as a result of which she and Cummings divorced. They remained on amicable terms.

Snowdon in evening dress, seated either side of a smiling Duchess. The Duchess was nervous about the visit, and wondered why they had come. She was left alone with them.

During her visit the Duchess gave an interview to Keitha McLean of *Women's Wear Daily*. The Duchess was described as nervous, twisting her rings, clasping and unclasping her hands, but fielding the questions with wit and candour. Pressed on comments quoted in Ralph Martin's forthcoming book, she said: 'I don't like his style of writing,' and asked if she had said she would have settled for being the Duke's mistress, she replied: 'It's absolutely untrue. Why would I settle for mistress when I could be his wife?' She volunteered that she thought Prince Charles would marry an English girl, adding: 'But if he does marry an American, let's hope it's not a divorced one.'[24]

On 5 June the Duchess sailed back to France in the *Raffaelo*. She arrived in Cannes on 14 June to be met by John Utter, wearing a black tie. He told her that the Duke of Windsor's last surviving brother, Prince Henry, Duke of Gloucester had died after a long illness. The Duchess hastily found a black jacket to wear, such were the demands of etiquette. A few days later she was represented by Lady Monckton at the funeral at Windsor.

The Duchess hoped that Grace Dudley would accompany her to Biarritz again that summer, but Lady Dudley was not overly excited by the idea of being a *dame de compagnie* to the Duchess and resisted committing herself. She said she might have to look after Peter Ward's children or go to Sardinia. The Duchess became more and more furious, especially when Lady Dudley ended up going to stay with Count and Countess Brandolini in Venice. Then she was afraid that she would not be able to afford the suite she once shared with Lady Dudley at the hotel. But all was well and the manager was sympathetic, telling her: 'Oh yes, I know these Dudleys – always booking the so-and-so suite then not appearing, then rebooking, then arriving unexpectedly, complaining about the wrong room etc.'[25]

Instead the Duchess went to Biarritz with Carol von Radowitz, John Utter going down at the end of her stay to pick her up. She returned to Paris on 3 September. For Christmas Miss Schütz suggested that she give her friends a new signed photograph. On 14 October a Mr Kuehn came to take photographs of her at the house and one was used for the card showing the Duchess in her upstairs sitting room with her pugs, Ginseng and Diamond.

*   *   *

Two biographies came out about the Windsors during this year. They were not popular in the Windsor household, though the Duchess read neither of them. The first, in August, was the one serialised the previous year, Ralph G. Martin's *The Woman He Loved*. The book was thoroughly researched, but tackled a number of scandalous issues, including Espil, as mentioned, and the late-life friendship the Duchess had with Jimmy Donohue, as well as perceived differences between the Windsors in their marriage. Given the nature of some later books on the subject the Martin book has almost settled down into respectability.

The other biography did not delve into gossip. This was Frances Donaldson's *Edward VIII*, a tough but well-written life that examined the former King's motives for abdicating and told for the first time the story of his affair with Freda Dudley Ward. It is arguably the most intelligent book on the Windsors and though it was not an official life – and thus Lady Donaldson was not allowed access to the Duke's papers – it was nevertheless perceptive. If I were to recommend one book to a reader new to the subject, I would still suggest this one, even thirty-five years later, and despite the mass of new information that has since come into the public domain. Like James Pope-Hennessy's *Queen Mary*, it is a masterpiece.

Frances Donaldson began her book while the Duke was still alive. She took it on because she recognised the subject in what she called 'some sphere which is a mixture of intellect and emotion'.[26] Freda Dudley Ward (by then the Marquesa de Casa Maury) agreed to help her. She had been the Prince of Wales's mistress in the 1920s, and dictated the terms on which she would assist Lady Donaldson. Though 'society' knew about her, the general public did not, so this was a major revelation in the Donaldson book. Lady Monckton then set about arranging for Lady Donaldson to meet the Windsors. She gave her access to Walter Monckton's papers, which led to a meeting between Lady Donaldson and Sir Godfrey Morley, who had charge of them.

Lady Donaldson did not know then that Morley was the Duke of Windsor's solicitor. Soon afterwards she learnt that James Pope-Hennessy was going to write the official life of the Duke, with his cooperation, but when this plan foundered for some unexplained reason Sir Godfrey suggested that she should take this project on. But Lady Donaldson told him that both the Duke and Duchess had written their own accounts – she wanted to write an 'objective' version, without giving them 'a veto'.[27] Sir Isaiah Berlin told her that it would be a better book if she did not go and meet the Windsors. 'Write it as history,' he said.[28]

In her memoirs, published many years later*, Lady Donaldson gave an excellent account of how she researched and wrote her book, referring to those who had helped her and those who had not – notably Sir Alan Lascelles, who had been the Duke's private secretary in the 1920s. Nevertheless, Lascelles conceded later that she had done a fine job.

Frances Donaldson's book was again not a favourite in the Windsors' household, but the Duchess herself never read it. Maître Blum wanted to sue Lady Donaldson, on what grounds it is unclear, but the Duchess wisely dissuaded her from this action, fearing that to do so would merely give the book additional publicity.

Blum would have done well to recall this advice when she acted independently of the Duchess's wishes a few years later.

Mountbatten came to the Duchess's house in the Bois for tea on 12 November, arriving promptly as ever at 4.30 p.m. He noted: 'As we had parted on slightly distant terms because she obviously wasn't going to take my advice about what to do in her Will, I was amazed at the warmth of her reception.'

According to him, the Duchess complained that he had not been to see her for so long. He said that she had been in New York when he was last in Paris.

Once again it was not long before Mountbatten was proffering advice. At this tea the Duchess apparently told him that she was considering giving up the house and moving into a suite at the Plaza Athéné for the times when she was not in New York. She spoke of the sale of The Mill, and how she found she now had a lot of money.

She volunteered that she was thinking of creating a Duke of Windsor Fund, and Mountbatten hailed this as 'a wonderful idea', not mentioning that this had been his idea in the first place. He said he would write to her with some suggestions, 'provided she could compete with Madame Blum, her French solicitor.'[29]

He stayed for an hour and a half and claimed to be 'back in business again' due to his tact in only responding to her questions. Mountbatten left full of plans:

I am now going to discuss this with Lilibet, Charles and Martin Charteris, as I have already suggested to her that the way to keep David's name green would be in Wales, and the best thing would be through the United World Colleges of which I am the International

* *A Twentieth Century Life* (Weidenfeld & Nicolson, 1992).

President now, and Charles, I hope, will succeed me. In any case she said she wanted us both to be associated with the Duke of Windsor's Fund, and hinted that she had already asked me to be an Executor of her Will though she has never mentioned it before.

She begged me to come and see her again and said she wants to come over and see David's grave next summer.[30]

Mountbatten was quick to follow this up with a letter to the Duchess:

Dearest Wallis,

I cannot tell you how much I enjoyed our long gossip over tea on the 12th and how delighted I was to find you looking so well even though your back was giving you trouble. I hope it is better.

It was lovely talking about David again and I quite understand that you will want to come and see his grave sometime when the weather is nicer in the summer. I will pass on a message from you to Lilibet to this effect and write again.

I appreciate your problem about whether to give up your lovely house in Paris and move permanently to a hotel or not. You asked my advice but the best advice I can give you is to have two budgets prepared, one to be marked 'Budget keeping the house' and the other to be marked 'Budget giving up the house'.

In both budgets the cost of your suite in the Waldorf Towers Hotel in New York would, of course, be the same, as you intend to spend as long as you can each year in the United States.

Since you don't want to take the risk of running over six months, I suggest that the budgets should be for five and a half months in New York and six and a half months in Paris and would include, of course, the cost of your fare to and from New York which would be the same in both. Then in the case of keeping the house you would have to put in the rent, the wages and expenses of all your servants all the year round. On top of that you would have to include the cost of your own food and entertaining while living in Paris and then you would add these together and that would give you the budget for the year for your living expenses keeping the house.

In the budget giving up the house you would substitute for the house and servants' expenses an item for what you would have to pay to your chosen hotel which I understand is the Plaza Athéné in the Avenue Georges V*. I presume you would get your representative to

---

* The Plaza Athéné is in Avenue Montaigne.

drive a good bargain with them for a suite for six and a half months of every year.

You said you wanted to take your best pictures and furniture into the suite, which would greatly enhance the value of the suite, and should be taken into consideration in reducing the hotel charges.

You then raised the question of what to do with all your other belongings and told me that you intended to sell all surplus furniture and pictures but were worried about what to do concerning the items which you were leaving to Lilibet in your Will in any case: that is, the Garter banner, the boxes which contained the Great Seal of England and all the other boxes that had the Prince of Wales's feathers or the insignia of David as King or Duke of Windsor, and any other particularly personal or family objects.

Surely, the simplest thing would be to ask Lilibet whether you could send them over to her at Windsor now to keep as they would be coming to her on your death in any case by your Will. If you would like to retain the right to recall any single item such as you could have struck out in your own Will, I am sure she would have no objection to your being able to recall any item in these circumstances. Thus they would be, as it were, on loan pending their passing over by means of your Will at your death. I can pass on all this to Lilibet after you have made up your mind.

Look after your health, please try not to do too much.

Very much love
Dickie[31]

Receiving no reply to his letter, Mountbatten telephoned the house on 4 December and spoke to Miss Schütz. Monsieur Amiguet happened to be there when the call came through. A note was made of the conversation. Mountbatten began to ask if the Duchess was satisfied with the information in his letter. He enquired about 'the other matter', meaning The Prince of Wales Fund. 'I talked to Prince Charles and he accepts to be the head of it with me. HRH told me to get in contact with Mr Amiguet. May I have his telephone number?' He was told that Amiguet 'always wanted to be in the background' and that the Duchess's permission would be needed before Miss Schütz could give out the number. Mountbatten asked that she or the Duchess call him.[32]

A few days later the Duchess wrote to Mountbatten in her own hand, a letter devised for her by Maître Blum:

Dear Dicky,

Thank you so much for [your] letter of November 25th and your kind suggestion on my behalf. I will let you [know] later on if I decide or not to give up my house in the Bois de Boulogne. As to the depositions in my will, I confirm to you once more, that everything has been taken care of according to David's and my wishes, and I believe that everyone will be satisfied. There is therefore no need of you contacting my advisor in Switzerland. It is always a pleasure to see you, but I must tell you that when you leave me I am always terribly depressed by your reminding me of David's death and my own, and I should be grateful if you would not mention this any more.

With love and do let me know when you are next in Paris. *Wallis*.[33]

Mountbatten retreated without entirely giving up hope. He never saw the Duchess again. Johanna Schütz managed to keep him away when a visit by him to New York coincided with the Duchess's stay there. When he visited Paris in 1975, the Duchess was in the American Hospital, and when he tried again in October 1976 he was told that the doctors permitted no visitors.

9

The Duchess's Decline – 1975–1976

John Utter officially 'retired' on 19 March 1975. It transpired that he and Miss Schütz did not get on well together, and gradually this lack of rapport intensified. Although I saw them together on several occasions I never saw a hint of this antipathy.

Later both spoke of it to me. Johanna Schütz thought John was too old and ineffectual, and blamed him for not standing up to Maître Blum.* He was, in turn, mistrustful of Miss Schütz. The Duchess had never been in rapport with him, though she relied on him in many ways. It seems that once the Windsors had hired Miss Schütz to work for them they hoped to dispense with Utter's services. But she was not sure how long she would stay and when she realised how seriously ill the Duke was she insisted that Utter should stay on.

As we have seen, the Duchess wanted to remove Utter at the time of the Duke's death but was persuaded by Sir Godfrey Morley to keep him on. There was an occasion at a dinner party at the Duchess's house with two tables of eight. Utter arranged the seating and placed himself in what would have been the Duke's chair. The next day Georges reported that the Duchess had pointed across the room angrily and said: 'Who is that man?' She was said to have resented the honorary CVO he received from the Queen in December 1972 for his services to the Duke.

There are several accounts suggesting that Miss Schütz effected Utter's departure. Maurice Amiguet, the banker, took the line that it was time to reduce the number of staff in order to economise. Blum would have seen Utter's departure as a step towards taking eventual control, because he was one of the few people who knew the previous limitations of her role and could gainsay her. Blum said later of John: '*Monsieur Utter manque une colonne vertébrale.*' She chose to believe that John handed over the Duke's papers, Orders and decorations in exchange for his CVO.[1] Hating the British as she did, Maître Blum was furious about John Utter's honour from the Palace.

* I visited Johanna Schütz in her office in September 1976. She asked if I'd seen Mr Utter or not. I said he seemed to be enjoying his retirement. 'I just wish he wouldn't go round saying nasty things about the Duchess,' she said. 'He hasn't seen her for two years.' I said that he hadn't said anything like that to me. 'I'm glad to hear it,' she replied [Hugo Vickers diary, 14 September 1976].

The well-known Paris based journalist Sam White noted his departure and hinted that relations between John and the Duchess had become
strained:

> Their differences have centred in the recent months on the Duchess's
> decision to launch an economy wave in her Paris establishment. This
> has involved the painful dismissal of many old servants . . .[2]

From Utter's point of view there was little more that he could do for
the Duchess. He was not in the best of health. He turned seventy in
1975, so retirement was how his departure was described. A year later
he told me his theories about what happened:

> John thinks the reason he was got rid of was that the Swiss banker
> etc. think he was 'too close to the Palace'. Miss Schütz is effective
> in keeping him away. He used to ring the Duchess every day and
> go to dinner about once every two months, and then one day
> Germaine [the concierge] told him that Miss Schütz had ordered
> the phone calls not to be put through.* 'She wants to be King-pin
> and be there as the secretary at the funeral etc, and the Palace are
> not too keen on her,' he said.[3]

In fact it was Blum and Dr Thin who kept him away. He never saw
the Duchess after March 1975.

Some years later, Walter Lees volunteered that the Duchess had been
livid when John received his CVO. He also recalled that once the Duke
and Duchess had declared: 'Utter has been disloyal.' He asked them:
'Oh, what makes you think that?' They replied: 'Dr Antenucci told us.'
To this he said: 'Well I dislike anyone who'd say such a thing.' Lees went
on to describe Antenucci as '*not* a good doctor, just a social one.'† He
thought John had been kind to the Duchess.[4]

The result was that Johanna Schütz, the Duchess's Swiss secretary, took
on the duties of Private Secretary. Blum and Amiguet instructed her not
to be in touch with Utter after he left, and they never saw each other again.

In the spring of 1975, or possibly in the late months of 1974, Prudence
Glynn‡ interviewed the Duchess for a fashion article in *The Times*. She was

---

* This harks back to the 1930s when Freda Dudley Ward rang the Prince of Wales, to be told by
the switchboard that they had orders not to put her through.
† Miss Schütz thought him an excellent doctor, and the Windsors relied on him heavily.
‡ Prudence Glynn (1935–86), fashion writer, married to Lord Windlesham (1932–2010).

taken there by a friend they had in common. The article is significant because there is more description of the house, the background, Glynn's slight apprehension at meeting the Duchess, than of anything the Duchess actually said to her. From it we learn that the Duchess was still surrounded by her pugs, that she was 'a little birdlike lady', anxious, yet considerate as a hostess. She told Glynn that she had spent all her morning with lawyers, adding 'not much sense of humour, lawyers'. Other than that her comments were confined to remarks such as 'I can't fit ready-to-wear because my shoulders are too broad.'

Glynn clearly struggled to fill her page. She hinted that the Duchess's mental powers had declined and that she found it novel having to deal with the financial and legal matters placed before her. But she found that the Duchess exuded a certain cosiness:

> The awesome veneer is certainly not cracked, but it turns out to be soft sculpture. She is not slick or glossy or point-scoring, though she is so tremendously gregarious. She is also very strong-minded – she does not sleep but will not take pills, because she disapproves of the habit.

Glynn concluded that the Duchess had acquired a strong resemblance to the ladies of the Royal House of Windsor.[5] Reading between the lines, it is clear that the Duchess was past saying anything worth quoting in an article.

On 9 April the Duchess went down to Cannes with Miss Schütz and they lunched with Maître Blum in her South of France residence before sailing to New York. Since giving up her villa on the Cap d'Antibes, Blum lived at L'Escareine, Moulin de la Vallée, some twenty kilometres from Nice.

Blum had recently bought a house, La Cormelière, Échiré, near her birthplace of Niort. Not having sold this South of France house, she asked if she could submit a bill to the Duchess, since she had not done so. This was agreed and it enabled her to make a down payment on the house in which she was settled by February 1976. Later Blum would always maintain that she never submitted any such bills.

In the South of France the Duchess generously gave her lawyer a small Cartier brooch made of rubies and sapphires, with an interlocking W & E.* Presently the Duchess sailed to the United States with Miss Schütz, arriving in New York on 19 April. They stayed until 26 June. The Duchess's office diary records a visit from her American lawyer, Hank Walter, on 6 May.

---

* Maître Blum put this brooch into the Geneva sale of the Duchess's jewels, as property of the Duchess of Windsor (Lot 43) and it sold for 132,000 Swiss francs.

The Duchess sailed back to Cannes, arriving there on 5 July and was back in Paris by midnight the same day. Regrettably, some items were stolen from some of her eleven suitcases during the train journey back to Paris.

On 12 August Miss Schütz went with her and Carol von Radowitz to Biarritz, and the Duchess suffered from an upset stomach. She came back from Biarritz on 3 September and on the eighteenth she dined with Sir Edward and Lady Tomkins at the British Embassy.

One of her staff once said that before the Duke died the Duchess knew everything, and after he died she knew nothing. It is a generalisation, but perceptive – for, while the Duke lived, she kept the show on the road, but after he died there was no longer the same incentive to sustain the myth. Of course, she continued to dress beautifully and have her hair done for as long as she could, to entertain and to be entertained, and to travel. But it cannot have been easy for her.

In times of decline, things begin to go wrong, not to mention missing. In November 1974 there had been an incident concerning the Duchess's jewels, when the key to the safe at the Morgan Bank went missing. A search was set in motion and presently the keys and some hairpins were found, apparently tucked behind the seat in the Duchess's black car.

On 12 September there was a dinner party at the house at which Lord Tennyson, Diana Vreeland, Tassos Fondaras and Ambassador and Mrs Henry Taylor* were present. Another visitor earlier that day had been Madame Metz, a secretary (formerly called Janine Spaner) who had worked for the Windsors in the early 1960s, before her marriage. On the Monday Georges noticed that two lacquer boxes (one of them a rectangular box with a blue enamel centre lid) had disappeared from the salon. Miss Schütz wanted to call the police but Blum and Amiguet said not to. Miss Schütz questioned all the guests. Fondaras later told friends that he had seen the Ambassador slip 'something valuable' into his coat pocket. He stared the Ambassador down and after dinner the object was returned. Miss Schütz's conclusion was that the Duchess may well have given the boxes as a present. This tended to happen and it is not uncommon for old people to do this. John Utter had noticed that if he praised a picture she was likely to tell him to take it. He never did, but was alert to the dangers.

During the lacquer-box weekend, Maria Costa also lost an imitation gold bracelet.

* * *

* Henry J. Taylor (1902–84), US Ambassador in Berne, broadcaster, writer and novelist, friend of the Windsors since 1943; m. 1970, as his second wife, Marion (Rikki) Richardson (d. 2010), artist & philanthropist.

By this time Miss Schütz was intensely worried by the growing influence of Maître Blum. She saw the direction in which things were heading, and thought it essential to rescue the Duchess from Blum's control. It was not possible to do this while the Duchess was in Paris. Therefore, on the return from Biarritz, a second trip to New York was arranged, the unstated plan being to effect a coup when the Duchess was safely the other side of the Atlantic.

A booking was made on the *Queen Elizabeth 2* for the Duchess to sail to New York in the third week of November. Assisting her was Nathan Cummings. He reserved an apartment for the Duchess at the Plaza Hotel.

On 15 October the Duchess went to dinner with Gaby Bentinck, one of the last times she dined out. John Phillips, a writer best known as the young friend of Violet Trefusis, was designated to collect her. He found her charm intact as she served him champagne and talked of San Francisco, China and her beloved pugs. She found it hard to remember where they were going for dinner and asked him the same question many times. Then, as the Duchess's chauffeur drove them through the Bois de Boulogne, she suddenly panicked: '*Mon bijou*, where is it?' An earring had fallen. '*On trouvera le bijou, Altesse Royale*' said the chauffeur. As they looked for it – and found it – the Duchess spotted the prostitutes in the Bois: 'Look. The girls! The girls! Is it good business?'[6] This is almost the last vignette of the Duchess before she fell ill.

Amongst Miss Schütz's many concerns was her knowledge that the Duchess had been made sick by Maître Blum continually worrying her over money issues. Not only had Blum turned her against her honourable English lawyer but she had suggested she might be thrown out of her house in the Bois de Boulogne, and pestered her about the cost of the wages of her staff and her other expenses. These were considerable, but the Duchess had plenty of money in Switzerland to pay for them.

The travel plans remained in place and the suitcases were prepared and packed. As usual when the Duchess travelled, her jewels were brought from the bank and laid out on her bed, creating a magnificent display. Maria held up the selected dresses, appropriate jewels were chosen to match the colours, these were insured, and the rest of the collection returned to the bank.

The proposed trip did not find favour with Blum, Amiguet or Georges. Throughout September and October the Duchess received numerous visits from her lawyer, which caused her great agitation.

Tragically, the Duchess never made this last journey. The strain of the impending voyage and the tensions of frequent visits from Blum wore her down. On 8 November she fell ill. Two days later Blum and Amiguet visited her again and then on 12 November she was well enough to accept an invitation to lunch with Blum and Hugh Fullerton, the former Governor of the American Hospital and Blum's ally when she fled from France in 1940.

In later years Blum boasted that the last time the Duchess ever went out was to lunch with her. This was true and in retrospect it was an unlikely and depressing finale to the Duchess's extended years of social life. At least Hugh Fullerton was there. He is remembered as an elegant and cultured man and would have enhanced any lunch table.

Unfortunatley the next day the Duchess of Windsor suffered a perforated ulcer which led to a severe internal haemorrhage. She was taken to the American Hospital where, according to John Utter, who continued to enquire about the Duchess's state of health as best he could, she was 'definitely on the way out'.

At that time the American Hospital was acquiring an increasingly poor reputation in the Paris medical community. Richard René Silvin, the management consultant assessing the way it was run, worried that the hospital was coasting on its former excellent reputation. Its Chief of Surgery, Maurice Mercadier, who had been consulted over the Duchess's health when she was in the hospital, had a bad track record of infections amongst his patients. Silvin recalled:

> Mercadier would bring his own instruments into surgery! He claimed he was a great surgeon because he could see the Eiffel Tower from 'his' operating theatre and be inspired! He hated me when I told him the new theatre block would have no windows and he would have to derive his inspiration elsewhere. 'En plus' all operating theatre instruments would be centrally sterilised by us.[7]

If suspicion of this surgeon's incompetence were needed, it had come earlier that year. Aristotle Onassis, the Greek shipping tycoon, had been operated on by Mercadier to remove his gall bladder. Onassis never recovered from the operation and died soon after in the American Hospital on 15 March 1975.[8]

The Duchess, who was gravely ill and dying, was patched up and sent home a wreck.

Paparazzi photographs were taken of the Duchess of Windsor in the American Hospital. These photographers must have spent hours outside the building, waiting to catch a glimpse of her. Finally she was captured in grainy photographs, being helped up from a chair or possibly a commode. These pictures were the last where she still resembled her former self. Her hair was well done, and still dyed auburn. She wore a shawl and retained her dignity and poise. This would not last much longer. Blum visited her in hospital on 28 November. And there were visits from Dr Antenucci, Robin Beare and Dean Oliver of the American Cathedral*.

After her return to the house in the Bois, the Duchess never fully recovered her health. It is easy to say in retrospect – and it was certainly said at the time – that it would have been better if the Duchess had been allowed to die in the hospital. Instead she was destined to live a pathetic existence for the next ten years, in which there were few, if any, moments of pleasure or happiness.

The Duchess returned to the house in the Bois in January 1976. Soon afterwards John Utter wrote to me:

The poor Duchess is back in the house after almost two months in the American Hospital. I fear her days of entertaining and being entertained are over, as the nurses have now taken over.[9]

In February 1976 he told me:

She is now so old and ill. She should have died soon after the Duke. She always thought everyone would shun her after the Duke's death. This didn't happen and a lot of the young people invited her and went to the house . . .

Not long ago the Duchess asked a Mrs Malone† to go to lunch there. She said the Duchess's head fell to one side. She picked at her food. Mrs M. left after 55 minutes and the Duchess went straight to bed.[10]

Nevertheless Nate Cummings still hoped that she might effect the move to the United States. He talked to her in January 1976 and told her that if she planned another visit, then Dr Antenucci would 'accompany her and hold her hand, etc.'.

The Duchess had a nurse assigned to her in the American Hospital who accompanied her back home in due course. While the Duchess was in

* Very Rev. Robert Oliver, Dean of the American Cathedral in Paris 1974–9.
† Mrs Halsey Malone, who lived in the Seizième district of Paris.

the hospital, this nurse found her having problems sleeping, which she thought was due to her being overstimulated by the drugs she was being prescribed. She found her at times completely confused, and worse during the night.

At one point the Duchess slept for two days in succession, after which her brain was less anxious and she began to talk in her normal voice.

The Duchess's three nurses from the American Hospital each had over ten years' nursing experience. They agreed that the Duchess had not been at all well since her return home from the hospital in January. She was tired and became anxious at the end of each day. They were concerned that she should not have to worry about anything, especially during what was still described as a period of convalescence. Her resistance had been drained by alcohol abuse, her nerves were tense, and none of this was helping her get over her gastric ulcer. Her mental health was poor and her blood pressure high.

The Duchess had conceded that she was now old and ill. Sometimes, when in pain, she pleaded with the nurses, hoping that 'the Good Lord would take her away', as one of the nurses put it. At other times she became more aware of her plight, seeing herself as an elderly invalid, and then her mind would wander back to more 'glorious' days. On these occasions she either worried that she should be entertaining friends or that she could no longer entertain. Her digestion remained poor, and her abdomen became swollen as a result of the Crohn's disease from which she was suffering.

The nurses volunteered their opinions from time to time, while recognising that Dr Thin was in charge.

During January Blum came to the house, Professor Buchet came to see the Duchess about her eyes, and she was well enough to dine downstairs with Lord Tennyson on 15 January and with Monsieur Amiguet and Johanna Schütz on 26 January.

By the end of January there was no marked improvement in her health. Therefore, on 6 February she was forced to cancel a dinner with Baron de Redé and went back to hospital, which she deeply resented.

The Duchess returned home after ten days, well rested. Once she was back, she was better physically but more confused mentally. She began to ask about entertaining friends for lunch and dinner. Sometimes she was restless at night and asked if she could get dressed to go home, despite being already at home. She went through phases when she was over-agitated, followed by times when she was subdued. All the doctors could do was to give her extra tranquillisers. The nurses requested that a hospital bed should be ordered as they found it difficult lifting her in and out of her normal one.

In March one of the nurses suggested that the Duchess's spinal chord had been damaged by excessive alcohol and that her muscles were slowly becoming paralysed. This meant that her heart muscles were affected – contracted and strained – which caused her to tremble. Her neck and spine were deformed.

The nurses detected a problem with visitors because they caused excitement. Sometimes the Duchess had three bad nights in a row, the nurse then deciding it was better to let her sleep late to catch up rather than sedate her. The Duchess would never submit to the routine they wanted for her, so they had to adapt to hers.

In April the Duchess's condition appeared critical for a while, but she was sustained by vitamin B12 injections. The three nurses all remained on duty over Easter. They thought that Easter depressed her. On Easter Sunday morning the Duchess asked the nurse on duty if anyone was going to church. One of them was going to the American Cathedral and promised to pray for her recovery, which seemed to please her. It was sad that the more lucid the Duchess was the more depressed she became.

All was not well among the nurses themselves. They complained that the Duchess's chef did not provide them with adequate meals, and they frequently suffered from stomach upsets. All they got to sustain them through the night were eight small sandwiches and some fruit. The bread was too thin and unevenly buttered, and often they found the sandwiches so dry that by the time they came to eat them they fell apart. They asked for the sandwiches to be augmented by some cake, a tart, a pudding, or a single yoghurt.[12]

They took the dogs away

One of the Duchess's pleasures in life was the presence of her pugs. In a television interview Sydney Johnson, the Duke's Bahamian valet, said the pugs were like the children the Duke and Duchess never had. They ate from their own bowls with their names on them. They travelled to New York with the Duchess, living below deck but being walked at regular intervals. In Paris they were very much in evidence and I saw them running about on my first visit in 1972. Sadly, one of them died in the summer of the Duke's death.

When the Duchess fell ill, the pugs called Ginseng (Chew) and Diamond (the Duke's black pug) were still in the house. Also on the property was the mongrel dog, Pompon, who lived at the gatehouse with Germaine the concierge. Presently, however, the nurses said they feared that the dogs might infect the Duchess. So they were taken from her. They lived elsewhere in the house, looked after by Georges and Monsieur Martin until they – the dogs – died. The Duchess never saw them again.

Another major issue was the question of visitors. The Duchess relied heavily on friends for stimulation. But for the remaining months of 1976 it was Maître Blum who decided who should be allowed to see the Duchess and for how long. Very often, though not always, she made a point of being present in order to hear what was said. None of this was pleasant for the Duchess.

Miss Schütz was still working at the house as secretary, and Georges was still monitoring the comings and goings, rare as these now were.

One of those who took an interest in the Duchess was Robin Beare, the same doctor who had been concerned with the Duke's illness. He was a very distinguished plastic surgeon, working with Sir Archibald McIndoe at East Grinstead. He was a friend of Lady Monckton, who considered herself the Duchess's best friend and had been a loyal visitor during these years of widowhood. She would have been surprised to know that the Duchess found her pushy and severe and her visits hard work.

Lady Monckton was anxious to see the Duchess, but by March 1976 Maître Blum and Dr Thin had imposed a ban on visitors.

Robin Beare realised that he had to deal with Maître Blum. He came over to Paris and had dinner with Blum at the Duchess's house, though the Duchess herself was not at the table. Also dining were General Spillmann, Dr Thin and his wife. Beare was allowed to see the Duchess. But in advance of his visit, Blum ensured that the Duchess was sedated so that she could not tell him anything. On his return to England he said that the only way he knew that she recognised him was that a single tear rolled down her cheek.[13] On his return to London, Beare wrote to Blum from Harley Street:

I have thought about this very carefully and I have come firmly to the conclusion that Lady Monckton *should* pay a visit to Her Royal Highness in the near future for the following reasons: –

Firstly, she is the Duchess's oldest and closest friend and indeed, she is the only person who might be regarded as a member of the family.

Secondly, I think it important that Lady Monckton should see for herself the tragic state of health which the Duchess now suffers.

Thirdly, there is always the possibility that this visit might be the last one possible.

Fourthly, it is impossible to predict whether such a visit would be beneficial or detrimental to the Duchess's health, and this can only be established by a 'therapeutical trial'. It might well do her a lot of good, and I do hope it proves to be so.

As a postscript Beare added: 'I feel that this visit should take place *regardless* of what the doctors say.'[14] To this Blum replied that when she had spoken to the Duchess about a visit from Lady Monckton a mere week before, the reply had been a categorical no. Blum said she was not sure if this was because the Duchess feared being tired, did not wish to evoke old memories, or to appear diminished. She assured Beare that she would not stand in the way of such a visit, and that she was motivated only by the fear that even a very short call might cause the Duchess to get over-excited or enervated, and that afterwards it would be difficult to calm her down.[15]

That summer Princess Ann-Mari von Bismarck* asked Diana Mosley to intercede with the Royal Household to get a message to the Royal Family to the effect that the Duchess was dying all alone and, as Princess Bismarck understood it, wanted her royal in-laws to know this.

The message came back that the Windsors were blamed for the Abdication in 1936, the death of King George VI in 1952 and 'that being K & Q not only killed him but half killed Cake'†. Diana Mosley commented:

Well, if Cake hated her spell as Q I'll eat my hat & coat, & then how about all the Christianity & chat about widows, the dying, & forgiveness of sins & loving one's enemy etc. Isn't it richly hypocritical . . . I never can get over Christians, their unkindness is so much deeper than ours. What could it all matter, we shall soon be dust & turned to clay.[16]

Not everything went badly. One day the Duchess had a visitor, and her nurse observed that she held herself straight-backed in her armchair in the boudoir, well made-up and well dressed. The manner in which she held her head indicated to her visitor that she was pleased to receive her. At other times the Duchess was annoyed to find herself looked after by strange nurses on the rare occasions when Maria had a day off.

---

* Ann-Mari Tengbem (1907–99), m. 1928. Prince Otto von Bismarck (1897–1975), grandson of the Chancellor. A rich, social lady, immaculately dressed by the best couturiers, she died in Marbella.
† The (Dowager) Duchess of Devonshire's nickname for the Queen Mother.

By the beginning of May the nurses noticed some improvement in the Duchess's health, due, they maintained, to vitamin-B-complex injections. The Duchess became more communicative, though she was still far from well. It began to be possible to take her out into the garden 'to make the days more pleasant and to enjoy a little bit of what life can offer her', as one nurse put it.

Unfortunately this led to trouble due to the paparazzi. They photographed and filmed the Duchess on several different days as she was carried out onto the terrace for an afternoon in the sun. She appeared weak and emaciated, her head hanging to one side, her hair pulled back in a bun. She was lifted from a wheelchair and placed on a garden bed. Another photograph showed a nurse feeding her from a medical bottle.

I first heard about this from John Utter, whom I saw in Paris at this time:

John was looking much better than when I last saw him. He had some horrifying news about the Duchess of Windsor. There'd been a film on the news and a picture in the paper of the Duchess being carried out onto the terrace. She looked frightful, ill and agonised. Miss Schütz was nearby, though not in the picture, Georges [in fact one of the outdoor watchmen], Maria (the maid) and a nurse were in evidence.

The Duchess nearly died last November when she had a bleeding ulcer. She has a strong heart, however, and has pulled through. The Duchess may have had a stroke, has problems keeping her head up at all, and is only lucid from time to time. Her party days are over, and she can only move with the aid of nurses, has to be carried through to the boudoir.

The picture certainly confirmed all one's fears. The doctor tries to prevent old friends seeing her as it upsets her. 'Biddy' Monckton got a fearful shock on a five-minute visit, and another time wasn't allowed in at all.

It is a thoroughly sad story altogether – the Duchess must realise in her lucid moments the state she is in yet maybe there is a will to live in it all somewhere.

There are tales of Maître Blum intervening . . .'[17]

A few days later I gave John a copy of *Hola*, which contained one set of the full-colour photographs of the Duchess. He said he would pass this on to Maître Blum. He did so and Blum litigated against the photographer

and any outlet that published the photographs for invasion of privacy (representing the Duchess 'as a helpless old woman'). She won damages reported
to total $32,000 from *France Soir* and French TV.[18]

One of the Duchess's nurses was particularly shocked to hear what
had happened while she was on leave, commenting: 'There are so little
pleasures left for HRH these days, even to enjoy a change of scenery and
the sunshine is menaced by the journalists and photographers . . .'[19]

On 5 June 1976 Lady Mosley wrote to Lady Monckton:

> Ann Mari Bismarck came on her way from Spain & we dined
> with her. She didn't see the Duchess this time. As you say it's
> up & down. I only hope she's not too wretched – perhaps *not*.
> One could only judge that if one were with her all the time. Poor
> little Duchess . . .
>
> I saw John Utter yesterday at a party at the Admiral's – the
> Sotheby Admiral*. He quite agrees that none of the Duchess's
> devoted servants would have told the television photographers that
> she was going to be brought down in the garden & that (as Bowyer
> said) one must suspect one of the nurses. Too bad really. I haven't
> seen [the] Spanish magazine but it sounds horrid.[20]

In June the Duchess turned eighty, thus entering the last decade of
her life. It was reported in the British press that the Queen had sent
congratulations to her.

The Duchess's state remained unchanged. Sometimes she talked of
receptions, invitations, or seeing the hairdresser. She spoke of whisky or
Martinis. She tended to become particularly confused in the evenings,
especially if she had had a visitor. One such visitor who was allowed to
call was Diana Mosley, who reported to Lady Monckton:

> They allow 2 visits a week of ¼ of an hour – all the rest of the time
> I suppose she just sits doing nothing, it is terribly sad. She looked
> incredibly frail & thin. She was absolutely all there but just reminds
> one of the person one knew, a sort of very sad shadow of her. Poor
> little Duchess. The nurse I saw seemed kind & gentle. I talked to
> Miss Schütz afterwards. It must be really awful for her, there all
> the time. I only wish John were there too, one feels they need a

* Rear-Admiral John Templeton-Cotill, CB (1920–2011), Commander British Forces, Malta 1972–3,
Director of Sotheby Parke Bernet (France) 1974–81; & Sotheby Parke Bernet (Monaco) 1975–81).

sensible clever man of the world – however no good thinking of *that*, & it can't be helped now. I asked her if she can sleep & she looked desperate & said NO. She never slept well at the best of times. One felt terribly sad & completely useless – nothing one can do, & I came away deeply depressed.[21]

By July the Duchess was calmer and sometimes smiling, able to have some normal conversations with her nurses, and to enjoy having her make-up applied while sitting in a chair. For some hours in the day she was even quite lucid. With the improvement sadness came again, as the Duchess became more aware of how ill she was and that she would never again lead a normal life. This proved an opportunity for one nurse to complain how another kept the Duchess in bed until four p.m. when it was not necessary. 'No wonder H. R. H. got irritable in curling-up positions, and also bad for her breathing.'

It was not long before the nurses became fractious. They demanded a pay rise which was not granted. They began to complain about each other. They argued about when each would take a holiday and who the replacement nurses would be when one or other was away. They complained that the nightwatchman had shouted at them during the night, using insulting language and making aggressive grimaces at them. At the beginning of August all three nurses handed in their notice in protest, though none left at that time.

In August the Duchess was making some progress, though when Ambassador Taylor and his wife proposed a visit they were warned that they would get a shock at the Duchess's decline since their last visit.[22] Towards the end of the month the Duchess was even trying to read a little, struggling with the newspaper print which she found too small. Magazines were better for her, as the pictures were colourful and she was interested to learn about the autumn and winter fashions. She could sit in her armchair a certain amount, which meant increased monitoring in case she tried to get up and then fell. For this reason bars were attached to her bed at night.

The nurses then complained about the kitchen boy and how unhygienic the kitchen had become. Not only were they having stomach problems but the Duchess was suffering too, and even the two pugs. One evening the Duchess was given langoustine for dinner and had to spit out hard shells. As the nurse commented: 'If she had swallowed them, they might have perforated the new tendered [sic] tissue lining of her stomach ulcer which might endanger her life.'

The nurses were fed boiled fish tails, which gave them indigestion and they complained that a lamb chop was contaminated with fly eggs. A living fly was discovered swimming in the sauce of an escalope placed in the refrigerator for the nurses' late meal. Another nurse offered to take on responsibility for cooking, but this was not deemed wise. The other two nurses were united against her. An English replacement was found and one nurse asked that Maître Blum and Dr Thin should consider her.

By the end of August it was decided that the team of three nurses should be replaced as they were giving too much trouble. Miss Schütz asked the Duchess which of the nurses she would like to keep. She replied that she did not need any of them*. The nurses were asked not to discuss their impending departure with the Duchess, but one day towards the end of August the Duchess was grumbling about being turned and complained that she had never had such bad nursing. In America the nurses were much better, she said. That nurse then said she knew that Miss Schütz had asked her which nurse she – the Duchess – preferred. The Duchess replied: 'Did she?'

When the same nurse said she needed a vacation, the Duchess said 'You do work hard, don't you?' Then the Duchess settled down, but the nurse was aware that sometimes she recognised her and sometimes she did not. Then the Duchess would fantasise that she was on a ship heading to the United States and ask the nurse what she should wear for dinner, and what time the ship would arrive in New York. The nurse humoured her with the kind of replies that she thought she would like.[23]

Presently the three nurses from the American Hospital were replaced by two nurses from the Danish Institute. Joining the team at this time was Elvire Gozin, who remained with the Duchess until she died and was soon advertising herself on her card as 'Assistante Médicale Privée – Interprète de son Altesse Royale La Duchesse de Windsor'.

Lady Monckton and Lady Mosley were allowed to visit the Duchess on 6 September and the Edmond Borys came on 22 September.

That same month I went to the house for the last time during the life-time of the Duchess, in order to borrow some items for an exhibition for the Queen's fiftieth birthday at the Guildhall in Windsor (which the Queen Mother opened). Miss Schütz arranged this and during my brief visit to the now very quiet house told me how the Duchess was:

The Duchess is much better now. For ten months from 13 November 1975 she had been terribly ill. Now with a proper diet, no alcohol etc.

---

* In the event one of the three nurses stayed on for a further year.

she is just beginning to get her sparkle back. She is very weak, that is the problem. She can only walk with help.

She said that the Duchess could live another ten years if nothing comes along to upset her . . . J.S. said she's now better mentally than since before the Duke died.[24]

At the end of the meeting, Johanna said she had to go to the Duchess:

As I left she told me that the Duchess remembered me (I've never met her, so that's very clever). She said: 'I don't know how she does, but she said she remembered you. I showed her the book you gave her.' Off I went.[25]

Miss Schütz later said that this was the kind of thing she invariably said to foreign visitors.

Towards the end of September the slight improvement in the Duchess's health was damaged by a sudden relapse. On 28 September Dr Thin wrote to Maître Blum, giving his opinion that he was sure that however much the Duchess improved she would never be able to resume a normal social life.[26] The Duchess was returned to the American Hospital where she stayed from 5 to 20 October, ostensibly suffering from food poisoning. In reality this was done to facilitate Blum's dismissal of her chef, gardener and Germaine at the gate.* This was effected on 14 October.

Lord Mountbatten tried to visit the Duchess on 27 October but was told that no visitors were allowed. Lady Monckton and Lady Mosley came on 13 December, and Lady Mosley again on 21 December, at which meeting Maître Blum was also present.

There was still no shortage of public interest in the Windsors. There were rumours of a book by Philippe Bouvard, in which one of the stories was a fabricated one concerning the Duke peeing down his leg at the Lido 'throne room' and having to be helped by the lady attendant. Charles Murphy was scouting around, gathering material for *The Windsor Story*.† J. Bryan III got hold of John Utter and told him: 'You & Aunt Bessie Merryman are the only nice people in the book.'[27]

The distinguished journalist, James Cameron was preparing a fifty-minute documentary for the BBC to mark the fortieth anniversary of the Abdication in December 1976, based on Frances Donaldson's biography.

* *See* Chapter 10.
† *See* Chapter 12.

This was aired on 10 December and I watched it at the time, thinking it excellent, in particular the tough contribution from Helen Hardinge and the more jocular one from the Earl of Carnarvon. He claimed that Prince George sent him round to see Edward VIII in December 1936, and that he said to him: 'Don't give up all this for a mess of pottage.' The King cried: 'How dare you call Wallis a mess of pottage!'[28]

To all this and more the Duchess was oblivious. She had declined terribly in the course of the year. By November 1976 her condition was described as 'feeble but stable'.[29]

As one of the departing nurses put it: 'It gives me great distress to see H.R.H. who was once a great lady, admired and fêted throughout the world, who showed courage which was widely respected – becoming little by little, a lady who suffers terribly, not only physically, but morally in her moments of sharp lucidity.'

10

The Machinations of Blum – 1975–1977

In widowhood Maître Blum had married the retired French general, Georges Spillmann. One day she brought the general to the Duchess's house. They arrived by taxi. The general looked around and said to Blum: 'My dear, this will be the apotheosis of your career.' By the time she had finished with the Duchess, Blum was being driven by the Duchess's chauffeur Monsieur Martin and had been twice advanced in the Legion of Honour by Jacques Chirac.

In her takeover of the Duchess, Blum was motivated by many things, not least an irrational hatred of the English that had developed during her sole visit to Britain. This extended to the British Royal Family, though not to the Queen herself.

Blum thought the Duchess was going to die while she was in the American Hospital. The lawyer wanted to know whether or not any of the British Royal Family had enquired about the Duchess's health. Miss Schütz assured Blum that she had informed Sir Edward Tomkins, the retiring British Ambassador, immediately the Duchess had gone into hospital. Since then nobody from the British court had asked how she was. Walter Lees informed Miss Schütz that Princess Margaret had been in Paris to attend the Soviet exhibition, but there had been no word from her during that visit. Prince Charles and Lord Mountbatten had been silent. On the other hand the Duchess had received dozens of letters of sympathy from well-wishers all over the world.

The Maître wanted an updated list of those who would be invited to the Duchess's funeral. She was particularly anxious that neither John Utter nor Sir Godfrey Morley should appear on it, even though that was none of her business.*

The plight of the Duchess was of long-term concern to the British Embassy in Paris. One of their main priorities was how to handle her

---

*The Duchess used to tell John Utter: 'One of your jobs will be to bury us.' But by the time the Duchess died John himself was dead. Despite Blum's efforts, Sir Godfrey Morley and his wife were invited to the funeral and seated in the Quire Blum's two envoys to the service, Maître Lisbonne and Michael Bloch (her pupil) were relegated to the Nave.

death and funeral. The Ambassador's Private Secretary had several files which became operational if a member of the Royal Family died while in France*. There was particular concern over the Queen Mother, who visited France most years in the early summer, and Lord Mountbatten, another regular visitor.[1]

Plans for the Duchess of Windsor, known as 'Operation Haze', had been updated in 1972. The Duke of Windsor had agreed the details of his funeral as early as 1961, with certain changes implemented in May 1962 and again in 1966. In those days various eventualities had to be considered. John Utter had mentioned to me that arrangements existed for flying the Windsors back from wherever they died, be it Paris, New York, Palm Beach, Spain or elsewhere. There was also the possibility that the Duchess might predecease the Duke. There were plans for that too, of particular concern: 'Some variation of procedure may however be necessary between the arrival at Benson and the funeral service at Windsor.'[2]

A few months after the Duke's death, when the Duchess was in a precarious state of health, the procedure to be implemented was reconfirmed, files being lodged at Buckingham Palace, the British Embassy in Paris, the Duchess's house, the Foreign Office and in other relevant places.

The file stated that both the Duke and Duchess had agreed to these plans, as had the Queen. The Windsors were to have funerals as similar to each other as possible. In the case of the Duchess, there would be no court mourning, only family mourning, flags would fly at half-mast on government buildings on the day of her death and the day of the funeral (this had been agreed, significantly, as early as 1961). The court circular would announce the death, but the State Bell at St Paul's Cathedral and the bell at the Curfew Tower at Windsor would not be tolled. There would be no Lying-in-State.

An RAF VC-10 would fly the body home. The Lord Chamberlain would go out to Paris, with others, and on arrival in Britain it would be met by a Royal Highness. Senior figures such as the Lord Lieutenant, a Cabinet Minister, the French Ambassador and others would be on the tarmac. The Royal Highness would travel behind the hearse to Windsor, where the body would lie in the Albert Memorial Chapel.

On the day of the funeral, the coffin would be carried into the Quire by a bearer party of the Welsh Guards (of which the Duke had been Colonel from 1919 to 1936), and guarded by the Military Knights. The instructions then declared:

---

* Such a file was produced in 1997 when Diana, Princess of Wales was killed in a car accident in Paris.

The Order of Service will be the same as for the Duke of Windsor with the omission of Insignia, Styles & Titles, Last Post & Reveille*.

Details were also given in respect of the attendance of the Royal Family, the interment, and the list of mourners by invitation. By 1972 the list for the Duchess's funeral had already been agreed by Sir Godfrey Morley in consultation with John Utter.[3]

In the days before Blum took control, the Lord Chamberlain's Office and the British Embassy in Paris honed the small details between them. British Ambassadors had entertained the Windsors over the years and accepted their hospitality, though in 1952 the Duke had complained, as he did from time to time, about perceived incivility from the then British Ambassador, Sir Oliver Harvey.[†]

Every such Ambassador was aware that one day he might have to implement the funeral procedure. The file was on hand for whoever was on night duty at the Embassy, or on standby for crises that occurred over the weekend.

In January 1973 Sir Edward Tomkins had been worried by the Duchess breaking her hip and noted that, despite a good recovery, 'her general state of health is not good'. He was concerned that the press might hear of her death before an official announcement. He was aware that 'the Press will be on the lookout for anything in the arrangements which they can interpret as an implied slight to the Duchess even after her death.' He was especially concerned by there being no guard of honour planned for her arrival at RAF Benson and by the possibility of comparisons being made between the way her funeral was planned in contrast to plans for that of the Duke. He continued:

> There is quite a lot of popular sympathy for the Duchess here in France and I think it will be both appropriate and expected that we should open a book of condolence at the Embassy when she dies, in which case the Consulates General will follow suit. It is also possible that, as a mark of respect, the French will want to provide a guard of honour at the airport when the Duchess's body is flown out. If they do suggest this, do you want us to discourage the idea, given that there will be no guard of honour at Benson?[4]

Sir Eric Penn, Comptroller of the Lord Chamberlain's Office, encouraged the book of condolence, but asked the Ambassador to discourage a French guard of honour, 'in accordance with the Duchess's wish'.[5]

---

* This instruction was too zealously adhered to at the actual funeral.
† See Part 2 – Chapter 8.

Sir Nicholas Henderson succeeded Tomkins as Ambassador in 1975. Aware of the well-prepared programme, he maintained contact with the Duchess's office and duly sent presents and messages to the Duchess at prescribed times. He understood that he should 'keep the royal family informed about the state of her health, a subject about which there was the closest interest.'[6]

Similarly his Private Secretary, Philip Nelson, kept in touch with Miss Schütz, inviting her to events such as the Queen's Birthday garden party. He never went to the Duchess's house but they met from time to time, just as she had occasionally had meetings with his predecessor, Howard Davies.*

Blum was as traditionally suspicious of the British Embassy as she was of any other representatives of Great Britain, but she was on civil terms with Lord Nicholas Gordon Lennox,† whose charm won her over to some degree. He took tea with her occasionally and remembered her as 'elderly, aggressive and highly litigious.'[7] He recorded that Blum 'professed profound admiration and respect for our queen, but the rest of the royal family was beyond her contempt. She reserved a special loathing for Mountbatten . . . her vituperation against him knew no bounds.'[8]

Gordon Lennox devoted a lot of time to dissuading Blum from entering into pointless legal action against the press, which he thought would upset the British Royal Family. At his meetings with her he was obliged to eat two large slices of a chocolate cake, produced by an 'ancient maid'. The chocolate cake was served on a silver plate but, 'by French standards or, indeed, any other, it was dry and disgusting.'[9] When Gordon Lennox left Paris in 1979, he invited Blum to his farewell party and introduced her to Philip Nelson, who was to be the new liaison. He told her that Nelson did not get much to eat and had a passion for chocolate cake. 'May you be forgiven!' mouthed Nelson in response.[10]

Blum's intense dislike of the Royal Family was confirmed by Diana Mosley. Blum and the general once lunched with the Mosleys at the Temple de la Gloire, and Blum launched into a vitriolic attack on the royals. Finally the general told his tyrannical wife to pipe down. Lady Mosley thought it discourteous to insult the Royal Family in the presence of British citizens, as the general fully realised.

Blum was so against the British that she even tried to persuade the

---

* On 2 April 1976 Howard Davies had lunch with Miss Schütz and they discussed the Ambassador's visit, the Duchess's state of health and other matters. Sir Howard Davies went on to be Director of the London School of Economics, resigning in 2011.
† Lord Nicholas Gordon Lennox (1931–2004), Counsellor and Head of Chancery at the British Embassy 1975–9.

Duchess to give up her annuity of £5,000 from the Queen. The Duchess was still well at that time and refused. She found Blum's attitude especially odd since Blum was forever instilling panic into her about overspending.

Blum was full of plans. In January 1976 she informed Miss Schütz that, two years before, the Duchess had given Monsieur Amiguet precise instructions, written and oral, about which silver and porcelain objects should be sold, as well as details of those pictures she no longer wished to keep. Her message was that Amiguet would introduce certain interested parties who might buy these things quietly, without publicity, and they would be introduced by him or by Blum's own intermediary. It would be for the best, declared Blum.[11] Amiguet supported this plan.

On 6 February 1976 and again on 26 February the Duchess was asked to sign new authorisations for Amiguet to replace his mandate of 26 June 1974, which did not cover certain points. The new letters would instruct Amiguet (1) to continue to sell objects that she might no longer wish to keep, and (2) to be in sole control of her interests in Switzerland. The Duchess was well enough to refuse to sign either of these. The unsigned letters still exist.[12]

Miss Schütz was worried about the selling and wrote several times to Amiguet for some written authorisation to make the sales concerned. At the end of February she asked for assurances regarding sales on 11, 21 and 24 February that she and Blum had made during one of his absences abroad. Together with this she sent a copy of Blum's charges to the Duchess. Eventually, in March 1976, Amiguet replied. He began by saying that he was pleased to find that the costs had been greatly reduced and took it upon himself to thank Miss Schütz on behalf of the ailing Duchess. He was angered by a communication from the Morgan Guaranty Trust Co. in Paris and terminated all contact with the bank, while telling Miss Schütz that this must be done without the Duchess's knowledge.

In reply to Miss Schütz's request for written authorisation, Amiguet explained that in the light of his 1974 mandate he was in sole charge of the fortune and well-being of the Duchess, and that she had authorised him to sell any of her assets or belongings, wherever they were, for her benefit. As we have seen, he was in quest of a new mandate. He told Miss Schütz that he was the Duchess's banker but, in a wider sense, he was also her adviser and intimate friend. He assumed that Miss Schütz knew this after her years as the Duchess's secretary. As before, with John Utter, Amiguet attempted to reassure her that the Duchess was lucky to be advised by Maître Blum, and that Blum would be overseeing the sale of any objects.

Amiguet went on to say that it was the role of Georges, the butler, to take responsibility for all the objects of value listed in the inventory prepared by John Utter and which were located at the Duchess's house in the Bois du Boulogne. It would be Georges's role to suggest to Maître Blum the items that could be sold.

Amiguet wrote to Miss Schütz to confirm she was not involved in this process of selling and that her role was to remain as secretary, receiving the information about the sales as and when they took place. He stressed that the sales should be undertaken without publicity, maintaining that this was the Duchess's express wish. He did not want staff members getting involved in this.[13]

The Dismissals

This was the precursor for the dismissal of some of the staff and the bribing of others. Rumours of sales had indeed spread in Paris and Maître Blum was furious that it appeared that the Duchess's staff might be responsible for these rumours. In April she addressed this issue aggressively, maintaining that the only things she had sold were orchids. She announced in a letter that if the staff wished to show their loyalty to the Duchess there were other ways of doing so, that she would take care of things in her own way, and that since the staff derided her and put perverse interpretations on her actions she would make no further efforts on their behalf. It was a most unpleasant letter.[14] She began to prepare to get rid of some of them.

The summer saw some disruptions in the household. On 25 August Philippe, the sous-chef, suddenly left without prior notice. Lucien Massy, the main chef, was still on holiday, so Monsieur Martin undertook the cooking, an arrangement that suited everyone. Georges no longer needed the valet Manuel (due to retire at the end of the year), so he was given notice to quit on 25 September.

For some time there had been talk of the Duchess giving up her house in favour of an apartment in the Hotel Plaza Athéné Paris, but this idea was immediately dropped when her health took a turn for the worse at the end of September. Dr Thin asserted that the Duchess would never again live a normal *mondaine* life. He was not keen that she should move from her house. Perhaps prompted by Blum, he put in writing his belief that the Duchess was aware how expensive everything was and that worrying about this was one of the reasons for the decline in her health.[15]

This enabled Blum and Amiguet to decide that the not inconsiderable expense of employing a staff of thirteen could no longer be sustained under such circumstances.

This was probably no surprise to the staff themselves. Loyal to the Duchess for many years, they had been obliged to put up with much. The house, once so full of life with dinner parties, was now virtually asleep. The Duchess was no longer leading an interesting life. She was an invalid. Many of them had little to do. The atmosphere had become tense and unpleasant. No one knew from one day to the next who would be staying and who would be going. A state of virtual internecine war had developed between the nursing staff and the kitchen.

Perhaps worst of all there was Maître Blum coming to the house and removing the Duchess's possessions with the help of Georges.

Thus the axe fell. First, the Duchess was sent to the American Hospital to get her out of the way. Then it was alleged that Lucien Massy, the chef, had tried to get the Duchess intoxicated, which all sounded like nonsense, although it was certified by Dr Thin. Massy was dismissed forthwith, along with Roland Gougault (the gardener) and Germaine Bowyer, all of whom had given twenty-five years of loyal service. These members of staff left on 14 October.

Dr Thin stressed that news of the dismissals should be withheld from the Duchess. He was concerned that she would be upset, as well she might have been. Nor did the Duchess like to see her advisers taking control and acting independently of her wishes. Amiguet was principally concerned that Blum should handle the legal aspects involved in any dismissals. He was delighted at the consequent reduction in annual costs.

Amiguet did not think the three dismissed members of staff would have a problem in finding equivalent or better jobs elsewhere. He urged Miss Schütz to calm Germaine down, pointing out that it was quite a leap from years of slavery to a life of total freedom.[16] To replace Germaine, an intercom system was installed at the main gate so that Georges could speak to would-be visitors from inside the house. In the attendant publicity Blum gave her verdict to the media. She was quoted as saying: 'Why have a porter who never has to open the door – or a telephonist who never has to answer the telephone?'[17]

One of the problems for dismissed staff was that only those still in the Duchess's employ at the time of her death would receive the bequests promised to them in the Duke's will. Maître Blum took it upon herself to inform them of the arrangements made for them. She also needed to reassure those who were staying. Thus she dismissed on the one hand, and bribed on the other. Georges and Ofélia were to be given 40,000 FF and six months' salary, M. Martin 20,000 FF plus six months' salary.

Those departing were in a sense paid off. Of these, Roland Gougault, the gardener, was particularly disgruntled. In December he attempted to have the Duchess of Windsor taken to court for wrongful dismissal and claimed 66,100 FF in compensation. Blum was forced to pay up.

A version of this saga reached the general public when one of the Duchess's biographers, Stephen Birmingham, published his book *Duchess* in 1981. He maintained that it was the Maître who dismissed 'the last three footmen, the sous-chef, the parlormaids, and the gardeners under conditions which, Maître Blum insists, were very generous.'[18]

Between September 1976 and December 1977 there was quite a distribution of spoils, none of which the Duchess would have been aware of. The gifts were listed on a document signed by Blum and Amiguet, confirming the items given. Furthermore the jewels given were listed as removed from the Duchess's inventory in a document presented by Miss Schütz to Amiguet on 12 December 1977.

Amiguet was given earrings, a bracelet and a necklace. Dr Thin received watches for himself and his son and two brooches and a bracelet (with his daughter in mind), and in March 1977, he was given a gold box (no 6 in the inventory). In the documentary that Prince Edward made in 1995, shown as *Edward on Edward*, Dr Thin can be seen on camera claiming that the Duke himself had given him one of these watches and made much of the fact that the Duke's father signed himself, 'G. R. I.' – which was in fact a perfectly normal way of signing by a monarch of that era.

Miss Schütz was given earrings, two bracelets and a ring*. Georges got a brooch, as did Vitoria Marques, a cleaning maid, and Monsieur Martin. Nathan Cummings was given a pair of cufflinks adorned with a crown of sapphire and diamonds.

Blum herself was given an amethyst brooch, but did not want this. She received a ring with an oval amethyst surrounded by turquoises and diamonds, an amethyst necklace and a Louis XV gold box (number 1 in the inventory).

Amiguet received various other gifts during these years. During the Duchess's lifetime he gave a friend of his, a Frau Schmöhl, a gilded ashtray adorned with a WW and a royal coronet. He was also given a tea service from the Duchess's collection. In July 1976 he was delighted to receive a present of some of the Duchess's wines.[19]

---

* In the will she was meant to receive a parure.

Meanwhile Amiguet had invested most of the Duchess's Swiss money in gold, because it was safe. This proved a wise and profitable investment. Her capital grew immeasurably.

The Sales

Maître Blum had received a promotion in the Légion d'Honneur in 1973 when she promised some of the Duchess's furniture to Versailles and the Louvre (two boxes and a red-leather chest – the latter originally destined for Lady Ednam). In July 1976 Blum was promoted Commandeur of the Légion d'Honneur. Miss Schütz wrote to congratulate Blum, describing the honour as '*un récompense largement méritée pour vos efforts pour la France*'[20] – an irony which probably escaped Blum. The Duchess was able to add a few words in her own hand, which Blum acknowledged in a prosaic letter of reply as a great display of sympathy which heralded, she was sure, the Duchess's rapid recovery.[21]

A party was given to celebrate Blum's honour at her home in the rue de Varenne. She asked Georges to send over all the Duchess's champagne to her house for this party and Georges himself was in attendance, waiting on the guests. Miss Schütz was so shocked by this that, with the collaboration of Georges, she sold the remaining contents of the Duchess's wine cellar for the benefit of the Duchess's budget.

The first of the sales had taken place as early as 28 January 1976 during Miss Schütz's absence. By March sales had produced a total of 186,000 French francs. In February Blum bought a silver tankard for herself. By August further sales had taken place, raising 2,188, 292.75 French francs, and 30,000 US dollars. Amiguet assessed the total value of sales to that date as being $470,000, which he deemed but a fraction of the expenses that the Duchess was incurring.

There were further sales. Blum's policy was to sell items in the house that the Duchess would not notice should she survive. On a lesser note, the remaining plants in the greenhouse were sold and the greenhouse heating was switched off on 14 November.

After the Duchess returned from hospital at the beginning of 1976, the message to the staff was that she had to be kept in the upstairs rooms. If she did come downstairs and noticed the absence of any item or piece of furniture, she would be told that the French government had asked for that particular piece to be restored. It would be returned presently. With luck, the Duchess would not notice, or she would not remember. Needless to say, the items never did come back.

As we have seen, visitors to the Duchess were now forbidden. This policy was said to be to protect her health and to save her from becoming flustered. There was another possible reason. Friends who came to the house might notice that pieces of furniture and other objects had gone. And then the rumours would spread.

I cannot possibly claim to list every sale that took place while the Duchess was ill, and I can only vouch for what happened up to the end of April 1978. Of course further sales went on during these years and in the years from 1978 until the Duchess's death in 1986. But the sales listed here are based on documentary evidence.

In March 1976 Georges went through some items and selected the following, which Blum later removed from the Duchess's house. On 13 July Blum sold a gold oval Louis XV box, marked E.B. 1760 (number 7 in the inventory); the same day she sold the following: an oval box of crystal, monogrammed in diamonds; a rectangular box of blue lapis; three round boxes with heads of kings, a gold rectangular box (*belette*); a long, very straight gold box with three feathers; two rectangular gold tooth-pick boxes and an Arabesque oval box.

On 30 September 1976 Blum gave the Louvre a gold box with diamonds, and a small rectangular box of Pompadour, in blue enamel in accordance with the Duchess's agreed donation (numbers 8 and 9 in the inventory). On 20 October she took away two more boxes (numbers 2 and 4 in the inventory), which she kept at the rue de Varenne as potential gifts.

Blum tended to sell things at low prices. Miss Schütz was a better salesman than the lawyer. She went to Kugel and sold an ancient watch adorned with a coat of arms, an owl on a piece of lapis, a Fabergé hippopotamus, a fat frog, a small green frog, and a Chinese dog on an ebony stand, achieving ten times the price offered by Blum's antique dealer.

On 5 May 1977 the following items were given to Blum, the ostensible purpose being that they would be given as presents: a pair of earrings made of rubies, emeralds and brilliants (for Margret Amiguet); a bracelet with round brilliants on platinum; a watch-bracelet with two snake chains; a gold Cartier watch; a gold cigarette box with a map of Europe, inscribed 'David from Wallis 1935 Christmas'; a gold tiepin with a blue enamel 'E' under a crown; along with various buttons and cufflinks, shirt studs, two evening bags in gold silk, and eleven shirt buttons.*

---

* Some of these items survived to go into the Geneva sale after the Duchess's death.

On 11 May 1977 Blum went to the bank with Miss Schütz and took away further jewels destined to be given to the Duchess of Kent and Princess Alexandra, and a brooch of a gold leopard, stretched out, with black and red enamel inlaid, to be given to Mlle. Hivet, a former secretary to the Windsors.

By the spring of 1977 possessions to the value of three million French francs had been sold. In 1976–77 sales of gold boxes achieved £66,000 and jewellery $100,000.

In November 1976 Amiguet had written to Miss Schütz about a sale to Estée Lauder, recapitulating that he would decide what would be sold and Blum would agree the items. He, Amiguet, was pleased to have escaped any mention in the press, and appreciated that Miss Schütz and to some extent Blum too were the ones exposed to the media. Johanna was to continue with discretion and circumspection, in the role of secretary and nothing more.

Miss Schütz reported more sales in October and November and informed Amiguet that Blum had taken jewellery and gold boxes. She had wisely obliged Blum to sign for these, much to Blum's irritation. Amiguet authorised the sale to Estée Lauder and so, on 30 August 1977, Estée Lauder paid $150,000 for a ring (no. 142 in the inventory – see frontispiece, p. vi). On 1 September £180,000 was transferred to the Duchess's account with Amiguet in Switzerland.

Miss Schütz was horrified at the ridiculously low prices that Blum was getting from her antique dealers. She therefore intervened when Blum was about to let a very fine Meissen *Tigre* dinner set go for $20,000, well below its value, and arranged a private sale to Nathan Cummings, who accepted the asking price of $100,000 without question. Anxious lest her selling activities were noticed, Blum was worried that Cummings might use this set at his dinner parties and that it would be recognised. He did not use it. Instead he displayed it behind glass in his apartment in New York. Pleased with this and other transactions, in August 1976 Cummings mentioned that he would like to buy the Duchess's Foujita of a small girl, a Dufy of a country scene, a Utrillo flower painting, two large paintings by Lorjou and a Capuletti.

Blum also used the Duchess's possessions as gifts. It must have given her a sense of enormous power to distribute the possessions of her client, at her whim rather than the Duchess's. Some of these have been mentioned above. After the Duchess died, her remaining jewels were sold by Sotheby's in Geneva.

As to the other jewels which did not survive to the Geneva sale, I identified three pairs of earrings, twelve brooches, eleven or twelve bracelets, two necklaces, two rings, two chokers, a vanity case, a tube for rouge, two scent bottles, a handbag and two watches.

And so it continued.

The Queen Mother

The Queen Mother came to stay with Sir Nicholas Henderson at the British Embassy between 25 and 28 October 1976 to open the British Cultural Centre. In the press at the time there was a suggestion that the Queen Mother might visit the Duchess, though this was never actually going to happen. It was a sop to the press. Such a visit would have given no pleasure to either party, nor was the Duchess in any state to receive a momentous visit of that kind. Instead, the Queen Mother, ever one to do the right thing, sent flowers with the message: 'In Friendship, Elizabeth.' Miss Schütz was also invited to a reception at the Embassy and was presented to the Queen Mother.

For a long time the British Ambassador did not see the Duchess because she was unwell. But in February 1977 Miss Schütz telephoned to say that she was a bit better and was ready for a visit from him. Sir Nicholas and Lady Henderson were invited to tea one afternoon at 4.30. He described how they were met by Georges at the door – 'A butler greeted us, looking a little sinister' – and how Miss Schütz told them not to accept tea if the Duchess offered it, because it would tire her. She took them to the Duchess's bedroom and as they did so a nurse sidled out of the room. Georges hovered outside, listening as ever to what might be said:

The Duchess was lying on a couch by the window. Her hands, which caught the eye immediately, were badly contorted in shape, and paralysed. Our handshakes were perfunctory. Unless we had known before whom we were meeting I do not think that we would have recognised her. There is nothing in the face to recall that very distinct and dominating look known to the whole world.

There was an exchange of small talk and the Duchess said she hoped she would be able to go to America. The Ambassador concluded:

I do not think she was in a condition to talk about anything seriously. Every now and again she took a deep breath which seemed to require considerable effort. She kept her hands under the rug. She was perfectly compos mentis but it was as though living was a big task and could only be coped with for short intervals at a time. She did not strike one as being comfortable or at ease with herself as she lay under those blankets.[22]

At least the Ambassador was reassured that the Duchess was alive and could report accordingly to Buckingham Palace.

Elvire Gozin became concerned about the advancing deformatory rheumatism from which the Duchess was suffering. She asked Dr Bruno Vuillemin of the Centre de Médecine Physique et Rééducation Fonctionelle to visit the Duchess and he did so on 16 January. He was concerned to prevent what he called a catastrophic evolution from the point of view of skin and muscular retraction. He proposed a course of action involving placing sandbags on the Duchess's hands, knees and feet. Elvire Gozin wanted to order eight sacks of sand of two kilograms each and five sacks of one kilogram from the Établissement Couverchelles. Vuillemin believed this was the only way to prevent further deterioration.

When Dr Thin heard about this he was furious, accusing Dr Vuillemin of professional discourtesy in not consulting him. He pointed out that he had been the Duchess's doctor for fifteen years and he alone would decide what treatment she would undergo. He told Vuillemin to abstain from further recommendations unless invited by Thin himself. Vuillemin told Miss Schütz that, following this surprising reaction from Thin, he had no choice but to withdraw.[23] So the Duchess was left to her decline. Nor did Maître Blum sanction any other mooted suggestions for improving the Duchess's health. She deemed these too expensive.

The Duke's Papers

In February 1977 an article appeared in the *Daily Express* in which Sir Robin Mackworth-Young was as good as accused of having taken the Duke of Windsor's papers to the Royal Archives without the Duchess's knowledge or permission. Blum seized on the idea that the Duchess had been tricked into sending the Duke's papers to Windsor. In fact the opposite was true.

Blum did not know about the Orders or decorations that had also gone to England or she would have made a fuss about them too. Miss Schütz did not enlighten her.

Blum obliged Miss Schütz to write to Sir Martin Charteris, then the Queen's Private Secretary, making accusations on the Duchess's behalf. The Duchess herself was by then completely unaware of any of the issues

raised, nor was she in a state to be concerned by such matters. It was
Blum who instigated the complaints:

> When the Duchess learnt, shortly before she fell ill in 1975, of the
> nature and importance of the documents abstracted from her home,
> she was deeply concerned and the article which appeared in the *Daily
> Express* has proved her fears well grounded; as the documents were
> removed without either her knowledge or her consent. With regard
> to the papers concerned, no list has ever been submitted to her for
> approval. The Duchess had previously given her consent for the
> transfer to the Royal Archives of documents of historical importance
> and was very upset to learn that a number of items, including her
> own divorce papers, personal letters and diaries of the Duke of
> Windsor were removed at the same time, a schedule of which is
> included herewith. The fact that these personal papers have been
> read, filed, controlled and indexed without her consent distressed the
> Duchess. Additionally, Her Royal Highness feels that judging from
> the tone of the article in the *Daily Express* there appears to be a
> considerable risk that these papers may be misused and compromise
> the memory of his late Royal Highness. The Duchess has instructed
> me to advise you that this interference is quite inacceptable [*sic*].
> The papers having been abstracted on instructions of Lord
> Mountbatten, the Duchess feels that H.M. the Queen could not
> possibly have been aware of the situation, thus she instructed me
> to request your assistance in acquainting H.M. the Queen with the
> facts regarding her papers, and have them returned to her.
> The announcement of a proposed visit by Lord Mountbatten,
> who wanted to discuss serious matters with her, caused the Duchess
> further emotional distress, and she remained deeply agitated.
> The Duchess of Windsor would greatly appreciate your help in
> again bringing the attention to Lord Mountbatten what Her Royal
> Highness has repeatedly stressed to him. The Duchess has made
> all necessary dispositions and this has been done in accordance with
> the wishes of His late Royal Highness and her own, therefore, the
> Duchess would appreciate if Lord Mountbatten would refrain from
> bringing this subject up again.
> In the name of the Duchess I thank you in advance for your
> assistance . . .[24]

Charteris replied in May. Hearing about this exchange and the threat
of a renewed onslaught by Mountbatten, Amiguet stressed the need to

be vigilant on any matters in which Mountbatten was involved. But he was grateful that Charteris was being cooperative over the return of certain papers. He emphasised that nothing must remain with Sir Godfrey Morley.[25]

Sir Robin Mackworth-Young put on record that the first consignment of papers had been handed over on 15 June 1972, in the presence of the Duchess's solicitor, that the Duchess was in residence at the house and had received him. 'The movement of the papers was carried out with her full knowledge and permission, and indeed she helped me in locating some of the papers.' The second consignment was handed over on 13 December 1972, again with her full knowledge and permission.

On 22 July 1977, as a result of the exchange between Miss Schütz and Sir Martin Charteris, Sir Robin collected a third consignment, returning some originals from Windsor 'by mutual agreement.' On that occasion the Duchess was again in the house but he did not see her, as she was unwell. It is worth quoting his last paragraph:

All these dates and transactions are confirmed by correspondence in the files of the parties concerned, and there is no truth in the allegation that some of His late Royal Highness's papers now at Windsor were removed from the Duchess's residence without her full knowledge when she was in England for the Duke's funeral. On the contrary it was on that occasion that the disposal of the papers was discussed by The Queen and the Duchess, and the subsequent arrangements to move the papers were the result of that discussion.[26]

In September that year Maître Blum was still vexed by the question of the Duchess's papers and demanded a written statement from Miss Schütz to the effect that the original papers had been removed by Sir Robin and John Utter on 15 June 1972 while the Duchess had gone with Miss Schütz to the beauty parlour. This, as we have seen, was nonsense.

At Windsor Castle one evening in 1981, I had the chance to talk to Sir Robin Mackworth-Young. His view was that it was fortunate that so many papers had come to the Royal Archives. He told me that he was 'a black figure' with Maître Blum.[27]

While the sales continued apace there was further activity in the Duchess's house, none of which involved her personally. While she languished upstairs, huge bonfires were taking place in the garden. In April 1977 Amiguet instructed Miss Schütz in writing to burn a great number of the Duke's financial papers in order that these should not be in the house when the Duchess died.

During the course of this operation, which took a long time, Georges, the butler, materialised in the office with a bundle of letters which the Duchess had consigned to him. He told Miss Schütz that the Duchess had asked him to destroy these after her death, and he now wondered if she should burn them along with the Duke's papers.

Miss Schütz took a cursory look at these documents and realised at once that they had historical value and should not be burned. They were the letters between the Duke and Duchess that had been written around the time of the Abdication and after.

These letters had not been sent to Windsor with the others that were deposited there in 1972. John Utter had drawn the Duchess's attention to them and asked her to look at them and decide what she wanted to do with them – whether she wanted to keep them, whether she wanted to send them to the Royal Archives, or whether perhaps she even wanted to destroy them. The Duchess never felt strong enough to look at them. Later she made her wishes known to Georges.

On 30 April Miss Schütz and Georges took the letters to Maître Blum at the rue de Varenne. Miss Schütz asked Blum what she intended to do with them. Blum told her that she would put them in a safe place. It never occurred to Miss Schütz that Blum would later cause these letters to be published or that she might benefit financially from their publication.

The handing over of these papers inspired Blum to take an interest in any other such items that might still be found in the house. In July 1977 she started to go through the documents that had come back from Windsor.

At the risk of restating matters, the Duchess herself was not troubled about where her papers were, any more than she cared about the contents of Frances Donaldson's biography of the Duke; she was completely unaware of the 1978 television series and of any of the other Windsors-related books and articles that appeared in her widowhood years.

But Blum was now in her stride. Regardless of the Duchess's views or state of health, Blum was ready to tell the world that the Duchess was furious. She would invoke her displeasure as an excuse for future litigation and to give her the brief to publish the series of books that would appear from 1982 onwards.

In May 1977 Amiguet thanked Miss Schütz for having organised an inventory of the Duchess's books, and again authorised her to destroy a considerable amount of bank receipts, bank statements and correspondence relating to financial transactions concerned with the United States, Canada, Great Britain and Switzerland. One day in July she spent twelve hours burning papers. None of them had historical value.

Everything was set for the Duchess to die. The plans were in place. But the Duchess did not die.

Miss Schütz came in on Saturdays to visit her. That summer she became so worried by what was happening that she sought Nate Cummings's advice and went to see Charles Torem*, Senior Partner of Coudert Frères in the Champs-Élysées. For an hour she told him what was going on. Torem did not offer much hope of rescue. The Duchess seemed to have no relatives of her own, or eventual heirs within her family. She was no longer an American citizen. Miss Schütz wanted legal intervention on the grounds that the Duchess was helpless and that someone was taking advantage of her, but Torem did not see how Johanna could pursue this herself. All he could do was to advise her how to protect herself over the jewels that Blum had taken.[28]

Lady Monckton had last visited the Duchess in January 1977, after which she asked that the Duchess's office should pay her travel expenses from London. Lady Monckton belonged to a pre-Blum era. She was considered grand and rather arrogant. Even the Duchess found her hard going, though Lady Monckton considered herself to be the Duchess's best friend. As to visits, these were inconvenient. Blum declined her request for expenses and made sure that she never saw the Duchess again.

In May the Duchess was briefly a bit better, replying to questions from her nurse, sleeping better and eating well. But the improvement did not last. Diana Mosley reported to Lady Monckton on what turned out to be her last visit in July:

> As George[s] will have told you, I went to see the Duchess & found her much worse than before. But in the house they said she was 'better' – she must have been in a very bad way. She was pathetic, just staring in front of her with mouth open in a sad expression. I was at a loss, Georges said to talk to her, & I did but there was hardly any reaction. Ann Mari Bismarck also went to see her &

---

* Charles Torem (1916–93), American attorney representing corporate clients. Represented the Walt Disney companies, Lockheed, the Sara Lee Corporation and figures such as Armand Hammer and Nathan Cummings. Collapsed and died of a heart attack near his home in Paris in July 1993.

found the same pathetic person. It really & truly wouldn't be worth you coming over unless she gets much better. I don't think she even enjoys seeing people – it's just an effort. The nurse I saw seemed very kind & gentle, & spoke English. Georges *perfect* as always. Thank heavens for him. I stayed 10 minutes.[29]

Another visitor was Mrs Gilbert Miller, an old friend of the Duchess's. In years past the story was told that the Duchess had once telephoned her to ask her to lunch. Kitty Miller said: 'I am sorry, but my new clothes haven't arrived.' The Duchess had replied: 'Oh Kitty, you are so clever. I don't even know where my last year's clothes are.'

It was Georges who took Kitty Miller to the Duchess's bedside in contravention of the ban imposed by the doctors and Maître Blum. I heard about this visit at the time, Kitty Miller telling a friend that the Duchess was 'in bed and making no sense at all'.[30] Kitty Miller later told a journalist from the *Daily Express* that Georges had urged her to give the Duchess a little smile. She was horrified that the Duchess no longer had monogrammed linen.*

The Duchess versus Blum

September 1977 was a turning point in the relationship between the Duchess and Maître Blum. The Duchess had clearly relied on Blum in her early widowhood, but she was also afraid of her, sometimes trembling when Blum was present. She was often made ill by Blum's visits with her continual doses of panic – panic about expenses, panic about whether she could stay in her house, panic about legal documents thrust in front of her for signature. If Blum deluded herself into thinking that she was the Duchess's friend and protector, she was in for an unpleasant surprise.

Blum came to see the Duchess, and the Duchess summoned up a sudden outburst of energy. She turned to the lawyer who had driven her to a state of such anxiety and illness and shouted at her: 'I HATE YOU!'

After that Blum was careful to avoid the Duchess – at least until she was beyond the power of speech. It explains a later statement that Blum gave to the press: 'Right now, she is in a pretty sad state and even I try not to bother her.'[31]

* * *

* Kitty Miller died in New York in October 1979, aged eighty-three.

Nor would Blum allow anyone else to 'bother' the Duchess, though some slipped past the cordon of security which she now had in place. As ever Georges was the one who occasionally let a visitor in.

Nate Cummings came to Paris in September 1977, and Miss Schütz suggested that he call Georges, who arranged for him to see the Duchess. Cummings had not seen her for two years and reported that he found her looking 'extremely' well, her health sustained by regular intake of food. Maria had made her up with a little lipstick and put some modest jewellery onto her, nevertheless, he wrote: 'When I came out of her room, I could not help but shed a tear, because, as you well know, she speaks just barely above a whisper. However, she was fully conscious of my visiting with her.' Cummings said he would tell any enquirers that he believed the Duchess's health was much as before. Referring to the Duchess's rebuke to Blum, he wrote that he was 'delighted' adding: 'I hope she doesn't forget what she said.' He hoped the Duchess would handle Blum with 'a firm hand', wishing Johanna and Amiguet could handle her affairs, perhaps helped by Charles Torem, but he recalled Torem telling him 'he had a lawsuit against Maître Blum several years ago.'[32]

The thought that the Duchess could be saved from Blum was a vain hope. The Duchess would pay heavily for her 'I hate you' remark. After that she was kept a virtual prisoner in her house, while Blum did exactly as she pleased.

Other visitors were less fortunate. Lady Monckton made a final attempt to see the Duchess. She wrote to Diana Mosley, who replied on 25 October:

Yes, it's quite true that the doctor won't allow anyone to visit the Duchess. It appears that 'la tension monte' when friends appear. I haven't seen her since June, & she looked terrible then, so sad, almost angry, she stared into space. Georges said I must tell her things, I tried but there was hardly a flicker of recognition in response. I feel terribly sorry for Georges because it must be deeply depressing, day after day.[33]

Diana Mosley remained concerned by the plight of the Duchess, blaming the doctors more than Blum. She told her friend, James Lees-Milne:

I am so horrified by what is happening to the poor Duchess of W. that I have joined the voluntary euthanasia society. I'm afraid nobody can do much about *her*, because all those cowardly doctors stick

THEIR DAY AT THE FAIR

(*Above*) *The first press cutting I ever saw of the Duchess.*
The Windsors at the World Fair in New York, 6 May 1964

(*Above*) The Funeral of Princess Marina, Duchess of Kent, 30 August 1968. The Queen and
the Duke of Edinburgh, with Members of the Royal Family, Princess Marina's Household,
and the Dean of Windsor (Robin Woods). In the background, the Duke of Windsor on his
last ever visit to Britain. Sir Philip Hay (hidden), Lady Rachel Pepyss, Major Peter Clarke,
the Duchess of Gloucester, the Duke of Windsor, Prince Richard of Gloucester, the Earl
and Countess of Pembroke, Madame Zoia Poklewska-Koziell. Princess Margaret and the
Earl of Snowdon. The Queen Mother, the Prince of Wales, Princess Anne.

(*Above*) The Duchess lunching with Paul Louis Weiller at 85 rue de la Faisanderie.

(*Right*) The Duchess on one of her daily visits to the Duke in the London Clinic, March 1965.

(*Below*) The Duke and Duchess talking to the Queen Mother after the unveiling of the Queen Mary memorial at Marlborough House, June 1967.

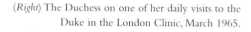

(*Right*) The Duke with his head on the Duchess's shoulder at the Mill, photographed by Robin Beare.

(*Above*) The Duke and Duchess in 1969.

(*Left*) The Duchess with Maurice Chevalier, arriving at the Lido, 11 December 1969.

(*Below*) Robin Beare with the Duke at the Mill. He visited the Duke when he was dying, in May 1972.

(*Above*) The Duchess watching the
Trooping the Colour procession from
her window at Buckingham Palace,
3 June 1972.

(*Left*) Lord Mountbatten with the Duchess
on her arrival at Heathrow Airport
for the Duke's funeral, 2 June 1972.

(*Above*) The Duke's Lying-in-State at St George's Chapel, 2–3 June 1972.

(*Above*) The Queen with the Duchess of Windsor and Prince Philip leaving St George's Chapel after the Duke's funeral, 5 June 1972.

(*Right*) Hon Mary Morrison (Lady-in-Waiting to the Queen) saying goodbye to the Duchess at Heathrow Airport after the interment, 5 June 1972.

(*Below*) Wreaths for the Duke at Windsor, June 1972.

(*Above*) The Prince of Wales and Admiral of the Fleet the Earl Mountbatten of Burma on the Royal Yacht *Britannia*.

FACING PAGE
(*Top left*) The Duchess arriving for a dinner at Maxim's in 1973.
(*Top right*) The Duchess at the Waldorf, New York in April 1974. (*Below left*) The Duchess in her Paris home, 1975 with the Duke's portrait by James Gunn, removed from the house by Maître Blum during the Duchess's illness. (*Below right*) The author in the same seat – the Gunn portrait had by then been replaced by one of the Duchess by Drian.

(*Above*) Maître Suzanne Blum, the lawyer, in 1980.

(*Right*) Release from torment. The Duchess's coffin arriving in England, 28 April 1986.

(*Above*) The Duchess's coffin leaving St George's Chapel for Frogmore, carried by the Welsh Guards. The Queen and Prince Philip, the Queen Mother, the Prince and Princess of Wales and Princess Anne on the steps, 29 April 1986.

together, & as long as the heart beats they pretend they're being brilliantly clever & 'saving life'. One day some brave Dr will have to break the spell. Until he does, Tito, Franco*, Duchess of Windsor – it doesn't bear thinking of.[34]

Some years after the Duchess died, Diana Mosley wrote to me:

I think at the very beginning of the Duchess's illness M*e* Blum did discourage visitors, but she was obeying the doctor. He was pestered by the nurses, who said visits tired & excited her so that she couldn't sleep (a bore for *them*. Ditto vodka. But at that stage I thought it a shame because if she enjoyed visit & vodka she should have them, heaven knows her life was dreary enough with the nurses & tiresome secretary for company). But quite quickly she was really far beyond visits. At my last one she never said a word, just stared looking wretched. After that to want to see her was only idle curiosity & no pleasure at all to her.

What I feel strongly is that her in-laws should have made a few efforts. *Not* to 'pull the plug out', but to make quite certain that she was having anything that made her less unhappy. You can tell by the expression, even when the person is a 'vegetable.' Only relations can do it. I had mobilised a world-famous neuro-surgeon to give a second opinion.[35]

To this she later added:

It's all *too awful*. I don't know, but I guess, there might have been drugs to make her less unhappy, but they might not have been 'good' for her in the sense that they might have shortened her life. So much the better of course, you or I would say, but possibly not the doctor . . . Doctors have quite different ideas & ambitions from us. They feel triumphant as long as the patient is 'alive'.[36]

At a certain point Lady Mosley sought a meeting with the Prince of Wales to inform him of the Duchess's plight. It might have been as a

---

* Marshal Tito (1892–1980). He was in hospital from 11 January 1980, had his left leg amputated and finally died from the gangrene on 4 May. The amputation inspired a cartoon in a British paper which showed an angel handing up the leg on a cloud and the caption: 'We are getting him in instalments.' General Franco (1892–1975) was whisked to hospital wrapped in a carpet. He suffered from heart illness, Parkinson's disease, peritonitis, lung congestion and a build-up of fluid in the abdominal cavity. He survived from 1974 until his death on 20 November 1975.

result of that meeting that Michael Mann, the Dean of Windsor*, took an interest in the Duchess and succeeded in visiting her. Michael Mann once described her condition to me as 'pitiable'.[37]

In a television interview with Russell Harty in 1980, Diana Mosley said she had not seen the Duchess for three years. She was 'pretty ill. I think she's very ill. She's not allowed to see her friends.' When Harty asked her if the Duchess knew, Diana Mosley replied: 'I doubt it.'[38]

---

* Rt Rev. Michael Mann (b. 1924), Dean of Windsor 1976–89. He was not especially interested in the Duchess as a person but took his duties towards the British Royal Family most seriously. His visit to the Duchess was probably made possible by the Dean of the American Cathedral.

11

Blum Closes In – 1977–1978

Johanna Schütz was still working in the house but she now only saw the Duchess for ten minutes each day, at times specified by the nurses. She found that the Duchess was frequently sedated. There was no chance for Johanna to have a proper conversation with her. In September there had been another outburst of animosity between the two nurses then in place, due in large measure to the long hours they had worked without a break. Their hours were re-arranged and they were both kept on.

Blum was becoming increasingly irritable. She told Miss Schütz that she preferred to get news of the Duchess from someone other than her, since she was always told that the Duchess was 'fine'. Blum complained that there were still too many staff employed and was toying with the menacing threat of putting the Duchess into a maison de santé.

Power of Attorney

Presently Maître Blum took action to secure final power. Worn down by the machinations going on around her, Miss Schütz was preparing to leave for a holiday in America. Blum told her that the postman could not deliver any registered letters until a new Power of Attorney was in place. She gave as a particular example the Christmas card that the Queen sent the Duchess each year. This always arrived by registered post. It does seem an odd example, since surely anyone at the house could have signed for it when the postman rang the bell.

But this was to be a Power of Attorney that would cover all the lawyer's past and future misdeeds. Miss Schütz was told that she would not be allowed to leave until this new Power of Attorney was in place.

In October Blum came to the house with a notary and his clerk bearing the relevant Power of Attorney document. Miss Schütz had to give them tea in her office, and the notary said to Blum: 'Maître, your wishes are my orders.' Blum sent the clerk up to the Duchess's room with Miss Schütz, while she hovered outside the bedroom door. The notary stayed downstairs in the office.

There was by now no question of the Duchess signing any documents since her hands were twisted with arthritis. The clerk was there on the pretext of gaining her verbal assent.

The clerk began to read the document in French. Not surprisingly, the Duchess could not understand the legal language. She stopped him and asked if he would mind translating this document into English. The clerk pretended that his English was not up to that, and obliged Miss Schütz to inform the Duchess that it merely confirmed existing arrangements. The Duchess said something like 'Oh, all right' at which point the clerk left the room and told Maître Blum that all was well. Blum had what she wanted.

Thus by October 1977 Blum's plans were in place. She was ready for the Duchess to die. Photographs of the salon and the beautiful objects could be sent to *Connaissance des Arts*. An article should be written, preferably by Axelle de Gaigneron*. Objects could be given to museums, but if they were, she insisted that it was on condition that they were described as a gift of 'Her Royal Highness the Duchess of Windsor to the Museums of France.' An explanatory note was to be appended, explaining that the highest legal authority in the United Kingdom had confirmed that no Letters Patent could confer or withdraw the title of HRH which was the Duke's right by birth and the Duchess's by marriage. In support of this, Blum asked for copies of tables of precedence from the Duchess's house, which she thought important.

Miss Schütz left for her month's holiday in America on 5 October and returned in early November to find the atmosphere little better, but she was able to report to Cummings: 'I am happy to tell you that I found the Duchess in good shape on my return and I feel Her Royal Highness is strong enough to cope with the coming winter.'[1]

By November Blum's attitude to Miss Schütz was becoming increasingly curt and disagreeable. She queried the arrival of Dr Antenucci, and in particular his charges and the arrangements for a proposed visit. At the end of a particularly sinister letter, Blum pointed out that she missed nothing when the Duchess's interests were involved, was aware of what she, Blum, was told and what she was not told. Sometimes, she said, she liked to appear to be deaf or an old dotard, but only when it suited her.[2]

Miss Schütz then had to write to Dr Antenucci asking him to inform Dr Thin when he was arriving, mindful of Thin's hurt feelings when

---

*Axelle de Gaigneron-Morin (1933–2004), author and writer for *Connaissance des Arts*, married 1957 Prince Aymon de Broglie, divorced 1971.

Antenucci had appeared without warning six months earlier. She also told him he would have to come at his own expense and that they could not house him in the Duchess's house 'since the conditions here are different and we had to close the guestrooms of the first floor'.[3] This was in the interests of sidelining Antenucci.

On 22 November Miss Schütz wrote to Blum, confirming that she and Monsieur Martin had destroyed a great number of papers consigned to them by Amiguet on his last visit to Paris, on which occasion he had ordered their immediate destruction. She did not know their precise contents. There remained other papers. John Utter had retrieved a collection of documents from Buckingham Palace (from the days when Victor Waddilove worked there for the Duke). These and other papers of the Duke's and various office papers, she pointed out, Blum had removed on a number of occasions, always at times when Johanna was away. All she knew for certain was that she had been told frequently that these were not her concern and presumably for that reason Blum had not felt the need to give her an inventory of what had been taken.

She also said that Amiguet had asked her to burn a number of documents but had not asked her to make a list of these.[4]

London Weekend Television had sought permission to use the Abdication speech in a programme. Blum said that this was not the sort of thing they authorised.[5]

At the end of the month the Duchess was sent to the American Hospital with a fever. Dr Thin thought she was going to die. He arrived unannounced at the house at three a.m. in search of a dossier he needed. When the Duchess once again did not die, he wanted to return her home on 2 December, but neither the Duchess's nurse nor the nurse at the hospital thought this was a good idea. The problem was, who was to make this decision? Miss Schütz finally called the night nurse, Elvire Gozin, and asked her to call Dr Thin, who agreed to keep the Duchess in hospital a few days longer. Robin Beare was expected for a meeting with Dr Thin on 12 December.

Blum also went to the hospital and told the nurses to communicate directly with Dr Thin on these matters. Blum maintained that Dr Antenucci always congratulated Dr Thin on what he was doing for the Duchess, and stressed her confidence in Professor Mercadier, who was still overseeing the Duchess while she was in the American Hospital.

The Duchess returned home and Amiguet spent three days in Paris in the middle of December in connection with her affairs. He was not supposed to see the Duchess, but one morning the nurse suddenly came down and asked him to come upstairs quickly. The Duchess was well

rested and was just able to wish him a good trip. Nevertheless Amiguet
concluded it was still very sad.[6]

Meanwhile the Duchess's Mercury car was sold because she no longer
used it. The cooking arrangements were reduced. It was noted that the
house was in bad repair, pieces of cement falling near the front door.

In January 1978 the Duchess was described as 'just about holding her
own,'[7] but by February, the news was bad: 'Her Royal Highness's health
is stable again but there is no hope of improvement.'[8] In March Maria
reported that the night nurse had failed to close the Duchess's bedroom
shutters.

Lord Tennyson made his last appearance at this time. When the
Duchess had her first stroke in 1977, Blum had asked him to be her
liaison with the Palace, to which he agreed for a while. He had tried to
see the Duchess in August 1977, but at the last minute Blum cancelled
the visit, causing panic in the nurse in charge. But he did visit the Duchess
in her room for the last time early in 1978: 'She could scarcely move,
but seemed pleased to see me and even talked about a future dinner
party.'[9]

After that no other callers were allowed to see the Duchess, though
some old friends still slipped past, thanks to Georges. A letter from the
doctor was kept in the hall, explaining that visits were forbidden. Georges
could brandish this if necessary.

There was one piece of positive news. The City of Paris extended the
lease on the house in the Bois de Boulogne so that the Duchess could
stay on there for the rest of her life.

The next few months were increasingly difficult for Miss Schütz. The
situation at the house was becoming intensely stressful. Blum and
Amiguet clearly wanted to get her out, and their method was to insist
on a new contract. When this was presented to her, it did not appeal,
not least because they wanted a reduction in her salary, a classic device
to oust someone. Miss Schütz refused to sign this and appealed for help
to Nate Cummings. On 25 January Cummings called Amiguet to inform
him that she would not sign the new contract and to propose a meeting
between himself, Johanna, Amiguet and Blum. Amiguet replied to him
that there was nothing to worry about and it would all be resolved
without newspaper publicity after the Duchess died. Cummings quoted
Amiguet as saying that he was Johanna's friend and wished to be 'impar-
tially helpful.' At that point Amiguet still thought Blum was 'a very
smart woman.'[10]

On 23 February Johanna left for Canada, informing Blum that she thought the Duchess's condition was stable and that she did not anticipate any problems in her absence.[11]

When she returned on 13 March she found the Duchess could no longer speak to her. By this time the Duchess was crippled with deformatory Rheumatism. Her hands were so twisted that for a time they were bound in an attempt to straighten them. Later they placed cotton wool under her fingers to prevent them digging into her palms. Her legs were likewise twisted. She could do nothing.

Johanna realised that her position as secretary was under threat. She told Nate Cummings that her salary had not been reduced, but that when she tried to call Amiguet she was instructed to call Blum.

She was planning a few days off early in March 'with Maître Blum's permission'. With all the tensions at the house, her health was suffering and she lost eight pounds.

The Duchess almost ceased to exist as a person. She could still communicate, speaking occasionally. But she could hardly move without assistance, being turned to the right and left, moved from her bed to a chair or couch, and then back again.

Miss Schütz's negotiations with Blum and Amiguet (then on a world cruise aboard the *Queen Elizabeth 2*) were making no progress. Amiguet could not attend to Johanna's problems since he was travelling the high seas:

> I received already two postcards from Mr Amiguet, but never any money in Switzerland. Anyhow we will discuss it when you are in Paris. Thank you for proposing Charles Torem as a lawyer but I don't think I could pay his fees. My lawyer up to now managed that I have no problems with Blum. I call her every day as she asked me to do, and we are quite friendly, but never a word on my subject. She only comes to the house when I am not here, which means she avoids seeing me.[12]

Miss Schütz had always promised the Duke that she would stay with the Duchess till the end, but the point came when she could be of no more assistance. The last few years had been unpleasant. The Duchess was now so ill that she did not recognise Johanna who was under pressure to sign the new and restricting contract, which Blum and Amiguet were confident she was unlikely to do.

Miss Schütz came to the point where she could no longer accept the working conditions imposed by Blum and Amiguet. Her lawyer pressed for the compensation due to her according to French law after working for eight years. Amiguet then made the surprising proposal that she accept a cheque for 100,000 French francs on Morgan Guaranty – but not declare it. She was suspicious, working out that by that method they could always denounce her in the future. No adequate explanation was ever produced for why they offered so much money.

Johanna refused their 'dirty' money, as she called it, and told them she would continue in her job. Legally Johanna was entitled to compensation of 45,000 French francs. The moment she refused their offer, she received a registered letter dismissing her.

She declined a reference from Blum, insulted that she was described as a 'secretary-*typist*'. But she did not forget that she was owed money in the Duchess's will and that if they dared to remove her from that, they would be 'committing themselves'.[13]

Nor was Johanna alone in being a victim of the new decisions that Blum was taking. The Duchess was no longer allowed flowers in her bedroom, an economy of about five dollars a week. The nightwatchman was dismissed, and there was a plan to replace the nurses with less expensive '*gardes-malades*'. Dr Thin was resisting the last proposal and in fact the nurses remained.

Nate Cummings was not pleased to hear that Johanna had been 'discharged' when she was needed 'so desperately.' He hoped for a copy of the inventory so that when the Duchess died, he could 'protect the estate' if necessary. He was anxious that there might be adverse publicity, and as he put it, 'I hate to think that anything will be done that might be questioned.'[14]

Blum put it about that the reason why Johanna Schütz had had to go was that she was 'unstable' and 'away a lot'. [15] The reason was rather different. Soon after she left, Monsieur Martin was driving Amiguet and Blum in the car together. Johanna told me that he overheard Blum say to Amiguet: 'Well, at least we won't have Miss Schütz to contend with.'[16]

On 11 April Amiguet wrote to Nate Cummings to thank him for the copious introductions that had made a long world trip in the *QE2* such a success. He added that the Paris situation was much the same, that the Duchess's health was not improving, and that Miss Schütz was leaving. The matter, he added, was in the hands of lawyers.[17]

To this Cummings responded that he would call Blum next time he was in Paris and that he hoped to see the Duchess, even if only for a moment. He said he did not understand why Miss Schütz was leaving the Duchess's employ and felt entitled to an explanation. He had always found her trustworthy and industrious. Pointing out that his involvement in the Duchess's affairs was 'a labor of love', he added that he had bought a number of items from the Duchess 'as a sentimental gesture' and always paid the prices suggested by Miss Schütz.[18]

Not surprisingly, Blum, the Duchess's over-energetic lawyer, devoted her energies to external matters. In September 1977, somewhat optimistically, Guy d'Arbois from TV Française had written to the Duchess inviting her to take part in a round-table discussion on 9 May 1978 to coincide with the release of the French version of the film *The Woman I Love**. The letter was passed to Maître Blum who became excited by the idea.

When Miss Schütz had returned from her skiing holiday in March 1978 she had found Blum ferreting about in the Windsors' private papers. Blum claimed that she needed to prepare for the television programme and she took away three envelopes of 1937 press cuttings, four 1936 scrapbooks and a 1936 Man Ray photo of the Duchess.

Among those taking part in the television discussion were Maurice Schumann (the French Foreign Minister from 1969–73, who had covered the Windsor wedding as a reporter), Lord Tennyson, Ambassador Henry J. Taylor, Edward Pope[†], and Audrey Russell (the well-known BBC commentator on royal occasions, and also, by coincidence, the niece of 'Fruity' Metcalfe)[‡]. Miss Schütz got the impression that Blum was 'preparing a book.'[19]

Ambassador Taylor wrote to the Duchess about this programme. Miss Schütz replied to say that the Duchess did not know about the television programme so she had not shown her his letter. She told him that Dr Thin now forbade visitors: 'Her Royal Highness's state of health is stable and she is quite lucid at the moment, but does not speak or only very rarely.' Johanna also told him she was leaving:

I will not take up another job immediately, as I hope to come and see Her Royal Highness from time to time, but I am afraid that this won't be possible. I feel I cannot help Her Royal Highness in her

---

* The 1972 film, starring Richard Chamberlain and Faye Dunaway, which was evidently banned in Great Britain.

† Edward Julius Pope (1919–95), a writer for MGM, and later an international business executive, who lived in Paris from 1955 to 1990 at 5 Lamartine Square. Later Managing Director of the international affairs of the National Association of Chain Drug Stores. He was one of the first to take the Duchess out to lunch in Paris in the early days of her widowhood. In 1963 he married Princess Niloufer of Turkey and Hyderbad (1916–89), granddaughter of Sultan Murad V.

‡ Audrey Russell (1906–89) was a friend and spoke a great deal about this programme, returning from Paris with the story that Lord Tennyson had told her that the Duke was 'difficult and crotchety' in the last two years of his life.

state and it breaks my heart to leave her, but I will always be at her disposal if Her Royal Highness needs me.[20]

At the end of April Johanna left the Duchess's employ. The locks of the house were changed so that she could no longer return there.

In May 1978 Dr Thin allowed Nate Cummings to visit the house and take a two-minute look through the Duchess's door: 'It really is heart-breaking to see her sitting in a chair, propped with pillows.'[21] In July Cummings reported that he had phoned Georges, who had advised him that the Duchess barely spoke 'above a whisper', but that otherwise she was much the same though 'gradually becoming weaker'. Cummings had then telephoned Dr Thin who said that no one could see the Duchess, but that if he called in September he hoped to meet me and perhaps he could then go to the house and 'at least look [in] on the Duchess.'[22]

Nate Cummings and Amiguet kept in touch. Amiguet told Cummings the latest news of the situation in Paris, pointing out that Dr Thin was right to restrict visits to the Duchess because it was wrong to allow visitors to see her in her present condition. He addressed the departure of Miss Schütz, adding they had called in the Notary Public to undertake an official check on some sales that she had organised.'[23]

Cummings worried about his purchases, though he had proper receipts. He wondered if 'Maître Blum had done anything that might be criticised?'[24] On 1 September Miss Schütz clarified the position:

Firstly I told you already that I handed everything over to the Duchess's attorney clerk, who incidentally has all powers since 1976 (and not Maître Blum). [He] as well as the attorney, who has the will, are at the feet of dear Suzanne! By the way, Amiguet, Blum and [the attorney clerk and his wife] had lunch together in the Duchess's dining room on July 19th [1977].

Secondly, I always protested about the procedure of sales which were handled by Maître Blum. [Where] I am concerned, I only acted on instructions from Maître Blum (you know that she never gave me anything in writing) or by Mr Amiguet, from whom I have a letter stating that I have to execute all instructions given by Maître Blum and that I am only the secretary and have no responsibility. The procedure generally was as follows: They told me what was to be sold, the amount to be paid. Georges then established a list of the items sold, and I added the amount paid by the purchaser. Copy

of this list went to Amiguet and Maître Blum. The amounts paid
to me I handed to the Bank with proper receipts and the amounts
paid to Blum or Amiguet I got a statement from Amiguet saying
how much he received. All this has been checked by the banking
expert, controlling the accounts each year and I have the letters
from him to the Duchess, saying the accounts were in order.

What they are up to now, I do not know. They can do anything
or say anything, who can prove them the contrary . . .[25]

12

Blum on the Attack – 1978–1979

'They can do anything or say anything, who can prove
them the contrary?'[1]

By April 1978 Blum had as near full control of the Duchess as she could have. She did not confine herself to running the Duchess's business life, making sure that the bills were paid and that she was properly cared for.

She continued to sell things. I have no precise details of these sales. But she certainly sold a rare set of twelve 1832 Rockingham dessert plates bearing the arms of King William IV surrounded by the Garter to Nathan Cummings, as well as a Royal Worcester breakfast set.* Givenchy was one of the Duchess's friends who was invited to the house for a possible purchase. Aubusson carpets were also sold.

But this was not enough for Blum. She now added the role of historian to her self-appointed duties. She considered that she had the right to present the Duchess to the world – to state what she perceived to be the Duchess's case.

Blum had several theories that she wished to promulgate – first and foremost that the Windsors had never had sex before marriage, which was frankly none of her business; and secondly, more interestingly, that the Duchess had not wanted to marry the Duke and had certainly not forced him to abdicate. There were other, lesser matters against which she protested. In pursuit of these claims she issued a great number of statements on the Duchess's behalf. Many of these contradicted each other. They also made Blum look ridiculous as when she pointed to the elegant Man Ray photograph of the Duchess that she had removed from the Duchess's house and told the author Stephen Birmingham: 'Look at that. Can you imagine a woman of such – dignity – ever agreeing to be the mistress of any man?'[2] Diana Mosley, who knew the Duchess considerably better, was one who poured scorn on Blum's campaign. She summed it up by saying: 'She invented a new Duchess. She even gave her back her virginity.'[3]

As an intelligent lawyer, Blum should have appreciated the danger of

---

* After his death these plates were sold at Christie's, New York, without their royal provenance, for \$30,800 [Lot 514, 8–9 October 1985].

making contradictory statements. The more people say, the more they incriminate themselves. An example of Blum projecting her ideas occurred at the time of the sale of the remaining jewels of the Duchess of Windsor in Geneva in April 1987. Blum, then aged eighty-eight, issued an extraordinary statement about the Windsors and their love for each other:

> The Duke was more taken at first. When he was nothing more than Prince of Wales, he wrote enflamed and very poetic letters to Wallis and she replied: 'You do not seem to have attained maturity in love.' For a long time he feared that Wallis would not go through with her divorce from Ernest Simpson. 'Finally, it was I who won,' he wrote in his memoirs. She became very in love after the Abdication.

The Maître continued:

> They were, however, separated by their tastes. She lived only at night, he was bored after ten o'clock. She hated fox-hunting, the aeroplane, everything he loved. He could not live without her. He showed himself nervous, agitated the moment she left. She was sometimes a little rude with him; everything in him showed much tenderness. They finally achieved the impossible.[4]

Thus the lawyer turned historian and gave her verdict on the 'love story of the century'.

Maître Blum had also made statements to the press concerning the Duchess's health. After the Duchess's death in April 1986, she was quoted in the *Sunday Times*:

> She was lucid to the last moment, although she had to be fed intravenously because she could no longer swallow. Her brain was very slow but she was not in a coma as some people have said.[5]

Yet some years before, in the autumn of 1982, the Maître had given an interview on television, in the BBC's *Timewatch* programme. On that occasion she had said:

> Everyone knows that for seven years now she has been bedridden, being only able to be taken in an armchair in front of the windows to look at the trees and hear the birds sing. She cannot read and she practically cannot move. She has been much better, though, in '76 and in the first part of 1977 so we had some hope that she would

maybe recover, but it was only hope and unfortunately now she's not able to have any talk with anyone. She's taken care of by very good doctors, in fact the best doctors I know, because no one else could have done such a thing.[6]

The Maître's line during the last eight years of the Duchess's life was that she had to be protected from the evil allegations made about her by authors and journalists, that the Duchess was frequently upset by such things, and that her reputation must be defended.

Lord Nicholas Gordon Lennox, Counsellor at the British Embassy, noted that anyone who suggested that there had been carnal relations between the Windsors before their marriage in 1937 'would find themselves at the wrong end of a legal process conducted with no quarter'.[7]

Blum's enthusiasm for litigation was also held in check by Amiguet. On my only ever face-to-face meeting with Blum, she told me that she hated *The Windsor Story*, the book written by Murphy and Bryan III. She said that she could win lawsuits against them, but the bankers would not let her sue. She was also aware that if she sued in the United States she would have to win in every state across the country and that might not work.

She also told me that she hated Lady Donaldson's book. Her version was that Lady Donaldson had written through the English lawyer asking for cooperation as the book would be published at the Duke's death. Blum claimed that Lady Donaldson had said she thought that would be a good time to publish, but since the Duke would be dead by then she saw no point in submitting her manuscript for approval.[8*]

The Duchess herself was beyond caring what people wrote about her, and even in the years before she became desperately ill any publications that might have upset her had been kept from her. Blum's crusade on the Duchess's behalf appeared to be based on high moral principles. In fact, as later became evident, she was protecting the market for herself.

Hardly had Miss Schütz been ousted than the Maître began to make the public statements for which she soon became well known. It was a television series and a book that preoccupied her and established her in the eyes of the general public as the Duchess's spokeswoman and a potentially litigious lawyer.

---

* As we have seen, Lady Donaldson's version was that when James Pope-Hennessy was dropped – or dropped out of the running as official biographer – Sir Godfrey Morley, who had met her when he allowed her access to the Monckton papers, suggested she might like to assume that role. But she decided she did not want to meet the Windsors or to write a book over which they would have the right of veto.

In September the Duke of Kent went to Thames TV's studios at Teddington to see the filming of Thames Television's series *Edward & Mrs Simpson*, which was broadcast in the autumn of 1978. It was well received by the critics, and considered to be interesting and dramatic without being sensational. Blum's first public attacks were against this television series. She told the world that the Duchess took exception to it, and some of the world believed this.

Like many others I watched this series at the time and soon became engrossed by it. Cynthia Harris played Mrs Simpson as a woman with strange and uncontrollable power over the King. Edward Fox was well cast except that I was not sure that Edward VIII had such a barrack-room attitude, nor that he was so considerate. Expressions like 'We couldn't ask Winston to do that' did not seem to fit. By 1978 I was convinced that Edward VIII would use and misuse everybody at whim. I have watched the series since and my overriding feeling is one of sadness as the car takes the couple away after the wedding into an uncertain future. I wished the story could have ended differently.

This proved to be the first time that the general public heard of the existence of the so-called love letters between the Duke and Duchess. My conclusion at the time was:

> I think Maître Blum is off her head wanting to publish the letters of Mrs Simpson. The Duchess of Windsor clearly knows nothing about the serial. She doesn't even know if it's day or night. So why? Or has Maître Blum succumbed to that power mania of all those who looked after the Windsors?[9]

As *Edward & Mrs Simpson* was screened on British television, a *Daily Express* reporter looked over the wall of the house in the Bois and secured an interview with Blum. She told him that the Duchess was semi-paralysed, unable to leave her bed unaided, seriously ill, but not in immediate danger. 'She eats well and is able to talk. She still wants to know what is going on in the world – but not too much.'

Blum insisted that the Duchess was aware of the TV series and had commented: 'I would have thought they had forgotten that old, old story by now.' This was fabrication. Blum announced that on her birthday and at Christmas the Duchess received sackloads of greetings cards, and that every day people wrote to her from New York, Rome, Nice and London, which was obviously an exaggeration.

On 20 November Blum issued a statement to the effect that the television series was 'largely and essentially a fable based on an incorrect or distorted interpretation of the facts.'[10] She said that the Duchess had received hundreds of letters of sympathy since the series had started. Blum's statements were muddled and contradictory. At one point Blum announced that the Duchess hated the film, and that she had authorised her to release her love letters in order to prove that her part in the saga had been different. Another time Blum said that the Duke had intended to tell the 'truth' in his memoirs but had been dissuaded from so doing. But he had consigned his 1936 letters to the Duchess 'at a time when they were linked only by friendship' to an historian in order that he should release them in a later publication.

Both of these statements were lies, as is proved by subsequent developments.

Blum complained that Thames Television had refused to allow her to see the script. 'I understand why now, after having read press reviews of the series,'[11] she added, reinforcing my view that she never actually saw the series. Blum was anxious to make the point that the Duchess was not a cheap adventuress; she asserted that Mrs Simpson was not the King's mistress before marriage: 'This legend is an absolute negation of the truth,' she said.

To Charles Laurence of the *Daily Telegraph*, Blum said:

> People all over the world will be amazed to discover how seriously they have been fooled. Mrs Simpson, the Duchess of Windsor, has been portrayed as a cheap adventuress determined to get hold of the Prince of Wales, determined to marry the King, and destroy the King.
>
> The reverse is true. She was the reluctant partner. She was happily married to Mr Ernest Simpson until he took up another woman. What has particularly distressed her – and myself – has been the allegations that she was the Prince's and then the King's mistress. This is quite untrue.
>
> The King did not want a mistress and if he had, no doubt he would not have abdicated. He wanted a wife and the support of this one woman for the rest of his life.[12]

In the *Evening Standard* that November Blum was quoted as saying it was a 'grotesque exaggeration' to call the letters love letters. She continued: 'They are letters of dissuasion rather than love letters.' She mentioned a letter from Mrs Simpson to the King, which read: 'Give up this mad idea. It is impossible. It will be a disaster.'[13]

This was the first time that the lawyer made the claim that the Duchess herself had agreed to the release of her letters. In *The Times* Blum further declared:

> Before the Duke's death he handed the letters to a friend and histor-ian intending that they should be published after he and his wife had both died.
>
> The friend, whom Maître Blum would not name, has decided to make the documents public now because of the image presented in the television series.[14]

In fact, as we now know, Blum was in possession of the letters since they had been brought to her office from the Duchess's house. No one besides the Windsors and Blum had read them.

After the Duchess's death, Lord Tennyson read about this 'friend and historian' being appointed to edit the Windsors' letters. He assumed it must have been him, but questioned Blum's version: 'The truth seems to me to be rather different to Maître Suzanne Blum's version'. He wrote that the Duchess never mentioned her papers to him. As we have seen, Lord Tennyson paid the Duchess a final visit early in 1978:

> It was after the meeting that Maître Blum said the Duchess wished me to look after her papers, and even that I should accompany her body to England. While I agreed to the second and told Nicholas Gordon Lennox of the Embassy that I would always help, if, I repeat, if this was thought to be suitable. The papers I *refused absolutely* to be responsible for and sent Maître Blum a letter making this quite clear. But with the proviso that she should tell me what she proposed doing with them before she took any action. This she clearly did not do.[15]

Soon after this meeting Lord Tennyson introduced Blum to Sir Nicholas Henderson, and the British Embassy acted as liaison from then on. This relationship did not always run smoothly. Henderson moved on in 1979 and was replaced by Sir Reginald Hibbert, a man known to speak his mind freely. He fell foul of Blum's wrath:

> I was in disgrace with Maître Blum for a long time when I ventured to indicate to her that I did not believe she had a power of attorney or had ever held one. In the end we resumed relations on practical

matters which had to be dealt with & the alleged power of attorney was never again invoked.

Maître Blum was a doughty crusader. It was surprising that an intelligent woman should have chosen so poor a cause.[16]

Meanwhile Blum's outbursts fuelled public interest in the television series. Thames Television was delighted. Verity Lambert, the producer, said she could not have hoped for such stirring publicity.

In December 1978 Blum threatened that the Duchess's letters would be ready for publication within six months or a year. This panicked Charles J.V. Murphy and J. Bryan III into pressing ahead with an unpleasant and vengeful book that had been gestating since before the Duke's death. *The Windsor Story* would be published in Britain on 22 November 1979.

The preparation of this book had been no secret. In the summer of 1976 Murphy told John Utter that his would be the 'definitive' study. He kept trying to get John to tell him things and John kept evading him until one day he was caught on the telephone at eight a.m. Murphy admitted that when he had contacted Maître Blum he had found her 'rather distant'.[17] Johanna Schütz also mentioned this book to me in September 1976 but said that Murphy had signed a confidentiality agreement when working on the Duke's memoirs, which effectively prevented him from publishing anything. She also thought he was so ill that he would predecease the Duchess.*

Bryan and Murphy had interesting pasts. They were close to Frank Wisner, who ran the covert action division, OPC, within the CIA – Bryan as a psychological warfare officer (also closely involved with Carmel Offie), and Murphy as a *Time Inc* journalist. Murphy had ghosted the Duke of Windsor's memoirs, *A King's Story*, and was asked to help the Duchess with her memoirs, but they fell out. J. Bryan III knew the Windsors a bit socially and had been asked to help the Duke with certain collaborations which had come to nought, including a proposed volume on the Duke's Hanoverian ancestors which foundered when the Duke discovered how badly they had all behaved. The association between the 'ghosts' and the Windsors went back a long way, and both men had been well paid and generously entertained by them. However, they became disillusioned.

As early as 1950, Charles Murphy was travelling to New York in the

---

* Charles J. V. Murphy (1924–87) died of lung cancer on 29 December 1987. His collaborator, Joseph Bryan III (1904–93), died of cancer in Richmond, Virginia on 3 April 1993.

Queen Elizabeth with the Duke of Windsor. Cecil Beaton was aboard. He found Murphy 'very indiscreet to all & sundry':

> The Windsor love story, one of the most extraordinary of our times, is a romance without love, a fairy tale that went off the rails, the little Cinderella, instead of bringing the Prince to live her sort of life, makes him give up his life, then tries to make her life as much like his as possible.[18]

As the 'ghosts' became increasingly bitter, they decided to use their position of privileged access to turn the tables on the Windsors. They were dishonest in their approach, as I saw first-hand for myself.

One of those interviewed for the book was Laura, Duchess of Marlborough*. Laura had been Countess of Dudley at the time of the famous jewellery theft at Sunningdale in 1946†. I had met her earlier in the year and was helping edit her memoirs. She had agreed to see Bryan III when he told her that the Duchess of Windsor had it in her will that they should publish this book. Bryan III had also promised that their book would only come out after the Duchess's death. Breaking these promises, they needed to 'fix' their sources. Bryan III materialised in London and sent a document round to Laura. He wanted her to sign an 'irrevocable consent' to their publication. She became alarmed.

I telephoned John Utter in Paris and told him what they said about it being in the Duchess of Windsor's will that the book was to be written. 'Balls!' he said. He told me that they had been pressing him for information, that he was fed up with them and that all he would do was to 'correct' information.[19]

Bryan III delivered the document containing her quotes to Laura. I soon judged these 'just another scurrilous load of journalese, inaccurate and in very poor taste.' I drafted a suitable letter of refusal for Laura to sign.

The next day Laura telephoned in panic. Lady Diana Cooper had rung her up and told her not to be so silly. She was sending Bryan round. I jumped into the car and arrived at her flat to find Mr J. Bryan III in the midst of his well-tried 'psychological warfare' technique. He looked worried but he was polite – at least to me:

---

* Laura Charteris (1915–90), four times married. Her second husband was the 3rd Earl of Dudley, her third Michael Canfield, and her fourth the 10th Duke of Marlborough.
† *See* Part 2, Chapter 7.

Clearly he wanted to leave at once and clearly he couldn't. He was saying: 'Well, we've sorted out our problems now, haven't we?' He hadn't, of course. He also said 'You're going to come out of this as a boring old crone.' Very rude. I said 'Well, we can change that in her own book.' He also said, 'The Duchess of Windsor was a hateful, terrible woman. Nobody likes her. Her family hate her,' and so on. I said I didn't see how he could produce the book in the Duchess of Windsor's lifetime. 'It *can* be done,' he replied. Evidently Lady Diana Cooper signed happily and he was on his way to see Mountbatten. There were fifty-one pages of his rubbish. 'Biddy' Monckton is now locked away at Newbury* through excess of drink and he was still chasing Lady Baba (Alexandra Metcalfe). Fortunately he failed to get Laura to sign and departed, looking thoroughly grumpy.

There was a sense of relief after he had gone – a feeling that a sinister presence had left us. I was sure he'd ring again and it's worth noting here that he did. He said he'd lost the papers i.e. he was going to feel free to publish whatever he wanted. So later we wrote him another letter – in fact addressed to the publishers which said all her quotes were to be removed.[20]

I sent all the relevant information over to John Utter, and he in turn passed it on to Maître Blum. No quotes from Laura appeared in the published book.

Lord Mountbatten was one of the few people who emerged well from *The Windsor Story*. He had been prepared to help the 'ghosts' since, once again, it provided him with an opportunity to put himself firmly in the centre of the story. A year earlier, on 25 April 1978, Bryan had written to John Barratt, Mountbatten's Private Secretary, with a view to getting the quotes from Mountbatten cleared. He said that the *Evening News* were intending to syndicate their story – either when the Duchess died, or perhaps even before. They had heard rumours that the Duchess was *in extremis* and so they needed Lord Mountbatten to sign off his quotes as soon as possible.[21]

Mountbatten told them: 'I remember the dreadful day of the Abdication, when his brothers and myself were alone with him trying to dissuade him.' But since this meeting was on 10 December, the Abdication had been settled, so Mountbatten's advice could have had no impact at all.

Speaking of his tribute to the Duke following his death, he wrote to them: 'I was told that my voice showed my feelings which of course were deep at that time as I was very moved.' Of course he was.

---

*Lady Monckton was an inmate of Edgecombe House, near Newbury. She died there in 1982.

There were moments of light relief in the correspondence. The ghosts asked him if he could explain the nickname: 'Batty Mountlouis'. Mountbatten responded: 'I have never heard anybody use it nor have I had my leg pulled about it. It sounds like an American newspaper invention.'[22]

He even told them a story about attempting to visit the Duchess in October 1976, in which he asserted that he had never had any contact with Dr Thin, a story contradicted in his own (now published) diaries.*

On 23 December 1978 Bryan III wrote to Mountbatten to say that their publishers both in London and New York were 'agog over Maître Blum's expressed intention to publish the Windsor love letters'. He said that neither Charles Murphy, nor himself, nor John Utter had ever heard them mentioned. He wondered when they had been written.[23] On 4 January 1979 Lord Mountbatten replied, following a visit to Paris:

> While there, I rang up to enquire about the health of the Duchess of Windsor and was put through to Maître Blum. She assured me that she was comfortable and resting in bed but was apparently not fit enough really to get up or to sign any letters or documents. She said that the Duchess was very distressed by the television serial *Edward and Mrs Simpson*. She told me that the Duchess was going to file her love letters to be published. I expressed some surprise at this but didn't press the matter. If she is unable to sign any documents, she can hardly have given written authority for their publication.[24]

Mountbatten did not live to see *The Windsor Story* published.

Blum spent much of 1979 trying to stop *The Windsor Story* coming out. But she failed to prevent its publication or its subsequent release as a paperback. This is the more strange since she was in possession of contract letters from Charles Murphy to both the Duke and Duchess of Windsor, appointing him to assist with their respective memoirs, which contained a clear confidentiality clause: 'I will at all times hold confidential and will not divulge or use in any way, directly or indirectly, without your express written permission, any information with respect to your life or the life of your family which I have obtained or may obtain by reason of my services hereunder.'[25]

In his contract with the Duchess, Murphy further agreed to 'deliver to you all notes, photographs and other data of any kind relating to the

* *From Shore to Shore*, p. 261.

subject matter of the Memoirs.'[26] When the Duke died, Sir Godfrey Morley went to some lengths to secure the return of Murphy's notes.

The Windsor Story was published in the autumn of 1979. The book attracted considerable attention. On 23 November Blum attacked it, accusing the ghosts of reviving discredited myths and breaking agreements, written and unwritten. She was interviewed by the *Daily Mail*. As usual she objected to suggestions that the Windsors had been lovers before marriage, that the Duchess dominated the Duke after the wedding, that he lingered in Lisbon rather than defend his country, and that the Duchess possessed Queen Alexandra's emeralds.

Blum was not wholly accurate or honest in her defence of the Windsors. She claimed that the Duke 'didn't need anyone to write his prose and the Duchess also had talent.' She said the ghosts made a lot of money out of the Windsors* – 'They helped to put a bit of order into things and to arrange the chapters' – and they tried to persuade the Duke into further collaborations.

Murphy responded that he stood by every word in the book. He denied that he had said the Windsors were lovers before marriage: 'It speaks very well of Maître Blum's affection for the Duchess that she attributes such virginal qualities to her, notwithstanding two previous marriages.' He stood by the German allegations: 'There is no question that the Duke bargained with the Germans in the hope of getting a better job for himself and a title for the Duchess.' He said Queen Alexandra's jewels were destined for a future Queen of England, and he accused Blum of forbidding him to quote from the Duchess's memoirs even though this would have portrayed her in a better light.

He claimed that it was the Duke who had sought him out for future work together. He argued that the reason for publishing now was that the Duchess had been non compos mentis since 1973 and that other books were coming out. 'We didn't want to waste four years of work,' he said.[27]

Presently Maître Blum allowed H. Montgomery Hyde to reproduce a letter written by Mrs Simpson in November 1936 to the Marchioness of Londonderry. Her line was that she was an innocent victim of press reports in the United States about her friendship with the King.

I was one of many reviewers who attacked the book in print (in *The Times*). I was in the same camp as Dame Rebecca West – 'their loathing of their subjects is pathological'[28] and John Grigg – 'an outrage . . .

---

* Murphy received twenty-five per cent of the main rights in the memoirs, a further ten per cent of other rights, and he received additional travelling and maintenance expenses.

a cruel revenge'[29] – though the maverick politician and journalist, Woodrow Wyatt, judged *The Windsor Story* 'entertaining.'[30]

In January 1980 John Utter telephoned about the book, telling me that Murphy had promised to submit the manuscript to him but had not done so. He wrote to Murphy, who replied that he had been ill and his wife had Parkinson's. John listed numerous inaccuracies in the text. Stephen Birmingham had also written a book which was due out soon. The conclusion was that Maître Blum had not handled any of this at all well.[31]

13

Last Years of the Duchess – 1978–1985

Those who sent Christmas cards to the Duchess, such as Diana Vreeland, either received a printed card in reply or sometimes a telegram. When the Duchess was well, she used to add a note herself: 'Much love and do come here soon though not exciting – W'.[1] Later the words were added in the handwriting of a nurse or some other figure. One year the printed message stated: 'THE DUCHESS OF WINDSOR appreciates your thought of her at Christmas time and wishes you a very happy New Year.' To this was added by an unknown hand: 'and thank you for your faithful thoughts.'[2] When Ambassador Taylor died in New York in February 1984, his widow received a telegram purporting to come from the Duchess: 'THINKING OF YOU LOVE WALKIS [sic] DUCHESS OF WINDSOR.'[3]

In October 1978 I saw John Utter in Paris, and he gave me news of the Duchess:

> She is still in the house in the Bois, which is now like a morgue. The Duchess has lost the use of her hands and her feet and has to be carried from her bed to one of those clinical couches. She now no longer speaks and has apparently put on 25 lbs. For ten months there have been no visitors at all, because they used to put her blood pressure up too much. So she lives in a world of her own, lingering on, spoon-fed, miserable. For everyone's sake, the sooner she dies the better – John says they should have let her die in 1976 when she lost fifty per cent of her blood and they just pumped more in.[4]

Visits to the Duchess were forbidden but Blum made an exception for royal visitors. In 1963 Prince Michael of Kent had lived in Paris while studying Russian. He had often dined with the Windsors in the house in the Bois and stayed with them for weekends at The Mill. He was keen to talk to his uncle as an important living link to his father, Prince George, who had been killed in an air accident when Prince Michael was but six weeks old.

In June 1978 Prince Michael married Baroness Marie-Christine von

Reibnitz, whose brief marriage to Tom Troubridge had been annulled by the Pope.

The year before, jewels had been taken from the bank to be given to the Duchess of Kent and Princess Alexandra, following Amiguet's premise that the Duke only wanted the Kents to receive something from his estate, on account of the close bond that had existed between himself and Prince George.

On their return from their honeymoon – a long trip to India and Iran – Prince and Princess Michael made their way home via Paris, arriving there towards the end of 1978. They were invited to tea with the Duchess, presuming that the Duchess would want to take a look at the bride but having no idea that she was so ill. The invitation was issued by Maître Blum and Amiguet.

Prince and Princess Michael duly arrived at the house and found the Duchess seated in a chair in her bedroom, fully dressed on this occasion. She had two nurses with her. They had tea together. She appeared to recognise her nephew, but Prince and Princess Michael could not understand anything she said. At a certain point the Duchess waved Princess Michael and the others away, appearing desperate to speak to Prince Michael on his own. He recalled that she was 'wide-eyed and very anxious to be understood by him' but, understandably, he could not make out what she was trying to say.

Meanwhile Princess Michael went for a walk in the garden with Maître Blum. As the Prince and Princess were leaving, they found a box waiting for them in the hall. It contained some letters from Prince George, Duke of Kent to the Duke of Windsor*, a cigarette box inscribed by Prince George to his brother, a small bag and a small Cartier box. This contained a diamond brooch in the shape of the Prince of Wales's feathers, and a pair of Cartier panther-shaped earrings. The earrings consisted of a small cabochon emerald, above which was a golden panther. These were valued in 1976 at $2,250†. Princess Michael realised she could never wear a brooch designed as the Prince of Wales feathers. She returned it and a different brooch was sent, which she later sold.

Obviously, as with the earlier jewels given to the Duchess of Kent and Princess Alexandra, it was not the Duchess who gave these gifts. They were given in her name by Blum and Amiguet.

* * *

* Prince Michael placed these in the Royal Archives at Windsor.
† These appear in the Duchess's inventory as: 'motif fils et cordes or centre I cabochon émeraude avec au-dessus I léopard or et émail noir'.

During the last years of the Duchess's life I went to the Bois de Boulogne several times and looked up at the house. One such visit was in January 1979:

> Over the wall through the grey misty atmosphere one could see a kind of living tomb. All the windows on the ground floor were shuttered from the outside world, but I thought the drawing-room window was open. Upstairs what remains of the Duchess sits, surrounded by nurses. There were two lights – one on the side, which I think is her bedroom and one in the far window of what I think is the upstairs sitting room. In one of those rooms sat the Duchess, unable to move her hands and feet, unable to speak, unable, it seems, to die, poor thing.[5]

A month later the Duchess was back in the American Hospital undergoing 'abdominal surgery' – an operation for an intestinal occlusion. She was 'slowly improving' but the recovery was proving 'long & difficult'. Her condition was said to be fair. I happened to be at St George's Chapel, Windsor on Sunday, 25 February on which occasion the Dean of Windsor said prayers for her: 'We pray for Wallis, Duchess of Windsor.' He stressed the words 'And if it be thy will, restore her to health . . .'[6] I record this because in April 1986 there was some fuss when the Duchess's name was not mentioned during her funeral in the same chapel.

In April 1979 John Utter, who was still getting news of the Duchess, reported:

> She had the operation and survived that but since then there's no change. He said that Bob Oliver, the American Dean, called on her – he thought at the suggestion of the Dean of Windsor. That was at the time of the operation and she was lying unconscious in the bed. He said, as so often before, they should have let her die when she had the ulcers.[7]

The Duchess went home, but in May she was back in the American Hospital again. This time she was suffering from 'an incident of a bacterial nature'. The operation undertaken was 'completely successful'. Her condition was 'stable'. A few days later John Utter explained: 'The Duchess of Windsor's hospital visit yesterday was only because she had been taken ill and it was a weekend. They thought it better to have her in there for more nursing.'[8]

One of the most unfavourable pieces of publicity to land on Blum's

desk was an article by David Pryce-Jones in the *New York Times* magazine section. He examined Blum's contradictory statements and
extracted from her a confirmation that the Duchess had had no idea
about the television series of *Edward & Mrs Simpson*. He quoted various
sources – anonymous, though easy for me to identify and therefore no
problem for Blum. One was John Utter to whom a remark about the
Duke's drinking after seven p.m. was ascribed: 'the sound of their
drunken bickering was unbearable.' I have to say he expressed it rather
differently to me.

One of the nurses who had left some years before told him that the
doctor had stopped the Duchess from having a drink. When he talked
to Édouard, the hairdresser from M. Alexandre, he found him 'in some
panic least Maître Blum should find out that I had contacted him.' He
spoke to Lord Tennyson, who said: 'I promised the Duke I'd look after
Wallis, and I'd like nothing better. But I can't get near her. Meanwhile,
explain to me why her possessions are apparently disappearing into the
blue.' When Pryce-Jones put this to Blum, she denied it categorically.
He put a great many other points to her and her response was always the
same. As Pryce-Jones put it: 'Maître Blum explodes with more vivid
imagery about vultures and garbage.'[9]

The reappearance of the Duchess's name in the press inspired the
well-known columnist Hebe Dorsey to take an interest in her. She spoke
to a number of the Duchess's friends and she spoke to Maître Blum. The
lawyer gave her a statement:

> The Duchess is neither sequestered nor cloistered. The decision to
> keep visitors away was strictly on doctor's orders. Now the duchess
> is unfortunately not in a position to see anybody, but up to a year
> ago, when friends came, they talked too much, often about parties,
> and that sent the duchess's blood pressure up. So the doctors decided
> to cut visitors out.
>
> Actually the duchess never recovered from her husband's death
> and, after that, from the massive haemorrhage she suffered two
> [*in fact four*] years ago. Right now, she is in a pretty sad state and
> even I try not to bother her. It's a matter of decency. Knowing
> the duchess, I'm sure she wouldn't like to be seen in the state
> she's in.[10]

As it happened, the Duchess of Windsor stayed in the American
Hospital for four months.
She was still there when Lord Mountbatten was blown up in Ireland.

That summer he took his usual holiday at Classiebawn Castle on his Irish estate at Mullaghmore, County Sligo. On the morning of 27 August 1979 he went out in his boat, accompanied by his daughter Patricia and her husband, Lord Brabourne, his twin grandsons Nicholas and Timothy, Lord Brabourne's mother Doreen, Lady Brabourne, and the boat boy, Paul Maxwell.

Mountbatten had eschewed police protection. But the IRA was lying in wait for him. Hardly had he cast off from the shore than the assassins detonated a bomb.

Mountbatten was killed as were Doreen Brabourne (who died from her injuries the next day), Nicholas, and Paul Maxwell.* After a grand funeral at Westminster Abbey, Lord Mountbatten was laid to rest in Romsey Abbey. Of this dramatic death, it need hardly be said, the Duchess of Windsor remained unaware.[†]

John Utter explained that one of the reasons that the Duchess was still in hospital was that Georges and Ofélia had gone on holiday, and Dr Thin was also away. He said she was now 'just like a baby'.[11] So, by this time, the Duchess was put into hospital in the same way that a pet is sent to the kennels – for the convenience of others at holiday time. On 14 September it was announced that she was home again. Soon afterwards the mongrel dog Pompon died – another link with the past severed.

In 1979 and 1980 I saw a lot of John Utter and the more unpleasantly he was treated by Maître Blum, the more he talked to me. In February 1980 I visited him at his flat in the rue de Champagny, lunching with him later in a Chinese restaurant:

> John looked well. He walks so well too. We started off on the Windsors and *The Windsor Story* and continued on that note for a long time. He is still enraged by the book and worse than that by the quote ascribed to him. He said if he did tell that story[‡], it was because he thought it was funny. That's all. He said Maître Blum was livid, had attacked him on that and later he showed me a letter from her in which she was frankly insulting. She said she had heard from 'amis' de la Duchesse, who were very displeased – that's Amiguet (the Swiss

---

* Miraculously Lord and Lady Brabourne and the other twin, Timothy, survived.
† Later the press speculated that the Queen might visit the Duchess to break the news of Mountbatten's death to her during a two-day visit to Paris from 24 October. For obvious reasons, no such visit took place.
‡ In *The Windsor Story* (p. 543), John was quoted telling a story about the Duke's meanness, apologising that he could not give him a Christmas present because The Mill had not been sold.

banker), Nate Cummings, etc. She had heard also that he enquired from Georges as to the health of the Duchess. And she wondered whether the Duchess would appreciate his enquiries after his various quotes of late. What a muddle.

The letter from the Swiss banker was even worse. It said that someone had come back from a telephone call from John in a restaurant. 'John says he is delighted to have been dismissed. Now he'll have more time for his roses and he'll be away from the *awful Duchess*. He also said the Queen had asked him to take care of the jewels.' Well, all this was rubbish, of course . . .

And still the Duchess lives on. In the house are Georges and Ofélia, Martin, Maria and various round-the-clock nurses. The house is still as it was but nothing's done. And a house built in 1927 needs certain redecoration from time to time. Upstairs the Duchess is moved from bed to couch. And that's it. Downstairs Georges dusts and does his best.[12]

In March John rang to tell me that Frances Munn-Baker had been allowed to see the Duchess. She 'now just lies in bed, her eyes staring at the ceiling and her jaw moving.'[13] Several people reported that Walter Lees had also been allowed to see her. He said she had a tube in her nose.

My last visit to John was on a Saturday in June 1980. He had just come out of hospital. We talked about Maître Blum, whom he did not trust. 'He is frightened of her, as is Diana Mosley who also believes her to be mad . . . John became quite heated on the subject of Maître Blum.' He also spoke of Georges as a result of which I concluded that Georges was a crook.[14] In August John wrote to tell me that he was in the American Hospital for more treatment. I only got this letter in September and immediately rang the hospital. I was told he was 'too tired' to speak or read a letter. It dawned on me that this was all more serious than I had realised. I rang Diana Mosley at the Temple.

She had seen John the day before and he was just lying in bed with his eyes closed, his mouth open and with a dreadful contraption on his head, quite unable to stir. This sounded grim and the awful thing was him being there all on his own. Diana seemed to think it might be an idea for me to try and come over to see him if possible and invited me to stay if I did:

She said: 'I didn't want to have him woken as I'm just an acquaintance, but he'd love to see you as he adores you.' I asked if she thought it looked as though he would never come out of the hospital and she said: 'I hate having to give you this news but I fear it does.'[15]

It was hard to get further news but two days later Walter Lees telephoned. He called the American Hospital and rang a few minutes later: 'I'm very sorry to have to tell you that John Utter died yesterday.' He continued: 'I haven't seen him lately, but of course I used to see him a lot with the Windsors.'[16]

I was much saddened by this news. Reflecting on eight years of friendship, I noted that every time I saw John I had felt it was awful that we only ever talked about the Windsors. The truth was that he could talk about global politics and many other subjects in which he was well versed but I could not. Somehow the conversation always gravitated back to the Windsors. In the last weeks I had been determined to reassure him that he was 'in the right and that Maître Blum was mad and evil. It is sad that his last days were clouded by her evil presence.'[17] The least I could do for him was to write an obituary. This was duly published in *The Times*.

When Walter Lees rang again, I said: 'I felt sorry for him that he had been, as it were, exiled from his job.' 'Well,' said Walter Lees. 'I'm afraid that does happen when you do jobs of that kind.'[18] Some time later Diana Mosley made a good point about John and Maître Blum. She reckoned that Maître Blum disliked John because he was the one person who could expose her as not being '*intime*' with the Duchess. 'She was asked once a year out of politeness.' Since John's death, Blum had had to admit that all his files were immaculate, but by then he was dead.

Nate Cummings never saw the Duchess of Windsor after 1978. In January 1981 he reported that he had heard from Blum and Dr Thin that the Duchess was 'just about the same'.[19] Ill health forced him to give up plans for a large eighty-fifth birthday party that October. In March 1982 he reported that the Duchess was apparently 'ever-so-slightly better.'[20]

At about this time Dr Thin was questioned and played down his role as doctor, saying he was but one of many. His line was '*elle se fatigue.*' He maintained that it was the Duchess herself who did not want to see visitors.[21]

The last reliable news I heard about the Duchess's health during her lifetime was from Dr Thomas Hewes, a senior doctor at the American Hospital. I met him at a wedding reception in Paris in October 1981. He told me that the Duchess had not been in the hospital for about six or eight months:

She is a vegetable. She is in a pitiable state. I don't believe she suffers anything at all any more. The trouble is she is too well looked after. He said that the young nurses were very upset when they saw her. He also said that when in the hospital the Queen's religious advisers* ring to find out how she is.[22]

There were of course other stories. In 1982 Kenneth Rose told me that Mona Bismarck had been allowed to see the Duchess, but not to cross the threshold of her room. Her report was that the Duchess's hands were bound on account of spasms which led to her digging her nails fiercely into her side.[23]

Some years later, Diana Mosley told me the worst story: 'how someone once passed a stretcher in the American Hospital with a dead body on it. "That was the Duchess of Windsor," they said – "alive". She thought a good doctor would have put her to sleep. "After all, that's what would happen with an animal."'[24]

Johanna Schütz kept in touch with the staff at the house, calling on them from time to time. One such visit took place in April 1982. They told her the Duchess was 'about the same, does not recognise anybody and is not suffering either.' She wrote to Cummings:

There is a new blow. I feel you should know about, or maybe you have already heard: Imagine that on May 11th there is a sale at Christie's Geneva including twenty-one snuffboxes of the collection of HRH the late Duke of Windsor! These boxes have been bought in 1976 by the dear friend and antique dealer of Maître Blum for less than FF 50,000 – and now are estimated at FF 500,000. – (What a deal they made!)† You remember my telling you that they were giving the things away for practically nothing. Well, it is no more my problem, but at least I have the satisfaction to hear that my fears were justified. I am glad I have this letter from Amiguet, discharging me from all sales made.[25]

In October she added: 'The Duchess you may have heard is exactly the same as years ago when I left, which will soon be five years. How lucky I was, I cannot imagine how I could have gone on so long with Blum.'[26]

---

* Rt. Rev. Michael Mann, Dean of Windsor.
† Three of the Duke's twenty-two gold snuffboxes (valued for insurance in 1970 at £66,150) appeared in that sale. Two were given by Blum to the Louvre. Blum gave one to Dr Thin. Nathan Cummings bought one for Blum and she handed it to her antique dealer for sale.

Nate Cummings had remained poised to step in after the Duchess's death and expose any perceived wrongdoings done by Maître Blum. But his health failed him and he could do no more for the Duchess or for Johanna. In January 1983 his secretary reported that he was putting up a stiff fight, but weakening. He did not live to see the provisions of the Duchess's will. On 19 February 1985 he attended a cocktail party in Palm Beach given by Douglas Fairbanks, Jr, and a dinner afterwards. He suffered a massive heart attack at the table and died in the Good Samaritan Hospital at the age of eighty-eight. He predeceased the Duchess by a little more than a year.

For many years, while both the Duke and Duchess of Windsor had been alive, Maurice Amiguet had been a welcome visitor to the house. From time to time, when money was needed Miss Schütz would send him scrupulous accounts and ask for the necessary sum. He would then send an emissary with cash in French Francs. After Miss Schütz's departure, when Maître Blum was in sole charge, it was she who asked for the money.

For some time Maître Blum had felt hindered by Amiguet's presence and the need to apply to him for funds. Eventually, according to the staff at the house, Blum and he fell out on the grounds that he refused to send her any more money from Switzerland.

As a result of this falling-out, Blum started to sell gold boxes in Switzerland.

What happened to the Duchess's many millions in Switzerland remains unclear. There was certainly no shortage of money there.

Easier to resolve is the mystery involving the portrait of the Duke of Windsor by James Gunn that hung in the downstairs salon on the left-hand wall leading towards the dining room. This picture had been painted at The Mill in 1953 and there exists a photograph of the Duke posing with it, dressed in the full robes of the Order of the Garter. At some point it disappeared, and authors like Suzy Menkes questioned its whereabouts.

In 1979 it was given to the Musée National de la Légion d'Honneur, where I found it on a visit to Paris in April 1996. Today it hangs in the Foreign Orders section on the ground floor (espace 5). Also there, equally described as 'Leg. de S.A.R. la duchesse de Windsor 1979', are the Duke's Field Marshal's baton, a naval sword, insignia of the Coldstream, Scots and Irish Guards, and a Scots Fusiliers's bagpipe player's sword-frog tray.

It is not hard to work out how this portrait and these military accoutrements found their way into the museum. Until his death in 1980 the President of the Museum was General Georges Spillmann. The general was the husband of Maître Blum.

Elvire Gozin was the Duchess's night nurse from 1976 to 1986. In the first years that she was with the Duchess she managed to have some conversations with her and in articles published after her death revealed the Duchess experiencing the same mixture of coherence and fantasy (with lapses of memory) which others observed during those years.

Elvire Gozin was more proactive than some of the nurses. She was horrified that visitors were turned away, even the wife of the British Ambassador, who called from time to time. Eventually Elvire took photographs of the Duchess lying in her bed, which were published in a tabloid paper after her death. One of the photographs showed the tiny head of the Duchess just visible over the sheets, with all the medical paraphernalia to the left of her bed – the machinery that kept her alive.

The bed was not the fine one of happier times, with a headboard covered in pale blue silk. It was a practical bed, not quite a hospital bed but small enough for nurses to move around it. On the table behind the Duchess was a photograph of the Duke of Windsor in his uniform of 1940 and, behind that, some framed miniatures.

The Duchess herself was lying on her side, with a tube attached to her nose. Through this she was fed. Her eyes and mouth were slightly open. Her arms appeared swollen and were crossed. Her grey hair was drawn back, and she was dressed in a '*bon marché*' speckle-patterned nightdress. The Duchess's head rested on two pillows. She looked grotesquely uncomfortable. This was a terrifying image, but it proved one thing – the Duchess was alive.

Elvire Gozin's article wanted to make the point that the Duchess 'died in a slum', due to 'her own penny-pinching regime' which was 'overzealously enforced by her powerful, ageing lawyer and protector, Suzanne Blum.' She told how the regular visits of Édouard from Monsieur Alexandre's salon were terminated, and the expensive creams and lotions from Estée Lauder were replaced by cheap make-up. The bedclothes became tattered. Elvire Gozin described her as 'a prisoner in her own home.'[27]

The nurse went twice to London in a quixotic attempt to inform the Queen of the Duchess's plight. She was horrified that the house was so run-down, that things were being sold around the Duchess, and said later: 'I thought that if only the Queen knew the conditions in which the Duchess was living something would be done to ease her suffering.'[28]

On her first visit in April 1980, Elvire arrived at the gates of Buckingham Palace but was not admitted. She tried again in 1983, by which time 'things had degenerated' and this time was sent to see the Dean of Windsor. Michael Mann told her that he would pass on her message to the Queen and would respond to her. He never responded, and when pressed on this matter in 1988 he admitted he remembered the nurse coming, said he could not remember why she came, but would have to consult his files. When asked to do so, he deployed an answer he was to give on other occasions: 'I can't do that, I'm afraid, because they are now in the Royal Archives. They are privileged information.*'[29]

I drove alone to the South of France in August 1983. On the way I decided to take another look at the Duchess's house:

There was a light on in the drawing room upstairs. The Duchess's window was not locked like the Duke's which is completely barred, as are the downstairs rooms. So I think she is still there. There was a small blue car in the drive and the lawn was not so badly kept. There was a thin yellow hose stretching across it. So the drama continues . . . It is strange but I was a little scared even looking at the house from the public road . . .

In the short interval between 8.20 & 8.50 the light in the drawing room went out & the Duchess's shutters came down. For my benefit? At least there's someone there . . . By the time I had driven off, the upper drawing-room light was on. I was struck by how normal the house [looked], just as it always had. It's dreadful to think that the lady, who on my first visit was planning a visit to the salon of one of her designers, is now a helpless cripple on a life-support machine. The shutters were probably always closed at 8.30. And they still are. May the drama soon end![30]

The Duchess had been the victim of publicity and speculation, but in these last years even this dwindled to nothing. There are scarcely any references to her in the index of the *New York Times* in the last few years of her illness. Inevitably, the world had moved on.

*   *   *

*Bishop Mann gave me the same response when I was researching an authorised biography of Princess Andrew of Greece. He had transferred her body for burial in Jerusalem. He told me he had given his papers to the Royal Archives. It may be true, but the Librarian at Windsor was surprised to hear of him lodging any papers there. In my case, I was fortunate to find copies of all the correspondence I needed in the papers of Princess Theimouraz Bagration in New York.

In 1985 there were, however, two press reports about the Duchess, one independent and the other by way of a rebuttal from Maître Blum.

On 18 January 1985 Brian Vine of the *Daily Mail* reported that the Duchess was: 'unable to speak, unable to see, she is kept alive in a twilight world of her own.' He revealed that she could no longer wear her wedding ring, and that her friends were concerned about her plight. Apparently the house and grounds were in poor condition – a coronet had tumbled from the gatepost, the main gates were rusty, the canvas shades over the windows badly stained. Diana Mosley told him she left flowers downstairs for her, and Jane Engelhard, an American friend of the Duchess's, complained that she had been barred from the house.

Vine managed to speak to a nurse, possibly Elvire Gozin, who told him the Duchess was in pain but could not express it. She said:

> I suppose if she couldn't afford all this nursing she would have died for lack of care a long time ago. One wonders if that would not have been better for someone whose great beauty and vitality made her a figure of history. I cannot think it's the sort of death she would have chosen for herself.[31]

It might have been this article which inspired Maître Blum to allow John Knight of the *Sunday Mirror* to enter the grounds of the house later in the year and to speak to Georges and to Dr Thin. Georges lied to him, saying that the Duchess had addressed a few words to him in French that morning. He repeated his line: 'She no longer wishes to see anyone except her staff. She is content with the recollections of her extraordinary life.' Knight extracted from Georges a fabricated story of the Duchess's daily routine, involving her hair being tied in a ponytail and make-up and scent applied.

Dr Thin was little better. He maintained that the Duchess was 'aware of what was happening' and would 'indicate her feelings with a shrug of the shoulder or facial expressions.' He always kept to his reason for keeping her isolated – that she became hyper-tense and suffered nightmares after visitors came. He told Knight:

> Some of her best friends were not pleased. It led to all sorts of gossip.
>
> It was even suggested that I was trying to get her money. Last year it was said that she was dead and I had paid a charwoman to play her role. It is *so* ridiculous.

Based on Dr Thin's account, and with his assistance, a drawing was commissioned, showing the Duchess sitting peacefully in a chair, her hair as of old. Knight was told of light lunches served to her, letters read to her and so forth.

Dr Thin did admit that the Duchess had serious arthritis and revealed that he had ordered that her wedding ring from the Duke of Windsor should be 'gently cut off'.[32]

At about this time the press received confirmation that the Duke and Duchess's love letters would be published after her death.

In the summer of 1985, two years after my previous visit, I went to look at the house again. It was about 7.30 p.m. The lawn was very green, but there was a profusion of barbed wire. 'As it was a warm night, the windows in the upper salon were open. I snooped & quite clearly saw a nurse in white attending to some papers or whatever. At first I thought I saw the Duchess slumped there, but rather think not. It meant at least that someone was at home. So the age-old story goes on . . .'[33]

During these last years, the Duchess had one other visitor – Rt. Rev. James Leo*, Dean of the American Cathedral in Paris. He arrived in Paris in 1980 and was Dean until 1991. Soon after his arrival he received a message from the British Ambassador, Sir Reginald Hibbert, that he was to report regularly to Buckingham Palace on the state of the Duchess's health. He established good relations with Dr Thin but claimed that he never met Maître Blum in person, though she telephoned him from time to time. Of her he wrote: 'This lawyer's ways are difficult, her manner brusque.'[34]

The Dean was admitted to the house and was allowed to visit the Duchess. How often he went remains unclear. He remembered regular visits over a number of years – the staff at the house say he only came once or twice. It is immaterial, since memory on such matters tends to be selective.

The Dean was never able to have a conversation with the Duchess since she could no longer speak. He spoke some verses to her. He recited the Lord's Prayer, and a suitable psalm or another prayer. He believed that she took this in: 'On each visit I explained who I was and why I was with her.'[35]

---

* Very Rev. James Leo (1933–2011), educated Bucknell University, served two years in the army, then attended the General Theological Seminary. Rector of several Episcopal churches in Pennsylvania before being appointed Dean of the American Cathedral in Paris. In 1991 he was appointed Dean of Christ Church Cathedral in Cincinnati serving there until he retired.

The Dean found the house depressing, the Duke's regimental drums gathering dust, sad relics 'under brooding stillness', the garden with its 'memories of lavish summer evenings' now 'weeds, crab grass, and ghosts.'[36]*

* After the Duchess's death the Dean was given a wooden cross and two candlesticks, which he maintained the Duchess wanted him to have. Again, it would have been Blum who gave them. The Dean sold them on Ebay for $1,975.00 shortly before his death on 14 December 2011.

14

Enter Bloch – 1979–1986

As Blum floundered in her attempts to squash the various films and books about the Windsors in the late 1970s, a new figure entered the arena in the form of a young English lawyer called Michael Bloch. He had been researching a book on the journalist Philip Guedalla, in the course of which he noted a connection with the Duke of Windsor and wrote to Maître Blum to ask if there were any letters from Guedalla among the Duke's papers. On 27 January 1978 Monsieur Martin took his letter and a photocopy of a letter from the Duke to Guedalla to Blum's office in the rue de Varenne.

The pair met and in 1979 Bloch became Blum's pupil. Later he described his role as having assisted Blum with the Duchess's affairs and those of her estate between 1979 and 1988.[1]

The Guedalla book was laid aside in favour of more mutually profitable projects – publishing books about the Windsors.

I had never heard of Michael Bloch until he addressed a note to me in the Paris hotel where I was staying in February 1980. I was staying there on the recommendation of Stuart Preston*, and Bloch was lodging there, I believe on the same recommendation.

Bloch owed his introduction to figures such as Stuart Preston to the writer and diarist James Lees-Milne. In February 1979 he had met Lees-Milne, who found him 'slim & willowy' with Brian Howard eyes. Lees-Milne, by then seventy years old, fell for Bloch and began a platonic relationship, which he thought might be the deepest he had ever experienced. Bloch wrote of experiencing a 'rush of delight' when he saw him, which he believed was reciprocated.[2]

The relationship developed, causing Lees-Milne joy and angst in equal measure to the point that he once expressed the wish that Bloch would die so that he could possess him for ever. 'M' or 'Misha' was a name that now occurred regularly in his diaries, and anyone who wishes to know more about it can read extensively on the subject in the four volumes by

---

* I first met Stuart Preston (1915–2005), the art critic, in New York in March 1976 when I was researching my biography *Gladys, Duchess of Marlborough*.

Lees-Milne that were edited for publication by his chosen literary executor – none other than Bloch himself. In these diaries they will also read of the considerable distress this platonic relationship caused Alvilde Lees-Milne, Jim's bisexual wife. At one point she tried to frighten Bloch off by writing to him, but he was not so easily unseated. Bloch has given his version of this in the biography he wrote of his old friend.*

Stuart Preston had been art critic of the *New York Times* for many years, but was best known as 'the Sergeant' in wartime London life. He featured prominently, if a little uncomfortably, in Lees-Milne's wartime diaries, and had made a memorable appearance as Lieutenant Padfield – 'the Loot' – in Evelyn Waugh's *Unconditional Surrender*: 'he expressed his thanks to his hosts and hostesses not with the products of the PX stores but with the publications of Sylvia Beach and sketches by Fuseli.'[3]

Stuart had possessed legendary good looks, with ear lobes that trailed lazily into his cheeks, huge eyes and a bassoon-deep voice. His physical attributes combined with a wide knowledge and appreciation of the arts, attentiveness to elderly hostesses, and what James Pope-Hennessy called a 'permanent smile of appreciation' on his face.[4] His star shone bright, but waned long. James Lord, another American expatriate, wrote that 'those few brilliant, exhilarating years of social glory during the war laid up a heavy burden of nostalgia for the decades to come.'[5]

In later life, inevitably, Stuart Preston felt neglected, even shunned and he complained of this regularly. While Walter Lees went from one French duchess to the next, Stuart stayed at home. His legendary looks had been tarnished by alcohol; he wore his fingernails alarmingly and unattractively long, and presented a rather dishevelled figure at literary memorial services in London. '*Oui, oui ... volontiers,*' he used to say. Never in the Windsors' circle, he was a kind and solicitous friend to Diana Mosley. He went to live in Paris in 1976, prompting Harold Acton to comment mischievously: 'What did Henry James say? All good Americans go to Paris to die.'[6]

Stuart surrounded himself with a coterie of young aesthetes who were genuinely fond of him, respected his encyclopaedic knowledge and lapped up his anecdotes. He could be funny. He joked that the worst social invitation that Sibyl Colefax might issue would be 'to come in after tea to meet her sister'.[7] One young man asked him: 'Stuart, were you really a G.I?' He replied that, yes, he had been, adding: 'but I was the *only one* who went to Panshanger.'[8]

* *James Lees-Milne – The Life* (John Murray, 2009), pp. 307–13.

At times his conversation was curious and gave glimpses into dark worlds in which he was at home and I was not. He told me once: 'Peter Watson was a masochist. He liked to find rough boys in bars who stole his gold cigarette case. Well, he was lucky. He found them.'[9]

Though I was ignorant of the precise details of Stuart's private life, it appears that he formed a strong affection for Colin McMordie, an expert on early nineteenth century furniture, from Oriel College, Oxford and whom I once met in Paris in 1983. An Oxford contemporary, John Martin Robinson, thought him 'dazzling', relished his 'Irish whimsy', his 'pre-war good looks' and his 'well-stocked mind'.[10] McMordie died, as the result of complications following a straightforward operation for tonsillitis, in 1985 at the age of forty-seven. James Lees-Milne was haunted by the image of this Adonis lying in his coffin like the effigy of Shelley at University College, Oxford,[11] and Stuart lamented his passing: 'Our close relationship was one I counted on to last for the rest of my life. And now I'll never see him again, a realisation hard to consider unemotionally.'[12]

Stuart Preston was a point of contact for me on my Paris visits: 'I count on seeing you,' he would say generously. Many years later he came to my wedding in a hilltop village in Lot-et-Garonne. Like a figure in a novel, he loomed in the doorway of an auberge, briefly obscuring the sun. His familiar bassoon voice enquired: '*Est-ce-qu'il y a le possibilité – de quelque chose à boire?*'

Michael Bloch was born in Northern Ireland on 24 September 1953, the son of a factory owner in the textile business. His family were Jewish and came from Poland. Educated at Portadown College, the well-known grammar school in County Armagh, he went on to St John's College, Cambridge where, along with the historian Andrew Roberts, he lodged with the well-remembered Cambridge landlady Sadie Barnett, who held aristocratic undergraduates in high esteem: 'He was such a gent,' she said of one. 'When he was sick he was always sick out of the window.'[13] Bloch gained an MA. From 1971 he worked on a doctoral thesis, which he never presented. He gained an LLB and in 1978 he was called to the Bar at the Inner Temple. Bloch emerged from Cambridge successful and ambitious.

The London phase of Bloch's friendship with Lees-Milne was interrupted when, in October 1979, he accepted Blum's invitation to work as her pupil. Presently she appointed him as what she described as the Duke of Windsor's official biographer, writing about the Duke's life after the Abdication with full access to those of the Duke's papers which Blum had in her custody. Blum took to telephoning Bloch daily. Not unnaturally he was excited by the prospect of his new employment and was soon heading off to take up his position with the Maître.

Lees-Milne introduced Bloch to Diana Mosley, who became fond of him and frequently invited him to the Temple de la Gloire. By this time Diana thought Blum 'rather mad'[14] and sought to warn Bloch about her, though he did not heed her warnings. By May 1980 Bloch was so *lié* with the Maître that when Lees-Milne came over to see him in Paris he apologised that he had been unable to secure the Duchess of Windsor's chauffeur to meet him at the Gare du Nord. Bloch presented his admirer to Blum, and Lees-Milne noted among other attributes the sharpness of the Maître's features and the strength of her eye.[15]

In 1985 there was an idea that Lees-Milne might take on the editing and publishing of a book ghosted for the Duke called *My Hanoverian Ancestors*, about the four King Georges in the eighteenth and nineteenth centuries. This book had had a somewhat chequered history. It was thought to have been inspired by Lord Beaverbrook, with the involvement of Kenneth Young* and none other than J. Bryan III. Bloch suggested to Lees-Milne that he should consult Sir Godfrey Morley, but warned him that Morley was a Buckingham Palace man and a mortal enemy of Blum's[16] who might be able to resolve some of the issues.

J. Bryan III even wrote to Bloch's literary agent, Andrew Best†, telling him that he had tried to work with the Duke but had found it impossible. The Duke would make no contribution whatsoever by way of anecdotes. Therefore he and Young worked on a manuscript and took it over to the Duke. Aware that he would not concentrate long enough to read it, they read him selected passages. Halfway through, the Duke cried out: 'Why, they were terrible people. *Terrible*! I had no idea they were anything like that! I can't possibly sign such a book!'

Bryan told him: 'Sir, they *were* like that, alas! In fact, they were rather worse. I have played down their crimes and follies as far as I dared. If I went any further, serious historians would laugh at you.'

'I don't care,' said the Duke. 'I won't sign it!'[17]

Therefore the project foundered. The drafts of *My Hanoverian Ancestors* remained in the Duke's papers and came to Blum's attention in 1981.

Blum told Lees-Milne that the rights in the book would remain the Duchess of Windsor's copyright, claiming control of her unpublished material.[18] She offered him thirty per cent against seventy per cent to

---

*Kenneth Young (1916–85), Political & Literary Adviser to Beaverbrook Newspapers, former editor of the *Yorkshire Post*, author & editor.
† Andrew Best (1933–2006), literary agent at Curtis Brown.

the Duchess. She informed him that he would have complete freedom as editor, but required him to present the book with nothing that could compromise the late Duke's 'honour, reputation and good intentions'.[19] Lees-Milne was briefly inclined to undertake the editing, but later changed his mind because nobody could work out how much of the work had been the Duke's and how much that of either Kenneth Young or J. Bryan III.[20]

Cross-generational friendships are often considered curious and none more so than the relationship between Blum and Bloch. He was devoted to her and admired her hugely. In time he would earn a large amount of money on her account. He now owns a smart London dwelling which contains a specially designed four-poster bed from Berkeley Cole in which to spend his nocturnal hours.

Blum's influence over Bloch was considerable. When he grew a moustache she ordered him to have it shaved off and he complied at once. In December 1980 Bloch presented Lees-Milne with the Duke of Windsor's specially bound and signed copy of Harold Nicolson's *George V*. This came with a letter from Blum to explain how he got it. Whether the lawyer had the right to give away the Duke of Windsor's books is highly questionable.

It was to Bloch that Blum assigned the task of editing the love letters. But first he was to produce two books, authorised by her.

Bloch was clearly not the historian cited by Blum in 1978. This was almost certainly Alain Decaux, the well-known French historian with an impressive list of books to his name. Blum certainly allowed Decaux access to papers for a proposed book on the Abdication. He worked on this in good faith and the book could have been published in 1982. However, by then she had found Bloch and she informed Decaux that Bloch's book of the Windsors' letters must come out first. Decaux was forced to withhold his book, which was not finally published until 1995, after Blum's death.

Bloch worked closely with Blum in her apartment and office in the rue de Varenne. She said of him: '*Michael sait tout*'[21], implying that he had her full confidence.

In the late 1970s and 1980s Blum went every Saturday to the Duchess's house. She would sit in the dining room at a small table, the large dining-room table having been purloined by one of the executors*, and would go through correspondence and other business matters with Georges.

---

* After the Duchess's death, Fayed bought it back for £120,000.

On a Saturday afternoon in 1980, Bloch went with her and was permitted his only ever glimpse of the Duchess from the door of her bedroom. Of this sighting he left two contradictory accounts. While Blum was alive, the Duchess was propped up on her pillows, with her hair done and, though thin, 'amazingly *soignée*'. He remarked on the brilliance of her blue eyes and how 'wide open and watchful' they were.[22]

After Blum died, Bloch changed this. Her eyes were blinking, her 'square' hands in 'constant agitated movement'. He reported that her hair was 'white and wispy' and her mouth a 'gash'. Terrifyingly, he suggested she might have recognised Blum.[23]

Bloch did not comment on the array of tubes that kept the Duchess alive. Walter Lees told me at that time of a visit that he had made before that of Bloch. There had been rumours that the Duchess was dead and, since he was well placed to spread the word in society circles, he was allowed to visit the Duchess:

> Bloch came to him one day & said: 'I bear a message from Maître Blum. Would you please call on the Duchess tomorrow afternoon?'
> So he went in and saw her. He didn't speak to her, but she was aware of his presence, didn't recognise him, but became flustered. There is a tube up her right nostril and one other tube.[24]

Having met Michael Bloch in January 1980, there was a phase during which he told me certain things. He was keen to engage my help versus Murphy and Bryan III and this I was happy to give. He described Maître Blum as 'a very powerful lady who likes to defeat her enemies by making them laugh'. He said the Duchess was on a life-support machine, having given instructions: 'Keep me alive as long as possible.' I noted Bloch's version at the time:

> Amiguet was furious that the Duke's papers had gone to Windsor, that the Duchess didn't care, but that the love letters were found in a shoebox. These will be published presently in France with a soppy covering text by a well-known French popular historian*. They have been trying to beat Murphy over the head – but the injunction didn't work as they had known about the book for too long.[25]

---

* Presumably Alain Decaux, though at the time I thought it was André Castelot.

The next day I told John Utter that I had met Bloch. Amongst other things he speculated that the historian mentioned might be Kenneth de Courcy.*

In March I saw Bloch again in London. I asked him if Maître Blum would attend the Duchess's funeral at Windsor, and he told me she had said: 'No, I don't think so. I don't like travelling in the winter.' At one point he said: 'Think of the millions who will live thanks to the operations performed on the Duchess.'[26]

The Duchess's friends tried to get news of her, even if they could not see her. In May 1980 I lunched with Diana Vreeland, the legendary former Editor of *Vogue* in the United States. She told me she hated going to Paris now because of what had happened to the Duchess. 'I haven't seen her for four years,' she said, 'for obvious reasons.' She said she sometimes rang Georges to ask how the Duchess was. '*Oh! Madame, c'est toujours la même chose*,' he replied. She mentioned a friend who had seen the Duchess [Frances Munn-Baker], who related that she had a soft complexion and sat staring out of the window. Diana Vreeland said that the Duchess should not see the visitor for if she did she would react – 'perhaps not at once, but hours later,' and this would have been bad for her.[27]

This was a more sympathetic response than that of another old friend of the Duchess's, Cee Zee Guest, who had once obliged Georges to let her past the gates. She had found the Duchess in a terrible state, but seemed to think it amusing that the Duchess had suggested giving a dinner party for her when she was clearly in no state to do so. When I spent a Sunday with Mrs Guest at her Long Island home in 1981, I raised the Duchess's plight with her. She replied: 'What's the point of worrying about her? No one can do anything. So why worry about it?'[28]

In May 1980 the Duchess was again in the American Hospital for a check-up. One of the Canons of Windsor had a daughter who was a nurse at the hospital. She was horrified by what she saw.

In the same month Stuart Preston told me that the British Ambassador was accepting no engagements as he expected 'to have to accompany the body any day now'.[29] Bloch then informed me that the Duchess had been semi-comatose for months but had suddenly become 'quite garrulous'. They worried that this might be a rally before the end.[30]

Shortly after this I was introduced to Lady Caroline Blackwood, who was writing a book on the world of Blum and the Duchess. She purported to be terrified of Blum who she said controlled the Duchess's house like

---

* Kenneth de Courcy (1909–99), self-styled Duc de Grantmesnil, a dodgy financier and editor, who occupied himself with the Duke of Windsor's plight in exile and spent time in Wormwood Scrubs, convicted of fraud, forgery and perjury.

Fort Knox and came out with sinister remarks: 'You should see her. Her body is so beautiful now.' Caroline mistrusted Georges, partly because she could not understand why a very social butler would stay on in the house when his love in life was dinner parties for eighteen guests.

Caroline went on to write *The Last of the Duchess*, with its devastating portrait of Blum, so sharp that the publishers had to wait until after the Maître's death before publishing it. In the next year or so Caroline told me many stories concerning Blum and Bloch. In May 1980 she related that Lord Snowdon had photographed Blum. While they were there, Lord Longford had telephoned in connection with a book. Blum sent Bloch to talk to them. When he returned, Blum grinned at him and asked: 'Will they do as we say?' He replied: 'They are acceding to our demands, Maître.'[31]

Not long after this, on 23 June, Maître Blum's husband, General Georges Spillmann, died aged eighty at her country house, La Cormélière, Echiré in Western France. Bloch persuaded *The Times* to publish an obituary of the general, under the device 'A friend writes'. After paying extravagant tribute to the general's 'sensitive diplomatic missions in the Middle East', his proverbial tact and his later years spent producing scholarly works, Bloch concluded: 'After the death of his first wife (by whom he had four children) he married Maître Suzanne Blum, the Duke and Duchess of Windsor's advocate, and with their charm and wit they were among the most popular people in Paris'.[32]

In July Bloch had a story about Maître Blum, draped in widow's weeds, and others (presumably Dr Thin and Amiguet) going to the Duchess's house for their 'ritual inspection' of the Duchess. He said they came down 'ashen-faced'. He concluded that she had but a few weeks to live.[33] But, as with so many predictions about the Duchess, this was wrong.

In December I had my only meeting with Maître Blum, arranged by Bloch. I had come over to Paris to attend John Utter's memorial service, the plan being that Diana Mosley would join me at the American Cathedral and take me back to the Temple de la Gloire for lunch. It was a strange occasion. Bloch had decided to be present. 'I deeply regret never having met John Utter,' he said. 'The least I can do is to attend his Memorial Service.' I asked Stuart Preston whether he would be there. 'Well, you know I think I might,' he said. 'I didn't know him well but the times I met him I always liked him very much'. Unbeknown to either of them, Caroline Blackwood would also be in the congregation.[34]

The day before the service, I went along to 53 rue de Varenne to meet Maître Blum:

She has the top flat. A minute lift made its way up and a sour-looking maid opened the door upstairs. I went into a brighter drawing room than I had expected. After a moment of waiting, Maître Blum came in, dressed in black. She was smaller than I had imagined, moved slowly and I really do think she is doing an impersonation of Queen Mary. She was of course much more charming than I had expected and said at once: '*Oh! J'ai attendu un vieux monsieur. Je suis contente de savoir que vous n'êtes pas un vieux monsieur.*' From that moment on she was perfectly friendly.

Bloch arrived just as she was explaining that he had overslept. It was interesting to watch the interplay between them. We began by talking about Caroline Blackwood's recent article in the *Sunday Times* supplement. Originally this had enraged the Maître, but now she was delighted. I praised the Snowdon picture. '*Ah! Il est vrai artiste. C'est la première fois que je trouve une photo de moi, que j'aime. Je trouve moi-même dans ce photo.*'

She told a story about an old Countess being photographed by Snowdon. '*Et elle est même plus agée que moi,*' said Maître Blum. '*N'est-ce pas, Michael?*' He didn't corroborate this statement, so the playfulness began. '*Vous auriez du dire qu'elle était beaucoup plus vielle,*' said Maître Blum, laughing. She told me she hated *The Windsor Story*. '*Lady Caroline a raison de dire que je m'enfâche quand on parle de ce livre devant moi,*' she said.

She went on to discuss how the book could be attacked and her dislike of Lady Donaldson's book. Presently a door opened behind me and the maid beckoned 'to summon Maître Blum who was leaving that day to resign from the Paris bar in order to have more time to devote to the affairs of the Duchess.'

Bloch then took me to his study in which he said the ghost of General Spillmann still lurked. It was filled with letters from the Duchess to Aunt Bessie Merryman . . . We looked at the file of *The Windsor Story* and I took away xerox letters. There was even a letter from me to John Utter in the file.

Bloch took me out to lunch.

At the restaurant Bloch told me he had seen the Duchess – 'succeeded in getting to see' were his words. He said that she looked startled when she saw him – but was beautiful, with the untroubled face of someone paralysed. He never sees the point that she is in pain and danger.

That evening I was due to dine with Stuart Preston, and so went to his apartment at the rue de Rivoli. His first words destroyed my plans for the following day: 'You've heard the news? Sir Oswald *is* dead.' Sir Oswald Mosley had died peacefully in his sleep:

The Sergeant was not on good form. He gave me a drink, told me he was taking me out to dinner and that we would be at the café he loves. He tended to repeat himself a lot and as the evening went on – snails, meat, plenty of red wine – he sank into a kind of stupor. He became repetitive, boring and from time to time blathered like an idiot, his eyes gazing like a mesmerised owl, his mouth open. When the waiters addressed him and asked him a question he just replied '*Oui*' – which was not the answer. '*Côtes du Rhône ou Beaujolais, Monsieur?*'
      '*Oui, oui.*'
      Then a friend of his approached the table and made a telling remark to him: '*La dernière fois que je t'ai vu, tu étais très fatigué. Ça va mieux maintenant?*'
      Stuart looked perplexed. '*Oui, oui, ça arrive.*'[35]

The following day was John Utter's memorial service:

The Cathedral was gloomy and heavily covered in plaques of one sort and another. I went in and sat alone. The congregation was a mixture of old French people with dignity, rich Americans, one or two people who might have been part of the Embassy, his god-daughter and her family who were attractive, Marcelle from Osmoy, and the occasional slightly dubious figure. Bloch came in and up to me: 'You've heard the news about Sir Oswald?' I had . . .
      The flowers were shoddy, there was no address, no printed sheet, no book to sign. Marcelle greeted some people in front of me: '*Pauvre John. Pauvre John. On se téléphonait chaque jour.*' That was as close to him as the service got . . .[36]

My last direct contact with Maître Blum occurred the following summer and involved a ridiculous law case in which she represented me and the Duchess of Windsor jointly against *Le Journal du Dimanche*, a tabloid French paper. This paper suggested that in my royal wedding book* I had written that the Duke of Windsor had been forced to abdicate because he was a Nazi. I had written no such thing.

Bloch came onto the telephone one Saturday afternoon, followed shortly by the Maître. She began: '*Monsieur Veek-aires, je veux vous remercier pour tout ce que vous faites pour le Duc et la Duchesse.*' She needed me to write a telegram to *Le Journal du Dimanche*. I was happy to do this, but the paper failed to print it. Therefore the Maître decided to go to court, representing me for no fee but with the possibility that I might be awarded some damages.

On Tuesday, 12 May I went to lunch with Bloch at the Oxford and Cambridge Club and various papers were prepared for me to send to Maître Blum. After that I went to America and forgot all about it.

On my return to London Bloch rang me. His sepulchral tones announced: 'Congratulations. You won your case.' I perked up, but he was quick to inform me that no damages would be forthcoming.[37]

The exercise had been pointless, but was indicative of Blum's obsessive interest in anything she could attach herself to which remotely involved her bedridden client.

During these years, and until the Duchess's death, Blum attempted to instil fear into any author publishing anything that remotely concerned the Windsors. In 1981 Stephen Birmingham's book *Duchess* was published in the United States by Little, Brown. It was subsequently published by Macmillan in London on 28 October 1982, but by then the last chapter had been closely rewritten on Blum's instructions. She insisted on the removal of passages concerning her dislike of Frances Donaldson's biography, of the television series *Edward & Mrs Simpson*, references to the forthcoming love letters, and passages relating to the Duke's stay in Portugal, the Duchess's jewels and the whereabouts of the Duke's papers. Also removed were many statements by Blum dismissing the views of others as 'malice' and 'lies'.

That this book was delayed until a month after the publication of Bloch's first book, *The Duke of Windsor's War* (Weidenfeld, 1982) may be significant, a point that did not pass un-noticed in *Private Eye*.

In his preface, Bloch described Blum as the executrix and guardian of the Duchess of Windsor's interests since as early as 1972. He thanked her for making copious documents from the Windsors' archives available to him. He paid tribute to his personal debt to her.[38] Even the publisher's

---

* *Debrett's Book of the Royal Wedding*, a book about Prince Charles and Lady Diana Spencer, which topped the best seller lists in Britain for several weeks in the summer of 1981.

blurb declared: 'Appointed on the Duchess of Windsor's behalf to write this book . . .'[39]

Though later on Bloch would describe his own work as hagiography[40], it was a competent book and Diana Mosley was one who praised it highly to Lees-Milne:

> I am bowled over by Michael's book. It is so cleverly organised & every nasty suspicion one had is confirmed by chapter & verse. There (to me) is terrible pathos about the fear of the Dook's mere shadow, felt by the royal family. With good reason. I wish Michael had known him & experienced the charm (Oh that word! What does it mean, & what does it convey to the reader & yet how can one do without it.) I am thankful the Master gave Michael & not me the archive because I couldn't have done the book *half* as well . . .
>
> I can't wait for the reaction. What can 'they' say? It was all too sordid for words. How lucky that archive didn't go to Windsor![41]

Soon after this, *Timewatch* staged a programme based on the book. According to Diana Mosley, Frances Donaldson, the Duke's biographer, refused to appear in it, which she thought 'very cowardly'[42], but, in order to promote her protégé's work, Maître Blum allowed cameras into the Duchess's garden, and Georges was filmed entering the house. Blum spoke, as quoted before, about the Duchess's health. There was then a heated discussion, conducted by John Tusa, between Bloch and the historian David Cannadine. The version as shown on television displays Cannadine making mincemeat of Bloch. However, it is not the original version. The discussion had to be reshot because the first version was deemed too cruel to Bloch to be aired on national television.[43]

The second book, *Operation Willi*, published in 1984, concerned the supposed plot of Hitler and von Ribbentrop to kidnap the Duke of Windsor in Spain in July 1940. In his preface, Bloch again acknowledged Blum's help and the 'privileged access' she had given him to the Duke's archives.[44]

Michael Thornton's book, *Royal Feud*, was published by Michael Joseph in 1985 after Blum had failed to squash it. Blum had obtained a proof copy of that book and discovered that Thornton was critical not only of the Windsors but also of herself and Bloch. She sent him a telegram warning him that Michael Joseph published at their peril. It was suggested in *Private Eye* that the precise wording of Thornton's reply was so insulting to Blum that she 'reportedly suffered a minor stroke from which she has never fully recovered.'[45]

Bloch then employed a firm of solicitors to claim that he was the 'exclusive licensee' of the Windsors. He threatened an injunction on grounds of breach of copyright and plagiarism. Legal opinion was sought by Thornton's publishers concerning Bloch's right to make a claim to the Duchess's copyright. Not unreasonably Bloch was asked for written evidence. This was not produced. Bloch's stand was made no easier by Thornton having written to Blum enclosing a list of the quotations he wished to make. To this she had raised no objection.

As the lawyers' letters went backwards and forwards, Thornton wrote to Bloch's editor, John Curtis:

> As a result of further information that has come into my possession, I have changed the instructions to my solicitors. 'I intend to contest this action to the utmost extent possible, since there are certain matters which I now feel warrant the fullest public scrutiny and clarification.[46]

Curtis consulted Bloch who then backed down on several points. Thornton stood his ground. He declared that he was happy to go to court in order to subpoena Blum and demand to see the document from the Duchess which authorised her to publish the letters. David Hooper, his solicitor, questioned the validity of Blum's Power of Attorney because, under French law, this lapsed if the person who authorised it lost command of their faculties. Blum and Bloch had no wish to answer these allegations in court. Most of the claims were dropped and they accepted a modest payment for the use of some material from the Bloch books in exchange for Michael Joseph's permission to Bloch to quote from the Duchess of Windsor's autobiography. Not a word of *Royal Feud* was changed.

Meanwhile work progressed on the editing of the letters. Once the book was ready, Bloch's agent Andrew Best went over to Paris and conducted secret negotiations between Blum and the publishers, Weidenfeld & Nicolson, as well as the *Daily Mail*. Then, in 1985, he sold the American book rights to Summit Books in New York, apparently for $500,000. It was said that Best's negotiations with Blum and Bloch over the Duke of Windsor's papers was worthy of the conductor of a five-part choir.

This deal might explain why a deed of authority, purporting to bear the Duchess's initials and dated 17 March 1975, was lodged by Blum with a notary on 6 May 1985, for why else would this suddenly happen? This document is highly important but, despite many requests, Blum never allowed it to be seen in order that it could be verified as authentic.

Some three years later, in September 1988, Blum showed Suzanne Lowry of the *Daily Telegraph* a letter from the notary, dated 3 June 1985, in which he confirmed that on 6 May 1985 Blum had deposited the letter dated 17 March 1975 in which the Duchess gave her permission to publish. A copy of the notary's acknowledgement was published in that newspaper. But even then Blum did not show the actual letter from the Duchess. I have now seen a copy of this document. It states:

> I authorise you, or anyone appointed by you, to publish all documents or letters in your possession concerning the Duke or myself which you consider as useful to our memory, or to answer our detractors.
>
> As to the royalties, I suggest to divide them equally between the author and I, or, should the publication occur after my death, between the author and my *légataire universel*.
>
> With love and gratitude,
> W.W.[47]

The document was attested by Maître Lisbonne, who worked with Blum. I first saw it in October 1996. I publish it on page 394. At the same time I was shown original documents initialled by the Duchess, where the 'WWs' were rather different. The '1975' document was not typed on the office typewriter kept at the house and on which all the Duchess's communications were written at that time.

The fact that the document was not lodged with a notary until 1985 is significant because it means that Blum had plenty of time in which to create it. It had to be dated before November 1975 since anyone with any knowledge of the Duchess would have been aware that she was incapable of signing anything afterwards. In 1975 John Utter was still just at the house. So too was Miss Schütz. It is near impossible that such a document could have been signed by the Duchess without either of them knowing about it.

Even if it were genuine, it cannot be deemed legal since it was only initialled.

Georges, the butler, was complicit in all this, and it is believed that he was paid a large sum of money for his part in producing the letters and 'forgetting' the Duchess's instructions to destroy them.

The date 17 March 1975 could have further significance. That was the day that John Utter left the Duchess's employ. Miss Schütz kept a precise diary of her time at the house, recording the comings and goings. All she noted for 17 March 1975 was that John Utter left and she had dinner that evening with the Duchess. She did record that Blum came to lunch on 13 March and that Amiguet visited on 19 March.

There is another interesting point to consider. The Duchess made a new will on 8 November 1972. Blum then sacked Morley and the Duchess made another will on 16 February 1973. Under an arrangement made with the Minister of Cultural Affairs on 30 March 1973, a great number of items were gifted to Versailles and the Musée de Sèvres*. There was a codicil dated 4 December 1973, and two further codicils dated 6 February and 10 April 1975 (at the time of the retirement of John Utter, annulling his bequest).

Miss Schütz's diary of 17 March 1977 (not 1975) records that Blum arrived at the house at 3.45 and the notary at 4.30. This is the date given for the final codicil.

So it is possible that Blum dated the letter of authorisation 1975 rather than 1977 to get around any arguments (raised by many including me in the 1980s) that the Duchess was not capable of authorising such things in 1977.

Blum also 'forgot' that in 1976 she had produced a document that was to be used to secure the return of some of the Duke of Windsor's papers from the Royal Archives at Windsor. She produced this statement which she said was one of the wishes expressed by the Duke of Windsor in several earlier versions of his will:

JE DEMANDE que mes Exécuteurs testamentaires brûlent ou détruisent par tout autre procédé, tous ceux de mes papiers et correspondances ou des papiers ou correspondances appurtenant à ma femme et dont j'aurais pu hériter, qui, à, leur avis, devraient être brûlés ou détruits.[†]

---

* A full list is given in Suzy Menkes, *The Windsor Style*, pp. 206–7.
[†] 'I ask that my executors burn or destroy by whatever means all those of my papers and correspondence or the papers and correspondence belonging to my wife which I might inherit, which, in their opinion, should be burnt or destroyed.'

She added that this phrase had been omitted from the final version of the Duke's will created for him by Sir Godfrey Morley and Senateur Jacques Rosselli in 1971.

The book and serialisation deals were made. Blum did not intend to publish the letters during the Duchess's lifetime, though with the 'attestation' now lodged with the notary, she could have done so.

The Duchess died within the year, on 24 April 1986.

15

Death of the Duchess – 1986

Maria Costa had become the Duchess's chief nurse during the long years of her illness. While others came and went, she remained constant in her devotion. During her long years of service, she lived through many changes, from the days when the Duchess was in control of the household and through the difficult Blum years. There came a day in April 1986 when she noticed that the Duchess's breathing had suddenly changed. She knew that the end was near.

By this time the world had largely forgotten the Duchess. It was therefore something of a surprise when, in the late morning of 24 April, Laura Marlborough telephoned me to tell me that she had heard on the radio that the Duchess had died. My immediate reaction was one of relief. It was perhaps more of a surprise to hear that a statement had come from Buckingham Palace. It read as follows:

> It is announced with great regret that the Duchess of Windsor died at ten a.m. today at her residence near Paris.

At the Duchess's bedside were Dr Thin, Maria, and Georges, her butler. In other reports, the doctor was quoted: 'I saw her last night and then again this morning. It was obvious that she was near the end. I saw her almost every day.' Maître Blum was described as being 'too distressed to speak.'[1]

Dean Leo was summoned by Dr Thin to perform the last rites. He told reporters: 'She squeezed my hand during the last rites and again as I read a short passage from the Bible – the eighth chapter of Paul's letter to the Romans. I had been seeing her on a regular basis for seven years. Although she never spoke we did learn to communicate in our own way. She always squeezed my hand'.[2] He remembered returning to the house after the Duchess's death. Daisy de Cabrol was apparently allowed in to see the Duchess's body laid out.

The long-held plans outlined in Operation Haze were now implemented. Sir John and Lady Fretwell, the British Ambassador and his wife, had paid several courtesy visits to the Duchess's house without ever seeing her. Lady Fretwell later told me that the Ambassador's Chef de Cabinet was there when the Duchess was put into her coffin to make sure it was really her body. The Fretwells knew it was important to be friendly towards Blum for fear that she might impound the body at the last minute.[3]

Mr Kenyon, the undertaker, had complained that the French Police insisted on having a gendarme present when he embalmed the Duke's body. In 1972 he stated that he hoped he could proceed without such a presence when the Duchess's time came but that, if it was necesary, he hoped it would be a female police officer or police surgeon.[4]

Inevitably the story of the Windsors was told and retold many times in the press over the next few days. Rather than analyse all the contradictions, it is more interesting to note the line taken by the various newspapers. The *London Standard* took the view that the Duchess had done the British nation a great service by removing 'from the throne a man who was so manifestly unsuited to its responsibilities'. The leader writer also said:

> Having done so, she protected and supported the Duke of Windsor in exile with the same dignity and loyalty she had shown him throughout the abdication crisis.

Her death was described as 'a merciful release.'[5] Sam White, the legendary Paris correspondent, noted that so forgotten a figure was she 'that to many in Paris it came as a surprise that she had still been alive until this morning.'[6] Another Paris correspondent was Sebastian Faulks before he became a well-known novelist. He took the same view a few days later in the *Sunday Telegraph*: 'She is seen as no more than the star of an old romantic film that most French have forgotten.'[7]

The Queen was at Windsor Castle, where she had recently celebrated her sixtieth birthday and had been hosting the State Visit of the King and Queen of Spain. She duly attended the return state banquet in London. Family mourning (there being no court mourning) was delayed until the end of the visit and, as had been agreed decades earlier, it was announced that flags would fly at halfmast on the day of the funeral.

Normally when a famous figure dies there are extensive tributes. This time there were few. There was analysis, a glance back at history, but little by way of reminiscence. Diana Mosley expressed her admiration for the Duchess and reminded people of the Duke's undying devotion to her. She then wrote:

The last years were terrible. She was alive, and yet not alive. Doctors have become very clever at keeping the heart beating. Who knows what she suffered? I do not mean so much physical pain, or even discomfort, but who can tell whether someone in her condition feels sorrow, has illusions or nightmares? Nobody knows. What we do know is that her nurses loved her.

So did her devoted couple Georges and Ofélia; their loving care of her was marvellous in its unselfish devotion.[8]

Frances Donaldson, the Duke of Windsor's biographer, wrote of the Duke's 'intense desire to be dominated and hers to dominate' while conceding that in a parlour game in Paris in his later years, when granted a wish, he said at once that all he wanted was a few more years with Wallis.[9] John Grigg, ever a controversial scourge of monarchy, particularly its occasional hypocrisies, declared: 'The Windsors' romance is an honourable part of the British monarchy's story, from which it has gained an enhancement of prestige.'[10]

The *Daily Telegraph* made the point that the Abdication had not come about as a great love story 'tragically thrown off course by prelates and premiers.' Their leader said:

The crisis was caused, not by an obdurate Establishment, but by the character of the King. It was compounded by the nature of the Duchess of Windsor, more intelligent than the King, yet drawn, step by step and knowingly, in the wrong direction.[11]

At this time, and only a few weeks before her own death in June at the age of ninety-three, Lady Diana Cooper was asked about the Abdication, and said:

He certainly didn't want to be King, that I know. He told me so several times. It was usually when we were alone, apart from Wallis. I remember on one public occasion telling him: 'The crowd loves you.' He replied: 'Yes, I'm all right as Prince of Wales, but I wouldn't be a good king.' He said that often. He may have had the thought of Wallis tucked away, but I don't think he used her as an *excuse* to abdicate. He was besotted in love. But it didn't agonise him to abdicate. I think he was delighted.

As for the Duchess, Lady Diana said: 'She certainly never saw herself as Queen. I didn't sense any sheer ambition in her.'[12]

*　　*　　*

A memorial service was held in Paris, attended by Maître Blum. In the last few years she had become visibly frail. In 1982 she confessed to Virgil Thomson that she was seeing very badly and by 1984 she was blind. To this service Bloch escorted her. Dean Leo of the American Cathedral spoke of the Duchess:

> She was a sinner as we all are, a struggler beset with all the temptations that we are. Her priorities were not always right. Her hat, so to speak, was not always on straight. Her face was sometimes faulty . . .
> . . . In Wallis's best moments, and there were many, in those moments she gave to the world and to us who knew and loved her.[13]

This service infuriated several of the Duchess's friends, for two reasons. French society resented the sinister Blum putting herself forward as chief mourner and 'receiving', and some, in particular the Comtesse de Rochambeau, daughter of Captain Ali Mackintosh, an old friend of the Duke's, thought the address inappropriate. As the Dean said later, he disliked hypocrisy at funerals – the deceased lying in the church, and the priest lying in the pulpit.[14]

The Duchess had not been out of her upstairs rooms for some years. Now her coffin was led out of her house by Dean Leo dressed in his scarlet cassock. Gathered to see her leave were the Lord Chamberlain, the Earl of Airlie, the British Ambassador, Sir John Fretwell and his wife, and Peter Hartley from the Lord Chamberlain's Office. On the other side were four men, including Paul-Louis Weiller. Bloch was there too, in a pale grey suit and black gloves.

The royal machine had clicked into operation. Any plans that Blum might have dreamt up were of no consequence now. The Lord Chamberlain's Office took over.

The Duchess's coffin was flown to Britain in an aircraft of The Queen's Flight and met at RAF Benson by the Duke of Gloucester, the requisite if reluctant Royal Highness.

The coffin was driven to Windsor Castle, which was closed to the public. Here it was met by a guard of honour and it rested overnight in the Albert Memorial Chapel. The Royal Vault was opened and the catafalque mounted onto it. The lift bore this up into the Quire and it was covered with a pall. The Duchess's coffin would rest on the same spot as that occupied by all the Kings and Queens of England back to George III, including Queen Victoria – and the former Edward VIII.

The next afternoon, just before the mourners were admitted into

St George's Chapel, the coffin was carried into the empty Nave on the shoulders of the Welsh Guards (the Duke of Windsor had been their first Colonel), borne under the organ screen and into the Quire. Then the doors opened and the non-royal mourners took their prescribed seats.

The Royal Family and the Duchess's staff and nurses sat in the Quire, as did survivors from amongst the Windsors' friends. Others were placed in the Nave. The senior members of the Royal Family were the Queen and the Duke of Edinburgh, the Queen Mother, the Prince and Princess of Wales, Princess Anne, Princess Alice, Duchess of Gloucester, the Duchess of Gloucester (her daughter-in-law), the Duchess of Kent, Prince and Princess Michael of Kent, and Princess Alexandra and Angus Ogilvy.

There were other members of the Royal Family present, several British Ambassadors to Paris, Lord Whitelaw (on behalf of the Government), the US Ambassador, Grace, Countess of Dudley*, Lady Alexandra Metcalfe (a survivor from the wedding), Lady Mosley and others†. Comtesse Romanones took a photograph, which had to be removed from her camera by the Chapter Clerk. She later wrote a scathing article about the service in *Vanity Fair*, complaining at not being allowed to go to the graveside.

St George's Chapel did its best for the Duchess. As Ghislaine de Polignac commented later: 'There was the Queen and the Royal Family, and the chapel beautifully lit and the choir singing. It was everything the Duke would have wanted for the Duchess.'[15] Unfortunately, due to what was described as an over-strict adherence to the form of service for burial, there was no mention of the Duchess's name during the service.‡ This came about because those organising the event removed the part from the Duke's service in which his style and titles were read out but inserted nothing new. The Queen was said to have been furious at the omission.

Sadly, few diarists were present at the Duchess's funeral. There was an exchange between the Duchess of Devonshire and her sister, Diana Mosley. The Duchess wrote:

> Well the Dss of Windsor. What a mercy. As for the poor old thing spending her last years gathering inf. which would rock the royal family I guess not. I wonder what actually finished her. You will be thankful

---

* Grace Kolin, third wife of the Earl of Dudley, who had been the Duchess's escort at the Duke's funeral. To her predecessor's annoyance, she was wearing the Dudley pearls.
† For a full list and seating plan, see pages 388–94.
‡ This was confirmed at the time by Peter Hartley of the Lord Chamberlain's Office and, many years later, by Canon John White, who read the Lesson at the service.

she can't be tortured by the drs. any more. Now I suppose old Maître Blum dare die, I bet she was keeping alive till the coast was clear.[16]

A few days later the Duchess of Devonshire was irritated to read accounts in the press that the Royal Family were to be concealed behind a screen at the service, this merely meaning that they would be seated in the Quire.

In return Diana Mosley gave her sister an account of the funeral:

Yes, as you say, the papers excelled themselves in spite & vileness. Nothing could have been more perfect & dignified than the funeral. Of course if one had been in the nave one wouldn't have seen much but that's the way the chapel is built. The idea that the royal family hid is such absurd rubbish. The choir (which sang too beautifully & so quietly) & the [Military] Knights of Windsor or whatever they're called in their splendid scarlet, & the Welsh Guards, & the archbishop, & the entire royal family – what more could have been done to give the poor little person an honourable funeral. The Queen in her clever way gave the best seats to Georges & Ofélia.

I was so glad I asked if Catherine could come with me (she was perfectly willing to wait in the car) because the whole thing was so interesting. We were opposite the Garter stall of Emperor Hirohito. I thought what on earth is that strange device of a sun, & the banner had just one huge chrysanthemum, & of course it was the dear little Jap. Mostly Paris friends, Anne-Marie Bismarck came from Hamburg, Hubert [Givenchy] had one of the grand places! & climbed across knees to hug me to (I think) the general surprise. Next to us was Laura Marlborough & the other side of her the present Duke. You know how they abominate each other so of course she whispered non-stop to me. I told Catherine [Neidpath] to be sure I gathered up what she said & it was, 'When I told Diana Cooper I'd hired a car to come, she said "Oh *do* take me", but I said "Sorry mate no way, I can't carry you up the steps."'

About two seats away from me were the Hendersons*, he busied himself with Tarmac papers while he waited for the Queen. Opposite was Gladwyn† also reading – a whodunnit. The ladies were very smart, mostly French . . .[17]

---

* Sir Nicholas and Lady Henderson. He had been British Ambassador in Paris. He and the Duchess of Devonshire were both directors of a building company, Tarmac plc.
† Lord Gladwyn, another former British Ambassador to Paris.

Of this occasion I have my own account, written at the time:

Today I am on duty for the funeral of the Duchess of Windsor, who died last Thursday at the age of eighty-nine.

I feel I have been involved with the story for a very long time . . .

The later story of her long illness and the veil of captivity which shrouded her from the world – the reign of Maître Blum – has been well covered in my journals, in books and in the press. My feeling when Laura told me that the Duchess was dead was only one of relief that her long years of suffering were at an end. The story of life-support machines was so awful, so grim, so prolonged that (alas for the frailty of human feelings) even I found that I gave up worrying about it. I tried at first to engage the attentions of the Queen's Household, but they were not really interested. They were interested but impotent – unwilling to do anything. Even Prince Johnny Lucinge* received the frostiest of looks from the Queen Mother when he raised the subject of 'the lady we all know and love in the Bois'. Queen Elizabeth merely said: 'I must talk to my daughter about it.'

The press has written such rubbish since her death. Never have I been more angered by the false rumours of the emeralds, the contradictory reports of her state of health in Paris – and more lately by the very premature publication of the love letters.

I was impressed by the way the Duchess's body was removed from her house (seen by me on television). It brought it all back to me as I watched the coffin come through those doors – past a line-up including Paul-Louis Weiller, erect and sombre at the age of ninety-two. Later he said he was the only one at the 'I don't know how you say it – *la levée du corps*.' In fact there was a group of them including the British Ambassador and his wife [the Fretwells], and the very elegant Lord Chamberlain, Lord Airlie (whom I nearly mistook for Prince George of Hanover at the Queen's Birthday Service).

The Garde Republicaine were as *Clochemerle*-ian as one could hope – their 'present arms' like a long ill-timed shuffle. Our RAF was brilliant putting the coffin into the aeroplane. Likewise at RAF Benson where the Duke of Gloucester (as the Queen's senior cousin) greeted the arrival.

In Windsor the streets were lined as the hearse arrived by way

---

* Prince Jean-Louis de Faucigny-Lucinge (1900–92), who used to conduct the Queen Mother on her visits to France and Italy.

of the Henry VIII Gateway. The Castle was closed and there was a kind of reveille salute from a bugler as she went past the guards lined up. I feel sure that St George's will do its best for the Duchess – treating her with the dignity due to the widow of one of the Queen's uncles.

It will be interesting to see who is there – even as I write a red helicopter takes off in the direction of Windsor (9.25) – and how it all turns out. I have had a grim time with Laura [Marlborough] ringing me at every minute of the day – about her hat, her ticket, her car, etc., etc. It's all been too much. It seems that the Duchess is giving her last party and all the ladies are thoroughly overexcited – Maureen Dudley* stamping her foot in Hardy Amies, now to appear in widow's weeds with veil – Aileen Plunket ringing up her daughter [Doon – Countess Granville] 20 times about whether or not she should wear her nice pink suit – and Laura discussing every detail of her outfit – all too mad.

But I write this only that I may continue it a little later on.

The Duchess of Windsor's Funeral

I joined Laura after 12.00 and Bolton [the chauffeur] arrived at 12.30. We drove to Windsor by a most curious route – I who go there nearly every week suggested Datchet. He knew better and then as good as got lost in Windsor itself. Laura and I had a rather grim lunch in the Castle Hotel.

Then I walked up the hill to the Castle and entered with no difficulty, despite having no ticket. I went to the Cloisters to look at the wreaths – there were large ones from the Waleses, 'Eddie & Katharine', Anne (rather formally written, not by her) – a very formal one from 'Her Royal Highness Princess Alice, Duchess of Gloucester and Their Royal Highnesses the Duke and Duchess of Gloucester'.

My flowers 'with gratitude for your kindness' were very good-looking. There was a huge one from Diana Vreeland, and a £250 effort from Estée Lauder – I found Laura's laurel wreath and some from Diana Mosley – there were a few official ones, and some from the general public, even one from a total madman, the Duke of Greatness or whatever. In all there were two rows of wreaths in the Cloisters.

---

* The Countess of Dudley – the former film star Maureen Swanson.

When the Duke died, the whole Cloisters were full and for the funeral the flowers were spread out down the lawn by the Chapel.

Inside, the Chapel was still and empty – just a few stewards and Roy Dixon, the Chapter Clerk. We were given our instructions. I was viewed with suspicion by my fellow stewards on account of the piece in *The Times* and also the flowers. John Handcock recalled the Duke's funeral and how I was suddenly thrown forward into the midst of the Gentlemen Ushers – the late General Sir Rodney Moore, etc.

Peter Hartley came down and said: 'There is one change of plan, thanks to Hugo's article in *The Times* this morning' (joke scowl at me) – 'Lady Alexandra Metcalfe will be seated in the Quire instead of the Nave.'* He told me later that it had jogged his memory and that she had been disappointed to be in the Nave last time. When I asked if Maître Blum was to be there or not, he very kindly gave me a seating plan. Evidently she was unable to come.

The stewards were present at one part of the service denied the mourners. We stood very still while four Military Knights marched down to the end of the Nave under the command of Sir Peter Gillett.

Then the coffin of the Duchess was carried under the Organ Screen into the Quire by a bearer party of the Welsh Guards. Evidently the coffin was very heavy, made of fine dark oak – possibly lead-lined because the Duchess herself can have weighed nothing – the bearers looked almost purple in the face. Then the Military Knights marched the full length of the Nave. They took it in turn to stand guard.

When the doors were opened, I spotted Lady 'Baba' and pointed her out to the steward on duty. I observed figures such as the Marlboroughs going in, Maureen Dudley, *chic* in her Hardy Amies suit, Aileen Plunket, her hair coiffed into her hat, unsteady on her feet – later on Diana Mosley and Catherine Neidpath [her granddaughter].

My job was to care for the Nave – the first clients dealt with were the Van der Kemps, then came Bloch, whose work on the letters has been in evidence these last days. I said to him: 'How are you, Michael?' – after the usual Bloch pause he said: 'Rather dazed.'

'Yes, I can imagine.'

I placed him in the front row of the Nave. Pilar [de la Béraudière]†

---

* My article recalled that Lady Alexandra was the last surviving guest from the Windsor wedding in 1937.
† Pilar de la Béraudière, granddaughter of Commandant Paul-Louis Weiller.

was there too, looking rather glamorous. Then Walter Lees came in
and gave himself away by demanding to sit with (as it turned out)
Diana Vreeland's grandson.

In due course it was possible to catch distant glimpses of
members of the Royal Family coming in by the North Quire
Door . . . I noted that Sir Godfrey Morley and his wife were seated
in the Quire while the French lawyers were seated in the Nave.
Very interesting. Of absent royals – no Princess Margaret – and
it is interesting to note that there was no royal coat of arms on
the Ceremonial.

Presently the service began. I sat at the back, behind the Press,
an unruly rabble including figures such as Jean Rook – we also had
a lot of community members in the Nave (since the overspill of the
Duchess's friends only took two rows).

The sentences were sung and the short service very beautifully
conducted, especially the anthem. The only point which was bad I
suppose was that there was absolutely no mention of the Duchess
by name. They never commended the spirit of 'our sister Wallis' –
perhaps at the Committal this occurred.*

At the end of the service, the Chapter Clerk and Tom Taylor
went to open the West Door. I therefore took an aisle seat and was
able to observe the slow procession coming out of the Quire. They
took a long time to turn the heavy coffin, then, to slow *Nimrod*, out
they came.

The Governor, leading the Military Knights, the Archbishop
of Canterbury in a black silk over-cassock, not cope, the Dean of
the American Cathedral, his Gucci shoes with a red band over
them winking from under his red cassock. The coffin of the
Duchess came by so close that I could have touched it, followed
by the austere figures of the Queen and Prince Philip – the Queen
Mother and Princess Anne, the Prince and Princess of Wales and
household officials.

Meanwhile the Duchess's staff and Grace Dudley were led out
of a side door to be in their cars to follow the Royal Family to the
Committal.

The sunlight blazed outside and I could see the coffin being eased
into the hearse. Silhouetted in the doorway were the Queen and
Prince Philip. I did notice that they remained close by the door
whereas normally they go down to be near it. Nevertheless they

* It did.

stood there with the supreme dignity with which the whole service had been conducted.

In death the Duchess had been afforded the dignity of a Royal funeral. The Windsor Castle establishment had pulled out all the stops. The atmosphere in the Chapel was charged with a moving stillness – one could not be sad that the Duchess's earthly life had come to an end, but there is always a sense of sorrow and regret on such an occasion. There had been so much pain, physical and mental, so much written about the curious woman from Baltimore – it was the final curtain on a most dramatic piece of history and I believe that the curtain could not have been lowered with more dignity.

It did occur to me to wonder how they would have handled it had the Duke outlived her. Could his family then have followed him in the same way? Or would he have had to bury her all alone? Mere speculation.

Duties over, I went to the Cloisters to find Laura, Catherine and Diana. The mourners were all looking at the wreaths and some were being seized by the press for quick comments. Then it was luxury to have the car, to be able to leap in and then be driven speedily away.

So now it was all over, bar the publications and the disposal of property.[18]

In the evening I went to see Diana Cooper. She listened avidly to stories about the funeral. She asked if the Duchess had been made an HRH in death, but that's just an old April Fool – from the *Observer*, I believe.

The following day's papers dwelt on the omission of the Duchess's name. In due course stories emerged of the Committal at Frogmore – in particular how the Queen had suddenly cried, which was most unusual in one normally so reserved. Possibly the whole thing had been a strain or she recalled the sadness of her father and her uncle. Maybe the enormity of the saga that was now finally closing and which had had such an effect on her own life caused this. Possibly someone said something upsetting, though this has never been suggested by any of those present at the graveside. But when a close friend rang in the evening to ask her how the day had gone, the Queen was still too upset to take the call. Dean Leo, who was at the Committal, recalled the Queen pointing to the Duke's grave and saying: 'That was the one that I loved.'[19]

And then of course there were the jokes. In the next days Alastair Forbes saw Mrs John Barry Ryan*. He took advantage of her daughter being married to Lord Airlie, the Lord Chamberlain, the man who scattered the earth on the Duchess's coffin as it was lowered into the ground.

It was typical of Ali's sense of humour to say to Nin: 'Imagine you being the mother-in-law of the last man to dish the dirt on Wallis!'[20]

---

* Mrs John Barry Ryan (1901–95), daughter of Otto Kahn, and mother of the Countess of Airlie.

16

The Letters, Georges and Fayed – 1986–1987

The beautiful funeral service was overshadowed in the media by the publication of the Duke and Duchess's so-called love letters, serialised in the *Daily Mail* at the behest of Maître Blum. Day after day, within four days of the Duchess's death and even before she was buried, more and more embarrassing trivia appeared. These were letters between the Duke of Windsor and Mrs Simpson, dating from his days as Prince of Wales and before he became king. There were many letters from Mrs Simpson to her aunt, Bessie Merryman, tracing the course of the romance.

The extracts ran for two weeks in the *Daily Mail*. Eventually the heavily embargoed book emerged, likewise authorised for publication by Blum, and edited by Bloch. It was called *Wallis & Edward: Letters 1931–1937*.*

As we have seen, Maître Blum had been planning this book for several years. She now insisted publicly that the letters were published to 'prove that the Duchess did everything she could to dissuade him [the Duke] from marrying her'.[1] Bloch went further, stating that it was the Duchess's wish that the letters be published after her death.[2]

The Duchess's cause was ill-served by the publication of the letters, and Bloch's editorial was exactly the kind of thing which normally threw Blum into a frenzy. He described the Duchess as 'a very ordinary woman . . . no longer young', neither beautiful, nor rich, nor even very well educated.[3] He addressed questions about whether she was a socially ambitious schemer, and 'bewitching the Prince with some kind of sexual sorcery,'[4] and speculated about whether the Prince had enjoyed sexual relations with her 'and, if so, of what sort.'[5] He wrote that the Duchess 'exercised a great fascination on lesbians'[6] and travelled with two such women, Gloria Vanderbilt and Nada, Lady Milford Haven. Did Maître Blum suppose this would enhance the reputation of her recently deceased client?

The letters were copyrighted in the name of 'The Legal Representatives of the Estate of the Duchess of Windsor'. It would be interesting to know where the money – of which there was a consider-

---

* Edited by Michael Bloch (Weidenfeld & Nicolson, 1986). Review copies were sent out 'in the strictest confidence' and embargoed until publication of the book on 15 May.

able amount from all the global publishing deals – went. Even taking into account the later announcement of a beneficiary chosen by the Duchess, any proceeds were certainly too late to be of the slightest benefit to the Duchess of Windsor.

Given the state of the Duchess's health over a number of years, I refuse to believe that she could have authorised the publication of these letters. Had she done so in writing, the evidence should have been produced in the book rather in the same way that a photograph signed by the Duchess to Maître Blum was published in the Sotheby's catalogue of her jewels.

Alastair Forbes was one reviewer who asked for it in the *Spectator*, but without success:

Mr Bloch has been so free with photostats that one wonders why he has not produced the one clearly dated document, with signature to study by graphologists that could clinch the argument.[7]

I reviewed this book in *The Times*. Bloch stated in his introduction that the Duchess was 'determined that, at the right moment, the truth should be known to the world in the form of the authentic contemporary record.'[8]

As I pointed out, the Duchess had not wished the letters to be published and I highlighted inconsistencies in statements made by Blum. The idea for publication was Blum's and Blum's alone. I also said that had the Windsors wanted to use these letters they could have done so in their ghosted memoirs: 'They were both sufficiently aware of their inexperience as writers to employ ghosts. Regrettably these love letters did not have the benefit of the ghost.'[9]

Following publication of my review, Bloch went to the offices of *The Times* in Wapping, demanding the right of reply, and threatened a writ from Maître Blum. *The Times* received a letter from him, but they did not publish it as they felt it added nothing.[10]

Despite what J. Bryan III had told Mountbatten, John Utter had remembered that the letters existed and that, when the Duke's papers came to light, he had asked the Duchess whether she wanted them to go to Windsor, or to keep them, or to destroy them. She was never up to making the decision.

Utter left and, as we have seen, while Miss Schütz was burning papers in 1977, Georges brought the letters to the office and asked if they should be burnt too. Realising the importance of the documents, Miss Schütz consulted Maître Blum and as a result she and Georges consigned them into the lawyer's care. In so doing Miss Schütz never thought for one moment that they would be misused or published. She asked Blum what she would do with them and the lawyer said she would put them in a safe place.

At that time Blum was not aware that the Duke's papers had gone to Windsor Castle, nor that his Orders and decorations had been sent to London. Presently she became interested in what other archival material there might be in the Duchess's house. She began to explore.[11]

One of the arguments that Blum extended, and which Bloch supported on her behalf, was that her actions on behalf of the Duchess were undertaken in order to pay the expensive nursing bills and keep the Duchess safely in her own home. It is not an unreasonable argument, but it is destroyed by the publication of these letters and by subsequent books.

The *Wallis and Edward Letters* were reviewed in *Private Eye* by an anonymous but well-informed reviewer (Peter McKay with input from Michael Thornton). That review emphasised that the Duchess had played no part in the publication of this book, that she had been unaware of Frances Donaldson's 1974 biography, and that she had been 'a cabbage for the last eight years of her life' and therefore completely unaware even of the 1978 television series, *Edward & Mrs Simpson*.

It told the story of how Blum and Bloch attempted to suppress publication of Michael Thornton's book, *Royal Feud*. *Private Eye* concluded:

> With the massive American advance from Summit Books, British publication by Weidenfeld and a reputed fee of £400,000 for serialisation in the *Daily Mail*, *The Wallis and Edward Letters 1931–1937* are liable to earn well over £1 million. Where is all the loot going? Certainly not to the Duchess of Windsor, who is no longer here to enjoy it*.[12]

At this time Lord Tennyson volunteered his version of events, inspired to do so by Alastair Forbes's reference to the unnamed historian to whom the Duke was said to have consigned his papers. After explaining how Blum had tried to entrust the papers to him, he concluded:

* The book was initially sold to Weidenfeld, the *Daily Mail*, and then to Summit Books. On the day the Duchess died, Andrew Best, Bloch's literary agent, was on his telephone all day long until late at night. He sold second serial rights to the *News of the World*. He sold Canadian rights to Methuen (Canada) with first serial to the *Toronto Mail and Globe*. He sold US serial rights to *People* magazine, and a second serial to Canada. The French rights were taken by Librairie Academique Ferrin, and serial by *Paris Match*. Book rights were sold in Germany and Italy and magazine rights in Finland, Norway, Holland, Italy, South Africa, Spain, New Zealand, Sweden and Portugal. Chinese world rights were sold in Taiwan. [*The Bookseller*, 24 May 1986].

As I see it, both she and Mr Bloch would have realised that I would never have passed the Duke's letters to the Duchess, because, while most men's love letters are not worth reading, these were 'enfantine' in the extreme. But first, they tested the water with the two Bloch books, which were not particularly well informed, and, as I said nothing, they considered that they were Home and Dry. At the same time, I have to say that Maître Blum had told me in her office that the Duchess wished to prove by her papers that she was not an adventuress and she had been relentlessly pursed. I think that this does emerge quite clearly, but also that the poor Duke appears to be 'sillier' than he really was.

P.S. I was only 'Liaison with the Palace' for a week or two when the Duchess had her first stroke. I then introduced Maître Blum to Sir Nicholas Henderson, our then Ambassador, and the Embassy acted from that moment onwards.[13]

As we shall see, this was not the end of the publishing partnership of Blum and Bloch.

Within a few days of the Duchess's death, Maître Blum announced that the bulk of the estate would go to the Louis Pasteur Institute. Blum refused to give details of the will, but stated that the Duchess's furniture would go to the Louvre and to Versailles and some fine china to the Sèvres museum. Minor bequests would go to the RNLI, the Guide Dogs for the Blind Association, the Claude Pompidou Foundation for the Handicapped, the American Hospital in Paris, and four British regiments. When asked if she thought the British Royal Family would challenge the will, Blum said: 'The British Crown ought not to raise any objections. Anything is possible but I do not believe they will do so.'[14]

In July 1986, a mere eleven weeks after the Duchess's death, their old friend Commandant Paul-Louis Weiller decided that I should see round the Duchess's house in the Bois.

This was the same Paul-Louis Weiller against whom Maître Blum had fought in the 1940s, representing his former wife Aliki Russell in the prolonged divorce and bigamy case.* Weiller was an extraordinary figure who used twentieth-century business enterprises in order to live like a seventeenth-century king. He had known the Windsors since the 1930s and had housed them in the late 1940s at 85 rue de la Faisanderie. He

*See Chapter 7.

was then nearly ninety-three and was destined to live to one hundred. In his early days he had been a distinguished flying ace (or 'ass' as he pronounced it – 'I was one of the greatest *asses* of the First World War' he used to say to our amusement). Later he had owned an aircraft company which was nationalised and is now known as Air France. He was a vigorous figure who continued to windsurf until within a month of his ninety-ninth birthday.

A highly intelligent, cunning and devious man, he loved to outwit those with whom he did business, and often to outwit his friends. He was a dextrous and energetic seducer of beautiful women, many of whom became famous stars thanks to his passing interest. He had one Achilles heel. He loved royalty and they could do no wrong in his eyes. As a result, a number of well-known royal exiles lived in luxury at his expense, including, for a time, the Windsors.

The visit to the house was the result of a cleverly waged campaign. On Saturday, 12 July I was with the Commandant in his office when he rang the house to try to speak to Georges. He reached a *femme de chambre* who told him that Georges was away. He promptly offered her a job and suggested that he should come round and interview her. This ploy failed, but we were told that Georges would be back on Monday.

I lunched with the Commandant on that Monday and he confirmed that the visit was arranged for later in the day. He had evidently reached Georges and offered him the post of butler. Georges told him that he was not seeking further employment but he knew a butler who had worked at The Mill. The Commandant made an appointment to interview the said butler in the house.

The Commandant's chauffeur picked me up from the rue de la Faisanderie, where I was staying, and then picked up the Commandant from his home in the rue de la Ferme at Neuilly. We arrived at 'Bagatelle', as the Commandant called the house. The gates, so long closed against the world, swung open to admit us, and the car swept us up the drive:

I had of course been inside the house several times between 1972 and 1976. Yet I thought all that was in the past. To be given another chance was a wonderful surprise.

I had only been permitted a glimpse before – one little tour of the downstairs rooms with John Utter in 1972, one visit to the terrace, through the drawing room later that summer, and several walks through the hall, to and from the office.

The Commandant is an amazing operator. He had come to see Georges and to meet a couple that might come and work at the rue de la Faisanderie. Georges met us at the door (quite informally dressed in a white housecoat). We entered the hall through those grille doors, hung with pale yellow drapes. On the right is the cloak-room (loo), on the left a cloakroom for coats etc. We sat down in the hall and talked for a while.

The hall is dimly lit with flickering electric candlelight in branches at the side. There are tables with eagles under them either side of the drawing-room door and two Maurs holding torches. The Duke's Garter banner as Prince of Wales hangs from the banister. Dating from 1911* it is now so fragile that you can see through it. The ceiling is fine & very high, and there is a huge screen by the study door. The study itself looked deserted.

Georges has changed a lot since I last saw him – and the years of isolation have done him no good. He is old now, pure white hair, very shaky of hand – very hesitant, very protective of the house, of course.

The Commandant did not remain seated for long. He was soon up & about – and presently there could be heard behind his back the crinkling of notes, some rustling – so that Georges knew he was in for a tip, and a big one. I would say that it was about £120 worth of French francs. But it was not given. There was just a lot of rustling.

The Commandant then asked a question by way of accusation. 'Is the portrait of the Duchess still in the library?' '*Ah oui, monsieur.*' The Commandant clearly expected to see it. Georges was clearly under instruction to let no one into those rooms, but despite his protestations, we were soon in the drawing room, which seemed to me very much as it had been on my earlier visit. As we went around, there was more rustling as the Commandant played with some crisp fresh notes behind his back. I saw this and heard it, and I could see that Georges had also taken this in.

The signed photo of the Emperor & Empress of Japan stood on the table – a Drian of the Duchess hung where the Duke used to be in Garter robes [the James Gunn], and the Brockhurst of the Duchess in blue was at the end in the library. There were endless bibelots everywhere, and plenty of books in the library – a very modern impression of the Duke to the right in the library and some other little sketches of the Duchess with a pug, etc.

The Commandant was clever. For him it was not to be the mere

---

* In fact the Garter banner of Edward VII, but he may have used it as Prince of Wales.

triumph of getting past Georges. We must inspect everything. He asked me to point out and explain a lot of the items to him, and thus much was absorbed.

There are quite a lot of tapestry cushions all over the house. The dining room at the other end was as I remember it, in Chinese pattern, with two little music galleries in each corner – a violin in one – but the big dining-room table has gone, and now there is just a small table with three chairs. Here I believe Maître Blum came to do her work.

Georges told us that Maître Blum was now in the country. She was all right, but had problems with her eyes. There was a Portuguese *femme de chambre* wandering around upstairs [Maria] – and also Ofélia who is now white-haired but looks more in control than Georges.

Everything, Georges said, belongs to the Louis Pasteur now – things are taken to the Musée du Louvre and elsewhere. Every item, big or small, had a little number on it – either white or dark blue.

Then we went back into the hall and met the couple. The husband was the man Georges thought might work as a butler to the Commandant. The wife was excellent but he was a bit scatty. He also told two silly lies. He said he was 48, when in fact he was 62. Then he said '*Je bois peu*' – and when a man says he drinks little, this surely means he drinks a lot. They used to work for the Windsors at the Moulin (Gif-sur-Yvette). To digress for a moment, they said the Duchess demanded perfection (and got it). She said 'If you break something you must own up at once. You mustn't hide it.' Mme C. admitted she once hid an ashtray that she broke.

After a brief interview in the hall, it appeared that we were about to set out for the rue de la Faisanderie, so that the butler and his wife could see where they might work. Then the Commandant turned to me and said quietly: 'Well, you have seen the downstairs rooms; you would like to see the room where died the Duchess, I suppose? I have to be very tactful.'

Tact played little part in what followed. There was a pause. '*Est-ce qu'on peut voir la chambre où est morte la Duchesse? Ça peut être très émouvant!*'

'*Oh, c'est tout fermé!*' said Georges. A further rustling of notes. The briefest of pauses and the Commandant was heading up the stairs. And I was following, with Georges in cold pursuit.

The door to the Windsors' own apartment is mirrored on the outside, and the first room is the Duchess's sitting room. I was very surprised by this. It was pure Elsie de Wolfe, very crowded, cluttered almost – and all dark browns – masses of photos, little chairs, tapestry cushions and so on. The door to the Duchess's own room was small – and suddenly we were in it.

Her room was powder blue – the double bed (quite small) was stripped of everything. Only the base, covered in blue silk, remained. An old white telephone was on the floor on the left. There were two shelves either side of the bed & under the glass of one there was a photo of the Duchess, very soignée in bed, holding her pugs, her auburn hair done to perfection. I would say 1972 or so. There was a painting of a girl at St Tropez on the right-hand wall – and the two dressing tables were absolutely covered in pictures – a signed photo of George V, the Duke & Bertie – photos of babies to whom she was godmother. At the foot of her bed, a blue sofa, with about nine rather amusing pug cushions – that's to say identical cushions in the shape of pugs. Her love of pugs was in fact the most prominent feature of the room.

I didn't see her bathroom – nor were there any signs of medical equipment, but there was a non-medical tube hanging over the picture, and about two feet above the bed (maybe less) were marks where things had been taped to the wall. I would say this indicated some kind of life-support or feeding drips or whatever. It was an attractive room, not large or spacious – far from it.

From the Duchess's room we went back into the little salon and through into the Duke's room. Georges lit this for us (which he didn't do in the others). The Duke's bedroom was huge in comparison with hers – it was open-plan with the sitting-room area. Here there abounded portraits of the Duchess. There were albums piled high on a desk, photos of him (one of which was cut out of the *Illustrated London News* after his death & framed in a modern Perspex frame). There were books everywhere, stacked up in piles, and photos of the Duchess as a young girl – 1916 or so – also in the Duke's rooms. I felt these rooms were exactly as the Duke had left them before his death fourteen years earlier.

His bed was covered with a huge tapestry cover with his cypher on it, the rather angular 'EP'. There was a large coat of arms – Stuart, I think – hanging magnificently behind his bed. The books were mainly historical – Nigel Nicolson's *Alex*, books by Churchill, etc. His rooms contained a spacious dressing room, quite sparse with big cupboards – and lots of copies of his own books all piled up – and in due course this led to his large bathroom which was at the front of the house. All marble, again very French – and altogether in perfect taste – austere, those back rooms.

No photos of the Queen, but I saw a signed Princess Mary – and a number of his mother & quite a few pictures of horses from his youth.

In the downstairs drawing room there was Queen Mary in Garter robes – this was reproduced upstairs (the Sir William Llewellyn portrait). Then we went onto the landing & to Georges's mild protests we continued round. There is a large Munnings of the Duke hunting (which you can glimpse from the hall) – and I found a Cecil [Beaton] drawing of the Duchess, which was once in *Vogue* – this was the drawing she asked him for. I have its pair. It hangs opposite some differently decorated stairs which lead to the few guest rooms above. This part was more white-walled and red-carpeted (with pattern) not like the golden, brown, bronzed look of the main part of the house.

As we prepared to go down the stairs, Georges was given his well-earned, much rustled tip. '*Un petit quelque chose pour vous, Georges . . .*' '*Ah, monsieur*! . . .' He didn't have the chance to inspect it, but he would be pleased. He looked such a sad man. Neither he nor Ofélia want to go on working. Ofélia said: 'We have enough. We do not have children. So why work?' Georges leaves for the country at the end of July.

Overall the house had a melancholy air, which has no doubt hung over it for many years now. Long gone are the days of John Utter and his ever-buzzing telephone, planning the Queen's visit – and Miss Schütz telephoning Dior: '*Son Altesse voudrait voir les robes qu'elle a choisi de la nouvelle collection dans votre salon cette après-midi . . .*'

After her long illness, the Duchess died just a little under three months ago. And it was curious for me to be in the back of a car, Georges and Ofélia having shaken hands, and waving to us as we left. How often I had seen the pictures of the Duchess on the same steps, waving to the Queen on her visit all those years ago.[15]

Presently Georges took his retirement. He did not leave empty-handed. Opinions vary as to his character, but it is agreed that he was devoted to the Duchess. Like many such figures this led him to devious ways. He looked over banisters, he told stories on other members of staff, and he was not wholly honest. The pressures of internecine warfare and the temptation of unguarded riches proved too much for him.

Lady Fretwell thought Georges had been shoddily treated, though he was given an honorary Royal Victorian Medal by the Queen in the New Year Honours list of 1987 to mark his long years of service. Georges was also in the Duke's will and presumably he received his inheritance. He was cut in on the deal over the Duchess's letters. Lady Fretwell encouraged him to tell his story if asked, though was worried when he seemed to invite people to take things. He pedalled his revelations of life with the Windsors to the *Sunday Mirror*, in which he claimed (nonsensically) that he had amused the Duchess by pinching the Empress of Japan's bottom on her 1971 visit, and related (truthfully) how the Queen had broken down at the Duke and Duchess's graveside at Frogmore.

Georges had had plenty of time to take possession of items from the Duchess's house. She had entrusted her most personal letters into his care, with instructions that he should destroy them. He had been employed there for thirty-eight years, and from 1976 his duties as butler had been no more than guardian and doorkeeper. From time to time he had admitted visitors to the Duchess, in defiance of orders from Maître Blum, but more often he told the Duchess's friends that visits were forbidden – '*Madame c'est interdit!*' or, when asked how the Duchess was: '*C'est toujours la même chose.*'

The next and last time I saw him was in Geneva. The Commandant and I ran into him and Ofélia on the way to the Richemond Hotel to inspect the Duchess's jewels. They were there as guests of Sotheby's. Ofélia was wearing a mink coat, which looked remarkably similar to the mink coat that the Duchess had been pictured wearing on her visits to the Duke in the London Clinic in 1965.

Georges died in the late 1990s, and Ofélia died some years later. I remember a curious remark made by Madame Janine Metz, secretary to the Windsors in the 1960s who later did occasional work for them when they were in New York. In 1998 she said that Ofélia had inherited a fortune. This might have been explained by the negotiations in which Mohamed Fayed engaged with her after he took over the lease of the house. He bought back a treasure trove of silver lions, gold boxes and other items.

But it did not all come back. In 2004, after both the Sanègres were dead, there were two sales. The first was in Rome and the second in Paris.

Christie's (Rome) produced Lots 531–718 of items belonging to Georges. These comprised a considerable collection of the Windsors' possessions. There were books signed by the Duke and Duchess to Georges, books signed by Queen Mary to the Duke, letters to the Duke from Queen Mary, the Princess Royal, Winston Churchill, Somerset Maugham, to the Duchess from Eleanor Roosevelt, the Aga Khan, Rose Kennedy and others, signed photographs of the Windsors, along with golf irons, ducal pipes, lighters, clocks and watches, vintage wine, cognac, whisky, champagne, a camera, a telescope, ashtrays, silverware, medals, snuffboxes and scent boxes, bracelets, cufflinks, some of the Duchess's clothes by Dior, five Hawes and Curtis shirts, suits and jackets belonging to the Duke, a mass of photographs (including a Man Ray of the Duchess), various oil paintings and aquarelles of ships, plates, glasses and porcelain bearing the Prince of Wales's coat of arms, monogrammed linen and more besides.

Most shockingly, in this sale were Lots 542, 543 and 544. Lot 542 comprised five letters to the Duchess from her first husband, Win Spencer. Lot 543 contained seventeen letters from Ernest Simpson to the Duchess, and Lot 544 sixteen letters from the Duke to the Duchess between 1936 and 1955. There was a further Lot of nineteen letters from Elsa Maxwell to the Duchess. All of these were of historical interest, but sadly for historians they passed into private hands. Either the Duchess consigned them to Georges for burning or he stole them.

The second sale was at Espace Tajan in the rue des Mathurins in Paris on 21 October. A hundred and two Lots were put up for sale, including sets of chairs, furniture, photograph albums, clocks, plates, ornaments, the address book from The Mill, and other such items.

The explanation for this treasure trove is that most of the things came from The Mill. This had been sold to Edmond Artar, but Georges had gone down there with a van and removed an enormous number of objects. These were stored, still in packing cases, in the house behind the main house in the Bois, where some of the staff lived. In the long years of the Duchess's illness Georges had had plenty of time to spirit these things away.

In Georges's defence, I doubt that possession of these things brought him happiness or peace of mind. When I saw him after the Duchess's death he looked a pathetic, broken man. The years of the Duchess's illness and the atmosphere imposed on the house by Blum had taken its toll on him.

Ever since the Duchess's death, Blum's team had been visiting the house regularly and removing documents and other items. In September, Michael Bloch went to dine with Diana Mosley. She reported to their mutual friend, James Lees-Milne what he was doing:

Michael Bloch dines, he is daily at the Windsors' old house clearing up papers. Heaven alone knows what he'll find. Of course the Windsor archive has no legal right to anything & M*e* Blum would LOVE to annoy the royal family. What a strange turn of fate that she & Michael are in complete control. I said 'Are there any nuggets among the dross?' & he said 'Yes, there are'.[16]

In November 1986 it was announced that the lease of the house had been granted to the Egyptian businessman Mohamed Al-Fayed, owner of Harrods in Knightsbridge and of the Ritz Hotel in the Place Vendôme in Paris, the restoration of which, in 1979, had greatly impressed the Mayor of Paris, Jacques Chirac. Fayed was inspired to take it on by Sydney Johnson, the Duke's former Bahamian valet, now in his employ, who told him that the house and the collection that it contained were unique. According to Fayed's biographer, Fayed opened negotiations with Blum before the Duchess died. Sydney went to the house in 1985 and met Blum there. He told her that his boss was especially taken with the story, had long been fascinated by the Windsors, and had promised to create a permanent memorial to the Duke and Duchess at the house. 'Blum nodded approvingly.'[17]

After the Duchess's death, and with the approval of Chirac, Fayed took possession of what now became known as 'the Windsor Villa'. Frank Klein, the manager of the Ritz, went to Blum's office with the lease for her to sign. He told me that Blum did not like having to sign: 'Never had a woman a sicker face.'[18]

On the day that the transfer of the lease was signed, Fayed ordered that the locks be changed, thus preventing Blum's team from entering the premises as indeed they tried to do that very day.

Fayed ringed the house with fierce security. There were many genial and smiling security guards, but as a visitor, you felt that one wrong move would provoke a swift change of mood. Likewise there were now huge cages to the right of the drive – wherein large guard dogs lived. These were presumably let out to roam at night.

Articles about the Fayed takeover began to appear in the press. Journalists and photographers were allowed in as early as November 1986. The story of Fayed's work in restoring the Ritz for the benefit of the City of Paris was heavily stressed. So too was the deep impression that the Abdication had made on him, though at the time he had been about eight years old and residing in the back streets of Alexandria.

Work proceeded swiftly. By November the house already looked fresher. Versailles had claimed items due to them under the Duchess's 'will'. These included Louis XV furniture, the chandelier in the drawing room and various clocks.

Fayed bought the rest of the furniture, paintings and belongings from 'the Duchess's trustees'. He was also successful in retrieving certain items that had vanished. One such was the dining-room table that had been absent when I visited the house the previous July. To secure its return Fayed said he paid £120,000.

He also reinstated Sydney Johnson. As we know, Sydney had been dismissed shortly after the Duke's death. Fayed believed the story that Sydney used to tell – that he had been at the Duke's bedside when he died in 1972. This was not the case and Fayed later felt deceived. Nevertheless, Sydney continued to work at the house as a kind of front man, with his easy charm and anecdotes, until his death in 1990.

The plan was that Fayed would take over an apartment at the top of the house while the ground floor and the Duke and Duchess's private suite of rooms, including bedrooms and bathrooms, on the first floor, would be preserved as a kind of museum.

In November 1986 it was reported in the *Daily Mail* that Fayed had offered the Queen a seventeen-century oil painting of a small child, originally at Hampton Court but lately in the Duchess's bedroom. Fayed also offered the Queen the Abdication desk. The latter was not returned to her.

At a certain point Mohamed Fayed invited Prince Charles to come over and see the house, in case there was anything he wanted. The Prince came over within three weeks of the invitation. The Ritz ran up some curtains for the drawing room in a rush.

In time the rooms were throughly restored. The office to the right of the front door was converted into a miniature museum, as were rooms in the basement. The restoration was done to perfection, though there were a few lapses of taste. The Duchess had always had a flair for lighting. Thus, in her day, the front hall was bathed in a soft honey-golden light, so subtle that I for one never spotted the door to a lift in the corner. Passing through the hall, there was the pale silvery blue light of the drawing room, with the large French windows overlooking the expansive, perfectly cut lawn. After Fayed's restoration, the hall was overly lit, every corner illuminated. He hung a Venetian chandelier in the downstairs salon, which would, I think, have had the Duchess spinning in her Frogmore grave.

Any articles written about the house were approved by the Fayed team. But they were fulsome in praise of what he was doing. Ivan Fallon wrote: 'The house at least will be preserved for posterity: echoing the great love for which, fifty years ago, King Edward VIII exchanged his throne and all the palaces that went with it.'[19]

In June 1987 an article about the house by the distinguished architectural historian John Cornforth was published in *Country Life*. His understanding of what Stephane Boudin had been aiming for was considerable. He concluded that it was an extraordinary creation, not untheatrical in effect, but he added: 'There is a distinct sense of shock and distaste that executors should have sold all the relics of the Duke's and Duchess's private life in this way.'[20]

It is interesting to compare three photographic images of the downstairs drawing room of the house in the Bois. The first was taken in the 1960s and the Duchess can be seen in the distance by the library. The room contained plenty of furniture and the tables were covered in bibelots. A second photograph was taken in November 1986. The Abdication desk had been moved from the hall, there was hardly any furniture and the magnificent chandelier had been replaced by a lesser one. The curtains were pale blue, the carpet worn and stained. The explanation given was that much of the porcelain and furniture had been distributed to French museums.

The third photograph showed the house after the Fayed restoration. It was not possible to retrieve the James Gunn of the Duke from the Musée National de la Légion d'Honneur, and now Queen Mary's portrait occupied that spot. The curtains had been restored to an earlier style and the furniture was appropriate if not identical.

If there were a few touches that were more Fayed and Harrods than Duchess and Jansen, it would be churlish to be critical. The overall restoration work was remarkable and the assurances that all this would be preserved as a memorial to the Windsors and their place in romantic history were commendable.

17

Blum's Last Stand – 1987–1996

Speculation about the Duchess's jewels began the moment she died. In the autumn of 1986 Maître Blum announced that there had been a number of bids for this collection, said in the press to be worth two million pounds. There was speculation that Fayed was one of those interested. Blum declined to confirm this, although it was true.

What she did not say was that the Duke did not want the jewels sold in the settings that the Duchess wore. The Duke did not want anyone to wear them as the Duchess had done. He wanted them broken up. Clearly, from a sales point of view, they had more value in the Duchess's settings.

Then came the sensational announcement that the jewels were to be sold at Sotheby's in Geneva. In 1976 they had been moved from the Morgan Guaranty Bank in the Place Vendôme to the Banque de France in the rue des Petits-Champs. But not all the jewels would be there.

Stories circulated to the effect that Blum was giving heirlooms to chosen friends of the Duchess – friends chosen by Blum, not by the Duchess.

Blum sold certain pieces to other people. Jacques Arpel, of Van Cleef & Arpel, noted that many of the pieces they had created specially for the Duchess were not listed in the sale. Apparently they found only fifteen out of their forty pieces. Elvire Gozin, the nurse, confirmed that many pieces had been sold. We know that in 1977 Estée Lauder bought a jonquil diamond shaped like a heart for $150,000.

The Duchess's jewels were sold at Sotheby's in Geneva on 2 and 3 April 1987 in 306 Lots. These included a number of items belonging to the Duke, such as swords, merries, sporrans and cufflinks. But how many of the items in the Duchess's personal inventory, made in the 1970s, had found their way into that sale?

The Duchess's inventory contained 235 listed items, consisting of jewels, brooches, bracelets, necklaces, rings, hatpins, tiepins, clamping bands, vanity cases and compacts, rouge tubes, scent bottles, combs, notebooks, bags, lorgnettes, watches, hand mirrors, belts, purses, medallions, pill boxes, and portfolios. There were a considerable number of further important items at the bank.

The Duchess had given away some of these pieces when she was well. As we have seen, she gave Oonagh Shanley, the Duke's nurse, an ivory brooch in the shape of a carnation with sapphire rings, pins and ovals, on 1 March 1972.*

Theft accounted for certain losses. When the Windsors entertained, it was not unusual for gold knives, forks and spoons to disappear. When she was still well, the Duchess had lost a gold basketwork powder compact with five brackets of brilliants, enamel and rubies while she was dining at Maxim's.

In May 1977 a large cache of jewels was consigned to Blum – envisaged as presents. Blum had gone to the bank with Miss Schütz and taken away jewels destined to be given to the Duchess of Kent and Princess Alexandra, and a gold leopard brooch for Mlle Hivet (the secretary before John Utter). Later certain jewels were given to Princess Michael of Kent.†

At the risk of repetition, I was able to identify three gold snuffboxes from the Duke of Windsor's 1970 inventory in a sale at Christie's, Geneva on 11 May 1982: Lot 105 – no. 18 (insurance value £250), Lot 106 – no. 22 (£200) and Lot 112 – no. 16 (£1,500). I know that of the other boxes in the inventory, numbers 2 and 4 were given to the Louvre, and number 6 to Dr Thin, while Blum herself took number 1.

I spent several days matching the jewels in the Geneva catalogue against the Duchess's inventory. This was no easy task as Sotheby's, Geneva listed them in English, whereas the Duchess's inventory was in French and the descriptions were slightly at variance. It was exciting to make a match, some pieces proving easy to find, others extremely difficult. I will spare the reader the details.

In undertaking this task, I confess that I was unable to extend my quest to the swords, kukris, studs, buttons and regimental badges, because they were not in the jewellery inventory. And I ran out of steam when it came to uncut stones, buttons, medallions, fashion jewellery, gold Statues of Liberty and other such items, as it was too complicated.

In conclusion it would seem that the jewels which disappeared in the Duchess's lifetime were not the most celebrated or most readily recognisable ones.

*   *   *

---

* It seems that Oonagh Shanley attempted to sell this brooch in the Geneva sale. A newspaper report suggests that it was estimated at £3,000 to £4,000. At the last moment, Ms Shanley raised her reserve to £30,000, and this it failed to reach. [Report by Geraldine Norman, *The Times*, 22 May 1987]. It was re-auctioned in 2011.

† See pp. 158–9.

The jewels were moved to Geneva before being displayed in New York between 17 and 22 March 1987, and then in Geneva before the sale.

They went to Sotheby's in a curious way. Princess Alexandra's husband Angus Ogilvy, who was a Director of Sotheby's, heard that Maître Blum was unhappy over her dealings with Fayed. He had offered to buy the jewels and a price was agreed. According to Fayed's biographer, Blum estimated these, conservatively, at six million pounds. Fayed seemed to think 'he was dealing with an old woman who could be snowballed.' At the last moment, he told her that his experts valued the jewels at £4.2 million, and 'adopting a method so favoured in the bazaar' offered her five million. Unimpressed by this lower price, she declined to sell.[1] The jewels would sell for thirty-one million pounds, twenty-five million more than Blum had asked for them.

Nicholas Rayner, the jewellery expert at Sotheby's, prepared a pitch for Blum, and presently went to see her at the rue de Varenne. He rehearsed and rehearsed his line, aware that he had to get his point over to this lawyer with 'a very fierce reputation' in the first five minutes of his talk. After that he would lose her attention. Arriving in the Maître's rooms, he was duly nervous.

Rayner was shown into Blum's presence and found her sitting on a sofa at the end of a room. '*Avancez*!' she commanded. She invited him to sit on the sofa beside her and he launched into his pitch. Part of this was to show her some catalogues. He opened one on her knees so that she could inspect how they laid out their images. He realised that he was getting nowhere.

She said to him: 'I am terribly sorry, but I am completely blind.' Rayner was so embarrassed that he burst into tears. He put his arm round Blum and she began to cry too. The jewellery sale went to Sotheby's.[2]

For this sale, Sotheby's produced a handsome catalogue, which sold 25,000 copies and made about £600,000 before the sale even started. It contained certain curious elements. Clearly it was the intention to show the Duchess wearing her jewels on special occasions. But Blum vetoed certain images, including the poignant one of the Duchess with a single drop pearl from her necklace looking out of a Buckingham Palace window in 1972, and a photo of the Duchess wearing her sapphire brooch during the Queen's visit to the house in the Bois to see the ailing Duke shortly before he died. Nor did Blum permit the image of the Windsors with the Royal Family at the unveiling of the memorial to Queen Mary in 1967 to be used. On that occasion the Duchess wore her panther brooch. Instead a picture of them leaving Claridge's was printed.

I flew to Geneva to inspect the jewels at the Hotel Beau-Rivage, making an early foray on the morning of 1 April. Arriving shortly after ten a.m. I found only a short queue and was able to spend an enjoyable hour, looking at the different items. The swords and sporrans were as nothing compared to the little boxes, Fabergé frames and cigarette boxes. I inspected some tiepins which I had earmarked and for which I intended to leave an excessive bid. I took them out to have a look at them. They were so fine and would look smart with morning dress. Best of all was one with a letter E in sapphires.

Laura Marlborough had asked me to inspect a particular bracelet. I liked the ERI despatch box, and the chalcedony necklace, one of the jewels I remembered the Duchess wearing in later life in a photo by Karsh. I examined an inscription that I was pretty certain related to Queen Alexandra. I was even more convinced later.

Spotting Michael Bloch, I informed him of this and later I told Nicholas Rayner, who was not that interested. I asked Bloch about the Silver Jubilee medal that was also for sale. Had it been presented to the Duchess? 'It would have been seen to that she got one,' he said.*

Suddenly a microphone was thrust in my direction by French television and I was interviewed in French. Why had I come? I was interested, I said, in the romantic aspect of the story – the connection of the jewels to the person. No man, said I, repeating Diana Cooper's view, had given up so much for a woman – '*une femme comme la Duchesse de Windsor*'.[3] Then I continued my inspection of the priceless collection, enjoying in particular the panthers, the flamingo and the really massive pieces.

After lunch I returned, this time with Paul-Louis Weiller, his daughter-in-law Olimpia† and Princess Valaya of Thailand. As we approached the Hotel, we saw Georges, who recognised the Commandant and remembered seeing me that time when we went round the house. He said that Fayed had wanted him to come and work for him, but he only wanted to retire. He too was staying at the Hotel de la Paix, as a guest of Sotheby's. As previously mentioned, Ofélia, his wife, was wearing a fabulous mink coat which must once have belonged to the Duchess – and, I think, an Hermés scarf.

A Sotheby's executive brought us in past the queue, and when a more switched-on Sotheby's figure recognised the Commandant as a man who was capable of buying a large percentage of the collection with no credit

---

* Later I asked Sir Nicholas Henderson, the British Ambassador, about this medal. It had nothing to do with him. So I asked Lord Charteris, who replied that the simple reason was that the Duchess was entitled to one, so one was sent. Sadly it would have meant nothing to her.
† Olimpia Weiller was a granddaughter of Queen Ena of Spain.

problems at his bank, we were taken behind the cabinets and presently emerald bracelets were being placed round Olimpia's wrist. The Sotheby's man explained the difference between these jewels and those of Mona Bismarck. He said the Duchess needed powerful jewels as a disguise because she was not beautiful. Mona had more delicate ones to complement her beauty. He asked: 'Have you noticed how spiky they are – to keep men away?'[4]

The exhibition was closing and as it did so one or two people arrived who were presumably known to Sotheby's and deemed worthy of a private view. One had a most arrogant step, another looked athletically energetic. Numerous people greeted the Commandant and as we were leaving an ITN man brushed forward and asked me: 'Is the old man a wealthy dealer?' I said: 'No, no!' rather unhelpfully.

The next day I returned alone to place my bids. I multiplied the estimate by nearly ten. When the Sotheby's man of the previous day saw my form, he said: 'Ah! So you really want those . . .' Even so, I was destined to be outbid by over £100,000. Then I returned to London – coincidentally for a dinner given by Maureen Dufferin for the Queen Mother.

The sale took place on that Thursday evening. Next morning I turned on Breakfast TV and astonishing sights met my eyes:

It was fantastic to see the crowd in the marquee with all the telephones and hands popping up. The Princess who'd arrived with two million dollars to buy the yellow diamond got up and walked out disconsolately. Nicholas Rayner looked animated, as well he might have done. What a week it's been in the salerooms – Christie's Van Gogh on Monday, now this.

I knew that the prices for the Duchess's jewels were going to be ludicrous. But I couldn't have encompassed the thought that they would reach thirty-one million pounds by the end of the day.

The dreadful truth is that giving the money to the Louis Pasteur Institute is the best solution. The Prince of Wales, the more natural and obvious recipient, did not need the jewels. Nor could he have sold them. In a museum they would have died.[5]

It was of course a good decision to devote the proceeds of the Geneva sale to the Louis Pasteur Institute – an extraordinary thirty-one million pounds (no doubt after numerous deductions) – but the Duchess can never have suspected her posthumous generosity. Blum had the nerve to go onto French radio shortly after the sale to speak of the Duchess's wish to find a research enterprise of world repute, and, added the Maître, 'contrary to what has been said, she was perfectly *au courant* with what was going on in this field.' She suggested that the Duchess had paid them a visit in about 1970.

The Pasteur Institute is situated at 15 rue du Docteur Roux, not unduly far from the Bois de Boulogne. Yet once again no photographic nor written evidence was produced to support the Duchess's interest. Blum had put the Institut Louis Pasteur in the Duchess's will, but the Duchess had no idea of the implications of them becoming her '*Légateur Universel*' and this of course contradicted the instructions in the Duke's will.

The proceeds of one item in the sale may not have wound up there – Lot 43 – a ruby and sapphire brooch (Cartier, 1936), designed with the initials W & E. As we have seen, this brooch was given to Maître Blum by the Duchess just before she sailed to America in April 1975.

Blum put this brooch into the sale, listed with the other jewels as the property of the Duchess of Windsor. Lot 43 would have fetched somewhat less had it been described as the property of Suzanne Blum, even with its earlier provenance. But that night it was sold to the *Daily Mail* for 132,000 Swiss francs (almost £62,000), one of seven items to be given away in a week-long competition*. I wonder if Maître Blum gave the proceeds to the Louis Pasteur Institute? I wonder where the money went.

At the time of the sale Fayed announced that he had found further jewels at the house in Paris. These he placed in his safe. Nigel Dempster reported: 'The philanthropic Al Fayed has decreed that this intimate collection will never come under the auctioneer's hammer. He is adding them to his collection of Windsors' prized possessions and they will only be available to academics studying the Windsor story.'[6]

These jewels, which were fashion jewellery, were later sold at Sotheby's in New York along with the rest of the Windsors' collection in February 1998.

The outcome of the jewellery sale, which earned so much for the Institut Louis Pasteur, undoubtedly enhanced the posthumous reputation of the Duchess of Windsor. But Blum and Bloch were not able to leave it at that. They had possession of more papers removed from the Windsors'

---

* The *Daily Mail* extracted a comment from Michael Bloch about this jewel. He said: 'You could ask for almost nothing more personal, or more representative of the deep nature of their love, than this piece of work.' He did not mention that it had been the property of Blum for twelve years. It was won by a couple called Percy and Vera Brindley, of Wolverhampton, who were duly photographed 'laughing with delight' and enjoying 'a sparkling celebration'. [*Daily Mail* cuttings, May 1987]. They sold it at Bonham's in 2000, and it sold again at Bonham's on 7 December 2006 for £36,000, just over half of the original sale price.

house and they could not resist the temptation to exploit these. Hardly had a year gone by than another book hit the bookstalls.

The motive for publishing this was that Blum and Bloch knew that Philip Ziegler's official biography of the Duke of Windsor would presently be published, with full use of the Duke's and other papers in the Royal Archives.* They wanted to get their version out first.

In 1987, just before he left Paris, the British Ambassador, Sir John Fretwell, invited himself for tea with Blum. She thought he was coming to thank her for her noble work on behalf of the Windsors. Fretwell had another mission. He did not come with his wife but with a Private Secretary who was clutching an important-looking envelope heavily encrusted with royal coats of arms. He told Blum that the Queen had appointed Ziegler to write the official life of the Duke of Windsor and hoped that she would oblige by allowing him to see any papers in her possession. She refused outright, declaring that she had her own chosen biographer – Bloch. The Ambassador nodded at his Private Secretary, indicating that the envelope should not be handed over: presumably it contained an honour that might have been bestowed on Blum.[7] Panic ensued in the Blum camp.

In July 1988 Bloch published *The Secret File of the Duke of Windsor*, this time with Bantam Press. It was advertised as 'based on fascinating secret papers from the Duke of Windsor's archives, confided many years ago to his lawyers with a view to their eventual publication.'[8] The PR handout further stated: 'It was always the Windsors' intention [*sic*] that the unknown story of their long exile should be told.' As we know, this was not true.

The Secret File was the book in which every possible grievance endured by the Windsors was aired. We learnt that the Duke and Duchess called the Queen Mother 'Cookie' and the Queen 'Shirley Temple'. Bloch quoted the Duke on the death of his mother: 'I'm afraid the fluids in her veins have always been as icy cold as they now are in death.'[9] The Duke was even ruder about his female relations: 'What a smug stinking lot my relations are and you've never seen such a seedy worn-out bunch of old hags most of them have become.'[10] It is unthinkable that either the Duke or Duchess would have descended so low as to put this into the public domain, a view supported by close friends such as Lady Mosley and Lord Tennyson.

Just before the book was published, there was a spat between Michael

---

* This is confirmed by a reference in James Lees-Milne's diary, 3 June 1987. [See *Beneath a Waning Moon*, pp. 186–7].

Thornton and Michael Bloch. In 1985 Michael Thornton had published his book *Royal Feud* (Michael Joseph), which sought to set the Queen Mother and the Duchess of Windsor as bitter adversaries. I assisted Thornton with his book, answering a number of his questions. His book was the cause of one of many enjoyable exchanges with Ali Forbes:

> Ali was on top form . . . I said that Thornton's book, *Royal Feud*, was not bad, but that it was based on a false premise. He agreed: 'A feud must be declared – like the Montagues and the Capulets. The Duchess of Windsor may have had some Montague ancestors, of course, and it may be that through those Bentincks, the Queen Mother had some Dutch Capulets!'
> This was followed by many minutes of laughter at his own joke.[11]

When, in 1983, Bloch heard that Thornton was writing his book, he wrote to him, welcoming what he called 'a demonology' of Queen Elizabeth.[12] In a letter to *The Times*, Thornton pointed out, as so many had before him, that according to long-standing friends of the Windsors, no instructions had been given to publish their correspondence.

Bloch responded that Maître Blum had 'clear authority', bearing the date 17 March 1975, to publish their papers and correspondence.[13] I joined the fray with a letter of my own to *The Times*:

> At last we are told by Mr Bloch (July 4) that a document exists authorising Maître Blum to publish the papers and correspondence of the Duke and Duchess of Windsor. I wonder if scholars will be allowed to see it? Clearly the Duke is absolved from any part in this posthumous publication since the document is evidently dated March 17, 1975 (nearly three years after his death). Likewise the Duchess, who was by then a victim of arteriosclerosis*. I fear the blame must rest with Maître Blum for appointing Mr Bloch to release these letters to the press.[14]

In due course Fayed also joined the attacks on *The Secret File*, accusing Blum of having no right to publish the Windsors' papers. He did so from a position of some strength as he still employed the more faithful members of the Duchess's staff – Sydney Johnson, Maria Costa and Gregorio Martin – all of whom produced signed sworn affidavits.

They stated categorically that the Duchess had not wanted her letters

---

* The popular view, which is denied by Johanna Schütz.

published and that these papers had been removed 'at a time when the Duchess was neither physically nor mentally competent'. Bloch countered with the suggestion that a valet, a chambermaid and a chauffeur could have no 'idea of the private instructions of either the Duke or Duchess'. Blum was tracked down to her country house and stuck to her story that the Duchess had told her and others that the facts needed to be put straight. An ITN crew went down to interview her but, according to the *Sunday Telegraph*, were forced to address her through an intercom until she set her dogs on them.[15]

Immediately Bloch gave a published interview to Catherine Bennett of the *Daily Telegraph*, in which he described the allegations as 'grotesque'. He said he had seen the March 1975 letter authorising Blum to publish. When asked for sight of it, he said: 'It is for Maître Blum to reveal that document.' He told Bennett that it was none of her business where the Duchess's papers were now. He said that the Pasteur Institute was delighted about the publication of his book as some royalties went to them. 'Would it not be a splendid thing' he mused, 'if a cure for AIDS were to be the final result of this book?'

Bloch launched an attack on Fayed. The interview concluded with a public declaration of his love for Maître Blum: 'I fell madly in love with her from the moment I saw her. I thought she was the most beautiful person I'd ever seen. She had amazing bone structure, incredible eyes . . . I love her, really love her. The idea of life without her is killing.'[16]

On 11 August my review of *The Secret File* was published in *The Times*. I referred to my request to see the document. 'I am not wholly surprised that, like previous such challenges, my request has been unanswered.' My conclusion was: 'The cause of the Windsors was ill-served by the publication of this book.'[17]

Michael Thornton declared that the material being published was 'disastrously compromising to both the Duke and Duchess', and went on:

> It seems the ultimate irony that the greatest disservice done to the Duke and Duchess of Windsor should have been performed by the very people who claim to be representing their interests.[18]

This provoked the response from Sir Reginald Hibbert, former British Ambassador in Paris, part of which has already been quoted. He told Thornton: 'My experience taught me in detail all the points which you make in your letter.' He wrote of how Maître Blum had tried to interpose herself between himself and Maître Lisbonne, and between himself and Dr Thin and how he had annoyed her by telling her he did not believe she had a power of attorney 'or had ever held one'.[19]

As to Bloch's publication of *The Secret File*, neither James Lees-Milne nor Diana Mosley was impressed, which was hard, for both were fond of Bloch in their respective ways.

In a diary entry, Lees-Milne opined that, by launching attacks on the Royal Family, Blum and Bloch risked making 'a disagreeable impression on some people'.[20] A few days later he received a letter from Diana Mosley on the same theme. She wrote:

I think Michael Bloch's book goes a bit too far, it would have upset the Duke terribly. Quite right to say how abominably the Windsors were treated but, I do *not* think the letters about his mother's death should have appeared. At least not yet. You see it harms the Duke, not Q. Mary, I'm afraid. I expect he wrote them mostly to amuse the Duchess but to the public they just seem spiteful towards his (admittedly awful) mother.[21]

She returned to the point a while later:

I'm afraid M*e* Blum thinks that any attack on the royal family helps the Windsors, which is of course not true. I regret the letters when horrid old Q. Mary was dying, because although she deserved them for being so ridiculous there's something rather awful about a son writing them at that juncture – I'm sure he only did it to amuse the duchess & never dreamed they'd be published. Anyway Michael says he couldn't as it were *edit* them, which is probably true.

Diana hated the way the reviewers had become increasingly nasty about the Duke, practically accusing him of being a traitor: 'However, posterity will see more clearly perhaps. The Duke was anti-war, *not* pro-German'.[22]

And where did the money from the book go? In his preface Bloch declared that one third of the royalties gleaned from that book would go to the Pasteur Institute for the fight against cancer and AIDS.*[23] Presumably the other two-thirds went to Blum and Bloch. As Ali Forbes put it without contradiction in his *Spectator* review:

---

* The Duchess of Windsor would never have heard of AIDS.

But Blum and Bloch, they 'don't say nothing', they just laugh their way to the bank, whither the money, like the Mississippi to the sea, 'just keeps on rolling along'.[24]

Finally Blum retaliated. She invited Suzanne Lowry, the *Daily Telegraph*'s Paris correspondent, to her country house in Western France to hear her version of the story. Blum told her:

I have a lawyer's mind and everything I tell you I have written evidence to prove. The letters were given to me by the Duchess. I never took anything. The Duchess gave me written authorisation to publish the letters. And, in another earlier letter, she charged me, without limitation of time, to defend her and the Duke's interests.

There is not a scintilla of truth in her declaration. Blum then quoted the Duchess: 'I authorise you, or any person appointed by you, to publish any papers or documents in your possession concerning the Duke or myself which you may consider necessary to defend our memory or reply to our detractors'.

Blum went on to say that the Duchess had been 'furious' about the serialisation of Frances Donaldson's book which made her out to be an adventuress. 'The letters prove the opposite.' She repeated the lie that when the TV series was announced the Duchess asked Maître Blum: 'Can you stop this?' Blum went on to claim that this clinched the Duchess's decision to assign her remaining papers to her. She said that the papers were still in France and belonged to the Pasteur Institute.

The question of the royalties was then aired. As advertised in the book, the Pasteur Institute received 'more than' one-third of the royalties from Bloch's books. Blum said she made no formal claim on profits from the book but received a share of Bloch's royalties in recognition of her 'time and assistance' in their preparation. Bloch said that he was happy to share his royalties: 'Maître Blum sacrificed herself for the Duchess in the last years and was paid little more than her expenses,' he said. As we have seen, she submitted several bills, one of which enabled her to make a down payment on her country house near Niort.

Blum reiterated the old line: 'They had always wanted a book written to tell the full truth of what had happened to them, using the words written at the time, which they thought would carry more weight with public opinion . . . The book that Michael Bloch has written would have pleased them very much.'

She then attacked Lord Mountbatten and accused him of trying to get rid of her. She said he wrote to the Duchess: 'I know you have taken a liking to your lawyer, but she has done nothing for you.'

She related how Mountbatten had tried to set up the Foundation. She retold her version of the Duke's papers going to Windsor, again blaming Mountbatten and asserting that Sir Robin Mackworth-Young had taken away a lorryload of papers without the Duchess's knowledge: 'On December 13th [1972] the Duchess entertained him to a good lunch. But she was not very well and retired to bed afterwards, telling him to search [for any documents] himself and take what he required.'

Blum said he did just that. She claimed that in 1975 the Duchess had discovered the extent of the haul and was furious. They even had the Duchess's divorce papers. In 1977, with the help of Lord Nicholas Gordon Lennox at the British Embassy, there was an exchange of papers. For the business of the papers, Blum was at pains not to blame the Queen. 'The Queen has always behaved perfectly with the Duke and the Duchess,' she said.

As to preventing people visiting the Duchess, Blum claimed that it was not her decision: 'It was the doctor, Jean Thin, who restricted the visitors, not I. The Duchess was very ill. But few people continued to inquire or send flowers. All they wanted to ask at the end was "What has she left me?"'

Blum then addressed the question of the 'clear authority' to publish the letters and papers. She showed Suzanne Lowry a letter from a notary, dated 3 June 1985, in which he confirmed that on 6 May 1985 Blum had deposited such a letter dated 17 March 1975, in which the Duchess gave her permission to publish. Significantly she did not hand over the actual letter or a copy of it.

The interview ended with Blum saying that she defended the Windsors 'because I knew them. Because I had every reason to esteem them. Everything I knew and saw caused me to admire them . . . It really is very difficult for me to understand the continued attacks on them. The Duchess was so simple, so full of goodwill, purity even. They were two innocents . . . I only wish I could have done more . . . The Windsors have many friends who cannot do anything active for them. Michael and I are the last pillars of their defence.'[25]

To state that the Windsors wanted these books published has not been proved and strikes me and many others who knew the Windsors closely as nonsense. Blum was right to attack Mountbatten for much that he did, although ironically what he aimed to achieve was in line with the Duke's wishes. The Duke wanted the money to return to England. Mountbatten's methods, as we have seen, were clumsy. Sir Robin Mackworth-Young behaved perfectly honourably and everything he did was done with the knowledge of the Duchess and her secretaries.

As to the 'clear authority', it was not signed by the Duchess. The initials it bore appear fake, even the typing was different from the way the Duchess's letters were produced. Since the document supposedly initialled by the Duchess in March 1975 was not lodged with the notary until May 1985, that gives a period of ten years in which such a document could be created.

Miss Schütz believed that the initials were written by another hand. For his part in the publication of the Windsor letters Georges was apparently paid a considerable sum, possibly as much as ten per cent of the proceeds.

Failing to abide by the terms of the Duke of Windsor's will, exploiting the Duchess, reinterpreting her wishes, selling her furniture and porcelain, keeping her in her room so that she did not notice what had gone, preventing her from seeing her friends, taking away her beloved pugs and denying her flowers in her bedroom – *this* was Blum's way of 'defending' the Duchess.

I respect most of those who were hostile to Maître Blum, in particular John Utter and Johanna Schütz. Likewise that devoted couple, Monsieur Martin and Maria, who dedicated themselves to the Duchess's day-to-day care. People around the Duchess fell into two categories – those who were loyal to and caring of her, and those who aimed to '*profiter*' from her. Maître Blum was in the latter category.

One more book emerged from the Blum-Bloch stable during the Maître's lifetime, though in the preface Bloch went to pains to state that this work was not one of Blum's commissions.[26]

Bloch had wanted to publish this book earlier, but was diverted by the death of the Duchess into publishing the embarrassing letters. *The Reign and Abdication of Edward VIII* finally came out in April 1990. Again the timing was aimed to pre-empt Ziegler's official biography*, due the following September.

The purpose of his book was to suggest that Edward VIII had decided to abdicate long before most people realised. Bloch made the usual accusations against the present Royal Family, persisting in the suggestion that the Windsors had given Blum their papers and that some of the Duke's had been taken to Windsor 'under irregular circumstances'.[27]

* *King Edward VIII* (Collins, 1990).

I have come to believe that Edward VIII did not want to be king and that the Duchess of Windsor did all she could to prevent the Abdication. Other historians disagree. Sarah Bradford, reviewing this book which she judged 'a bucket going to the well too often', took the line that the King could not believe that the British people would not let him do what he wanted – i.e. to marry the woman he loved and make her his queen. Bradford was harder on Mrs Simpson, blaming her for continually pressing the King to fight for his rights. In the end she thought Bloch was writing with 'a somewhat jaded pen, reworking material from his previous books'.[28]

Following Blum's last public interview, Bloch returned to live in London but remained in touch with his Master. In the summer of 1989 he persuaded her to meet Philip Ziegler who had come to Paris for a tour of the Windsors' house. Ziegler was deeply suspicious of Blum, telling James Lees-Milne that he thought her a woman who had done harm.[29] On this visit he recalled the tap-tapping of her stick and how, in her blindness, she found her way through the apartment by guiding her hands along a rope, stretched from one end to the other. 'It was all very sinister,'[30] he said.

Blum soldiered on. On her ninety-first birthday in November 1989, Bloch found her in excellent form.[31] But in the last three years of her life, from 1991 or so she entered a twilight world of her own beyond conversing. The Duchess was dead, the house had gone to Fayed, the jewels had been sold.

Maître Blum died in Paris on 23 January 1994, at the age of ninety-five. She was accorded substantial obituaries in the British press. The *Daily Telegraph* obituary claimed that she had taken no fees from the Duchess, which was untrue, and she had only survived by selling off an art collection acquired due to the many artists who had been her clients and friends. It conceded that it was mainly in France that she was able to protect her client's privacy, and that her attack on the TV production of *Edward and Mrs Simpson* 'presented its producers with welcome publicity'. It also admitted – at last – that Blum had commissioned Michael Bloch to produce the books – contrary to the many lies that she had told between 1978 and 1988. The most significant line was:

> With characteristic drama she revealed her client had bequeathed her entire estate to the Pasteur Institute, an international medical foundation based in France – *a decision in which Blum may have been influential**.[32]

* My italics.

This is as close to an admission that the Duchess of Windsor had nothing to do with that decision as we will ever achieve. It may explain why Blum never produced a single photograph of the Duchess going round the Pasteur Institute nor any documents signed by the Duchess.

The Times described Blum as 'the self-appointed guardian of the Windsors' privacy', and went on to describe the pre-wedding letters of the Windsors as her counter-offensive to Thames Television's series *Edward & Mrs Simpson*. Their obituarist went on to say that after protracted negotiations the *Daily Mail* 'eventually paid a very large sum of money for the serialisation of the love letters.'

Blum's motives in the publication of these and other 'favourable' biographies of the Windsors was described thus: 'Her constant aim was to prove that the Windsors had been very much more in love to the end of their days and that the Duke had entertained no regrets over abandoning the throne. In this sense, she was a romantic as well as a very hard-headed lawyer.'[33]

I took a sterner line in a signed piece in *The Independent*, describing how Blum took the Duchess over, became 'the guardian of the Duchess in her long decline' and claimed she was 'the Duchess's friend'. I pointed out – then, as now – the contradictions in the statements she made over the years and reminded the readers that by her own admission she profited from the royalties of Bloch's books for her 'time and assistance'. But she might have liked my description of her as 'a striking-looking woman, with the dignity of Queen Mary, her forceful personality veiled by an old-world French courtesy which soon disappeared when journalists telephoned.'[34]

In November 1995 Bloch was summoned to Paris to attend what would have been Blum's ninety-seventh birthday, in the unenticing company of her niece and nephew and her secretary. He dreaded this posthumous party. He heard that her stepdaughter (who was also her heiress) had cleared out Blum's possessions (including his own books which he had left in Blum's office) without consulting him.[35]

Bloch was also concerned by the imminent publication of Caroline Blackwood's book *The Last of the Duchess*. He was annoyed with Diana Mosley for having suggested that the Duchess longed to die but that Blum had been keeping her alive. When he saw the finished product he was horrified, while conceding that Caroline had a gift for identifying what was absurd in peoples' character. He thought he emerged as the kind of aesthete parodied in Gilbert and Sullivan's *Patience*. As for Blum, he thought Blackwood's loathing of her was frightening, but admitted the portrait contained 'a grain of truth.'[36]

Soon afterwards he found himself the object of mirth at lunch in his favoured club, the Savile*. There was worse in store than Caroline's book. When Bloch next went to Paris, he discovered that Blum's papers had been burnt, many of her wishes had been ignored, her heiress had died in a horrible way aged fifty-two and her estate now rested with people she did not like.[37]

It is impossible not to conclude that history had repeated itself.

When the Duchess's centenary loomed, Bloch sniffed the possibility of a substantial advance to write a biography of her to mark this significant anniversary. He was not excited by the prospect, but reckoned he could write a chapter every two days or so.[38] Rereading his works on the Windsors, he was amazed that he had devoted so much of his time to writing about the Duchess whom he now thought shallow and selfish. He had done so because he had been in love with her 'High Priestess' [Maître Blum], who, he maintained was 'neither.'[39]

Unfortunately for Bloch and his agent Andrew Best, no publishers were especially excited by the prospect of a new biography – unless Bloch could come up with a new angle. So Bloch duly produced a new angle. He decided to promote the idea that the Duchess had been a man. He informed James Lees-Milne that Blum believed this and he gave it credence, claiming that it explained why her birth had not been registered and why her first marriage had turned sour so quickly. He proposed to present the Duchess as a modern-day Elizabeth I.

Quite possibly Bloch might not have believed any of this. He was aware, correctly, that he was laying himself open to ridicule. He was not even sure that the money would make his efforts worthwhile.[40]

Bloch went to Paris in November that year with two plans. He hoped to collect a table that had belonged to Daisy Fellowes – said to have been Nelson's map table in the *Victory* – bequeathed to him by Blum, and he intended to visit the Duchess's doctor, Dr Thin, on 8 November. He informed Lees-Milne that he hoped that the Doctor would set him right as to whether or not the Duchess was a man.[41]

In the final version of his book, Bloch made no mention of any visit to Dr Thin, so presumably Thin told him the idea was nonsense. It was certainly what Thin informed James Fox when he was tackled on this issue in *Vanity Fair* some years later: 'That's ridiculous. She was a woman.'[42]

* See Bloch to James Lees-Milne, 26 February 1995 [GEN MSS 476 James Lees-Milne Papers, Beinecke Rare Book and Manuscript Library, Yale].

Bloch's centenary tribute to the Duchess was published in the summer of 1996. I reviewed the book in *The Independent*:

How low can he stoop to gain serialisation for his book? A man who says he is a serious historian cannot make such claims and expect to be taken seriously. Trained as a lawyer, he should have delved a little deeper and had his story categorically denied. Why did he not consult Dr Jean Thin who contributed to his book *The Secret File of the Duke of Windsor*? Thin had the Duchess at his mercy for many years while she was a patient locked from the world in her house in the Bois de Boulogne. He must have examined his comatose patient. He could have clinched the matter at once.

We live in an age of sensation and wherever there is a celebrated story, there is an opening for ludicrous exaggeration. Bloch must have known that his suggestion is rubbish but he cannot resist the tabloid shilling.

I concluded:

What is needed now is not another rehash of the abdication, wrapped up in bizarre theories impossible to substantiate, but a clinical analysis of exactly what did happen in the last days of the Duchess when Maître Blum held sway. It will not make pleasant reading.[43]

Wallis Simpson, sketched by Cecil Beaton on 20 November 1936.

The Duke of Windsor in 1970.

(*Right*) The Duchess, President Richard M. Nixon and the Duke at the White House dinner, 4 April 1970.

(*Left*) The Windsors leaving New York, June 1971. In the background, a security officer and Johanna Schütz.

(*Right*) Empress Nagako of Japan saying farewell to the Duke and Duchess, 4 October 1971. John Utter in the background.

(*Left*) Johanna Schütz with the Duchess, being entertained by the Captain, on board *Michelangelo* in 1974.

(*Right*) The Duchess waving goodbye to the Queen, with Georges and John Utter in the background, 18 May 1972.

(*Left*) The Duke of Edinburgh, the Duchess, the Queen and the Prince of Wales after the visit to the dying Duke.

(*Right*) Johanna Schütz dining with the Duchess on board *Michelangelo* in 1974.

Five photographs of
4 route du Champ
d'Entrainement.
FACING PAGE:
(*Above left*) The staircase
in the hall.
(*Above right*) The staircase
and ceiling.
(*Below*) The library
with the portrait of
the Duchess by
Gerald Brockhurst.
THIS PAGE:
(*Above*) The upstairs
sitting room with the
chair in which the Duke
sat when the Queen
visited him.
(*Right*) The downstairs
salon.

(*Left*) The Duchess at the Duke's grave at Frogmore, with Lord Mountbatten and the Duke of Kent, 11 July 1973.

(*Above*) The last photograph of the Duchess in Britain. The Duke of Kent leading the Duchess from the Royal Burial Ground. Also in the picture, John Utter, Commander Michael Wall, James Fitch and Lord Mountbatten, 11 July 1973.

(*Above*) Return to France, June 1974. Johanna Schütz, John Utter, and the Duchess, all wearing mourning for the Duke of Gloucester who had just died.
(*Below left*) The Duchess's desk in the upstairs sitting room
(*Below right*) Behind Closed Doors. The front door seen from the hall.

(*Above*) The house where she was born.
The cottage at Monterey Inn,
Blue Ridge Summit, Pennsylvania.

(*Left*) The house in the Bois du
Boulogne in which she died.

(*Right*) The bedroom in which the
Duchess spent her last days.

18

The Sale of the Century

When does a story end? Perhaps it never does. I was invited to the Windsors' house in the summer of 1989 to research an article about a little First World War diary of the Duke of Windsor's, which made a slight but entertaining article in *The Mail on Sunday*. By this time Fayed had the lease of the house, and the restoration was well under way.

By then Michael Cole was working for Fayed. He was the bouffant-haired former BBC Court Correspondent who, among other duties, had reported on the Duchess's funeral in April 1986.

Cole had got into trouble at Christmas 1987 when he let slip the contents of a rather controversial Queen's Christmas broadcast, in which she was to refer directly to the IRA's Poppy Day massacre at Enniskillen. Privileged with advance knowledge of the contents of the broadcast, Cole let the cat out of the bag at a lunch attended by a bunch of royal correspondents, including several from tabloid papers. One of the journalists was Andrew Morton, who would later acquire wealth and notoriety as the conduit for the Princess of Wales's revelations about her crumbling marriage.

Morton did not hesitate to go to press with the scoop. Presently the contents of the broadcast, which had been embargoed until Christmas Day, were spread across six tabloids. 'Cole the Mole', as he was inevitably nicknamed by a tabloid, apologised:

I have never been a mole and I never shall be. From the very moment I knew my confidentiality was being betrayed I told the BBC the full facts. I acted with honour whatever others may have done.[1]

Cole was soon 'switched to other duties', but his career at the BBC was effectively over. He was soon lured to work for Fayed. He proved a master at presenting Fayed's case in favourable light to the world, something which would later be put through a test of fire following the death of Fayed's son Dodi, in the car accident with Diana, Princess of Wales in 1997.

Also working for Fayed was Joe Friedman, who was in charge of the redecoration programme. One day in 1989, at the house in the Bois, he told me of the antipathy that Fayed nurtured towards Blum and Bloch. He urged me to stay and meet Fayed:

> The afternoon continued. Al Fayed was due at one, then at four. Eventually he appeared, striding in, alert and energetic in a grey suit. It was not long before we were in the drawing room and he was railing against the lawyers: 'That fucking Maître Blum and that fucking Bloch – what did he do? Was he fucking that woman?' etc. The room into which I first went in May 1972 while the Duke was dying upstairs and the Duchess was trying to get someone for Bridge was now the scene of this energetic Egyptian letting off steam about everything under the sun – the things he was trying to do, the efforts he made, the unfair way the British press treated him – he never drew breath. He would give me the story and I could tell the world. Joe was a bemused witness, never having seen him so animated, and Michael Cole stood in the wings – or once rather crazily lifted his jacket & bent over for Fayed to kick his backside, a gesture of bizarre subservience that was probably more real than it looked.[2]

The display cabinets containing the Windsors' treasures and memorabilia had been beautifully dressed but Fayed wanted everything changed. I watched him go round with Joe, causing hearts to sink left and right. The labels had to be redone, the clothes cabinets must be crowded with gloves; more cabinets were to be placed in the hall. It was like a whirlwind – everyone jumping around and all for no point. In the end nothing would change that much. In due course Fayed departed, his two girls in tow, Michael Cole at hand. Joe breathed a sign of relief and the Duchess's servants collapsed in the kitchen, sitting around in an end-of-day huddle.[3]

Later in 1989 the house was ready for its grand opening. Jacques Chirac, then Mayor of Paris, presented Fayed with a Grande Plaque and a generous speech: 'In 1986, the Duchess died, and with her the last symbol of a great love story which set the whole world dreaming. Through you, Mr Al Fayed, a fragment of the history of Paris and that of England has been restored, reinstated – indeed, rescued – from what would have been, without your intervention, a disastrous loss.'[4]

As a result of meeting Fayed's curator Christiane Sherwen I was invited to write a book about the house, eventually entitled *The Private World of the Duke and Duchess of Windsor* (published in 1995). By this time Georges and Ofélia were long gone from the house, Sydney had died, and Monsieur Martin, the former chauffeur, was more benignly in charge, with Maria, who had nursed the Duchess during her long illness.

The inspiration for that book was the discovery of a cache of photographs in the Duke of Windsor's bath. When the Duchess fell ill, her bedroom was converted into a kind of hospital room as a result of which much of her furniture was piled up in the Duke's bathroom. As the Duke never took a bath, preferring a shower, his bath was covered with a wooden lid. In the bath were concealed a huge number of photographs. The inaccessibility of the room prevented Maître Blum from finding these pictures. It is curious that Georges was not aware of them, though Monsieur Martin, never a great fan of Maître Blum or her team, clearly was.

The writing of the book gave me the opportunity to explore the house from top to bottom, though I never went into the top-floor rooms. I spent many hours in the main rooms, including the Duke and Duchess's bedrooms and bathrooms. I looked in the cupboards, and I spent a long time inspecting the items that had been placed in glass cabinets in the museum part (the former office and the basement rooms). It was like returning to the stage of a theatre after the curtain had fallen and the principal actors had gone home. In my enjoyable task I was much supported by Christiane Sherwen, an able and straightforward editor.

In due course the book was finished and went to Mr Fayed for his scrutiny. Soon afterwards Christiane had to rescue the project when one of Fayed's team – possibly Dodi Fayed – criticised my text on the grounds that the Duke of Windsor should be made to appear more like James Bond. The text was eventually published as written.

It was apparently never possible to open the house to the public as a museum but certain groups were allowed to make special visits. Anyone who saw it had the opportunity to observe at first hand the vestiges of a miniature court in exile, filled with the symbols of royalty, and the place where two people who had rocked the world in 1936 had spent their twilight years. After my book, *The Private World*, came out, I conducted two tours around the house for the benefit of Parisian journalists. I was allowed to invite Johanna Schütz whom I had not seen for twenty years. She returned to the house and was warmly greeted by Monsieur Martin and Maria. She said later that the visit had helped to exorcise the unpleasant memories of her last years working there.

Why did Fayed undertake this restoration? Reading the well-controlled publicity, it is clear that by so doing he believed he was doing something that would endear him to the British Establishment and the Royal Family.

The restoration was completed in 1989 and my book was published in 1995. I had not realised that *The Private World* had been commissioned to drum up interest in the Windsors and their collection in advance of a proposed sale of all these effects in 1997. Fayed may well have wanted to preserve it all. In one sense understandably, he tired of living above a museum. For whatever reason, he decided to dispose of the contents.

In the summer of 1997 my wife and I were invited to a dinner to be given by Mr Fayed at the house. A quarter of a century after the Duchess had been looking for a spare man, here was my chance to dine at her table, albeit not with her as hostess. In addition to this, Michael Cole invited me to record some words for a 'home movie' about the Windsors to be made by Desmond Wilcox. We arrived in Paris and were given a magnificent room at the Ritz, overlooking the Place Vendôme.

While my wife went to have her hair done at Monsieur Alexandre's famous salon, I was taken to the house and placed in a chair in the Duke of Windsor's library. I was then interviewed about the Windsors, the Abdication and their later life. Anyone who appreciates my long years of interest in the Windsors will understand how surreal this was. Wilcox was a good interviewer, and although I was annoyed to find out later that this was for no home movie but for a TV documentary entitled *Going, Going, Gone* . . . I was pleased with the way the interview had gone. In no way do I regret doing it.

But it was an odd experience to give a filmed interview in that house which had occupied my thoughts for so long. I had seen it when the Duke was alive, when the Queen was expected; I had seen it in the days when the Duchess was a widow, but still active; I had once been there when she was lying ill upstairs; I had looked over the wall so many times in the dark years; and finally I had been allowed in to explore it.

Fayed hosted the dinner party that evening. Before dinner he came into the salon and launched into a diatribe against the Windsors. I thought at the time that that was probably why he needed Michael Cole as his PR. Cole could translate his words into elegant phrases for the world at large – as 'Mohamed's deep respect for the greatest love story of the century.'

One of the guests was Ghislaine de Polignac*, a friend of the Windsors. I had met her several times at Paul-Louis Weiller's villa in the South of

---

* Princesse Ghislaine de Polignac (1918–2011), Ghislaine Brinquant, m. 1939 Prince Edmond de Polignac (1914–2010), divorced 1946. Veteran of the social world of Paris, and at one time a mistress of Duff Cooper. In 1947 she was sent to America to launch Dior's New Look. She stayed with Mr and Mrs Norman Winston, had an affair with the former. As Lady Diana Cooper put it: 'I'm awfully sorry for her. True, in 100,000,000 Americans she was foolish to pick Mr Winston, but poor girl to have to crawl back to Rheims, tail gripped between those ungovernable legs. Humiliation.' [Lady Diana Cooper to Cecil Beaton, 30 January 1948].

France. She was more canny than I. She wondered why we were all dining there. Of our host she said: 'He is an Egyptian. When you and I give a party, we give a party. With an Egyptian there is always a reason. They are very complicated. We may never find out what the reason is, but you be sure, there is a reason. *Ah oui!*'[5]

The reason soon became clear. This was to be the last-ever dinner party at the Windsors' table, with their plates and glasses. The following day, the packers arrived and took the house apart, boxing up most of the Windsors' contents for the secretly planned sale in New York.

The house would have cause for one last flurry of attention when, a few weeks later, on 30 August, Dodi Fayed brought Diana, Princess of Wales, to have a brief look round it, on the fateful Saturday afternoon before the night of the tragic accident in which they both lost their lives.

The Duke and Duchess of Windsor sale in New York was postponed until February 1998, on account of the death of Diana, Princess of Wales and Dodi Fayed. It was not without controversy. Maîtres Jean Lisbonne and Paul Bailly, both of whom had worked with Blum and described themselves as '*Exécuteurs Testamentaires de la Duchesse de Windsor*' made a joint eleventh-hour protest against the sale. They claimed that when Fayed took over the lease of the house and bought the furniture, allegedly for fifteen million French francs, he had promised to retain the house as an historical monument in memory of the Windsors. Evidently he was prevented by contract from selling furniture for five years, and if he did so thereafter it was to be without publicity. There were questions about the terms of the transfer of the lease to Fayed.[6] Nothing came of any of this.

Before I flew to New York a journalist asked me if I thought the Queen would buy the Abdication desk. I replied: 'The Queen needs a desk to work on, not to abdicate on.'[7]

The sale had been well hyped. Parties had been given to lure the bidders in. One was for New York ladies who owned pugs. Behind the rostrum hung the Munnings of the Duke on horseback; his Garter banner hung high in the room and there were two huge images of the Duke and Duchess, ironically printed back to front.

The punters were a mixture of dealers (some respectable, some creepy), eager amateurs (practising how to bid, putting their paddles up before the sale began in order to see how it was done), and one or two smart people as well as some sweet-looking couples hoping for whatever they might get. There were many 'Hicksville' types, too – the overall effect was depressing.

Watching the sale, I concluded that for whatever reason many of the punters just wanted to grab something, anything. They did not know what it was but they knew they had to have it. Items with coronets sold well, as did things bearing the initials 'E' or 'W'. So did anything symbolising or representing pugs. Cecil Beaton's two sketches made new world-record prices ($134,500 and $178,500), which was pleasing to those of us like me who already owned Beaton sketches of the Duchess of Windsor from the same sitting*.

The Munnings went for $2,312,500, and a girl from the National Portrait Gallery in London bought the Brockhurst of the Duchess for $107,000, the Gallery claiming that they were keen to own a good Brockhurst. There were the crazy bids – a ducal telephone fetching $5,500. I spotted the green sign announcing '*chien méchant*' in French and English. It was not in the catalogue. It was now planted in a flowerpot. I remembered it from my first-ever walk up the drive to the house in 1972. Surely that would slip through the net? But alas! 'Wait till you see what this goes for!' announced the auctioneer, and after heated bidding the hammer fell at $4,000. My paddle was not even raised.

A Dior scarf went for $2,000 and the funeral hat by Givenchy for $9,550. It was bought by a youngish man with a pale green face. On the way out, he volunteered that he had tried to buy the inscribed box containing some 1937 wedding cake (which went for $29,900): 'I tried to buy into the beginning of the story but failed, so I bought into the end of the story instead.'[8] I shared a Lot containing towels and bathmats with a friend, paying rather over the odds for them.

I wanted a Dmitri Bouchène gouache from the Duchess's bathroom. In 1990 I had bought one that belonged to Garbo; in 1991 I had bought three in Monte Carlo in the Boris Kochno sale. Then I had discovered that this curiously talented yet largely unknown Russian artist, who had worked with Diaghilev and the Ballets des Champs-Élysées, had decorated the Duchess's bathroom in Paris.

The Bouchène lots came up for sale. I let one lot go by for $2,250, then got the next two Lots for $2,750 each and finally another lot for $750. The Bouchènes did not appeal to the souvenir hunters who quested and bid for porcelain pugs and items with obvious royal connections. I went specially to New York determined to buy one Bouchène but the competition was slight. I came home with twenty. I notice them every day and will take them – or good copies of them – with me to the old folks' home, if that is my eventual fate.

---

* I bought mine in London in February 1983 for £270.

To me they symbolise the best of the Parisian taste of the Duchess of Windsor, a woman of style and elegance – a woman who had suffered too long, but who was at last beyond the grasp of those who had harmed her.

Part Two – The Life

Miss Wallis Warfield

Wallis Simpson was one of the most maligned women of the twentieth century. In many quarters she was held responsible for causing the Abdication. She was blamed as 'the woman who stole the King'. When an event of such magnitude occurred, everyone with a passing knowledge of her, or acquaintance with her, had the perfect excuse to advance a theory, usually to her discredit.

Inevitably biographers have criticised her. The intelligent and Establishment writers are well educated, they read serious books and some enjoy the arts in their highest form. They have a tendency to look down on one whose main literary enjoyment was a detective story, who eschewed the opera, who was no great attender at art galleries and did not involve herself in cultural activities.

Philip Ziegler, the Duke of Windsor's official biographer who did not care for her much, nevertheless believed that she had been the victim of 'so much speculation, so much lurid and unbridled fantasy'.[1] Ziegler, who was obviously more concerned in his book with Edward VIII himself, portrayed Mrs Simpson as ambitious, harsh and ruthless.

Greg King, an apologist biographer, went perhaps too far in the other direction, particularly when comparing the Duchess to the Queen Mother during the Second World War. The gist of his message was that Queen Elizabeth was 'richly attired' during her visits to the East End, seldom took her gloves off and did not attempt to involve herself in the kind of unpopular projects that the Duchess tackled in the Bahamas: 'The smiling face of the Queen, with her steely determination, was featured around the world in photographs and newsreels . . .'

Wallis, by contrast, 'rarely carried out any of her work in the public eye; she certainly never publicised – in ways which the Royal Family, with their advisers, actively sought to do – her work as an example of her personal sacrifice and devotion to the war effort. She saw what needed doing and did it without concern for the consequences to her reputation'.[2]

Reading the Abdication papers today, all of which are now available in the National Archives, it is interesting to see the contempt in which Mrs Simpson was held, even in the minds of sober-minded rational figures operating in public life. There are times when she is portrayed as some sort of Mata Hari figure. Sir Horace Wilson, the distinguished civil servant who was Stanley Baldwin's personal adviser throughout the crisis, wrote of the King's 'subservience to Mrs Simpson's wishes', how 'the King's infatuation with Mrs Simpson was such as to make him quite oblivious of the realities of the situation and to make him incapable of seeing any other considerations in the proper perspective,' and suggested that she was the reason that there had been no intimate meetings between the Prince of Wales and his brothers for two years prior to the Abdication.

Sir Horace went on to ask how a woman who had 'real affection' for a man could allow him to make such a mess of his life. Though she offered to 'fade away' during the crisis, she immediately withdrew the offer. Wilson believed that she only renounced the King in a public statement as she was frightened for her safety in Cannes and wanted to be sure that the King took sole responsibility for the Abdication. Sir Horace maintained that she showed no affection for Edward and was only trying to feather her nest. He thought she dominated his mind, that he lavished jewels on her on her demand, that she boasted she could do 'what she liked' with the King yet held him in contempt. 'There are those', he noted, 'who called her a gold-digging adventuress'. Sir Horace concluded:

> To know all is to forgive all, and all is not known: but subject to that, the conclusion seems to be – selfish, self-seeking, hard, calculating, ambitious, scheming, dangerous.[3]

Wilson was not a man given to exaggeration. Many shared these views which he consigned to paper in 1936 or soon after. Over a great many years intelligent people have advanced bizarre theories about this woman, the craziest being that of Lady George Cholmondeley who appeared to believe that Mrs Simpson was sent to Britain by an alien power to hypnotise the Prince of Wales, that he was terrified of her and begged people to keep her away from him but that eventually she managed to insinuate herself into his bedroom and, following that, he was enslaved to her and obsessed by her for life.[4]

Fortunately, there are contradictory versions from others who knew Wallis personally. At the time, Winston Churchill wrote: 'No one has been more victimised by gossip and scandal.' He was impressed by her effect on the King:

He delighted in her company, and found in her qualities as necessary to his happiness as the air he breathed. Those who knew him well and watched him closely noticed that many little ticks and fidgetings of nervousness fell away from him. He was a completed being instead of a sick and harassed soul.

Churchill believed: 'The association was psychical rather than sexual, and certainly not sensual except incidentally.'[5]
Cecil Beaton wrote of the Windsors:

History will make his story into a romance. In fact, for us so close it is hard to see that. Wallis has been a good friend to me. I like her. She is a good friend to all her friends. There is no malice in her. There is nothing dislikeable. She is just not of the degree that has reason to be around the Throne.[6]

At the Duke's funeral Beaton blamed him for what had happened:

The most moving sight was to see carried on cushions the orders that he now in death had to give up – the diamond-embroidered Garter.
These of such inherent grandeur, such dignity, that one was reminded of Shakespeare's Kings and Princes, and they made one feel that the fair-haired Prince had not been the stuff of history, that he was the perfect young Prince of Wales, with charm and a smile for all, but that his tastes and life were not of a high quality and that it was inevitable that he should fail in his duty.[7]

Many give testimony to Wallis's style and consideration. Marjorie Merriweather Post's granddaughter was in serious trouble with her grandmother and about to be cut out of her will for a series of youthful crimes at school. A lunch was arranged in New York at which the child was to be told her fate. The Duchess of Windsor was in the same restaurant and, after talking to the child briefly, she extolled her virtues to Mrs Post, as a result of which she was given a vital second chance.[8]
Lady Diana Cooper said that people sharpened up when Wallis Simpson entered a room. She brought out the best in them, and her last secret-

ary, Johanna Schütz, recalled the effect she had on strangers even in old age. There were times when people saw the Duchess, this small, not beautiful woman and, though they had no idea who she was, they were mesmerised by her.[9]

Birth

Wallis's father, Teackle Wallis Warfield (known as T. Wallis), was born on 8 February 1869 and lived in Baltimore with his young wife Alice Montague. Frail in health, he was virtually unemployable and the family looked after him by giving him a job as a clerk in one of their businesses. Many were surprised and some thought it unwise when he married Alice, albeit in a quiet ceremony in Baltimore, on 19 November 1895. Alice was soon pregnant. One Warfield relation suggested it was a shotgun wedding.

In the summer of 1896, to avoid the heat of Baltimore, T. Wallis and his pregnant wife left the city and took the little train up into the hills where the air was purer and life more tranquil. Baltimore is hardly a bustling place these days, but Blue Ridge Summit was far from the everyday stresses of that life. The Warfields took over a cottage in the grounds of the Monterey Inn.

I was working in the Maryland Historical Society in Baltimore, to which I had allocated two days in my quest to discover more about the young Wallis. Robert Nedelkoff, whose encyclopaedic knowledge has enriched many a book, proposed that we should make the journey to Wallis's birthplace on the Saturday afternoon. He and his wife picked me up and we drove for about an hour and a half into Pennsylvania, a gentle climb into the hills. There are not many residents in the vicinity, and none were in evidence, but we happened on Mr Ed Orndorff who announced that he was one of the few people living there who knew where the 'Wallis Warfield foundation' was. I had never heard of such a thing. But he meant the site of the old house.

He took us to a neighbour's garden where once the cottage had stood, a detached two-storey building built of wood, with a balustraded balcony on the upper floor. All that remains now are a few slates scattered in the undergrowth.

Wallis was born at the cottage near the Monterey Inn on 19 June 1896. Her paternal grandmother was at the Inn itself and Aunt Bessie Merryman (Alice's sister) and her husband were lodged nearby. Wallis and her parents returned to Baltimore at the end of September. T. Wallis, suffering gravely from tuberculosis, passed his last days in a wheelchair and died soon afterwards on 15 November at his mother's house, 34 East Preston Street. The local paper reported: 'Mr Warfield had been in failing health for about a year, and his death was not unexpected.'[10]

The day after my visit to Blue Ridge Summit, Zippy Larson, who conducts a Duchess of Windsor tour in Baltimore, drove me to Green Mount Cemetery, not far from Wallis's old home in Biddle Street. There we found a cache of Warfield graves, right in the centre of the cemetery with views down a sweeping hill. A large cross marked WARFIELD stands in the centre. Gathered round it were the small, unremarkable gravestones of Wallis's grandfather, Henry Mactier Warfield, her father (though not her mother), and various uncles and aunts. Had things evolved differently the Windsors might have lain there too.

In the 1950s the Duke and Duchess came to Baltimore by train and asked their friend, Clarence W. Miles*, for a private discussion. Miles engaged a private dining room at the Elkridge Club. The Duke then told him that they had decided they wished to be buried together in that cemetery. Miles recorded:

> They wanted to purchase a large lot in a good location. The lot was to be large enough for landscaping around the edges. To say I was astounded by the request is putting it mildly, but the next day I put one of my law associates to work on the request. Under his name, I purchased an appropriate lot in a good location and informed the Windsors.[11]

Had the Windsors died in the 1950s the Duchess would have returned to her home town. I had always thought that while the Duke was in the London Clinic in 1965 he had asked the Queen if he could be buried with the Duchess in a private mausoleum at Frogmore. But records in the National Archives now prove that his funeral plans had been fully resolved as early as 1961. Yet maybe there was still some tweaking of the final arrangements. In 1968, when watching Princess Marina's coffin being lowered into the ground in the Royal Family's private burial ground at Frogmore, the Duke was drawn to the quiet tranquillity of the place, in the shadow of Queen Victoria's Mausoleum. In August 1970 it was agreed that both the Duke and Duchess would be buried there instead, near the graves of his family – closest, as it happens, to his brother the Duke of Kent.

---

*Clarence W. Miles (1897–1977), married Eleanor Addison Williams (1902–99), widow of Wallace Lanahan. They are both to be found in Green Mount Cemetery.

Ancestry and Relations

The Duchess descended twice over from Henry III on her father's side. I can trace the Warfields back to 1465 or so in Berkshire, and the Montagues to about 1505, also in Berkshire (see Appendix I and Appendix II). Casting his Proustian eye towards the Duchess of Windsor's antecedents, Alastair Forbes commented that they came from a higher stratum in American society than 'say, Princess Grace of Monaco, Jacqueline Bouvier or the Jerome or Vanderbilt ladies of the nineteenth century. By present English standards [1974] she might rank rather below two recent royal duchesses and rather above two others*.'[12]

The Warfields were a prominent Maryland family, who had been among the early Anne Arundel settlers who came up from Virginia. Scott Watkins, one of the Duchess's distant cousins, spoke of the Warfields' pride in their heritage:

The geography of Maryland is often described as America in miniature. The same is true of its history. In military, civil, commerce, medicine, agriculture and social, the Warfields were great leaders and contributors to Maryland. Bessie Wallis and all Warfield descendants are the sum total of early British immigrants who helped build an empire in the New World.

Being brought up with that sense of history allowed them to overcome many barriers, both social and economic. In Maryland, as in Britain, it was not so much about money but more about background.[13]

Cleveland Amory[†], a respected historian of social America, wrote: 'The Warfields had a certain amount of Yankee prominence, having made their money after the unpleasantness of the 1860s.'[14] Their fortunes prospered in the care of Hon. Henry Mactier Warfield, Wallis's grandfather, a successful grain merchant, imprisoned in 1861 for his Southern sympathies. One of those in prison with him was Severn Teackle Wallis, after whom he named Wallis's father. There is a statue of him in Mount Vernon Square in Baltimore.

---

* I surmise that Ali referred to Princess Marina, Duchess of Kent and Princess Alice, Duchess of Gloucester as the first two, and the present Duchesses of Kent and Gloucester as the other two.
† Cleveland Amory (1917–98), author of *The Proper Bostonians* (1947), *The Last Resorts* (1952), and *Who Killed Society?* (1960). In 1955 he worked as ghost on the Duchess's memoirs, but withdrew from the commission, one of the reasons being that every time he put a joke into the text the Duke struck it out. Also a keen animal rights activist.

Later Wallis's grandfather became a director of the Baltimore & Ohio Railroad and one of the first Presidents of the Chamber of Commerce. He travelled all over the world and was one of the first Americans to establish a business house in Australia. He established the Baltimore and Havana Steamship Company.

In 1850 he married Anna (Gittings) Emory, of Manor Glen and My Lady's Manor, whose family had come from England in 1666. They had seven children. Like Henry, Anna descended from Henry III.

When Henry Mactier Warfield died on 17 January 1885, a contemporary report declared: 'Always bright, always cheery, always seeking to do what he could to advance the interests of the city, he numbered among his friends many of the most prominent citizens of Baltimore of both political parties, and was especially liked by the working people whose cordiality he had won by his frank and genial ways and by his liberality, to the extent of his means.'[15]

Of Wallis's uncles, two were significant – Uncle Sol and Uncle Harry. Solomon Davies Warfield went into manufacturing (corn cutters and silkers) and later into politics and banking. Among considerable business interests, he was involved in the formation of the Seaboard Air Line Railway Company in 1900.

Significantly, he lived as a bachelor with his mother at 34 East Preston Street. When he died in October 1927 he had, as we shall see, a nasty surprise for Wallis and her cousins. Sol's obituary highlighted interesting contradictions in his character:

> A remarkable man. Not free from deserved criticism, sometimes approaching the ruthless in his methods, he was one of the constructive forces produced by this community, and the work of his hand is to be found far beyond the borders of his Native state.[16]

Uncle Harry – General Henry Mactier Warfield, Jr – was the Baltimore representative of the Royal Fire Insurance Company. He had served in Cuba in the Spanish War of 1898. He and his wife Rebecca Denison lived at Salona Farms, a working farm near Long Crandon, in Harford hunting country.[17] Their daughter Anita* was to be Wallis's closest childhood companion.

Wallis came from a well-off family, though sadly her father was not one of the rich ones. Ill health prevented him from earning a good living

---

*Anita Warfield (1892–1969), married Zachary R. Lewis. The Windsors once stayed at their farm on Jarrettsville Pike. The Elkridge-Harford Hounds hunt through the property.

as many of them did and his early death from tuberculosis left Wallis's mother dependent on the kindness of disapproving in-laws.

Alice or Alys Montague, Wallis's mother, came from a no less well-born family, though Cleveland Amory was dismissive, describing them as 'an old but unimpressive Virginia clan'.[18] In England an ancestral cousin was Richard Montague, Bishop of Norwich and a Canon of St George's Chapel, Windsor. He would have been surprised by the circumstances that brought Wallis to St George's Chapel for the Duke's funeral in 1972 and her own in 1986.

Wallis's maternal grandfather, William Latané Montague, moved to Baltimore when he was twenty-four and became a clerk with Harrison & Co., a packaged dry-goods house. In 1852 he went into the insurance business. On 25 February 1858 he married Sally Howard Love and they began their married life in Baltimore.

In 1865 William moved into sugar and coffee trading, and then, in 1867, he moved to New York and became a stockbroker. William and Sally had two sons and three daughters amongst whom was the famous Aunt Bessie, who was born on 19 August 1864, and Wallis's mother Alice, born on 30 November 1869. At the time of Alice's birth the family were living at Hackensack, Bergen County, New Jersey, but in 1876 William returned to Baltimore where he continued to be a stockbroker. Then in 1891 he returned to Richmond, Virginia, to engage in mercantile pursuits.

Sally died in New York in 1876. Like the Warfields, she is buried in Green Mount Cemetery, Baltimore. William remarried in 1888 and died in 1909.

Doug St Denis, granddaughter of Wallis's cousin, Corinne Mustin, says of the family:

> A trait of Montague women was that they were adventurers. Alice and her daughter, Wallis, wanted so much to be a part of and live up to the Montague family legacy but were thwarted at nearly every turn by uncertainty and reduced financial circumstance ... Aunt Bessie's life's work was to support and defend Wallis. She could depend on her. So too could her cousins, Corinne Mustin and Lelia Montague Gordon Barnett.[19]

Lelia and Corinne were sisters and they were Wallis's first cousins once removed. They were two of the three famous Montague beauties of Richmond and Baltimore. Lelia was considerably older than Corinne who, in turn, was nine years older than Wallis. As she grew up, Wallis formed a bond of sympathy with the two sisters that she never achieved with her Warfield relations. There was a lot of fun and witty conversation. She felt she could trust them and they liked her.

Both sisters led fulfilling lives with distinguished husbands and both played an important role in Wallis's early life. They were daughters of Walter Powhatan Montague ('Uncle Pow'), the very much younger brother of Wallis's Montague grandfather.

Lelia was first married in 1895 to the immensely rich Basil B. Gordon, State Senator in Virginia, Chairman of the State Democratic Committee and a poet. He died in 1901 and, as a young widow, Lelia then married in 1908 Major-General George A. Barnett, twelfth Commandant of the US Marine Corps during 1914–20. Their country home was a substantial house, Wakefield Manor in Huntly, Rappahannock County, which Lelia inherited from Gordon and where they entertained extensively, giving weekend parties, balls and garden parties. Mrs Barnett, it was said, 'was never happy unless she is in the midst of excitement.'[20] She had two daughters, another Lelia and Anne, a poet like her father, both married. At one time Anne fell in love with Newbold Noyes, associate editor of the *Washington Evening Star** (and likewise married), but in 1935, after multiple divorces, he married her sister Lelia instead.

Corinne was first married in 1907 to Captain Henry C. Mustin, First Commandant of the Naval Air Station, Pensacola, and Naval Aviator no. 11, known as 'the Father of Naval Aviation'. In 1915 he became the first man to climb into a plane and be launched by a catapult from the deck of a ship. He died due to the effects of an accident when rescuing a drowning sailor.

After his death in 1923, the stylish Mrs Mustin, known as an inveterate traveller, married in 1925 Admiral George D. Murray, US Navy, also a pioneer aviator and a friend of Henry Mustin. In May 1942 he was awarded the Navy Cross by Admiral Nimitz for a raid that his ship, the *Enterprise*, had conducted on the Marshall Islands. George Murray accepted the Japanese surrender on behalf of the C-in-C Pacific Fleet in the Second World War.

* * *

* Noyes had a sister, Ethel, a great friend of Wallis's in Washington – she married Sir Willmott Lewis, Washington correspondent of *The Times*. At the time of the Abdication Noyes offered to help improve her image in the US press. The King thought this might help and Noyes was invited to the Fort where he had off-the-record discussions with both Wallis and the King. After the Abdication, he saw the chance of a scoop and published a series of articles which appeared to be an authorised account of the love affair. The Duke of Windsor was furious and the Duchess issued a disclaimer. She never spoke to Noyes again.

Much has been written about the difficult childhood that Wallis endured. Short of money, she was left in little doubt that she was the poor relation. Biographers tend to blame her and her mother for this. It was hardly her fault, but they see her as growing into a jealous girl, determined to improve herself and shine among her contemporaries. Doug St Denis said: 'Whatever was going on at every stage of Wallis' life (and let's face it, she WAS an adventurer, and a fairly fearless one at that – a trait of Montague women!) she always knew she had family she could depend on – not on the Warfield side, however, according to my Montague forebears'.[21]

It is hard to establish the truth about the young Wallis. Most biographers rely on her memoirs, which were ghosted. I too found them a useful source, but quite soon warning bells began to sound. First there was Frances Donaldson, still the best biographer of the Duke, who was swayed by reading the volumes of the Duchess's published letters. Until then she had thought that the Duchess had found a safe harbour with Mr Simpson: 'I thought her sights were not set inordinately high, and that, but for the accident of meeting Lady Furness and through her the Prince of Wales, she might have been content with her second husband for the rest of her life.'[22] After reading the published letters, Frances Donaldson wrote: 'I realise that I believed exactly what she wanted me to believe.'[23]

I was made suspicious by reading Cleveland Amory's account of his attempts to ghost the Duchess's memoirs. His project began badly when he suggested that the book should be called 'Untitled'. For obvious reasons this hit a raw nerve with both the Duke and the Duchess.

Amory only worked with the Duchess during the summer of 1955, after Charles Murphy dropped out. Then he too abandoned the project. He found that the Duchess would tell him contradictory versions of the same story. He outlined his main problem as ghost – 'how to get rid of the Duchess's two husbands prior to the Duke . . . they were the real stumbling block to her becoming Queen of England.'*[24] Amory claimed that he told the Duchess that faults should be assigned to her two husbands, 'faults so terrible that the reader would not only understand why she eventually had to divorce them, but would also understand how, in contrast to them, the Duke, who, though he had a fair share of faults of his own, would somehow be believable as the true love of her life.'[25] Though the Duchess finally worked with yet another ghost, it is likely that the accounts in her memoirs were still exaggerated.

---

* I do not believe that she wanted to become Queen of England.

Cleveland Amory knew survivors of Wallis's Baltimore childhood. He was told that while other children said 'Ma-Ma' she said 'Me-Me', that her dolls were called Mrs Astor and Mrs Vanderbilt, and that the reason that she was spoiled was because her mother indulged her, where richer children had stern governesses to discipline them.[26]

As Wallis grew up, she was spoken of as something of a magnet to boys. In later life, one old boyfriend called Carter Osburn told biographers that he had found Wallis an expensive date.

On a visit to Baltimore in the early 1970s Frances Donaldson met a number of the Duchess's surviving girlfriends and concluded that none of them had liked her much though they kept on terms with her because she drew the boys. Like other biographers, Frances Donaldson detected 'a strong desire to dominate . . . the evidence of the Duke's willing subjection to her is extremely convincing and spoken of in all the books of those who knew them personally.'[27] She discussed the psychological issue of the relationship with Peter Scott, the psychologist who advised the police on psychological warfare against men holding hostages, and his theory was that the Duke of Windsor would have needed to find a woman who had the same kind of bullying father as he had.

Wallis's father was rather gentle and died too young to have any influence on her. In her case the bullying role fell to her bachelor Uncle Sol, who adored his mother and to whom it fell to educate her, either pay for parties or deny them, and later to inform her that she had brought disgrace on the Warfield name.

Frances Donaldson had more to say on all this, leading to the conclusion that Wallis grew up seeking protection and failed to find it with her first husband, who was an alcoholic, or even with nice Mr Simpson. Finally she found financial security with the Duke of Windsor, but in the end, as we shall see, she believed that the Duke of Windsor also let her down.

Following the death of her father, Wallis and her mother lived with old Mrs Warfield at her home on Preston Street where Uncle Sol also resided. Wallis found Uncle Sol 'reserved, unbending, silent'. But despite having absorbed much of the Warfields' strict approach to life, she found that her grandmother 'retained within herself some of the Emory softness and gentleness that warmed what otherwise would have been a cold house.'[28] The young Wallis was fond of an old Irish nurse called Joe and Uncle Sol's valet-footman, the asthmatic negro Eddie.

The family were presently on the move, the Duchess of Windsor attributing this to Uncle Sol having fallen in love with her frivolous mother. They transferred to an hotel and later lived with Aunt Bessie. They spent some time in the Preston Apartment House, finally settling at 212 East Biddle Street, a small red-brick house in a pleasant residential area. These houses all had marble steps, which the coloured maids washed down every morning.

The novelist Upton Sinclair was a nephew of Lelia Sinclair, wife of Wallis's great-uncle, 'Uncle Pow' Montague. He attributed Wallis's sense of humour to Uncle Pow, a figure of some romantic interest, who had entered the Confederate Service at the outbreak of the Civil War and served until General Lee surrendered. He was hopeless at making or keeping money but full of fun and mischief. Hearing that Wallis was later an imaginative cook, preparing 'strange and thrilling things for after-theater supper parties at her home', Sinclair recalled that Uncle Pow's greatest gift was as a chef. Sinclair summed up Baltimore life at that time:

> It seems to me that there were just three subjects talked about in Baltimore; the first was who married whom, and the second was clothes, and the third was good things to eat.

Expanding on this, he recalled Maryland beaten biscuits, and how, when Uncle Pow asked his black cook how she made them, she replied: 'Ah wuks 'em till dey pops, Marse Pow, Ah wuks 'em till dey pops'.[29]

The activities of the Warfields were duly recorded in the society pages of the Baltimore papers – Lelia and Anne Barnett at Mrs Barnett's country home in Virginia, Wakefield Manor, and 'their young cousin, Wallis Warfield, of Baltimore, and several of their schoolmates . . .' When her cousin Lelia, a young widow, married Lt-Colonel George Barnett, US Marine Corps, at a brilliant society wedding at Christ P. E. Church in January 1908, the outfits of the guests were noted in full, including that of Wallis's mother, Mrs T. Wallis Warfield, dressed, surely without prescience in a 'handsome gown of pale gray satin striped chiffon and duchess lace, embroidered in silver; black picture hat'.[30] Wallis was listed as one of the representatives of Baltimore society attending this wedding.

The Warfields disapproved of Wallis's mother Alice, especially when she moved in with the man who became her second husband, John Freeman Rasin, son of the Democratic Party leader in Baltimore. Wallis liked him until she heard that he was to become her stepfather. Her mother married him in 1908. Later it was known that he drank. And later still Wallis's mother moved to Atlantic City, where Rasin, suffering from Bright's Disease, died on 4 April 1913, after which their financial situation became precarious.

Another American Duchess, Gladys Deacon, Consuelo Vanderbilt's successor at Blenheim, was disparaging about Wallis and her mother, and indeed the Duke of Windsor:

> He was a miserable fellow – his mother too much for him, had George V (an idiot) by the ear – he was attracted by the newness of America as presented by Mrs Simpson – he would be able to be free there. She was just a common American making her way in the world – not all bad – amusing and with a good sense of dress – but common. Her mother ran a boarding house – not an hotel – a boarding house – well, you can imagine what that was. Edward was a *coureur* and *impuissant*, perhaps once or twice, but nothing more. They had to get rid of him to secure the succession.[31]

At the end of this disdainful diatribe, she added mysteriously: 'Mrs Simpson and her little red pills.' The pills remain as one of those unsolved mysteries.

Education

Wallis attended Miss O'Donnell's school, then situated at 210 East Chase Street, Baltimore. Miss Ada O'Donnell had founded the school as a debutante in 1891. It appears that during one lesson Miss Ada asked who had tried to blow up the Houses of Parliament. A boy called Jesse Webb answered on a rare occasion when Wallis knew the answer. She was so cross that she hit him over the head with her pencil box. When Wallis married the Duke of Windsor, Miss Ada (by then Mrs R. Sanchez Boone) wrote to send her good wishes. Aunt Bessie replied because the new Duchess was swamped with mail: 'You would have been proud of your pupil yesterday as she brought to bear on the momentous event all the dignity and poise which the occasion demanded.'[32] In 1941 the Duchess wrote to Miss Ada personally, recalling her 'struggles to put something into my empty head.'[33]

Later she went to Arundell School on St Paul Street, near Mount Vernon Place, spending summer holidays with her Warfield uncles on their various farms. Wallis was confirmed at the age of thirteen on the third Sunday after Easter, 17 April 1910. In 1912 she followed her mother and aunt Bessie to Oldfields, a secondary school at Glencoe, Maryland, staying there until 1914.

Oldfields was a secondary school (more a finishing school) for smart young ladies, about twenty-five miles from the centre of Baltimore, founded by Mrs John Sears McCulloch in 1867. Many years later, in 1976, by which time the Duchess was in poor health, there was a plan to establish a Duchess of Windsor Museum and Fine Arts Center in honour of their 'most famous graduate'. She would serve as Honorary Chairman. On 29 March 1976 a committee including Diana Vreeland, Nathan Cummings, Florence van der Kemp, Joseph Moore and Janine Metz (a former secretary) gathered to launch the scheme at the Bijou Restaurant in New York. Mario Buatta, the fashionable interior decorator, would design the museum which would recreate the library of the house in the Bois and would be the perfect repository for items of 'great personal interest' which the Duchess herself would select. It would thus celebrate the Windsor style, house the definitive collection of their things, and would furthermore have a building dedicated to the study of fine arts by the students.

Needless to say, this came to nought, as by 1976 Maître Blum had other plans for the Duchess's possessions. But there was another reason. The alumnae of Oldfields were not keen on the idea.

Despite Frances Donaldson's claim that the girls who knew Wallis at this time did not like her that much, two particular lifelong friendships were forged at Oldfields, one with Mary Kirk, her room-mate, the daughter of Henry Kirk, owner of the Kirk silversmith company in Baltimore, and another with Ellen Yuille, a smart girl from New York, who invited Wallis on her first visit to that city. Both were to play an important part in her later life, Mary marrying Jacques Raffray and succeeding Wallis as the third Mrs Ernest Simpson, and Ellen marrying William Sturgis in November 1915, and later the Wall Street broker Wolcott Blair.

Another lifelong friend was Cordelia Biddle, daughter of Anthony J. Drexel Biddle, an eccentric millionaire, about whom Cordelia wrote a book, *My Philadelphia Father*. She remembered that at school, 'Wallis fondled another girl's mink cape as if it gave her physical pleasure.' She said Wallis 'was well brought up but always liked bums – vulgar people. She was always a flirt and had more determination than anyone she had ever known. If she wanted something, she went after it'.[34]

Wallis emerged from Oldfields with no particular distinction. With Mr Rasin dead, Wallis and her mother had little to live on. They moved into an apartment in a large forbidding-looking building on the corner of St Paul and Preston Street. Uncle Sol provided some financial support and he made it possible for Wallis to be presented at the Bachelor's Cotillion. In October 1914 she found she was to be one of the forty-seven chosen girls. When she was dressed for the party, her mother allowed her to apply some rouge to her pale face. As the Duchess later recorded: 'Even at that late date the use of rouge was considered a little fast.'[35] She was escorted to the event by her cousin Henry and by Major-General George Barnett, Lelia's husband. Having made her curtsy, she was officially 'out' and the next months followed the traditional round of tea dances, dinner parties and balls.

Uncle Sol had arranged the Cotillion but he would not stretch to a ball as he had done for Wallis's cousin Anita a few years earlier. This was wartime and he was supporting Allied causes. He went so far as to explain that he did not 'consider the present a proper time for such festivities, when thousands of men were being slaughtered and their families left destitute in the appalling catastrophe now devastating Europe.'[36] Instead, Lelia gave a dance for Wallis at the Marine Barracks in Washington in April 1915.

Soon after her debutante year ended, Wallis's Warfield grandmother fell and broke her hip. She became bedridden. When Wallis visited her, she gave her a lecture about conscience, telling her that it was like a mirror. She must look into it with thought once a day. On 17 December 1915 Anna Warfield died. The Warfields were plunged into a prolonged period of mourning and any hope of fun was at an end.

Relief came in the form of an invitation to Pensacola, Florida from her cousin Corinne Mustin. A family council was held, and Aunt Bessie agreed that it would a good idea if Wallis saw a wider world. So in April 1916 Wallis left Baltimore for the West Coast.

I spent some days in Baltimore in May 2009. It is a fine city and it was interesting to visit the places where Wallis grew up, the houses where she lived and the Belvedere Hotel, where some of the debutante events had taken place. I had not realised how strongly drawn she was to Baltimore during her years with the Duke and how often they returned there.

If the theory is right that the Duchess was ever-anxious to avenge early slights, then to return as Duchess of Windsor and be widely fêted would have seemed attractive to her. Many were pleased to see her, but by no means all. Nancy T. Wehr* was a cousin of Wallis's and recalled that her grandmother would speak of Wallis without mentioning her name: 'She married a foreigner and left town for good.'[37] Diana Warfield Daly, a distant cousin, stated proudly in a television programme, *The Demonised Duchess*, that when she asked about Wallis Warfield she was firmly told that they were not related.†

---

*Nancy T. Wehr (1904–2005), born Nancy de Wolf Theobald, married 1924, Frederick Louis Wehr.
† There is a confused message here. Despite denouncing Wallis as 'a bad egg', this lady apparently displays a portrait of the Duchess in her house.

But the attraction that Baltimore continued to hold for Wallis was surely more than just a matter of her being able to return as a Duchess with a former King in tow. However anxious she might have been to escape in 1916, and to find a new life, there was clearly genuine affection for her old city.

In the Maryland Historical Society, I found her writing to Miss Ada, her old schoolteacher, that on receiving a special plate from her son, 'it made me quite homesick'.[38] Another letter to Eleanor Miles referred to images of Maryland: 'I must say it gives me nostalgia.'[39]

In advance of their first visit to Baltimore as a married couple in 1941, the Duke wrote to Wallis's uncle, General Warfield, saying how honoured he was to be meeting a member of the family, echoing his later statement to Kenneth Harris: 'I've always considered myself a Southerner by marriage.'[40] On that first visit there was a parade through the city and a reception. The general found them too much of a handful with their copious luggage and their Cairns terriers and would not have them again, so they invariably stayed with Clarence and Eleanor Miles at Blakeford. In 1959, Wallis thanked Eleanor for a visit to their home, Blakeford, as 'one of the pleasantest we have ever had'.[41]

The Duchess of Windsor was not the first girl from Baltimore to make a prestigious international marriage. The Catons had produced Marianne (1788–1853), who married the widowed Marquess Wellesley before becoming Vicereine of Ireland and later a lady-in-waiting to Queen Adelaide. Her sister-in-law Betsy Patterson (1785–1879) married Jerome Bonaparte, brother of Napoleon I, and then, in February 1913, Elinor Douglas Wise married the eighth Duc de Richelieu (son of Alice Heine, Princess of Monaco) in Baltimore Cathedral, a union which cannot have escaped Wallis's notice.

The Windsors appeared frequently, staying at the Belvedere or the Mount Vernon Club. In 1955 they supported a fund-raising drive by attending the Cancer Crusade Ball. The following year they attended the Assembly Ball. The Duchess gave one of her dresses to the Maryland Historical Society. So she surely kept a special place in her heart for Baltimore.

2

San Diego and China

San Diego

Wallis told Cleveland Amory: 'Every generation has its own set of heroes, and mine were flyers'.[1] She met her first husband at Pensacola, Florida in April 1916. The day after her arrival, her cousin Corinne Mustin held a lunch party at which Wallis met the man whom she described as the 'world's most fascinating aviator.'[2] This was the man who, somewhat to Corinne's dismay, became Wallis's first husband, Lieutenant (junior grade) Earl Winfield Spencer, Jr, of the US Navy.

He was born in Kinsley, Kansas on 20 September 1888, and after college in Wisconsin he graduated from the United States Naval Academy in 1910. He was a pioneering pilot in the US Navy and served as the first commanding officer at the Naval Air Station, San Diego, setting up a permanent naval air station for training exercises.

Clearly Wallis was drawn to this dashing figure with his Clark Gable looks. But equally there was a desire to escape from her home life. Her cousin Lelia Barnett later told her that she thought she had married Win out of curiosity, to find out if all those strange stories about the facts of life were true. She was meant to stay a month, but after he proposed she wanted to stay longer. It is said that her first disappointment in what became a difficult marriage was to discover that in Chicago his family lived at Lake Forest, not Highland Park.

They were officially engaged in September and married by the Rev. E. B. Niver at Christ Church, Baltimore on 8 November 1916 with her mother, General Barnett, his wife Lelia and Ethel Spencer as witnesses.[3] Mrs Barnett, it was noted in the society pages of the day, 'took as much interest in the wedding of her niece Wallis Warfield and Lieutenant Winfield Spencer as though Wallis were her own daughter, and gave big parties and little parties before the wedding in Baltimore.'[4]

On that day, Uncle Sol gave her away, Ellen Yuille Sturgis was her maid of honour and Mary Kirk was one of her bridesmaids.

It is generally accepted that the problem with Win Spencer was that he was a drinker and there is evidence in his later life to support this. Wallis claimed to have discovered on their honeymoon that her husband had a predilection for gin. Aged only twenty, she had never had an alcoholic drink in her life. Yet Cleveland Amory stated that he was determined to accentuate Winfield Spencer's faults in her memoirs, painting him as selfish, bossy, demanding and, above all, drinking. The Duchess warmed to the idea of this portrayal and assigned more and more drinking episodes to Winfield until Amory reminded her 'if we did not let up a bit we would not be able to stop the reader from wanting to join him.'[5] Furthermore, it was stretching credulity somewhat to have Winfield Spencer teaching young naval air cadets to fly while being simultaneously permanently drunk.

Corinne Mustin told her granddaughter that those early aviators 'lived life on the edge – fearless gutsy guys risking their lives in these wacky flying machines while at the same time fighting tooth and nail against a Washington that insisted aviation had no future in the Navy'.[6]

The Spencers were not unhappy at first and settled into life at the Air Station at Pensacola, the United States' sole naval aviation station at that time. They and the Mustins had some good times together. The war was still raging in Europe and all officers wondered when they would take part. But Win, promoted to lieutenant in 1917, was disappointed to be posted to Boston to set up the Squantum Air Base. He responded well to the job, worked hard and was successful. He hoped to be posted overseas, but instead was sent to North Island, near San Diego, his brief to establish a permanent Naval Air Station for training purposes, to include ground-school and flight-school courses for qualification as Naval Aviators, and to instruct listed personnel to qualify as machinists' mates and quartermasters. He began duty on 8 November 1917.

In those days the station was little more than a strip of beach. Nevertheless, Spencer was furious if the flight instructors reported for duty without white gloves and swords. He was commended for doing a remarkable job in his two years there, creating the station from nothing and helping build it up despite numerous squabbles with the Army. By 1918 there were 363 qualified aviation personnel, 345 students under training and 237 awaiting instruction, while 191 trained and qualified machinists' mates had been transferred to foreign stations.

The Spencers began life in San Diego at the Hotel del Coronado, known locally as 'The Del'. This hotel is perhaps best known as the Hotel Seminole-Ritz in the film *Some Like It Hot*, starring Marilyn Monroe, Jack Lemmon and Tony Curtis. In that film the hotel was located in

Florida, but by 1958 most such hotels had been pulled down. Billy Wilder turned to Southern California for an appropriate-looking one. I stayed there in October 2009.*

Presently the Spencers found a typical Californian bungalow to live in, where Wallis could entertain. But after a year of marriage Wallis realised, at least subconsciously, that the marriage was not working. By the time war ended on 11 November 1918 she could tell, despite the success of Win's work, that his self-confidence had been badly damaged by the Navy Department's decision not to send him overseas.

Wallis maintained that this was when his drinking began and no doubt it was one of the problems of the marriage. Others have suggested that he drank because she was such a flirt. He became sarcastic towards her and fiercely jealous. While he remained devoted to the Navy she soon became disenchanted with naval life. She was also afraid when he went on flying expeditions. She feared he might not return, and it left her with a deep fear of flying for the rest of her life.

Life in Coronado was not stimulating. The small houses in which they lived were undistinguished. There was not a lot of entertainment on offer. Even in 2009, when Mark Gaulding staged the first Duke and Duchess of Windsor conference there, he concluded that San Diego was 'Iowa by the sea'.

Wallis tried to enliven their life with social activity. Much of this centred round The Del, where she met the great actors John Barrymore and Charlie Chaplin. And on 7 April 1920 the hotel was the place where Edward, Prince of Wales was entertained to a magnificent banquet on a stopover during his voyage to New Zealand.

Historians have disagreed for years over whether or not this was the occasion on which Wallis first met or at least saw the Prince. The background is this: the Prince of Wales sailed into San Diego in HMS *Renown*, on a refuelling stop on his way to New Zealand and Australia. The cruiser had left Portsmouth on 16 March, stopped at Bridgetown, and made her way through the Panama Canal. *Renown* would then sail to Honolulu, Suva and on to Auckland. Accompanying the Prince was his ambitious young cousin Lord Louis Mountbatten, who had positioned himself carefully, 'pulled every string at his disposal'[7], and finally been invited on the voyage by the Prince himself. He was serving as Flag Lieutenant to the royal party, but in effect was there as the Prince's ally, minder and friend. It was on this trip that genuine intimacy grew between the two cousins,

---

* I addressed the first conference of the Duke and Duchess of Windsor Society, and familiarised myself with Wallis's life on the West Coast.

which only ended in 1937 when Mountbatten failed to accept the Duke of Windsor's plea to be his best man.

As a naval officer, Win Spencer would have merited an invitation to at least a reception during the Prince's visit and Wallis would have been invited as his wife.

The myth that Wallis met the Prince arose for a variety of reasons. Not unnaturally, residents and journalists of San Diego wanted to claim the meeting as their own. The Duke of Windsor did not mention San Diego in his memoirs, while the Duchess denied any such meeting in hers. Mountbatten later told the ghosts Charles J. V. Murphy and Joseph Bryan III that Wallis had been there and used to chide them in later life for not having noticed her: 'She was dressed to kill . . .'[8] In 1936 the San Diego *Sun* quoted Win Spencer as saying:

> Practically all navy officers stationed here were present with their wives. We all went down the receiving line. My former wife was with me most of the evening. Of course, I'm not quite sure but what she may have been introduced to him. As I recall she slipped away for a few minutes and may have been received by the Prince . . .[9]

But a local historian, Benjamin Sacks, established for once and for all that no meeting could have taken place since Wallis was in Monterey staying with her friend Mrs Jane Selby Hayne, a prominent social figure in San Francisco, to watch polo matches. She left San Diego on 31 March 1920 and did not return until 13 April, her departure and return being duly recorded in the society column of a local paper, the *Union*. Evidently, on account of his wife being away Win Spencer took no part in the Prince of Wales's visit either.

Nor did the Prince of Wales enjoy his trip. He was upset not to have received a letter on shore from his then mistress, Freda Dudley Ward. His prime memory was that Mildred Harris, a movie star, the estranged wife of Charlie Chaplin, had bribed the Mayor so she could meet him. Though they tried to prevent her attending the dance, she got in and he told her that Mountbatten infuriated him by dancing with her, while contemporary accounts suggest that he danced with her too. Perhaps because of not getting any mail from Freda, the Prince referred to the dinner as 'the most bloody awful dinner & dance at the Coronado Hotel; I've never hated a party as much as I did this evening's . . .'[10]

By 1920 the Spencer marriage was unhappy. Win was occupied in flying instruction and was often serving in other parts of California while Wallis stayed in Coronado. He was sent to Pensacola in November 1920 where a winter of some uncertainty followed. His appointment to the Navy Department in Washington in May 1921 offered what appeared to be a chance for a new start, but any hopes of happiness proved short-lived. As the Duchess wrote: 'our move to Washington only made the wreckage complete'.[11]

Spencer was unhappy in his desk job, longing for a more active serving life. He became demoralised. He fell out with a fellow officer, and he took this out on Wallis. They lived in a service apartment in the Hotel Brighton and it was here, apparently, that Spencer locked her in the bathroom on a Sunday afternoon, only releasing her when he returned home late that night. The next morning she resolved to leave him.

In contradiction to this, Wallis told Cleveland Amory that the reason she left Win was because she discovered that she had 'a real and truly extraordinary gift for being able to see through people'. She used to dissect the characters of people they met, warning Win that certain people did not like him or 'boded him no good'. She claimed to be right on almost all occasions but, she said, 'when I saw he simply did not possess the perspicacity to see what I was doing for him, I gave up.'[12]

Whatever the circumstances, she relayed her decision to her mother and her aunt Bessie Merryman, neither of whom left her in any doubt about the problems that lay ahead. Neither the Warfields nor the Montagues would countenance divorce. Wallis was told she must seek an interview with her Uncle Sol. His line was equally strict: 'I won't let you bring this disgrace upon us!' He informed her that there had never been a divorce in the extended Warfield family since his first records of them in 1662.[13] Yet he conceded that, though a bachelor himself, he could understand how some marriages might become unbearable.

Wallis returned to Win for a while and to a relatively tranquil phase, but soon she was telling him that she needed a divorce. His old courtesy briefly returned to him and he said: 'Wallis, I've had it coming to me. If you ever change your mind, I'll still be around.'[14] Wallis moved in with her mother. She informed her family of her irrevocable decision and wrote to Uncle Sol. He replied that he would offer no help with the costs of any divorce action. She was on her own.

Win Spencer was sent out to Hong Kong as Commander of a gunboat on the Asiatic Station. His duties did not involve flying, so again he was unhappy. He kept in touch with Wallis who, meanwhile, settled into the Washington social scene as a single woman. It was at this time that she had an affair with Felipe de Espil, a young diplomat and lawyer, attached to the Argentine Embassy, an affair she later denied through her lawyers when Ralph Martin made the details public in 1972.

This was clearly important to her, Cleveland Amory describing it as 'the one genuine love affair of her life' and stating that 'to Wallis's credit, the break-up of this affair seemed to have been one thing in her life which moved her very deeply.'[15]

In 1922 Wallis ceased to live with her mother as she had done since the separation and moved into an apartment in Georgetown with a friend whose husband was abroad with the Navy. The following year, Corinne Mustin was widowed and invited Wallis to join her on a trip to Paris. For this trip she needed funds. She went to see Uncle Sol at his New York apartment. Here she found evidence of another side to his life. The reserved uncle in Baltimore, devoted to his mother and a paragon of respectability, lived in an apartment filled with photographs of actresses and opera singers. He explained to his niece that banking was an expedient way to earn a living, but extremely dull. These ladies lifted his life to a more enjoyable plateau.

In a difficult interview, Wallis pointed out that if she went abroad she would at least be far away from Baltimore when her divorce came through. Despite enormous reservations on several counts, Uncle Sol handed over five hundred dollars.

The visit to France was a success, Wallis and Corinne soon finding escorts and enjoying their time there. Corinne eventually returned to America but Wallis stayed on. Meanwhile ideas of divorce became less attractive when she was told it would cost her several thousand dollars. Win kept writing from China, and she began to balance her uncertain freedom with these pleas from her husband to return to him. In a curious twist, she agreed to join him and so, on 17 July 1924, she set sail for China in the company of several naval wives.

China

Win Spencer was on the quayside to greet her. Wallis found her estranged husband looking better than she had expected. He told her that he had not had a drink since she had written agreeing to come to Hong Kong. Therefore she was dismayed to find two half-empty gin bottles in his apartment in Kowloon but was somewhat reassured by the houseboy telling her that these were for washing his teeth.

The marriage went through its now habitual phases of happiness and unhappiness. A honeymoon period was quickly followed by the all too familiar disappearance of Win and his reappearance drunk. Then he was solicitous in nursing Wallis after she suffered a kidney infection (as she put it in her memoirs), followed by a high temperature. Some have suggested that this was no illness but that Spencer had kicked her in the stomach, causing internal bleeding. His jealousy soon returned. Finally she had had enough and they agreed to admit failure. Nevertheless, he resumed her monthly payments and saw her off on the steamer to Shanghai.

Wallis's life for the next few years was one of drifting. She settled at the Palace Hotel on the Bund in Shanghai and was soon being taken out by Harold Robinson, a British diplomat to whom an introduction had been sent from Washington. Presently she moved on to Peking, settling at the Grand Hôtel de Pékin. Wallis had longed to see Peking as her Aunt Bessie and cousin Lelia had been there. She intended to stay for a fortnight but by chance she met Katherine Moore Bigelow, who had been a friend in Coronado as a young widow and was now in China, remarried to Herman Rogers, a successful banker on Wall Street. Instantly a strong friendship with Katherine was rekindled, while Herman and Wallis became equally close. Herman Rogers was devoted to Wallis and had circumstances been different he might have married her, in which case history would have taken a different turn. As it was, he remained happily with his wife.

Wallis moved in with the Rogerses and spent a year in their house. A happy year it proved to be. In her memoirs, she described it as 'the most carefree, the most lyric interval of my youth – the nearest thing, I imagine, to a lotus-eater's dream that a young woman brought up the "right" way could ever expect to know.'[16] Years later Cy Sulzberger asked her if she learnt to speak any Chinese. She replied: 'Yes, I studied it a little, but all I learned were a few phrases such as "Could I have a bit more champagne, please?"'[17] In the spring of 1925 Wallis returned to the United States.

Wallis's visit to China was to lead to many a rumour in her later life, fuelled by the assertions of biographers from the lower echelons of the trade. There were suggestions that she learnt special sexual techniques in Shanghai – there being a joke that where other girls picked up pennies, she was so proficient that she picked up a sovereign. Needless to say there is nothing to substantiate this, nor has any evidence ever been produced to suggest the existence of the so-called China Dossier. All this was but another attempt to blacken her name. But it will never be easy to assert the more reasonable. The truth is surely that she was a mildly ambitious woman trying to make a life for herself, but continually thwarted by circumstances.

The Warfields hardly helped her, while the Montagues came frequently to her rescue. She had detractors but she had loyal friends. This was not a phase in her life when she was making an impact. If she was a schemer, then she was not a very good one.

Wallis returned to the United States, where she found herself once again ill with 'an obscure internal ailment'.[18] She had to undergo an operation in Seattle. Win learned of her condition. He insisted on joining her in Chicago, boarded the train with her, and accompanied her to Washington. Despite this last act of kindness, they never met again and presently Wallis began the quest for divorce. She settled on desertion as the declared cause of complaint. This required three years of separation.

There is no evidence that Wallis took any interest in what happened to Win after that time. He married his second wife, Miriam, on 4 September 1928. Within a week she was accusing him of dismantling their home in Beverley Hills and was locking him out of the house. In 1931 Wallis returned some furniture to him with the help of her aunt, and heard that his wife was finding his drinking difficult. Spencer's second marriage ended in divorce in 1936.

Needless to say, when the Abdication crisis occurred the press located Winfield Spencer and from that day on irritating references to him appeared from time to time in newspapers. He was described, predictably, as 'ex-mate of the king's friend'. As a naval officer, he felt that the press jibes cost him esteem in the eyes of those of senior rank. During the crisis, reporters tracked him down to a hospital after he had broken his leg during a hunting trip. He spoke of his ex-wife: 'She is most attractive and has one of the strongest characters I have ever known any person to possess.' He refused to discuss her romance with the King: 'That would be untactful as a gentleman and undiplomatic as an officer.'[19]

Win's third wife was Norma Reese, widow of Homer Stuyvesant Johnson, a Detroit manufacturer. She was born in 1889 and had known him since his Coronado days with Wallis. She was a widow and grandmother, grey-haired and sweet-natured. They married soon after the Windsors on 4 July 1937 but divorced in 1940, both parties citing cruelty and Norma blaming Win for 'habitual intemperance'. He claimed the same of her.[20]

In later life Spencer returned for two more spells of duty on North Island, but avoided the former social acquaintances from his days there with Wallis. He married a fourth wife, Lilian Phillips (1892–1981). Then, on 29 May 1950, during a nostalgic visit to Coronado, Commander Spencer, as he had by then become, died of a heart attack in his room at the El Cordova Hotel. He was sixty-one. He was buried at Fort Rosencrass, San Diego.

In Washington Wallis returned to her mother's house, finding her about to marry (in 1926) Charles Gordon Allen, a lawyer's clerk in the Veterans' Administration.* In her quest for freedom from Win, Wallis found that if she lived in Virginia she could obtain her divorce in three years. She made her base at the Warren Green Hotel in Warrenton, Fauquier County, Virginia, a little way south of Washington.

Here she settled, eating at the same table alone in the hotel, observing the commercial travellers who passed through and talking to the only other regular inmate of the hotel, an Englishman in his sixties called Jack Mason.

If Wallis had drifted before, now she became virtually static. She spent a year in that hotel, doing little other than walk, read novels by John Galsworthy and Somerset Maugham, and occasionally travel into Washington to see her mother or to dine with friends. She had little money and no taste for adventure. Yet on her visits to Washington she sometimes went on to New York to buy clothes, where she stayed with her former bridesmaid Mary Kirk and Mary's husband Jacques Raffray in their apartment on Washington Square. They dined out, went to the theatre or played bridge.

It was while visiting the Raffrays that Wallis met a couple they knew – Mr and Mrs Ernest Simpson.

* They were married in 1926. He died in 1931.

3

Mr Simpson

Ernest Simpson made no public statements and escaped being quoted by the diarists of his day, but a few of his letters survive. Some have been published and others sold. Punters pored over his letters when they were on view before being sold at auction in Rome.* I saw them before they passed into private hands.

When the Duchess of Windsor was writing her memoirs she wrote to Ernest to check details of the flat they shared at Bryanston Court in London. He replied that he deeply disapproved of people trying to justify themselves in this way. He had been called everything under the sun and, as he put it, the truth lay somewhere at the bottom of a well and as far as he was concerned there it could remain, should anyone be interested to search for it[†][1].

Simpson emerges as a man made desolate when his marriage to Wallis came to an end. He was beyond tears when he left their flat in Bryanston Court for the last time, feeling that something inside him had died. Even when all was lost he hoped she might return to him. They were still in touch a year after the marriage, when he felt he had been shamed in his club.

Cleveland Amory met him by chance at a cocktail party in New York in the 1950s. Simpson approached him. 'I thought you might like to talk to me. My name is Ernest Simpson.'[2] In a brief exchange, Simpson told him that he did not accept Wallis's version of their marriage as expressed in her memoirs, and he said:

> Wallis never had dignity nor proportion. She never could take even minor criticism. She needed a strong man with judgement. If she was hurt she would fly into a tantrum. She was wild when she was

---

* Twenty-eight letters were sold for 28,000 euros ($31,000). Seventeen of these were from Ernest Simpson, and five from Win Spencer. They had fallen into the hands of Georges Sanègre, the Duchess of Windsor's butler. After his death they were sold by his nephew.

† But he did mind lies. In January 1937 he brought a suit for slander against Mrs Joan Sutherland, wife of Lt-Colonel A.H.C. Sutherland, MC, when his sister Maud Kerr-Smiley overheard her suggesting, in a West End restaurant, that he had accepted money for permitting Wallis to divorce him. The matter was settled out of court.

angry and there was no end to her hate or temper. I think the Duke has always been mortally afraid of her.[3]

In a later version, Amory had Simpson adding: '. . . I know most of the time I was'.[4]

When working on the Duchess's memoirs, Amory decided to present Ernest Simpson as stuffy, stuck-up, stubborn and stodgy, which he later conceded was hardly fair. Amory explained that the real problem was that when Wallis first met him he was 'happily married to someone else'.[5]

There are still people who remember him. The author Kenneth Rose was entertaining the novelist Anthony Powell to lunch at the old Guards' Club at 16 Charles Street in the 1950s. Seated alone at the bar was another member of the club. Rose recalled: 'His clothes were a bit too smart. The cuffs of his coat were a little too narrow; he wore a double-breasted waistcoat with a watch chain; there was a stickpin in his tie. At that time men were resorting to soft collars. Not he.'[6] It was Mr Simpson.

Others remember him as a lone school father picking up his boy from prep school or later from Harrow. Somehow this brings him closer to us, but still he has succeeded in disappearing as little more than a footnote in history since he wisely forbore from giving his story to the world.

Ernest Simpson was really a Solomon, his father having been a British citizen who went to America and changed his name. This curious fact was resurrected at the time of the Duke of Windsor's death in the *Jewish Chronicle*. Ernest was born on 6 May 1895, son of Ernest Louis Simpson, one of the founders (in 1880) of the international shipbroking firm of Simpson, Spence & Young. His mother was Charlotte Woodward Gaines, a New York lawyer. Ernest was born in New York and educated at Harvard. He was drawn to Great Britain, and when he was eighteen his father asked him to choose between being American and British. He chose to be a British citizen and, while still an undergraduate, crossed to Europe in 1917 and served in the First World War as a second lieutenant in the Coldstream Guards.

In 1905 his sister Maud had married Peter Kerr-Smiley, the younger son of Sir Hugh Smiley, 1st baronet, a soldier in the British Army, who served as MP for North Antrim from 1910 to 1922. This marriage of a Simpson into the British aristocracy creates some curious and unlikely links to the world of the Duke of Windsor and Wallis, and to modern times. In February 1918 the Prince of Wales attended a party that Maud gave at her London home, 31 Belgrave Square. Air-raid warnings sounded and the partygoers went down to the cellar. Mrs Freda Dudley Ward and a companion called 'Buster' Dominguez (some kind of Latin American diplomat in London) were passing by and took shelter in the doorway. Maud invited them to take sanctuary in the cellar. After the air raid, the party resumed. Freda was persuaded to stay on, danced all evening with the Prince, and soon afterwards became his long-standing mistress.

Furthermore Maud was the mother of Betty Hussey, wife of the architectural historian Christopher Hussey who lived at Scotney Castle in Kent (where for a time Denis and Margaret Thatcher rented a country retreat). Peter Kerr-Smiley was the uncle of Sir Hugh Smiley, 3rd baronet, who married Cecil Beaton's sister. By 1928 Maud was separated from her husband.

At the time Wallis met him, Ernest was working in New York. In 1923 he had married Dorothea Parsons Dechert, a divorcee and the daughter of Arthur Webb Parsons, a lawyer from New England. She was descended from Judge Theophilus Parsons, Chief Justice of the Massachusetts Supreme Judicial Court and a President of Harvard. They had one daughter, Audrey, and Dorothea had an older daughter, Cynthia, by her first marriage. Neither of these children played any part in the joint life of Ernest and Wallis Simpson.*

According to the Duchess's memoirs, Ernest's marriage was already in trouble. Mary Kirk Raffray used to invite him on his own for dinner and bridge, and Wallis was sometimes there. Wallis later wrote that 'with each of us caught up in a personal dilemma of some complexity, the friendship for a long time was nothing more than one of those casual New York encounters between the extra man and the out-of-town friend.'[7]

Given the way things finally turned out, it is not impossible that Wallis 'stole' Ernest not only from Dorothea but also from her friend Mary. This theory gains weight when, after the Abdication, Raffray and Mary got divorced and Ernest married her, some suggesting that an affair between Ernest and Mary was in some part a cause of the breakdown of the Simpson marriage, which is unlikely. But the attraction was probably already in place, even if not acknowledged.

Reading the Duchess's memoirs, it is hard to see her other than in her chosen role as a drifter. Occasionally she contemplated a job and once she even went to Pittsburgh to see if she could work in the tubular steel business. She had many friends and there were many parties. She caused a certain amount of havoc from time to time. As she approached her thirtieth birthday Wallis seemed unaffected by the occasionally changing circumstances of her life.

---

* In August 1935 Wallis was afraid that Ernest intended to bring Audrey back to England to live with them. She dreaded the discomfort and the expense. Nothing came of the plan.

Ernest began to take on a more prominent role. He was something of an educator, conducting her round museums and galleries and giving her books to read. In due course he proposed, asking her to marry him when they were both free. There is not a hint in anything written by Wallis or her contemporaries that she was in love with Ernest, but he was there. Dorothea, his wife at the time, considered her life ruined by Wallis. In later life, a gentle white-haired lady with a wry smile, she told Cleveland Amory: 'The Duchess was a very helpful woman. First she helped herself to my apartment and then she helped herself to my clothes, and then she helped herself to my husband.'*[8]

In 1927 Wallis's aunt Bessie invited her to accompany her to Europe, which both of them enjoyed. As was her habit, Wallis lingered on and there was more drifting: 'The trip . . . was enlivened by the presence of a very amusing young Irishman named Rowland Byers . . . .'[9] The drifting ceased for a while when Uncle Sol died on 24 October 1927. Wallis read the news in the *Paris Herald* and then received a cable from her mother.

Instead of leaving his fortune divided between Wallis and her Warfield cousins, Uncle Sol established a fund to benefit elderly women. To this he bequeathed 'the bulk of what I may own.' He did so in memory of his adored mother, who had died twelve years earlier on 17 December 1915. In his will he stated:

My mother represented to me all I really had in life, which I did not entirely realise until her death . . . It is to my Mother therefore – to her memory – I wish to establish this memorial – the Anna Emory Warfield Home for Aged Women.[10]

The foundation, now called the Anna Emory Warfield Memorial Fund, Inc., was incorporated in 1928 and still benefits old folk in Baltimore to this day.† Uncle Sol also left the foundation his home, Manor Glen, in which to house them.

Wallis was to receive the income from a trust of $15,000, which would cease if she remarried. She and some cousins contested the will and 'an equitable settlement was made with the executors'.[11] Far from inheriting a share of Sol's great fortune, she was left little more than adequately well off.

Wallis's divorce from Win Spencer came through on 6 December 1927.

---

*By 1936 Dorothea was running a domestic employment agency in New York.
† In 2006 it had assets of $5,803,178 and made sixty-eight individual grants, usually of $4,000 a year.

Ernest was about to set off to run his father's London office, fulfilling a long-held dream to settle in England. He proposed again and Wallis appeared to accept, not without doubts. She went to stay with her firm friends, Herman and Katherine Rogers, at Villa Lou Viei, on the hillside above Cannes. While there, she wrote to Ernest giving him a firm acceptance. They were married in London on 21 July 1928.

Thus began their married life. In her memoirs Wallis claimed that it was a 'blissful existence' and that 'for the moment, I felt a security that I had never really experienced since early childhood.'[12]

Having travelled through the Duchess of Windsor's life in the company of authors good and bad, I see her as something of a victim. In his official biography of Edward VIII, Philip Ziegler listed all the insults hurled at her in life and posthumously – she had been called illegitimate, both a lesbian and a nymphomaniac, a spy for the Nazis and probably the KGB, Ribbentrop's mistress, and there was a claim that she had mothered a child by Count Ciano; 'she learnt her sexual techniques in the brothels of Hong Kong, or was it perhaps Shanghai?' Ziegler concluded: 'It is notoriously almost impossible to prove that something did not happen, but the evidence for all these charges seems, to say the least, unlikely to hold up in court'.[13]

She was also a victim in the circumstances of her life. She could have expected to enjoy an easy childhood with better treatment from her father's family. She escaped into her first marriage, with which she could not cope, and after several attempts to save it she gave in. Then she drifted. She might not have been the single woman that a wife would have wanted her husband to run into while he was travelling. Drifters can be dangerous; they have little to lose.

Above all, Wallis's was a quest for security. Her marriage to Ernest Simpson set her off on a new track: the reasonably well-off wife of a perfectly nice if unexceptional Anglo-American businessman. In due course they settled in a flat in Bryanston Court and Wallis began honing her talents as a minor figure in London society. At domestic virtues she had a natural talent and this was now fostered. But it did not take wing fully until she entered the Prince of Wales's circle in 1931.

On this matter Cecil Beaton is a key observer. When he first met her in the early 1930s in 'a box full of American bums at the Three Arts Club Ball', he judged her 'a brawny great cow or bullock in sapphire blue velvet'. He continued: 'To hear her speak was enough. Her voice was raucous and appalling. I thought her awful, common, vulgar, strident, a second-rate American with no charm.'

Beaton wrote this as an introduction to the transition she underwent, as those in proximity to royalty so often do. Following her meeting and involvement with the Prince of Wales, he commented: 'Now she is all that is elegant. The whole of London flocks after her as the mistress and possible wife of the King . . . I am certain she has more glamour and is of more interest than any public figure.'[14]

Maud Kerr-Smiley provided the gateway for Wallis into this society. She introduced her new sister-in-law to her friends and instructed her in every aspect of social life, from the language to be used in society to the way to eat in company. Some of this she adopted, some she resisted. Reading between the lines of Wallis's memoirs, it emerges that she did not consider herself instantly co-opted into the bosom of English society.

While Ernest ran the business side of their life, Wallis was the *maîtresse de maison*. She developed a flare for entertaining and showed initiative as a hostess. She kept a hostess book, listing the guests, the food they ate, and the imaginative menus she devised. Ernest worked hard and enjoyed modest entertaining, reading, going to the theatre and playing bridge. Wallis was content, yet sometimes she was lonely as she adapted to this new life.

A crisis occurred in May 1929 when her aunt Bessie telegraphed Wallis to say that Wallis's mother was gravely ill. She and Ernest set sail to America. Wallis did indeed find her mother's health very poor, but she was well enough to meet Ernest for the first and only time. When her mother's condition became relatively stable, Wallis was advised to return to England. Soon afterwards, on 2 November 1929, her mother died.

Frances Donaldson believed that Wallis had been 'at her best and most attractive'[15] when married to Ernest. His cultural interests, his fondness for weekends away, good food and visits to cathedrals and castles clearly appealed to her. The impression given was of a young American wife enjoying creating and improving the marital home. She did indeed appear settled. But Frances Donaldson was horrified by the revelations made in the subsequent published letters.

In contrast to the self-portrait in her memoirs, Wallis's letters revealed her as insecure, the Simpsons often in need of money and unable to maintain their increasingly ambitious social lifestyle, dominated by a mean father-in-law in Mr Simpson senior (who cut down a loan he had made to them), and so forth. With her customary unsentimental approach to these matters Frances Donaldson judged Wallis harshly:

No explanation is necessary for the fact that the royal family, with their enormous sense of dedication, their almost religious belief in the consecration of the crowning ceremony, and their upper-class attitude to life, could possibly have liked this wise-cracking, purely pleasure-loving, twice-divorced woman.[16]

Yet even Frances Donaldson accepted, at least in part, that Wallis's sights were not set high, and had it not been for her meeting with Thelma, Lady Furness, she might have been content with Mr Simpson to the end.

Had she stayed with Ernest, she would have become a widow in 1958 when she was sixty-two. She might have been one of any number of elderly widows living in a flat at Marble Arch or Cranmer Court in Chelsea. Her Smythson's diary would have been filled with predictable invitations. She would have had friends in for cocktails and gone to a number of similar such entertainments. Finally, one day she would perhaps have fallen, broken her hip and her life would have ended unremarkably. But fate had other plans for her.

Wallis became a close friend of Benjamin Thaw, Jr and his wife Consuelo. Benny was First Secretary at the US Embassy. Wallis had known his brother Bill in their Coronado days. His wife, Consuelo or Connie, was the elder sister of the Morgan twins, Gloria Vanderbilt and Thelma, Viscountess Furness*. Thelma was the current girlfriend of the Prince of Wales. By mischance, Benny's mother was taken ill and Connie had to go to Paris to see her. Benny (detained in England on diplomatic business) was to go to stay with Thelma when she entertained the Prince of Wales and Prince George for a hunting weekend at Melton Mowbray. She asked Ernest and Wallis to accompany Benny. Ernest liked the idea and Wallis experienced a mixture of excitement and terror. But they accepted.

There have been several accounts of the meeting, the date now being fixed as 10 January 1931. Wallis sat next to the Prince of Wales at lunch, and was not convinced that she had made a good impression on him.

According to her memoirs, Wallis came away struck by 'the odd and indefinable melancholy that seemed to haunt' the Prince. She thought him a remote figure 'not quite of the workaday world'.[17] Nor was he.

---

* Thelma Morgan (1904–70), twin with Gloria Vanderbilt and younger sister of Consuelo Thaw. She m. (1) 1922, James Vail Converse (divorced 1925), & (2) 1926, 1st Viscount Furness (1884–1970) (divorced 1930). She died in New York in a doctor's waiting room, with the teddy bear that the Prince of Wales had given her in her handbag.

4

The Prince of Wales

Edward, Prince of Wales remains one of the most enigmatic figures of the twentieth century. Thousands of pages have been devoted to him, and in particular to his extraordinary action in 1936 when he abdicated the Throne in order to marry Mrs Simpson. Frances Donaldson asserted rightly that he was three different men – the Prince of Wales, the King, and the Duke of Windsor. The first was the best of the three, though even here there are reservations.

He was born towards the end of the reign of his great-grandmother Queen Victoria, thus assuring her three generations in line to the Throne. Prince Edward Albert Christian George Andrew Patrick David was born on 23 June 1894, the eldest son of Prince George, Duke of York, and his wife, Princess Victoria Mary of Teck (later King George V and Queen Mary). His father was the son of Albert Edward, Prince of Wales (later Edward VII) and his wife, Princess Alexandra of Denmark (later Queen Alexandra).

The child, known in the family as David, was heir to a rich heritage. When Queen Victoria celebrated her Diamond Jubilee in 1897, troops arrived in London from every part of her vast Empire. She reigned over nearly two-thirds of the world's population. The Prince retained only dim memories of his great-grandmother, largely concerning her peregrinations round her estates at Windsor, Balmoral or Osborne, either in a low-slung carriage or in her wheelchair, followed by a vast retinue of relations and courtiers.

Queen Marie of Romania, a granddaughter of Queen Victoria, thought the Prince was 'an adorable youth with golden hair'. He had a legendarily unhappy childhood, terrified of his severe father and not adequately protected from that gruff old naval officer by his nervously reserved mother. There were stories of governesses pinching the boy before he was presented before his parents so that he made a bad impression by crying his head off. No one would suggest that he was a bright or perceptive child. His brain retained facts for only a short time. He lacked the gift of analysis. He was far from attentive in his lessons and he never acquired a love of books or learning. It is significant that he who travelled the world in the 1920s had remarkably little of interest to say about it, barring a few entertaining anecdotes about characters met on the way.

The young Prince loved his grandfather, Edward VII, and was indulged by Queen Alexandra in a way that did not happen with his parents. For playmates he had his siblings, who arrived in his life between 1895 and 1905. His next brother, Prince Albert, or Bertie (1895–1952), was shy and afflicted with a painful stammer. They were close as children and later, for a time, Prince Albert followed his elder brother into the raffish set whose company he enjoyed, though never very comfortably.

He was also close to his sister, Princess Mary, born in 1897 and likewise shy. He blamed his father for keeping her too strictly within the family circle and not giving her the chance to find a suitable husband. When eventually she married the somewhat older Viscount Lascelles, later sixth Earl of Harewood, he considered it something of a waste. Princess Mary remained close to him even after the Abdication, protesting slightly at his action but then resuming normal relations. One of her last acts was to visit him in the London Clinic ten days before her sudden death.

Prince Henry, Duke of Gloucester, born in 1900, was not his natural soul mate and later they fell out irreparably in 1927 when the Prince heard that Prince Henry had told someone he thought he would never be King. He tackled him on the issue and Prince Henry admitted he had said it. A terrible row ensued.

To Prince George, Duke of Kent, the next brother and the artistic one, born in 1902, he was the best friend a brother could hope for, something Queen Mary never forgot even in the bitterness of the post-Abdication period. David cared for Georgie and saw him through more than one serious crisis, of which more later.

Then there was a younger brother, Prince John, born in 1905, who developed epilepsy and was largely kept away from his family, living in his own establishment at Sandringham. When John died in 1919 the Prince showed himself at his least sympathetic, his main regret being that family mourning would cut out the chance to go to parties – 'this poor boy had become more of an animal than anything else & only a brother in the flesh & nothing else!! . . .'[1]

Despite these sibling playmates, in later life the Prince would reminisce: 'I had a *wretched* childhood! Of course, there were short periods of happiness but I remember it chiefly for the miserableness [*sic*] I had to keep to myself.'[2]

He was raised first at Marlborough House and later at Buckingham Palace, Windsor Castle, Balmoral, and on the Sandringham estate in York Cottage. He was tutored by Henry Hansell, a Norfolk man of limited imagination, and in 1907 he was despatched to the Royal Naval College, Osborne, while still not thirteen years old.

There he was roundly bullied as the scion of a royal House. His fellow cadets poured red ink on his hair so that he missed 'quarters' or evening parade. Another time they pushed his head out of the window and rammed the lower sash down on his neck in a mock guillotine-style execution. In the mornings he woke to be summoned to a freezing shower. Yet Lord Esher, a court adviser, thought that Osborne freed the young man from his inherent shyness and that there he learnt good manners. From Osborne in 1909 he moved to Dartmouth.

When Edward VII died in 1910, King George V and his family moved to Buckingham Palace, and the Prince became Duke of Cornwall and presently Prince of Wales. Royal duties of a distasteful nature impinged on his naval life. He was invested as a Knight of the Garter at Windsor and walked in the Garter procession. In his Garter robes he was prominent at the coronation of his father, the last coronation he would ever attend. At Caernarvon Castle he was publicly invested as Prince of Wales in a mock-medieval ceremony, devised by Lloyd George for political reasons. In the summer of 1912 he was sent to France for four months in a vain attempt to get him to learn French.

In October that year the Prince went up to Magdalen College, Oxford, where the sporting life of the university took precedence over academic endeavours. He was there for two years until the outbreak of the Great War. During his holidays he went often to Germany, visiting his godparents, the King of Württemberg and Karl Eduard, Duke of Saxe-Coburg, who was also his cousin and had been raised as Charles Edward, Duke of Albany. The Kaiser, that most difficult of Queen Victoria's grandsons, played a part in his life at various times.

When war broke out he was immediately commissioned into the Grenadier Guards at his own request and with the full consent of his father, George V. He undertook a two-week training course in Brentwood. He longed to go to the front but Lord Kitchener would not allow it. The Prince declared he had four brothers and that it would not matter if he were killed. He received the well-known reply from Lord Kitchener that he could not risk him being taken prisoner – 'If I were sure you would be killed, I am not sure if I should be right to restrain you.'[3] Despite this, the Prince of Wales made every effort to see action and reach the front. He succeeded in seeing more grim action than the authorities would have wished and this, above all, made an impression on him.

The Prince had disposed of his virginity at some date before the end of 1916, having been consigned to the care of a French prostitute called

Paulette by two fellow Grenadiers and later members of his household, Lord Claud Hamilton and Piers 'Joey' Legh. The following year he enjoyed a dalliance with a 'pol' called Maggy and unwisely wrote her some indiscreet letters, after which she made an attempt to blackmail him. He matured slowly and some suggest that he might have been rendered sterile by an attack of mumps at Dartmouth in 1911. This unsubstantiated rumour could be a contributory factor in his subsequent Abdication. Why be a stopgap King if he could not have an heir? Why stand between the throne and his popular niece, Princess Elizabeth? This view was promulgated by that unlikely romantic, George Bernard Shaw.*

Thereafter easy conquests became a part of his staple diet. When once I suggested to Lady Diana Cooper that possibly the Prince might have been homosexual, she replied in forthright manner: 'Don't be ridiculous. He was never out of a woman's legs!'[4]

There were, of course, girlfriends. He pined for Viscountess Coke and pursued Hon Sybil (Portia) Cadogan. In 1918 Lady Rosemary Leveson-Gower, daughter of the Duke of Sutherland, appeared a suitable candidate, though Queen Mary warned him against marriage with her, considering there to be 'a taint in the blood of her mother's family'[†].[5]

Above all there was Freda Dudley Ward, whom his brother Prince Henry thought was the best friend the Prince ever had, though he did not realise it. Freda was born on 28 July 1894, the daughter of Colonel Charles Birkin, a rich lace manufacturer from Nottinghamshire. In 1913 she had married William Dudley Ward, a nephew of the 1st Earl of Dudley and a Liberal MP, who was Vice-Chamberlain to the Royal Household from 1917 to 1922. They had two daughters, Penelope (Pempe) (1914–82) who married the film director Carol Reed, and Angela (Angie) (1916–99) who married Major-General Sir Robert Laycock.

Freda and the Prince of Wales met while sheltering in the doorway of 31 Belgrave Square during an air raid. The Prince's letters to Freda have largely been published.[‡] After a few formal letters addressed to Mrs Ward in March 1918, she became by 26 March 'My Angel!!' By September

---

* Shaw gave this view when interviewed on film while on a transatlantic crossing in 1936. Jack Le Vien included it in the Duke of Windsor's 1965 film *A King's Story*.

† In the mid-1920s Cecil Beaton was told that the Prince dined with her frequently when she was married to Viscount Ednam, later 3rd Earl of Dudley, and believed her to be his mistress.

‡ There were 263 letters between 3 March 1918 and 12 January 1921, some of which were published in Rupert Godfrey's *Letters from a Prince*. This collection was sold at Bonham's in 2001 for £36,750. These had been in suitcases in possession of descendants of Freda Dudley Ward. A further 2,000 letters were seen by Philip Ziegler when writing the official biography of Edward VIII. And there were said to be other letters in the collection of the family.

he was hinting at how nice it would be to have a house to share with her. By October he had passed the phase of being madly in love with her, and now he knew her well. Soon he was relying on Freda, sometimes addressing her as 'my very own darling beloved little mummie'.[6] Perhaps the most telling letter concerns his perception of what he needed in a satisfying relationship:

> You know you ought to be really foul to me sometimes sweetie & curse & be cruel; it would do me worlds of good & bring me to my right senses!! I think I'm the kind of man who needs a certain amount of cruelty without which he gets abominably spoilt & soft!! I feel that's what's the matter with me.[7]

But there were relaxed times. Sheila Milbanke used to see them both towards the end of the war when she lived with her first husband, Lord Loughborough, at a Gothic-revival lodge called Lanks Hill, near Winchester. Years later she found it while driving with Sir Charles Johnston, and told him:

> We used to have such fun in the garden with Prince Bertie, and the Prince of Wales, and Freda and Jeannie (Norton), and there were masses of American soldiers in a camp nearby, and we were fascinated because nobody had seen an American before, except for a few American wives, and they all had such extraordinary names, there was one called Easter Day, and Ali Mac (Mackintosh) used to call him New Year's Eve and he didn't think it was funny at all.

Johnston thought this 'curious as an account of the first impact of the Americans on the Prince of Wales and what was already beginning to be his set'.[8]

Freda was a great support to the young prince, almost mothering him, never minding his random infidelities, and never a threat to him for his future. As a royal mistress she knew the rules. Besides, while being undoubtedly fond of him, she was not in love with him. He was too abject as a person. He aroused a maternal form of pity and the need for boosting and protection.

Later on she took a lover in Michael Herbert, a cousin of the Earl of Pembroke and a man occasionally mentioned in these letters as a rival to the Prince.

* * *

Until the end of the war the Prince was serving in France and Italy with occasional periods of leave. In 1919 he was in Germany and France. On his return to England the Prince found the country riven with social discontent. The war was won, the Germans defeated and Britain declared itself a land fit for heroes. He was aware that it was no such thing. He set about trying to ameliorate the lot of the working man. Sincere as he was in this aim, the plan was frustrated by external circumstances. It has never been easy to map out a path for the heir to the throne. He waits in the wings for the death of the monarch, his uncertain future dependent on a heartbeat. The problem has always been the question of how to occupy and prepare the heir. In the case of the future Edward VIII they sent him travelling.

Between 1919 and 1931 the Prince of Wales undertook extensive trips around the world.* From the outset he made a good impression. Meeting the wife of Colonel House in Paris, he told her: 'Oh, this is a bedazzlement to me.'[9] But the effect of the travelling was that he never settled for long into English life. Arguably anyone has time to fall in love and find a wife, but he blamed the demands of travelling for making this impossible in his case. It was while he was away on these journeys that his letters to Freda Dudley Ward became especially revealing, particularly after he left for Canada on 5 August 1919, remaining away until December. The letters are also interesting during his visit to New Zealand and Australia from March to October 1920.

What emerges is how depressed the Prince was while overseas. He was idolised by the general public on these tours, yet returned nightly to his room or cabin to pour out his heart to his mistress back in Britain. These long years away contributed to his despair and the decline in his character. He declared over and over again his distaste for his role as Prince of Wales, his dislike of the tedious duties meted out to him, how at odds he was with the stultifying formality of George V's court, how often he was berated by his father, but how he remained devoted to his mother, longing for letters from her. In May 1919 he told Freda his father was not 'worth working for though it's a foul thing to say & you know I'd never say it to anyone else!!'[10]

In July he identified that there was a difference 'between official capacity and private life; it's that difference which none of those ——— old courtiers realise, it's so so vast that their pompous minds can never grasp it'.[11]

He questioned whether the monarchy would survive and gave several strong hints that he longed to escape. This surely anticipated his

---

* There were further European travels in 1932 and from 1934 to 1936.

eventual Abdication and supports the theory that the real reason for the Abdication was that he did not want to be King.

On 18 August, while in Canada, the Prince complained to Freda about his endless official duties and ended by saying: 'If only WE could settle West (British Columbia or Alberta) darling what heaven & we could be the very happiest couple in the whole world'.[12] In September he spoke of Canada 'as the country & life for me, sweetheart, if we could live together'.[13] By October he was declaring: 'Christ I am fed up with the job of P. of W.'[14]

Serious thoughts of chucking it all in had formed in the Prince's mind. He did not believe it to be an impossible plan: 'I do get so terribly fed up with it & despondent about it sometimes & begin to feel like "resigning"!! And then I should be free to live or die according to how hard I worked though I should have you all to myself sweetheart & should only then be really happy & contented'.[15]

On the way to Australia he showed remarkable callousness when a private of marines fell overboard but was given up for dead after an hour's search – 'Of course one man's death means nothing . . .'[16] He was also happy to relate that he was using his cousin Dickie Mountbatten to procure partners for him '& only take on a "young woman" that he has vetted as being possible!!'[17] He came to rely on Mountbatten and declared that he would 'always be a great help to me',[18] adding that he would never have liked him had it not been for Freda's approval of him. His closeness to Mountbatten caused Dickie some problems as others on board became intensely jealous of him. This firm friendship between the Prince and Dickie survived the shipboard jealousies.

Their voyage to Australia took them to the celebrated stopover in San Diego, during which the Prince did not meet Wallis Spencer.

The Prince spent most of 1921 in England so that he could have a rest after the strenuous schedules of Canada and Australia. Then on 25 November he departed for an eight-month tour of India and the Far East (including Japan), returning in July 1922.

While the Prince was in India, another figure entered the picture: Major Edward (Fruity) Metcalfe, appointed to look after the Prince's polo ponies and very soon a key member of his staff and a close friend. A year or so later, from Balmoral, the Prince wrote to him. After news of his stalking and other activities, he continued:

> But enough balls & ragging. Honestly & you must know by now, I miss you terribly when you are away, & somehow I want to say I'm

ever so grateful to you for being the most marvellous friend to me
you have ever been ever since we left India; I don't count so
much *before* March do you? As we saw so very little of each other
as compared to now. Oh! I can't write what I want to say but I am
oh! *so very* grateful to you for *everything*, your marvellous friendship at first & then all your help with the horses & ponies & the
running of my stables. But I'm not going to write a soppy letter
though I *insist* on your *driving* out of your silly old head any ideas
or thoughts of returning to India when your year's leave is up. As
a matter of fact there's been no mention of your name up here as
yet but that don't make a scrap of difference. I'm just not going to
let you go back to that god forsaken country & life & insist on you
staying on with me (officially) to run my stables etc but actually to
————— well to carry on being what you've always been to me & are
now my greatest man friend. I can't just explain why you hold that
'position' and mean so much to me, right here on paper it is just
YOU!! But now I'm getting sloppy again and you'll hate me if I get
like that & besides I must dress for dinner for which it is an even
a far greater crime to be late than at Badminton!! But you know
what I mean!![19]

Thus was forged another friendship that would be severely tested by
later events.

In 1923 the Prince's relationship with Freda settled into something
more platonic than romantic. He returned to Canada and visited New
York. In March 1925 he set off on a tour of South Africa and South
America. In the summer of 1927 he took Prince George on a visit to
Canada, and in 1928 was in East Africa with Prince Henry, returning
home reluctantly when he was told his father might be dying.

Another figure who knew him well and who lost faith in him as these
years passed was Alan Lascelles, invariably known as 'Tommy'. He had
joined the Prince's staff in 1920, believing him at that time: 'the most
attractive man I've ever met.'[20] Eight years later Lascelles was wholly
disillusioned. In the 1960s Lascelles gave James Pope-Hennessy a thor-
ough character analysis of the Prince of Wales. 'It was impossible to be
angry with him, and very difficult to disagree with him. His favourite
slogan was: 'You know I can get away with it', and he did get away with
practically everything until he came to the throne,' he wrote. He loved
all forms of violent physical exercise – anything that would give him 'a
real good sweat', thus foxhunting and riding in point-to-points, even big-
game hunting. Hunting and golf were the passions of his outdoor life,

and 'for perspiratory purposes' squash-racquets. He practised hard at golf and got his handicap down to eight. (He even had a golf-driving cabin in a bedroom at York House, St James's.)

Lascelles realised that the Prince had been poorly educated, his tutor taking him only as far as Euclid and arithmetic. Tutoring had been followed by the Royal Navy; thus books played little part in his life. As a result he grew up frivolous, spending his evenings in nightclubs. He could exist on little sleep, but every now and again he slept round the clock to catch up. He was highly sexed and was always passionately (not romantically) attached to one lady after another – 'Society' ladies' rather than the *demi-monde*. He lived within substantial means, spending less than half his Duchy of Cornwall income of £50,000 to £80,000 a year:

There was much in him that was likeable, even lovable; yet at times he could be horribly selfish and ungenerous – latterly, he became distressingly mean over petty money matters. He was in fact 'an archangel ruined' – though ruined by what, God only knows. One theory was that he was an arrested adolescent – mentally and morally. There were, so doctors who knew him well said, certain physical signs to support this idea – e.g. the fact that he hardly ever had to shave; his ability to sleep, as if drugged, for many hours on end; his childish habit of strumming eternally on such instruments as the bagpipes, accordion, etc., his mulish obstinacy if asked to change any plan on which he had set his heart. Another theory was that the shock of plunging straight from Magdalen into the war, and seeing his contemporaries killed in droves, had warped his whole mental machinery. But whatever the cause, it was a fact that general ideas had no meaning for him, and that his only moral yardstick was the aforesaid 'Can I get away with it?' – which is really the yardstick of the average boy. In his case too, the consciousness of his own boundless charm disposed him to that particular form of egoism.

There never was a public figure with so many 'might-have-beens' in his life.

Later on, the saddest of all Shakespearian lines used sometimes to be applied to him – 'Lilies that fester smell far worse than weeds.'[21]

The Prince of Wales started his public life in 1919, full of charm, loved by everybody, but gradually degenerated into a fractious, worrying figure until, by the end of the 1920s, worn out by incessant travel, he had become a character who was already causing concern to his family and staff. Lloyd George can be blamed for some of this, since he insisted on the unending schedule that exhausted and disillusioned him. The Prince once asked Winston Churchill: 'How would you like to have to make a thousand speeches, and never once be allowed to say what you think yourself?'[22]

By the end of the 1920s the monarchy was in a curious situation. The Prince of Wales was still unmarried and his private life was the subject of some concern. His next brother, the Duke of York, had been happily married to Lady Elizabeth Bowes-Lyon since 1923. She was a supportive sister-in-law to the Prince, once describing George V to him as a 'narrow-minded autocrat'.[23] The Yorks had one little girl, the popular Princess Elizabeth, born in 1926. Another daughter, Princess Margaret, would complete their family in 1930. Princess Mary had married Viscount Lascelles and produced two sons. The other two brothers would not marry until the mid-1930s. Since 1928 King George V had been in indifferent health. He very nearly died from a condition that developed from congestion on his lung to a weakening of his heart and septicaemia. In December 1928 there were real fears that he might die. He recovered slowly, travelling to Bognor in February 1929 and returning to Windsor in May. Further recuperation followed and he remained effectively out of action for a whole year. From the late summer of 1929 until he died in January 1936, the King was nursed by Sister Catherine Black.

In 1929 the Prince took on Fort Belvedere, near Sunningdale. This little fort, perched on high land and surrounded by falling acres of garden, became his haven, the one home he loved over all others. Freda Dudley Ward helped him with its initial decoration.

During this phase the Prince took considerable responsibility for Prince George, who had retired from the Navy due to 'ill health' in March 1929. At that time he had engaged in a liaison with 'Kiki' Preston*, known as 'the girl with the silver syringe', who was considered such a bad influence on him that she was banned from England. An addict of heroin, cocaine and morphine, Kiki Preston soon had Prince George hooked on drugs. It was no easy business to get him off them, and much of the credit for this goes to the Prince. He invited his brother to move into his London home – York House, St James's – with him. There he acted as a mixture

---

* Alice ('Kiki') Gwynne (1898–1946), m. (1) 1919, Horace R. Bigelow Allen (divorced 1924). She m. (2) 1925, Jerome ('Gerry') Preston (1897–1934). She was a member of the Happy Valley Set in Kenya. Later, after many personal tragedies including the death of her son, and after years of mental instability, while in a state described as 'in ill health, depressed and nervous', she jumped to her death from a window in the Stanhope Hotel, 5th Avenue, New York on 23 December 1946.

of 'doctor, gaoler and detective combined'.[24] There was also a detective assigned to keep an eye on Prince George, and at certain times his outside telephone line was cut to isolate him from the outside world.

I was once taken to see Freda Dudley Ward – she was by then the Marchesa de Casa Maury. She was eighty-five and living at 86 Old Church Street, just off the King's Road. The house was smart and I noticed a 1945 drawing by Princess Marina of her daughter, Angie Laycock, in the hall.

Upstairs in a small room sat the Marchesa, a tiny, elegant little lady with fine bone structure and fair-tinted hair who was quite strongly made-up like an actress. She was very thin but had a rather swollen tummy due to having been immobile for days on end. There was a huge stick beside her and she was evidently in some pain. Beside her was a Campari, and a remote for the television. She smoked continually and her cigarette seemed to have more ash than tobacco. Somehow the ash always fell before it reached the ashtray. Later, in the hall downstairs, her Filipina maid explained: 'She can't move at all, the Marchesa. I do everything for her.'

The Marchesa spoke of the Duke of Kent and his brothers. She said that they all lived in fear of their parents – King George V was terrified of doing the wrong thing by them, and yet he did nothing *but* wrong. The Duke of Gloucester once went to a party and came home at four a.m. The poor man was spotted by a courtier. He was two minutes late for breakfast and the King looked at him and he went into 'a dead faint'. The other brothers saw him and told Freda; they thought it was very funny. Freda remembered the Duke of Kent as 'weak but charming', recalled Kiki Preston as 'very bad – he had a spell of her,' and said that Prince George was '*narcissiste*'. She was able to help him, however, knowing a doctor who could treat him.[25]

Another who was involved in this saga was the Countess of Dalkeith, the former Mollie Lascelles and later Duchess of Buccleuch,* who, as a young debutante, had lured James Stuart from Lady Elizabeth Bowes-Lyon when he was meant to be her boyfriend. She saw a lot of the Prince of Wales when, in her words, he was 'anchored' to Thelma Furness,[26] and she had an affair with Prince George. In later life (1961) the Duke of Windsor complained to the Duke of Buccleuch that he had disapproved

---

* Mary Lascelles (1900–93), married 1921, Walter, Earl of Dalkeith, later 8th Duke of Buccleuch & Queensberry (1894–1973). She was known as 'Midnight Moll' on account of her nocturnal peregrinations round the stately homes of England and Scotland. Among her other conquests were Major Tommy McDougal, Claus von Ahlefeldt, Sir Derrick Dunlop etc.

of Mollie and of her friendship with Prince George. But at the time it was a different story. In fact, if Mollie was with him she was considered so reliable that Prince George's detective was allowed off duty.

One night at York House, St James's Palace, Mollie was to dine with Prince George but discovered that he had told her a serious lie and so left 'in a disillusioned fury'. Prince George tried to telephone her but found that his line had been cut. The next morning, at 7.30 a.m., the Prince of Wales telephoned Mollie in person and asked her to come round and see him. The night had been one of terrible drama. Mollie arrived to find both brothers in 'a sorry state'. The Prince persuaded Mollie to forgive Prince George and help him 'make good'. She did so and took him to stay with her at Eildon, one of the many Buccleuch houses in Scotland, after which he never returned to 'dope' again.[27] In 1931 the Prince took Prince George with him on his tour of South America – not somewhere one would take a recovering drug addict these days.

The care that the Prince gave to his brother Prince George at this difficult time stands as a shining example of the very best of his qualities. When Prince George was killed in a flying accident in the war in August 1942, Queen Mary wrote to her estranged son in the Bahamas to thank him for a kindness to Georgie that she would never forget. Prince George's death was such a shock to both of them that it heralded something of a rapprochement between mother and son.

The Prince's affair with Viscountess Furness began in 1929. Thelma Furness knew him slightly, having once danced with him at Londonderry House, but caught his eye when he came to pin rosettes on cows at the Leicester Fair. At this depressing event he congratulated her on the birth of her son (the previous March) and enquired if she was ever in London. Recently deceived by her husband, she told him she was and very soon found herself invited alone to York House. They had cocktails together and later he took her to the Hotel Splendide for dinner and to dance. He asked if he might call her again.

Presently they were dining out frequently and began their affair*. The relationship flourished in 1930 when she was in Kenya with her husband and the Prince came out on safari. She joined him while her husband stayed away. After that she was recognised as the Prince's mistress in London society. Helen, Lady Dashwood recalled disapprovingly that 'Thelma Furness used to light the cigars for the Prince very publicly.'[28]

In January 1931, as recorded, it was Thelma's sister Connie who

---

* In March 1930 the Prince wrote to 'G' Trotter to say he was disturbed to get a cable from her saying she was a bit under the weather. He was concerned that she might be pregnant. She wasn't.

arranged for the Simpsons to join the Prince of Wales and Prince George at Burrough Court for a weekend. Thelma was later dismissive of Wallis's account of what happened – and dismissive of Wallis herself. Her line was that none of the dialogue about central heating and so forth ever took place: 'At that moment Wallis Simpson was as nervous and as impressed as any woman would have been on first meeting the Prince of Wales.'[29]

Wallis Simpson's meeting with the Prince in January 1931 did not sweep her overnight into his immediate circle. They did not meet again until the following May, after his return from South America.

She did not realise that she was involving herself with a man who was depressed and fed up with his royal duties, already a worry to his father and proving exasperating to his courtiers. She in turn was a woman of thirty-four, on her second marriage and making her way in London society, fuelled by the ambition to widen her group of friends. But her social ambitions took second place, as ever, to her quest for security. She had overcome a number of difficulties in her life and had reached a relatively stable plateau. Her letters to Aunt Bessie, published after her death, show a woman dealing with minor money worries and servant problems, relishing an invitation to tea at Knole with Lord Sackville and his American wife Anne Bigelow, or battling with the Lord Chamberlain over being a divorced woman who wished to be presented at court.

Wallis hoped to see the Prince of Wales again and moved closer to his set when she was befriended by Nada, Marchioness of Milford Haven, Dickie Mountbatten's sister-in-law. The second meeting was also at the instigation of Thelma Furness, who included Wallis in a tea party. When she was presented at court in her white dress and ostrich feathers the following month, Thelma helped her dress for the occasion. At the Palace itself Wallis happened to overhear the Prince complaining that the lighting made all the women look ghastly.

She had the opportunity to tease the Prince about this when they met that evening at Thelma's house. The Prince complimented her on her gown. 'But sir,' she said, 'I understood that you thought we all looked ghastly.' He was taken by surprise and then smiled: 'I had no idea my voice carried so far.'[30] When they left the party the Simpsons found the Prince on the doorstep. He offered to drop them home in his car. Wallis invited him in for a drink. He did not accept but told her that he would love to come in another time.

One of the Duchess's later friends said that Wallis treated the Prince as if he were some kind of movie star or American business tycoon. There is no doubt that her provocative manner appealed to him. He liked to be treated badly as he had made clear to Freda Dudley Ward. It is an exaggeration but the example used to be given that Wallis would say to him: 'Hold the dogs while I have my hair done,' and that he loved it. Nobody had spoken to him in that kind of way before, and he felt that at last he was being treated as a real person. But it was not Wallis who 'Americanised' him. It was Thelma. She fuelled a fascination for the New World that had first been inspired in him on his 1919 visit. Later in life he became entranced by American tycoons and their ways. Unlike Freda Dudley Ward, Thelma Furness was not considered a good influence on the Prince's character.

Thelma also maintained that no 'electric tension was set up'[31] between Wallis and the Prince. Thelma considered Wallis her best friend and thus the Simpsons met the Prince regularly in her company. In fact there were only four encounters with the Prince in 1931. In January 1932 he dined at Bryanston Court for the first time, Thelma and her sister Connie being among the guests. This was swiftly followed by the first of many invitations to Fort Belvedere. 1932 was not Wallis's best year, however, as she suffered intermittent bouts of ill health, which were not helped by a serious decline in Ernest's business. 1933 proved little better, though she was drawn more frequently into the Prince's company. Between 1931 and 1934 the friendship developed somewhat gradually.

However, in 1934 a major change occurred after which Wallis's fate was virtually sealed. Thelma left for America on 25 January 1934. Just prior to her departure Wallis lunched with Thelma at the Ritz. According to Thelma's memoirs, Wallis suddenly said to her: 'Oh, Thelma, the little man is going to be so lonely.' And Thelma replied: 'Well, dear, you look after him while I'm away.'[32]

Musing on this many years later, Gladys, Duchess of Marlborough commented: 'Mrs Simpson was left in charge by Thelma Furness – a nice person – a bit better than the rest, not as gossipy. "Can you imagine? – Knowing what he was, and what she was?"'[33]

According to both the Duke and Duchess of Windsor, the relationship took wing at a dinner he gave at the Dorchester, when he began to talk about his work and Wallis showed sympathetic interest and support. Suddenly he took to popping into Bryanston Court, staying for a few minutes or the whole evening. Ernest took to excusing himself and retiring to another room with his papers. At weekends at the Fort, the Prince danced more often with Wallis than with anyone else. As early as 12 February 1934 she was telling Aunt Bessie that she had 'inherited' the Prince (the 'young man') from Thelma Furness.[34] Inevitably there was gossip and a week later Wallis protested to her aunt that she was 'not in the habit of taking my girlfriends' beaux'.[35]

While she was away Thelma had been pursued by Prince Aly Khan, the playboy son of the Aga Khan. He was a legendary womaniser, blessed, so it was said, by the ability to sustain his endeavours in bed almost indefinitely. He inspired Alastair Forbes to one of his equally legendary jokes: that Aly Khan was like Father Christmas – he came but once a year.[36] No one made such claims for the Prince of Wales.

On Thelma's return to Britain in March 1934 she found that the atmosphere at York House and the Fort had cooled. Conveniently, the Prince was able to attach his rather distant attitude to Thelma to the rumours about Aly Khan. Concerned, Thelma invited the Simpsons to the Fort the next weekend and was quick to observe little jokes passing between the Prince and Wallis. Wallis slapped his hand playfully. Thelma wrote of her realisation as follows:

> Wallis looked straight at me. And then and there I knew the 'reason' was Wallis – Wallis of all people . . . I knew then that she had looked after him exceedingly well. That one cold, defiant glance had told me the entire story.[37]

After a brief, unsatisfactory exchange with the Prince, Thelma left the Fort the following morning. On 15 April Wallis reported to her aunt that Thelma's 'rule' was over and that she was avoiding seeing the Prince alone due to his being very attentive.[38]

Wallis also claimed that the Prince was still seeing just as much as ever of Freda Dudley Ward. Frances Donaldson, however, related that Freda had been concerned with the illness of her daughter and had not spoken to the Prince for a while. When she attempted to do so on the telephone not long after the split with Thelma, around May 1934, a deeply apologetic switchboard operator at St James's Palace told her that the orders were that she should not be put through. Freda Dudley Ward and the Prince never spoke again. By then, whether she realised it or not, and whether she truly wished it or not, Mrs Simpson held sway.

5

The Road to Abdication

The Abdication in December 1936 was a personal tragedy for those involved in it. Edward VIII departed in a state that Queen Mary described as 'absolutely unhinged'.[1] Though he professed never to have regretted his decision, one look at his eyes told a sadder story. His consolation was that he married the woman by whom he was so besotted and stayed married to her for the next thirty-five years, contrary to the expectations of the British court in 1936. Yet since the only issue that concerned the departing King was his quest for personal happiness, he passed through the drama with single-minded resolve.

For Wallis Simpson it was certainly a tragedy. There is no doubt that she enjoyed being the 'friend' of the Prince of Wales, and perhaps even more so when he became King. As to the word 'friend' the interpretation put on that word is of no great consequence. She was his favourite. The great men of the age sought her company as a conduit to the King. The society hostesses of the day vied to entertain her. If she gave a dinner party, the King sent gold plate and flowers and footmen to her flat at Bryanston Court. It cannot have been other than intoxicating.

But it got out of hand. Wallis Simpson was fond of Edward VIII but she was not in love with him. Therefore the Abdication is not one of the great romances of the twentieth century, it is one of the great tragedies. There came several points in 1936 when Wallis realised the dangers and panicked. She tried to escape. How hard she tried is a matter for speculation. But she always considered the Abdication a terrible mistake that should have been avoided. She used to say, in later life, that she aged ten years in 1936, and that the one thing for which she never forgave the Duke of Windsor was abdicating.

She was then condemned to a life of self-imposed exile, looking after a man who had been busy every day of his life but who now had nothing to do other than play golf, travel from one hot spot to another, eat admittedly delicious meals and ruminate over the past, which he did endlessly, though he maintained in public that he and the Duchess never spoke of the Abdication again. Cleveland Amory wrote:

Almost every conversation I had with the Duke would have at least one time in it the preface, 'When I was King', and then a story about that. As for the Duchess, she did not know the first thing about the British government, nor indeed about the British people. All she knew was how to get a man, and how to get ahead.[2]

Amory was an embittered witness to the lives of the Windsors, but nevertheless he had a point. Wallis did not understand what she was getting herself into. She misinterpreted the motives of the King. She also thought that a king was a king and could do as he pleased. Her self-perception was in marked contrast to how the world viewed her. She saw herself as the scion of two highly respected Southern families in Baltimore and Virginia, as a girl who had been denied her birthright, had suffered an unfortunate first marriage and had found some stability in her second marriage. She had then enjoyed the social success of being the King's favourite.

The Abdication propelled the Prince's brother, the Duke of York, to the Throne. He felt inadequate for the task of kingship ahead. He had never seen a state paper, found public speaking terrifying since he suffered from a bad stammer, and both he and the Duchess seriously believed that the British public might not want them as King and Queen. For Queen Mary, too, it was a tragedy. She was devoted to her eldest son, but could not accept his wish to put the path of personal happiness before that of duty. This was best summed up in her line to him: 'It seemed inconceivable to those who had made such sacrifices during the war that you, as their King, refused a lesser sacrifice.'[3]

For Britain and the Empire it was the opposite. They acquired a dedicated King and Queen, who soon won the hearts of the people – for the people of Britain preferred the kind of monarchy represented by George VI and Queen Elizabeth: Sunday lunch, a walk in the park and a cup of tea, as opposed to the brittle nightclub and cocktail-shaker life represented by Edward VIII and Mrs Simpson. To this day there are those who jest that the Duchess of Windsor should be allocated a statue on the fourth plinth of Trafalgar Square for taking Edward VIII away.

Between the spring of 1934 and the death of King George V in January 1936, the romance between the Prince of Wales and Wallis solidified to a point where he considered her to be indispensable to his future happiness. Wallis was aware that she was now the favourite but still considered herself a married woman whose duty was to keep two men as happy as possible. Ernest was acquiescent in this, undoubtedly unhappy but continuing to hope that this would be just an episode that would pass, as other such romances with the Prince were known to have done, and that his wife would return to him. According to Wallis, in May 1934 she would have given the Prince up if Ernest had raised any objections. Meanwhile Thelma Furness consoled herself with the rigorous ministrations of Prince Aly Khan.

The Royal Family noticed a change in the Prince at this time. In December 1936 the Duke of Kent told Colonel Thomas Dugdale, Baldwin's Parliamentary Private Secretary, that 'since Mrs Simpson had entered the King's life neither he nor his brothers had ever seen him as in days gone by and that he had talked to him during the morning for a longer time than he had enjoyed for over two years'.[4] During the summer of 1936 Edward VIII told his brother: 'As I made up my mind two years ago, why should I change now?'[5] And yet he could still show sparkle. When the King's niece, Princess Elizabeth, knocked on his door one morning, the King called out: 'You may come in, but don't forget your bloody curtsy.'[6]

Aunt Bessie was still Wallis's confidante and in the summer of 1934 she became her chaperone, first in Biarritz and later on a yacht to Cannes which sailed on to Genoa. They stayed on Lake Como, making it a holiday of virtually seven weeks. When Wallis returned to Southampton, Ernest met her and asked how it had been. She said she had been 'Wallis in Wonderland'. He thought she had been in Peter Pan's Never-Never Land, and called the Prince 'Peter Pan' from that day on.[7]

Canon Alec Sargent, chaplain to the Archbishop of Canterbury, first heard about Mrs Simpson in 1934, when George V 'poured it all out to C.C. in a long talk at Balmoral', and the Archbishop's clergy gathered that there was some 'dreadful common American woman'[8] always in the Prince's company.

The wedding of the Duke of Kent and Princess Marina of Greece was the only occasion when Wallis met Queen Mary. For Wallis, there was what she called 'the excitement of the Prince bringing the Queen up to Ernest and self in front of all the cold jealous eyes',[9] itself a telling description.

1935 was to be the last carefree year, the year of the Silver Jubilee, soon after which George V became exhausted. His health broke down and he deteriorated yet further after the death of his favourite sister Princess Victoria in December.

Wallis was happy enough and there was still no hint of the impending crisis. She saw her role as being supportive, almost maternal to the Prince. Wallis helped him with redecoration work at the Fort and their life, such as it was, settled into a routine. Yet others were confused by her, Chips Channon finding her 'surprised and rather conscience-stricken by her present position and the limelight which consequently falls upon her.'[10] By April Channon thought she had 'complete power over the Prince of Wales.'[11]

Ernest became irritated when Wallis went to Kitzbühl with the Prince rather than accompany him – Ernest – to New York and soon their marriage was in serious trouble. Conveniently, however, the marriage of Wallis's girlhood friend Mary Kirk and Jacques Raffray came unstuck at the same time, affording Ernest some distraction.

Wallis attended the Silver Jubilee ball on 14 May, invited with Ernest. And in the summer she stayed with the Prince at Villa Le Roc at Golfe-Juan. According to the Duke of Windsor, it was after this holiday that he began to consider marriage to Wallis as his determined path, though contemporary evidence suggests he was set on this idea a year before.

A recently released Metropolitan Police file at the National Archives includes a report dated 3 July 1935, suggesting that Mrs Simpson had a secret lover called Guy Marcus Trundle. Superintendent A. Canning of Special Branch wrote confidently of his information, suggesting that Mr Simpson was having his wife watched and that 'in consequence she is very careful for the double purpose of keeping both P.O.W. and her husband in ignorance of her surreptitious love affairs.'[12] I hesitate to question Special Branch's findings but it is most unlikely that this was true, not least because no independent witness (including members of the Trundle family) has ever hinted at such a thing and it does not fit psychologically. I do not believe it.

It has often been suggested that the Prince intended to talk to his father about Wallis. Sir Horace Wilson's account of the Abdication reveals that the Duke of York told Stanley Baldwin on 8 December 1936 that 'the King, then Prince of Wales, had so definitely made up his mind to marry Mrs Simpson that he had determined to offer to give up his position as Prince of Wales.'[13] Sir Horace continued: '(It is, I think, known to several people that for some time previously the King, then Prince of Wales, had remarked to his friends that he had no wish to become King and that it would be preferable if his brother, the Duke of York, could succeed King George V.) He had postponed speaking to his father about this, realising how much it would upset the King. Before anything had been said on the matter the death of King George V occurred.' Baldwin came to attribute the 'hunted' look on the new King's face as evidence of his realisation that 'he had missed his opportunity to get out and would now find it much more difficult to do so'.[14]

Sir Horace recorded two points of criticism that an historian of the future might make in relation to the way Baldwin, along with his ministers and advisers, had handled the Abdication. The first was that Lord Wigram, the old King's Private Secretary, had warned Baldwin early in 1936 that the King was determined to marry Mrs Simpson.* Baldwin's answer to this was that he could not believe that 'whatever might have been the King's intention beforehand, he would propose to go on with the matter now that he had become King.'[15] The second concerned the King's brothers, who had not been allowed to exercise any influence upon him, having scarcely seen him since Mrs Simpson came on the scene. Sir Horace's verdict was: 'Mrs Simpson had, in fact, as frequently happens in this sort of case, come between the Prince of Wales and the members of his family.'[16]

The latter point is a hard one. There is no evidence that Wallis consciously tried to isolate him from his family but she was acutely aware of their unwillingness to accept her. It was more a division of the ways. Once with Wallis, and keen to join her café-society world, the Prince found his own family more antiquated than ever. None of them showed any inclination to meet Wallis and George V instructed the Lord Chamberlain that she was not to be invited to the Silver Jubilee Ball or to Ascot, although the Prince circumvented the first instruction. As we have seen, the Duke of Gloucester had drifted away from his brother. The Yorks went skating with Wallis once, but when the Duchess of York met her at Royal Lodge in 1936 she showed no enthusiasm to repeat the encounter. Though they were sometimes thrown together, the Duchess let it be known that she did not wish to meet Mrs Simpson.

Prince George was still in the Prince's company to some extent, though his bride, Princess Marina of Greece, was not in the least inclined to include Mrs Simpson in her circle of friends.

Through 1935 the relationship between the Prince and Wallis crystallised. In the summer they had a row and she was sufficiently sure of her hold over him to rebuke him. By October her marriage to Ernest was nothing more than a public façade. Christmas gave way to the New Year and the Prince of Wales was summoned to Sandringham as the King was dying. George V's life was ended, with decisive help from the needle of his doctor, Lord Dawson of Penn, on 20 January 1936.

* * *

* The Archbishop of Canterbury's chaplain, Rev. Alan Don, recorded that in February Wigram had warned them about the King: 'Wigram regards the poor fellow as "mad" and would not be surprised if he did away with himself, for he is dominated by that woman who does what she likes with him and sometimes reduces him to tears by her treatment of him. It is all utterly pathetic.' [Rev. Alan Don diary].

The Prince of Wales became the head of his family and was proclaimed as King Edward VIII. Almost immediately he changed the Sandringham clocks to the normal time – in his father's reign they had been set half an hour fast. For those who deal in omens, two sinister things happened. Soon after Edward VIII's accession, the flagpole on Sandringham House broke in a storm. This was not reported in the press. The second incident *was* widely reported: during the ceremonial funeral procession from King's Cross to Westminster Hall, the Maltese cross fell off the Imperial State Crown that had been placed on top of George V's coffin. It was retrieved by the sergeant-major of the Grenadier escort.

The Accession was heralded, as new reigns are, with laudatory comments about the new King. Inevitably he acquired many new duties, receiving mourners, dealing with state papers and later with all the attendant business of a new monarch. Though the courtiers, members of his family and other well-informed figures had considerable reason to be concerned on his behalf, the general public still thought of him as the good-looking young Prince of Wales who had so consistently charmed them. But there was cause for concern. The Archbishop of Canterbury's chaplain, Rev. Alan Don, heard an odd rumour on the day that George V died to the effect that the King had become a Roman Catholic in order to escape the throne: 'That the P. of W. would like to make way for the Duke of York and his charming Duchess I do not doubt, but that there is truth in this rumour I refuse to believe. The next few hours may enlighten us,'[17] wrote the chaplain.

King Edward VIII had one overriding worry – how to resolve his personal crisis. He was determined to marry Wallis and to his credit he realised that he must resolve this issue before taking the Coronation Oath, in which he would promise to uphold the beliefs of the Church of England. He knew that the moment he took that oath he would lose any chance of marrying a twice-divorced woman.

As to Wallis, she had been told often enough that she was a good influence on the new King and she intended to remain so. One of the things she had achieved was a control of the aspect of his character that most worried Queen Mary. She had curtailed his excessive drinking and he was now happily limited to whisky and water. In that respect she fulfilled the duty of a best friend. During most of 1936 she had no hint that he might surrender his throne. She wanted him to excel as a King and believed she could help him from the wings. She told her aunt she thought he would make 'a great King of a new era.'[18]

In March Wallis sidelined Ernest by suggesting that one day he might marry her old friend Mary Kirk Raffray, telling Aunt Bessie that he had always loved her and thus supporting the theory that she might have stepped between them earlier in their lives.

By May the King had settled a considerable sum of money on Wallis, enough to spare her financial worries for the rest of her life. In a long letter to Aunt Bessie, she confessed to being overwrought and under considerable stress. She said she could not go back to Ernest and life at Bryanston Court, though she was not contemplating divorce. She considered her position with the King as powerful but tenuous. If he fell for a younger woman she would lose her power base. But she began to worry that the King was forming a graver plan from which he must be dissuaded.

While Wallis remained married to Ernest there was no direct reason why Ministers or courtiers should worry unduly because, self-evidently, the King could not marry her. But the King decided that he wanted her to divorce. He might have felt that, as King, it was wrong to be involved with another man's wife, but by setting the divorce in motion he precipitated the Abdication crisis.

Despite imminent separation, the Simpsons were invited jointly to dinner with the King and their names appeared in the Court Circular for the first time. On 28 May 1936 the Prime Minister and Mrs Baldwin were guests at York House. Presently there was another dinner at York House when Wallis dined and the Duke and Duchess of York were present. A few days later Ernest Simpson conveniently made himself the guilty party in the divorce by spending a night at the Hotel de Paris at Bray. Soon afterwards followed the *Nahlin* cruise, during which the King, Wallis and various guests sailed the Mediterranean. This cruise attracted considerable attention in the foreign press, especially in the United States. By tacit agreement no hint of the affair was mentioned in Britain, causing the curious situation that a few people knew all about it while the majority knew nothing.

The attitude of the overseas press was responsible for Wallis's anxious letter of 16 September to the King, in which she said she needed to renounce him and return to Ernest. She made the point that he (the King) had been 'independent of affection' all his life and rightly predicted: 'I am sure you and I would only create disaster together.'[19]

The King would have none of this and a few days later Wallis was heading to Balmoral to stay with him there. Some months previously he had been asked to open the Aberdeen Royal Infirmary, but in June he declined on the grounds that the Court was still in mourning and he was therefore undertaking no engagements of that kind. He felt he could not make an exception but offered them the Duke of York instead (despite the fact that he too was in mourning). Unfortunately the day of the opening coincided with the King going to the station to collect Mrs Simpson. This unfortunate incident was said to have lost the King the affection and respect of Scotland to a man.

Many have left accounts of how the Abdication saga progressed. One of the most compelling is the report by Sir Horace Wilson, recently released and available to be read in the National Archives along with all the Abdication papers.

Sir Horace was one of the great public servants of the twentieth century, praised for his 'intelligence, clarity of mind and expression, skill in conciliation, impartiality, and integrity,'[20] He had been appointed special adviser to Stanley Baldwin ('seconded to the Treasury for special service with the Prime Minister') and was thus at the Prime Minister's right hand throughout the crisis, with an office next to the Cabinet Room in 10 Downing Street. Shortly after the Abdication, he wrote a forty-five-page account of it, which makes for gripping reading even all these years later when the eventual outcome is known. His version, though quite hostile to Mrs Simpson, is important since it strengthens the views of many of the central protagonists – that nobody wanted the King to abdicate, that nobody tried to force him to do so and that everyone worked hard to prevent the final tragedy.

This was certainly the opinion of Alan Lascelles, then the King's Assistant Private Secretary. He told James Pope-Hennessy:

> Since about 1925, Mr Baldwin, to my certain knowledge, had been a warm admirer & a devoted friend of the Prince of Wales, & his R.H. cordially reciprocated his friendship.
> To those of us who were closely associated with the tragedy of the Abdication, the idea that Mr Baldwin or anybody else ever, in any way, wished the King ill, has always been preposterous.[21]

When the Duke of Windsor died in 1972, Helen Hardinge, widow of the King's Private Secretary, Alec Hardinge, supported this view. She told Frances Donaldson: 'I don't mind what the Press said & all the hysteria at all. They can pretend the Duke of W. was the greatest King since Alfred & the greatest lover since Cleopatra's Antony provided they do not question the *loyalty* of his servants & his Government during the 10 months' reign.'[22]

The Abdication was brought on by the obstinacy of one man and one man alone – King Edward VIII. He was the only person in Britain who wanted Mrs Simpson to be Queen. Not even Mrs Simpson herself entertained the idea.

Sir Horace pointed out that Baldwin became increasingly anxious about the King's association with Mrs Simpson in the summer of 1936 despite there being no specific event or aspect of the association which forced him to take action. He hoped that the King's 'good nature, his capacity for getting on with other people, and his obvious pleasure in understanding ordinary people, in particular work people'[23] would 'make such an appeal to him that he would decide in the end that the only course open to him was to do his utmost to be that King which the people of this country had come to expect.'[24] Lord Wigram was the first to sound alarm bells shortly before his resignation as Private Secretary. His concerns were that the King appeared subservient to Mrs Simpson, was extravagant in his generosity to her, treated his staff badly and allowed Mrs Simpson to see state papers. He thought it pointless to attempt to reason with the King. Sir Horace Wilson believed that Mrs Simpson might be in touch with 'certain political factions' in Germany and thought this might explain why 'she urged the King to show his authority, to govern, to dictate.' He believed she was keen to have a position of influence for herself and to influence public affairs.[25]

There were political matters to preoccupy Baldwin in 1936 and the issue of Mrs Simpson did not become a particular concern until the late summer. Towards the end of July the Prime Minister's doctor, Lord Dawson of Penn, advised him to take three months of complete rest. Baldwin began his holiday in Wales and later in Norfolk. Photographs of the *Nahlin* cruise appeared in British papers, and anxious letters of concern began to reach Downing Street. As related, agreement was reached in the British press that there should be no comment about the King's private life. When Baldwin returned to Downing Street in October he was very worried. The following day, 13 October, he had an audience with the King at which no mention was made of the press comment, but before and after it Alec Hardinge, the Private Secretary, warned him that trouble was brewing.

On 15 October the press learned of the impending Simpson divorce case, after which it was clear that the silence could no longer be maintained indefinitely. Baldwin decided he must see the King and he did so at Fort Belvedere on 20 October. This proved a friendly meeting at which no formal advice was offered. Baldwin simply wanted to warn the King about the course he was taking and its possible consequences. The Prime Minister brought some correspondence and press cuttings with him to support his case. The King came away from the meeting with the impression that the Prime Minister had told him 'he was embarking on a course which would affront the people of the country and would arouse their opposition.' As Sir Horace commented with hindsight:

At the time it looked as if the Prime Minister might perhaps have been so anxious not to break the contact between the King and himself as to have given the King the impression that he, the Prime Minister, did not take a grave view of the consequences of the continuance of the King's association with Mrs Simpson. We now know, in the light of later events, that the King's infatuation for Mrs Simpson was such as to make him quite oblivious of the realities of the situation and to make him incapable of seeing any other considerations in the proper perspective. I was myself very much perturbed at what I heard the King had been saying after the interview; it did not seem to square at all with what the Prime Minister had told me he had said to the King. I am satisfied myself that the explanation is the one that I have just stated.[26]

At the meeting the King told the Prime Minister that he could not live without Mrs Simpson and nor could he intervene with the private affairs of his subjects. Baldwin, in turn, told him that Mrs Simpson should not proceed with the divorce suit which would 'accentuate the already growing volume of public anxiety.'[27]

The divorce case proceeded and was granted – decree nisi with costs – on 27 October. Ernest left Bryanston Court. He wrote to Wallis:

I think something in me quietly died when I closed the door of the flat for the last time this evening. I have no tears left to shed. I know that somewhere in your heart there is a small flame burning for me. Guard it carefully my darling and don't let it go out – if only in memory of the sacred lovely things that have been. Someday I pray God will fan it into a blaze again and bring you back to me.[28]

Wallis evidently reimbursed Ernest for the costs of the divorce. About three weeks later Victor Cazalet, a Conservative MP, had the chance to ask Wallis why she had gone through with the divorce. She told him 'it was not her fault. Simpson had divorced her; she wanted to be free, if she ever had to make her life again.' Nevertheless Cazalet thought Wallis was 'the one real friend he [the King] has ever had. She does have a wonderful influence over him, but she knows how stubborn he is, and how difficult to influence.'[29]

On 3 November the King drove to Westminster to open Parliament and took the prescribed oath to be a 'faithful Protestant'. Mrs Simpson, fresh from her divorce, watched part of the ceremony from the Royal Gallery, which caused Alan Don to comment: 'She must be a brazen-faced woman to appear thus among the assembled aristocracy within a week of the divorce which has set everyone talking.'[30]

Following discussions with senior cabinet colleagues, Baldwin decided that this was not the moment to offer the King formal advice. The King attended Armistice Day celebrations and inspected the Fleet. Then he was going on a tour of depressed areas in South Wales. Baldwin thought that a further informal talk would be more productive after these visits, 'each of which must have raised "Kingly" thoughts in the mind of the King.'[31]

Events were accelerated by the actions of Major Alec Hardinge, the King's Private Secretary. He had learned of the fears of the press and the anxiety of government ministers, and he felt obliged to let the King know about this information. He wrote the King a letter on 13 November and brought it to the Prime Minister for his scrutiny. Wilson's interpretation of this letter was that if Ministers tended formal advice to the King and it was rejected, it would lead to the resignation of the Government. He added a plea on his own behalf that the King should arrange for Mrs Simpson to leave the country forthwith. Sir Horace was present when Hardinge met Baldwin.

It was pointed out to Hardinge that he was taking a considerable personal risk. Hardinge replied that he would face any consequences since he was 'gravely concerned by the course that events were taking', believed the King should be warned of the constitutional implications, and felt that as his Private Secretary it was his duty to impart the information that had reached him. The Prime Minister agreed that the letter should be sent. As a result of receiving the letter there was a further meeting between Baldwin and the King.[32]

This time Baldwin told him that the public opinion in the United Kingdom and the Dominions would not accept the marriage since Mrs Simpson would automatically become Queen. The King told the Prime Minister that he was set on marrying Mrs Simpson, that he accepted that Baldwin was right about public opinion and therefore he was prepared to abdicate. Baldwin mentioned possible problems over Mrs Simpson's divorce and asked the King to think it over. The next day he visited Queen Mary, while the King had meetings with Sir Samuel Hoare and Duff Cooper, as well as with Winston Churchill and Esmond Harmsworth, the press baron.

Now Walter Monckton entered the picture. He was a lawyer who served as Attorney General to the Duchy of Cornwall. He was such an arch negotiator that he managed to retain the King's confidence during and beyond the Abdication. He acted as the intermediary between Baldwin and the King. As Wilson put it:

> He was able to interpret to the Prime Minister what was in the King's mind and went so far as anyone could possibly go to explain to the King the consequences of his proposed action and at the same time the feelings of his many friends as to the unwisdom of his actions.[33]

The press remained the greatest danger during these days. The Government wanted to take all the major editors into their confidence. They did not know that 'influences' were at work in the Harmsworth and Beaverbrook press which might favour the King against the Government.

When Baldwin finally met Harmsworth he wanted to know what information was reaching him and how long the press was likely to remain silent. Harmsworth then advanced the idea of a morganatic marriage, which, Wilson thought, might have originated with Winston Churchill.

On 25 November the King and Baldwin met again and the King asked him to examine the Harmsworth proposal of a morganatic marriage. Baldwin was doubtful whether the House of Commons would accept this idea, but said he would consult the Cabinet. He warned the King that, while at present he enjoyed undoubted popularity, 'there was every reason to suppose that persistence in his present course of action would cause a revulsion of feeling, a good deal of which would be directed against Mrs Simpson.'[34]

After that events moved swiftly. There was a Cabinet meeting on 27 November at which it was agreed that the Dominion Governments should be informed and consulted. A telegram was sent to them. Their response was eagerly awaited. Baldwin did not impose his views upon them. Since the Statute of Westminster became law in 1931 all the Dominion Prime Ministers resisted any form of interference from Whitehall, genuine or perceived. Independently they all declared themselves against the morganatic proposal. This was significant as the political situation was already unstable in Europe and there was the fear that war might come, in which case, as in the Great War, their support would be needed. Mackenzie-King, Prime Minister of Canada, was a dour figure – a Presbyterian Scot. He would never have supported such a marriage, nor did he.

On 1 December the Bishop of Bradford* addressed his diocesan conference on the forthcoming Coronation service. In a long speech about the way the Coronation should be approached, he highlighted a divide between the King's personal approach to religion, including his attitude to the service he was to take part in, and his 'public capacity' at his Coronation. He ended by saying:

> First, on the faith, prayer, and self-dedication of the King himself; and on that it would be improper for me to say anything except to commend him to God's grace, which he will so abundantly need, as we all need it – for the King is a man like ourselves – if he is to do his duty faithfully. We hope that he is aware of his need. Some of us wish that he gave more positive signs of such awareness.

A reporter from a local paper returned to his office with his notes and, after consulting a colleague, wired the story to the Press Association. Leaders appeared in papers such as the *Yorkshire Post*, all assuming that the bishop had referred to Mrs Simpson. The national papers could no longer hold their silence. Later, the stunned bishop maintained that though he had briefly heard of Mrs Simpson, he did not have her in mind. His concern had been the King's indifference to churchgoing, which he felt sat uneasily with his role as head of the Church of England. Canon Sargent thought the disclaimer 'unwise' and recorded the Archbishop's annoyance: 'Why can't he hold his tongue? If he had only known all that I know?'[35]

The following day the King asked Baldwin if he could make a broadcast appeal to his people on the question of his marrying Mrs Simpson and then retreat for a time while the British people considered the proposal. Baldwin was against this plan, as was Clement Attlee, Leader of the Opposition. Nothing came of it.

Meanwhile some areas of the press promoted the morganatic suggestion so the Prime Minister squashed it in a statement to the House of Commons on 4 December. This left Edward VIII with but two alternatives – to renounce Mrs Simpson, or to abdicate. There was never any doubt in his mind concerning his choice. But timing was an issue: Parliament was becoming restive and the King was anxious to make his views known, while Baldwin was playing for time, hoping against hope that the King might see sense.

---

* Rt. Rev. Alfred Blunt (1879–1957), 2nd Bishop of Bradford, a scholar who preferred pastoral work. He suffered several nervous breakdowns due to overwork and adopted a rabid form of socialism.

In the next few days the King asked if Mrs Simpson's decree nisi could be made absolute at once. Although there were many sensible reasons for expediting this – which was, after all, the cause for the Abdication – the matter got tangled in questions of the Government interfering with the law of the land, and after prolonged and complicated negotiations nothing came of that notion either.

Meanwhile the King asked Baldwin if he might see Winston Churchill, a friend since boyhood. Fearing that he might be accused of attempting to isolate the King, Baldwin agreed. Later, aware of various moves by Churchill and the Harmsworth and Beaverbrook press, he said: 'I have made my first blunder.'[36] His cabinet colleagues assured him that they would have taken the same action. Churchill's line (which also emerged in those elements of the press) was that the King needed time. Churchill wrote to Baldwin that he found the King 'under the very greatest strain and very near breaking point.' The King had lost the thread of the conversation at least twice. 'It would be a most cruel and wrong thing to extort a decision from him in his present state.'[37]

Churchill urged the King to fight his corner and was disappointed when the King did not rise to the challenge. Possibly he was afraid he might win. Churchill claimed later that he had no intention of supporting the idea of Mrs Simpson as Queen but had thought the King was suffering from 'a temporary passion'. Along with Lord Beaverbrook, he hoped that Mrs Simpson could be frightened away. If that were successful, the King could be detained at Windsor Castle with his doctors Lord Dawson of Penn at the front gate and Lord Horder at the back and, given time, he would recover from his infatuation.

Years later Churchill told his Private Secretary Sir John Colville that threatening letters would be written to Mrs Simpson and bricks thrown through her window. Colville was horrified and asked: 'Do you mean you did that?' Churchill said that Beaverbrook had done so. Beaverbrook denied this but conceded that some of his journalists at the *Daily Express* might have done such things.[38]

On the other hand, Sir Horace Wilson was another who thought the press were being manipulated. He was convinced that Mrs Simpson was briefing elements of the American press, in particular the Hearst press. He credited her with evolving 'the lines of the campaign for the marriage', attempting to lay down terms concerned with her title and to secure the right to return to Fort Belvedere and 'adequate financial provision'.[39]

A brick was thrown and Wallis duly took fright. She had not expected to become a vilified woman. She retreated to the Fort with her Aunt Bessie, who had come from America to protect her. Then, on 3 December, she set off in secret to France, escorted by Lord Brownlow, a former Grenadier and a Lord-in-Waiting to the King, and driven by the King's chauffeur, George Ladbrook. Her departure left the King free to implement his decision on his own.

While the King waited at the Fort, the King's Proctor then emerged with concerns about the Simpson divorce. These involved 'association between the King and Mrs Simpson' and 'collusion between Mr and Mrs Simpson as to the divorce proceedings'.[40]

Mrs Simpson was in France and unlikely to return. Monckton now suggested that her solicitor, Theodore Goddard, should stand ready to go out to Cannes where 'he might be able to put before her considerations which would induce her to stay away.'[41]

Goddard felt that Mrs Simpson had misled him over her divorce, having told him of her plan to fade away after the proceedings, something which she failed to do. His mission now was a last-ditch attempt to persuade her to give the King up. When Goddard had a meeting with Sir Horace Wilson, the civil servant got the impression that the lawyer was asking whether there might be a financial incentive in her 'clearing out'.[42] Wilson was taken aback and reminded Goddard that it was the lawyer's duty to establish the wishes of his client. No more was heard of that matter. At this point, on 7 December, Mrs Simpson issued a statement, which read:

> Mrs Simpson, throughout the last few weeks, has invariably wished to avoid any action or proposal which would hurt or damage His Majesty or the Throne.
> Today her attitude is unchanged, and she is willing, if such action would solve the problem, to withdraw forthwith from a situation that has been rendered both unhappy and untenable.[43]

Goddard flew out to France and discussed the situation with Mrs Simpson.

Goddard was urged by Wilson to remain with Mrs Simpson. but he telephoned to say that he wanted to return to Britain as quickly as possible. A message was due from the Chancellor of the Exchequer (Neville Chamberlain) and the Home Secretary (Sir John Simon) to drum home that if the King 'were to affront public opinion by abdicating, it was very doubtful whether Parliament would be prepared to grant money to the King after he had gone.'[44] Goddard's message was that Mrs Simpson was 'ready to do anything that would ease the situation', but that 'the other end of the wicket was determined'[45]. He prepared a statement which he took back to Britain:

I have today discussed whole position with Mrs Simpson – her own – the position of the King, the country, the Empire. Mrs Simpson tells me she was and still is perfectly willing to instruct me to withdraw her petition for divorce and indeed willing to do anything to prevent the King from abdicating. I am satisfied beyond doubt this is Mrs Simpson's genuine and honest desire. I read this note over to Mrs Simpson who in every way confirmed it.[46]

It was signed by J. Theodore Goddard and countersigned by Lord Brownlow. The document was never implemented and the cynical interpretation put on it was that Mrs Simpson wanted the King to take full blame for the action he was about to take.

Goddard reported on his actions. He had warned Wallis that there was likely to be an intervention over the divorce and that it was 'his duty to advise her to withdraw her petition'.[47] But it was clear that whatever he said to her was countermanded in telephone calls from the King. She therefore felt that she could not accept his advice.

The drama was drawing to its now inevitable conclusion. Yet on 8 December the Prime Minister went down to the Fort, determined to give it one last chance and prepared to stay overnight. He told Wilson: 'He must wrestle with himself now in a way he has never done before and if he will let me I will help him. We may even have to see the night through together.'[48]

Unfortunately there were other guests at the Fort, making a heart-to-heart with the King impossible, but Baldwin soon concluded that further arguments or discussion were useless. The King was set on his terrible path. It was on this evening that the Duke of York told Baldwin that the King had long resolved to marry Mrs Simpson and to give up his position as Prince of Wales.

With the King isolated at Fort Belvedere, bizarre rumours circulated in London society. Lady Ottoline Morrell was convinced she had worked out why it was happening:

I believe really that the poor little fellow has found at last a woman with whom he could be sexually happy & think this has never happened before – so his whole being is tied up with her . . . Will it compensate for the loss of Kingdom, power, & all his interests in the people of England?

Lady Ottoline also speculated: 'He had injections to make himself more virile & they affected his head & made him very violent.' When the

Abdication was announced, she met Virginia Woolf in the street, they fell into each other's arms and agreed 'this was wicked & a tragic moment'.[49]

All kinds of issues were discussed. At the Cabinet meeting on 9 December the question of the ex-King's precedence arose. On that day it seemed he would be a Royal Highness and as 'the eldest brother of the Sovereign' he would rank before the Dukes of Gloucester and Kent, but they agreed: 'It seemed improbable, however, that he could claim to take precedence over Princess Elizabeth and Princess Margaret. In certain circumstances the matter might be of very great importance.'[50]

It was but a matter of time before the Instrument of Abdication was drawn up and signed by the King at the Fort. It was witnessed in turn by his three brothers, the Dukes of York, Gloucester and Kent. At Lambeth Palace Alan Don commented:

Thus it came about that a King with an Empire at his feet nine months ago has gone into the wilderness as an exile from his native land for the sake of a woman who has already made a failure of two marriages!

Here is a theme for a dozen tragedies. Here too is a demonstration for all the world to see that the British Democracy demands from those in high places an exacting standard of life and character. It is that and that alone which counts in the long run.

Tonight there is almost everywhere, at any rate among responsible people, a sense of relief. The crisis is passed . . .[51]

The former King dined with his family at Royal Lodge, and was then driven up the Long Walk to Windsor Castle to give his Abdication broadcast to a stunned nation. One who heard the speech was Wallis Simpson herself, cowering under a rug at Villa Lou Viei in Cannes. Lord Brownlow witnessed her 'moaning and sobbing while King Edward gave his farewell broadcast.'[52]

After delivering his broadcast, the former King bade farewell to his family and was driven away. Alan Don concluded:

A couple of hours later the poor fellow was hurrying through the darkness to Portsmouth where he boarded the ferry for an unknown destination. Will he ever set foot on these shores again? I doubt it, if he ever marries Mrs. S. Feeling has hardened against poor King Edward very noticeably . . . His was a dual personality, a mixture of much that was good and attractive and charming with much that was rotten and unstable. His infatuation for 'the woman I love' (as he called Mrs. S. in his broadcast talk) descended to something akin to madness. What will be the end thereof?[53]

6

The Realisation

'The choice before the ex-King is either to fade out from the public
eye or be a nuisance. It is a hard choice, perhaps, for one of his
temperament, but the Duke of Windsor would be wise to fade out.'
 – *Herbert Morrison, Labour MP and Leader of the GLC*

'The only part possible for him to play is that of a private gentleman.'
 –*Harold Laski, Professor of Political Science at London University*[1]

His Royal Highness The Duke of Windsor, for such he was created by
the new King, George VI, settled in Austria to eke out a lonely waiting
period until the Simpson divorce became absolute. He was the guest of
Baron Eugen de Rothschild at Schloss Enzesfeld, somewhat south of
Vienna. He allowed himself to be photographed in the garden wearing
a bow tie and looking rather irritated. 'I think that will do,'[1] was all he
would say. Later there were occasional snaps of him playing golf, his
familiar pipe gripped in his teeth. Queen Marie of Romania ran into
him at the British Legation in Vienna and found the Duke rested, less
jumpy than in the past, but rather fat. He had Wallis's Cairn terrier,
Slipper*, for company. He did not get on particularly well with his
hostess.

The news that the former King was staying with Kitty de Rothschild[†]
caused the novelist Edith Wharton some mirth. She wrote to her friend,
the author Louis Bromfield:

Don't you think the fiction writers, poor things, had better go out
of business, seeing the class of goods the royalties are supplying
us with? The idea of Edward VIII taking refuge in the Schloss of

---

*Slipper's life ended tragically that April. The Duke sent Slipper to Candé. Shortly before he joined
Wallis there, Slipper ran off into the woods in quest of a rabbit. A viper bit him and Wallis found
him in spasms of agony. He died at the vet's. In her memoirs the Duchess wrote: 'His loss on the
eve of my reunion with David seemed to me a frightful omen. He had been my companion in joy
and trouble; now he was gone. Was everything that I loved to be destroyed?' [*The Heart Has Its
Reasons*, p. 294].
[†] Kitty Wolf, m. 1925 Baron Eugen de Rothschild. She died in 1946.

the Brooklyn dentist's ex-wife delights me mightily, for I remember her Parisian début, at the Opera, about 1908, when she was still Mrs Spotswood, & divided by several divorces from the lofty eminence she now occupies! (When I say 'début at the Opera' I mean in a box, when all the old first-nighters 'bracked' their glasses on her florid beauty. If Edward R. had been grown up then, I don't believe Mrs Simpson wd have had a look-in. Don't you think the 1st act of MacBeth, with Mrs Spotswood, Elsa Maxwell & Lady Maud [Cunard] as the three witches would fill the house for a season?[2]

This was the kind of jibe that the ex-King would have to face or which would be made behind his back from then until his dying day. He was forced to realise, gradually, that he had done a terrible thing. Certainly he had abdicated quite honourably, without inspiring division in the country or acting unconstitutionally. But, unquestionably, he had let the nation down, and such a thing would not be forgiven.

It was not long before he wanted to come back to England, to settle once more at Fort Belvedere and reinvent himself as a younger brother of the new King, undertaking certain royal duties on his own terms. Of him it was said: 'It is one thing if he wants to go and dwell in a garden with Mrs Simpson. But now he wants to come back.' Alan Lascelles was one who realised early in the new reign that there could be no room for two kings in the same country.

In Britain the Private Secretaries made sure that the new King and Queen were seen as widely as possible throughout Britain to establish them in the minds of their people. The more they were seen, the more the Duke of Windsor faded into the background. After his marriage to the Duchess, which none of his family attended, the Duke had two major preoccupations – the first was to obtain the title of Royal Highness for the Duchess, and the second to have her received by the King and Queen and for this reception to be recorded in the Court Circular. Indeed, he appeared to make it a condition that these two things should happen before he would return to Britain. This was not inconvenient. The new court had no intention of granting either request – and as a result the Windsors stayed in voluntary, self-imposed exile.

As the years went by, the Duke of Windsor rejigged his version of history in his head. He attributed the Abdication to an Establishment plot against him and turned his hatred on Baldwin, for one. When Baldwin died in 1948, the Duke told a friend 'I have one less enemy.'[3] He began to believe that Queen Elizabeth (later the Queen Mother) had led a campaign against him. She played no part in the Abdication. He had particular disdain for the two Private Secretaries, Alec Hardinge (to whom he did not say goodbye on leaving England) and Alan Lascelles, believing they had conspired against him.

Lascelles's view was that no one – neither Baldwin, nor Queen Mary, nor Lascelles himself – ever dreamed even until the last moment that the Duke could or would abdicate. When he heard it on that fateful evening in December 1936, he was so stunned that he 'went & walked 3 times round St James's Park in the darkness, thinking of James II.'[4]

Bitterness came easily to the Duke and, since he had nothing to do, he had time to mull it all over. Years later, the Duke of Windsor told Kenneth Rose 'in that cockney voice of his': 'Twenty years I worked for my country and they kicked me out on my *ass*.'[5]

James Pope-Hennessy, Queen Mary's official biographer, tackled the Duke's perception of the Abdication when he was asked to be an adviser on the Duke's film *A King's Story*. He asked the film-makers:

> Is it to be, like *The Finest Hours*, an important visual contribution to the history of our times; or is it to project, and so to speak publicly confirm, the Duke of Windsor's private mythology? As the years have gone by, the Duke has become more and more convinced that he was the victim of a plot, and a martyr of the Establishment. His conviction is perfectly understandable, but it is not historically accurate.[6]

The after-effects of the Abdication took a long time to settle. The attitude of the Royal Family towards the Duke was something he found it hard to come to terms with and arguably never forgave.

The most positive support came from his sister, the Princess Royal, who told her brother she was amazed at him leaving everything, sent him a prayer book with his name printed in it as King and after that communicated with him as though nothing untoward had happened. But she made no reference to his future wife, whom she did not meet until she and the Duke were about to leave New York in 1953 by sea together just before Queen Mary died. The Princess told her son she had found the Duchess charming, leaving him bemused by 'the moral contradiction between the elevation of a code of duty on the one hand, and on the other the denial of central Christian virtues – forgiveness, understanding, family tenderness.'[7]

Queen Mary was only able to remain in touch with the Duke by letter, but when she referred to the Abdication it was in terms of the dreadful last evening at Royal Lodge, her grief at parting and the cause for that, tempered by her relief at how dignified it had all been and how well the country had settled down to the new reign after such a terrible upheaval.

The Duke's great-uncle, the Duke of Connaught, a son of Queen Victoria, who combined a life in the company of beautiful ladies with a strict devotion to royal and military duties, believed that once the King had resolved to marry the lady of his choice he had had no alternative but to abdicate. He was most disappointed at the way things had turned out since he had entertained such high hopes for the new reign. Nevertheless, he kept in touch with his errant great-nephew, sending him his usual Christmas card, fearing that he must be sad and lonely in exile. The Duke of Connaught's sister Princess Louise, Duchess of Argyll, was preoccupied by the press continually dragging the Duke of Windsor's name into everything.

The new Queen Elizabeth said she would always remember him in her prayers, though she soon got irritated by his demands. Years later she told Henry Gillespie, a friend from Australia: 'The two people who have caused me the most trouble in my life are Wallis Simpson and Hitler.'[8] The Duchess of Gloucester wished him happiness. Other members of the Royal Family wrote to him as if he were crossing the divide. His aunt, Princess Alice, Countess of Athlone, professed profound shock while hoping that he would now discover that happiness which he had so long sought yet never found. His cousins Princess Helena Victoria, Princess Marie Louise and Lady Patricia Ramsay wrote to bid him farewell as sovereign and cousin.

Dickie Mountbatten was more concerned at repositioning himself. He had, after all, been closely associated with the Duke of Windsor when he had been heir to the Throne. Now he needed to change tack. His attitude to the Abdication was: 'The King is dead. Long live the King.'[9] He was quick to express his loyalty to the new King and Queen. He welcomed a new Sailor King and told George VI that the Duke of Windsor had asked him to give him some help on naval matters. Meanwhile he thanked the Duke of Windsor for fixing things so that he, Mountbatten, should be appointed a Personal Naval ADC to the new King (something he himself had clearly raised) and attributed his promotion to GCVO to support by the Duke. Mountbatten visited the Duke at Enzesfeld in March and involved himself in negotiating dates for the Duke's wedding that would suit George VI. But by May he was reporting that although he had found a date that suited the King and the Duke of Kent, 'other people' had stepped in and prevented any members of the Royal Family from attending.

There were numerous judgements on the Abdication, a subject on which most people had strong views. Thelma Furness wrote:

> I assumed that when he acquired his royal authority he would use it dynamically and progressively – to the best interests of England and the whole world. Or perhaps he never wanted to be king . . . It seems to me that he should have known that the British Empire could not and would not accept as their King a man who deliberately flouted the most deeply rooted traditions of church and state.[10]

Chips Channon gave his verdict. He thought Wallis had been an excellent influence on the King. She had never once hinted that she wanted to be Queen. 'Not until too late did she realise the gravity of the position and then even she could do nothing with the King.'[11] He noted her strong social ambitions and credited her with making the King interested in society. His conclusion was: 'I have known her do a hundred kindnesses and never a mean act. There is nothing sordid or vulgar in her make-up, but she is modern certainly. She has a terrific personality and her presence grew as her importance increased: we are far from being done with her yet . . . She would prefer to be grand, dignified and respectable, but if thwarted she will make the best of whatever position life gives her.'[12]

Robert Bruce-Lockhart, another noted diarist of the day, thought the Duke suffered from *dementia erotica*. His verdict was: 'He is not a strong man. To have resisted the pressure which has been brought to bear on him must have meant that he was completely obsessed by one thought.'[13] Many years later this theme was taken up by Lady Gladwyn who saw the Windsors from time to time in Paris when her husband, Sir Gladwyn Jebb, was Ambassador. She told me:

> The Prince had sexual problems. He was unable to perform. It was all over before it began – she called it a hairpin reaction. She said that the Duchess coped with it.

I commented: 'She was meant to have learned special ways in China.' 'There was nothing Chinese about it', said Lady Gladwyn. 'It was what they call oral sex.'[14]

Victor Cazalet, the Conservative MP, decided that the King had been trying to have the best of both worlds, 'being a good and gracious King, sympathising with the miners and so on, while on the other hand he wanted everything that a rich idle bachelor desires in material pleasures – lavishing jewels on his mistress while at the same time getting rid of his father's servants.' He felt that Mrs Simpson had 'played her cards with a folly and stupidity almost unbelievable' and predicted a dismal fate for the Duke: 'The thought that he might have to spend the rest of his life wandering from one international centre to another, longing for home, is a very sorrowful picture.'[15] It was a sternly accurate forecast.

Stanley Baldwin, who presently stepped down as Prime Minister, told Victor Cazalet that the ex-King's only criterion was 'his personal happiness'. He said he had never met a person 'who had absolutely no spiritual or religious background to the same degree.'[16] The society hostess Sybil Colefax said Wallis 'thought she was in command of the situation and could do what she liked with the King. She never thought he would abdicate. She did not want to be Queen.'[17]

Walter Monckton was a close observer. He told Alan Don that he had never met a man as obstinate as the Duke of Windsor. 'In Mrs S.'s presence Edward was like a rabbit in the presence of a ferret – she had a quite abnormal hold over him and though she did him good in some ways . . . she could not bring herself to leave him, as W.M. implored her to do when he saw how things were working themselves out.'[18] He reflected that the Duke was still infatuated with her, but was gradually realising 'what he has given up and what the life of an exiled King means – if the infatuation wears off, as well it may when they are married, the poor man will be in a sorry state.'[19]

In the United States opinion was quite different. Elsa Maxwell, a clear-headed observer, influenced a great number of readers with her perceptions of Wallis's character. These were reprinted in the *Sunday Express* which noted that the one element Miss Maxwell chose to overlook was the two inconvenient divorces in the Duchess's past.

Elsa dismissed the descriptions of the Duchess as a modern-day Cleopatra, Diane de Poitiers, Madame de Pompadour or Dixie version of Madame du Barry. She pointed out that she was neither beautiful nor plain, but had a good figure, wore little make-up and no rouge and had what the French would call 'chic'. Elsa thought the Duchess's success with the Duke lay in the contrast she offered to his formal upbringing. She gave him 'gaiety and warm friendship'. Her success came about because she was not 'overawed by his rank'. She did not 'junk old friends' when he entered her life. She taught him to enjoy Southern dishes, awakening a pleasure for food in him, and once took him to a small restaurant off the Faubourg St Honoré so that he could taste genuine, simple fare, rather than banquet-style food. Elsa Maxwell mused on how a professor might tell the story of the Abdication to his class in 2037. She hoped he would say:

> The most remarkable thing about this pathetic case was not its outcome, which was wholly to be expected, but the fact that in an age which was supposed to be an age of enlightenment, a King was called to task by his Ministers, not for dissolution and reprehensible conduct, but merely because he wanted to marry a woman he loved.
>
> Let us be thankful, my friends, that we were not born a century too soon.[20]

George VI did not allow the Duke of Kent to visit the Duke of Windsor at Enzesfeld in January 1937, but in February the Princess Royal and Lord Harewood made the journey. Lord Harewood found the Duke living in a 'Merry Widow' castle, perched on a rock, decorated in pseudo-Louis XV style. He was astonished by the American luxury of the bathrooms. He discovered to his horror that the Duke thought his family would receive his wife with open arms the moment they married and he reported his concerns to George VI.

On Easter Monday the Duke moved to the White Horse Inn, Villa Appesbach, on the shores of the lake between Salzburg and Bas Ischl while he waited for the Simpson divorce to become absolute.

There was relief in some quarters that the wedding was definitely taking place. Though there had never been any serious suggestion that Mrs Simpson would not marry the Duke when her divorce became absolute, some observers had dreaded the devastating effect it would have had on him if she had let him down. Before the Abdication Wallis had wanted to escape. She had cringed under a blanket when she listened to the Abdication speech over the wireless in Cannes.

Cecil Beaton, with his unerring ability for being in the right place at the right time, had become something of a friend of Mrs Simpson. He first photographed her in the summer of 1935. He photographed and sketched her in November 1936 just before she fled from London. On that day she told him that ideas of marriage to the King were 'absolute rot'.[21] In the months following the Abdication she was much in touch with him, writing to him from Villa Lou Viei:

Everything is lovely and *dull* here, with the strangest English people filling the place and taking themselves and their Rolls (*sic*) quite seriously. I hope for a change of scene next month.[22]

The change came when Wallis moved from Cannes to the Chateau de Candé, the home of Mr and Mrs Charles Bedaux*, near Monts, Indre & Loire. She invited Beaton for the weekend to photograph her for *Vogue* in order to present a softer image of her to the world. He thought her a trapped animal. One evening he talked with her till almost dawn. He recorded:

I was amazed at the clarity and vitality of her mind and went to bed, eventually, feeling that I had spent the evening with someone who not only has individuality and personality, but is a personality, a strong force. I find she is intelligent within her vast limitations. Politically she may be ignorant, aesthetically she is so, but about life she knows a great deal.[23]

She told Beaton that she had been taken by surprise by the Abdication, that she had signed papers withdrawing the divorce and that the King had been prepared to delay talk of marriage until after the Coronation. She said there were times when she was tempted to hang herself from the antlers adorning the walls of the chateau. Beaton concluded that she was 'determined to love him though I feel she is not in love with him. She has a great responsibility in looking after someone who, so essentially different, entirely relies upon her.'[24]

Diana Vreeland said the Duchess had had no one to talk to during the Abdication crisis: 'She begged him to let her go, saying "I'll go to South America; you'll never hear from me or see me again." But he wouldn't let her go. After that, what could she do? She entered into marriage wholeheartedly.'[25]

Wallis did not relish her position. Just before she moved to Candé she wrote to the Duke, fed up with 'all of England taking cracks at me and no decent society speaking to me'. Plaintively she asked: 'What have I done to deserve this treatment?' She suggested that the new King should offer her some protection by letting it be known that the Royal Family approved of their wedding. This, she thought, would make a great difference. 'I do feel utterly down. It has been a lone game against the world

* Charles Bedaux (1887–1944), made a fortune out of scientific management, later economic adviser to the Reich. He was arrested during the war, charged with treason, and committed suicide while in prison in Miami, Florida.

for me and a woman always pays the most.'[26] As Frances Donaldson put it: 'And then to the poor wretch who had given up so much for her: "And you, my sweet, haven't been able to protect me".'[27]

As soon as the divorce became absolute, the Duke made his way to Candé to begin preparing for the wedding. Various guests appeared, none more unlikely than Constance Coolidge, then Comtesse de Jumilhac*. She was a wild Bostonian, the cousin of Frank Crowninshield, Editor of *Vanity Fair*. When she was married to Ray Atherton, a diplomat in China (and later an Ambassador), she was known as 'the Queen of Peking' or 'the Lady of the Golden Horse'.[28] There she had become friends with Herman and Katherine Rogers, later meeting Wallis with them. Among many love affairs, Constance was intensely involved with the dissolute Harry Crosby – who committed suicide with one of his girlfriends in 1929 – and at this time with H. G. Wells. Always keen on racing, she now lived partly in Paris and spent the summer season at the Negresco Hotel in Nice. Wallis invited her for a night, apologising that the wedding was restricted to a handful of guests.

Constance observed the scene at Candé where Winston Churchill's son Randolph was a fellow guest. The Duke, she thought, was 'like a boy let out of school . . . gay, carefree, laughing and terribly in love.' She was amused that when Wallis asked him to fetch her handkerchief, 'he springs up and goes and gets it and sits down close beside her on the sofa. A little shy of her, and adoring.' After dinner he noticed that her slipper was undone and knelt down to tie it up. 'I caught Randolph Churchill's eye at this moment, and his expression was amusing to say the least.'[29]

During the Abdication crisis Constance had invited Wallis to come and stay with her in Paris 'if she wanted to get out of the limelight.'[30] She did not believe that Wallis had ever been in love, and came to describe the marriage 'as the greatest tragedy in the world'. Her view was that there was no worse fate than 'to have to face, morning, noon, and night, a middle-aged boy with no purpose in life other than a possessive passion for you.'[31] Nor did her views change with the passing of time. In December 1938 she observed: 'Only one woman exists for him. All others are just bores.'[32]

Like so many other elements in the lives of the Duke and Duchess after the Abdication, the wedding was rife with problems. Wallis wanted

* Constance Coolidge (1892–1973), m. (1), 1910, Ray Atherton (div. 1924, d. 1959); (2), 1924, Comte de Jumilhac (div. 1929, d. 1932); (3), February 1930, Eliot Rogers (div. 1930); & (4) 1940, André Magnus (d. 1995). Amongst her numerous sexual conquests were the gardener, Russell Page, & the exiled Earl Beauchamp.

a dignified marriage ceremony and Walter Monckton worried to what ends the Duke would go to obtain this for her. The religious aspect was complicated because the Church of England forbade marriages in church for those with previous partners still living. A Canon Andrews from the Home Farm Parish of the Duchy of Cornwall offered to officiate, but he was advised that in so doing he would be acting contrary to the deliberate decisions of Convocation.

The next blow came when the King decided that no member of the Royal Family would attend the wedding. This precluded someone like Canon Andrews presiding. The fear was that the Duke would now 'get hold of some notoriety-seeker among the clergy'. The Duke did precisely that. A 'Kensitite* clergyman by the name of Jardine[33] offered to perform the ceremony. Alan Don dismissed him as 'an entirely insignificant vicar in Darlington' acting 'without any ecclesiastical authority and in defiance of what he knows to be the mind of the Church of which he is an accredited minister.'[34]

The Bishop of Fulham, under whose jurisdiction the Anglican Church in France lay, immediately published a statement to the effect that the proposed action by Rev. R.A. Jardine was being taken 'without his consent or even his knowledge'. The bishop then sent a telegram of protest to Jardine. It did not take the press long to discover that the bishop had been talking to the Archbishop of Canterbury, who had already been in trouble for his post-Abdication broadcast in which he had criticised Edward VIII and his friends. Alan Don concluded: 'It is really rather tragic that the Duke should demean himself by accepting the services volunteered by a poorly educated and wholly obscure cleric whose record is anything but impressive'.[35] When the wedding took place the press rounded on the Church of England, accusing the clergy of being unnecessarily harsh on the poor Duke. The clergy's line was that they were merely being consistent.

When the Duke realised that his brothers would not be joining him for his wedding and acting as his 'supporters', he asked Dickie Mountbatten to be his best man. The Duke never forgave him for not accepting and Mountbatten never ceased to insist to anyone who would listen that he had offered to do as he had been asked but had been turned down by the Duke.

As to the question of the Royal Family attending the Duke's wedding, the Duke of Connaught was astonished that his great-nephew could ever have imagined that they might contemplate such a thing.

---

* Kensitites were puritans who objected to new High Church ways, deeming them to be idolatry.

As the wedding approached, the Duke of Kent wished both Wallis and the Duke well after their terrible ordeal and apologised that he could not be with them on the day. Princess Marina also wrote but reserved her wishes for the Duke's happiness, without any reference to his wife. The Duke of Gloucester sent a box as a present. Stanley Baldwin wrote the Duke a particularly generous letter confirming that he had accomplished what he wanted with dignity, that he had always been 'dead straight' with him, that he had done nothing to embarrass his successor or unduly harm the monarchy.

On 17 May the Duke invited his old friend Fruity Metcalfe to his wedding, and more specifically to be his best man: 'I want to say that I hope you will be my Best Man, so that even if Baba is unable to get away that week, you will anyway come yourself and play this important part at the ceremony.' The Duke confided he could not believe the months of separation from Wallis were over: 'It seems too good to be true. Our plans are working themselves out gradually despite the withholding of a single helping hand from England, not that we ever expected one. But the behaviour of some people is utterly amazing.'[36] The Duke told Fruity that he would be wearing a black coat with striped trousers but that if Fruity preferred a grey tailcoat suit that would be fine.

Fruity Metcalfe and his wife, Lady Alexandra ('Baba') arrived at Candé on 2 June. Baba Metcalfe kept a diary of the wedding, beginning by saying that she had never dreaded a visit more. They ran the gauntlet of the press and Ladbrook drove them to the Chateau, which Baba found 'ordinary and rather ugly'. Her heart sank:

> Before long Wallis appeared. Not having seen her for a while, I had forgotten how unattractive is her voice and manner of speaking. The rest of the party consists of Mrs Merryman (Aunt Bessie), who must have had a stroke as half of her face does not function; Herman Rogers, a nice, quiet, efficient man but unknowledgeable about how to handle the press; Mr and Mrs Bedaux, the owners of the chateau, who are infinitely better than I expected: she is like a borzoi dog, thin and elegant; he is clever and very astute and unattractive: they are very retiring and might be guests instead of host and hostess. Dudley Forwood, the Duke's equerry, is a dapper little guardsman, very loyal and very unsuitable for the job.

The party sat in the library until the Duke appeared after dealing with letters and telegrams. Lady Baba found the Duke looking well and in excellent spirits. At dinner he was in 'marvellous form, obviously happy and very much at ease. He has made no allusion to England, family, staff or friends. After dinner Wallis and he disappeared. The rest of us carried on a desultory conversation until we went to bed.'

Baba thought the presents 'rather pathetic', and noted 'The Duke sees through Wallis's eyes, hears through her ears and speaks through her mouth.' The Rev. Jardine arrived and the house party turned a chest into an altar, covering it with a tablecloth, and improved it with flowers by Constance Spry. They fetched a cross from a local church.[37] Cecil Beaton arrived to take wedding photographs on the day before the ceremony. He found Wallis 'today especially unlovable, hard and calculating and showing an anxiety but no feeling of emotion.'[38] Until the wedding Wallis curtsied and called the Duke 'Sir'.

There were disappointments – Piers 'Joey' Legh and Lord Brownlow not coming, the latter backing out at the last minute. But the worst blow was Wallis not being given the right to be a Royal Highness and a member of the British Royal Family. The title of Royal Highness was to be restricted to the Duke alone and could not be enjoyed by his wife or any children of the marriage.

The Duke minded this more than Wallis did and insisted that his staff call her 'Your Royal Highness'. But it meant that no lady had to curtsy to the Duchess, though many did, Lady Diana Cooper explaining that she always did so 'to please him'. There was also irony in the fact that the Duke had suggested the morganatic proposal as a solution to his marriage – that Wallis should become his wife but not his Queen. He was told that the wife of the King is always the Queen. But now she had an unequal status, though George VI thought he had been adequately generous in granting her the rank of a British duchess, the highest degree in the peerage. For the rest of his life the Duke appealed over and over again to have this decision reversed.

In practice the Royal Family could do as they pleased. They took steps to prevent the Duchess becoming a Royal Highness partly out of fear that the marriage would not last. At the time it was said that they did not want a lot of divorced Royal Highnesses 'floating around the cafés of Budapest'[39].

At the Chateau de Candé Baba Metcalfe observed the couple:

I have never seen HRH happier or less nervous but looking at her, and trying with all one's might and main, one is unable to register that she is the cause of the whole unbelievable story. One almost begins to think there is nothing incredible, unique or tragic about it, as they are so blind to it all. If it were not for the press, who are only allowed as far as the gate, one might be attending the wedding of an ordinary couple.

The day of the wedding dawned and Baba noted that there was bitterness in both of them:

He had an outburst to Fruity while dressing for dinner. He is through with the family. He will be loyal to the Crown but not to the man, his brother. He blames him for weakness in everything. The friends, staff and Perry [Brownlow] have been awful. He intends to fight the HRH business as legally the King has no right to stop the courtesy title being assumed by his wife. Walter and Allen [the solicitor] agree. Wallis has lots to say about the behaviour of family and friends. She realises there is no insult they have not heaped on her. She thanked me effusively, three or four times, for having come and said she thought it was very sweet of me.

A scene never to be forgotten, perhaps more than the actual ceremony, was the rehearsal in the small green drawing room, with the organist from Paris trying out the music in a room next door. Fruity walks in with HRH and stands on the right of the altar. Wallis, on Herman's arm, comes in under the tutelage of Jardine, a large-nosed, bulgy-eyed, red-faced little man. They go over the service, HRH's jaw working the whole time, exactly the same as I saw the King's, all through the Coronation Service. Walter, Allen and I watched with such a mixture of feelings. The tune played for *O Perfect Love* was not the proper one, so I sang it to the organist and he wrote it down as easily as I am writing this.

Kitty, Eugene de Rothschild and Randolph Churchill came to dinner. Seven English people present at the wedding of the man who, six months ago, was King of England. The Rev. Jardine told Wallis that one reason for his coming was that the time will come when HRH will be needed and a religious ceremony was essential.

It is over and it is true. I felt all through the ceremony that I must be in a dream. It was hard not to cry. In fact I did. Jardine came in first, followed by HRH and Fruity. They stood two yards from me. Wallis, on Herman's arm, came in by the other door. She was in a lovely blue dress with a short, tight-fitting jacket and wore a blue straw halo hat with feathers and tulle. On her arm was the loveliest diamond and sapphire bracelet, which was her wedding present.

Jardine read the service simply and well: 'Do you Edward, Albert,

Christian, George, Andrew, Patrick, David take . . .' etc. His responses were clear, firm and very well said. Her voice: 'I Bessie Wallis' was much lower, but very clear. It could be nothing but tragic to see an idealistic Prince of Wales and King of England buried under these circumstances; and yet, pathetic as it was, his manner was so simple and dignified, he was so sure of himself in his happiness that it gave something to this sad little service, which is impossible to describe.

Afterwards, we shook hands in the salon. I knew I should have kissed her but I just couldn't. In fact I was bad all day: my effort to be charming and to like her broke down. I don't remember wishing her happiness or good luck. If she occasionally showed a glimmer of softness, took his arm, looked as though she loved him, one would warm towards her but her attitude is so correct and hard. The effect is of an older woman, unmoved by the infatuated love of a younger man. Let's hope she lets up in private.

During the service Fruity held the prayer book Queen Mary gave HRH when he was ten: 'To darling David from his loving mother.' HRH had tears running down his face as the service finished.[40]

Reports of the wedding were not well received in the clubs of London or at court. The eccentric Duke of Argyll* wrote to a friend:

I had a long talk to the [Japanese] Ambassador & other Japs & had the Brazilian Ambassadress next me who said how utterly that odious woman seemed to have mesmerised that nitwit. It is an extraordinary case . . .

I had a talk to Lady Airlie†. All the Court very angry about that self-advertising Jardine, a Durham Diocese vicar who rushed over to Touraine – impelled by his 'conscience'. He is of the Kensit faction & had been an agnostic & then a dissenter. She said to me & did you see those dreadful photos & her very middle-class clothes 'and to think it is for a creature who looks like that, that he has behaved in this way'? She also told me of some impudence about the Bps that creature Rothermere had put into recent evening papers. I had not seen it. I told her the Club talk was that in 2 years time she will, after leaving him de-plumaged, caper off with a

---

* 10th Duke of Argyll (1872–1949), a devout Anglo-Catholic and bachelor, who 'met any challenge to his opinions with a wealth of invective, sometimes humorous, sometimes deeply serious, but always devastating' [*The Times*, August 1949].

† Mabell, Countess of Airlie (1866–1956), Lady of the Bedchamber to Queen Mary.

cowboy! Admiral Meade* says he hears there is a very rich American who wants to get hold of her so the nitwit's future is likely to be a queer one.[41]

A few days later he pursued this theme:

[Lady Londonderry]† told me how angry all the family are about the odious Jardine man rushing off in that very vulgar way to Touraine. I am sending you two papers with horrible photos of the wretch. Read certain bits carefully & judge what some of these pestiferous paper Lords are up to.[42]

There remained a genuine fear of the Duke of Windsor within certain sections of the aristocracy – that he might attempt to reclaim his birthright, that his charisma was a threat to the new King, and that he could now no longer be trusted.

Relations between the Duke and his family suffered irreparable damage as a result of the family's non-attendance at his wedding. From that day on he lay in wait for slights and succeeded in finding them at every turn.

The Windsors honeymooned in Europe, stopping in Venice for a day, then staying at Schloss Wasserleonburg, Count Paul Munster's home in Carinthia, and moving on to Venice again, Vienna, Salzburg and Yugoslavia. While at Wasserleonburg, Wallis wrote to her cousin Lelia Barnett:

Here I am at last with my king sitting on a mountain in Austria – where it is really lovely and peaceful – we hope here to gather strength for future battles . . . Please write me and say you still love me and that we may come to Wakefield one day.[43]

The Yugoslavian stay caused more family problems since the Duke and Duchess of Kent were also in Yugoslavia in August. The Duke of Windsor was furious to hear that only his brother would come and visit them, and that the Duchess of Kent would not accompany him. The Duke demanded to know if Marina did not want to come or had been forbidden from so doing. Prince George confessed that she did not want to meet Wallis.

---

* Admiral Hon. Sir Herbert Meade-Fetherstonhaugh (1875–1964), Extra Equerry to King Edward VIII.
† Edith, Marchioness of Londonderry (1879–1959), celebrated political hostess.

This caused upset. The Duke of Kent asked George VI's advice and was told that they should both go. Princess Marina was then cross because she thought she would be criticised in the press and reckoned it looked as if they were giving in. In the end the Kents did not visit the Windsors.

After the honeymoon the Duke and Wallis settled in Paris, where presently they appeared at a few public events together. In the autumn the Duchess coped well when confronted with some duchess's Coronation robes in the British Pavilion at the World Fair.

Fortunately the Windsors were not aware of instructions sent by the King's Private Secretary to the Foreign Office concerning future diplomatic arrangements. The message was that the Windsors would have 'no official status' in countries they visited. There were to be no official interviews, and they would play no part in any official ceremonies. The Ambassador should send a member of his staff to meet the Duke (and Duchess) at the station. Private invitations were at the discretion of individual Ambassadors, but they were not to be invited to stay at embassies or legations. Regarding private entertainment, 'care should be taken in the invitation of guests, as the Duchess of Windsor should be placed on the right of His Majesty's Representative on every occasion. This is an important point to remember, and one which will help the Ambassador or Minister in limiting the number of guests.'[44]

In other words no guest could be of higher status than an English duchess. This stricture was confirmed by Tommy Lascelles in 1945 and was still in place in 1952.

In October 1937 there was considerable controversy when the Duke and Duchess travelled to Berlin to visit Hitler. This idea resulted from a letter to the Duke from Oscar Selbert, who had been Military Attaché at the United States Embassy in London between 1919 and 1924. He had acted as the Prince of Wales's ADC on his 1924 visit to the United States. On 27 April Selbert wrote from New York urging the Duke to head up a global peace movement, what he called 'A League of Peace at Geneva' to match the League of Nations and the International Labour organisation.

Selbert was in touch with only two men – Thomas J. Watson, President of the American Section of the International Chamber of Commerce and a Swede, Axel Wenner-Gren, a millionaire captain of industry. Selbert assured the Duke that both these men were hard-hearted and practical and that Wenner-Gren would put a considerable amount of money towards the plan.

Just as the Duke was feeling neglected and regretting that there was nothing for him to do, this opportunity arose. He jumped at it. The Duke was deeply concerned about the fear of another war and he believed that if he visited Hitler he might be able to prevail upon him to support peace. In this he exaggerated his own importance and failed to consider the implications such a visit might have or to assess the publicity benefits for the Fuehrer. He refused to see anything controversial in it, since all he was doing was going to Germany to inspect housing and industrial conditions.

The millionaire industrialist Paul-Louis Weiller knew the Windsors in Paris. His view was that the Duke made bad judgements, one of them being the visit to Hitler. He said:

> The Duchess, as Mrs Simpson, was very pro-German because she was not accepted by the true society, but only by those of pro-German persuasion – for example Ribbentrop (the Ambassador), the Londonderrys and the Mitfords. He said that the Duchess fixed up the Hitler meeting. Hitler made the Duke travel a long way to see him and received him in his mountain hideaway. The Duke was extremely impressed with him and came back after a long talk of 1 1/2 hours believing him a pacifist. But the Duchess was furious because she was left out completely.[45]

Weiller saw the Windsors on their return to Paris. The Duchess wanted nothing more to do with Hitler.

Winston Churchill wrote to the Duke to say that he was glad the visit had gone well, having been worried that anti-Nazis might misinterpret it. The Duke was slightly indignant, stressing that he had gone there without political considerations and entirely as an independent observer. But unquestionably the visit did harm him. When he was photographed waving, it looked as if he was giving a Nazi salute. Herbert Morrison, leader of the GLC and a Labour MP, was one who criticised him: 'If the Duke wants to study social problems he had far better quietly read books and get advice in private, rather than put his foot in it in this way.'[46]

Meeting the Windsors in November 1937, soon after their return, Ambassador William Bullitt, a shrewd observer, reported to President Roosevelt that he thought the Duke was 'taking as serious an interest in housing and the other problems connected with the life of the industrial workers as his royal intelligence will permit.' The Duchess told him of Hitler's intense interest in architecture, and that he had said to her: 'Our buildings will make more magnificent ruins than the Greeks.' Bullitt thought: 'That seemed to me about as revealing psychologically as anything I ever heard. The curse of the Germans is that they have swallowed the *Niebulungenlied* and do not recoil even before the *Götterdämmerung*.'[47]

The Duke was meant to undertake another such tour of the United States, but shortly before setting off he realised that he been taken in by Wenner-Gren and indeed his host at Candé, Charles Bedaux. He backed away.

Such incidents have been exaggerated into the theory that the Duke was an incipient Nazi. He was no such thing. But he was naive, and having been brought up with people to advise him all his life until December 1936 he was hardly competent or equipped to deal with men like Hitler. Nor should he have undertaken this trip independently.

Ambassador Bullitt judged the Duke 'obviously intensely in love with his wife'. He noted:

> The girl, on the other hand, behaved like a person whose insides have been taken out and replaced by an idea of what a king's wife should be like. She has gone English in a big way so far as her accent is concerned, and indeed, at the moment is talking a rather nasal cockney which is more English then her husband's rather good pronunciation. She has lost that spontaneous wit and twinkle which used to make her very attractive; instead she is 'gracious'. I had the feeling that if one had her alone for a few minutes she would probably say: 'Isn't this a hell of a mess but don't you think that I am doing it well?'

Bullitt thought that Wallis's mistake was that she had 'stopped being herself and is engaged in trying to be exactly what she thinks he wants her to be.'[48]

This is perceptive. It was perhaps Wallis's mistake to allow the Duke to fall into the trap of being a royal-in-exile and establishing a mini-court around him with liveried footmen. He found himself surrounded by the many accoutrements of royal life, coronets on plates and so on – symbols of all he had sought to escape.

She should perhaps have offered him a life in America. Later he told the actress Lilli Palmer: 'When I first set foot on American soil as a very young man, it came to me like a flash: this is what I like. Here I'd like to stay. And when I married an American, I hoped we would live in America. But as fate would have it, my wife hates America and only wants to live in France.'[49]

Cecil Beaton was given the same impression by Charles Murphy who was ghosting the Duke's memoirs in the 1950s: 'The Windsor love story, one of the most extraordinary of our time, is a romance without love, a fairy tale that went off the rails – the little Cinderella, instead of bringing the Prince to love her sort of life, makes him give up his life, then tries to make her life as much like his as possible.'[50] Many years later Lady Diana Cooper told me: 'If I had taken him on, I would have taken him to Virginia.'[51]

A major preoccupation of the Duke's over the next two years concerned his right to return to Britain. As early as September 1937 he began to plan a visit, but the new King was advised on all sides that the Windsors must not come back. As with the Duchess's title, this would be an issue that would dog them for the rest of their lives. The Duke had been hugely popular in his youth. James Pope-Hennessy wrote that he failed to realise that, by abdicating, he had flung himself from this 'pinnacle of popularity'. Pope-Hennessy concluded: 'To be a hero-king one minute, and to find oneself the object of nation-wide if unsympathetic condemnation the next, might well have been warping.'[52]

In December 1937 the Duke complained to Neville Chamberlain, the new Prime Minister, that while he accepted that it had been a dignified and sensible course of action to leave Britain for a while after his Abdication, he had never intended or agreed to stay away for ever. He was alarmed to find that if he arrived in Britain without obtaining the King's permission – on the advice of his ministers – private financial arrangements made for him by the King could be cancelled. Despite having turned his back on Britain, he still felt that his long years of service as Prince of Wales, and even as King, should have convinced the powers that be that he was a man of his word. The Duke's proposed solution was always the same: if the Royal Family would give evidence of a less strained atmosphere between themselves and himself and his wife, then there would be no chance for negative publicity. Meanwhile he and the Duchess felt 'acute pain' at the treatment meted out to them by both the Royal Family and the Government.

Petty slights included there being no mention of his marriage in the 1938 *Seasons Kalendar* issued by the Lord Chamberlain. The Duke duly complained.

In August 1938 he tried again to arrange a private visit to Britain for himself and the Duchess in order to sort out some of his belongings stored at Windsor, reckoning that by now George VI must feel secure as King.

As a litmus test, George VI asked the Duke and Duchess of Gloucester to visit the Windsors at the Hotel Meurice in Paris on their way back from

Kenya. The King wanted the visit to be a purely private one, with no publicity, since the Gloucesters had been on safari and might not have smart clothes. George VI considered this visit to be a good opportunity to break the ice. The Duke of Windsor replied, slightly irritably, assuring his brother that he had no intention of informing the press. He then wrote to Walter Monckton suggesting ways that the press could cover the visit with dignity.

The press were poised for the visit. The Duke of Windsor was malevolently amused that Godfrey Thomas (formerly on his staff but now working for the Gloucesters) had not engaged rooms for them at the Hotel Meurice. He consigned all enquiries from journalists to Thomas.

The Gloucesters arrived and there were photographs taken of both couples on the steps. Following the visit, the Windsors received some hate mail, most of it anonymous and some of it deranged. The Duchess of Gloucester was similarly bombarded, as was Buckingham Palace. The Duke of Gloucester told his brother that some of the letters were extremely rude. The reaction was used as evidence that the Windsors should not return to Britain that autumn but should postpone their trip until March 1939.

Perceived slights continued to beset the Duke. He was not invited to the Armistice Day service at the Anglican Church in Paris. Then he was hurt that he and his wife were not invited to a memorial service in Paris for his aunt, Queen Maud of Norway, who had died in London on 20 November 1938.

Neville Chamberlain called on the Duke during a visit to Paris in November 1938. Later he told him that when the idea of a visit by the Windsors had been mooted in the press, he had received over 150 hostile letters, and even his wife had received thirty. In December the Duke's brother-in-law, Lord Harewood, urged him not to visit Britain in the spring in order to avoid unpleasant indignities. The Duke then began to bombard the Prime Minister with memoranda about his plans to come to Britain, complicating the issue by suggesting that they should stay in a royal residence, preferably in rooms at Windsor Castle.

He saw the only problem that could arise as the refusal of the Royal Family to meet them but chose to assume that this was not in fact going to be a problem. When it seemed that it was, the Duke told Chamberlain that he was not prepared to let their hostility keep him out of his country indefinitely. But on account of the forthcoming trip by the King and Queen to Canada and the United States, once again the Duke agreed to stay away. As the Duke told Lord Beaverbrook, he was well aware that the attitude of his mother and Queen Elizabeth was such that it might cause adverse criticism of the visit.

* * *

None of this was helped by a row between the Duke and Queen Mary. In the summer of 1938, when the question of his visit to London was in the forefront of his mind, he asked his mother to make clear her views on the Abdication. It was then that she made the point about all the young men who had given their lives in the Great War, and how the Duke had not been prepared to make a lesser sacrifice.

The Duke waited a long time to reply. I have a copy of this letter, but for some reason permission has never been given for it to be published. The Duke stuck to his guns, stated that he needed his wife at his side and could not have undertaken his duties as King without her. In these circumstances he sincerely believed that he had done the right thing by his country.

In March 1939 the Duke exploded with rage. He had offered to pay £4,000 as half the cost towards his father's tomb in St George's Chapel, with its effigy by Sir William Reid Dick. The Duke realised that he would not be invited to its dedication but made a point of telling his mother that he expected his financial contribution to be publicly acknowledged. He was therefore furious to read in the paper that the tomb had been dedicated in the presence of all the Royal Family and there had been no mention in the press of the Duke's financial contribution.

As so often is the case, the Duke needed something on which to pin his real anger over the mean treatment he felt that he and the Duchess had endured during the last two and a half years. He wrote his mother a blistering letter and from that moment on he ceased to communicate with her.

He ignored her birthday on 26 May each year, which caused her great distress. She sent him presents for his on 23 June, which he did not acknowledge. He remained silent until the tragic death of the Duke of Kent in 1942.

(*Above*) Miss Wallis Warfield of Baltimore, about 1907.

(*Above*) Wallis with her mother, Alys
Montague Warfield in January 1897.

(*Above*) Wallis's grandmother,
Mrs Henry Warfield.

(*Above*) The grave of Wallis's father, Teackle Wallis Warfield,
at Green Mount Cemetery, Baltimore.

(*Left*) Wallis as a bride at her first wedding, 8 November 1916.

(*Below*) Wallis and Earl Winfield Spencer in Coronado, San Diego.

(*Above*) Wallis in Peking about 1925.

(*Right*) Wallis riding a donkey in China, escorted by Freddy Mills about 1925.

(*Above*) Mr & Mrs Ernest Simpson and a friend at their second London home, 12 Upper Berkeley Street, where they lived from 1928 to 1929.

(*Right*) On her way to court. Wallis Simpson as a debutante, with Ernest Simpson in the uniform of the Coldstream Guards, 1931.

(*Above*) The Prince of Wales with Lt-Generals Sir Henry Wilson, Sir Charles Harington and the winner of the King's Cup, Bisley, 8 July 1926.

(*Above*) Mrs Arthur Crichton, the Duchess of York (later Queen Mother) and the Prince of Wales at Sandwich in about 1927.

(*Right*) Wedding at the Chateau de Candé, 3 June 1937.

(*Left*) Fort Belvedere, the Prince of Wales's favourite home.

(*Left*) Le Chateau de la Croë, Cap d'Antibes.

(*Right*) The Duchess in her Red Cross uniform

(*Below*) The Duchess in the Bahamas with Red Cross nurses and survivors, who had spent 33 days on a raft.

(*Left*) The Duke and Duchess at 85 rue de la Faisanderie.

(Below) The Duke in the garden of the Mill.

(*Above*) The Duke with Lord and Lady Monckton at the Mill.

(*Right*) The Duke walking with Queen Mary in the garden at Marlborough House, October 1945.

(*Above*) The Duke at a press conference on board *Queen Elizabeth*, as he arrived
at Southampton on 12 March 1953, shortly before his mother's death.
(*Below*) The Duke and Duchess in their garden at the Mill.

7

Wartime and After: (1939–1952)

The Windsors had two homes in France. In Paris they lived at 24 Boulevard Suchet, settling there late in 1938. They also took on the Chateau de la Cröe on the Cap d'Antibes, in the South of France. Both properties were leased since they fully intended to resume life at Fort Belvedere, at least for part of each year. Elsie Mendl advised on the decoration of La Cröe, while Jansen adorned the Paris house. The Duchess attended to the decorating and the entertaining, while the Duke enjoyed his golf. The Windsors might have continued this gentle way of life had war not intervened.

Like many who had witnessed the destruction during the First World War, the Duke believed that anything possible should be done to prevent a second one. He had been dismayed when reading Sir George Arthur's biography of Lord Kitchener to learn that the general had approached war as a glorious adventure, almost as one might a holiday. The Duke's attitude to the latest horror was soon fixed: 'One wonders,' he wrote, 'if the generation of that age of today feel as we did, or are they convinced of the appalling consequences of another World War and its futilities. No! Far worse than that: how it would utterly destroy civilisation.'[1]

The Windsors were at La Cröe when war broke out, and after some more prevarication, this time on his side, the Duke agreed to return to Britain without insisting on terms. Mountbatten came over to Cherbourg in his destroyer, HMS *Kelly*, and brought the Duke and Duchess across the Channel, where they found no member of the Royal Family to meet them and no royal car. The Metcalfes therefore housed them at South Hartfield, Sussex and at Wilton Place in London. Lady Alexandra Metcalfe noted: 'The Duke never once gave the impression of feeling and sensing the sadness of his first return after the drama of his departure. A blind has been drawn down on the past and all memories have been forgotten.'[2] At 16 Wilton Place the Duchess did her hair in Baba's bedroom, they ate sandwiches and drank tea from a thermos. On leaving, the Duchess realised 'there was no place ever for him in this country and said she saw no reason for him ever to return.'[3]

Queen Elizabeth made it clear in advance that she had no wish to meet the Duchess of Windsor, believing that if she did, it would be no time before the pair would be wriggling their way into court functions. The Duke had one lone meeting with his brother, the King, at which various options were discussed concerning his future in wartime. In the end it was decided that he should serve as a liaison officer for the British Mission at the French Army General Headquarters in France. This suited the British since it meant he would be out of Britain. In this new role, his aura as the former Prince of Wales served him well and he was warmly received. For the duration of his service he temporarily surrendered his rank as Field Marshal and became a Major-General.

The Duchess also took on war work. She wanted to help the British but found herself 'far from welcome', so offered to help the French who were 'polite and charming'.[4] She joined the Colis de Trianon relief organisation, started by Elsie de Wolfe, which distributed comfort kits to the troops – sweaters, socks, gloves and soap. The Duchess helped to put these packs together. She then joined the Section Sanitaire Automobile, the motor branch of the French Red Cross, donating an ambulance to them. She made many trips to hospitals delivering items such as bandages and cigarettes. This occupied her through the winter of 1939.

The Duke sent some interesting reports back to Britain and took his role seriously but, as so often after the Abdication, there were petty disagreements. In November 1939 he complained that there was a network of intrigue against him and that he was not allowed to visit any British divisions. He demanded to see the King but his brother would not receive him. Winston Churchill, then First Lord of the Admiralty, who had more important matters to concern him, was forced to intervene, pointing out to the Duke that offence had been taken when he insisted on taking the salute at GHQ when the Commander-in-Chief was present and when the Duke of Gloucester, a senior Major-General, was also there. Churchill was also annoyed when the Duke suggested visiting the RAF and wearing an Air Chief Marshal's uniform. He urged the Duke to discharge his duties and thanked him for his valuable contribution to date. Churchill made a valid point:

Having voluntarily resigned the finest throne in the world, and having been for so many years Prince of Wales and afterwards King-Emperor, it would be natural to treat all minor questions of ceremony and procedure as entirely beneath your interest and dignity: otherwise one merely gives opportunity for slights from those who are unfriendly.[5]

Soon afterwards, however, this liaison work petered out. The Duke was sent down to the South of France. He asked permission to prolong his stay until April and promised to continue to send reports on the frontier defences. Without doubt the Duke was now happier, especially when he rejoined the Duchess at La Cröe. In May he wrote to Churchill to congratulate him on succeeding Neville Chamberlain as Prime Minister.

Just before Paris fell in the summer of 1940 the Duke escorted the Duchess to Biarritz and settled her there. He then returned to Paris, only to depart again at the beginning of June, giving Fruity Metcalfe, who was then on his staff, no advance warning, a matter which many cite against the Duke as evidence of his total preoccupation with himself and of course the Duchess.* Winston Churchill later questioned this sudden departure, hinting that it had been done without permission.

The Windsors stayed uneasily at La Cröe. Queen Mary wrote to her son with family news and wished him well for his birthday, while telling him that she had been hurt by his silence on hers. Then the Italians declared war on France and German forces drew close to the frontiers in the South of France. The Windsors fled, presently reaching Spain.

There has been much speculation about this period. Suffice it to say that while, undoubtedly, German plots developed around them and plans were devised which could use them to German ends, the Windsors themselves were not a party to these. The Duke behaved in a manner both difficult and foolish, but he was not disloyal.

There were problems ahead. The Windsors arrived in Lisbon to find Churchill summoning them to return to Britain forthwith. The Duke wasted no time in informing Sir Samuel Hoare, then serving as British Ambassador in Spain, of his latest conditions for so doing – an announcement in the Court Circular that he and the Duchess had lunched or dined with the King and Queen, a better job (on an equal footing to those undertaken by the Dukes of Gloucester and Kent), assurance that if he were forced to spend the war in Britain his non-resident tax status would be respected and, if not, that any financial difference suffered would be reimbursed from the Civil List. Hearing this, Churchill sent the Duke an angry telegram:

---

* In January 1942 the Duchess wrote to Baba Metcalfe, saying she was sorry not to have had a word from her, 'even if the Duke and Fruity have agreed to disagree, I hope we haven't. I am afraid British Mission No. 1 was never Fruity's affair'. [letter of 31 January 1942]. Baba was furious: 'I know nothing about the Duke and Fruity agreeing to disagree & I'm sure this explanation would come as a complete surprise to Fruity . . . True friendship is very rare & I feel it calls for better treatment than this . . .' [David Metcalfe papers].

Your Royal Highness has taken active military rank and refusal to obey direct orders of competent military authority would create a serious situation. I hope it will not be necesary for such orders to be sent. I most strongly urge immediate compliance with wishes of Government.[6]

This message contained a veiled threat of court martial. The Prime Minister left the Duke to stew it over. The Duke wrestled with the situation and drafted various replies, one of which proposed sending his ADC, Major Gray Phillips, to discuss the issue with the Prime Minister, and stating that if this were not acceptable then he would resign all the ranks he held in the Forces.

On 4 July Churchill sent him a further telegram, informing him that it was in his power to offer him the Governorship of the Bahamas. This was classic Establishment behaviour. The Prime Minister cornered his man and then gave him an escape route. He propelled him across the Atlantic to the Bahamas to keep him out of harm's way for the duration of the war. The Duke accepted, adding: 'I am sure you have done your best for me in a difficult situation'.[7]

Nobody was excited about the appointment, the Duke and Duchess considering it another form of exile and Queen Elizabeth trying to squash the appointment on account of the Duchess. The main problem was that the British thought they were getting the Duke out of the way, whereas there were some sinister figures lurking in the Bahamas who had retreated there to avoid the war, including the Swedish industrialist Axel Wenner-Gren. Effectively they were dropping the Duke into a nest of sharks.

The King told his brother that he was pleased that he would be taking on the post of Governor and arranged to send him the necessary accoutrements for ceremonial dress – the Garter, other Orders and the Royal Victorian Chain. On 1 August 1940 the Windsors sailed from Lisbon to Nassau. The Duchess commented: 'the story of Lisbon is too bad – but I am afraid our book will be filled with chapters like that so long as we have anything to do with officialdom and naturally the war has placed us in that position.'[8]

The Bahamas

The Duke was Governor of the Bahamas for five years between 1940 and 1945. As it turned out, he was not a bad Governor, though he had received no training for such a role. He hoped that being Governor some official recognition would be granted to the Duchess, but the Secretary of State for the Colonies sent a memorandum stating that no one was to curtsy to her, and she was to be addressed as 'Your Grace'.

They arrived in Nassau in August 1940 and were soon busy undertaking all the jobs that befell them, despite finding the Bahamas distinctly provincial. The Duchess became President of the Red Cross and started up two infant welfare clinics on New Providence Island, paid for by the Bahamas Assistance Fund (a trust which the Duke had set up as Prince of Wales). These clinics were modern and well run and they were supervised by the medical staff of the Bahamas General Hospital. The Duchess bought a car for the visiting welfare nurse. She attended clinic days to interview particularly needy or urgent cases.

The Duchess organised the United Services Canteen for British and American servicemen, and arranged social events for them. Throughout the war it was housed in the fashionable Bahamian Club owned by Frederick Sigrist, a friend of the Windsors. The Duchess herself oversaw the organisation and redecoration of the club with RAF staff, helped with funds from Lord Nuffield and donations from Sir Harry Oakes, Herman Rogers and others. The club was available to non-commissioned officers and men of all forces stationed on the island, and there was a grand opening on Christmas Eve 1942. The Duchess also became President of the Nassau Garden Club and a welfare group called the Dundas Centre.

The Duke set about doing all he could to help the island – he saw a large part of his efforts as the improvement of Anglo-American relations. He also wanted to modernise and to ameliorate race relations in the islands. Though encouraged by the Colonial Office, he was never adequately supported and he had to battle with 'the semi-tropical indifference and the natural resentment of the few powerful islanders who held political power and were very rich men'.[9] He also found that the House of Assembly was dominated by twenty-nine members of the Bay Street merchants and a few embittered and vindictive coloured men. Most of the members had got themselves elected by bribery. This led to a virtual dictatorship by the Bay Street Boys.

One scheme the Duke promoted was the Windsor Farm to encourage the raising of crops. This was met with indifference and nicknamed 'Windsor's Folly'. He was annoyed if the Executive Council blocked some progressive measure that he proposed. But he remained diligent in sending reports to the Colonial Office and worked long hours on his opening and closing speeches to the Bahamian Legislature. He chaired the Bahamian Economic Commission, trying to promote fish and sisal exports to the United States. He arranged for Bahamian labourers to work in Florida, travelling to Washington to undertake the liaison work in person.

The Windsors found that their presence on the island acted like a magnet for tourists, especially to the Americans. Gradually they changed the local perception of them as the romantic lovers exiled by the Abdication acquiring reputations as respected and conscientious administrators.

The Duchess set about redecorating Government House, which earned her an unlikely word of praise in the memoirs of the Duke's aunt, Princess Alice, Countess of Athlone, who found it 'much improved . . . by the Duchess of Windsor'.[10] Her aim was to transform a rather cold official residence into a tropical mansion more suited to its locality. She rearranged the furniture and ornaments, hung her recently painted portrait by Gerald Brockhurst and filled the rooms with royal photographs, which inspired great interest in visitors.

The drawing room, library and dining room were formal, but the couple's own suites of rooms were distinctly informal. Hers was decorated in French provincial style, Wallis-blue and white. The Duke's rooms were more masculine and relied heavily on bamboo. There he displayed the symbols of much that he had given up – the red leather box marked 'THE KING', his Field Marshal's baton, both of which were taken daily to his office and returned each night. There too stood his illuminated globe. The overall effect was of a lounge in a tropical club, comfortable and relaxing.

At large dinners the Windsors usually sat opposite each other but one place to the side, in order to be able to talk to as many guests as possible. The Duke often left these dinners at 10.30 p.m. if he had letters to dictate. He would then stride back and forth, still wearing his kilt and puffing at a cigar, dealing with the matters to hand.

In 1941 the Windsors visited the United States, which included a return to Baltimore. This was the occasion when they stayed with General Henry M. Warfield, the Duchess's uncle, at Salona Farms. Anita and Zack Lewis were much in evidence. A reception was given by the Mayor of Baltimore at the Baltimore Country Club in honour of the Windsors and they attended a party for wounded soldiers. They went on to New York and stayed at the Waldorf Towers. A profile in *The American Mercury* described the Duchess:

> Her extraordinary blue eyes are just as keen and her figure just as trim, but her face has taken on harsher lines, lines born of bitter experience, of attack and of defence. Her jaw, if anything, is squarer because of decisions which have been hers, not David's. Her smile is more downward and her eyebrows more satirical in

their upward rise. However, there is still humour in her face;
humour in the tiny wrinkles around her eyes and in the quirk of
her mouth.[11]

That was no doubt a fair description, but the author, Helen Worden,
who had addressed the subject of the Windsors before, then upset the
Duchess and her staff by making exaggerated claims about how many
dresses Wallis bought, how she never wore the same dress twice and so
forth, none of which was true.

There is an unpublished account by Miss Jean Drewes who worked
for the Windsors as their private secretary, living with them at
Government House for nearly four years. She observed them closely and
found that the Duke was secretive, locking cases and metal trunks in
which he kept his private papers. But he was never secretive in his devotion to the Duchess. When he came in from golf he rushed to find her.
He was forever checking where she was and when she was due home.
He dropped whatever he was doing to welcome her back. Equally he
worried about the safety of his mother in Gloucestershire and when he
sent typed messages to the King he left spaces for personal handwritten
additions.

The Duchess told Miss Drewes that she thought the British were
afraid of the Duke's 'vitality and awareness' and for this reason kept him
away from Britain. Miss Drewes detected: 'a lonesomeness about the
couple – a lonesomeness they shared, and because of it, I felt that there
was a selfishness in their devotion to each other.' She thought the strongest
link between the couple was 'mutual respect for each other's ability'[12].
The Duchess considered the Duke dynamic while he thought the Duchess
indomitable.

The Duchess reserved her complaints about the insularity of the
Bahamas for the letters she wrote to friends. She wrote of the 'same
people – behaving same way – and the RAF not producing any Don
Juans',[13] how she felt 'rather ragged after months of this heat', and
complained that the RAF 'was a thing apart – mentally – best explained
in R. Hillary's little book, *The Last Enemy*'.[14] After two years in the
Bahamas she feared 'My mentality is getting very dire.'[15]

She encouraged friends to visit and she kept in touch with her
Montague relations. She was concerned at Corinne's husband George
Murray and her son Lloyd Mustin both serving in the Pacific. She wrote
to Corinne: 'I think of them always and include them in my prayers.'
She regretted being so far removed from everything but added: 'We are
busy caring for survivors that fetch up on these shores from torpedoed

ships and I have plenty of Red Cross work and my Infant Welfare Clinics to keep me busy – but this is a small place and one longs for contact with people in the know.'[16]

Unbeknown to them, J. Edgar Hoover of the FBI was monitoring the couple's activities. Reports listed people they met or entertained, but among this there were rumours that the Duke had a secret deal in place with Goering, and then with a curious Würrtemberg relation of the Duke's. Dom Odo*, a funny, fat monk, told the FBI absurd stories suggesting that Queen Mary had told him that the Duchess had been a mistress of von Ribbentrop, that she had been overheard in Paris saying that the Duke was impotent and that only she could handle this and that Lord Baldwin had 'allegedly asserted that the Duke wanted to suppress Parliament and head a party which would effectively make him the Dictator of England'.[17]

There were stories that the Duke was afraid that he would be kidnapped and traded for Rudolph Hess, then in custody in London – such is the nature of monitoring public figures. The kidnap rumour certainly circulated in the Bahamas at the time.

In 1942 the Duchess produced a book of her favourite Southern recipes, giving all the royalties to the British War Relief Society. Eleanor Roosevelt contributed the foreword.

In January 1942 the Duke was saddened to hear of the death of his ninety-one-year old Uncle Arthur, the Duke of Connaught. Then, late one evening in August, an urgent cable arrived from London, was decoded and delivered to Government House. The Duke of Kent had been heading towards Iceland in a flying boat on 25 August. It had crashed. The Duke of Windsor was shattered by the news and found it hard to compose the requisite cables to his family.

The Duke of Kent had been killed along with the pilot and the other passengers on board. The plane had taken off from Invergordon at 2.30 for what was meant to be an eight-hour journey. It was a wet and foggy night. There was no news of the flight until 6.30 when a farmer saw the plane crash near Wick. The Marquess of Titchfield (later Duke of Portland) had been shooting nearby and he joined the search. The Duke of Kent had been thrown out of the plane, his head injured at the back, both his legs broken and one arm. Death was thought to have been instantaneous. His body was taken to Dunrobin, where the Duchess of

---

* Dom Odo was a curious figure. Formerly known as Prince Carl Alexander of Württemberg (1896–1964), he had become a Benedictine monk. He was a distant cousin of Queen Mary and lived at Altshausen, Germany, but was in the United States during the war.

Sutherland gave it a temporary resting place.' Then it was taken to Windsor, where the young, widowed Duchess of Kent received it.

The King and Queen and Royal Family attended the funeral service and Queen Mary came over from Badminton in Gloucestershire, where she was spending the duration of the war. The Duke of Windsor's cables to his mother paved the way for a slight rapprochement between mother and son.

Not long before this accident, Bishop John Dauglish, the Bishop of Nassau and Chaplain to the Navy, was recalled to Britain by the Archbishop of Canterbury. Aware that Queen Mary might receive him, the Duchess of Windsor plucked up courage and wrote her a letter saying how sorry she was that she had been the cause of separation between mother and son. She told Queen Mary that the Bishop could inform her about the Duke's activities in the Bahamas.

The Bishop was received. Queen Mary listened with interest to stories about her son, but when he mentioned the Duchess he met 'a stone wall of disinterest'.[18] Nevertheless, when Queen Mary wrote to the Duke about the Duke of Kent's death and funeral she added a cryptic line: 'Please give a kind message from me to your wife. She will help you to bear your sorrow.'[19]

This was quite a sea change, possibly inspired by the intensity of the grief shared by Queen Mary and the Duke of Windsor. In such moments, perhaps, family squabbles fall into more modest perspective. But it highlighted another problem. The Duke immediately replied, speaking of the love and comfort that Wallis had given him, how Georgie had been the only member of the Royal Family she really knew at all, telling her that his long silence had been as painful for him as he was sure it was for her but then saying that he hoped he would have 'the intense pride and pleasure of bringing Wallis to see you'.[20] On this point, however, Queen Mary was not prepared to yield.

As related, the Bahamas was full of sinister figures and the Duke was naturally thrown into contact with them – men such as Harold Christie, Axel Wenner-Gren and Maximino Comachi. The Bay Street Boys held local power, and the atmosphere was not always pleasant.

Then there was Sir Harry Oakes, who had made a considerable fortune in mining. He moved from Canada and made his home in the Bahamas. On 7 July 1943 he was murdered in his bed. There were four large holes in his head, and there was evidence that his body had been set on fire, possibly while he was still alive. The Duke had never had to handle a violent murder. He did not do so especially well. He tried to impose a local censorship of the news but rumours were soon widespread on the mainland. He bypassed the local police and consigned the case to two detectives who had looked after his security in Miami. It was said that he should have called in the FBI or the CID.

After the murder the Duchess commented: 'You can imagine what the 'Rumour Clinic' is doing to the sad Oakes case. It really is too tragic.'[21] When the trial took place Major Gray Phillips commented:

> Poor Lady O. was down for 2 nights & looked *miserable*, but her daughter* is made of iron with apparently a thirst for publicity. I'm afraid a conviction will be hard to come by as I cannot visualise the Bahamians arriving at a unanimous conclusion about anything.[22]

The Duchess and Major Phillips were right. So many blunders followed that the case is officially unsolved to this day, though many claim to know who was responsible for the murder.

Towards the end of their time in the Bahamas, in 1944, the Windsors spent four months in America from July until October – the Duchess needed to have her appendix removed.

At the end of the war, the Duke's appointment as Governor came to an end. He had undertaken his duties most conscientiously and had impressed the Colonial Office as one of the more inspired and better-informed of colonial governors. Even Philip Ziegler paid him a striking tribute:

> The Duke had not been transformed miraculously into a paragon of public-spiritedness and devotion to duty; what he did show was that, to an extent Hardinge and Lascelles would have felt inconceivable, when given a job of work to do and with his wife to support him, he would do it faithfully and with considerable ability.[23]

Post-War

There was some talk about the Duke becoming Governor of Bermuda but he declined the offer. The Duchess hinted in letters that he had been offered Australia but had declined it and that he hoped to be sent to Canada. The latter appointment would take him near his ranch and suit him for reasons of tax and finance. Nothing came of either suggestion.

---

* In 1942, when she was eighteen, Nancy Oakes married Alfred de Marigny (1910–98) as his third wife. He was tried for the murder and acquitted. However, he was deported from the island, the Duke of Windsor describing him as 'an unscrupulous adventurer [with] an evil reputation for immoral conduct with young girls'.

On returning to Europe, the Duke was irritated that following their time in the Bahamas neither he nor the Duchess was received at Buckingham Palace, the right of every colonial Governor and his wife.

Towards the end of the war, the Duchess had complained to a friend: 'I can't see why they don't just forget all about the Windsors and let us be where we want to be – in obscurity.'[24]

For a time the Duke drifted. He continued to be concerned about Britain. He was discomforted by the political situation. He found it ironic that the troops of Soviet Russia had not taken part in London's Victory Parade in 1945 since they were, in his opinion, the real victors. He feared that the newly elected Socialist government would ruin Britain. Then he came over to England on his own in quest of another job. Here he met a stone wall.

In May 1944 the question of what the Duke might do next had been raised in London. Tommy Lascelles, by then the King's Private Secretary, told the Prime Minister's office that nothing had given him so much worry over a quarter of a century as the problems associated with the Duke of Windsor.

There were four possibilities, of which only one seemed plausible – that the Duke should settle in the USA, buy his own home and devote his fortune to some charitable cause*. Lascelles did not want him in England and made the devastating point that it would be 'a constant agony (I use the word advisedly) to the present King, which might have really serious consequences.'[25]

In October 1945 the Duke came to London and stayed with his mother at Marlborough House, during which time they chatted about old times and mutual interests. At some point in the 1950s he told the actress Lilli Palmer that he had never liked England: 'My mother was the only person I missed in England.'[26]

While the Duke was at Marlborough House, Tommy Lascelles came to see him. The Duke asked him if the King or Queen Mary would receive the Duchess. He was told most forcefully that they would not. Nor did Lascelles think he could find another job for them. He commended the Duke's work as Governor of the Bahamas, but said that that had been an emergency solution to find him something to do in the war. Lascelles refrained from adding that it was also to keep the Windsors out of Britain. The situation had changed and no equivalent job would now be appropriate. Lascelles then made a personal appeal to him:

---

* The others were another ambassadorial role abroad; a role as a quasi-younger brother of the King in Britain, undertaking some royal duties; or living in Britain as a private citizen.

In 1936 you made a tremendous sacrifice on behalf of your wife, who, you have told me, has made you far happier than you have ever been before; could you not now make another sacrifice, on behalf of your brother, who, in order that you might lead your own life, took on, in your place, the most difficult job in the world, and saddled himself for life with cares and responsibilities which he had never expected to assume, but for which you have always been prepared; could you not now, to save him embarrassment, accept the two decisions once and for all, and not continually go on arguing against them, which could only make things difficult for him?[27]

Effectively Lascelles was suggesting that the Duke should go away. To some degree he did.

The Duchess's Jewels

The next time the Duke came over he brought the Duchess with him. They came to stay at Ednam Lodge in Sunningdale on 11 October 1946. Their hosts were the Earl and Countess of Dudley, living in what Lady Dudley referred to as their 'suburban villa'.[28] This visit was overshadowed by the theft of the Duchess's jewels.

There have been several versions of this story, not least that of Lady Dudley herself in the memoirs she wrote as Laura, Duchess of Marlborough*. Since 2003 the police files have been open and an accurate contemporary account is available. The Windsors brought their luggage in three army lorries under the command of an officer in the Royal Army Service Corps. The Duchess used to travel throughout Europe and other parts of the world with three identical suitcases, deliberately treating them all the same in order not to draw attention to the one that contained her jewel box. Only her maid knew which suitcase it was in. The Windsors were given rooms on the first floor of Ednam Lodge, overlooking the front.

The servants had a communal supper at 5.30 p.m. The Duchess's maid, Joan Martin, took the jewel case to the room of Miss Blaisdell (the Duchess's American secretary) on Tuesday, 15 October with the help of Rowe, their second valet. On the night of the burglary – Wednesday, 16 October 1946 – the Dudleys were not at home. Nor were the Duke and Duchess. All had gone to London. Miss Martin went down to supper at 5.35 p.m. and on returning at 6.45 p.m. she found the jewel case open.

* *Laughter from a Cloud* (Weidenfeld & Nicolson, 1980).

Thieves had entered by an open upstairs window while the staff were dining downstairs.

At eight a.m. the next day, the jewel case was found on the golf course just outside the boundary of Ednam Lodge, about two hundred yards from the drainpipes. Numerous items of jewellery were found in the bottom of the case and in some of the trays, and further items were found scattered in the long grass. A string of valuable pearls, once the property of Queen Alexandra, had been dropped in the grass. The police thought the pearls had been left because they were so large that they would have been hard to dispose of. The value of the recovered jewellery was estimated at £5,000.

The Duchess's staff were considered loyal and trustworthy. They included Sydney Johnson, the Bahamian boy who would stay with them until the Duke died. The Dudleys vouched for the good characters of their own staff. The police report said of the Dudleys: 'They naturally assumed that the Duchess would have brought some jewellery with her, but neither had any idea that she had brought such a large quantity as was stolen. They, like Bullock the butler, mentioned that there were two safes at Ednam Lodge which could have been used, and they gave the impression that they thought anyone handling valuable jewellery in such a manner deserved to lose it.'

The press exaggerated what the stolen jewels might be worth, claiming it could be as much as £500,000. The Duke thought it was more like £20,000. A reward of £2,000 was offered. Inspector J. R. Capstick of Scotland Yard reckoned the theft had been carried out by 'one or more of the many expert London housebreakers'. Since no information had been volunteered, he concluded that they were 'seasoned and cunning thieves who have kept very silent about the theft, and will undoubtedly be very cautious in disposing of the jewellery'.[29] Reports of the theft and details of the jewels were relayed to the FBI and the Argentine and Uruguayan police, and were sent to Switzerland, France, Belgium, Holland, Ottawa and Washington.

Eleven pieces of jewellery were stolen: a diamond bird clip, a diamond and aquamarine brooch, a platinum and diamond bracelet with six large aquamarines, an aquamarine and diamond bracelet, an aquamarine ring with solitaire aquamarine, a gold ring with a golden sapphire, a solitaire square-cut emerald ring, a pair of diamond and sapphire earrings, a pair of diamond ball earrings, a pair of earrings in the shape of a shell (one set with a blue sapphire, the other with a yellow one), and a double gold-chain necklace with a large blue sapphire and a yellow one.

The Windsors left for New York in the *Queen Elizabeth* on 6 November with the case unsolved. The file remained open for many years. One suspect told the police that he got to the golf course, put the jewels in his overcoat pocket, got lost and ended up in Southampton. He then called his friend at Sunningdale Railway Station and handed them over in exchange for £30,000. With the professional pride of one in his trade, he took credit for a big robbery at Blenheim Palace in 1939. As late as 1960 a man called Harry Larkin was charged with indecent assault on a fifteen-year-old girl. While being questioned, he appeared to admit to the previous crime, and Detective Chief Inspector White noted that he knew more about the jewel theft than he could have gleaned from the newspapers. But nothing was ever proved and nor did the jewels ever surface. The file remained open until 1961.

There were, of course, persistent rumours that the Royal Family had staged the robbery to retrieve some jewels. Though there is no evidence for this it was believed by figures such as Georges, the butler. It was fuelled by the strange situation of the Duchess going to London for the night but leaving her jewel case behind.

The insurance company reimbursed the Duke and consequently he spent the next few years acquiring more jewels for the Duchess. She ended her life with a legendary collection, much of it specially designed for her, including the Cartier panther bracelet, clips and brooches, the bracelet so beautifully articulated that it literally slunk over the wrist. She favoured imaginative fashion jewellery such as the gold and enamel necklace with cultured pearls, tourmalines and quartz designed for her by Tony Duquette, and the collection included some impressive diamonds, emeralds, sapphires, rubies and pearls.

The Duke was next in London at the time of Queen Mary's eightieth birthday on 26 May 1947, for which a family lunch was given at Buckingham Palace. To this he was not invited though he called on her at Marlborough House later in the day. Nor were the Windsors invited to the wedding of Princess Elizabeth to Prince Philip in November that year.

The following year they accepted the offer to rent 85 rue de la Faisanderie, a deceptively enormous house in Paris, which belonged to Paul-Louis Weiller. They did so because they thought it would be cheaper than staying in hotels. I stayed often in this house between 1984 and 1993 and on my first visit concluded that if this was the kind of place the Windsors were forced to live in, then it was far from the pathetic exile described by some historians.

The house was like a palace concealed behind the unimposing doors of a Paris street. An outer hall led to a huge hall with gilt sofas yards long, a vast organ to the left and a grand piano. An imposing marble staircase led to a small landing where an immensely historical marble horse (of national museum quality) looked down the stairs. But the Duchess did not like the horse and concealed it behind a screen. Upstairs there was an enormous drawing room next to a dining room, and on the floor above were the large bedroom used by the Duchess and the smaller suite of rooms for the Duke, along with Paul-Louis Weiller's bathroom – adorned with shells since the 1930s. Some of the decoration, such as the leopard-skin walls in one of the bathrooms, was the work of Elsie de Wolfe. Elsewhere the house was packed with treasures: eight chairs that had belonged to Marie Antoinette, Marcel Proust's desk and other rare pieces collected during the long life of Paul-Louis Weiller.

The Windsors never liked the house, which they found depressing and gloomy, though the Duchess did her best to make it attractive and comfortable. But it remained their principal home until they moved to the Bois de Boulogne in 1953.

They kept the lease on La Cröe until 15 August 1948. During the war it had been occupied by Italians and then by Germans. It was shelled from the sea by the British and during the course of this bombardment the Windsors lost more than a few possessions. After giving up La Cröe, they had no country house for a time.

New York was a feature of the Windsors' lives for part of the year, Cecil Beaton reporting in 1948: 'The Windsors being much fêted & I went to a party last night very late where the Duke was dancing by himself a bit worse for wear.'[30] The Duchess had more medical tests, joking to Ambassador Taylor: 'At the moment I am going through the repair shop – every day a doctor for some "part" . . .'[31] Their travelling continued in the early 1950s, taking them to Tallahassee and in 1950 to Mexico to a ranch belonging to a friend of Bob Young's – 'we are to shoot everything in sight',[32] on to Mexico City, and later to Texas, New Orleans, the ranch in Alberta, Canada and then to Biarritz.

Tycoons entered the Duke's life in force and in a very short time he made a considerable sum of money, based on their advice.

In August 1950 the Duke received a letter from the Rt. Rev. Spence Burton, Bishop of Nassau. Burton was a well-known missionary among coloured people and the first American ever to be consecrated a Bishop of the Church of England. He had succeeded Bishop Dauglish as Bishop of Nassau in 1942 and endeared himself to the Duke by sending him a prayer he had written when his brother had been killed in the First World War, in order to comfort the Duke after the death of the Duke of Kent.

The Bishop noted the death of the Duchess's first husband, Win Spencer, on 29 May 1950. He pointed out that Spencer's death altered the Windsors' marital status in the eyes of the Church:

> As both of them [Win Spencer and the Duchess] were baptised Christians at the time of their marriage they were united in Holy Matrimony 'till death us do part'. Now death has parted them and that sacramental bond is thereby broken.

The Bishop affirmed that the Duchess's subsequent marriages were legal ones only, completely honourable according to civil law but not recognised by the church*. He now believed that it was 'the duty, according to the teaching of the best moral theologians, to bless your marriage and administer to both of you the Sacrament of Holy Communion.'[33] The Bishop hoped that the Archbishop of Canterbury might administer this blessing.

In 1953 Burton sent a copy of his letter to the Archbishop of Canterbury's chaplain at Lambeth Palace. The reply stated that Archbishop Fisher had no direct jurisdiction over the Duke since the Duke lived abroad, besides which he would need to be satisfied on several points – that they would 'come to it in a spirit of penitence and faith' and that they had never taken Holy Communion in the years since their marriage.[34] With that the Archbishop allowed the matter to rest. Nor was the Duke inclined to pursue the issue when the Bishop of Fulham raised it with him.

The Duke had not planned to write his memoirs, considering that a dignified silence was the best route forward. But salacious books like *Coronation Commentary* annoyed him, stirring him to successful litigation. Other participants in the Abdication crisis had begun to make their versions known. And on his travels, he was made many enticing offers by newspaper magnates. Finally *Time-Life* encouraged him to write some articles about his reign. In 1948 he began work on his memoirs with the help of Charles J. V. Murphy (the man who would later turn against him and use his privileged position to poison his memory by collaborating on *The Windsor Story*). In due course these were widely serialised and were published as *A King's Story* in 1951. Even while employed by the Duke,

* The Bishop clearly did not take the Rev. Jardine seriously.

Murphy did not hesitate to complain to Cecil Beaton, describing the Duchess as 'the most voracious woman' he had ever met. Beaton questioned Murphy about the relationship:

> When they are together they are like two automata. They have no intimacy – they seldom talk of anything at all serious. They drift. Meanwhile the Prince is happy in his relationship with her. He depends on her utterly. It is a mother-mistress relationship. She looks after him like a child, & yet makes entertainment for him as she did in the days when he was the Prince coming to her home for relaxation at the end of a long day. She now gives him the antidote to hard work but he has none of the hard work. He has nothing to do. She is nearly driven mad trying to find ways of amusing him. He has no interests. He thought he was bored as being a Royalty & he has no reason since to consider he has stopped being bored. He has no intellect. He never opens a book, & in many ways his memory has gone. Steam baths & brandy have made him very weak. The years as Prince have gone by in a flash. He has a 'train driver's' memory of places he has visited but remembers nothing of what happened in any of them.[35]

In May 1951 the Duchess had to undergo an operation at the New York Medical Centre for the removal of a fibroid tumour. It was a shock to her system and gave the Duke an anxious time, but she made a full recovery.

That summer the Windsors were in Biarritz and Elsa Maxwell gave a big dinner for them. Sir John Balfour was on one side of Wallis and a Frenchman from the Levi Mirepoix family on the other. During the dinner an American friend of hers passed a note down the table: 'Who is the Frog seated on your left?' She replied at once: 'I've often been accused of avoirdupois, but this is the first time I've sat next to a Levi Mirepoix.' When Sir Jock stooped down and picked up her handbag, she thanked him: 'I like to see the British grovelling to me.'[36]

The Duke was in England in September 1951 when his brother the King was undergoing his serious lung operation. Returning to Paris, he and the Duchess dined with Margaret Biddle. Cy Sulzberger was another guest: 'The Duke clearly adores her ... After dinner we were sitting together talking and every now and then he would look across at the Duchess and say: 'It's so wonderful to see her. You know, I haven't seen her for a week. Isn't she charming?'[37]

The following year, on 6 February 1952, George VI died and the Duke came to London alone for the funeral. He soon discovered that the new reign was not going to make his life easier and among the differences he lost his allowance of £10,000 a year, a voluntary allowance given him by his brother. The Duke was shocked at this and claimed he would have to adjust his standard of living while trying to live as befitted the son of an English sovereign.

8

The New Reign: 1952–59

A mere four days after the death of King George VI, Queen Mary sent a request to Queen Elizabeth, beseeching her and 'the girls to see [The Duke] & bury the hatchet after 15 whole years'.[1] They did see him, though, as her official biographer put it, 'Queen Elizabeth was not enthusiastic.' Queen Mary thought, rather over-optimistically: 'So that feud is over, I hope, a great relief to me.'[2]

But, alas, the feud was not over. The Duke soon realised that there was no future for him in Britain and that he would not be offered another job. He was consigned to an aimless life of travel.

It would be wrong to suggest that the Windsors did nothing of use. They attended many charity events, usually in the United States. And, during these years, the Duke appealed on US radio on behalf of the Salvation Army – 'the only army that is always welcome in every land'*.[3] The Windsors were special guests at an Army and Navy Citizens Party in aid of wounded servicemen, and they also attended several charity functions in Baltimore, which helped raise money including the Cancer Crusade Ball in 1955, at which they welcomed five hundred guests. They founded the Windsor Awards to help young artists to study abroad, allocating them funds for travel and living expenses.

The Duchess's school friend Ellen Yuille, now Mrs Wolcott Blair, often had them stay, and in 1962 the Duchess worked with her on events for the American Heart Association. The Duchess was Co-Chairman of the Heart of America Ball, with Mrs Lyndon B. Johnson and Ellen Yuille Blair serving on the committee.[4]

The Windsors put down roots for the last years of their lives. They moved from 85, rue de la Faisanderie to no. 4 Route du Champ d'Entraînement, in the Bois de Boulogne. This was a lovely house with formal rooms downstairs and bedroom suites for the Duke and Duchess on the first floor, joined by an informal sitting room. There was a large lawn and various outbuildings. The house belonged to the City of Paris and was given to the Windsors for a small rent.

---

* Ambassador Taylor helped the Duke with this speech.

They also purchased the Moulin de la Tuilerie at Gif-sur-Yvette outside Paris. This had been the home of the artist Drian, who painted a portrait of the Duchess. She claimed to have fallen for The Mill when she first saw it in 1950. This was a cluster of houses gathered in several acres and gave the Duke the chance to work long days in his garden, amid the small rocks and stream. The Duke's French gardener, Édouard Kruch, preferred working for the Duke who was quite laid back in his approach, while he found the Duchess more demanding. In the 1960s the Duke used to 'escape' from the main house and come and read comics with Kruch's sons under an Indian tepee which he had bought for them.[5]

In order to buy The Mill, the Duke had to obtain funds from Britain where strict currency-exchange regulations were in place. The Labour Government had allowed him to take out £80,000 and the new Conservative Government were happy to let him take another £20,000 on the grounds that 'if it is in the public interest that the Duke of Windsor should make his home outside the United Kingdom, it was unreasonable that he should be denied facilities for transferring his own money from the United Kingdom to the country in which he proposed to establish himself.'[6]

These were to be the homes of an ageing couple, locked together by the act perpetrated by the Duke in 1936. They muddled along well, although their interests were very different. He liked golf and gardening and reminiscing with his cronies. She liked high society, haute couture and interior decorating. Unlike the Duke, she was prepared to decry the Abdication. It was hard to live out the myth of 'the greatest love story of the twentieth century'.

Diplomatic slights continued to occur. In the summer of 1952 Sir Oliver Harvey, the British Ambassador in Paris, invited the Windsors to come to a reception after a dinner given for Maurice Schumann. The dinner was said to be political and the reception social. The Duke was furious. He declined, and furthermore he refused an invitation to lunch at the Embassy on the grounds that the Court was in mourning. Presently Anthony Eden, the Foreign Secretary, took the matter up with Winston Churchill, the Prime Minister: 'It did not seem to me that there was any discourtesy to the Duke, and certainly none was intended.'[7]

Churchill thought differently. He felt that the Windsors should not be given a 'second-class social status' and examined the instructions issued by Sir Alec Hardinge in 1937. It will be recalled that these subtly curtailed potential guest lists by stating that the Duchess of Windsor must always sit on the Ambassador's right, which meant that no one with higher

precedence than a non-royal duchess could be invited to an Embassy
dinner at which she was to be present.

Churchill suggested that the Ambassador should not invite the
Windsors again for the time being and concluded: 'His invitation will
certainly not be accepted if they take the insulting form of relegating
him and the Duchess on social occasions to a position inferior to that of
the unofficial notabilities of French society.'[8]

In November the Duke was again in London and was invited to be present
at the lunch at Buckingham Palace to celebrate the fifth anniversary of the
wedding of the Queen and Prince Philip. The following spring he heard that
his mother had been taken gravely ill. He and the Princess Royal crossed
from America together. They arrived before Queen Mary died on 24 March
1953. As the Duke again marched through the streets of London, he realised
that his last strong link with Britain had now been severed.

However, there was one relation whom he used to visit when he came
to London in the mid-1950s, his cousin Princess Arthur of Connaught*.
She lived in Avenue Road, just north of Regent's Park, and since 1946
had been crippled with rheumatoid arthritis. She took no part in public
life and was never seen by the general public though she was taken out
for occasional drives in a specially designed ambulance car.

The Duke of Windsor used to visit her and, with the approval of her
doctor, provided her with the drugs Hydrocortone and Meticorten from
the USA. These helped her condition. It was an act of kindness with
which he is seldom credited.

The Windsors were not invited to the Coronation of Elizabeth II. Sir
Winston Churchill told the Cabinet that whereas it was understandable
that the Duke of Windsor might attend a royal funeral, it was completely
inappropriate for a King who had abdicated to attend the Coronation of
one of his successors. The Cabinet endorsed this view. Therefore in June
1953 the Windsors watched the new Queen being crowned on television,
Elsa Maxwell jesting that it was much more *chic* to watch the ceremony
on a black and white set in the company of the Duke and Duchess than
to be seated in the Abbey.

The diplomat Charles Johnston[†] and his wife Natasha saw the
Windsors when they visited Paris that autumn. They were invited to a

---

* HRH Princess Alexandra (1891–1959), elder daughter of Princess Louise, Duchess of Fife, and
thus a granddaughter of Edward VII. She was Duchess of Fife in her own right. In 1913 she married
Prince Arthur of Connaught, and they had one son, the Earl of Macduff (later 2nd Duke of
Connaught), who died of hypothermia in Canada in 1943.

† Sir Charles Johnston (1912–86), First Secretary in Madrid (1948–55), and later High Commissioner
in Australia. He was married to Princess Marina's Georgian cousin, Princess Natasha Bagration.

dinner given in their honour by Sir Keith Officer, the Australian
Ambassador to France:

> He [the Duke] manages to look fresh and wizened at the same time,
> like a very young man preserved in a bottle for years and years, and
> slightly shrunk in the process. After the usual blast against the
> Foreign Office, which he dislikes as much as the late King did, he
> was very agreeable to talk to . . . The Duchess is better than in her
> photographs, not so desiccated and nutcracker-ish, with a curious
> physical magnetism about the eyes that the camera doesn't catch at
> all. I had a long talk with her. She likes cracking metallic jokes about
> her situation, for instance we were talking about Austria and she
> said (trying to remember when she had been there): 'We were
> married in 1937 . . . as if anybody in the world didn't know.' She
> asked Lord Granard*, who was also at dinner, who he thought had
> been the best-looking member of the Royal Family at the Coronation
> and, when he said Lady Harewood†, she replied: 'Oh, you mean the
> Duke's Jewish relations?' Apart from that she likes gossip about the
> American upper crust and explained to me about two families called
> Biddle and Duke who had intermarried – going into it with a tremen-
> dous seriousness and thoroughness which would have made *Debrett*
> look like an amateur by comparison. Natasha and I didn't bow, curtsy
> or 'Ma'am' her, but she didn't seem to mind, which is a point in
> her favour. Otherwise I should say more light than warmth, and
> more charm than solidity.[9]

There is a further cryptic reference to the Windsors in Johnston's
diary the following July, when he met Fruity Metcalfe on the steps of
White's in St James's Street:

> He [Fruity] was upset because of the way things are going with the
> Windsors. Fruity, as a survivor of the Windsor court, an almost
> legendary relic of the last reign but one and two, feels this bitterly.
> His world collapsed a long time ago, but now the ruin isn't even
> picturesque any more. The whole thing distresses me too. As long
> as it was 'all for love' it made sense, but this squalid petering-out

* The 9th Earl of Granard (1915–92), a very rich Irish peer who lived in Paris with his wife,
formerly married to a Prince de Faucigny-Lucinge.
† The Princess Royal had had to appeal to George VI for permission for her son, the Earl of
Harewood (the Duke's nephew), to be allowed to marry Marion Stein in 1949. They were divorced
in 1967 and she married Jeremy Thorpe in 1973.

is lamentable. It could be a Lear-like tragedy, and the really tragic thing is, it isn't that either.*10

This was almost certainly a knowing reference to the Duchess's infatuation with Jimmy Donahue, a relationship largely based on their shared love of nightclubs and parties.

Donahue was a rich homosexual playboy, and a member of the Woolworth dynasty. No doubt he was a highly entertaining companion. Philip Ziegler dismissed him as a 'flamboyant vulgarian' and an 'epicene gigolo'11 and no doubt those descriptions fit too. There were stories of parties at which the Duchess and Donahue flirted, the Duke was miserable and at least once left early in tears. Lady Diana Cooper told me of one such occasion:

Diana spoke of the night when she dined with Donahue and the Windsors. The Duke persuaded her to come. 'Aw, come on, Diana!' At the dinner everyone got presents from Donahue. The Duchess put her ostrich fan in the middle of the roses: 'The Prince of Wales's feathers in Mr Donahue's roses.' Diana thought it the height of vulgarity. On the pavement later Donahue said to Diana: 'Don't you think *she*'s the best Duchess you know?' Diana riposted with: 'Well, my mother was my favourite Duchess.' She was certain the Duchess didn't love the Duke.12

Though the Duke tolerated Donahue, he became fed up at the end of a Portofino holiday and summoned him for a farewell discussion. There are numerous versions as to how the relationship ended. The most reliable is that of the Duchess's close friend, Cordelia Biddle Robertson. Cecil Beaton cross-questioned her in 1955, describing Cordelia as dressed 'like a flapper in the Twenties. She's raucous, she's graphic, she's an original.' He prised her version of the Donahue affair out of her soon after it ended:

She fell in love with Jimmy Donahue, and he, strange to say, with her. They fooled the Duke in a most terrible way. 'Isn't Jimmy a stinker?' she'd say. 'He's named his boat the *Walla Walla*. Isn't he a swine? I'm not going to speak to him. (They are all at the violin place in Paris!) You're not going to speak to him either.' The Duke

---

* Fruity Metcalfe died in November 1957. The Duchess wrote a rather scatty letter of sympathy to his widow, Baba, saying 'we never had a better friend and the Duke really loved him as you well know'. She went on to write of the deaths of two other close friends, Helen Fitzgerald and Herman Rogers. [Duchess of Windsor to Lady Alexandra Metcalfe, 22 November 1957].

gets tired. Wallis says she'll wait a bit longer. The Duke goes, Jimmy and Wallis fall screaming with laughter into each other's arms.

But the Donahue affair is all over.

'I'll tell you exactly for why. Now Wallis knew about Jimmy's taste for boys but she put up with it. There is one thing she loathes and that is garlic, and sometimes Jimmy would come to her smelling of garlic and there'd be the most awful row. Well, maybe they'd had enough of each other. It didn't end as we all thought it would with a terrible scandal on the front pages. It just ended one night when Wallis had a date with Jimmy for midnight. She went downstairs to wait for him arriving in the car and he turns up ten minutes late. She is cross – and what is more she is furious because he is smelling of garlic. "And so what?" shouts Jimmy. "Yes, I do like garlic – and you know it and I'd much rather go off with my boyfriend than hang about you." From that day to this not a word between them. It is over, over, over.'

Cordelia added: 'The Duke and she are happy enough now. He's bored to death. He only lives for her, but there's going to be trouble when she gets bored. If she finds a man who is a man, the Duke is going to be sore! He believes he married the most angelic creature on earth and if he thought she wasn't he'd blow his brains out.'[13]

In October 1954 Charles Murphy, who had ghosted the Duke's memoirs, went to Paris to work with the Duchess on hers. The book progressed well and the publishers liked those chapters which Murphy completed. But the Duchess was not satisfied and fired him. In April 1955 she took on Cleveland Amory but, as previously related, that relationship also came unstuck, whereupon the Duchess tried to get Murphy back again. In the end Joseph Bryan III (the other ghost in *The Windsor Story*) took the project on. The memoirs were published in 1956. By and large English reviewers ignored them, but the distinguished historian Roger Fulford wrote of them: 'This book explodes one myth generally believed at the time and still widely held – namely, that the Duchess was a designing and ambitious woman playing a game with all the skill and recklessness of a Pompadour or a Lola Montez.'[14]

The Marburg Papers

In the summer of 1953 an issue arose which dogged the Duke for the next decade and more. It would be wrong to give this undue prominence but it was nevertheless a great nuisance to him. This concerned the publication of German documents and included a number of suggestions concerning his wartime activities. The threat had been brewing since the end of the war. On 18 July 1953 John Colville, Churchill's Private Secretary, went to tea with Lord Beaverbrook to show him some papers about Spain and Portugal which purported to show that von Ribbentrop proposed to make use of the Duke if Britain was successfully invaded. In August a document was prepared for the Cabinet, and Winston Churchill was set on suppressing the papers.

In May 1954 Churchill invited the Duke to lunch at 10 Downing Street to discuss the Americans publishing some 'beastly documents' in their eighth volume of German foreign-policy papers. Churchill's view was that 'they will do no harm' and had been 'put in to add some sensationalism to what would otherwise be a very boring book'.[15]

In November *German Documents on German Foreign Policy, Series D, Volume VIII* was published with the claim that Count Julius von Zech-Burkersroda, German Minister to the Hague, had reported that the Duke had given him Allied defence plans for Belgium in 1940. The Duke wrote to Churchill:

> The initial mistake, of course, was the failure of the Foreign Office to issue a statement coincident with the publication of 'Documents on German Foreign Policy 1918–45' Series D, Volume VIII in which the two letters concerning me appeared, clearing me of these allegations.
>
> While it is a bore that Washington insists on the publishing of the 'Lisbon Documents'. Walter Monckton and I examined them very thoroughly over the week-and and will have a 'dementi' prepared by the Spring in advance of their publication. As a matter of fact it would be difficult to enlarge or improve on Bobbety Salisbury's* admirable and objective memorandum on the subject which he and I discussed at Hatfield on Sunday.[16]

On 10 November the Duke issued a formal denial. A few days later, in Parliament, Churchill backed the Duke's statement.

Perhaps it was knowledge of these various accusations that caused Queen Helen of Romania and Prince Paul of Yugoslavia to tell James Pope-Hennessy (in 1956) that the Duke of Windsor 'should be shot as a traitor'. Pope-Hennessy added that 'whether as a traitor to his country or to the concept of royalty' he could not understand. Prince Paul also told him: 'The Duke of Windsor is simply a masochist & King Leopold

---

* 5th Marquess of Salisbury (1893–1972), senior Conservative polician and Leader of the House of Lords 1951–7.

[III of the Belgians] who likes [his unpopular second wife] "Liliane's being rude to him in public" is another.'[17]

In July 1957 Tommy Lascelles, no admirer of the Duke's, told James Pope-Hennessy that the so-called Marburg papers would be released any day now. It had proved impossible to prevent it. He said these documents contained conversations with the Duke in Portugal to the effect that he had agreed to come back as King of England if the Germans conquered Britain. He said the Duke attributed the Abdication to 'that scheming woman my brother Bertie married' and that when he was Governor of the Bahamas he had applied for a special German code to keep in touch with the Reich. Lascelles declared: 'He will deny it all, of course, but I am afraid it is all true.'[18]

On 1 August 1957 the latest papers were released and the Duke did indeed deny them. The accusation was that he had been tempted by the Germans to aid them against Great Britain in 1940. The Duke was confident of his innocence and felt that at both times of publication the matter had been dealt with 'in the most satisfactory and dignified manner'.[19]

The Duke was therefore upset when on 28 December 1962 a third volume was released covering the years 1935 to 1936, which alleged that when he was King he had contemplated a British alliance with Germany in thirty-six memos to his Nazi cousin, the Duke of Coburg. The Duke complained to the Foreign Secretary, Lord Home, that he had been 'placed in a very embarrassing and undignified position vis-à-vis the Press last Friday'. He asked Home to ensure that if more papers came out he would be forewarned 'and able to deal with the Press which, now without any official support, I have to do personally'.[20]

The Duke issued another denial. He conceded that he had sought an 'understanding' with Germany, but said the Coburg documents gave a false impression.

On 8 December 1966 more papers were released, including a dispatch dating from March 1936 from Leopold von Hoesch reporting that the King had played a notable part in banning Great Britain from going to war over the German reoccupation of the Rhineland and another report that the King demonstrated 'profound regret that such serious tension should have developed' in British-Italian relations on account of the Italian invasion of Ethiopia.

As Philip Ziegler put it: 'Many other fantasies have been voiced in the last thirty years. The laws of libel mercifully ensured that the most grotesque have been published only after his [the Duke's] death and thus did not trouble him.'[21]

The conclusion must be that the Germans had their sights firmly fixed on the Duke. They might have made plans to kidnap him. They might have believed that they could use him as a figurehead. But that does not mean that the Duke was complicit in this. He remained loyal to the country of his birth.

Throughout these years the Duke clung to the belief that he had been wronged by Great Britain. In 1954 he replied to a stranger:

> The fact that I did work very hard for the furtherance of British interests was conveniently erased by my enemies and detractors in 1936. Overnight they switched from their former fulsome and exaggerated praise to a smear campaign of vilification of my character. However, when one's conscience is clear such hypocrisy can be ignored. Anyway it's nice to know one still has a lot of friends, which is pleasingly evident wherever the Duchess of Windsor and I happen to go.[22]

From time to time the Windsors were subjected to vicious books such as *Gone with the Windsors*, written by Iles Brody who claimed to 'view the situation as a cool, unbiased observer, undisturbed by chauvinism and hero-worship'.[23] It was published in 1953, a particularly virulent example. Soon afterwards Brody dropped dead in the street, after which the Duchess commented: 'At last I can believe in God.'[24] Passing on this story, her old friend Constance Coolidge commented: 'She looks wonderfully, really, & is amusing. One can forgive a lot for that.'[25]

The endless travelling continued. Between 19 and 23 March 1955 the Windsors went to Cuba to visit Arthur Gardner, the United States Ambassador, and his wife Susie. They dined with the British Ambassador, Wilfred Gallienne, at the Residence, met members of Cuban society and on 22 March the Duke called on President Batista (a few years before Castro overthrew him). In September they were in Venice. In 1956 they visited Vienna.

Having lost her first husband in May 1950, the Duchess lost her second on 30 November 1958 when Ernest Simpson died in the Middlesex Hospital in London following an operation for throat cancer. As previously mentioned, the Duchess had kept in touch with him, particularly when writing her memoirs earlier in the decade.

After his divorce in 1937 Ernest had married Mary Kirk Raffray, one of the Duchess's bridesmaids at her first marriage in Baltimore in 1916. They married at the Brooklawn Country Club in Fairfield, Connecticut on 19 November 1937. They had one son, Ernest Henry Simpson, who was born on 27 September 1939 and christened at the Guards Chapel.

He was educated at Harrow. Mary died of cancer at the Simpsons' family home, also in Wiltshire, on 2 October 1941.

Then, on 12 August 1948, the widowed Ernest married Avril Mullens, daughter of Sir John Mullens, a London stockbroker. Born in 1910, she had been twice married, first to Prince George Imeritinsky and then to Brigadier Hugh Leveson-Gower. She was the sister of the notorious Elvira Barney, who was tried for the murder of Michael Stephen in 1932 and was acquitted by the court, if not by the media. She died of a mixture of drink and drugs in 1936. Avril survived Ernest, dying in a car crash in Mexico on 28 November 1978.

When Ernest died, a friend commended him in *The Times* for having maintained 'the highest standard of personal conduct. In an age of commercialisation he refused all offers to write his reminiscences or to give interviews to the Press. He shunned any form of publicity, preferring dignified silence. The courage with which he faced his last illness was typical of the man.'[26] Evidently his greatest joy as a host was to show his friends his books and pictures, his old furniture and his garden.

Within a week a large congregation gathered at St Peter's, Eaton Square for Ernest Simpson's memorial service. There was a respectable smattering of London society and a great number of representatives from shipping companies (including the Chairman of Niarchos in London), the Baltic Exchange and other city organisations. Bernard Rickatson-Hatt, former Editor-in-Chief at Reuter's, represented the Guards' Club.

The day after Ernest died, James Pope-Hennessy was driving back to Paris with the Duchess from The Mill. The Duchess asked him if she should send flowers or a cable to the widow. He advised her to write a 'nice, private note'. The Duke had advised the same. She told Pope-Hennessy that she had seen Ernest a few times but had never met his wife. She had suggested he bring her to see her, but he never did. Pope-Hennessy could not resist mentioning that the death of Ernest finally resolved the issue of 'two divorces' or 'two husbands living'. The Duchess thought about it for a moment and then said: 'Do you think that we can all become Catholics and get married again?'[27]

James Pope-Hennessy had entered the lives of the Duke and Duchess when researching his authorised biography of Queen Mary. He visited them in 1958 and spent a memorable weekend at The Mill, leaving one of the best accounts of the Windsors together at that phase of their life. It is sympathetic, witty and entertaining.*

---

* *See* Peter Quennell (ed), *A Lonely Business* (Weidenfeld & Nicolson, 1980), pp. 209–224.

When Pope-Hennessy met the Windsors, he described them in a letter written (bravely) in his room at The Mill. He found the Duke very friendly and looking like 'Ernest Thesiger as the Dauphin in *St Joan* . . . she an amiable Southerner, large-jawed, funny and like her book, naïve, basically – sort-of surprised to be here, so to speak – they are like people after a cataclysm or a revolution, valiantly making the best of infinite luxury . . . I am much taken by both of them . . .'[28]

During his stay the Duchess expressed her intense irritation about a recently released song called 'Love, Love, Love', which the Duchess thought undignified and potentially libellous. Pope-Hennessy saw no libel, but she said she was going to call her lawyers all the same. Some of the words in Harry Belafonte's song ('It Was Love, Love Alone'), she found especially irritating:

> You can take his money, you can take his store
> But leave him that lady from Baltimore
> It was love, love, love, love, love alone
> Caused King Edward to leave his throne
>
> I don't know what Mrs Simpson got in her bone
> That caused the king to leave his throne
> It was love, love, love, love, love alone
> Caused King Edward to leave his throne
>
> On the 10th of December 1936
> The Duke of Windsor went to get his kicks
> It was love; love alone
> Caused King Edward to leave his throne . . .

The Windsors were likewise taken with Pope-Hennessy and it did not take them long to decide that he would be the ideal person to help the Duke with a new project they were cooking up. Pope-Hennessy described to his brother what happened:

> The telephone rang at midnight last Wednesday just when Dr John Robertson Unwin had hypnotised me so thoroughly I was comatose; we were discussing a thing in my dream (since identified as the effigy of the Duke of Clarence) which was pursuing me through a rocky Sienese landscape. The telephone was the Duchess. 'Naow, James, we have a project which we think may appeal to you because, well, because it's QUITE DIGNIFIED.'

'Yes, Duchess?'

'You couldn't fly over tomorrow?'

'No, Duchess'.

'It's also financially REWARDING'.

'Ah-ah-ah, Duchess' (suspiciously)

Mr Walter 'our American lawyer' then got on the line and talked without drawing breath for twenty minutes saying how competent, brilliant, and intelligent, and to-the-Duke indispensable I was and will be ('Mr Walter was in a funny mood, he'd just been jetted from New York' the Duke said on the telephone next morning). The words 'Express' 'collaboration' and 'financial rewards' frightened me so much I declined on the spot.[29]

The next morning the Duke persuaded Pope-Hennessy to change his mind, apologising for the lateness of the call and making it clear that the articles would be published under his name. The articles were to reflect the changes in male fashion since the First World War with illustrations from the Duke's albums, 'and with himself as pioneer of these alterations of the Mode'.[30] The Duke was keen to work with Pope-Hennessy. He refused to collaborate with anyone else.

The plan developed in 1959 but the Duke then discovered that his Private Secretary, Victor Waddilove, 'was not up to our required standard'. While resolving that matter, he did not have time 'for reflection on past and present fashions'.[31] Presently Pope-Hennessy had a meeting with William Aitken*, Managing Director of London Express News & Features. From this it became clear that the project was to have a strong political bias and an advertising slant. Aitken told him he wanted a lot about policemen in collars and ties: 'The Duke had remarked that this showed the Socialists' lack of understanding of the working-class, since police constables could not afford to change their collars every day.'

Pope-Hennessy backed out, explaining that he would not help the Duke 'who should be above politics' in 'absurd Tory propaganda', nor was he prepared to write anything 'to be used for advertising purposes for a textile firm'.[32] On 5 May he formally resigned from the project, claiming 'personal prejudice against the Beaverbrook newspapers'.[33]

At the end of 1959 the Bank of England quietly confirmed the Duke of Windsor's status as a non-resident for tax purposes, which pleased him.

---

* Sir William Aitken (1905–64), nephew of Lord Beaverbrook; journalist & politician; father of Jonathan & Maria Aitken.

9

Twilight Years: 1960–1971

The 1960s found the Duke involved in creating more self-serving articles. Despite his protestations that he never discussed or thought about
the Abdication in later life, these issues continued to hang over him. They
had been revived in the memoirs which both the Duke and the Duchess
wrote with help from ghost writers; they found their way into books and
articles about them and occasional television interviews.

The Duchess gave a frank interview to *McCall's* in January 1961 in
which she accused the British Monarchy and Government of persecuting
the Duke for twenty-four years. One who disapproved was the Palm
Beach hairdresser Rex Wighton, a society hairdresser with his own salon
in West Palm Beach. He noted the recent departure of the Windsors:

> The Windsors have come and gone ere this – he bathed in the
> pool at the Colony and gossip says he is a skinny chap – thin arms
> – and only splashed about – no swimming and a face full of
> wrinkles – while his Mrs – W. has her face well lifted and a jaw
> like a horse – and dyed hair – looks like Q. Eliz.1st – very high
> forehead and a very determined chin – she really is the boss
> I think, wish she would stop cheapening them – by her silly
> articles in the books and papers . . . I think they are all a mess –
> including Mrs. Winston Guest.[1]

In July 1961 the Foreign Office got concerned about a mooted television series on the Duke of Windsor in which he was going to be asked
to read the Abdication speech. Lord Monckton prevailed on the Duke
not to sign the contract, and warned Sir Michael Adeane, the Queen's
Private Secretary, what was afoot.

In June 1962 the Windsors marked their Silver Wedding. The Duchess
wrote tellingly to Lady Alexandra Metcalfe:

> It is as you say almost impossible to believe the scene at Candé was
> 25 years ago – I sometimes wonder how the Duke and I have
> survived the trying years that followed – but now they too are

forgotten and life is as serene as it can be living as we all do – with costs mounting and running a house a trial instead of a pleasure.[2]

Presently the Duke did indeed reread the Abdication speech, in the film documentary *A King's Story*, in which he and the Duchess both appeared. This came about for the simple reason that, as with his film on Churchill, *The Finest Hours*, Jack Le Vien was smart enough to ask the Duke to do it. At one point James Pope-Hennessy was going to be the historical adviser but, as we have seen, he objected to the Duke exploiting the film to give substance to his private mythology. Pope-Hennessy, much influenced by Tommy Lascelles, thought that 'a more detached relation of the facts would bring the Duke of Windsor into a better light than that cast by his reminiscences'. He questioned the portrayal of the Archbishop of Canterbury, Cosmo Gordon Lang, a man who had felt that he was not consulted enough during the Abdication crisis: 'Lang was sententious, sycophantic and a royal snob, but he was not the Machiavellian creature, which, to the Duke, he now seems to have been'.[3]

Viewing the film today, it can be seen to have dated badly. Both Windsors are hesitant readers of the autocues and much of it appears staged and artificial. But at the time it was compelling viewing, enhanced by the grave-voiced commentary of Orson Welles.

In June 1964 the Duke of Windsor turned seventy, with a flood of presents and a telegram of congratulation from the Queen. In celebration of this milestone, James Pope-Hennessy wrote a long profile for the *Sunday Times*, in which, among other things, he suggested that the Queen and Royal Family should relax their distant attitude and invite the Windsors to lunch. The article caused outrage. Viscountess Davidson, a lady life peer in her own right, was furious, failing to understand how a man with his connections to the Palace and the Crown could write such a piece. She was sure he must realise why it was 'essential to keep the Duchess away from England & how dangerous it would be even now after all these years to reverse the original decision'. She wrote that it was not petty-mindedness but that 'sensible knowledgeable people' would know 'what would happen if that woman was allowed to live in England'. The Throne would be undermined.[4]

Another man enraged was Tommy Lascelles, a long-time admirer of Pope-Hennessy's but someone who had been concerned when Pope-Hennessy fell, to some degree, under the Windsors' spell. He warned him that a great many people, not connected in any way with the Palace, were now describing Pope-Hennessy as 'a stooge of the Windsors' and asking 'Who the Hell does he think he is, to dictate to the Queen or to anybody else, whether or no they should invite their aunts to luncheon?'[5]

This was not the only family birthday being celebrated. Out in Huntly, Virginia, Aunt Bessie Merryman reached the age of one hundred on 19 August 1964. She had remained robust, on the ball, and game for new adventures. She told a reporter that no one had asked her to go to the moon, but if she lived long enough she might try it. Lelia Newbold Noyes gave a dinner for her at Wakefield Manor. As Aunt Bessie surveyed the scene she commented: 'I always feel when I look over Wakefield that I never want to be closer to Heaven than I am here.' Speeches were made and she was much complimented. 'You're all dressed up!' one of her relatives said. 'Well, I'm clothed,' replied the centenarian. The Duchess of Windsor, who owed her aunt so much, was not present at the celebrations as neither she nor the Duke were well, but she sent a telegram.[6]

Aunt Bessie did not give up after reaching this great milestone. She said she had a burial plot but was not ready to use it yet. But Aunt Bessie died soon afterwards on 28 November. The Duke attended her funeral while the Duchess was stuck in New York, recovering from surgery to her right foot.

The Duke's health was poor. His eyes were causing problems and then he suffered an aorta aneurysm. In December 1964 he was admitted to the Methodist Hospital in Houston, Texas, as a patient of the celebrated Dr Michael DeBakey, for surgery to remove the aneurysm. The Queen and the Princess Royal sent him flowers, and the Queen asked for daily reports on his condition. When he was examined, the doctors found that the aneurysm was the size of a large grapefruit and that the arterial wall to the heart was very thin.

The Duke made a good recovery from his operation but remained in hospital over Christmas and was finally discharged in the New Year. He and the Duchess sailed for Europe on 29 January 1965. Sir Winston Churchill had died on 24 January and they were at sea on the day of his State Funeral. Suitable comments on Churchill's friendship and support were issued to the press. In an interesting touch of protocol, both the Duke and Duchess were officially represented by Sir John Aird at the service at St Paul's Cathedral.

Hardly were the Windsors back in Paris than the Duke suffered a detached retina on a Sunday night in late February. They were whisked into London, avoiding the press, and soon settled with their staff at Claridge's.

The Duke underwent two operations conducted by the Queen's physician, Sir Stewart Duke-Elder. The Duke was in the London Clinic for some weeks and each day there were photographs of the Duchess arriving and leaving.

The Queen visited him twice (once at the Clinic and again at Claridge's). His sister, the Princess Royal, went to the Clinic to see the Duke and Duchess ten days before her sudden death, and Princess Marina, Duchess of Kent was another visitor. The Windsors walked in Queen Mary's Garden in Regents Park and the Duke walked in the gardens of Buckingham Palace as he recovered.

Both attended a public memorial service for the Princess Royal at Westminster Abbey on 1 April which was also the day of the funeral in Yorkshire, the first official engagement in Britain in which they both took part. The Duke was still wearing his dark glasses and entered by a side door to avoid flash photography. Figures such as the Duke of Beaufort, Lord Mountbatten and Lady Monckton were in the congregation. Audrey Russell, coincidentally the niece of Fruity Metcalfe, was the BBC commentator. She watched as the Duchess guided the Duke through the service: 'The Duchess found the places in the hymn books for him, pointing to the exact page with a black-gloved hand, holding a pair of marcasite lorgnettes. Her hands made gentle helpful gestures which he clearly took for granted.'[7]

The Windsors were flown back to Paris in an aircraft of The Queen's Flight. The Duchess wrote to a friend: 'It has been a dreadful winter – but the eye operations were much more difficult to bear than the Texas one. However, we are now back here and I feel a miracle has occurred, that the Duke can see and quite well, not 100% vision but very well . . . We shall take it easy as crowds rather upset him for the moment . . .'[8] It was not long before once again the pair were to be seen enjoying the Paris high life, notably at a white-tie ball given by Don Carlos de Beistegui.

In October the Duke returned to Houston for a check-up, in advance of which the British Consul, Gerald Simpson, became overexcited. He pointed out to the Foreign Office that there was a dearth of VIPs visiting Houston and hoped the Duke could be invited to address the English-Speaking Union. The Foreign Office did not like this and consulted Buckingham Palace. A message came back: 'Her Majesty entirely agrees with your views . . . namely that while nobody can prevent a body like the English–Speaking Union inviting HRH to a Banquet or other function, this is entirely a matter between the inviting body and the Duke of Windsor. Her Majesty does not think it would be either kind or wise for any such suggestion to come from the Government or from the Consulate-General in Houston.'[9]

The Duke arrived in New York in early October on his way to Houston, but was angered when he did not receive the customary visit from the Consul-General. The Duke told his English lawyer, Sir Godfrey Morley, to ask the Foreign Office if he had been 'purposely cold-shouldered' and to tell them that he was 'worried as to the reasons.' Morley hoped there had not been a change of policy in respect of the Duke.[10] Lees Mayall at the Foreign Office apologised, explaining that the Duke's arrangements had not been known and hoping that more notice could be given in the future.[11] The British Ambassador in Washington, Sir Pat Dean, was livid, pointing out that a 'rather gossipy Washington hostess' had told him that the Duke had felt that the Ambassador 'had treated him rather discourteously and had not enquired about his progress at the hospital.' Much of this was 'complete nonsense' but he added: 'From this it is clear that HRH or someone on his staff has been talking to the Americans. If you think it useful I should not object if you let Morley know sometime what I feel about this.'[12]

Once again the Foreign Office was obliged to consider how to handle the Windsors when they were travelling. A few months before this they had planned to go to Morocco. The Consul sought advice. He was told he should help the Duke with practical arrangements and ensure his 'proper treatment, his comfort and convenience, on entering and passing through Moroccan territory.' He should be met at the station or airport, a call should be paid to him as soon as convenient at his hotel, he could be given informal hospitality in order to meet local Moroccan personalities, and some official should be 'on hand to speed him on his way and to render any on-the-spot assistance which should be necessary.'

It was recognised that the Windsors presented a diplomatic problem. 'By the act of Abdication the Duke relinquished his status as a public figure, abdicated from his royal duties and assumed an entirely private life . . . Her Majesty's Government have no official contact with the Duke, or his household . . .' It was made more difficult because 'the Duke is a Royal Highness and the Duchess is not.' The Consul was told that any assistance given the Duke in an official capacity 'must be confined to that demanded by courtesy, and for humanitarian reasons.'

The Foreign Office added: 'Needless to say, when the Duchess of Windsor accompanies His Royal Highness, the same courtesies should be extended to her.'[13]

In other words, she could expect no such help if she were on her own.

Between 17 and 20 November 1966 the Windsors visited Austria, staying at Schloss Enzesfeld where the Duke had languished in the early months of 1937. The castle had been bought by Baron Hubert Pantz and converted into a luxury hotel for wealthy sportsmen. Pantz was a kind of front man for the operation, described by Sir John Pilcher, the British Ambassador, as 'the only Austrian anyone in Paris or New York has ever met and the only one whom nobody in Vienna has ever heard of.'[14]

The Windsors were being used for publicity purposes but with a certain discretion. A hunt ball was given for them and was attended by the 'international set of playboys and lady killers (who now seem to centre round Marbella).' When the Windsors arrived by train in Vienna they told John Utter, their Private Secretary, that they would have to face the inevitable gauntlet of press photographers and were then surprised and disappointed when none materialised. They fared better on their departure, on the same train as the Countess of Paris. They left as President Podgorny of Russia* was arriving. The Ambassador reported: 'There were more people interested in the Windsors' departure than in the arrival of the Russian President. We dealt with their luggage and offered any facilities, which seemed to give pleasure.'[15]

Sir John Pilcher praised the Duke for knowing exactly how to deal with Austrians of all income brackets. He made himself 'very popular at Enzesfeld by going for a walk with the local priest and addressing all and sundry in the local idiom.'[16] Back in Paris the Duke went out of his way to tell the British Ambassador, Sir Patrick Reilly, how much they had liked the Pilchers and how grateful they were for all that they had done for them.

This exchange was in marked contrast to earlier communications and showed how well the Duke responded to spontaneous civility. Miss Westwood, at the Foreign Office, circulated the reports: 'You may like to see. We do not inform the Palace of the activities of the Duke and Duchess of Windsor which are seldom taken note of officially and are usually regarded as private matters.'[17]

June 1967 saw one of the Duke's wishes fulfilled – a formal meeting for the Duchess with the Queen and the Royal Family. It took place, ironically, at Marlborough House when a plaque was dedicated to the memory of Queen Mary. Originally it was hoped to unveil the plaque on Queen Mary's centenary, 26 May 1967, but the Windsors could not come from New York for that date so the event was postponed until 7 June.

They arrived at Southampton from Le Havre in a ship that contained a certain amount of wily press men who had had the foresight to book themselves accommodation on board. They stayed overnight with Dickie Mountbatten at Broadlands and the next day were driven to Claridge's.

---

* Nikolai Podgorny (1903–83), Chairman of the Presidium of the Supreme Soviet 1965–7.

On the day of the ceremony there were no processions. The Windsors arrived by car. The Royal Family were there in force. The Queen and Prince Philip were joined by the Queen Mother, the Duke and Duchess of Gloucester, Princess Marina, the Duke and Duchess of Kent, the Earl of Harewood, Mr and Mrs Gerald Lascelles, the Duke and Duchess of Beaufort and others. They were lined up – the Windsors on the far end, next to the Gloucesters.

The Queen could be seen shaking hands with the Duke and Duchess and chatting briefly to them. The Queen Mother surprised the courtiers by suddenly kissing the Duke on the cheek. As the Duke of Gloucester's Private Secretary said: 'Consummate actress. She wouldn't have him to lunch.'[18] On the two days when the Windsors were in London they lunched with the Gloucesters one day and Princess Marina the next. When he arrived at his old home, York House, St James's Palace, then occupied by the Gloucesters, the Duke of Windsor rushed over to talk to his former valet Alfred Amos before greeting his brother or sister-in-law. For her lunch, Princess Marina invited the Duke's aunt, Princess Alice, Countess of Athlone, who was most reluctant to attend, not having forgiven the Duke for the sorrow which the Abdication caused Queen Mary.

In retrospect it does seem extraordinary that the Queen could ask the Windsors to such a ceremony and not invite them to lunch at Buckingham Palace (even though it was also Derby Day). But she did loan them an aircraft of The Queen's Flight to take them back to Paris.

In the late summer the question of the Duchess's title arose yet again, and caused some concern to Sir Michael Adeane, the Queen's Private Secretary, then at Balmoral. *Burke's Peerage* published an article by an academic, Philip Thomas, about the indignity suffered by the Duchess 'unique in the annals of British History, of being denied a social status and a status of precedence equal to that of her husband'.[19] Thomas's case was that the Windsor marriage was not even a morganatic one. The Duchess, he wrote, had been officially relegated 'into a twilight for which there is no position'.[20]

Thomas pointed out that when Edward VIII abdicated he had automatically become HRH Prince Edward, since he was a son of a Sovereign of the House of Windsor. Therefore his wife would automatically become a Princess and an HRH. But the Letters Patent that created him Duke of Windsor specifically restricted the Royal Highness title to him, not allowing it to be enjoyed by his wife. These Letters Patent, dated 27 May 1937 (published in the same edition of the *London Gazette* in which Stanley

Baldwin's earldom was gazetted), claimed falsely that the Letters Patent of 1917 restricted the title of Royal Highness to those members of the Royal Family in line of succession to the Throne, which clearly the Duke no longer was. Thomas suggested that the Duke of Windsor was fully aware of this loophole but did not choose to pursue it 'only for the avoidance of further acrimony and in order to protect the dignity of the Throne.'[21]

Over the years others argued the case from both sides. Baldwin's biographer, H. Montgomery Hyde, pointed out that Sir John Simon, the Home Secretary, Lord Hailsham, the Lord Chancellor, and Sir Donald Somervell, the Attorney General, had all approved the Letters Patent in 1937, and that even Walter Monckton had not disputed them.

Sir Michael Adeane consulted Sir Godfrey Agnew, the Clerk to the Privy Council. Agnew replied that the Letters Patent were made on ministerial advice and therefore fell into 'the political field'. He did not think it 'right that The Queen should now be asked, as a personal matter, to exercise Her Prerogative in favour of the Duchess of Windsor', but he added: 'If, on the other hand, the Prime Minister were to advise Her Majesty to issue further Letters Patent the position would be, of course, different.' Agnew took the line that only those in line to the Throne were Royal Highnesses under Letters Patent issued by Queen Victoria. Therefore Thomas was wrong to call the 1937 Letters Patent a 'depriving Act'. They were the opposite.[22] Sir Michael was content to let the matter lie, on the grounds that Letters Patent were only issued following ministerial advice, and the 1937 Letters Patent were not a depriving act, but 'a positive act of clemency'.[23] At least they considered the matter, even if they did nothing about it.

On 27 August 1968 Princess Marina died at Kensington Palace from an inoperable brain tumour. The Windsors were in Paris, about to go to Lisbon to attend some balls 'but', the Duchess told a friend, 'due to the death of Princess Marina we have of course cancelled'.[24] The Duke flew over to Windsor alone for the funeral, his last-ever visit to Britain. The Duke of Kent met him at the airport and he lunched at Coppins, the Kents' home in Iver. After the service he had tea in the Deanery at Windsor Castle, which gave him a chance to have his first proper talk to Prince Charles and Princess Anne. He asked his great-niece why she did not hunt since she loved riding so much. 'Blood sports,' she replied. The Duke flew back to Paris the same day on a standard Air France flight.

In March 1969 the Queen invited the Duke to the dedication of the King George VI Memorial Chapel at St George's Chapel, for which he had made a contribution to the John Piper windows, a gift from the Knights of the Garter. He did not come and nor did he attend the Investiture of the Prince of Wales at Caernarvon Castle, preferring to stay at home and watch it on television. That year both Windsors appeared in a significant interview for the BBC by Kenneth Harris, broadcast in January 1970.

Kenneth Harris took many years to persuade the Duke to take part and even the night before it was recorded, when all the crew were in Paris, the Duke tried to back out. It is the most revealing interview that he and the Duchess ever gave and bears rewatching even now, the Duke reminiscing and the Duchess taking part from time to time, talking about their life at that time. There is one especially telling moment when the Duchess announces: 'We're very happy' and the Duke, taken by surprise, looks suddenly relieved and fumbles uncomfortably for her hand, which he then holds. Over eleven million viewers watched the programme. I was one of them.

In 1970 the Windsors dined with President and Mrs Nixon at the White House. Richard Nixon had been elected President of the United States in 1968. The Duchess approved:

> I personally like Nixon and think he will be good and very sound. No one in public office is perfect but I do not think he panics and perhaps he will do less supporting of the world. We should be known for ourselves and not financial resources which every one wants a bit of without doing much to develop their own countries.[25]

Richard Nixon had dined with the Windsors in Paris in 1963, and remembered that what had most impressed the Duke about America was 'the way parents obeyed their children'. His admiration for the Windsors inspired him to issue his invitation to the White House.

The dinner was flagged up as a 'private-type dinner'.[26] Dates were discussed, the Windsors being in the United States from about 24 March until the end of May, their visit including stays with Mrs Arthur Gardner in Palm Beach and the Youngs. It was soon decided that this should be the first dinner of their stay, and Saturday, 4 April was agreed upon.

On 2 March H.R. Haldeman stressed that the President wanted the party to be 'fun and gay. There should be dancing and it should have a great flare ... good-looking young men and girls – so that we get across the subtle point of the youth in our staff and make this a swinging party.'[27] Society figures would not be precluded, and the Duchess particularly asked for Mrs Mildred Hilson, Mr and Mrs A. Britton Browne, George Baker, Sr, and Mr and Mrs Winston Guest. The names went back and forth. John Freeman, the British Ambassador, famed for his challenging *Face to Face* interviews, was included, as were the Charles A. Munns from Palm Beach, the Engelhards, and Dr and Mrs De Bakey from Houston.

The Nixon family was to be there in force. Mamie Eisenhower, Vice-President and Mrs Spiro Agnew, Henry Kissinger, Alice Roosevelt Longworth, Peter Glenville (the British producer), Estée Lauder, Henri Claudel, the Reagans, Kirk Douglas and his wife, Mr and Mrs William Paley, Barbara Stanwyck, Fred Astaire, Frank Borman and his wife, Ambassador and Mrs Watson, Perle Mesta, and Congressman George Bush and his wife were also guests. Names were added and names were deleted. On 10 March Rose Mary Woods asked that Paul-Louis Weiller not be put on the list 'unless he asks for an invitation'.[28] Walter Cronkite and his wife and the Munns were amongst those who refused.

American relations of the Duchess were invited – Mr and Mrs J. Davidge Warfield (he being Economic Development Administration, Department of Commerce and a distant cousin), and Vice-Admiral and Mrs Lloyd M. Mustin (son and daughter-in-law of the Duchess's cousin Corinne Murray, who was not well enough to attend) were added to the list. Bobby Short and the Young Saints were invited to entertain the guests. There were to be no after-dinner guests.

The dinner proved a magnificent occasion, the Duke in white tie, dapper as ever but now leaning heavily on a stick, the Duchess in a cream silk crêpe evening dress by Givenchy, with a pink belt adorned with beads. Afterwards the Duke drafted the Duchess's thank-you letter for her.

From time to time the idea of further reconciliation between the Royal Family and the Windsors was mooted. The 1967 meeting at Marlborough House had broken the ice and paved the way for the inevitable day when the Duke would die and the Duchess would join the Royal Family for the funeral. One year Sir Edward Ford, Assistant Private Secretary, suggested that the Windsors might be invited to Royal Ascot. This idea was not adopted.[29] In 1970 the young Prince of Wales, somewhat influenced by his great-uncle Lord Mountbatten, thought they should come over for a weekend. He suggested as much to the Queen Mother but met with a negative response. The Queen Mother reserved her communications with the Windsors to an annual Christmas card, on which she occasionally wrote a brief personal note.

Three of her Ladies-in-Waiting have attested that the Queen Mother did not hate the Duchess of Windsor. Visiting the Royal Burial Ground at Frogmore with Lady Penn in about 1978, the Queen Mother saw the Duke's grave and said: 'And I suppose the poor old Duchess will be here one day?' The Queen Mother's line was that you have to know someone to hate them, and the Queen Mother hardly knew the Duchess.[30] Dame Frances Campbell-Preston said: 'I will go to my grave trying to convince people that the Queen Mother did not hate the Duchess of Windsor.'[31] And Lady Jean Rankin told me years ago that the Queen Mother just wanted peace.[32] But equally the Queen Mother kept her distance.

In 1971 the Windsors received visits from the Prince of Wales and from Emperor Hirohito and Empress Nagako of Japan at their home in Paris. The Prince of Wales was taken to the house in the Bois late on a Saturday evening, 3 October, not long before the Duke's final illness. He found the duke 'rather bent and using a stick' and with one eye closed most of the time, and he spoke while clutching an enormous cigar. The Prince observed the Duchess: 'flitting to and fro like a strange bat. She looks incredible for her age and obviously has her face lifted every day.'[33] A few days later Emperor Hirohito and his Empress visited them in the course of their State Visit to Paris, the last time the world saw a photograph of the Duke. It was widely published at the time.

The Windsors had grown old, the Duke suffering from a bad hip which forced him to walk with a heavy cane, the Duchess ageing more elegantly. The pattern of their lives was set. They were in France for most of the year, the Duchess preferring the city and the Duke happiest at The Mill. They spent the early spring in New York or Palm Beach. And from time to time they travelled elsewhere.

In New York the Windsors stayed at the Waldorf. Years later Joanne Cummings, wife of the Duke's later life friend, Nathan Cummings, told me about these visits:

> She said she'd leave the Duke & Nate together at the Waldorf with a bottle of whisky and it would go down. The Duke loved to drink whisky all through dinner. They called her 'Duchess' always. She said that she never knew how the Duchess kept the food hot coming up from the kitchen on a dumb waiter – and at The Mill she'd see the staff carrying a tablecloth from another building on high. It was never creased. They'd have a late breakfast and a long lunch and then high tea – the servants standing around, but the Duke handing out the cups with a shaky hand. The highlight of his day was cocktail hour, when he served the drinks and there were no servants.
>
> She thought the Duchess beastly to the Duke, that he must have secretly wondered: 'Think what I gave up,' yet he brainwashed himself into thinking that all was well. He wanted the Duchess so much that he didn't think of the sacrifices until later.

She concluded that the Duchess had not wanted to marry the Duke. King, yes; Duke, no.[34]

Lady Mosley thought the Duke 'a sweet little man'. She said: 'If because of him (pointing to Sir Oswald) we went to dine, then they made huge efforts to get interesting people, journalists & writers. So it was not all café society, though of course at times it was.'[35]

The Duchess was always spoken of as a supreme hostess. Princess Ghislaine de Polignac was one who saw the Windsors frequently in those last years:

> She said the Duchess of Windsor was always served first and always took a little food. She never praised the chef – always criticised him a bit to keep him on his toes. She thought the Duchess was the best host she knew.
>
> She said that the Duchess taught the French a lot about lighting. The hall in Paris was softly lit and the dining room all candlelit. The table would be covered with gold boxes. After dinner the Duke would stay with the men. The Duchess used to tell the Duke and the men not to be too long with their port: 'Not too long, David!' She said that Englishmen liked to talk to other men. They don't like women. The Duke did not like to talk to women. He preferred to dance. At the Duchess's there was often a little band.[36]

Not all dinners went well. Sir Alec Guinness, the actor, remembered the Duke being somewhat surly:

> The Duke asked him for a whisky in a small glass – but none was available so he had to bring it in a large glass. The Duke swore at him: 'How dare you? I told you not to bring it in a fucking large glass . . .' (that kind of thing). Alec Guinness just turned away. But at the end of the evening the Duke had the grace to apologise.[37]

Relations with other royal houses provided another problem for the Duchess. There are stories of her being over-solicitous of the Duke and upsetting royal hosts, worrying that the Duke might be sitting in a draught. She felt insecure with the Duke's European royal hosts.

One host who produced many royal guests was their Paris friend, Commandant Paul-Louis Weiller. He had the habit of accommodating many such figures and naturally entertained them to lunch or dinner.

Paul-Louis's daughter-in-law Olimpia was the daughter of the Infanta Beatrix Torlonia and the granddaughter of Queen Ena of Spain:

> The Commandant had invited Olimpia and her mother with the Windsors to a dinner to meet Robert Massie after his *Nicholas & Alexandra* book was published [in 1967]. Massie had a haemophiliac son. It was not the easiest of evenings because the Infanta had close haemophiliac relations – two brothers. The subject came up and was pressed by the Duchess. 'Tell us, "Baby" you have two brothers who were haemophiliac?' She went too far. Finally – and Olimpia said it was the only time she ever saw her mother pull rank – the Infanta snapped in Spanish: 'Who is the woman? She's a coconut that should have stayed in a tree!' The Duke understood, of course. The subject was rapidly changed.[38]

A flavour of the Duchess's style can be found in her letters. On her return from a visit to Biarritz she wrote to Diana Vreeland: 'I will be ready for Lichfield* when he telephones and we'll try hard to see that you get what you want – but with "oldies" it is not so easy!'[39] She was photographed wearing Kenneth Jay Lane jewellery and enjoyed the session, but she warned: 'It is an old face and even he can't put the clock back.'[40]

Fashion remained a strong interest for the Duchess. Presently she toured the collections: 'When I look at the fashions I feel a million. This is really a trend that makes the old stay where they belong. Otherwise we (meaning me) look like a clown.'[41] She perused *Women's Wear Daily* with care: 'W.W.D. gives me a strange picture of N.Y chic'[42] and 'Can't stand any more pants in W.W.D.'[43]

She remained game and sprightly, largely for the Duke's benefit 'I found the German Ambassador most interesting to talk to', she told Mona Bismarck, 'and I may add quite handsome!'[44] And she told Diana Vreeland:

> There have been some amusing parties. I do not count those ghastly premières. We are too old to go anyway. Seems the last one there were nearly fisticuffs between Burtons & Harrisons!†[45]

Her letters frequently touched on ageing and the difficulties of life in Paris, the cost of living, the problems of staff, and so too did her conversation. Mary Soames, wife of the British Ambassador, dined with the

---

* Patrick, 5th Earl of Lichfield (1939–2005), photographed the Windsors at The Mill.
† Richard Burton and Elizabeth Taylor; Rex Harrison and Rachel Roberts.

Windsors and recalled the Duchess saying: 'People are always telling me to look up my old friends. Look 'em up? Dig 'em up!'[46]

Diana Vreeland wrote of life in New York and the Duchess thanked her for the letter 'which showed such a different slant on life than the French pursue . . .'

> Or it may be different when they do not have to bother to speak a foreign language which is always a handicap – no matter how good you are, the whole thinking is different. England would be O.K. – but here you change your personality and wonder if you'll ever be your natural self again. I find this a lonely country for foreigners whereas the US is not.[47]

On 3 December the Duchess went alone to Marie-Hélène de Rothschild's famous Proust Ball at the Chateau de Ferrières. Richard Burton observed her at dinner: 'She had an enormous feather in her hair which got into everything, the soup, the gravy, the ice-cream, and at every vivacious turn of her head it smacked Guy [de Rothschild] sharply in the eyes or the mouth and at one time threatened to get stuck in Guy's false moustache which was glued on.'[48]

A few days later the Burtons dined with the Windsors: 'He is physically falling apart, his left eye completely closed and a tremendous limp.'[49] The last press photograph I remember seeing of the Duke was when he and the Duchess went to the Lido in the same month.

At the end of August 1971 there was the first hint that things were not good. The Duchess was beginning to admit to being unwell.

In a letter to Diana Vreeland, she wrote: 'I was so sad not to be up to dining with you and Hugh but this elitis (spelt wrong) [Ileitis] goes and comes and there seems to be no real cure.' She ruminated about Gloria Guinness: 'all her houses seem always to be running – whereas I have domestic crises from time to time!'[50]

The Duchess was ill. Presently the Duke would be diagnosed with inoperable throat cancer. Within a few months he would be dead. The firmly held reins were slipping from the Duchess's hands.

A Satanic figure was waiting and watching – narrow-eyed and dangerous, wearing the mantle of good intention to disguise her inner malevolence: Maître Suzanne Blum, lodged in her eyrie in the rue de Varenne. Her hour had all but come.

THE MONTAGUES

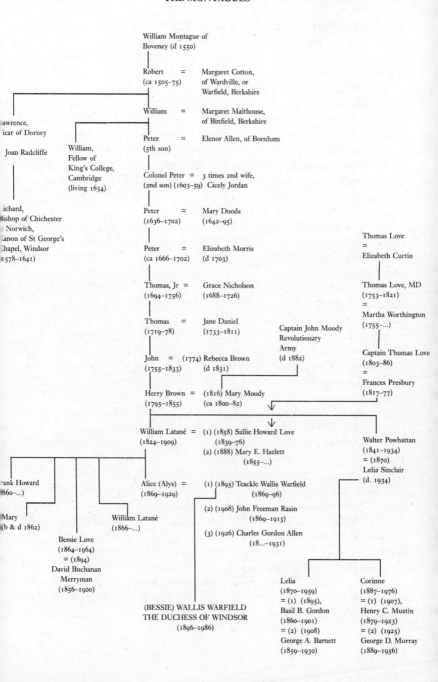

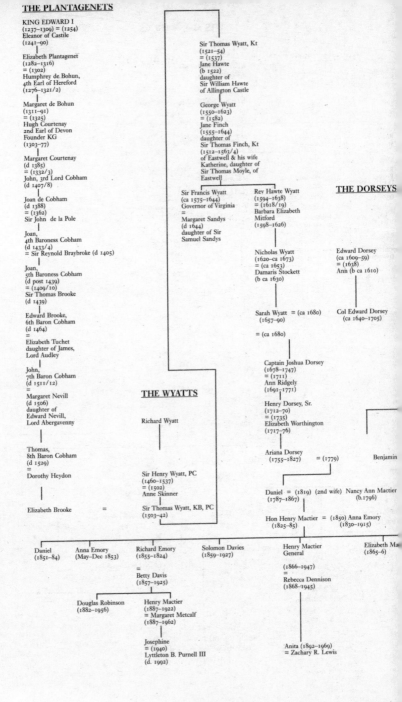

THE PLANTAGENETS

KING EDWARD I
(1237–1309) = (1254)
Eleanor of Castile
(1241–90)

Elizabeth Plantagenet
(1282–1316)
= (1302)
Humphrey de Bohun,
4th Earl of Hereford
(1276–1321/2)

Margaret de Bohun
(1311–91)
= (1325)
Hugh Courtenay
2nd Earl of Devon
Founder KG
(1303–77)

Margaret Courtenay
(d 1385)
= (1332/3)
John, 3rd Lord Cobham
(d 1407/8)

Joan de Cobham
(d 1388)
= (1362)
Sir John de la Pole

Joan,
4th Baroness Cobham
(d 1433/4)
= Sir Reynold Braybroke (d 1405)

Joan,
5th Baroness Cobham
(d post 1439)
= (1409/10)
Sir Thomas Brooke
(d 1439)

Edward Brooke,
6th Baron Cobham
(d 1464)
=
Elizabeth Tuchet
daughter of James,
Lord Audley

John,
7th Baron Cobham
(d 1511/12)
=
Margaret Nevill
(d 1506)
daughter of
Edward Nevill,
Lord Abergavenny

Thomas,
8th Baron Cobham
(d 1529)
=
Dorothy Heydon

Elizabeth Brooke

Sir Thomas Wyatt, Kt
(1521–54)
= (1537)
Jane Hawte
(b 1522)
daughter of
Sir William Hawte
of Allington Castle

George Wyatt
(1550–1623)
= (1582)
Jane Finch
(1555–1644)
daughter of
Sir Thomas Finch, Kt
(1512–1563/4)
of Eastwell & his wife
Katherine, daughter of
Sir Thomas Moyle, of
Eastwell

Sir Francis Wyatt
(ca 1575–1644)
Governor of Virginia
=
Margaret Sandys
(d 1644)
daughter of Sir
Samuel Sandys

Rev Hawte Wyatt
(1594–1638)
= (1618/19)
Barbara Elizabeth
Mitford
(1598–1626)

Nicholas Wyatt
(1620–ca 1673)
= (ca 1653)
Damaris Stockett
(b ca 1630)

Sarah Wyatt = (ca 1680)
(1657–90)

= (ca 1680)

THE DORSEYS

Edward Dorsey
(ca 1609–59)
= (1638)
Ann (b ca 1610)

Col Edward Dorsey
(ca 1640–1705)

Captain Joshua Dorsey
(1678–1747)
= (1711)
Ann Ridgely
(1691–1771)

Henry Dorsey, Sr.
(1712–70)
= (1735)
Elizabeth Worthington
(1717–76)

Ariana Dorsey
(1755–1827)   = (1779)   Benjamin

THE WYATTS

Richard Wyatt

Sir Henry Wyatt, PC
(1460–1537)
= (1502)
Anne Skinner

Sir Thomas Wyatt, KB, PC
(1503–42)

Daniel = (1819) (2nd wife) Nancy Ann Mactier
(1787–1867)   (b.1796)

Hon Henry Mactier = (1850) Anna Emory
(1825–85)   (1830–1915)

Daniel
(1851–84)

Anna Emory
(May–Dec 1853)

Richard Emory
(1855–1824)
=
Betty Davis
(1857–1925)

Solomon Davies
(1859–1927)

Henry Mactier
General
(1866–1947)
=
Rebecca Dennison
(1868–1945)

Elizabeth Ma
(1865–6)

Douglas Robinson
(1882–1956)

Henry Mactier
(1887–1922)
= Margaret Metcalf
(1887–1962)

Josephine
= (1940)
Lyttleton B. Purnell III
(d. 1992)

Anita (1892–1969)
= Zachary R. Lewis

THE WARFIELDS

Richard Warfield, Englishman
(b.1465)

|

John
(b. 1490)

oger = (1545)   Elizabeth Pinson
522–90/91)   (1526–1602)

ichard = (1590)   Elizabeth Carter
ector of   (1573–1619/20)
ry Drayton,
ambridgeshire
558–1619/20)

John = (1640)   Rachell Clarke
(1613–65)   (1619–post 1665)

ain Richard, Sr. = (1670) Elinor Browne
1646/7–1703/4)   (1649/50–1704)

John, Sr. = (1696) Ruth Gaither
(1674–1718)   (1679–1728)

Richard, Sr. = (1720) Marian Coldwell
(1698–1765)   (1701–26)

Seth, Sr. = (1750) Mary Gaither
(1723–1805)   (1722–77

THE GAITHERS

John Gaither, Sr
(1646–1702)
= (1676/7)
Ruth Beard
(ca 1650–1719)

John Gaither Jr
(1677/8–1739) = (1719)

THE DUVALLS

Tomas Duvall,
from a family
found in France
In 1490
(b France 1600)
=
Nicola Staggard
(b ca 1600)

Mareen Duvall
The Emigrant
(1627–94)
= (ca 1659)
Marie-Bouth Parran
(1630–70)
(from whom descend
Presidents Truman &
Obama)

Captain John
'Jean' Duvall
(1660–1711)
= (1685)
Elizabeth Jones
(b 1665)

Elizabeth Duvall
(1687–1770)

Teackle Wallis
(1869–96)
= (1895)
Alice (Alys) Montague
(1869–1929)

(BESSIE) WALLIS WARFIELD
THE DUCHESS OF WINDSOR
(1896–1986)
= (1) 1916 (div. 1927)
Earl Winfield Spencer
(1888–1950)
= (2) 1928 (div. 1937)
Ernest A. Simpson
(1895–1958)
= (3) 1937
HRH THE DUKE OF WINDSOR. KG

APPENDIX I

The Warfields, the Plantagenets, Wyatts and Duvalls

The Duchess descends from early Anne Arundel settlers. The Warfield family was amongst the families that came up to Maryland from Virginia. A charter for Maryland Colony, named after Queen Henrietta Maria was granted to 2nd Lord Baltimore by King Charles I in 1632. A man called Richard Bennett, a rich merchant in England, had become interested in trade in Virginia. He organised a company with two nephews and three others to send two hundred settlers from England to Virginia. They arrived in 1620, and in 1622 several were murdered by Indians. Richard Bennett himself came over in 1642.

Captain Richard Warfield (1647–1703/4), a direct ancestor of Wallis, was to be found on a large estate at Crownsville, Anne Arundel, reaching a beautiful sheet of water called Round Bay, of the Severn as early as 1662. He had come from Middlesex in England, where his family can be traced back five generations to Richard Warfield.

The Warfields married well, they moved into the unexplored territory of Anne Arundel County and their holdings increased. And so it continued through the generations. Benjamin (Beni) Warfield (1755–1829) married in 1779, Ariana Dorsey, from another well-known Anne Arundel county family. In about 1680 Ariana's great-grandfather, Colonel Edward Dorsey, Keeper of the Great Seal of Maryland, Colonel of the Horse and a member of the colonial legislature, had married Sarah Wyatt, daughter of Nicholas Wyatt.

It is through the Dorsey and Wyatt families that the Duchess had descent from King Edward I of England (also known as Edward Longshanks and Hammer of the Scots) and his wife, Queen Eleanor of Castile. As indicated on the family tree, Sir Thomas Wyatt married Elizabeth Brooke, daughter of 8th Baron Cobham. The 3rd Baron Cobham married Margaret Courtenay, daughter of Hugh Courtenay, 2nd Earl of Devon, KG, 12th founder Knight of the Garter, appointed in 1348, who had fought at the Battle of Crécy. Devon was married to Margaret de Bohun, a granddaughter of Edward I.

This line produced some interesting figures, particularly in the Wyatt family. Sir Henry Wyatt of Allington Castle (1460–1537) resisted Richard III's pretensions to the English throne and in consequence was arrested, spending two years in the Tower of London. He was said to have been put on the rack in the presence of Richard III, and forced to eat mustard and vinegar. A painting – and his well-known love of cats in later life – suggest an unconfirmed myth – that a cat visited him daily in his cell, bringing a pigeon from a nearby dovecote and thus saving him from starvation. When Henry VII acceded to the throne in 1485, Sir Henry was appointed to the Privy Council and became a guardian to the future Henry VIII. He was also appointed a Privy Councillor to Henry VIII, and a Knight of the Bath.

His son, Sir Thomas Wyatt (1503–42), the famous poet (who introduced the sonnet to England from Italy), courtier and Ambassador, was accused of being the lover of Anne Boleyn before she became involved with Henry VIII. Some say he attempted to warn the King of Anne's blemished character. He was sworn of the Privy Council in 1533, and poured scented water on Queen Anne Boleyn's hands at her Coronation. Sir Thomas was appointed Clerk of the King's Jewels. Later, he was briefly imprisoned in the Tower of London on account of Anne Boleyn's supposed infidelities. Important diplomatic missions followed and in 1540 there was another brief sojourn in the Tower. He shares one honour with his descendant, the Duchess of Windsor. His portrait (after a sketch by Holbein) is in the National Portrait Gallery. Her 1940 portrait by Gerald Brockhurst is also in that gallery.

Sir Thomas's wife, Elizabeth Brooke, the daughter of 8th Baron Cobham, was in her turn romantically involved with Henry VIII, and was considered a possible candidate to be the King's sixth wife.

The son of the poet and of Elizabeth, Sir Thomas Wyatt the Younger (1521–54), of Allington Castle and Broxley Abbey in Kent, was a rebel leader in the reign of Mary I. He denied being involved in the plot to put Lady Jane Grey on the Throne, but when Queen Mary planned to marry Philip of Spain, he rallied support against the Queen in Kent in what became known as 'Wyatt's Rebellion'. He led 4,000 men on London, arriving in Southwark, aiming to take St James's Palace. But his plot failed and he gave himself up. He was dispatched to the Tower of London and executed on 11 April 1554. Subsequently his head was displayed on gallows on Hay's Hill and his severed limbs were placed on gibbets in various locations across London. On 17 April his head was stolen.

Sir Thomas Wyatt's grandson, Sir Francis Wyatt (ca 1575–1644) became interested in the Virginia Company and was elected Governor of Virginia in the USA. He sailed from Britain, arriving at Jamestown at the end of October 1621. He was accompanied to America by his younger brother, Rev. Hawte Wyatt, Rector of Maidstone in Kent. It was Hawte's granddaughter, Sarah, who married Colonel Edward Dorsey, and from whom, as stated earlier, the Duchess descended.

Beni Warfield's son, Daniel, moved to Baltimore and entered the milling firm of Francis Mactier, a Scottish immigrant, operating the Monumental Flouring Mills. In 1819 he married, as his second wife, his boss's daughter, Nancy Ann Mactier.

Their fortunes prospered in the care of Daniel Warfield's son, Hon. Henry Mactier Warfield (1825–85). In 1850 he married Anna (Gittings) Emory, of Manor Glen and My Lady's Manor, whose family had come from England in 1666. Henry and Anna were Wallis's grandparents.

Amongst her other ancestors, the Duvalls are worth noting. Tomas Duvall came from a family originally to be found in France in 1490. His son was Mareen Duvall (1627–94), known as 'The Emigrant'. He settled on the south side of South River in Anne Arundel County in about 1655. A planter and merchant, he was a leader in the Jacobite Party and was responsible for laying out town and ports of entry in the interests of stimulating trade.

He is particularly relevant since a number of other figures of note descend from him, including US Presidents, Harry S. Truman and Barack Obama. So too does the actor, Robert S. Duvall, and former Vice-President, Dick Cheney. Details of these descents are well documented in the public domain. Obama owes his descent to his mother, Stanley Anne Dunham, and back through Armours, Overalls and thence to the Duvall family.

The Duchess also descended from King Henry III, the Plantagenet King, via his son, Edmund 'Crouchback'. His son, Henry, had a daughter, Joan, who married John De Mowbray. John married Elizabeth de Segrave and their daughter, Eleanor, married John de Welles.

Their son, Eudo de Welles married Maud de Greystoke and was father to Lionel de Welles, 6th Lord Welles, KG (1457) (ca 1406–ca 1434), who married Margaret Beauchamp, widow of John Beaufort, 1st Duke of Somerset, KG (1439), bringing more Garter ancestry into the Duchess's line.

Their daughter, Cicely (d. 1466), married Sir Robert Willoughby, of Parham, Suffolk. Their great-granddaughter, Elizabeth (ca 1516–80) married Thomas Totteshurst. Their daughter, Ann, married Richard Thomas, whose son Christopher Thomas went to Virginia in 1635.

His granddaughter, Anne Thomas (1677-1721), married Arthur Emory, Jr, and this line went down via Thomas Emory (ca 1700–ca 1755), Thomas

Lane Emory (1751-79), Richard Emory (ca 1798-ca 1855), and thence to Anna Emory (ca 1830-85), the Duchess's grandmother.

Pushing the line back beyond Henry III, the Duchess therefore descended at least twice over from Charlemagne (742-83). In the Emory line she was 38th in descent.

APPENDIX II

The Montagues

The Montagues trace their ancestry back to Virginia in the 1600s and before that to England in 1505. According to George William Montague's *History and Genealogy of Peter Montague* (published in 1894), there is reason to suppose that they can be traced back to the time of the Norman Conquest, though the direct link between the Montagues of Boveney and Drogo de Montagu, progenitor of the Montagus, has not yet been proved.

G.W. Montague makes a strong case for a link – the two families living close by in the same county, very similar coats of arms 'which alone would seem to silently but surely denote that they are a branch of the same family.'[1] But he conceded the genealogy lacked 'two generations, possibly three, to make a perfect record back to the conquest of England, AD 1066.'[2]

The earliest certain progenitor of Wallis's mother was William Montague (d. 1550), the elder of two brothers living in the parishes of Buckingham and Burnham. William lived at Boveney, a hamlet on the Thames near Eton College. His second son, Robert (d. 1575), married Margaret Cotton, of Wardville (thought to be Warfield) in Berkshire, and was the Duchess's ancestor.

William's elder son Lawrence had in turn a son, Richard (1578-1641), who was well known as Bishop of Chichester and later of Norwich. It may well be that Richard Montague was Wallis's most significant English relation. In the *Dictionary of National Biography*, he was described as a 'controversialist and bishop', who supported the Church of England against its enemies on both sides. Of him it was also said: 'In theological literature he was probably at least as powerful an influence as Andrewes or Jeremy Taylor.'[3] Richard Montague was a King's Scholar and later Fellow of Eton, was appointed a chaplain to Charles I and was a Canon of St George's Chapel, Windsor between 1617 and 1628. Wallis's mother did not descend from the Bishop and Canon.

Robert Montague's son, William, married Margaret Malthouse, of Binfield, Berkshire. Their fifth son, Peter, married Eleanor Allen, and it was his second son, Peter, who voyaged to Virginia.

Alice descended from Peter Montague (1603–59), an early settler in

Jamestown, Virginia, who arrived there very young, on board the *Charles* in 1621. Some say he was rather wild, ran away from home and could not pay his way, so was sold for his passage money. He came to America as an indentured servant and by 1624 was settled on the plantation of Samuel Matthews, later Governor of the Colony. He rose to be a plantation owner, patenting his acres in Upper Norfolk, Nansemond County, which he represented in the House of Burgesses in 1652 and 1653, moving to Lancaster County where he was variously Commissioner from 1656 to 1657, Burgess in 1658, and in the same year became Sheriff. By trade he was a planter, with crops of wheat, barley and tobacco which were exported to England.

By then he was styled as Colonel Peter Montague and was without doubt a large landowner and leading citizen. He died in 1659 and was buried in Lancaster, Virginia, near where his old house stood.

Peter married three times, and by his second wife, Cicely, he produced many descendants who proved themselves distinguished in colonial Virginia.

Of his descendants, John Montague was born in Orange County, Virginia in 1755. He moved to Cumberland County, was a soldier in the Revolutionary War defending Washington and was wounded by a British soldier. He married Rebecca Brown in Spottslyvania County, Virginia in 1774. Later he moved to South Carolina where he died in the Abbeville District in 1831.

One of his descendants, William Latané Montague (1824–1909), was Wallis's maternal grandfather.

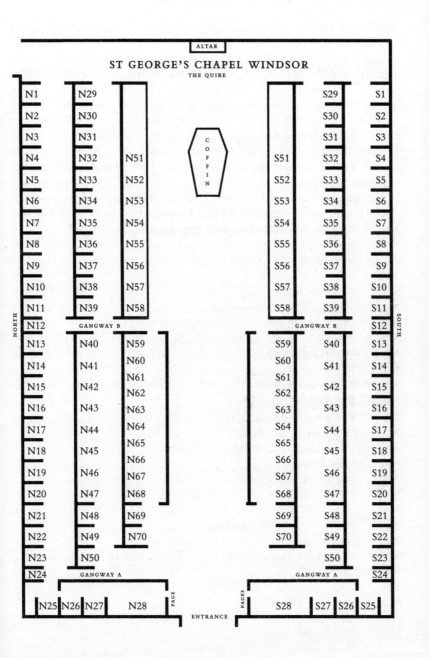

The Funeral of HRH The Duke of Windsor
St George's Chapel
Monday 5 June 1972

Those named in bold attended both funerals. Those in italics did not arrive in time.

Mourners at the Funeral of H.R.H. The Duke of Windsor

Garter Stalls (Left)

N1	The Earl Waldegrave
N2	The Countess Waldegrave
N3	The Lord Butler of Saffron Walden
N4	The Lady Butler of Saffron Walden
N5	The Lord Hailsham
N6	The Lady Hailsham
N7	The Prime Minister
N8	The Rt Hon The Speaker
N9	The French Ambassador
N10	La Baronne de Courcel
N11	The High Commissioner for Jamaica
N12	Lady Lindo
N13	The Lord Shackleton
N14	The Lord Byers
N15	The Lady Byers
N16	Rt Hon Harold Macmillan
N17	Lady Helen Smith
N18	Major Hon David Smith (Lord Lieutenant of Berkshire)
N19	Lady Adair
N20	Major-General Sir Allan Adair
N21	Sir Denis Greenhill
N22	Lady Greenhill
N23	Mrs Bowes-Lyon
N24	Major-General Bowes-Lyon

Royal Stalls (left)

N26   Captain Lord Hamilton
N27   Lady Hamilton
N28   The Lord Nugent

Top Centre (left)

N29   HRH Princess Alice, Countess of Athlone
N30   Hon Gerald Lascelles
N31   Captain Alexander Ramsay
N32   Hon Mrs Ramsay
N33   The Marquess of Cambridge
N34   The Marchioness of Cambridge
N35   The Duchess of Beaufort
N36   **Lady May Abel Smith**
N37   **Sir Henry Abel Smith**
N38   The Lady Brabourne
N39   The Lady Maclean

Lower Centre (left)

N40   Mrs Reginald Maudling
N41   The Home Secretary
N42   The Foreign Secretary
N43   Lady Douglas-Home
N44   Rt Hon Harold Wilson
N45   Mrs Harold Wilson
N46   Rt Hon Jeremy Thorpe
N47   The Chancellor of the Duchy of Lancaster
N48   Mrs Geoffrey Rippon
N49   Rt Hon Frederick Peart
N50   Mrs Frederick Peart

Top Front (left)

N51   The Lord Maclean
N52   Garter King of Arms
N53   **Sir Godfrey Morley**
N54   **Lady Morley**
N55   Mrs Michael Ramsay

N56   Mrs Donald Coggan
N57   **Grace, Countess of Dudley**
N58   ADC (King of Norway)

Lower Front (left)

N59   Mr John E. Utter
N60   Rt Hon Sir Ulick Alexander
N61   Lady Priscilla Aird
N62   Sir John Aird
N63   M. Le Senateur Rosselli
N64   Mrs Loel Guinness
N65   Mr Loel Guinness
N66   Mme Edmond Bory
N67   M. Edmond Bory
N68   *Dr Jean Thin*
N69   M. Henry Bertrand

Garter Stalls (Right)

S1   The Duchess of Norfolk
S2   The Duke of Norfolk
S3   The Earl of Avon
S4   The Countess of Avon
S5   Field Marshal Sir Gerald Templer
S6   Lady Templer
S7   The Viscountess Cobham
S8   The Viscount Cobham
S9   The Marquess of Cholmondeley
S10   The Marchioness of Cholmondeley
S11   Sir William Armstrong
S12   – – – –
S13   – – – –
S14   Admiral Sir Michael Pollock
S15   Lady Pollock
S16   General Sir Michael Carver
S17   Lady Carver
S18   Marshal of the RAF Sir Denis Spotswood
S19   Lady Spotswood
S20   Major-General Sir George Burns
S21   Lady Fitzalan-Howard

S22	Major-General Sir Michael Fitzalan-Howard
S23	The Lady Elworthy
S24	The Lord Elworthy

Royal Stalls (right)

S25	The Duchess of Buccleuch
S26	The Duke of Buccleuch
S27	Mrs Lancelot Fleming

Top Centre (right)

S29	**HM THE QUEEN**
S30	The Duchess of Windsor
S31	**HRH The Duke of Edinburgh**
S32	HM The King of Norway
S33	**HM Queen Elizabeth The Queen Mother**
S34	**HRH The Princess Anne**
S35	HRH The Princess Margaret, Countess of Snowdon
S36	The Earl of Snowdon
S37	**HRH The Duchess of Gloucester**
S38	**HRH The Duchess of Kent**
S39	**HRH Princess Alexandra, The Hon Mrs Angus Ogilvy**

Lower Centre (right)

S40	Hon Mary Morrison
S41	Brigadier Douglas Greenacre
S42	Lady Trend
S43	Sir Burke Trend
S44	The Hon Lady Charteris
S45	Rt Hon Sir Martin Charteris
S46	Mme Hervé Alphand
S47	Hervé Alphand
S48	Lady Eugster
S49	General Sir Basil Eugster
S50	*Johanna Schütz*

Top Front (right)

S51	**HRH The Prince of Wales**

S52   HRH Prince William of Gloucester
S53   HRH Prince Richard of Gloucester
S54   **HRH The Duke of Kent**
S55   **HRH Prince Michael of Kent**
S56   Admiral of the Fleet the Earl Mountbatten of Burma
S57   The Duke of Beaufort
S58   **Hon Angus Ogilvy**

Lower Front (right)

S59   Mrs Frances Munn–Baker
S60   Commander Colin Buist
S61   Mrs Colin Buist
S62   M. Reinhard Henschel
S63   Mr David Bowyer
S64   Mr. Sydney Johnson
S65   **M. Gaston Sanègre (Georges)**
S66   M. Lucien Massy
S67   **M. Gregorio Martin**
S69   M. Roland Gougault
S70   **Mr. Ronald Marchant**

The Nave

The Countess of Sefton, Viscount Rothermere, Lord and Lady Brownlow, Lady Diana Cooper, **Lady Alexandra Metcalfe,** Hon Bruce Ogilvy, Countess Munster, Baron & Baronne de Cabrol, Sir Cecil Beaton, Rose Bingham, Duc & Duchesse d'Uzès, Mr & Mrs Winston Guest, Mrs Leo d'Erlanger, **M. Alexandre Raimon,** Dr Arthur Antenucci, Mlle Giselle Deberry, 5 godchildren, representatives of Regiments, Mayor & Mayoress of Windsor, representatives of civilian organisations, staff & ex-staff, press, Gentlemen Ushers, Lay Stewards (including **the present author**), & many others.

The Funeral of the Duchess of Windsor
St George's Chapel
Tuesday 29 April 1986

Mourners at the Funeral of the Duchess of Windsor

The Quire

Garter Stalls (Left)

N1	Lt-Col Sir John Johnston
N2	The Viscount Whitelaw
N3	The US Ambassador
N4	Mrs Charles Price
N5	The French Chargé d'Affaires
N6	Madame de Lacoste
N7	Sir John Fretwell
N8	Lady Fretwell
N9	Mr Derek Foster
N10	The Lord Gladwyn
N11	Madame Agostino Soldati
N12	Gentleman Usher
N13	**Grace, Countess of Dudley**
N14	The Earl of Dudley
N15	The Countess of Dudley
N16	**Lady Alexandra Metcalfe**
N17	Mrs David Metcalfe
N18	Mr James Fitch
N19	Mrs James Fitch
N20	Baronne de Cabrol
N21	Hon Mrs Brinsley Plunket
N22	Madame Gaston Palewski
N23	Baron Guy de Rothschild
N24	Madame Antenor Patiño

Royal Stalls (left)

N25   Canon Derek Stanesby
N26   Canon John White
N27   Canon John Treadgold
N28   Canon David Burgess

Top Centre (left)

N29   Constable and Governor (Sir John Grandy)
N30   Lady Grandy
N31   Sir Patrick Reilly
N32   Sir Edward Tomkins
N33   Lady Tomkins
N34   Military Knight
N35   Military Knight
N36   Military Knight
N37   Military Knight
N38   Military Knight
N39   Military Knight

Lower Centre (left)

N40   Minor Canon
N41   Canon Bryan Bentley
N42   Lay Clerk
N43   Lay Clerk
N44   Lay Clerk
N45   Lay Clerk
N46   Lay Clerk
N47   Lay Clerk
N48   **Sir Godfrey Morley**
N49   **Lady Morley**
N50   Mr Alan Fisher

Top Front (left)

N51   **Dr Jean Thin**
N52   **M. Gaston Sanègre**
N53   Mme Gaston Sanègre

N54	Mme Elvire Gozin
N55	Mme Maria Costa
N56	Mme Marques
N57	**M. Gregorio Martin**
N58	Mlle Ada Leroy

Lower Front (left)

N59–	Choristers
N68	
N69	Baronne Eugene de Rothschild
N70	Baron de Redé

Garter Stalls (Right)

S1	**HRH Princess Alexandra, The Hon Mrs Angus Ogilvy**
S2	**Hon Angus Ogilvy**
S3	**Hon Gerald Lascelles**
S4	The Duke of Fife
S5	**Lady May Abel Smith**
S6	**Sir Henry Abel Smith**
S7	Rt Hon Sir William Heseltine
S8	Lady Heseltine
S9	Lady Susan Hussey
S10	Mr Kenneth Scott
S11	Major Hugh Lindsay
S12	Lt-Colonel Sir Julian Paget
S13	Sir Peter Miles
S14	Lady Miles
S15	Sir Nicholas Henderson
S16	Lady Henderson
S17	Comte Romanones
S18	Comtesse Romanones
S19	Hon Lady Mosley
S20	Lady Neidpath
S21	Laura, Duchess of Marlborough
S22	The Duke of Marlborough
S23	The Duchess of Marlborough
S24	M. Hubert de Givenchy

Royal Stalls (right)

S25   Canon's wife
S26   Mrs Robert Runcie
S27   Mrs James Leo

Top Centre (right)

S29   **HM THE QUEEN**
S30   **HRH The Duke of Edinburgh**
S31   **HM Queen Elizabeth The Queen Mother**
S32   **HRH The Prince of Wales**
S33   HRH The Princess of Wales
S34   **HRH The Princess Anne**
S35   **HRH Princess Alice, Duchess of Gloucester**
S36   HRH The Duchess of Gloucester
S37   **HRH The Duchess of Kent**
S38   **HRH Prince Michael of Kent**
S39   HRH Princess Michael of Kent

Lower Centre (right)

S40   Minor Canon
S41   Lay Clerk
S42   Lay Clerk
S43   Lay Clerk
S44   Lay Clerk
S45   Lay Clerk
S46   Lay Clerk
S47   Lay Clerk
S48   Rt Rev Richard Millard
S49   Rev Robert Oliver
S50   Virger

Top Front (right)

S51   Princesse Edmond de Polignac
S52   von Bismarck
S53   Princess Otto von Bismarck
S54   Prince Otto von Bismarck

S55   The Countess of Airlie
S56   The Earl of Airlie

Lower Front (right)

S59–   Choristers
S68
S69   **M. Alexandre Raimon**
S70   **Mr Ronald Marchant**

The Nave

M. Gérald van der Kemp
Mme Gérald van der Kemp
Major Walter Lees
Diana Vreeland's grandson
Maître Jean Lisbonne
Mme Jean Lisbonne
Mme Pilar de la Beraudiere
Mr Michael Bloch

Press
Castle community
Lay Stewards (including **the present author**)
& others

Analysis of the seating of the two funerals

The Duke of Windsor's Funeral

The Duke's funeral was almost a state occasion. Had he looked around
at the mourners in the Quire, he would have recognised the extended
Royal Family who were there in force (with the notable exceptions of
his brother, the Duke of Gloucester, who was not well enough to attend,
and the Earl of Harewood, who was not invited due to his recent
divorce). Amongst those present was his aunt, Princess Alice, Countess
of Athlone, one of two surviving granddaughters of Queen Victoria.
She was then in her 90th year. Of those names less easy to recognise,
Gerald Lascelles was the Duke's nephew (son of the late Princess
Royal), Captain Alexander Ramsay was a grandson of the late Duke of

Connaught, the Cambridges and Beauforts were the Duke's first cousins (through his mother, Queen Mary), Lady May Abel Smith was the daughter of Princess Alice, and Lady Brabourne the daughter of Lord Mountbatten.

Many seats were assigned to Knights of the Garter, and to the Prime Minister, Members of the Cabinet, Leaders of the Opposition parties, and the various senior figures in the Navy, Army and Air Force. There were some Ambassadors, past and present, and the Lord Lieutenant of Berkshire. Many of these he would never have met.

Members of his household and staff were seated in the Quire, and some old friends from days gone by – Sir Ulick Alexander, Colin Buist, Sir John Aird and the Duke and Duchess of Buccleuch. Loel Guinness and his wife were more recent friends. The French were furious that M. et Madame Edmond Bory were given seats in the Quire. Bory owned Fauchon and thus they thought him 'a grocer'. Also hard to understand is why the former German diplomat, Reinhard Henschel, was placed there.

Seats were saved for Dr Thin and Miss Johanna Schütz, but their plane was delayed, coming from Paris.

The Duchess of Windsor's Funeral

The Duchess's funeral was more personal and she would have recognised a number of close friends in the Quire. Of the extended Royal Family present, not previously mentioned, the Duke of Fife was a great-grandson of Edward VII.

There were several former British Ambassadors to Paris, Lord Whitelaw, the US Ambassador, the French Chargé d'Affaires and his wife, Grace, Countess of Dudley and the Earl and Countess of Dudley; Lady Alexandra Metcalfe and her daughter-in-law; Lady Mosley and her grand-daughter; Laura, Duchess of Marlborough (a former Countess of Dudley), and the Duke and Duchess of Marlborough; Hubert de Givenchy (the couturier), Alexandre (the hairdresser), Guy de Rothschild, Baronne Eugene de Rothschild (formerly an actress called Jeanne Stuart, and before that called Ivy Sweet), Madame Patiño, Baronne de Cabrol, Aileen Plunket (a Guinness), Violet Palewski (Duchesse de Talleyrand, daughter of Anna Gould), the Baron de Redé, Prince and Princess Otto von Bismarck, Princesse Ghislaine de Polignac, and from happier days, Sir Godfrey and Lady Morley, Mr & Mrs James Fitch, retired butler Alan Fisher, and Ronald Marchant, one of the Duke's chauffeurs, now living in Leicestershire.

Comte and Comtesse Romanones were there. Aline Romanones later wrote a scathing article about the service in *Vanity Fair*, complaining at not being allowed to go to the graveside for the interment.

March 17, 1975

Dear Suzanne,

I authorize you, or anyone appointed by you,
to publish all documents or letters in your possession
concerning the Duke or myself which you consider as use
ful to our memory, or to answer our detractors\

As to the royalties, I suggest to divide them
equally between the author and I, or, should the publication occur after my death, between the author and my
legataire universel.

With my love and gratitude,

W. W

Wallis, Duchess of WINDSOR

The 'Letter of Authorisation' 17 March 1975

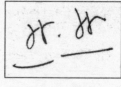

| December 1972 | 16 September 1975 | 24 September 1975 |

I believe the letter of authorisation to be fake. The three 'W. W.'s are genuine.

Notes

Source Notes for Chapter 1

1 Walter Savage Landor, poem.
2 *Daily Express* cutting (1964), Hugo Vickers scrapbook, volume 1.
3 *Daily Express* cutting (March 1965), in Hugo Vickers scrapbook, volume 2.
4 *Daily Express* cutting (March 1965), in Hugo Vickers scrapbook, volume 2.
5 John E. Utter to Hugh Montgomery-Massingberd, Paris, 27 April 1972 [HV papers].
6 Hugo Vickers to Mrs Gerhard Neumann, 15 May 1972 [HV papers].

Source Notes for Chapter 2

1 Rt. Hon. Edward Heath to Sir Robert Armstrong, 7 November 1971 [PREM/1184–National Archives].
2 *The Times*, 19 May 1972.
3 *Paris Match*, May 1972, Hugo Vickers Scrapbook, Volume 52.
4 John Utter to author, Paris, 17 February 1980.
5 Oonagh Shanley-Toffolo, *The Voice of Silence* (Rider, 2002), pp. 96–7.
6 *Inventaire des Bijoux appurtenant S.A.R. la Duchesse de Windsor*, Broches – no 56.
7 John Utter to author, 17 September 1972.
8 Hon. Lady Mosley to author, Paris [Hugo Vickers diary], 31 January 2000.
9 Hon. Lady Mosley to Mona Bismarck, 6 June 1972 [Mona S. Bismarck papers, The Filson Historical Society, Louisville, KY, USA].
10 Oonagh Shanley-Toffolo, *The Voice of Silence* (Rider, 2002), p. 101.
11 Hon. Lady Mosley to Mona Bismarck, 6 June 1972 [Mona S. Bismarck papers, The Filson Historical Society, Louisville, KY, USA].
12 Note by Dr Jean Thin quoted in Michael Bloch (ed.), *The Secret File of the Duke of Windsor* (Bantam Press, 1988), p. 301.
13 Note by Dr Jean Thin quoted in Michael Bloch (ed), *The Secret File of the Duke of Windsor* (Bantam Press, 1988), p. 302.
14 Rt. Hon. Sir Martin Charteris to author, 1980s.
15 Private information.
16 Oonagh Shanley-Toffolo, *The Voice of Silence* (Rider, 2002), p. 105.
17 Press cuttings, British newspapers, 19 May 1972 [Hugo Vickers scrapbook, volume 52].

18 Mrs Susan Shaw to author, 14 March 1982.

19 Note by Dr Jean Thin quoted in Michael Bloch (ed.), *The Secret File of the Duke of Windsor* (Bantam Press, 1988), pp. 302–3.

20 Oonagh Shanley-Toffolo, *The Voice of Silence* (Rider, 2002), p. 109.

21 Oonagh Shanley-Toffolo, *The Voice of Silence* (Rider, 2002), p. 109.

22 *Illustrated London News*, July 1972.

23 Charlotte Mosley (ed.), *The Letters of Nancy Mitford* (Hodder & Stoughton, 1993), p. 516.

24 Noted in letter from Lt-Colonel Sir John Johnston, Lord Chamberlain's Office, to John Curle, Foreign Office, 14 December 1972 [National Archives, FCO 57/524].

25 Memorandum concerning the funerals of the Duke and Duchess of Windsor, May 1962 [National Archives, DO 161/213].

Source Notes for Chapter 3

1 Mountbatten's diary, 25 May 1972, quoted in Philip Ziegler (ed.), *From Shore to Shore* (Collins, 1989), p. 250.

2 Mountbatten's diary, 29 May 1972, quoted in Philip Ziegler (ed.), *From Shore to Shore* (Collins, 1989), p. 251.

3 Mountbatten's diary, 1 June 1972, quoted in Philip Ziegler (ed.), *From Shore to Shore* (Collins, 1989), p. 251.

4 Mountbatten's diary, 2 June 1972, quoted in Philip Ziegler (ed.), *From Shore to Shore* (Collins, 1989), p. 251.

5 Hon. Lady Charteris to author, 29 July 2010.

6 Jonathan Dimbleby, *The Prince of Wales* (Little, Brown, 1994), pp. 180–1.

7 Mountbatten's diary, 3 June 1972, quoted in Philip Ziegler (ed.), *From Shore to Shore* (Collins, 1989), pp. 253–4.

8 Hugo Vickers to Mrs Gerhard Neumann, 1 August 1972 [HV papers].

9 Hugo Vickers (ed.), *The Unexpurgated Beaton* (Weidenfeld & Nicolson, 2002), p. 256.

10 Hugo Vickers (ed.), *The Unexpurgated Beaton* (Weidenfeld & Nicolson, 2002), p. 256.

11 Private information, 24 March 2010.

12 Mountbatten's diary, 5 June 1972, quoted in Philip Ziegler (ed.), *From Shore to Shore* (Collins, 1989), p. 254.

13 Walter Lees to author, London, 30 September 1980.

14 John Utter to author, 17 September 1972.

15 *The Times*, 6 June 1972.

16 *The Times*, 6 June 1972.

17 Frances Donaldson, *Edward VIII* (Weidenfeld & Nicolson, 1974), p. 411.

18 Oonagh Shanley-Toffolo, *The Voice of Silence* (Rider, 2002), p. 110.

Source Notes for Chapter 4

1 Christiane Sherwen to author, 1994.
2 Kenneth Pendar, *Adventure in Diplomacy* (Cassell, 1966), p. 20.
3 Robb, *Lifestyle* (Elm tree Books, 1979), p. 45.
4 Hal Vaughan, *FDR'S 12 Apostles* (Lyons Press, 2006), p. 244.
5 Hal Vaughan, *FDR'S 12 Apostles* (Lyons Press, 2006), p. 244.
6 Hugo Vickers unpublished diary, 9 September 1979.
7 John Utter, letter to author, Paris, 29 September 1972.
8 Hugo Vickers unpublished diary, 15 October 1978.
9 Hugo Vickers unpublished diary, 14 June 1980.
10 Confirmed in a handwritten note by Mrs Henry J. Taylor, on a telegram of sympathy from Maître Blum and Georges, 29 February 1984 [Henry J. Taylor papers – Herbert Hoover Presidential Library, Iowa].
11 The Duchess of Windsor to Major Gray Phillips, 1960.
12 Hugo Vickers unpublished diary, 15 October 1978.

Source Notes for Chapter 5

1 Helen, Lady Hardinge of Penshurst diary, 28 May 1972.
2 The will of HRH The Duke of Windsor, 6 January 1972.
3 The will of HRH The Duke of Windsor, 6 January 1972.
4 The Duchess of Windsor's document of dispositions, 1950s.
5 Sir Godfrey Morley to the Duchess of Windsor, 23 June 1972.
6 Sir Godfrey Morley to the Duchess of Windsor, 6 June 1972 [Allen & Overy copy].
7 Captain Andrew Yates to author, 1980s.
8 John Utter to author, Paris, 17 September 1972.
9 Lady Alexandra Metcalfe's unpublished (but privately printed) diaries, p. 190 [David Metcalfe papers].
10 Mountbatten's diary, 22 February 1970, quoted in Philip Ziegler (ed.), *From Shore to Shore* (Collins, 1989), p. 190.
11 Mountbatten's diary, 2 March 1972, quoted in Philip Ziegler (ed.), *From Shore to Shore* (Collins, 1989), p. 190.
12 Philip Ziegler, *Mountbatten* (Collins, 1985), p. 679.
13 Hugo Vickers unpublished diary, 4 September 1979.
14 Hon. Lady Mosley to the Duchess of Devonshire, 5 June 1972, quoted in Charlotte Mosley [ed.], *The Mitfords – Letters Between Six Sisters* (4th Estate, 2007), p. 583.
15 Gregorio Martin in *Going, Going, Gone* (1997 TV film).
16 Richard René Silvin to author, 16 August 2009.
17 Sir Godfrey Morley to Maurice Amiguet, 10 July 1972 [Allen & Overy copy].
18 Sir Godfrey Morley to Maître Suzanne Blum, 13 November 1972 [Allen & Overy copy].

19 Hon Lady Mosley to the Duchess of Devonshire, 4 December 1972, quoted in Charlotte Mosley (ed.), *The Mitfords – Letters Between Six Sisters* (Fourth Estate, 2007), p. 585.

20 Derived from *The Times & Daily Telegraph*, 21 December 1972.

21 Johanna Schütz to author, 5 December 2009.

Source Notes for Chapter 6

1 Sir Godfrey Morley to Maurice Amiguet, 24 January 1973 [Allen & Overy copy].

2 Hank Walter to Sir Godfrey Morley, 25 January 1973 [Allen & Overy copy].

3 The Duchess of Windsor to Sir Godfrey Morley, 26 January 1973 [Allen & Overy copy].

4 Sir Godfrey Morley to D.R. McMaster, QC, in Montreal, 27 February 1973 [Allen & Overy copy].

5 The Duchess of Windsor to Charles Patry, 16 February 1973.

6 Mountbatten's. diary, 8 February 1973, quoted in Philip Ziegler (ed.), *From Shore to Shore* (Collins, 1989), p. 259.

7 Mountbatten's diary, 8 February 1973, quoted in Philip Ziegler (ed.), *From Shore to Shore* (Collins, 1989), p. 261.

8 Lord Mountbatten to John Utter, 13 February 1973.

9 Lord Mountbatten to the Duchess of Windsor, 19 February 1973.

10 Derived from Maître Suzanne Blum to Joe Burrell, 22 February 1973 [Duchess of Windsor's copy].

11 Derived from Maurice Amiguet to John Utter, Zurich, 19 February 1973.

12 Maître Suzanne Blum, letter to author, Paris, 4 April 1985.

Source Notes for Chapter 7

For this chapter, I would most particularly like to thank Mary Dearborn for her help in obtaining the papers of William C. Bullitt, Carmel Offie, Hugh S. Fullerton and Virgil Thomson, and for her advice; also Barbara Will, Thomas Dilworth and Edward Burns for their help with the Bernard Faÿ issue.

1 William C. Bullitt to President Roosevelt, Paris, 6 February 1939, quoted in Orville C. Bullitt, (ed.), *For the President – Personal and Secret* (Andre Deutsch, 1973), p. 310.

2 John Julius Norwich (ed.), *The Duff Cooper Diaries* (Weidenfeld & Nicolson, 2005), (entry for 11 May 1947), p. 438.

3 Suzanne Blum, *Vivre Sans la Patrie 1940–1945* (Plon, 1975), p. 54.

4 Burton Hersch, *The Old Boys* (Tree Farm Books, 2002), p. 237.

5 Suzanne Blum to Carmel Offie, New York, 27 January 1943 [William Bullitt

papers, MS 112, Box 10, Folder 206 – Yale University Library, New Haven, USA].

6 Suzanne Blum, *Vivre Sans la Patrie 1940–1945* (Plon, 1975), p. 35.

7 Hon. Lady Mosley to author, in Paris [Hugo Vickers unpublished diary, 31 January 2000].

8 William C. Bullitt to President Roosevelt, 30 May 1945, quoted in Will Brownell & Richard N. Billings, *So Close to Greatness* (Macmillan, 1987), p. 254.

9 Suzanne Blum, *Vivre Sans la Patrie 1940–1945* (Plon, 1975), p. 53.

10 Virgil Thomson, *Virgil Thomson* (Knopf, NY, 1966), p. 320.

11 Virgil Thomson, *Virgil Thomson* (Knopf, NY, 1966), p. 320.

12 Suzanne Blum, *Vivre Sans la Patrie 1940–1945* (Plon, 1975), pp. 130–135.

13 Suzanne Blum to Carmel Offie, Hotel Concord, New York, 12 May 1941 [William Bullitt papers, MS 112, Box 10, Folder 205 – Yale University Library, New Haven, USA].

14 Carmel Offie to Louis B. Wehle, Esquire, New York, 24 January 1941 [William Bullitt papers, MS 112, Box 10, Folder 205 – Yale University Library, New Haven, USA].

15 Suzanne Blum to Carmel Offie, New York, 22 September 1943 [William Bullitt papers, MS 112, Box 10, Folder 206 – Yale University Library, New Haven, USA].

16 *Undernews*, 30 September 2003.

17 Janet Malcolm, *Two Lives* (Yale University Press, 2007), p. 99; & Susan Holbrook & Thomas Dilworth (eds.), *The Letters of Gertrude Stein & Virgil Thomson* (Oxford University Press, 2010), p. 280.

18 Virgil Thomson, *Virgil Thomson* (Knopf, NY, 1966), p. 388.

19 Derived from Suzanne Blum to Virgil Thomson, Paris, 18 January 1947 [Virgil Thomson papers, Yale].

20 Derived from Suzanne Blum to Virgil Thomson, Paris, 13 December [undated – thought to be 1954 or 1955] [Virgil Thomson papers, Yale].

21 Thomas Dilworth to author, 13 April 2010.

22 Susan Holbrook & Thomas Dilworth (eds.), *The Letters of Gertrude Stein & Virgil Thomson* (Oxford University Press, 2010), p. 297.

23 Lady Diana Cooper to author, Paris, 1 May 1984.

24 Suzanne Blum to Carmel Offie, Paris, 3 March 1949 [William Bullitt papers, MS 112, Box 10, Folder 206 – Yale University Library, New Haven, USA].

25 Suzanne Blum, *Ne Savoir Rien* (Bibliothèque du Temps Présent, 1973), p. 12–13. Photo by M. Brodsky.

26 Virgil Thomson to Suzanne Blum, 9 June 1949 [Virgil Thomson papers, Yale].

27 Virgil Thomson to Suzanne Blum, 13 April 1951 [Virgil Thomson papers, Yale].

28 Virgil Thomson to Suzanne Blum, Boxing Day 1955 [Virgil Thomson papers, Yale].

29 Alice B. Toklas to James Merrill, Paris, 5 January 1956 [Edward Burns (ed) *Staying on Alone – Letters of Alice B. Toklas* (Angus & Robertson, 1973. p. 330.

30 Hon. Mrs Raymond Bonham Carter to author, London, 10 May 2010.

31 Caroline Blackwood, *The Last of the Duchess* (Pantheon Books, NY, 1995), pp. 148–50.

32 Sir Reginald Hibbert to Michael Thornton, Powys, 4 July 1988 – copy in author's possession.

33 Johanna Schütz to author, 9 December 2009.

Source Notes for Chapter 8

1 Hugo Vickers unpublished diary, 3 June 1976.

2 Ralph Martin, *The Woman He Loved* (Simon & Schuster, 1974), p. 9.

3 Ralph Martin, *The Woman He Loved* (Simon & Schuster, 1974), p. 12.

4 Hugo Vickers unpublished diary, 12 July 1973.

5 Hugo Vickers unpublished diary, 28 July 1973.

6 Hugo Vickers unpublished diary, 14 September 1976.

7 Duchess of Windsor to Lord Mountbatten (her office copy, undated but September 1973).

8 Derived from Maître Suzanne Blum to Joe Burrell, 10 October 1973.

9 Lord Tennyson to Alastair Forbes, Paris, 18 July 1986.

10 Walter Lees to Mona Bismarck (1 Avenue de Tourville, Paris), 22 September 1973 [Mona S. Bismarck papers, The Filson Historical Society, Louisville, KY, USA].

11 *Time-Life*, November 1973, and *New York Times*, 17 November 1973.

12 *Daily Telegraph*, 24 November 1973.

13 *Time*, 18 October 1943.

14 Ralph G. Martin, *The Woman He Loved* (Simon & Schuster, NY, 1974), p. 72.

15 Walter Lees to Mona Bismarck, 11 September 1974 [Mona S. Bismarck papers, The Filson Historical Society, Louisville, KY, USA].

16 Derived from Maurice Amiguet to John Utter, Zurich, 18 February 1974.

17 Derived from Hugo Vickers unpublished diary, 16 March 1974; & a letter to Mrs Gerhard Neumann, 26 March 1974.

18 Janice Petterchak, *To Share – The Heritage, Legend and Legacy of Nathan Cummings* (Rochester, IL: Legacy Press, 2000), p. 5.

19 Janice Petterchak, *To Share – The Heritage, Legend and Legacy of Nathan Cummings* (Rochester, IL: Legacy Press, 2000), p. 25.

20 *Selections from the Nathan Cummings Collection* (National Gallery of Art, Washington, 1970), p. 8.

21 Janice Petterchak, *To Share – The Heritage, Legend and Legacy of Nathan Cummings* (Rochester, IL: Legacy Press, 2000), p. 113.

22 Hugo Vickers unpublished diary, 1 January 1995.

23 The Earl of Snowdon to author, 1994.

24 Quoted in *Chicago Tribune*, 13 May 1974.
25 John Utter to author, 3 June 1976.
26 Frances Donaldson, *A Twentieth Century Life* (Weidenfeld & Nicolson, 1992), p. 192.
27 Frances Donaldson, *A Twentieth Century Life* (Weidenfeld & Nicolson, 1992), p. 194.
28 Frances Donaldson, *A Twentieth Century Life* (Weidenfeld & Nicolson, 1992), p. 194.
29 Mountbatten's diary, 12 November 1974, quoted in Philip Ziegler (ed.), *From Shore to Shore* (Collins, 1989), p. 293.
30 Mountbatten's diary, 12 November 1974, quoted in Philip Ziegler (ed.), *From Shore to Shore* (Collins, 1989), p. 294.
31 Lord Mountbatten to the Duchess of Windsor, Broadlands, 25 November 1974.
32 Transcript of Mountbatten telephone call to Johanna Schütz, 4 December 1974.
33 Duchess of Windsor to Lord Mountbatten, 9 December 1974 [copy in Duchess of Windsor papers].

Sources for Chapter 9

1 Hugo Vickers unpublished diary, 15 March 1980
2 *Evening Standard*, 21 February 1975.
3 Hugo Vickers unpublished diary, 27 May 1976.
4 Walter Lees to author, London, 30 September 1980.
5 'Lunch with the Most Elegant Woman in the World' by Prudence Glynn, *The Times*, 15 April 1975.
6 Diary of John Nova Phillips, 15 October 1975.
7 Richard René Silvin to author, 16 August 2009.
8 Richard René Silvin to author, 16 August 2009.
9 John Utter to author, 30 January 1976.
10 Hugo Vickers unpublished diary, 15 February 1976.
11 Nathan Cummings to Johanna Schütz, 27 January 1976.
12 Derived from private nurses' reports, 1975–76.
13 Edward Fox to author, 26 September 2008.
14 Robin Beare to Maître Blum, 149 Harley Street, London W1, 25 March 1976.
15 Derived from Maître Blum to Robin Beare, 1 April 1976.
16 Hon Lady Mosley to the Duchess of Devonshire, 21 May 1976 [Charlotte Mosley [ed], *The Mitfords – Letters Between Six Sisters* (Fourth Estate, 2007), p. 622.
17 Hugo Vickers unpublished diary, 27 May 1976.
18 *New York Times*, 14 October 1976: & an article by Bernard Valery – *New York Daily News* [undated but October 1976].

19 Nurse letter, 20 May 1976.

20 Diana Mosley to Lady Monckton, 5 June 1976.

21 Diana Mosley to Lady Monckton, Temple de la Gloire, 3 July 1976.

22 Derived from Maurice Amiguet to Ambassador & Mrs Henry J. Taylor, Zurich, 14 August 1976 [Henry J. Taylor papers – Herbert Hoover Presidential Library, Iowa].

23 Derived from private nurses' reports, 1976.

24 Hugo Vickers unpublished diary, Paris, 14 September 1976.

25 Hugo Vickers unpublished diary, Paris, 14 September 1976.

26 Dr Jean Thin to Maître Blum, 28 September 1976.

27 Hugo Vickers unpublished diary, 4 September 1979.

28 Hugo Vickers unpublished diary, 10 December 1976.

29 Johanna Schütz to Maurice Amiguet, 11 November 1976.

Source Notes for Chapter 10

1 Philip Nelson to author, 3 February 2010.

2 Plans for the funerals of the Duke and Duchess of Windsor [National Archives, DO 161/213].

3 Lt-Colonel Sir John Johnston, Lord Chamberlain's Office, to John Curle, Foreign Office, 14 December 1972 [National Archives – FCO 57/524].

4 Sir Edward Tomkins to Sir John Johnston, Paris, 19 January 1973 [National Archives – FCO 57/524].

5 Sir Eric Penn, Lord Chamberlain's Office, to Sir Edward Tomkins, 5 February 1973 [National Archives – FCO 57/524].

6 Nicholas Henderson, *Mandarin: The Diaries of an Ambassador 1969–1982* (Weidenfeld & Nicolson, 1994), p. 135.

7 Nicholas Gordon Lennox, *The Tiddly Quid And After* (The Book Guild, 2006), p. 128.

8 Nicholas Gordon Lennox, *The Tiddly Quid And After* (The Book Guild, 2006), p. 128.

9 Nicholas Gordon Lennox, *The Tiddly Quid And After* (The Book Guild, 2006), p. 129.

10 Nicholas Gordon Lennox, *The Tiddly Quid And After* (The Book Guild, 2006), p. 129.

11 Maître Suzanne Blum to Johanna Schütz, 30 January 1976.

12 Letters in possession of the author.

13 Derived from Maurice Amiguet to Johanna Schütz, Ostbühlstrasse 69, 8038 Zurich, 11 March 1976.

14 Derived from Maître Suzanne Blum to Johanna Schütz, 5 April 1976.

15 Dr Jean Thin to Maître Blum, 28 September 1976.

16 Derived from Maurice Amiguet to Johanna Schütz, 3 October 1976.

17 Miscellaneous cutting from *Hola* [undated, but 1976] – *Mas Trabajo Para la Abogada de la Duguesa de Windsor*.

18 Stephen Birmingham, *Duchess* (Little, Brown, USA, 1981), p. 308.
19 Derived from Maurice Amiguet to Johanna Schütz, 1 July 1976.
20 Johanna Schütz to Maitre Suzanne Blum, 20 July 1976.
21 Derived from Maitre Suzanne Blum to the Duchess of Windsor, 26 July 1976.
22 Nicholas Henderson, *Mandarin: The Diaries of an Ambassador 1969–1982* (Weidenfeld & Nicolson, 1994), p. 136.
23 Derived from letters from Dr Bruno Vuillemin, 17 January 1977 & 21 March 1977, & a prescription dated 5 February 1977; a letter from Dr Jean Thin 24 February 1977; and a note from one of the nurses.
24 Johanna Schütz to Rt. Hon. Sir Martin Charteris, April 1977.
25 Maurice Amiguet to Johanna Schütz, Zurich, 14 May 1977.
26 Sir Robin Mackworth-Young to Duc de Grantmesnil, Kenneth de Courcy, Windsor Castle, 11 April 1979 – copy in possession of author.
27 Sir Robin Mackworth-Young to author, Windsor, 30 September 1981.
28 Derived from Charles Torem to Nathan Cummings, 15 August 1977.
29 Hon Lady Mosley to Lady Monckton, 22 July 1977.
30 Hugo Vickers unpublished diary, 19 June 1977.
31 *International Herald Tribune*, 19–20 May 1979.
32 Nathan Cummings to Johanna Schütz, 29 September 1977.
33 Hon. Lady Mosley to Lady Monckton, 25 October 1977.
34 Hon. Lady Mosley to James Lees-Milne, 9 April 1980 [GEN MSS 476 James Lees-Milne Papers, Beinecke Rare Book and Manuscript Library, Yale].
35 Hon. Lady Mosley to Hugo Vickers, Orsay, 17 March 1995.
36 Hon. Lady Mosley to author, Orsay, Easter 1995.
37 Rt. Rev. Michael Mann to author, London, 11 February 1997.
38 Russell Harty television interview with Lady Mosley, 1980.

Source Notes for Chapter 11

1 Johanna Schütz to Nathan Cummings, 7 November 1977.
2 Derived from Maître Suzanne Blum to Johanna Schütz, 21 November 1977.
3 Johanna Schütz to Dr Arthur Antenucci, 15 November 1977.
4 Derived from Johanna Schütz to Maître Blum, 21 November 1977.
5 Derived from Maître Blum to Johanna Schütz, 2 December 1977.
6 Derived from Nathan Cummings to Johanna Schütz, 24 February 1978.
7 Nathan Cummings to Johanna Schütz, 8 January 1978.
8 Johanna Schütz to Nathan Cummings, 14 February 1978.
9 Lord Tennyson to Alastair Forbes, Paris, 18 July 1986.
10 Nathan Cummings to Johanna Schutz, 23 January 1978.
11 Johanna Schütz to Maître Blum, 23 February 1978.
12 Johanna Schütz to Nathan Cummings, 23 March 1978.
13 Johanna Schütz to Nathan Cummings, draft of letter, 22 May 1978, and letter, 6 June 1978.

14 Nathan Cummings to Johanna Schütz, 6 April 1978.

15 John Utter to author, 8 October 1978.

16 Hugo Vickers unpublished diary, 8 October 1996.

17 Derived from Maurice Amiguet to Nathan Cummings, 11 April 1978.

18 File copy of a letter from Nathan Cummings to Maurice Amiguet, 28 April 1978.

19 Johanna Schütz to Nathan Cummings, 23 March 1978.

20 Johanna Schütz to Ambassador and Mrs Henry J. Taylor, 21 April 1978 [Henry J. Taylor papers – Herbert Hoover Presidential Library, Iowa].

21 Nathan Cummings to Johanna Schütz, 19 May 1978.

22 File copy of letter from Nathan Cummings to Maurice Amiguet, La Reserve, Beaulieu, 6 July 1978.

23 Derived from Maurice Amiguet to Nathan Cummings, Zurich, 10 August 1978.

24 Nathan Cummings to Johanna Schütz, 24 August 1978.

25 Johanna Schütz to Nathan Cummings, 1 September 1978.

Source Notes on Chapter 12

1 Johanna Schütz to Nathan Cummings, 1 September 1978.

2 Stephen Birmingham, *Duchess* (Little, Brown & Co, New York, 1981), p. 321.

3 *The Oddest Couple* by James Fox (*Vanity Fair*, September 2003), p. 292.

4 *Timewatch*, BBC television, 29 September 1982.

5 *Sunday Times*, 27 April 1986.

6 *Timewatch*, BBC television, 29 September 1982.

7 Nicholas Gordon Lennox, *The Tiddly Quid and After* (Book Guild, 2006), p. 128.

8 Hugo Vickers unpublished diary, 3 December 1980.

9 Hugo Vickers unpublished diary, 20 December 1978.

10 *The Times*, 21 November 1978.

11 *The Times*, 21 November 1978.

12 *Daily Telegraph*, ca 27 November 1978.

13 *Evening Standard*, 26 November 1978.

14 *The Times*, 27 November 1978.

15 Lord Tennyson to Alastair Forbes, 18 July 1986.

16 Sir Reginald Hibbert to Michael Thornton, Powys, 4 July 1988 – copy in author's possession.

17 Hugo Vickers unpublished diary, 27 May 1976.

18 Cecil Beaton diary, November 1950.

19 Hugo Vickers unpublished diary, 21 April 1979.

20 Hugo Vickers unpublished diary, 23 April 1979.

21 Joseph Bryan III to John Barratt, 25 April 1978 [Mountbatten Archives, K10 – Broadlands/Hartley Library, University of Southampton].

22 Lord Mountbatten to Joseph Bryan III, 17 May 1978 [Mountbatten Archives, K10 – Hartley Library, University of Southampton].
23 Joseph Bryan III to Lord Mountbatten, 23 December 1978. [Mountbatten Archives, K10 – Hartley Library, University of Southampton].
24 Lord Mountbatten to Joseph Bryan III, 4 January 1979 [Mountbatten Archives, K10 – Hartley Library, University of Southampton].
25 Charles J.V. Murphy to H R H The Duke of Windsor, Paris, 25 July 1950.
26 Charles J.V. Murphy to the Duchess of Windsor, Washington, August 1954.
27 *Daily Mail*, 23 November 1979.
28 *Sunday Telegraph*, ca. 2 December 1979.
29 *The Listener*, 13 December 1979
30 *Sunday Times*, ca. 2 December 1979.
31 Hugo Vickers unpublished diary, 6 January 1980.

Source Notes for Chapter 13

1 Card to Diana Vreeland, ca. 1972–4.
2 One of three such cards in Diana Vreeland's papers.
3 Telegram to Mrs Henry J. Taylor, 29 February 1984 [Henry J. Taylor papers – Herbert Hoover Presidential Library, Iowa].
4 Hugo Vickers unpublished diary, 8 October 1978.
5 Hugo Vickers unpublished diary, 21 January 1979.
6 Hugo Vickers unpublished diary, 25 February 1979.
7 Hugo Vickers unpublished diary, 21 April 1979.
8 Hugo Vickers unpublished diary, 21 May 1979.
9 *New York Times* magazine section, 18 March 1979.
10 *International Herald Tribune* 19–20 May 1979.
11 Hugo Vickers unpublished diary, 4 September 1979.
12 Hugo Vickers unpublished diary 17 February 1980.
13 Hugo Vickers unpublished diary, 19 March 1980.
14 Hugo Vickers unpublished diary, 14 June 1980.
15 Hugo Vickers unpublished diary, 9 September 1980.
16 Hugo Vickers unpublished diary, 11 September 1980.
17 Hugo Vickers unpublished diary, 11 September 1980.
18 Hugo Vickers unpublished diary, 12 September 1980.
19 Nathan Cummings to Johanna Schütz, 26 January 1981.
20 Nathan Cummings to Johanna Schütz, 12 March 1982.
21 Hugo Vickers unpublished diary, 9 February 1981.
22 Hugo Vickers unpublished diary, 17 October 1981.
23 Hugo Vickers unpublished diary, 6 May 1982.
24 Hugo Vickers unpublished diary, 31 January 2000.
25 Johanna Schütz to Nathan Cummings, 12 March 1982.
26 Johanna Schütz to Nathan Cummings, 12 October 1982.
27 *Sunday Mirror*, 6 March 1988.

28 *Sunday Mirror*, 6 March 1988.
29 *Sunday Mirror*, 6 March 1988.
30 Hugo Vickers unpublished diary, 22 August 1983.
31 *Daily Mail*, 18 January 1985.
32 *Sunday Mirror*, November 1985.
33 Hugo Vickers unpublished diary, 28 August 1985.
34 James R. Leo, *Exits and Entrances* (Xlibris, 2008), p. 14.
35 James R. Leo, *Exits and Entrances* (Xlibris, 2008), p. 12.
36 James R. Leo, *Exits and Entrances* (Xlibris, 2008), p. 11.

Source Notes for Chapter 14

1 *Debrett's People of Today*, 2009.
2 Michael Bloch, *James Lees-Milne – The Life* (John Murray, 2009), p. 309.
3 Evelyn Waugh, *Unconditional Surrender* (Penguin, 1964), p. 25.
4 James Lees-Milne, *Ancestral Voices* (Chatto & Windus, 1975, p. 155.
5 James Lord, *Some Remarkable Men – Further Memoirs* (Farrar Straus Giroux, New York, 1996), p. 23.
6 Sir Harold Acton to author, London, 25 November 1977.
7 Stuart Preston to author, ca 1976.
8 Simon Blow to James Lees-Milne, [undated, but 1980s] [GEN MSS 476 James Lees-Milne Papers, Beinecke Rare Book and Manuscript Library, Yale].
9 Hugo Vickers unpublished diary, 7 May 1980.
10 John Martin Robinson, *Grass Seed in June* (Michael Russell, 2006), pp. 158 & 160.
11 Michael Bloch (ed.), *Beneath a Waning Moon* (John Murray, 2003), p. 41.
12 Stuart Preston to James Lees-Milne, 2 August 1985 [GEN MSS 476 James Lees-Milne Papers, Beinecke Rare Book and Manuscript Library, Yale].
13 Hugo Massingberd (ed.), *The Daily Telegraph Book of Obituaries* (Macmillan, 1995), p. 250.
14 Michael Bloch, (ed.), *Deeply Romantic Chasm* (John Murray, 2000), p. 76.
15 Michael Bloch, (ed.), *Deeply Romantic Chasm* (John Murray, 2000), p. 84.
16 Michael Bloch to Lees-Milne [GEN MSS 476 James Lees-Milne Papers, Beinecke Rare Book and Manuscript Library, Yale – Box 24, Folder 968].
17 Derived from J. Bryan III to Andrew Best [copy in GEN MSS 476 James Lees-Milne Papers, Beinecke Rare Book and Manuscript Library, Yale – Box 24, Folder 968].
18 Maître Suzanne Blum to James Lees-Milne, 7 September 1985 [GEN MSS 476 James Lees-Milne Papers, Beinecke Rare Book and Manuscript Library, Yale – Box 24, Folder 968].
19 Maître Suzanne Blum to James Lees-Milne, 7 September 1985. [GEN MSS 476 James Lees-Milne Papers, Beinecke Rare Book and Manuscript Library, Yale – Box 24, Folder 968].

20 Michael Bloch (ed.), *Beneath a Waning Moon* (John Murray, 2003), p. 52 & n.

21 Hugo Vickers unpublished diary, 3 December 1980.

22 *Daily Mail*, 25 April 1986.

23 Michael Bloch, *The Duchess of Windsor* (Weidenfeld & Nicolson, 1996), p. 225.

24 Hugo Vickers unpublished diary, 30 September 1980.

25 Hugo Vickers unpublished diary, 17 February 1980.

26 Hugo Vickers unpublished diary, 15 March 1980.

27 Hugo Vickers unpublished diary, 21 June 1980.

28 Hugo Vickers unpublished diary, 29 November 1981.

29 Stuart Preston to author, 5 May 1980.

30 Hugo Vickers unpublished diary, 15 May 1980.

31 Hugo Vickers unpublished diary, 7 May 1980.

32 *The Times*, 4 July 1980.

33 Hugo Vickers unpublished diary, 10 July 1980.

34 Hugo Vickers unpublished diary, 2 December 1980.

35 Hugo Vickers unpublished diary, 3 December 1980.

36 Hugo Vickers unpublished diary, 4 December 1980.

37 Hugo Vickers unpublished diary, Ca 13 June 1981.

38 Michael Bloch, *The Duke of Windsor's War* (Weidenfeld & Nicolson, 1982), p xi.

39 Michael Bloch, *The Duke of Windsor's War* (Weidenfeld & Nicolson, 1982), dust-jacket copy.

40 Michael Bloch to James Lees-Milne, 31 December 1995 [GEN MSS 476 James Lees-Milne Papers, Beinecke Rare Book and Manuscript Library, Yale].

41 Hon. Lady Mosley to James Lees-Milne, Temple de la Gloire, 22 September 1982 [GEN MSS 476 James Lees-Milne Papers, Beinecke Rare Book and Manuscript Library, Yale].

42 Hon. Lady Mosley to James Lees-Milne, Temple de la Gloire, 2 October 1982 [GEN MSS 476 James Lees-Milne Papers, Beinecke Rare Book and Manuscript Library, Yale].

43 Sir John Tusa to author, Cumberland Lodge, Windsor, 28 May 2009.

44 Michael Bloch, *Operation Willi* (Weidenfeld & Nicolson, 1984), p. ix.

45 *Private Eye*, April 1986.

46 Michael Thornton to John Curtis 25 June 1985.

47 Duchess of Windsor, 'letter of authorisation', 17 March 1975.

Source Notes for Chapter 15

1 *London Standard*, 24 April 1986.

2 *The Star & Daily Express*, 25 April 1986.

3 Hugo Vickers unpublished diary, 20 June 1989.

4 Noted in the Duchess of Windsor's funeral file [National Archives – FCO 57/524].

5 *London Standard*, 24 April 1986.

6 *London Standard*, 24 April 1986.

7 *Sunday Telegraph*, 27 April 1986.

8 *The Times*, 25 April 1986.

9 *The Times*, 25 April 1986.

10 *The Times*, 25 April 1986.

11 *Daily Telegraph*, 25 April 1986.

12 *Daily Express*, 29 April 1986.

13 *London Standard*, 28 April 1986.

14 Dean James R. Leo to author, Cincinnati, 7 May 2009.

15 Princesse de Polignac to author, South of France, August 1986.

16 Duchess of Devonshire to Hon. Lady Mosley, 25 April 1986 [Charlotte Mosley [ed], *The Mitfords – Letters Between Six Sisters* (Fourth Estate, 2007), p. 711.

17 Hon. Lady Mosley to the Duchess of Devonshire, 1 May 1986 [Charlotte Mosley [ed], *The Mitfords – Letters Between Six Sisters* (Fourth Estate, 2007), pp. 712–3.

18 Hugo Vickers diary, 29 April 1986.

19 Dean James R. Leo to author, Cincinnati, 7 May 2009.

20 Hugo Vickers diary, 7 June 1986.

Source Notes for Chapter 16

1 Press statement by Blum.

2 Michael Bloch (ed.), *Wallis and Edward Letters 1931–1937* (Weidenfeld & Nicolson, 1986), p. ix.

3 Michael Bloch (ed.), *Wallis and Edward Letters 1931–1937* (Weidenfeld & Nicolson, 1986), p. 1.

4 Michael Bloch (ed.), *Wallis and Edward Letters 1931–1937* (Weidenfeld & Nicolson, 1986), pp. 107–8.

5 Michael Bloch (ed.), *Wallis and Edward Letters 1931–1937* (Weidenfeld & Nicolson, 1986), p. 109.

6 Michael Bloch (ed.), *Wallis and Edward Letters 1931–1937* (Weidenfeld & Nicolson, 1986), p. 39.

7 *The Spectator*, 7 June 1986.

8 Michael Bloch (ed.), *Wallis and Edward Letters 1931–1937* (Weidenfeld & Nicolson, 1986), p. x.

9 *The Times*, 15 May 1986.

10 Philip Howard, Literary Editor of *The Times*, to author, 16 June 1986.

11 Johanna Schütz to author, 24 August 2009.

12 *Private Eye*, ca. May 1986.

13 Lord Tennyson to Alastair Forbes, 18 July 1986.

14 *Daily Express*, April 1986 [Hugo Vickers scrapbook. 236].

15 Hugo Vickers unpublished diary, 14 July 1986.

16 Hon. Lady Mosley to James Lees-Milne, 30 September 1986 [Lees-Milne papers, Beinecke Library, Yale].

17 Tom Bower, *Fayed – The Unauthorised Biography* (Macmillan, 1998), pp. 172–3.

18 Hugo Vickers unpublished diary, 22 May 1997.

19 *Sunday Times* magazine, 21 December 1986.

20 *Country Life*, 25 June 1987.

Sources for Chapter 17

1 Tom Bower, *Fayed – The Unauthorised Biography* (Macmillan, 1998), p. 173.

2 Hon James Stourton to author, Sotheby's, London, 28 April 2009; Nicholas Rayner interview with Matthew Weigman, *Exceptional Jewels & Precious Objects formerly in the Collection of the Duchess of Windsor* (Sotheby's sale catalogue for 30 November 2010, p. 14).

3 Hugo Vickers unpublished diary, Geneva 1 April 1987.

4 Hugo Vickers unpublished diary, Geneva 1 April 1987.

5 Hugo Vickers unpublished diary, Geneva 3 April 1987.

6 *Daily Mail*, 5 April 1987.

7 Derived from Michael Bloch (ed.), *Beneath a Waning Moon* (John Murray, 2003), p. 183.

8 Advertising text, Michael Bloch (ed.), *The Secret File of the Duke of Windsor* (Bantam Press, 1988).

9 HRH The Duke of Windsor to the Duchess of Windsor, Paris, 27 March 1953, quoted in Michael Bloch (ed.), *The Secret File of the Duke of Windsor* (Bantam Press, 1988), p. 277.

10 HRH The Duke of Windsor to the Duchess of Windsor, London, 31 March 1953, quoted in Michael Bloch (ed.), *The Secret File of the Duke of Windsor* (Bantam Press, 1988), p. xiii.

11 Hugo Vickers unpublished diary, 1 July 1988.

12 Quoted by Michael Thornton in a letter to *The Times*, 30 June 1988.

13 *The Times*, 4 July 1988.

14 *The Times*, 7 July 1988.

15 *Sunday Telegraph*, 24 July 1988.

16 *Daily Telegraph*, 27 July 1988.

17 *The Times*, 11 August 1988.

18 *The Times*, 30 June 1988.

19 Sir Reginald Hibbert to Michael Thornton, Powys, 4 July 1988 – copy in author's possession.

20 Michael Bloch (ed.), *Ceaseless Turmoil* (John Murray, 2004), p. 50 – entry for 27 July 1988.

21 Hon. Lady Mosley to James Lees-Milne, Temple de la Gloire, Orsay, 29 July 1988 [GEN MSS 476 James Lees-Milne Papers, Beinecke Rare Book and Manuscript Library, Yale].

22 Hon. Lady Mosley to James Lees-Milne, Temple de la Gloire, Orsay, 9 August 1988 [GEN MSS 476 James Lees-Milne Papers, Beinecke Rare Book and Manuscript Library, Yale].

23 Michael Bloch (ed.), *The Secret File of the Duke of Windsor* (Bantam Press, 1988), p. xiii.

24 *The Spectator*, 10 September 1988.

25 Derived from Suzanne Lowry's interview with Maître Blum and Michael Bloch, published in the *Daily Telegraph*, 16 September 1988.

26 Michael Bloch, *The Reign and Abdication of Edward VIII* (Bantam Press, 1990), p. xiii.

27 Michael Bloch, *The Reign and Abdication of Edward VIII* (Bantam Press, 1990), p. xv.

28 *Sunday Times*, 8 April 1990.

29 Michael Bloch (ed.), *Ceaseless Turmoil* (John Murray, 2004), p. 108 – entry for 1–3 July 1989.

30 Philip Ziegler to author, 30 October 1989.

31 Derived from Michael Bloch to James Lees-Milne, 26 November 1989 [GEN MSS 476 James Lees-Milne Papers, Beinecke Rare Book and Manuscript Library, Yale].

32 *Daily Telegraph*, 26 January 1994.

33 *The Times*, 26 January 1994.

34 *The Independent*, 26 January 1994.

35 Derived from Michael Bloch to James Lees-Milne, 31 October 1995 [GEN MSS 476 James Lees-Milne Papers, Beinecke Rare Book and Manuscript Library, Yale].

36 Derived from Michael Bloch to James Lees-Milne, 16 February 1995 [GEN MSS 476 James Lees-Milne Papers, Beinecke Rare Book and Manuscript Library, Yale].

37 Derived from Michael Bloch to James Lees-Milne, 31 May 1995 [GEN MSS 476 James Lees-Milne Papers, Beinecke Rare Book and Manuscript Library, Yale].

38 Derived from Michael Bloch to James Lees-Milne, 16 August 1995 [GEN MSS 476 James Lees-Milne Papers, Beinecke Rare Book and Manuscript Library, Yale].

39 Derived from Michael Bloch to James Lees-Milne, 18 September 1995 [GEN MSS 476 James Lees-Milne Papers, Beinecke Rare Book and Manuscript Library, Yale].

40 Derived from Michael Bloch to James Lees-Milne, 2 October 1995 [GEN MSS 476 James Lees-Milne Papers, Beinecke Rare Book and Manuscript Library, Yale].

41 Derived from Michael Bloch to James Lees-Milne, 31 October 1995 [GEN

MSS 476 James Lees-Milne Papers, Beinecke Rare Book and Manuscript Library, Yale].

42 'The Oddest Couple' – *Vanity Fair*, September 2003.

43 'An outcast, yes . . . but a man?' by Hugo Vickers, *The Independent*, 16 May 1996.

Source Notes for Chapter 18

1 *The Times*, 22 December 1987.

2 Hugo Vickers unpublished diary, 13 July 1989.

3 Hugo Vickers unpublished diary, 13 July 1989.

4 Hugo Vickers, *The Private World of the Duke and Duchess of Windsor* (Harrods Publishing, 1995), p. 235.

5 Princesse de Polignac to author, 22 May 1997.

6 *Liberation Fr.*, 13 February 1998.

7 *Sunday Telegraph*, 22 February 1998.

8 Hugo Vickers unpublished diary, 25 February 1998.

Source notes for Part 2 – Chapter 1

1 Philip Ziegler, *King Edward VIII* (Collins, 1990), p. 224.

2 Greg King, *The Duchess of Windsor* (Aurum Press, 1999), p. 373.

3 Sir Horace Wilson, (Most Secret) *King Edward VIII – Notes by Sir Horace Wilson, at 10 Downing Street* (1936/7), National Archives, PREM 1/466.

4 Sir Humphrey Wakefield to author, Sotheby's, London, 28 April 2009.

5 Winston Churchill, *The Abdication of Edward VIII – December 1936 –* Martin Gilbert (ed), *Winston S. Churchill – Companion Volume V – Part 3 – The Coming War 1936–1939* (Heinemann, 1982), pp. 450–1.

6 Hugo Vickers (ed.), *The Unexpurgated Beaton* (Weidenfeld & Nicolson, 2002), p. 256.

7 Hugo Vickers (ed.), *The Unexpurgated Beaton* (Weidenfeld & Nicolson, 2002), p. 257.

8 William Wright, *Heiress* (Pocket Books, NY, 1979), p. 234.

9 Johanna Schütz to author, London, 8 July 2010.

10 *Baltimore News*, 16 November 1896.

11 Clarence W. Miles, *Eight Busy Decades* (White Banks, Queenstown, Maryland, USA, 1986), p. 113.

12 Alastair Forbes, *Times Literary Supplement*, 1 November 1974, quoted in Frances Donaldson, *A Twentieth Century Life* (Weidenfeld & Nicolson, 1992), p. 207.

13 Scott Watkins to author, 25 July 2010.

14 Cleveland Amory, *Who Killed Society?* (Harper & Brothers, New York, 1960), p. 235.

15 H.M. Warfield obituary.

16 Warfield, Solomon Davies clipping of October 1927 obituary in the Dielman–Hayward file, source & publication unknown [Maryland Historical Society].

17 Information from J. D. Warfield, *The Founders of Anne Arundel and Howard Counties, Maryland* (Heritage Books, USA, 2008), *passim.*

18 Cleveland Amory, *Who Killed Society?* (Harper & Brothers, New York, 1960), p. 235.

19 Doug St Denis to author, 29 June 2010.

20 Press cutting in Corinne Mustin's album [courtesy of Doug St Denis].

21 Doug St Denis to author, 29 June 2010.

22 Frances Donaldson, *A Twentieth Century Life* (Weidenfeld & Nicolson, 1992), p. 208.

23 Frances Donaldson, *A Twentieth Century Life* (Weidenfeld & Nicolson, 1992), p. 208.

24 Cleveland Amory, *The Best Cat Ever* (Little, Brown & Co, New York, 1993), pp. 131–2.

25 Cleveland Amory, *The Best Cat Ever* (Little, Brown & Co, New York, 1993), p. 132.

26 Cleveland Amory, *Who Killed Society?* (Harper & Brothers, New York, 1960), p. 235.

27 Frances Donaldson, *A Twentieth Century Life* (Weidenfeld & Nicolson, 1992), p. 206.

28 The Duchess of Windsor, *The Heart Has Its Reasons* (Michael Joseph, 1956), p. 21.

29 Upton Sinclair article in Corinne Mustin's album [courtesy of Doug St Denis].

30 Baltimore press cutting, January 1908 in Corinne Mustin's album [courtesy of Doug St Denis].

31 Gladys, Duchess of Marlborough to author, Northampton, 21 May 1976.

32 Mrs Bessie Merryman to Mrs R. Sanchez Boone, Candé 4 June 1937 [MS 2356, Ada O'Brien Papers – Maryland Historical Society].

33 The Duchess of Windsor to Mrs R. Sanchez Boone, Bahamas, 23 February 1941 [MS 2356, Ada O'Brien Papers – Maryland Historical Society].

34 Cordelia Biddle Robertson to Cecil Beaton, recorded in Cecil Beaton's unpublished diary, 1955 [St John's College Cambridge].

35 The Duchess of Windsor, *The Heart Has Its Reasons* (Michael Joseph, 1956), p. 53.

36 The Duchess of Windsor, *The Heart Has Its Reasons* (Michael Joseph, 1956), p. 58.

37 *Baltimore Sun*, 11 May 2005.

38 The Duchess of Windsor to Mrs R. Sanchez Boone, Bahamas, 23 February 1941 [MS 2356, Ada O'Brien Papers – Maryland Historical Society].

39 The Duchess of Windsor to Eleanor Miles, Moulin, 16 February 1962

[MS 1772, Wallis Warfield Windsor Collection. Maryland Historical Society].

40 Kenneth Harris Interview with the Duke and Duchess of Windsor, BBC television, January 1970.

41 The Duchess of Windsor to Eleanor Miles, Moulin, 17 May 1959 [MS 1772, Wallis Warfield Windsor Collection. Maryland Historical Society].

Sources for Part 2 – Chapter 2

1 Cleveland Amory, *The Best Cat Ever* (Little, Brown & Co, New York, 1993), p. 132.

2 The Duchess of Windsor, *The Heart Has Its Reasons* (Michael Joseph, 1956), p. 59.

3 Register of Christ Church, Baltimore.

4 Press cutting in possession of Doug St Denis, Coronado.

5 Cleveland Amory, *The Best Cat Ever* (Little, Brown & Co, New York, 1993), p. 132.

6 Doug St Denis to author, 26 July 2010.

7 Philip Ziegler, *Mountbatten* (Collins, 1985), p. 54.

8 Charles J.V. Murphy & Joseph Bryan III, *The Windsor Story* (Granada, 1979), p. 67.

9 Benjamin Sacks, Ph. D, *The Duchess of Windsor and The Coronado Legend, Part II* (Journal of San Diego History, Winter 1988, Volume 34, Number 1) (reprint), p. 1.

10 Rupert Godfrey (ed.), *Letters from a Prince* (Little, Brown & Co, 1988), p. 269 (letter of 8 April 1920).

11 The Duchess of Windsor, *The Heart Has Its Reasons* (Michael Joseph, 1956), p. 86.

12 Cleveland Amory, *The Best Cat Ever* (Little, Brown & Co, New York, 1993), pp. 133–4.

13 The Duchess of Windsor, *The Heart Has Its Reasons* (Michael Joseph, 1956), p. 91.

14 The Duchess of Windsor, *The Heart Has Its Reasons* (Michael Joseph, 1956), p. 91.

15 Cleveland Amory, *Who Killed Society?* (Harper & Brothers, New York, 1960), p. 237.

16 The Duchess of Windsor, *The Heart Has Its Reasons* (Michael Joseph, 1956), p. 114.

17 C.L. Sulzberger, *A Long Row of Candles* (Macmillan, New York, 1969). p. 673.

18 The Duchess of Windsor, *The Heart Has Its Reasons* (Michael Joseph, 1956), p. 121.

19 *The Sunday Oregonian*, 16 January 1938.

20 *Time* magazine, 5 August 1940.

Source Notes for Part 2 — Chapter 3

1 Derived from a letter from Ernest Simpson to the Duchess of Windsor, early 1950s, which I saw before it was sold.

2 Cleveland Amory, *The Best Cat Ever* (Little, Brown & Co, New York, 1993), p. 136.

3 Cleveland Amory, *Who Killed Society?* (Harper & Brothers, New York, 1960), p. 238.

4 Cleveland Amory, *The Best Cat Ever* (Little, Brown & Co, New York, 1993), p. 135.

5 Cleveland Amory, *The Best Cat Ever* (Little, Brown & Co, New York, 1993), p. 135.

6 Kenneth Rose to author, 25 June 2010.

7 The Duchess of Windsor, *The Heart Has Its Reasons* (Michael Joseph, 1956), p. 125.

8 Cleveland Amory, *The Best Cat Ever* (Little, Brown & Co, New York, 1993), p. 136.

9 The Duchess of Windsor, *The Heart Has Its Reasons* (Michael Joseph, 1956), p. 136.

10 Brochure of the Anna Emory Warfield Memorial Fund, Inc.

11 The Duchess of Windsor, *The Heart Has Its Reasons* (Michael Joseph, 1956), p. 138.

12 The Duchess of Windsor, *The Heart Has Its Reasons* (Michael Joseph, 1956), p. 139.

13 Philip Ziegler, *King Edward VIII* (Collins 1990), p. 224.

14 Cecil Beaton's unpublished diary, ca. 20 November 1936 in Hugo Vickers, *Cecil Beaton* (Weidenfeld & Nicolson, 1985), p. 193.

15 Frances Donaldson, *A Twentieth-Century Life* (Weidenfeld & Nicolson, 1992), p. 208.

16 Frances Donaldson, *A Twentieth-Century Life* (Weidenfeld & Nicolson, 1992), p. 209.

17 The Duchess of Windsor, *The Heart Has Its Reasons* (Michael Joseph, 1956), p. 172.

Source Notes for Part 2 – Chapter 4

1 The Prince of Wales to Freda Dudley Ward, 20 January 1919 [Rupert Godfrey (ed.), *Letters from a Prince* (Little, Brown & Co, 1998), p. 129].

2 Charles J. V. Murphy & Joseph Bryan III, *The Windsor Story* (Granada, 1979), p. xvii.

3 HRH The Duke of Windsor, *A King's Story* (Cassell, 1951), p. 109.

4 Lady Diana Cooper to author, London, ca. 1983.

5 Philip Ziegler, *King Edward VIII* (Collins, 1990), p. 94.

6 Rupert Godfrey (ed), *Letters from a Prince* (Little, Brown & Co, 1998), p. 169.

7 Rupert Godfrey (ed), *Letters from a Prince* (Little, Brown & Co, 1998), p. 245 (letter of 14 January 1920).

8 Sir Charles Johnston unpublished diary, ca. 4 July 1958.

9 Wade Chance, *The Truth About the Duke of Windsor* (CBC broadcast, October 1937).

10 Rupert Godfrey (ed.), *Letters from a Prince* (Little, Brown & Co, 1998), p. 148 (letter of 31 May 1919).

11 Rupert Godfrey (ed.), *Letters from a Prince* (Little, Brown & Co, 1998), p. 160 (letter of 15 July 1919).

12 Rupert Godfrey (ed.), *Letters from a Prince* (Little, Brown & Co, 1998), p. 174 (letter of 18 August 1919).

13 Rupert Godfrey (ed.), *Letters from a Prince* (Little, Brown & Co, 1998), p. 189 (letter of 8 September 1919).

14 Rupert Godfrey (ed.), *Letters from a Prince* (Little, Brown & Co, 1998), p. 208 (letter of 12 October 1919).

15 Rupert Godfrey (ed), *Letters from a Prince* (Little, Brown & Co, 1998), p. 215 (letter of 24 October 1919).

16 Rupert Godfrey (ed.), *Letters from a Prince* (Little, Brown & Co, 1998), p. 260 (letter of 24 March 1920).

17 Rupert Godfrey (ed.), *Letters from a Prince* (Little, Brown & Co, 1998), p. 261 (letter of 26 March 1920).

18 Unpublished extract from The Prince of Wales to Freda Dudley Ward, 8 May 1920.

19 The Prince of Wales to Major Edward Metcalfe, Balmoral Castle, 15 September 1922. (David Metcalfe papers].

20 Diary of Sir Alan Lascelles, 29 November 1920, quoted in Philip Ziegler, *King Edward VIII* (Collins, 1920), p. 163.

21 Sir Alan Lascelles document for James Pope-Hennessy, *E. P. – period 1920 to 1936 only* [Pope-Hennessy Papers, Getty Museum, Los Angeles].

22 Winston Churchill, *The Abdication of Edward VIII* – December 1936 – Martin Gilbert (ed.), *Winston S. Churchill – Companion Volume V – Part 3 – The Coming War 1936–1939* (Heinemann, 1982), p. 451.

23 Philip Ziegler, *King Edward VIII* (Collins, 1990), p. 172.

24 Philip Ziegler, *King Edward VIII* (Collins, 1990), p. 200.

25 Freda Dudley Ward (Marchesa de Casa Maury) to author, London, 8 February 1980.

26 Mary, Duchess of Buccleuch to Alvilde Lees-Milne, 12 January 1985 [GEN MSS 476: James Lees-Milne Papers. General Collection, Beinecke Rare Book and Manuscript Library, Yale University].

27 Derived from Mary, Duchess of Buccleuch to Alan Pryce-Jones, 9 December 1961 [GEN 513: Alan Pryce-Jones Papers. General Collection, Beinecke Rare Book and Manuscript Library, Yale University].

28 Helen, Lady Dashwood to author, 25 March 1984.

29 Gloria Vanderbilt and Thelma Lady Furness, *Double Exposure* (Frederick Muller, 1959), p. 275.

30 The Duchess of Windsor, *The Heart Has Its Reasons* (Michael Joseph, 1956), p. 175.

31 Gloria Vanderbilt and Thelma Lady Furness, *Double Exposure* (Frederick Muller, 1959), p. 275.

32 Gloria Vanderbilt and Thelma Lady Furness, *Double Exposure* (Frederick Muller, 1959), p. 291.

33 Gladys, Duchess of Marlborough to author, Northampton, 21 May 1976.

34 Wallis to Aunt Bessie, The Fort, 12 February 1934 [Michael Bloch (ed.), *Wallis & Edward Letters 1931–1937* (Weidenfeld & Nicolson, 1986), p.87].

35 Wallis to Aunt Bessie, 18 February 1934 [Michael Bloch (ed.), *Wallis & Edward Letters 1931–1937)* (Weidenfeld & Nicolson, 1986), p.89].

36 Derived from Alastair Forbes's review of Michael Wishart, *High Diver* (Blond & Briggs, 1977) in *The Spectator*, 28 January 1978.

37 Gloria Vanderbilt and Thelma Lady Furness, *Double Exposure* (Frederick Muller, 1959), p. 298.

38 Wallis to Aunt Bessie, The Fort, 15 April 1934 [Michael Bloch (ed.), *Wallis & Edward Letters 1931–1937* (Weidenfeld & Nicolson, 1986), p. 92].

Source Notes for Part 2 – Chapter 5

1 Letter from Queen Mary to Sir Alexander Hardinge, 12 December 1936 [quoted in Hugo Vickers, review of Philip Ziegler's *King Edward VIII – The Times*, 29 September 1990].

2 Cleveland Amory, *The Best Cat Ever* (Little, Brown & Co, 1993), p. 137.

3 Queen Mary to The Duke of Windsor, 5 July 1938 [quoted in Philip Ziegler, p. 385].

4 Sir Horace Wilson, (Most Secret) *King Edward VIII – Notes by Sir Horace Wilson, at 10 Downing Street* (1936/7), National Archives, PREM 1/466; various pages [*passim*].

5 Sir Horace Wilson, (Most Secret) *King Edward VIII – Notes by Sir Horace Wilson, at 10 Downing Street* (1936/7), National Archives, PREM 1/466; various pages [*passim*].

6 Wade Chance, *The Truth About the Duke of Windsor* (CBC broadcast, October 1937).

7 The Duchess of Windsor, *The Heart Has Its Reasons* (Michael Joseph, 1956), p. 202.

8 Canon Alec Sargent, *King Edward's Abdication* (written 13 December 1936) (Lambeth Palace Library).

9 Wallis to Aunt Bessie, 30 December 1934 [Michael Bloch (ed.), *Wallis & Edward Letters* (Weidenfeld & Nicolson, 1986), p. 105].

10 Robert Rhodes James (ed.), *Chips – The Diaries of Sir Henry Channon* (Weidenfeld & Nicolson, 1967), p. 23 – entry for 23 January 1935.

11 Robert Rhodes James (ed.), *Chips – The Diaries of Sir Henry Channon* (Weidenfeld & Nicolson, 1967), p. 30 – entry for 5 April 1935.

12 Superintendent A. Canning (Special Branch) Air Vice Marshal Sir Philip Game, Commissioner, Metropolitan Police, 3 July 1935 [National Archives – MEPO 10/35].

13 Sir Horace Wilson, (Most Secret) *King Edward VIII – Notes by Sir Horace Wilson, at 10 Downing Street* (1936/7), National Archives, PREM 1/466; pp. 43–4.

14 Sir Horace Wilson, (Most Secret) *King Edward VIII – Notes by Sir Horace Wilson, at 10 Downing Street* (1936/7), National Archives, PREM 1/466; p. 44.

15 Sir Horace Wilson, (Most Secret) *King Edward VIII – Notes by Sir Horace Wilson, at 10 Downing Street* (1936/7), National Archives, PREM 1/466; p. 44.

16 Sir Horace Wilson, (Most Secret) *King Edward VIII –Notes by Sir Horace Wilson, at 10 Downing Street* (1936/7), National Archives, PREM 1/466; p. 45.

17 Rev. Alan Don diary, 20 January 1936 [Lambeth Palace Library].

18 Wallis to Aunt Bessie, 9 February 1936 [Michael Bloch (ed.), *Wallis & Edward Letters* (Weidenfeld & Nicolson, 1986), p. 159].

19 Wallis to Aunt Bessie, Hotel Meurice, Paris, 16 September 1936 [Michael Bloch (ed.), *Wallis & Edward Letters* (Weidenfeld & Nicolson, 1986), p. 194].

20 *Dictionary of National Biography 1971–1980*, profile by Robert Armstrong, p. 916.

21 Sir Alan Lascelles to James Pope-Hennessy, 18 January 1965 [Pope-Hennessy Papers, Getty Library, Los Angeles, USA).

22 Helen, Lady Hardinge of Penshurst diary, 5 June 1972.

23 Sir Horace Wilson, (Most Secret) *King Edward VIII – Notes by Sir Horace Wilson, at 10 Downing Street* (1936/7), National Archives, PREM 1/466; p. 1.

24 Sir Horace Wilson, (Most Secret) *King Edward VIII – Notes by Sir Horace Wilson, at 10 Downing Street* (1936/7), National Archives, PREM 1/466; p. 1.

25 Sir Horace Wilson, (Most Secret) *King Edward VIII – Notes by Sir Horace Wilson, at 10 Downing Street* (1936/7), National Archives, PREM 1/466; p. 9.

26 Sir Horace Wilson, (Most Secret) *King Edward VIII – Notes by Sir Horace Wilson, at 10 Downing Street* (1936/7), National Archives, PREM 1/466; p. 9.

27 Sir Horace Wilson, (Most Secret) *King Edward VIII – Notes by Sir Horace Wilson, at 10 Downing Street* (1936/7), National Archives, PREM 1/466; p. 10.

28 Ernest Simpson to Wallis Simpson, October 1936 [quoted in the national press].

29 Robert Rhodes James, *Victor Cazalet* (Hamish Hamilton, 1976), p. 186, entry for 19 Nov. 1936.

30 Rev. Alan Don diary, 4 November 1936 [Lambeth Palace Library].

31 Sir Horace Wilson, (Most Secret) *King Edward VIII – Notes by Sir Horace Wilson, at 10 Downing Street* (1936/7), National Archives, PREM 1/466; p. 13.

32 Sir Horace Wilson, (Most Secret) *King Edward VIII – Notes by Sir Horace Wilson, at 10 Downing Street* (1936/7), National Archives, PREM 1/466; p. 14.

33 Sir Horace Wilson, (Most Secret) *King Edward VIII – Notes by Sir Horace Wilson, at 10 Downing Street* (1936/7), National Archives, PREM 1/466; p. 17.

34 Sir Horace Wilson, (Most Secret) *King Edward VIII – Notes by Sir Horace Wilson, at 10 Downing Street* (1936/7), National Archives, PREM 1/466; p. 20. Check.

35 Canon Alec Sargent, *King Edward's Abdication* (written 13 December 1936) [Lambeth Palace Library].

36 Sir Horace Wilson, (Most Secret) *King Edward VIII – Notes by Sir Horace Wilson, at 10 Downing Street* (1936/7), National Archives, PREM 1/466; p. 30.

37 Winston Churchill to Stanley Baldwin, London, 5 December 1936 contained in Sir Horace Wilson, (Most Secret) *King Edward VIII – Notes by Sir Horace Wilson, at 10 Downing Street* (1936/7), National Archives, PREM 1/466; p. 31].

38 Sir John Colville diary, June 1953 – John Colville, *The Fringes of Power – Downing Street Diaries 1939–1955* (Hodder & Stoughton, 1985), p. 716.

39 Sir Horace Wilson, (Most Secret) *King Edward VIII – Notes by Sir Horace Wilson, at 10 Downing Street* (1936/7), National Archives, PREM 1/466.

40 Sir Horace Wilson, (Most Secret) *King Edward VIII – Notes by Sir Horace Wilson, at 10 Downing Street* (1936/7), National Archives, PREM 1/466; p. 32.

41 Sir Horace Wilson, (Most Secret) *King Edward VIII – Notes by Sir Horace Wilson, at 10 Downing Street* (1936/7), National Archives, PREM 1/466; p. 33.

42 Sir Horace Wilson, (Most Secret) *King Edward VIII – Notes by Sir Horace Wilson, at 10 Downing Street* (1936/7), National Archives, PREM 1/466; p. 35.

43 *The Times*, 8 December 1936.

44 Sir Horace Wilson, (Most Secret) *King Edward VIII – Notes by Sir Horace Wilson, at 10 Downing Street* (1936/7), National Archives, PREM 1/466; p. 38.

45 Sir Horace Wilson, (Most Secret) *King Edward VIII – Notes by Sir Horace Wilson, at 10 Downing Street* (1936/7), National Archives, PREM 1/466; p. 39.

46 Sir Horace Wilson, (Most Secret) *King Edward VIII – Notes by Sir Horace Wilson, at 10 Downing Street* (1936/7), National Archives, PREM 1/466; Appendix IV.

47 Sir Horace Wilson, (Most Secret) *King Edward VIII – Notes by Sir Horace Wilson, at 10 Downing Street* (1936/7), National Archives, PREM 1/466; p. 40.

48 Sir Horace Wilson, (Most Secret) *King Edward VIII – Notes by Sir Horace Wilson, at 10 Downing Street* (1936/7), National Archives, PREM 1/466; p. 42.

49 Lady Ottoline Morrell diary, December 1936 [British Library].

50 Cabinet minutes, 9 December 1936 [CAB 127 – 156–7 (446–60) – National Archives].

51 Rev. Alan Don diary, 10 December 1936 [Lambeth Palace Library].

52 Lord Brownlow to Leopold Amery (Barnes, John & Nicholson, David (eds.), *The Empire at Bay – The Leo Amery Diaries 1929–1945* – Hutchinson, 1988).

53 Rev. Alan Don diary, 11 December 1936 [Lambeth Palace Library].

Source Notes for Part 2 – Chapter 6

1 *Daily Herald*, 1937 [press cutting in author's collection].

2 Edith Wharton to Louis Bromfield, 17 December 1936 (Daniel Bratton (ed), *Yrs, Ever Affly* (Michigan University Press, 2000), p. 88.

3 Paul-Louis Weiller to author, South of France, 26 August 1983.

4 Sir Alan Lascelles to James Pope-Hennessy, notes entitled *E.P. – period 1920 to 1936 only* [Pope-Hennessy papers, Getty Library, Los Angeles].

5 Hugo Vickers unpublished diary, 29 January 1979.

6 James Pope-Hennessy, notes on *A King's Story* (film), 1964 [Pope-Hennessy papers, Getty Library, Los Angeles].

7 The Earl of Harewood, *The Tongs and the Bones* (Weidenfeld & Nicolson, 1981), p. 117.

8 Henry Gillespie to author, 16 December 2009.

9 Captain Andrew Yates to author, ca 1979.

10 Gloria Vanderbilt and Thelma Lady Furness, *Double Exposure* (Frederick Muller, 1959), p. 328.

11 Robert Rhodes James (ed.) *Chips – The Diaries of Sir Henry Channon* (Weidenfeld & Nicolson, 1967), p. 51 – note entitled *Mrs Simpson (the Duchess of Windsor)* 1936.

12 Robert Rhodes James (ed.) *Chips – The Diaries of Sir Henry Channon* (Weidenfeld & Nicolson, 1967), p. 51 – note entitled *Mrs Simpson (the Duchess of Windsor)* 1936.

13 Kenneth Young (ed.), *The Diaries of Sir Robert Bruce-Lockhart* (Macmillan, 1973), p. 361.

14 Hugo Vickers unpublished diary, 2 June 1982.

15 Robert Rhodes James, *Victor Cazalet* (Hamish Hamilton, 1976), p. 189 – entry for 7 January 1937.

16 Robert Rhodes James, *Victor Cazalet* (Hamish Hamilton, 1976), p. 189 – entry for 7 January 1937.

17 Kenneth Young (ed.), *The Diaries of Sir Robert Bruce-Lockhart* (Macmillan, 1973), p. 372.

18 Rev. Alan Don diary, 5 April 1937 [Lambeth Palace Library].

19 Rev. Alan Don diary, 5 April 1937 [Lambeth Palace Library].

20 Elsa Maxwell, syndicated article, republished in the *Sunday Express*, 1937 [cutting in author's album].

21 Cecil Beaton diary, 20 November 1936 [Hugo Vickers, *Cecil Beaton* (Weidenfeld & Nicolson, 1985), p. 194].

22 Wallis Simpson to Cecil Beaton, 19 February 1937 [Beaton papers, St John's College, Cambridge].

23 Cecil Beaton diary, spring 1937 [Hugo Vickers, *Cecil Beaton* (Weidenfeld & Nicolson, 1985), p. 197].

24 Cecil Beaton diary, spring 1937 [Hugo Vickers, *Cecil Beaton* (Weidenfeld & Nicolson, 1985), p. 198].

25 Diana Vreeland to author, London, 21 June 1980.

26 Michael Bloch (ed.), *Wallis & Edward Letters 1931–1937* (Weidenfeld & Nicolson, 1986), p. 263.

27 Frances Donaldson, *A Twentieth Century Life* (Weidenfled & Nicolson, 1992), p. 212.

28 Geoffrey Wolff, *Black Sun* (Random House, New York, 1976), p. 214.

29 Constance Atherton to 'Crownie' [her cousin, Edward Crowninshield], Paris, 28 May 1937 [MS 1772, Wallis Warfield Windsor Collection, unsigned typescript. Maryland Historical Society].

30 Letter to David Coolidge, quoted in Andrea Lynn, *Shadow Lovers – The Last Affairs of H.G. Wells* (the Perseus Press, NY, 2001), p. 311.

31 Constance Coolidge (anonymously) to Helen Worden, *Liberty Magazine*, 10 April 1937.

32 Andrea Lynn, *Shadow Lovers – The Last Affairs of H.G. Wells* (the Perseus Press, NY, 2001), p. 321.

33 Rev. Alan Don diary, 2 June 1937 [Lambeth Palace Library].

34 Rev. Alan Don diary, 2 June 1937 [Lambeth Palace Library].

35 Rev. Alan Don diary, 2 June 1937 [Lambeth Palace Library].

36 HRH The Duke of Windsor to Major Edward Metcalfe, 17 May 1937 [David Metcalfe papers].

37 Lady Alexandra Metcalfe's diary, 2–3 June 1937 [David Metcalfe papers].

38 Cecil Beaton diary, 2 June 1937 [Hugo Vickers, *Cecil Beaton* (Weidenfeld & Nicolson, 1985), p. 199].

39 Frances Donaldson to author, 1973.

40 Lady Alexandra Metcalfe's diary, 2–3 June 1937 [David Metcalfe papers].

41 10th Duke of Argyll to Rev. Bartholomew Hack, 5 June 1937 [Letter in possession of the author].

42 10th Duke of Argyll to Rev. Bartholomew Hack, 13 June 1937 [Letter in possession of the author].

43 The Duchess of Windsor to Mrs George Barnett, 10 July 1937.

44 Hon. Sir Alexander Hardinge to Sir Robert Vansittart, Permanent Under-Secretary for Foreign Affairs, Balmoral, 2 September 1937 [PREM 11/5219 – National Archives].

45 Paul-Louis Weiller to author, South of France, 26 August 1983.

46 *Daily Herald*, ca. October 1937 [cutting in author's album].

47 Ambassador William Bullitt to President Roosevelt, Paris, 4 November 1937 [Franklin D. Roosevelt Library, Hyde Park, New York].

48 Ambassador William Bullitt to President Roosevelt, Paris, 4 November 1937 [Franklin D. Roosevelt Library, Hyde Park, New York].

49 Lilli Palmer, *Change Lobsters and Dance* (Macmillan, 1975), p. 207.

50 Cecil Beaton diary, on voyage to New York, November 1950 [Cecil Beaton papers, St John's College, Cambridge].

51 Hugo Vickers unpublished diary, 27 September 1981.

52 James Pope-Hennessy, draft obituary of the Duke of Windsor, *The King Who Could Not Be* [Pope-Hennessy papers, Getty Library, Los Angeles].

Source Notes for Part 2 – Chapter 7

1 HRH The Duke of Windsor to Sir George Arthur, 12 May 1938.

2 Diary of Lady Alexandra Metcalfe, September 1939 [David Metcalfe papers].

3 Diary of Lady Alexandra Metcalfe, September 1939 [David Metcalfe papers].

4 The Duchess of Windsor to Lady Alexandra Metcalfe, 30 November 1939 [David Metcalfe papers].

5 Winston Churchill to the Duke of Windsor, 17 November 1939 [CHAR 19/2A/84–86 – Churchill papers, Churchill Archive Centre, Cambridge].

6 Winston Churchill to the Duke of Windsor, 1 July 1940 [Foreign Office telegram, FO 458 – CHAR 20/9A/11–12 – Churchill papers, Churchill Archive Centre, Cambridge].

7 HRH The Duke of Windsor to Winston Churchill, July 1940 [CHAR 20/9A/11–12 – Churchill papers, Churchill Archive Centre, Cambridge].

8 The Duchess of Windsor to Lady Alexandra Metcalfe, 31 January [1942] [David Metcalfe papers].

9 Jean D. Hardcastle-Taylor (formerly Drewes), *The Windsors I Knew* (unpublished account of her years with the Duke and Duchess of Windsor in the Bahamas) [courtesy of Michael and Gloria Hardcastle-Taylor, & © The Heirs of Jean D. Hardcastle-Taylor, 2010].

10 HRH Princess Alice, Countess of Athlone, *For My Grandchildren* (Evans, 1966), p. 271.

11 Helen Worden, *The Duchess of Windsor* (*The American Mercury*, 4 June 1944), p. 675.

12 Jean D. Hardcastle-Taylor (formerly Drewes), *The Windsors I Knew* (unpublished account of her years with the Duke and Duchess of Windsor in the Bahamas) [courtesy of Michael and Gloria Hardcastle-Taylor, & © The Heirs of Jean D. Hardcastle-Taylor, 2010].

13 The Duchess of Windsor to Edith Lindsay, 19 January 1942 [MS 1772, Wallis Warfield Windsor Collection. Maryland Historical Society].

14 The Duchess of Windsor to Edith Lindsay, 18 September 1942 [MS 1772, Wallis Warfield Windsor Collection. Maryland Historical Society].

15 The Duchess of Windsor to Edith Lindsay, 17 October 1942 [MS 1772, Wallis Warfield Windsor Collection. Maryland Historical Society].

16 The Duchess of Windsor to Corinne Murray, 13 April 1942 [courtesy of Doug St Denis].

17 Dom Odo report in Memorandum to Mr Ladd from L.L. Laughlin, 29 September 1941.

18 The Duchess of Windsor, *The Heart Has Its Reasons* (Michael Joseph, 1956), p. 356.

19 Queen Mary to the Duke of Windsor, 31 August 1942 [slightly mis-quoted in Philip Ziegler, *King Edward VIII* (Collins, 1990), p. 484].

20 The Duke of Windsor to Queen Mary, 12 September 1942 [quoted in Philip Ziegler, *King Edward VIII* (Collins, 1990), p. 485].

21 The Duchess of Windsor to Edith Lindsay, 23 July 1943 [MS 1772, Wallis Warfield Windsor Collection. Maryland Historical Society].

22 Major Gray Phillips to Eleanor Lindsay, 3 September 1943 [MS 1772, Wallis Warfield Windsor Collection. Maryland Historical Society].

23 Philip Ziegler, *King Edward VIII* (Collins, 1990), p. 451.

24 The Duchess of Windsor to Edith Lindsay, 23 April 1943 [MS 1772, Wallis Warfield Windsor Collection. Maryland Historical Society].

25 Sir Alan Lascelles to John Martin (Churchill's Private Secretary), Buckingham Palace, 30 May 1944 [Churchill Archives Centre, Churchill Papers, CHAR 20/148/37-9].

26 Lilli Palmer, *Change Lobsters and Dance* (Macmillan, 1975), p. 207.

27 Sir Alan Lascelles diary, 9 October 1945 [quoted in Duff Hart-Davis (ed.), *King's Counsellor* (Phoenix paperback, 2007), p. 359.

28 Recalled in a letter from the Duke of Windsor to the Countess of Dudley, 26 April 1949 [in the possession of the author].

29 J. R. Capstick to the Superintendent, Metropolitan Police, 6 December 1946 [National Archives – MEPO 2/9149].

30 Cecil Beaton to his mother, [undated, but 1948] [Cecil Beaton papers, St John's College, Cambridge].

31 The Duchess of Windsor to Ambassador and Mrs Henry J. Taylor, 2

January 1950 [Herbert Hoover Presidential Library, West Branch, IA, USA].

32 The Duchess of Windsor to Mona Harrison Williams, later Countess Bismarck, 17 January 1950 [Mona S. Bismarck papers, The Filson Historical Society, Louisville, KY, USA].

33 Rt. Rev. Spence Burton, Bishop of Nassau, to the Duke of Windsor, 29 August 1950 (copy) [Lambeth Palace Library].

34 Derived from Rev. E.G.T., Chaplain to the Archibishop of Canterbury, to the Bishop of Nassau, 16 July 1953 [Lambeth Place Library].

35 Cecil Beaton's diary, voyage to New York, November 1950 [Cecil Beaton papers, St John's College, Cambridge].

36 Sir John Balfour, *Encounters with the Duke and Duchess of Windsor* (unpublished notes, June 1972) (Prince Paul Arranged Correspondence, Balfour, J.) – [Columbia Rare Book and Manuscript Library, New York].

37 C.L. Sulzberger, *A Long Row of Candles* (Macmillan, New York, 1969), p. 673.

Source Notes for Part 2 – Chapter 8

1 Queen Mary to Queen Elizabeth, 10 February 1952 – quoted in William Shawcross, *Queen Elizabeth The Queen Mother – The Official Biography*. (Macmillan, 2009), p. 660.

2 Queen Mary to the Earl and Countess of Athlone, 23 February 1952 – quoted in William Shawcross, *Queen Elizabeth The Queen Mother – The Official Biography* (Macmillan, 2009), p. 660.

3 Draft speech by the Duke of Windsor, 3 January 1947.

4 *New York Times*, (Heart Association Opens Fund Drive), 29 November 1962.

5 Elisabeth Kruch to author, 27 August 2010.

6 Cabinet minutes, 20 November 1952 [CAB 128/40 – National Archives].

7 Rt. Hon. Anthony Eden to Rt. Hon. Winston Churchill, 14 October 1952 [PM 52/123 – National Archives].

8 Rt. Hon. Winston Churchill to Rt. Hon. Anthony Eden, 15 October 1952 [PM 504/52 – National Archives].

9 Sir Charles Johnston Diary, 25 October 1953.

10 Sir Charles Johnston Diary, 14 July 1954.

11 Philip Ziegler, *King Edward VIII* (Collins, 1990), p. 521.

12 Lady Diana Cooper to author, 27 September 1981.

13 Cordelia Biddle Robertson to Cecil Beaton, recorded in Cecil Beaton's unpublished diary, 1955 [St John's College, Cambridge].

14 Review in the *Manchester Guardian* (1956) – on cover of The Duchess of Windsor, *The Heart Has Its Reasons* (Michael Joseph, 1956).

15 Martin Gilbert, *Never Despair* (Heinemann, 1988), p. 979.

16 The Duke of Windsor to Sir Winston Churchill, 17 November 1954 [CHUR2/202 A-C – Churchill papers, Churchill Archive Centre, Cambridge].

17 James Pope-Hennessy to John Pope-Hennessy, 20 October 1956 [Pope-Hennessy papers, Getty Library, Los Angeles].

18 Notes of a conversation with Sir Alan Lascelles, by James Pope-Hennessy, 25 July 1957 [Pope-Hennessy papers, Getty Library, Los Angeles].

19 The Duke of Windsor to the Earl of Home, [undated but December 1962/January 1963] [copy found in Duke of Windsor's house, 1994].

20 The Duke of Windsor to the Earl of Home, [undated but December 1962/January 1963] [copy found in Duke of Windsor's house, 1994].

21 Philip Ziegler, *King Edward VIII* (Collins, 1990), p. 555.

22 The Duke of Windsor to Dr D. Anderson, Neutral Bay, Sydney House, 23 June 1954 [copy in possession of the author].

23 Blurb for Iles Brody, *Gone with the Windsors* (The John C. Winston Company, NY, 1953).

24 Reported in a letter, Constance Coolidge to Caresse Crosby, 1954 – quoted in Andrea Lynn, *Shadow Lovers – The Last Affairs of H.G. Wells* (the Perseus Press, NY, 2001), p. 322.

25 Constance Coolidge to Caresse Crosby, 1954 – quoted in Andrea Lynn, *Shadow Lovers – The Last Affairs of H.G. Wells* (the Perseus Press, NY, 2001), p. 322.

26 *The Times*, 1 December 1958.

27 James Pope-Hennessy, unpublished notes on the Windsors, December 1958 [Pope-Hennessy papers, Getty Library, Los Angeles].

28 James Pope-Hennessy to John Pope-Hennessy, the Moulin, Gif-sur-Yvette, France, 28 December [? November] 1958 [Pope-Hennessy papers, Getty Library, Los Angeles].

29 James Pope-Hennessy to John Pope-Hennessy, the Moulin, Gif-sur-Yvette, France, 26 November 1958 [Pope-Hennessy Papers, Getty Library, Los Angeles].

30 James Pope-Hennessy to John Pope-Hennessy, 26 November 1958 [Pope-Hennessy papers, Getty Library, Los Angeles].

31 The Duke of Windsor to James Pope-Hennessy, 5 February 1959 [Pope-Hennessy papers, Getty Library, Los Angeles].

32 James Pope-Hennessy to John Pope-Hennessy, 23 April 1959 [Pope-Hennessy papers, Getty Library, Los Angeles].

33 James Pope-Hennessy to the Duke of Windsor, 5 May 1959 [Pope-Hennessy papers, Getty Library, Los Angeles].

Source Notes for Part 2 – Chapter 9

1 Rex S. Wighton to Hon. Stephen Tennant, Palm Beach, 2 May 1961 [Stephen Tennant papers, in possession of the author].

2 The Duchess of Windsor to Lady Alexandra Metcalfe, 11 July 1962 [David Metcalfe papers].

3 James Pope-Hennessy, notes on *A King's Story* (film), 1964 [Pope-Hennessy papers, Getty Library, Los Angeles].

4 Viscountess Davidson to James Pope-Hennessy, 21 June 1964 [Pope-Hennessy papers, Getty Library, Los Angeles].

5 Sir Alan Lascelles to James Pope-Hennessy, 23 January 1965 [Pope-Hennessy papers, Getty Library, Los Angeles].

6 *New York Times*, 20 August 1964.

7 Audrey Russell, *A Certain Voice* (Ross Anderson, 1984), p. 138.

8 The Duchess of Windsor to Edith Lindsay, Paris, 19 April 1965 [MS 1772, Wallis Warfield Windsor Collection. Maryland Historical Society].

9 Sir Edward Ford to Dugald Malcolm, 6 August 1965 [National Archives – FO 372/8010].

10 Sir Godfrey Morley to Earl Cairns, 11 November 1965 [National Archives – FO 372/8010].

11 A.L. Mayall to Sir Godfrey Morley, 22 November 1965. [National Archives – FO 372/8010].

12 Sir Pat Dean to Lees Mayall, 29 November 1965. [National Archives – FO 372/8010].

13 Sir Dugald Malcolm to R.A. Beaumont, Consul in Rabat, Morocco, 12 March 1965 [National Archives – FO 372/8010].

14 Sir John Pilcher, British Embassy, Vienna to H. A. F. Hohler, Foreign Office, 25 November 1966 [National Archives – FO 372/8166].

15 Sir John Pilcher, British Embassy, Vienna to H. A. F. Hohler, Foreign Office, 25 November 1966 [National Archives – FO 372/8166].

16 Sir John Pilcher, British Embassy, Vienna to H. A. F. Hohler, Foreign Office, 25 November 1966 [National Archives – FO 372/8166].

17 Note by Miss Westwood, 2 December 1966 [National Archives – FO 372/8166].

18 Sir Michael Hawkins to author, 5 Febuary 1973.

19 Philip M. Thomas, *The Duchess of Windsor – Her Position Reappraised* (*Burke's Peerage*, 1967), p. xxi.

20 Philip M. Thomas, *The Duchess of Windsor – Her Position Reappraised* (*Burke's Peerage*, 1967), p. xxi.

21 Philip M. Thomas, *The Duchess of Windsor – Her Position Reappraised* (*Burke's Peerage*, 1967), p. xxii.

22 Sir Godfrey Agnew to Sir Michael Adeane, 1 September 1967 [National Archives – PC 21/5].

23 Sir Michael Adeane to Sir Godfrey Agnew, Balmoral, 2 September 1967 [National Archives – PC 21/5].

24 The Duchess of Windsor to Eleanor Miles, Paris, 31 August 1968 [MS 2012, Mrs Clarence Miles (Eleanor Addison Williams Lanahan) Miles Collection. Maryland Historical Society].

25 The Duchess of Windsor to Diana Vreeland, Paris, 4 January 1969 [Diana Vreeland Papers, Manuscript and Archives Division. The New York Public Library, Box 19, folder 21–15] [copy in author's possession].

26 Dwight Chapin to Rose Mary Woods, 6 January 1970 [Richard Nixon Library, Yorba Linda, California – President's Personal File].

27 H.R. Haldeman to Connie Stuart, 2 March 1970 [Richard Nixon Library, Yorba Linda, California – President's Personal File].

28 Rose Mary Woods to Lucy Winchester 10 March 1970 [Richard Nixon Library, Yorba Linda, California – President's Personal File].

29 Sir Edward Ford to author.

30 Lady Penn to author, 2009.

31 Dame Frances Campbell-Preston to author, 2006.

32 Lady Jean Rankin to author, 1984.

33 Jonathan Dimbleby, *The Prince of Wales* (Little, Brown, 1994), p. 179.

34 Mrs Joanne Cummings to author, Carlyle Hotel, New York, 26 February 1990.

35 Hon. Lady Mosley to author, 18 September 1979.

36 Princesse Ghislaine de Polignac to author, South of France, August 1992; & Paris, 22 May 1997.

37 Sir Alec Guinness to author, London, 18 March 1986.

38 Hugo Vickers unpublished diary, Geneva, 2 April 1987.

39 The Duchess of Windsor to Diana Vreeland, Paris, 10 September 1967 [Diana Vreeland Papers, Manuscripts and Archives Division, The New York Public Library – Box 19, Folders 21–15] [copy in author's possession].

40 The Duchess of Windsor to Diana Vreeland, Paris, 17 February 1968 [Diana Vreeland Papers, Manuscripts and Archives Division, The New York Public Library – Box 19, Folders 21–15] [copy in author's possession].

41 The Duchess of Windsor to Diana Vreeland, Paris, 18 November 1967 [Diana Vreeland Papers, Manuscripts and Archives Division, The New York Public Library – Box 19, Folders 21–15] [copy in author's possession].

42 The Duchess of Windsor to Diana Vreeland, Paris, 10 November 1968 [Diana Vreeland Papers, Manuscripts and Archives Division, The New York Public Library – Box 19, Folders 21–15] [copy in author's possession].

43 The Duchess of Windsor to Diana Vreeland, Paris, 24 November 1968 [Diana Vreeland Papers, Manuscripts and Archives Division, The New York Public Library – Box 19, Folders 21–15] [copy in author's possession].

44 The Duchess of Windsor to Countess Bismarck, 29 November 1968 [Mona S. Bismarck papers, The Filson Historical Society, Louisville, KY, USA].

45 The Duchess of Windsor to Diana Vreeland, Paris, 24 November 1968 [Diana Vreeland Papers, Manuscripts and Archives Division, The New York Public Library – Box 19, Folders 21–15] [copy in author's possession].

46 The Lady Soames to author, London, 28 June 2010.

47 The Duchess of Windsor to Diana Vreeland, Paris, 4 January 1969 [Diana Vreeland Papers, Manuscripts and Archives Division, The New York Public Library – Box 19, Folders 21–15] [copy in author's possession].

48 Richard Burton's diary, 3 December 1971 [quoted in Melvyn Bragg, *Rich* (Hodder & Stoughton, 1988), pp. 390–1.

49 Richard Burton's diary, 7 December 1971 [quoted in Melvyn Bragg, *Rich* (Hodder & Stoughton, 1988), p. 393.
50 The Duchess of Windsor to Diana Vreeland, Paris, 27 August 1971 [Diana Vreeland Papers, Manuscripts and Archives Division, The New York Public Library – Box 19, Folders 21–15] [copy in author's possession].

Source Notes for Appendix 2 – The Montagues

1 George William Montague, *History and Genealogy of Peter Montague* (Carpenter & Morehouse, Amherst, Mass, USA, 1894), p. 31.
2 George William Montague, *History and Genealogy of Peter Montague* (Carpenter & Morehouse, Amherst, Mass, USA, 1894), p. 32.
3 *Dictionary of National Biography*, Volume XIII (1921–22), pp. 713–7.

Acknowledgements

I owe an enormous debt of gratitude to a great number of people who have made this book possible.

Above all, I would like to thank Johanna Schütz, the Duchess of Windsor's secretary from 1970 to 1978. I first met her in 1972 and many years later she said to me: 'You must write this book and I will help you.' I visited her several times in Paris and Geneva. She came twice to London, and at the time of writing I note I have received 222 emails from her in connection with this book. She provided me with vital material and was forever ready to answer every kind of question and to help me with my research. This book would not have been possible without her help and her patience. She and Jean Pigois offered me considerable hospitality during this quest, and I am more grateful than I can say to both of them.

Acknowledging help for this book presents me with a problem, since many of the conversations about the Windsors were conducted long before I had any intention of writing it, but were fortunately recorded in my diary. I transcribed 65,000 words from that diary and was thus able to recreate the story as it unfolded. I called the file 'the bran tub' and dipped into those 65,000 words from time to time, taking out the best and discarding the rest.

Amongst those to whom I spoke during the last 40 years, I would particularly like to thank the late John E. Utter, Private Secretary to HRH The Duke of Windsor, who took me into his confidence in many conversations between 1972 and 1980. Also Lady Mosley, whom I met with John, for conversations spread between the years 1974 and 2000. I was lucky as a young man to be asked to assist Lady Donaldson with her research on her biography, *Edward VIII*. My great friend, the late Hugh Montgomery-Massingberd, first sent me out to Paris in 1972. I was able to talk often to those who knew the Duchess well: the Marchesa de Casa Maury (Freda Dudley Ward), Lady Diana Cooper, Mrs Joanne Cummings, Helen, Lady Dashwood Mrs Winston Guest, Sir Alec Guinness, Sir Nicholas Henderson, Major Walter Lees, Jack Le Vien, Gladys, Duchess of Marlborough, Laura, Duchess of Marlborough, Lady Alexandra Metcalfe, Mrs Aileen Plunket, Princesse Ghislaine de Polignac,

Baron de Redé, Lady Tomkins, Diana Vreeland, and Commandant Paul-Louis Weiller (who arranged the memorable 1986 visit to the Windsor house).

Christiane Sherwen was a superb editor when I wrote *The Private World of the Duke and Duchess of Windsor*, published by Mr Mohamed Fayed. At that time I was able to talk to Gregorio Martin and Maria Costa, Sydney Johnson and others at the house, as well as Joe Friedman who was overseeing the restoration.

Over the years I also talked to Lady Caroline Blackwood, Sir John & Lady Fretwell, Alastair Forbes (who gave me important documents and the best jokes in this book), Kenneth Harris, Stuart Preston and Audrey Russell.

Amongst relations of the Duchess: Mrs Doug St Denis (granddaughter of Corinne Mustin) & her husband, Dale St Denis, Doug's brother, Tom Mustin, Scott Watkins (a member of the Warfield family), & Mary Groff (a relation of Anita Lewis).

I would like to offer special thanks to Mark Gaulding, hon Secretary of the Duke and Duchess of Windsor Historical Society for his enthusiastic support, the loan of photographs, for arranging a magnificent conference at Coronado and introducing me to numerous contacts. Also to John Wieneman, to Richard René Silvin for his help and wise counsel throughout the writing of this book, and to Lena Farugia & Robert Davies (for their recreation of the Duchess on stage). Mark led me to Zippy Larson, who was a superb guide in Baltimore, and in turn to Philip Baty and his Duchess of Windsor Museum in Biddle Street.

For interviews specifically for this book: Mr Julian Beare & Mrs Robin Beare, the Hon Lady Charteris, Mrs Perry Culley, Henry Gillespie, the late Dean James R. Leo & his wife, Patsy (who kindly entertained me in Cincinnati), Suzy Menkes, & Mr Philip Nelson.

Special thanks to Robert Nedelkoff for his encyclopaedic knowledge, for papers relating to the 1970 Nixon dinner, and for taking me (with his wife, René) to Blue Ridge Summit, Pennsylvania for the afternoon, Mr Ed Orndorff for showing us the site of the house where the Duchess was born, Mike & Gloria Hardcastle-Taylor for sharing the Bahamas memories of Mike's mother and allowing me access to her unpublished memoir of that period. John Nova Phillips for an extract from his diary. Martina Hall (Pier Productions) who perhaps inadvertently inspired this book to resume life in 2008, Richard Jay Hutto for help with elusive Americans, Andrea Lynn for help with Constance Atherton, Jane Tippett for many archival clues, documents and other material which would have eluded me, Claire Singer for resolving what had become a deeply complicated issue, Mark McGinness, Ian Shapiro, & Francisco Alvarez for elusive material, Mary Dearborn, Barbara E. Will, Thomas Dilworth, Edward Burns for their help with source material in America and advice, Michael Thornton for his help with the *Royal Feud* feud, and Veronica Read for giving me access to her father's papers relating to the Duke's funeral.

On the point of finishing the bulk of this book, I was hired as historical advisor on the film, *The King's Speech*, which was a tremendous boost for me in many ways. It was a huge privilege to work with Tom Hooper, Colin Firth, Helena Bonham Carter, Claire Bloom, Derek Jacobi, Guy Pearce, Francesca Budd and the cast and crew, and frankly I cannot resist dropping their names in this way!

Then Sotheby's sold a selection of the Duchess's jewels. Great thanks to Lucinda Blythe for inviting me to come and see the jewels privately and to help promote them for the sale; also to Alexandra Rhodes, David Bennett & Alice Montagu-Douglas-Scott. I received great hospitality from Sotheby's and at a boardroom lunch, James Stourton told me how the original sale came to them in 1987.

I have greatly enjoyed working with Paul Sidey, my editor, who has been a constant support at all times and put up with almost daily reports and questions from me. I have extracted some 448 emails from him and the figure is rising.

I would also like to thank Amanda Telfer for her wise advice over legal issues, and at Hutchinson, Emma Mitchell, Paulette Hearn and Neil Bradford. My typescript and complicated proofs were tackled in good spirits by Nick Austin, Anne Wegner and Joanna Taylor.

Help came in many ways – sometimes 'massive' and sometimes small, but always help – from:

Timothy F. Beard (with Warfield descents), Wolcott Blair, the Hon Mrs Raymond Bonham Carter, Tom Bower, Sarah Bradford, Tillie Page Laird Brown, Michael Burrows, Dame Frances Campbell-Preston, Charles Cator, Lady Catto, David Patrick Columbia, Annie Crawford (costume designer on Madonna's film, *WE*), Lady de Bellaigue, Anne de Courcy, Bertrand du Vignaud, Charles Duff, Oliver Everett, Edward Fox, Joseph Friedman, Lindsay Fulcher, Robert Golden, John Handcock, Peter Hartley, Nicky Haslam, Lady Selina Hastings Jim Holmberg (The Filson Historical Society), Lizzy Jamieson, James Knox, Elisabeth Kruch, Carol A. Leadenham (Hoover Institution Archives), Timothy McCahill, Michael Mallon, Katherine Marshall (Cecil Beaton Collection, Sotheby's), Charlotte Mosley, Tim O'Donovan, Jennifer Namsiriwan & Marc Thomas

(Maryland Historical Society), Ben Newick, Dr Alastair Niven, the Viscount Norwich, Charlotte Office, Lady Penn, Jonathan Petropoulos, Andrew Roberts, Kenneth Rose, Philip & Jane Rylands, Taylor Smith (Oldfields School), the Lady Soames, Diane Solway, Lyndsey Spence, Professor Peter Stansky, Will Swift, Sir John Tusa, Sir Humphrey Wakefield, Lavinia Wallop (who showed me letters to the Dowager Viscountess Monckton of Brenchley), the Rev Canon John White, and Philip Ziegler.

Gillon Aitken has been my agent and protector for over 33 years and I am, as always, grateful to him, and also to his team at Aitken, Alexander in particular Leah Middleton, who has lately tackled a great number of challenging issues on my behalf.

My family has had to put up with the long hours I have spent working on this book, with occasional absences on research trips abroad. Mouse has again proved a wise reader of my text, and Arthur, Alice and George have come to know the Abdication saga rather well. I even sat them through the whole of *Edward & Mrs Simpson*. They have been saintly.

This book has been a long time in gestation. I know how easy it is to be offended when help is not acknowledged. If I have inadvertently omitted anyone, it is not intentional. I have received such wonderful help, and I say a huge thank you.

Hugo Vickers
February 2011

P.S. I am grateful to those who pointed out small errors in the first edition. These have been corrected.

I am particularly grateful to Michael Reynolds who provided me with a considerable cache of papers from Allen & Overy. This enabled me to sharpen some points relating to Sir Godfrey Morley and how Blum and Amiguet prised the Duchess from his care.

December 2011

Copyrights

I have made strenuous efforts to trace all the copyright holders in respect of the many private letters quoted in this book. I apologise to any copyright holder who I have been unable to reach, and promise to rectify the matter in future editions.

Copyright in the letters of HRH The Duke of Windsor and the Duchess of Windsor rests with the Institut Louis Pasteur in Paris.

I am grateful to the following for permission to quote:

Her Majesty The Queen for a letter from Sir Robin Mackworth-Young, Librarian at Windsor Castle; Mrs Robin Beare, and to Mr Julian Beare, for a letter to the Duchess from Robin Beare; The Literary Executors of the late Sir Cecil Beaton for extracts from his diaries; The Lady Brabourne for the letters and diaries of the late Admiral of the Fleet Earl Mountbatten of Burma; The Hon Mrs David Erskine and Mrs Lavinia Hankinson for the letters and diaries of their father, Rt Hon Sir Alan Lascelles; Michael and Gloria Hardcastle-Taylor and the estate of the late Jean D. Hardcastle-Taylor for quotes from her unpublished memoir, *The Windsors I Knew*; Viscount Hardinge of Penshurst for extracts from the diary of his grandmother, Helen, Viscountess Hardinge of Penshurst; The Literary Executor of the late Sir Charles Johnston for extracts from his unpublished diary; The executors of the late Major Walter Lees for extracts from his letters to Mona Bismarck; Mr David Metcalfe for access to the papers and photographs of his mother, Lady Alexandra Metcalfe, and permission to quote from her diaries and letters; The estate of the late Diana Mosley for her letters to the Dowager Duchess of Devonshire, James Lees-Milne, Mona Bismarck and the Dowager Viscountess Monckton of Brenchley, and to myself; Mrs Dale St Denis for letters and documents belonging to her grandmother, Corinne Mustin; The estate of John Pope-Hennessy for the letters of James Pope-Hennessy; Natalia Sciarini, Beinecke Rare Book and Manuscript Library, Yale University Library, New Haven (papers of James Lees-Milne & Alan Pryce Jones); British Library (papers of Lady Ottoline Morrell); The Churchill Archive Centre, Cambridge (Winston Churchill Papers); The Filson Historical Society, Louisville,

Kentucky for material in the Mona S. Bismarck Collection; The Getty Library, Los Angeles (James Pope-Hennessy papers, within the John Pope-Hennessy papers); Matt Schaefer, Herbert Hoover Presidential Library, Iowa (for correspondence between the Windsors and Ambassador & Mrs Henry J. Taylor); Lambeth Palace Library (papers of Rev Alan Don, & Canon Alec Sargent); The London Library; The Maryland Historical Society for letters and cuttings in their possession; The National Archives at Kew; The Richard Nixon Library, Yorba Linda, California; The Franklin D. Roosevelt Library, Hyde Park, New York (letter of Ambassador William C. Bullitt).

Photo Credits

<u>The Duchess of Windsor's Collection (now in the possession of Hugo Vickers)</u>
Section 1 – pages 2 (top left); 7 (top left – photo by
Michel Giniès, & right – photo by Robert McElroy);
Section 2 – pages 4 & 5 (all, photos by Gérard Maré);
Section 3 – pages 1; 2 (top, left & right); 3 & 4 (all);
5 (top left & below); 6 (top right & below)

<u>Mrs Robin Beare Collection © Mrs Beare</u>
Section 1 – pages 2 (below right); & 3 (below right)

<u>Mark Gaulding Collection</u>
Section 1 – pages 3 (below left); 5 (below right); 7 (below left); 8 (top right & below)

<u>David Metcalfe Collection © David Metcalfe</u>
Section 3 – pages 5 (top right); 6 (top left); 7 (top right & below left); 8 (below)

<u>Tim O'Donovan Collection</u>
Section 1 – pages 2 (top right & below left)

<u>Ed Orndorff Collection</u>
Section 2 – page 8 (top)

<u>Johanna Schütz Personal Collection © Johanna Schütz</u>
Section 1 – page 5 (below left);
Section 2 – pages 1 (top right); 2 & 3 (all); 7 (top)

<u>Elizabeth Vickers Photographs © Elizabeth Vickers</u>
Section 1 – page 7 (below right);
Section 2 – pages 7 (below left); 8 (below right)

Select Bibliography

Amory, Cleveland, *Who Killed Society?*, Harper & Brothers, NY, 1960
　　The Best Cat Ever, Little, Brown & Co, NY, 1993.
Athlone, HRH Princess Alice, Countess of, *For My Grandchildren*, Evans, 1966.
Birmingham, Stephen, *Duchess – The Story of Wallis Warfield Windsor*, Little
　　Brown & Co, New York, 1981.
Blakeway, Denys, *The Last Dance; 1936: The Year of Change*, John Murray,
　　2010.
Bloch, Michael, *The Duchess of Windsor*, Weidenfeld & Nicolson, 1996.
　　The Duke of Windsor's War, Weidenfeld & Nicolson, 1982.
　　Operation Willi, Weidenfeld & Nicolson, 1984.
　　The Reign & Abdication of Edward VIII, Bantam Press, 1990.
　　The Secret File of the Duke of Windsor, Bantam Press, 1988.
　　Wallis & Edward Letters 1931–1937, Weidenfeld & Nicolson, 1986.
Blum, Suzanne, *Le Printemps Foudroyé*, Presses de la Cité, Paris, 1973.
　　Quand le scandale éclate, Librairie Académique Perrin, Paris, 1971.
　　Ne Savoir Rien, Bibliothèque du Temps Présent, Paris, 1973.
　　Vivre Sans La Patrie 1940/1945, Plon, Paris, 1975.
Borkin, Joseph, *Robert R. Young – The Populist of Wall Street*, Harper & Row,
　　NY, 1969.
Bower, Tom, *Fayed: The Unauthorised Biography*, Macmillan, 1998.
Bradford, Sarah, *George VI*, Weidenfeld & Nicolson, 1989.
Bratton, Daniel (ed), *Yrs, Ever Affly*, Michigan State University Press, USA,
　　2000.
Brody, Iles, *Gone With the Windsors*, The John C. Winston Company, USA, 1953.
Bullitt, Orville H. (ed), *For The President – Personal and Secret*, Andre Deutsch,
　　1973.
Burke's Peerage, 1967.
Burns, Edward M., Dydo, Ulla E., & Rice, William (eds),
　　The Letters of Gertrude Stein & Thornton Wilder, Yale University Press, 1997.
Colville, John, *The Fringes of Power – Downing Street Diaries 1939–1955*,
　　Hodder & Stoughton, 1985.
Decaux, Alain, *L'Abdication*, Perrin, Paris, 1995.
Dimbleby, Jonathan, *The Prince of Wales*, Little, Brown & co, 1994.
Donaldson, Frances, *A Twentieth Century Life*, Weidenfeld & Nicolson, 1992.
　　Edward VIII, Weidenfeld & Nicolson, 1974.
Fraser, Nicholas, & others, *Aristotle Onassis*, Weidenfeld & Nicolson, 1978.

Gilbert, Martin, *Never Despair*, Heinemann, 1988.

Gloucester, Princess Alice, Duchess of, *The Memoirs of Princess Alice, Duchess of Gloucester*, Collins, 1983.

Godfrey, Rupert (ed), *Letters from a Prince*, Little, Brown & co, 1996.

Goldsmith, Barbara, *Little Gloria . . . Happy at Last*, Alfred A. Knopf, NY, 1980.

Harewood, the Earl of, *The Tongs and the Bones*, Weidenfeld & Nicolson, 1981.

Hart-Davis, Duff (ed), *In Royal Service*, Hamish Hamilton, 1989.
   King's Counsellor, Weidenfeld & Nicolson, 2006; & Phoenix Paperback, 2007.

Hersch, Burton, *The Old Boys*, Tree Farm Books, 2002.

Higham, Charles, *Wallis*, Sidgwick & Jackson, 1988; & 2004.

Holbrook, Susan & Dilworth, Thomas (eds), *The Letters of Gertrude Stein & Virgil Thomson*, Oxford University Press, 2010.

Kelly, Jacques (ed), *Eight Busy Decades: The Life & Times of Clarence W. Miles*, White Banks, Maryland, USA, 876 1986.

King, Greg, *The Duchess of Windsor*, Aurum Press, 1999.

Lynn, Andrea, *Shadow Lovers – The Last Affairs of H.G. Wells*, The Perseus Press, USA, 2001.

Mainwaring, Marion, *Mysteries of Paris – The Quest for Morton Fullerton*, University Press of New England, 2001.

Malcolm, Janet, *Two Lives – Gertrude and Alice*, Yale University Press, 2007.

Marlborough, Laura, Duchess of, *Laughter from a Cloud*, Weidenfeld & Nicolson, 1980.

Martin, Ralph G., *The Woman He Loved*, Simon & Schuster, NY, 1974.

Menkes, Suzy, *The Royal Jewels*, Harper Collins, 1985.
   The Windsor Style, Grafton Books, 1987.

Murphy, Charles J.V., & Bryan III, Joseph, *The Windsor Story*, Granada, 1979.

Murphy, Robert, *Diplomat Among Warriors*, Collins, 1964.

Palmer, Lilli, *Change Losters and Dance*, Macmillan, 1975.

Pope-Hennessy, James, *Queen Mary*, George Allen & Unwin, 1959.

Quennell, Peter (ed), *A Lonely Business – A Self-Portrait of James Pope-Hennessy*, Weidenfeld & Nicolson, 1980.

Rhodes James, Robert, *Chips – The Diaries of Sir Henry Channon*, Weidenfeld & Nicolson, 1967.
   Victor Cazalet, Hamish Hamilton, 1976.

Rose, Kenneth, *King George V*, Weidenfeld & Nicolson, 1983.

Russell, Audrey, *A Certain Voice*, Ross Anderson, 1984.

Sacks, Ph. D., Benjamin, *The Duchess of Windsor and the Coronado Legend, Part II*, Journal of San Diego Historical Society, 1988, Volume 34, Number 1.

Shawcross, William, *Queen Elizabeth The Queen Mother*, Macmillan, 2009.

Sotheby's, *Exceptional Jewels & Precious Objects formerly in the Collection of the Duchess of Windsor, 30 November 2010*.
   The Duke and Duchess of Windsor, New York, 11–19 September 1997.
   The Jewels of the Duchess of Windsor, 2–3 April 1987.

Sulzberger, C.L., *A Long Row of Candles*, Macmillan, NY, 1969.

Thomson, Virgil, *Virgil Thomson*, Alfred A. Knopf, 1966.

Thornton, Michael, *Royal Feud*, Michael Joseph, 1985; & Pan Books, 1986.

Tommasini, Anthony, *Virgil Thomson on the Aisle*, W.W. Norton, 1997.

Tremain, Rose, *The Darkness of Wallis Simpson*, Chatto & Windus, 2005.

Vanderbilt, Gloria & Furness, Thelma, Lady, *Double Exposure*, Frederick Muller, 1959.

Vaughan, Hal, *FDR's Apostles*, The Lyons Press, Connecticut, 2006.

Vickers, Hugo, *Cecil Beaton*, Weidenfeld & Nicolson, 1985.
   Elizabeth The Queen Mother, Hutchinson, 2005.
   The Private World of the Duke and Duchess of Windsor, Harrods Publishing, 1995.

Wake, Jehanne, *Sisters of Fortune*, Chatto & Windus, 2010.

Warfield, J.D., *The Founders of Anne Arundel and Howard Counties, Maryland*, Heritage Books, USA, 2008.

White, Sam, *Sam White's Paris*, New English Library, 1983.

Wiesinger, Véronique, *Chefs d'oeuvre du Musée National de la Légion d'Honneur*, Carte Segrete, Paris, 1994.

Williams, Susan, *The People's King*, Allen Lane, 2003.

Windsor, The Duchess of, *Some Favorite Southern Recipes*, Charles Scribner's Sons, NY, 1942.
   The Heart Has Its Reasons, Michael Joseph, 1956.

Windsor, HRH The Duke of, *The Crown and the People 1902–1953*, Cassell, 1953.
   A Family Album, Cassell, 1960.
   A King's Story, Cassell, 1951.

Wolff, Geoffrey, *Black Sun*, Random House, NY, 1976.

Wright, William, *Heiress*, Pocket Books, NY, 1979.

Young, Kenneth (ed), *The Diaries of Sir Robert Bruce-Lockhart*, Macmillan, 1973.

Ziegler, Philip, *Mountbatten*, Collins, 1985.
   From Shore to Shore – The Final Years, Collins, 1989.

Index